ARAB SPRING

ARAB SPRING

Negotiating in the Shadow of the Intifadat

Edited by I. William Zartman

The University of Georgia Press
Athens and London

Athens, Georgia 30602
www.ugapress.org

Set in Minion Pro by Graphic Composition, Inc., Bogart, Georgia
Printed and bound by Sheridan Books
The paper in this book meets the guidelines for
permanence and durability of the Committee on
Production Guidelines for Book Longevity of the
Council on Library Resources.
Most University of Georgia Press titles are
available from popular e-book vendors.

Printed in the United States of America
19 18 17 16 15 P 5 4 3 2 1

Library of Congress Cataloging-in-Publication Data

Arab spring : negotiating in the shadow of the intifadat / edited by I. William Zartman.
pages cm. — (Studies in security and international affairs)
Includes bibliographical references and index.
ISBN 978-0-8203-4826-1 (ebook) — ISBN 978-0-8203-4824-7 (hardcover : alk. paper) — ISBN 978-0-8203-4825-4 (pbk. : alk. paper) 1. Arab Spring, 2010– 2. Negotiation—Political aspects—Arab countries. 3. Revolutions—Arab countries—History—21st century. 4. Protest movements—Arab countries—21st century. 5. Democratization—Arab countries—History—21st century. 6. Arab countries—Politics and government—21st century. 7. Arab countries—Armed Forces—Political activity—21st century. I. Zartman, I. William.
JQ1850.A91A797 2015
909'.097492708312—dc23

2015008709

British Library Cataloging-in-Publication Data available

This book is dedicated to those who made the Arab Spring and to their dreams of dignity, liberty, work, and citizenship.

CONTENTS

Process of International Negotiation (PIN) group members are marked with an asterisk.

ABOUT THE PROCESSES OF INTERNATIONAL NEGOTIATION (PIN) PROGRAM

Since 1988, the Processes of International Negotiation (PIN) Program—formerly at the International Institute of Applied Systems Analysis (IIASA) in Laxenburg, Austria, and now located at Clingendael, The Hague, Netherlands—has been conducted by an international Steering Committee of scholars and practitioners, meeting three times a year to develop and propagate new knowledge about the processes of negotiation. The Steering Committee conducts one or two workshops every year devoted to the analysis and improvement of the practice of negotiation, involving scholars from a wide spectrum of countries, in order to tap a broad range of international expertise.

It also offers miniconferences on international negotiations in order to disseminate and encourage research on the subject. Such "Road Shows" have been held at the Argentine Council for International Relations, Buenos Aires; Beida University, Beijing; the Center for Conflict Resolution, Haifa; the Center for the Study of Contemporary Japanese Culture, Kyoto; the School of International Relations, Tehran; the Swedish Institute of International Affairs, Stockholm; the University of Cairo; the University Hassan II, Casablanca; the University of Helsinki; and the UN University for Peace, San Jose, Costa Rica.

The PIN Network publishes a semiannual online newsletter, *PINPoints*, available at www.pin-negotiation.org, and sponsors a network of over four thousand researchers and practitioners in negotiation. Past projects and the PIN Program have been supported by the William and Flora Hewlett Foundation, Smith Richardson Foundation, the U.S. Institute of Peace, UNESCO, Carnegie Corporation, and Carnegie Commission for the Prevention of Deadly Conflict.

Members of the PIN Steering Committee are Cecilia Albin, Uppsala University; Mark Anstey, Nelson Mandela University; Guy Olivier Faure, University of Paris V–Sorbonne; Paul Meerts, the Netherlands Institute of International Relations, Clingendael; Mordechai Melamud, CTBTO, Vienna; Valerie Rosoux, Catholic University of Louvain; Rudolf Schüssler, Bayreuth University; Mikhail Troitskiy, MGIMO, Moscow; I. William Zartman, the Johns Hopkins University; and Wilbur Perlot, Clingendael. Emeritus members are Rudolf Avenhaus, the German Armed Forces University, Munich; and Gunnar Sjöstedt, the Swedish Institute of International Affairs.

Selected Publications of the PIN Program

Anstey, Mark, and Valerie Rosoux, eds. 2015. *Reconciliation and Negotiation.* (Pending)

Melamud, Mordechai, Paul Meerts, and I. William Zartman, eds. 2014. *Banning the Bang or the Bomb? Negotiating the Nuclear Test Ban.* Cambridge: Cambridge University Press.

Faure, G. O., ed. 2012. *Unfinished Business: Why International Negotiations Fail.* Athens: University of Georgia Press.

Zartman, I. W., M. A. Anstey, and P. Meerts, eds. 2012. *The Slippery Slope to Genocide: Reducing Identity Conflicts and Preventing Mass Murder.* New York: Oxford University Press.

Zartman, I. W., and G. O. Faure, eds. 2011. *Engaging Extremists.* Washington, D.C.: U.S. Institute of Peace.

Faure, G. O., and I. W. Zartman, eds. 2010. *Negotiating with Terrorists.* London: Routledge.

Avenhaus, R., and G. Sjoestedt, eds. 2009. *Negotiated Risks: International Talks on Hazardous Issues.* Heidelberg, Germany: Springer-Verlag.

Bercovitch, J., V. A. Kremenyuk, and I. W. Zartman, eds. 2008. *The SAGE Handbook of Conflict Resolution.* London: Sage Publications.

Avenhaus, R., and I. W. Zartman, eds. 2007. *Diplomacy Games: Formal Models and International Negotiations.* Heidelberg, Germany: Springer-Verlag.

Zartman, I. W., and G. O. Faure, eds. 2005. *Escalation and Negotiation in International Conflicts.* Cambridge: Cambridge University Press.

Zartman, I. W., and V. A. Kremenyuk, eds. 2005. *Peace versus Justice: Negotiating Forward- and Backward-Looking Outcomes.* Lanham, Md.: Rowman and Littlefield.

Spector, B. I., and I. W. Zartman, eds. 2005. *Getting It Done: Post-Agreement Negotiations and International Regimes.* Washington, D.C.: U.S. Institute of Peace Press.

Meerts, P., and F. Cede, eds. 2004. *Negotiating European Union.* Basingstoke, UK: Palgrave Macmillan.

Sjöstedt, G., and W. Lang, eds. 2003. *Professional Cultures in International Negotiation: Bridge or Rift?* Lanham, Md.: Lexington Books.

Faure, G. O. 2003. *How People Negotiate: Resolving Disputes in Different Cultures.* Dordrecht, Netherlands: Kluwer Academic.

Avenhaus, R., V. A. Kremenyuk, and G. Sjöstedt, eds. 2002. *Containing the Atom: International Negotiations on Nuclear Security and Safety.* Lanham, Md.: Lexington Books.

Kremenyuk, V. A., ed. 2002. *International Negotiation: Analysis, Approaches, Issues.* 2nd ed. San Francisco: Jossey-Bass.

Zartman, I. W., ed. 2001. *Preventive Negotiation: Avoiding Conflict Escalation.* Lanham, Md.: Rowman and Littlefield.

Sjøstedt, G., and V. A. Kremenyuk, eds. 2000. *International Economic Negotiation: Models versus Reality.* Cheltenham, UK: Edward Elgar.

Zartman, I. W., and J. Z. Rubin, eds. 2000. *Power and Negotiation.* Ann Arbor: University of Michigan Press.

Berton, P., H. Kimura, and I. W. Zartman, eds. 1999. *International Negotiation: Actors, Structure/Process, Values.* New York: St. Martin's Press.

Zartman, I. W., ed. 1994. *International Multilateral Negotiation: Approaches to the Management of Complexity.* San Francisco: Jossey-Bass.

Spector, B. I., G. Sjöstedt, and I. W. Zartman, eds. 1994. *Negotiating International Regimes: Lessons Learned from the United Nations Conference on Environment and Development (UNCED).* Dordrecht, Netherlands: Graham and Trotman/Martinus Nijhoff.

Faure, G. O., and J. Z. Rubin, eds. 1993. *Culture and Negotiation: The Resolution of Water Disputes.* London: Sage Publications.

Sjöstedt, G., ed. 1993. *International Environmental Negotiation.* London: Sage Publications.

ACKNOWLEDGMENTS

We are indeed grateful for support from many quarters for the accomplishment of this project of the Processes of International Negotiation Program in Clingendael, Netherlands. Initial and timely support came from the Council of American Overseas Research Centers (CAORC), followed by the Smith Richardson Foundation, the International Development Research Institute (IDRC), the African Development Bank (AfDB) in Tunis, and the Institute for Research in Stability and Conflict (IRISC). Meetings were generously hosted by the Centre d'Études Maghrébines à Tunis (CEMAT), the United States Institute of Peace (USIP), and the Bahçe Şehir University in Istanbul. Isabelle Talpain-Long provided solid administrative assistance, Sarah Cooper and Sabina Henneberg gave good research assistance, and Elizabeth Parker-Magyar prepared the index.

ARAB SPRING

Negotiations in Transitions

A Conceptual Framework

I. WILLIAM ZARTMAN

> A people does not rise up if it does not feel
> Impelled by a robust decision to live, when
> Life awakes in it.
> Abulqasim al-Shabbi, "Ser al-Nawhud," 1933

BEGINNING IN JANUARY 2011, the Arab world exploded in a vibrant demand for dignity, liberty, and achievable purpose in life, rising up against an image and tradition of arrogant, corrupt, unresponsive authoritarian rule over an alienated population. The Tunisians' slogan was "Dignity, Liberty, Work, Citizenship"; the Egyptians' was "Dignity, Freedom, Bread, and Social Justice," later ensconced in their constitutions. To be sure, the material source of this outcry was unemployment, and its agent was the youth bulge that shows up in quantitative analyses, but it all added up to a *cri du coeur* for respect and meaningful life as a human being.[1] The outburst pursued the truncated promise of democracy that came with the anticolonial movement after World War II, when nationalist parties took over government in the name of the people but prevented the people themselves from participation in accountable, responsive, and responsible self-governance. The people then came to be known as being inimical to democracy. The *intifadat*'s[2] target was not a failed state but, to the contrary, a hard and brittle state whose narrow authoritarian center was buttressed from behind by a pervasive *mukhabarat* (secret intelligence) apparatus that tamed parties and swallowed opposition (Luciani 1990; Dawisha and Zartman 1988; Jebnoun, Kia, and Kirk 2013). In some cases the uprising completed the collapse; in others it salvaged, revived, and reformed the state; and in still others it hardened the brutal authoritarian apparatus.

As a measure, one can set up a model or ideal type: one could see a busy interaction of the political forces push aside the Old Order and in a burst of political participation and commitment negotiate a consensual constitutional formula for a New Order, engaging the galvanized energies and building a new sense of trust and citizenship. No ideal type is an accurate portrayal of reality, and this one is no exception. Models serve as templates that help us understand what works and why, when it works, and why not. None of the eight cases of the Arab Spring discussed in this volume—Morocco, Algeria, Tunisia, Libya, Egypt, Yemen, Bahrain, and Syria—has been a good fit to the model; some are better, some worse than others. An analysis of their processes of interaction tells why and when.

To build a new state in whole or in part, societies needed to construct—to negotiate—a broad coalition of forces in order to devise—to negotiate—a consensual formula for a social contract. The more the process involves widespread integrative rather than narrow distributive negotiations, the better societies can fashion a consensual sociopolitical contract for a stable future. This they have not done, at least as yet. But humanity does not deal in perfections, only, at best, in approximations, and perhaps more often in missed opportunities and failures. This study presents an analysis of the ways different societies and groups of societies in the Arab world have attacked this challenge in its first four years (2011–2014), of why they have fallen short thus far, and where the possibilities lie for more fruitful approximations.

In the transition, there is little else beside negotiation. Long ago, it was noted that "negotiation is appropriate when there is a change in the structure of affairs and a new order must be created or problems managed in its absence" (Zartman 1982, 48). Even where there is violence, it is as an adjunct to the negotiation process, until it escalates to the point of open civil warfare; there the goal is no longer an agreement with the opponent but its elimination, after which the survivors again turn to negotiation (Nieburg 1969, 78–79). What is special about the use of negotiation in the Arab Spring is that it is characteristic of the entire exploded political system in transition, from the bottom up. The *intifada* negotiated its way up, among people and toward goals, and continued to do so as the resistance continued and then, where it happened, as the New Order was being clumsily put into place.

Negotiation is the important process of politics in general, in differing locations (Dahl 1955; Casper and Taylor 1996; Kolb and Williams 2000). In the closed and irresponsible system of the authoritarian Old Order, it was limited to a small group, with the rest of the system outside looking in or laying low. Against this hard order, negotiation rose from the bottom of society, among the dissatisfied individuals and groups, making coalitions around ideas for action, pulling in violence as an adjunct to bargaining, coalescing into more organized groups and parties, and finally working as the means for the establishment of electoral systems and constitutions, where it hands over decisive action to another form of decision making, the vote, in elections and legislation (Carr 1949, 212; Dahl 1955, 47; Rappoport 1960; Arrow 1974, 69; Zartman 1978, 68–71). The Arab Spring transition is the outburst of negotiation bubbling up through the social system and seeking to fill with a New Order the institutional vacuum that the *intifada* created. Since negotiation requires parties and moves from goals to outcomes, the process can be divided analytically into *negotiation for coalition* (by *whom*?) and *negotiation for formulation* (for *what*?). It takes place between government and uprising but more importantly among uprisers themselves.

This study seeks to identify patterns or courses of negotiation in the cases of the Arab Spring and explain why and how they occur. The eight countries in the throes of the Arab Spring are all different in their experiences, yet their idiosyncratic uniquenesses can be overcome by careful analysis. The approach shows how *Short Track Transitions* (relatively rapid and negotiated overthrow) evolve through negotiated courses struggling to stay pluralistic, how *Long Track Transitions* (periods of violence eight months and longer before overthrow) produce highly fractured systems scrambling over the *who* bearing the *what* in their holsters, and how *Short Track Reactions* undercut the *intifadat*, leaving a renewed challenge of reform.[3] As they continue, the Tracks further divide into divergent lines: a gradual return to "normal politics" where institutionalized competition focuses on substantive electoral and welfare politics, a bipolar system of pacting and seesaw instability that collapses under an overriding need for order, and an unstable fractured congeries of violence and extremism that implodes the state and fights for its control, plus two other Short Track patterns of repression and adaptation where the *intifadat* are preempted in different ways.

The analysis shows that it is the parties' attitudes toward negotiation that determine the role that they will play and their use of bargaining power that determines the outcome of the encounters into the different patterns. The extent to which the political system can get over dominance by a single force or by a bipolar contest between two large forces, and can develop a sense of undominated pluralism will determine their ability to negotiate a New Order, either integrative or distributive. If there is a long and violent struggle for overthrow, the contesting forces will splinter into small identity-bound pieces, making stalemate and effective negotiations lengthy and difficult until one side coalesces and achieves effective dominance, or the country breaks up into pieces. If these two forms of pluralism—political or violent—break down, the human need for order will be seized by a single dominating force.

It may appear odd to do a conceptual analysis of the Arab Spring at this point. The successive *intifadat* are works in progress and will not hold still long enough to be subject to the normal research methods. The various cases are each at a different stage in their trajectories, and it is not yet certain how they will turn out (if there is a time limit for turning out). It is a story without an end. The study begins in 2010 (or a bit before, although historians will later document its roots, in a different project) and continues through 2014, with elections and a constitution as the conceptual cutoff where possible. It is also a study based on ephemeral data, participant observation by many of the coauthors, and diligent research into ongoing events. Although it is impossible to say when the subject is over, there is real value in an initial attempt at an analysis that seeks to find common patterns and deviations and explanations for them, and hypothetical insights to be tested and supported or invalidated in later analysis.

THE APPROACH: NEGOTIATION ANALYSIS

Negotiation analysis is the study of joint decision making, the process of arriving at a common outcome from conflicting positions under a decision rule of unanimity (Zartman 1978). It is a communication exercise of statements, demands, and contingent promises to produce specific actions. It ranges from direct, face-to-face exchanges to tacit bargaining (Schelling 1960, 56–67, 99–111). It differs from voting, in that the decision rule is unanimity among equal parties and the project is flexible, and from judicial or executive decision, in that hierarchy and authority among parties are absent (Carr 1949; Dahl 1955; Rappoport 1960; Arrow 1974; Zartman 1978). The process can be divided into two types—*distributive* or value-taking negotiations and *integrative* or value-making negotiations (Follett 2012; Walton and McKersie 1965; Lax and Sebenius 1986). The first brings the parties to focus defensively on party identity and payoffs to the exclusion of others; the second brings the parties to focus creatively and constructively on joint benefits, consensual agreements, and overarching identities. This distinction is of major significance for an understanding of the Arab Spring negotiations.

Negotiation is the process of giving something to get something rather than clear winning and losing, and so involves identification of terms of trade (Nieburg 1969, 57). The giving and getting can be conducted by concessions over the same item, compensation or trade-offs of one item for another, or construction of a newly reframed picture of the issue to the advantage of both sides. Concessions are the hallmark of distributive negotiations and are bought by promises and predictions, threats and warnings, including the threat or use of force. Compensation can be used for both integrative and distributive negotiations, depending on whether it follows a coherent formula (Nash 1950; Homans 1960; Raiffa 1982, 2002), while construction is the favored process of integrative negotiations (Schelling 1960; Walton & McKersie 1965; Zartman 1978, 2008). Parties do not give to get unless they perceive that they cannot get without giving, that they would be getting (in their own evaluation) more than they give, and that their inability to get by themselves causes them frustration and discomfort. Subjective recognition of a mutually hurting stalemate and the perceived inability to impose unilateral outcomes are important conditions for engagement in negotiations; these perceptions have to be maintained throughout the negotiations until a mutually enticing opportunity is devised, and they are periodically evaluated during the process (Druckman 1986; Zartman 2000, 2006). Negotiation can also be done tacitly, with limited exchanges of offers and no direct contact (Schelling 1960; Rubenstein 1982).

The process moves from a gathering of information or *diagnosis* on such matters as the nature of the problem, risks and costs, parties and agendas, and issues, to the *formulation* of a common identification of the problem or a common sense of justice and then application of the formula to the determination of specific *details* (Zartman and Berman 1982; Zartman et al. 1996; Hopmann 1996; Zartman 1997b). These phases can be pursued deliberately or implicitly, but also inductively (details first, as in uncoordinated compensations to create an ad hoc formula) at the cost of incoherence. Each side seeks to develop its own prospective formula, sets about to convince the other of its or their validity, and then works to combine formulas if the first efforts do not succeed (as they rarely do). If the parties do not propose or agree on a formula, negotiation becomes ragged and results delayed or disorganized. Formulation is a trial and error process, carried out by persuasion and power.

Persuasion utilizes the logic and symbols that are meaningful to the target (Schopenhauer 1896). Bargaining power is the ability to move a party in an intended direction (Dahl 1957; Jonssön 1981; Habeeb 1988; Zartman and Rubin 2000); its sources, in Arab Spring negotiations, are *legitimacy*, *organization*, and the threat or use of *violence*. "Institutions are not established to be socially efficient but rather to further the interests of those with more bargaining power" (North 1990). An *intifada* is a struggle for legitimacy, violence, and organization to achieve the interests of the parties, comprising mobilization of the symbols of legitimate authority, the exercise of street and eventually militia violence, and the structure for the command of group relations. Without legitimacy, violence, and organization, parties are not players in the negotiation process and hence in the transition from the Old to the New Order. Legitimacy turns raw power into authority and enables the bearer to use the structures of politics and governance (Lasswell and Kaplan 1953). In the absence (to date) of a charismatic figure, the countries of Arab Spring exemplify better than most conflicts the clash between Weber's traditional (religious) and legal-rational (liberal) sources of legitimacy. Part of the struggle in the *intifada* is therefore over the definition of the terms of legitimacy, which in turn establishes the use of violence deemed appropriate and the nature of the New Order deemed proper. Violence is an integral part of negotiations, used as a goad and a threat. Its threat or use does not mean that negotiation is ended or interrupted, to the contrary. Nor does its use necessarily mean bloodshed; violence means physical contact that carries with it the threat or danger of bloodshed (Tilly 1978, ch. 6).

Organization is often assumed and not analyzed as a component of negotiation. Political settlements are "bargaining outcomes among contending elites. . . . [that] are shaped by political organization (DiJohn and Putzel 2009, 4–5; OECD 2011). Organizations are necessary to conduct negotiation, and negotiation is required to produce organization. Internally, organization provides a motor to give the uprising form and direction and a framework for internal negotiations; externally, it gives the other side someone with whom to negotiate and to whom to relate in terms of power in the vacuum of the transition. "An organization is a set of people who are combined in virtue of activities directed to common goals" (Russell 1938, 107), a structure for the command of group relations. It is hence essentially tied to negotiation of both coalition and formulation, requiring leadership, structure, and doctrine. Negotiation is a choice of partners; to negotiate means to make a pact or coalition—of short or longer duration—for the choice and implementation of formulas (Zartman 2009).

Although negotiations between a state and an insurgent movement are usually termed asymmetric because the state claims the legitimate monopoly of force, in an *intifada* the government is severely weakened as an organization and delegitimized as a government. However, for all its new legitimacy, the uprising has great problems getting itself an organization (Donohue and Cristal 2011). It is usually a lumpy conglomerate of a few organizations and masses of disorganized uprisers, leaving the one or more parties—often an Islamist body in the Arab Spring—standing out among the uprisers as the ones able to negotiate a New Order. Other, less well organized groups of uprisers are able to convene their troops for demonstrations but not maintain their cohesion; the organized part of the uprising benefits from the threat and use of violence by the less organized masses, who are then left out of the negotiations (Roberts 2011; Hostrup Haugbølle and Cavatorta 2011; for a similar case, see Payne 1965).

Let it be firmly understood that negotiation is not just a "nice" practice or a diplomatic exercise. It should be obvious, even by now, that negotiation as used here is not simply or often a formal exchange of proposal around a table by constituted parties. The Egyptian and Algerian cases, analyzed by Heba Raouf Ezzat and Aly El Raggal and by Hugh Roberts, respectively, emphasize particularly this aspect. Negotiation literature in general has gone way beyond that caricature, and the treatment here goes even further, to include any process where positions are developed and then made to fit into a joint decision by parties at any level. The process can indeed include an exchange of positions leading to trade-offs but can also be simply a statement of views with one party stating a concession/decision that it calculates will gain the acceptance of the other(s). "[Bargaining is] a process of adjusting conflict through threatened or actual escalation and counterescalation—an equation of sliding scales whose points of respite and tentative balance (agreement or accommodation) result from a mutual testing (whether symbolic or actual) of mutual capabilities and cost-risk constraints" (Nieburg 1969, 75). In the surging *intifadat* of the Arab Spring, that process begins with individuals and small inchoate groups, moves en masse to a focus on overthrow of the Old Order (usually spaced over time and depth), then shifts to the formation of parties and the consolidation of larger groups, along with the formulation of steps and plans for the New Order, marked by tests of strength of coalitions in elections, and culminating (for analytical purposes) with the negotiation of a constitution and elections. Thus it is dynamically multilevel, as the people, liberated from an inability to make their own decisions about the Old Order, negotiate their roles and views and then hand up the power to negotiate to new decision makers and institutions of the New Order.

THE APPROACH: CONTENTION, REVOLUTION, DECOLONIZATION, PACTS, AND NEGOTIATION

In a world of social analysis where little is new, the Arab Spring nonetheless distinguishes itself from other identifiable types of events previously well analyzed. Nonetheless, much can be borrowed from such analyses before they are traded in for a different analytical approach. The most relevant literature concerns contentious politics, revolutions, anticolonial struggles, and pacted transitions.

The contentious politics of social movements move from demonstrations to violence and involve demands, participants, and commitment (Tilly 1978; 2008, 120–121). Demands or claims (like everything else) can be procedural, referring to recognition of the protestors and their inclusion in governance, or substantive, referring to adoption of specific policy changes, essentially on welfare and security. Participants act in prolonged, organized campaigns, producing change only incrementally, and in interaction with political opportunity structures of governments (Morris and Mueller 1992; Tarrow 1998, 73, 199; Freeman and Johnson 1999; Tilly 2008, 91, 208; Tilly and Tarrow 2007, 45–87). Commitment gives orientation and coherence to developing social action, turning mob into movement (Tilly 2008, 121–122). To apprehend this social action, "systemic study of performances requires close description of interaction among participants rather than simple identification and counting of whole episodes," pointing to negotiation analysis (Tilly 2008, 206).

Social movement theory is quite relevant to understanding membership and support in evolving structures. Opportunity structures, resources mobilization, and cognitive framing are social movement concepts that are useful in seizing the dynamic nature of the Arab Spring, but the analysis needs to go a step further and examine the communications among individuals and structures, notably in regard to the knotting together of coalitions and the elaboration of frames (Salame 1994; Clark 2004, 2012; Wiktorowicz 2004, 2004; Beinen and Varel 2011; Zartman 2011; Brynen et al. 2012). The focus on the rising movement of protest needs further focus on the personal and programmatic relations among the uprisers during and after the revolt. Contentions politics generally refers to protest and revolt leading up to the climax rather than the decision making among protestors as they conduct their overthrow and then move on to set up a New Order. Unlike most contention politics cases, at least, *intifadat* were designed to overthrow the government; even though they started with substantive grievances, they moved rapidly to a procedural agenda. Analysis of the gradual build-up would be enlightening but turns attention away from the inchoate event itself and the perpetrators' efforts to find order and orientation in their organization and goals.

Literature on revolution is relevant in its focus on the climactic event and its aftermath (Brinton 1965; Huntington 1969; Gurr 1970; Tilly 1978; Skocpol 1994; Coser 2000; Eckstein 2001; Sanderson 2010). *Revolution* is the term used in Tunisia (with some debate) and in Egypt (with some disillusion), although the characteristic violence of a revolution was absent in these two cases (at least in the first two years), whereas the term is less frequently used in Libya, Bahrain, and Syria, where violence is the name of the events. Paradoxically, if a revolution is an appropriate term, events in the two nonviolent countries resemble a Western model of a regime with clay feet that is rapidly overthrown, whereas the others would be following the Eastern model where the countryside rises in a long struggle to overthrown a regime well entrenched in the capital (Huntington 1969). Most treatments of the Arab Spring (e.g., Gelvin 2012; Noeihed and Warner 2012; Lynch 2012) refer to the events as a revolution, undefined. Only Dawisha (2013, 66) defines it, in Hanna Arendt's (1963) terms, as "en entirely new story . . . of freedom" and decides that liberation has indeed occurred but not achieved the essential element of freedom, and Larémont (2013) identifies the background events as political revolutions at best and more likely as revolts.

Skocpol's (1979, 1994) analysis of the classic revolutions as social movements focuses on class relations, peasant revolt, marginalized elites, and modernizing effects on social relations, all crucial elements in the sociopolitical upheaval. But if a revolution is considered as a violent overthrow of the social-political structure in a compressed period of time, the reversal of the social pyramid, necessary to the definition, is quite absent in the Arab Spring. What is overthrown is not a social class but a ruling clique, often initially drawn from a middle social class itself, leaving at best a political but not social revolution (Zartman 2014). And where protracted violence does occur in the Arab Spring, it tends to evolve into ethnic, tribal, or sectarian conflict, denaturing the revolutionary characteristic of social upheaval.

A much closer parallel can be found in the nationalist anticolonial struggles of the 1950s and 1960s, particularly in North Africa (Micaud 1964; Quandt 1969; Zartman 1980, 1987a, 1997b; Mezran 2007). The nationalist movements went through a similar evolution of demands, ending with a delegitimization of colonial rule and a concentration of all demands—in a "funnel phase" of negative, procedural calls for its withdrawal, which also supplied the negative definition of nationalist identity. The unity of demands was supported by a great coalition of social forces, traditional and modern, behind the single goal; after independence was achieved, this unity of demands suffered fissures and was often held together only by an authoritarian single party claiming to incarnate the nation.

The goal was achieved by negotiation; in the relatively few cases where colonial resistance was prolonged, the violent struggle ended in negotiations, followed by military rule. Quandt's (1969) study of the Algerian nationalist movement focuses not only on its anticolonial protest and its politico-military evolution but also on the relations among factions within the National Liberation Front and Army (FLN/A). Nationalist movements took decades to develop, however, and did not explode in a single *intifada*, unlike almost all movements of the Arab Spring, and their unity of forces, although imperfect, was still more encompassing than the *intifada* coalitions. Nonetheless, the anticolonialist experiences—and also memories—are instructive and relevant to the current uprisings.

A quarter of a century ago, attention was drawn to a different type of transition from authoritarian rule occurring in Mediterranean Europe and Latin America (O'Donnell and Schmitter 1986). The common characteristic of these upheavals was analyzed as a process of pacting between incoming and outgoing leadership groups. Pacting refers to "an explicit . . . agreement among a select set of actors which seeks to . . . redefine rules governing the exercise of power on the basis of mutual guarantee for the 'vital interests' of those entering into it." Identified as moving "the polity toward democracy by undemocratic means," such agreements are negotiated by a small number of people, reducing competition along with conflict, limiting accountability, controlling the agenda of concerns, and constraining the players, especially the excluded. "Actors agree to forgo or underutilize their capacity to harm each other by extending guarantees not to threaten each others' corporate autonomies or vital interests. . . . The authoritarian rulers may be compelled by pressure or anticipated reaction to abandon power without the exchange of mutual guarantees, the outcome being left open to the subsequent uncertainty of factional struggle" (O'Donnell & Schmitter 1986, 37–39). However, the pacting process as analyzed is an elite affair in which a "popular upsurge" may only follow the pacting, if at all, and "is always ephemeral" (54–56). There was no reformist pacting going on in Arab Spring countries before the uprisings.

A case where the parties consciously studied and adopted the findings of the pacting literature was South Africa, presented here in Mark Anstey's chapter as a comparison, where the mechanism of negotiation has been studied with useful results (Sisk 1995; Zartman 1995). For several reasons, most current transitions have not followed the pacting path. The parties and even the sides that characterized transitional pacts are absent or inchoate in the current revolts. The authoritarian rulers have left, carrying legitimacy for their supporters with them, and the uprising is typically disorganized, leaving no clear sides to be represented in a pact. There are no or few functioning political parties to join a pact or pick up the pieces, and the old parties are sufficiently delegitimized to be unable to make a pact. The military is a significant but independent actor, the deus ex machina whose decisions whether to shoot its own people and to tell the ruler to retire constitute crucial turning points (O'Donnell and Schmitter 1986, 54–56). In a few cases—Egypt and Yemen—the army did play a pacting role, but their different societies produce different outcomes than in South Africa. In Tunisia and Egypt, however, the old elites, bereft of their retired autocrat, returned, at least as a sociopolitical class; in Morocco, Algeria, Syria, Bahrain, and Yemen, they never left, in each case under different conditions. They were more likely cases of soft pacting, mainly with themselves, neither revolution nor restoration but *plus ça change*, . . .

All of these approaches are structural, focusing on the movement of constituted groups, but not on how they are formed and how they move. Analysis of the *negotiation process* focuses on the process of forming decision groups and of their interaction. "The key to understanding political violence and projecting methods for its management must be found in the dynamics of bargaining relationships rather than in the chance issues of the conflict" (Nieburg 1969, 59–60). Analysis concerns the relationships between all sorts of heteroclite proto parties as they consider their own identity and the requirements of finding others of their same type in order to take the action they deem necessary (McAdam, Tarrow, and Tilly 2001, 56). This search for partners faces the Tactical Question (TQ) of whether to use violence or political means, and the breadth of their negative demands also plays into introspection about their own nature, their grievances with the Old Order, and then the type of New Order they seek (Zartman and Alfredson 2010). If the government offers to negotiate, the uprisers need to consider—diagnose—the extent of their demands and how much they will concede in order to attain how much of their goals. They also need to negotiate the relationships among themselves and both the principles—formulas—and the details of the future they are seeking to create when the past is overthrown. The longer the struggle continues, the more the uprisers face competing pressures—whether to fall back on the narrower nature of their group and its interests, or to drop their differences in order to concentrate of the single overriding goal.

So what are the possibilities and patterns? What are the turning points in these evolutions? And what can the Arab world tell about this type of event, and what can previous similar events tell about the evolution of the Arab countries?

NEGOTIATION IN THE ARAB SPRING

Negotiation for Formulation in the Insurgency

The Arab Spring negotiations began at the bottom. The spontaneity of the *intifadat* is incontestable, but they were preceded by a long history of grievances and demands. The negative substantive grievances—unemployment, food shortages, high prices, limited opportunities, but above all the arrogance and contempt from those in authority (*la hogra*)—were articulated and repeated, and the inability of the Old Order to meet them only augmented the negative procedural demands over who should redress the grievances (Roberts 2011; Blidi 2012; Hogra en Algerie n.d.). Increasingly, the incumbent regime was seen as the problem, not a source of a solution, and its removal became the focus of the uprising. None of this process brought out as yet any formulation of what the New Order should look like once the Old was gone.

For all their spontaneity, the uprisings still had their dry runs. In January to early April 2008 in Tunis, Redayef, and Gafsa and again in "Tunisie en Blanc" on 12 May 2010, labor and censorship protests took place, opening contacts and establishing relations that were ready for consummation the following year (Puchot 2011; Chomiak and Entelis 2011, 13–15). In Egypt the 2004 call for civil disobedience by jurist Tariq al-Bishri against President Hosni Mubarak's plans to run again, the formation of the Ghad (Tomorrow) Party for the 2005 elections, and the Kefiya (Enough) Movement, followed by strikes at the Mahalla al-Kubra textile factory by the illegal Independent Textile Workers' League, which then persisted as the 6 April Movement, not only preceded the eruption of demonstrations on Police Day (commemorating the killing of policemen in 1952 in Ismailiya) but actually prepared the organizations and contacts that made the Liberation Square uprising possible (Beinen 2010; Joffe 2011, 520–22). In Algeria a pre-*intifada* occurred in 2008, as the chapter by Hugh Roberts shows (Chomiak and Entelis 2011, 10–11). The *intifada* in Yemen was actually the second stage of the "six wars in six years" against the Houthi rebellion in the north that began in 2004, as fully analyzed in Abdullah Hamidaddin's chapter, and in Bahrain the confrontation with the Haaq movement in 2007 culminating in 2010 in violent repression, as analyzed by Roel Meijer and Maarten Danckaert, was a succession of "cycles with a cycle." Even in Syria, where the *mukhabarat* state was most active, a movement for the revival of civil society committees rose in the first decades of the 2000s; although it was nonviolent, it was to play an important role as the *intifada* broke out in 2011, as Samir Aita's chapter discusses. These various movements and events were generally not seen as harbingers of the 2011 *intifadat* because they were a normal part of the political scenery and were all focused on substantive grievances, not overthrow.

There were also growing but positive procedural demands for greater accountability and participation, from meaningful multiparty competition and multicandidate presidential elections. Multiparty systems existed in every country but Libya, but the parties were controlled, tamed, and emasculated, and some were banned. Presidential electoral competition also existed in Algeria, Tunisia, Yemen, and Egypt—Morocco, Bahrain, and Jordan are family monarchies, and rulers in Algeria, Tunisia, Egypt, Yemen, and Libya implicitly wished they were too—but the incumbent was always overwhelmingly popular, by official count. When positive demands for meaningful participation went unanswered, the substantive demands turned procedural—attention to what was to be done was overshadowed by rising protest for a change in who was to do it.

Once the *intifada* breaks out and then goes on and on, commitment increases and euphoria decreases; the uprising has now become serious, life-endangering business. When the protests are not effective in overthrowing the autocrat within a short time, the uprisers settle in for the long and violent haul, and the demands become fully focused on the single call for resignation. Whether the overthrow is early or later, that focused demand soon broadens to include the entire entourage and institutions of the Old Order, and each step in defining that broadening goal is the subject of negotiations among the uprisers. As in any conflict negotiations, bargaining over creeping demands continues under the pressure of violence, with the uprisers returning to the streets when the progress toward an agreement or the trial agreement itself is judged unsatisfactory; they then return to the "table" to resume negotiations (Druckman 1986). Repeatedly, violence has been an adjunct to negotiation; there is little negotiation by an exchange of favors or by reframing a mutually beneficial outcome, but only in a successive extraction of concessions, as expressed in the following proposition:

> **P1.** Negotiations with the government are conducted by civil society groups mainly over concessions extracted by popular disapproval expressed through the threat or use of violence.

In Short Track uprisings that produce an overthrow within a month, demands start with reduction in the autocrat's tenure and rapidly rise to his and then to his entourage's removal. In Egypt, "the demands of January 25 were [for] at least [Interior Minister Habib] al-Adly's resignation. The demands of January 28 were the removal of the regime. . . . Well, let him delegate to the vice president. He delegated too late" (Hamzawy 2011, 113; Fahmy 2011, 101–106). After a week of violent protests, President Hosni Mubarak announced that he would not run again for election; the protests abated, then returned to violence until he agreed to resign ten days later, and then revived again until he was indicted on criminal charges in late May and then subject to an on-again-off-again trial, as developed in the chapter by Raouf and El-Raggal. In Tunisia, the protests in dispersed order throughout the country in early January 2011 focused on a mixture of substantive grievances, which turned into grievances against police action and finally only on 9 January became the cry "Get out!" ("*Dégage*!" or "*irhal*!") (Weslati 2011; Puchot 2011; Bettaieb 2011), which President Zine el-Abadine Ben Ali did do five days later, as discussed in the chapter by Abdelwahab ben Hafaiedh and I. William Zartman. Within the week, the Caravan of Liberty had left the interior and reached the Kasba square in Tunis, demanding the dissolution of ben Ali's party and the resignation of its ministers, which happened on 21 February and 27 January (Weslati 2011).

In the Long Track uprisings, prolonged negotiations lead to splits among the uprisers' demands over partial offers from the authoritarian ruler. Negotiations in Libya, involving foreign mediation from Russia, the United States, Turkey, the African Union (AU), Britain, and France, worked on a wide variety of options for the end of Muammar Qadhafi's regime, involving exile within Libya, exile outside Libya, and amnesty from domestic trial and from the International Criminal Court (ICC), among others, none of which were entertained by Qadhafi and some of which were not entertained by various rebel groups either (Lamen 2011), discussed in the following chapters by Karim Mezran and Alice Alunni and by Johannes Theiss. In Yemen, a range of poorly formulated demands soon boiled down to one that dominated the scene for all of 2011 into 2012, the total removal of President Ali Abdullah Saleh and his replacement by a national transition council government of technocrats to organize elections, as Abdallah Hamidaddin develops in his chapter. There were no effective negotiations in Syria until the end of 2013, if at all, although President Bashar al-Asad called a negotiating session on 20 July 2011 to which he presented his conclusions, rejected by the opposition; the chapter by Aita records the escalation of demands in the revolt's slogans. Negotiations among the uprisers involved mainly the Tactical Question and became more and more heated and divisive as the uprising entered 2012 and headed into open civil war. At the end of the year, when the National Coalition of Syrian (COS) Revolutionary and Opposition Forces was formed, it refused negotiations with Asad, even under UN mediation, but insisted on total removal, all the way until the negotiations for a Geneva II meeting at the end of 2013, when conditions for negotiation were long gone (Zartman 2015; Hof 2014). In Bahrain, the demands of the largely Shiʿi protesters were for greater rights, political freedoms, and amnesties, and negotiations with the king continued on this agenda after mid-February under repeated pressure of violent demonstrations, as Roel Meijer and Maarten Danckaert's chapter analyzes. In Morocco and Algeria, as Amy Hamblin and Hugh Roberts indicate, protesters' demands never became procedural, understanding that the removal of the single leader was an unpromising goal, and it was better to seek redress of grievances from the incumbent rather than seek his removal.

Negotiations for Coalition in the Insurgency

A gamut of actors is involved in this situation. Negotiations begin with an informal, personal type of exchange as individuals and groups seek to find their most comfortable allies, to determine their attitudes and thresholds on the Tactical Question (TQ), to form their visions and hopes for a New Order. Insomuch as they do this in discussion with others, exchanging and shaping their views, they are negotiating to pursue joint actions and visions. Behind the spontaneous aspect of the uprisings lies a network of informal organizations and contacts, circulating around the conditions and grievances even if not actually preparing for street action or formulation of a New Order. Most of these contacts are merely occupational, amical, familial, or incidental expressions of feelings; a few of them involve planning for a political future that unexpectedly appears within their grasp. These contacts are rapidly galvanized, in supersaturated solution awaiting its speck of dust, when the coalescing event occurs. The authoritarian atmosphere in which these contacts take place and their informal, covert, and social-media nature contribute to rendering structure difficult and unstable, an important characteristic that will become salient as events move on.

Although the uprising is characterized above all by an absence of organization, the inchoate masses who joined the Caravan of Liberty from the interior to Tunis on 22 January or who came together in Tahrir Square on 25 January or who were galvanized to protest in Deraa in Syria on 18 February and elsewhere or who gathered at the Pearl Roundabout in Bahrain or Court Square in Benghazi or Change Square in Yemen at the same time had plenty of informal network contacts already in place that could be activated for political protest. These include football fan clubs, neighborhoods and informal associations, school classes and student unions, labor union locals operating with functional autonomy from the government-controlled national organization, workplace associations and wildcat strike committees, café socializing, mosque prayers, and, as the protests intensified, wakes (the more suicides and security deaths the more wakes, the more connections, and the more motivating anger). These all intermesh to form the basis for negotiations toward action-oriented coalitions unimpeded by weakening state control.

The next level of negotiations for coalition occurs between constituted groups and bodies over decisions with public outcomes, confrontations where the elements of violence and organization are the key to the bargaining power of the parties, first against the Old Order and then among themselves in setting up the New. Like any riot, the insurgency itself begins as a moment of enthusiasm, and its challenge is to get itself organized. Unless it emerges as one or more coherent organizations, it remains a street demonstration, useful only as a flash of demonstrative violence and an adjunct to other organizations' negotiations. "As restraints fail and conflict is escalated by tactics of greater cost and risk, the parties mobilize all their resources in order to endure as independent bargaining units" (Nieburg 1969, 79). The organization of the insurgency takes place on the job, a work in progress, and parties seek to come together on the basis of the two criteria of means and ends (Broom and Selznick 1958). The first refers to the Tactical Question again: How much pressure is required to achieve the goal, and indeed what is the immediate goal—the removal of a person, of his cronies, of his supporters, or of the whole system, which is the second criterion of ends. That question in turn involves estimates of success, operational plans, further risks and costs, consideration of allies, and the resistance of the other side. However, operational leadership tends to be localized, requiring negotiation for strategic coordination and coalitions among disparate bands (Quandt 1969).

Early protests and demonstrations that petered out or were repressed left a training experience and continuing communications contacts for future uprisers. Short of a galvanizing act, these contacts would scarcely be recognized as groups until coalesced when—literally—the speck of dust fell—Khalid Said killed in police custody in Alexandria in June 2010 in Egypt (Badrawi 2011, 84; Seif el-Dawla 2011, 119; Joffe 2011, 520), Mohammed Bouazizi immolated in Sidi Bouzid in December 2010 in Tunisia, lawyer Fathi Tarbil Salwa and journalist Idris al-Mismari arrested in February 2011 in Benghazi (Joffe 2011, 523), Ali Abdalhadi Mushayma and Fadel al-Mabrook shot in February 2011 in Bahrain, Hamza al-Khatib tortured in Deraa in March in Syria. In Syria, "an amorphous group of young activists operating mainly online" had difficulty in organizing a broad protest until an incident involving the boys in Deraa and subsequent repression ignited the broader protest (Zoepf 2011).[4]

That was the first trigger. The second was the contagion effect, endogenous to each uprising and then exogenously reinforcing. As people flocked to join the demonstrations, they found increasing security in numbers, increasing the solidarity and decreasing the danger, and more people flocked to join. Again, usually some incident lifted the fear and opened the door to demonstrating, such as the YouTube image of the army refusing to fire in Tunis on 13 January 2012. Thereafter contagion became a remarkable tsunami that swept from Tunisia on 17 December 2010 and 14 January 2011 to Algeria on 3 January, to Egypt on 25 January, to Yemen on 27 January, to Bahrain on 14 February, to Libya on 17 February, to Morocco on 20 February, and to Syria on 15 March. Nabil Fahmy (2011, 108) used a different metaphor about Egypt: "Oil was spilled out there on the street waiting to be lit up. It was lit up by Tunis." Once the match was thrown and the tinder (or oil) burst into flames, the uprisings drew in weak, potential, disorganized groups that already existed before the time of the uprising and activated them to form the *intifada*.

In their most organized forms, these groups included students, labor unions, and political parties. The predominant population of all the uprisings was made of students, from both higher and secondary education, and the *intifadat* were often initially dismissed as "just student riots." But labor and professional groups, especially lawyers, were just as much involved. Students may well be of a more volatile and not yet fully disillusioned age, but they also benefit from ready-made networks, relations, and often organization. The presence of a new spirit of optimism and universality, consciously free of ethnic, religious, or sectarian divisions, has often been noticed, notably in Tunisia, Egypt, and Syria, although as the protest proceeds, the divisions tend to resurface, revived by elders and leadership rivalries, and again by the Tactical Question.

Notably missing was a core organization for the uprising, leaving a vacuum readily filled by the latecoming Islamist movements. In spirit the former opposition political parties were often close to the uprisers in their call for a liberal democratic New Order and might have been expected to supply the needed organization. But they were weak and discredited, left in shambles by the *mukhabarat* (secret intelligence) organization of the Old Order. Those who had cooperated with the repressive regime were delegitimized, even if they retained any effective organization, but even those who had tried to maintain their integrity in these conditions were weakened at the base. The work of the *mukhabarat* left a lasting legacy for the uprisings, years after the disappearance of the authoritarian regime. Previous treatments of Arab authoritarian regimes have come in for criticism for being so ill-prepared to foresee an Arab Spring because of their focus on the *mukhabarat* state (Luciani 1990; Hinnebusch 1990; Bellin 2004; Cook 2007; Heydeman 2007; Schlumberger 2007). This criticism misses the persistent impact of the *mukhabarat* after the overthrow of their regimes: they had effectively destroyed both the structures and the skills of the political parties, leaving them unable to rebound when the repression was lifted. The only well-organized party was that of the Old Order; it was dishonored and disbanded but was ready to reappear with its skills and experience in diverse forms in the New Order, as in the Mubadara (Intiative) coalition and Nida Tunis (The Call of Tunisia) in Tunisia, the National and Freedom parties and the National Salvation Front in Egypt, the General Peoples Congress in Yemen, and of course the *makhzen* in Morocco, the junta and camp followers in Algeria, and the Alawites in Syria.

The political Islamic groups were effectively organized despite the repression under the old regime and had a significant effect on the negotiations. Because of their beleaguered position and because of the nature of the *intifadat*, these groups were not fomenters of the uprising, but they rushed to recover their organization and to run after the uprising train to get on board when it appeared to gain speed; the memory of their repression gained them popular sympathy and the fact that they represented a broad, unifying national identity gave them positive strength. Above all, their purposeful, dedicated organization was a crucial asset, meeting a high internal and external need. Internally, their organization gave them an immediate means of mobilization, putting them far ahead of other parties, and externally, it made them capable of negotiating and holding their deals with the government (in Tunisia) or with the army (in Egypt), who needed an organized body to talk to. But most significantly, their predominant position had a determinant impact on the formulation of a vision for the New Order by inserting the identity issue into early elections and debates. The October 2011 elections in Tunisia and the 2011–2012 elections in Egypt were fought on the single issue of identity at an abstract level: Islamic (not Islamist) versus secular, but not on its implications for a New Order. As late as July 2011 (after the original election date), al-Nahdha (the

Renaissance) Party had no positive electoral platform, and only in September did it agree on a 365-article program (Nahdha 2011), too much for a focused vision.

The next best organized civil group was the labor union, which contained a number of contradictory characteristics. It is the segment of civil society that has the best experience in negotiation, whatever its political position, using that experience to defend the interests of its members and to secure a place for itself in any given political system. It also has the most ready and organized mass of potential participants in an uprising, and its members have been in the forefront of demonstrations in Tunisia above all and in Egypt. It was also certain to be infiltrated and coopted by the authoritarian system, leading to deep splits between Old and potential New Order supporters. Thus, it was usually the workers, often in locals, rather than the national union organizations, that helped make the uprising. The General Union of Tunisian Workers (UGTT) was tolerated by the ben Ali regime and tried to negotiate its interests within the system; in January 2011 it met with ben Ali and proposed a government of national unity under his presidency, calling for a general strike only after the *intifada* had actually begun. Its leadership was ousted in January 2012 elections, but its negotiating experience served as training for the incoming leaders, and its members played an important role in the uprising. Later, in the negotiations for a constitution, it was the UGTT, along with the lawyers', business, and civil rights unions, that organized the National Dialogue to consummate the transition to elections in 2014. Workers, organized and disorganized, were prominent participants in the Liberation Square demonstrations in Cairo, even though the Egyptian Trade Union Federation (ETUF) was under strict government control. "The entry of the working class as an independent social force with its independent general strikes [on 9–10 February is] . . . what ended the regime" (el-Hamalawy cited by Sallam 2013, 253). Other groups include professional unions and associations, among which the bar associations are most prominent, and other civil society groups. All of these potentially demand-bearing groups struggled to regain activity and recover from the authoritarian regime, as they negotiate within themselves over appropriate participation and tactics in the uprising and among themselves over appropriate alliances to form.

A crucial role is played by the military, whose corporate nature and possession of the means of force necessarily make it a political player. The military have their own interests, above all in making their own transition to the new situation, still unfolding. They have to negotiate their position in the evolving events and at the same time make their best guess on how the events are going to evolve. As the best organized of the groups in a disorganized situation, they always remain a potential savior from the evolving anarchy. In Tunisia the military was trained to be absent from the political scene, whereas in Egypt, Syria, Yemen, and Algeria they are part of the politico-economic system, with interests in preserving their economic as well as political position. The other players are necessarily disorganized, uncertain of their goals and visions, unclear about their interests, and divided over the Tactical Question, all subjects on which the military have clear views.

SHORT TRACK NEGOTIATIONS

Thus the *first pattern* concerns the length of the uprising and the negotiations required to accomplish the overthrow. The model would suggest that a rapid overthrow would produce a smoother and more moderate transition and would maintain a role for personnel and programmatic leftovers from the Old Order. The difference between the Short and the Long Track depends on five factors: (1) a contextual condition, the incumbency of an aged leader awaiting replacement anyhow and sporting an illegitimate, unacceptable heir; (2) the collapse of the repressive machinery, represented by the refusal of the military to fire on civilians; (3) the willingness of members of the Old Order to negotiate a transition that will lose them their jobs; (4) the presence of an ostensibly moderate organization within the uprising; and (5) the desire of all sides to maintain the institutionalized state. Thus Short Track negotiations begin with the expeditious removal of the authoritarian figure.

In both Short Track cases of Tunisia and Egypt, the ruling autocrat was an aged figure facing a new term election possible only through a doctored constitution and the grooming of an illegitimate, unaccepted heir for his succession, providing a clay head at the top of the autocratic state (McIntyre 1988). Ben Ali and Mubarak were going out anyhow, at some not too distant point, and the uprisers did not want to go through the usual rigged plebiscitary methods of the Old Order to pick a designated successor; they wanted to do it their way. This condition alone is not defining; even in Long Track cases, the same characteristics facilitated the uprising, against Muammar Qadhafi in Libya and against Ahmed Ali Saleh in Yemen. The three exceptions—negative and positive—are Morocco, Syria, and Algeria. In Morocco the wily autocrat, Hassan II, had died a decade ago, leaving his less wily son, Mohammed VI, the opportunity to come to power as the "King of the Poor" and pull a new and more liberal constitution out of his crown and wave it at the more timid uprisers. In Syria, the old autocrat, Hafez al-Asad, had already been succeeded by his younger, unpopular son, Bashar al-Asad, setting up a Long Track uprising, whereas in Algeria, the aged leader Abdelaziz Bouteflika sat sickly atop the military junta iceberg, and his overthrow would do little to change the Old Order. He did what his peers could not—change the law to allow himself to be re-reelected in 2014. So there was no track at all (Roberts 2011).

Second, if the government uses the army to shoot the uprising people, as in Syria, Libya, and Bahrain, there is no Short Track (O'Donnell and Schmitter 1986).[5] The army did not fire on civilians in Tunisia and Egypt (in the initial *intifada*) or Morocco, or in the comparative cases of Serbia and South Africa presented by

Siniša Vuković and Mark Anstey; it split in Yemen, Libya, and Syria; in Algeria and Bahrain, the army stood firm against the uprisers, killing an effective *intifada*. Furthermore, the armies that did fire on their civilians tended to use helicopters, tanks, and artillery, as in Syria or Libya, where the targets are anonymous, rather than standing face-to-face, eye-to-eye in combat. It has been suggested that the defining characteristic is whether the army is part of the political system or not, but this is ambiguous as an indicator (Dorsey 2011). However, the army did not fire in the Short Track cases for different reasons—in Tunisia because it was deliberately not part of the system, and in Egypt because it was the backbone of the system, looking out for its own interests, which it saw in salvaging the Old Order, supporting the uprising first against Mubarak and then against Morsi.

Even this defining point involved various forms of negotiation. In Tunisia, the decision was rather clear: Gen. Ammar's refusal to obey ben Ali's orders (Barrouhi 2011a, 2011b; Indigo 2011). In Libya Gen. Abdul Fatah Younis on 20 February refused Qadhafi's order to fire and joined the uprising in Benghazi (then was shot five months later by a rebel offshoot) (Brahimi 2011, 617). In Egypt, "the Egyptian Army does not fire on the Egyptian people" (Fahmy 2011, 105; El-Menawy 2012)), although it later did, when defending its own coup. In Yemen, negotiations within the military led to a split, with the faction of Gen. Ali Mohsen al-Ahmar refusing to fire on the uprisers in March 2011 and joining them against the forces of President Saleh, producing the lengthy impasse. In Syria as in Algeria, the people are the only thing the army fires on.

A third characteristic of the Short Track is a government of the Old Order that, bereft of its authoritarian leader, is willing to negotiate its own transition (Joffe 2011, 517). In the process, members of the previous government gradually move out of office in response to the broadening demands of the uprising. They appear simply to be willing to be part of an interim government and then be discarded, albeit maybe only temporarily. This attitude was characteristic of both Egyptian and Tunisian transition figures. In Tunisia they saw their participation in the transition as a contribution to stability and a control against excess, a role a few notable figures such as Beji Qaid es-Sebsi and Kamal Morjane played til the end of the transition. In Egypt, Prime Minister Kamal Ganzouri and Vice President Omar Soleiman stayed on until after the 2012 presidential election, Mubarak's military were primary Old Order participants in the New Order, and the High Court judges of Mubarak played a crucial role in the pacting relations (Joffe 2011, 529, 555; O'Donnell and Schmitter 1986).

Fourth, Islamic groups with a large following had developed a formidable organization going into the *intifada*; they then rode along with the uprising until they could profit from it in the elections, but they protested their moderation so as to make the post-overthrow evolution appear less dangerous and to provide an acceptable organization for transition negotiations. Rachid Ghannouchi carefully spelled out how al-Nahdha was "just like any other party" and was deeply opposed to the Salafis and al-Qaeda in the Islamic Maghrib (AQIM);[6] he seems to have been genuinely seeking system participation as a legitimate political party rather than system takeover. The Muslim Brotherhood in Egypt repeatedly declared its democratic character, at least until it won the election. Islamist groups were certainly not protesting their moderation in the other cases.

A fifth characteristic that appears during and after the initial uprising is the commitment of all parties to the maintenance of the state. Continuity of the state, respect for the state, restoration or correction of the state are all themes that appear in the course of the Tunisian and Egyptian *intifadat*, as they do in the comparative cases of Serbia and South Africa. There are exceptions in the discourse, but they remain exceptions, and the course of the Short Track uprisings, as opposed to the Long Track *intifadat*, has been marked by a respect of constitutional provisions as long as possible (including the constitution's implicit use later as a "single negotiating text" for the new document) and the continued functioning of state institutions as much as possible throughout the transition. Probably the most striking case is the continuity of the Egyptian court system, with its Mubarak-appointed judges, throughout the transition period, and also the Tunisian courts.

> **P2a.** In the context of a worn-out autocrat expected to go anyhow, the army's refusal to fire on the people, the government officials' willingness to accept a negotiated transition removing them from their positions, the primary opposition organization's emphasis on its moderation, and all parties' expressed commitment to state (not Order) continuity combine to create the conditions for negotiation, producing a Short Track outcome.

Still, success on the Short Track brings a vacuum; uprising forces are not organized well enough to take over actively, and the quick success of the "funnel phase" of demands focusing on takeover allows the many fissures in the movement to rise to the surface when the unifying goal is achieved. There was no single dominant organization to emerge from the uprising. This situation is an important consequence of the rapid, spontaneous mobilization accomplished by the use of social media. Social media are excellent for bringing people together and for flexible strategies; they are inappropriate for structured organization. The three elements necessary for effective organization—leadership, structure, and doctrine (ideology)—are difficult to achieve, if not incompatible with the widespread use of electronic messaging. With Facebook, Twitter, and cellphones, leadership, message nodes, and direction are shifting, transient, and replaceable. Structure is multimode networking but not established line and staff with clear command and control. Ideology and visioning is under continual and disjointed discussion. In classical revolutionary terms, in the Arab Spring uprisings there is no Convention and no Jacobin Club as in France, no Communist Party as in Russia, no mullah network as in Iran, and were there one it would be deconstructed by the social media. Neither an organization, a network, or even a movement, the *muntafadin* are best seen as an energy, a powerful powder without a cannon, a rhizome as portrayed in the Raouf and El-Raggal chapter. In this situation, negotiation is difficult, conclusions are transitory, and implementation is chancy. The opportunity is open for a group outside the social media networks to fill the vacuum with an organization that has leadership, structure, and doctrine to dominate negotiations.

Aftershocks are to be expected as the insurgency works out its ideas of how much stable cleansing is required for the Old Order to be removed. Some of the most explicit negotiations occur on the issue. In Tunisia the interim government followed a path indicated by the constitution for filling a vacant presidency, then extended deadlines for electing an assembly to draft a new constitution and govern at the same time. Under the pressure of the Kasba II demonstrations, the interim government made a number of decisions to further purge the state apparatus of relics of the Old Order; at first ministers and then members of the Democratic Constitutional Rally (RCD) were prohibited from participation in government and then in the elections, although Qaid es-Sebsi, transition premier, returned to lead disorganized secular forces for the 2014 elections.

In Egypt, demands spread on several levels. As normally occurs in riots, objectives continued to grow after Mubarak's resignation on 1 February 2011 to cover incidents emerging from the protests themselves. "The second wave of the revolution" on 8 July—the Friday of Persistence—targeted judicial leniency toward the interior minister and police who repressed the demonstrations, but a liberal manifesto, Revolution First, highlighted economic demands as well as police and judiciary reforms. Protests continued to press for the dissolution of municipal councils elected under the old regime, which was not accomplished until the end of July. By November, negotiations shifted to focus on the role of military rule as a continuation of the Old Order, with repeated outbreaks of street violence, but in the end, a year later, the military returned.

Thus, the notion of a short uprising is somewhat misleading. Aftershocks concern procedural demands over elections and constitutions, but there can also be a revival of the uprising because satisfactory responses to substantive demands—notably for jobs—are not immediately forthcoming, as they are certain not to be. The collapse of order always leads disparate groups to relish the situation where the wraps are off and to test the new limits of possibilities. This "overflow" effect of the uprising is typical of reform as well as revolutionary situations (O'Donnell and Schmitter 1986, 59–60). After all, liberty was one of the major demands of the uprising, and now all groups feel they have the liberty to express themselves forcefully. Since security is weak, the police delegitimized, and the rules of the New Order unclear and unestablished, both gangs and newly liberated demand-bearing groups continue to disturb the public order and pose their own exactions on the population. In Egypt, the *muntafadin* continued to protest the shortfall of the uprising, demonstrating against both the Muslim Brotherhood and the military regimes. In Tunisia, Salafi students raised new demands for the right to wear the *niqab* (women's black total covering), including during exams, in the name of liberty, and then for all students to enjoy the same liberty (i.e., be obliged) to wear the *niqab*. Elsewhere workers practiced strikes and sit-ins that were forbidden under the Old Order and embarrassing to the New and then, in Tunisia, protested against a new government order banning protests. In Egypt, personal security was literally up for grabs, in both residential neighborhoods and downtown. The focus on identity in the first (2011) round of elections, paradoxically, brings out violence against outgroups that may have benefited from the old regime's protection. The solidarity of "everyone" swept up in the uprising turns into the solidarity of "everyone of us" against those—such as Christians, Jews, Alawites, and others—protected by the Old Order before its overthrow. Confused between responsibility for order and devotion to potential electoral supporters, the new governments dithered, prolonging the efforts to ascertain limits and to benefit from the free space for action, until, in Egypt, the government cracked down hard on popular protests and was ousted by the army, and in Tunisia, it cracked up under popular pressure and was replaced by a technocratic caretaker government. Having not yet finished setting up the New Order, transitional governments are obliged to act like normal democrats and respond to diverse demand-bearing groups whose votes they need for the upcoming elections.

> **P2b.** The Short Track pattern followed by the Arab *intifadat* involves a few weeks of intense negotiations over rapidly rising procedural demands producing the overthrow of the autocratic ruler and a series of negotiated moves to fill the institutional vacuum and shape a New Order. Popular violence remains to force these negotiations into productive results, until the demand for order of any stripe drowns out the difference between the Old and the New.

LONG TRACK NEGOTIATIONS

The Long Track takes months and more of violence accompanying stalled negotiations to complete the removal of the autocrat and his associates, as in Yemen and Libya, and far down the road in Bahrain and Syria. But negotiation is no less characteristic of Long Tracks; it merely operates in different conditions, under different constraints, with different demands that may or may not be met.[7] Long Track negotiations can be for removal of the ruler and for reform, as in Yemen, but in the longer cases such as Libya and Syria, negotiation was quickly pushed aside as a means of removal and turned instead to coalitions and formulations among the *muntafadin* themselves. As the uprising continues, it loses its character as a revolt of the youth and of civil society and develops a military wing, composed of the youthful uprisers but also growing numbers of defectors from the military and local and tribal militias. The heterogeneous nature of the rebel army poses the challenge of unity and command both to the rebel military and to a National Transitional Council (NTC) aspiring to replace the government. Rebel military activity continues to serve as an adjunct to negotiation, but its mission also creeps into an effort to destroy both the old regime directly and rival groups, and to bypass negotiation, just as the old regime seeks to eliminate the rebellion through military violence.

Negotiations occur primarily within the uprising, as two counter tendencies develop. On one hand, as noted, factions crystallize and harden, focusing inwardly on their internal characteristics and interests and on their differences regarding the Tactical Question. The conflict of militias against the government's army spawns a structure of autonomous local groups with secret organizations eluding any central command. Because of the danger of infiltrations from the government, there is as much distrust among the rebel groups as there is between the rebels and the government (Quandt 1969). The government has its back against the wall, refusing to acknowledge a hurting stalemate, seeing its situation in zero-sum terms, and engaging in negotiation only to destroy the rebellion. On the other hand, it becomes necessary for the uprisers to develop a common organization, both for its own effectiveness in the uprising and in preparation for filling the vacuum to be left by the government when defeated. Because of the tendency to factionalize, building an NTC is a difficult challenge. Like the Tunisian NTC that was formed within a month of the January 2011 uprising and oversaw a Short Track until ben Ali's resignation a week later and the National Constituent Assembly (NCA) elections in October, the Libyan National Transitional Council was self-appointed in late February 2011 and functioned effectively through the overthrow of Qadhafi in October until the election of the General National Congress (GNC) in July 2012. It was theoretically to be composed of delegates of local councils throughout the country, in a pyramid quite similar to Qadhafi's government structure, but even a year later its composition was not publicly known, and some eight hundred local militias came to contest its authority. When it handed over power to the GNC, the factional divisions reemerged to destroy budding order. The Syrian *intifada* broke out in mid-March 2011; by the end of June the country was spotted with Free Syrian Army (FSA) militia and local coordinating committees, with little contact with each other, and it took until mid-October, after "incredibly intense negotiations" under strong foreign pressure, for an SNC to be formed, as Aita chronicles (Tanir 2012; al-Zubaidi 2011–2012). Plans for union with a rival leftist coalition, the National Coordinating Body for Democratic Change (NCB), were denounced by the SNC over the Tactical Question (NCB's willingness to negotiate, rejection of the FSA, and opposition to foreign intervention) (Shahid 2011). It was not until November 2012 that the National Coalition of Syria was constructed under heavy foreign pressure, which then continued to be necessary to keep it together. Both "national" councils lacked control over various tribal, religious, military, and then religious militias, for reasons involving both the Tactical Question and the distribution of power.

Yet every war must end, either by victory or by stalemate, or by the emergence of new forms and forces, all involving negotiation. Victory of the insurgents is the setting for negotiation, but among the victors. The opponents have rallied together against the Old Order, but their success leaves them with strong factional interests, until a new pecking order and central structure are negotiated. Long after the Long Track is over, the parties continue to face sharp problems of antagonisms and entrenchment in their midst. They have accumulated accounts to settle and affronts to resolve as a result of the prolonged disorganized and often clandestine conflict; they also fall back into a defense of their own piece of hard-fought territory and autonomy and as an assertion of their specific brand of identity. Frequently, as in Syria and Libya, local militias develop with little interest in taking over central control but rather seek only to dominate their neighborhood. Yet the rebels are under pressure to coalesce in order to be effective. In some areas, this pressure takes a form halfway between local and national, in regional identity formations—Kurdistan in Syria, Cyrenaica in Libya, Huthis and Hirak in north and south Yemen, respectively. Still others try to pick up the ultimate unifier (and divider), a form of political Islam, to produce a New Order. On the other hand, insurgent disunity can be so debilitating that it allows the Old Order to prevail, as in Syria. As a result, negotiations for formulation and for coalition before and after Long Track victories tend to be prolonged and bitter, heading in uncertain directions. The assassination of Abdel Fatah Younis in July 2011 in Libya is an early case of winners' infighting alongside negotiations; the Syrian civil war between the FSA and the Islamic Front (formally created in November 2013 of Jebhat al-Nusra and the Islamic State of Iraq and Syria [ISIS] by al-Qaeda, another external imposition that did not last) is a prolonged example.

As positions harden, there is increasing need for external help. Encompassing, reconciling negotiations are required to keep the great coalition together as long as possible in order to give direction to the uprising and prevent settling of accounts and a return to authoritarianism. Almost inevitably, this requires outside intervention, as mediators or as supporters of one party or another. Mediators have been tried in a number of cases, generally without effect because of the obstacles noted, making the Long Track longer. Western powers and NGOs such as the Finnish Conflict Management Initiative (CMI) tried mediating in Libya once the NTC handed over power to the fractious GNC. The Arab League, a broad international Coalition of the Willing, and former UN secretary-general Kofi Annan and special envoy Lakhdar Brahimi, and finally the United States and Russia cooperating for the purpose of mediating in Syria, in the absence of a mutually hurting stalemate but facing the common enemy of emerging al-Nusra and ISIS, all failed, as discussed in Aita's chapter. As the mediators stumbled, other states threw their weight behind the Shi'i government (Russia, Iran) or the Sunni insurgents (Saudi Arabia, Qatar), while others (United States, EU) intervened negatively by withholding support for the COS. Foreign embassies tried mediation with Mohamed Morsi in Egypt to broaden his consultations to others than the Brotherhood, but failed, and so did Morsi. The existence of a hurting stalemate, brought home by the work of the Gulf Cooperation Council (GCC), the U.S. ambassador, and UN special envoy Jamal ben Omar aided by the UN Security Council, distinguishes the Yemeni case, which then collapsed. As Hamidaddin's chapter brings out, parties who have invested so much in overthrowing the Old Order are not likely to give up their investments even to their coalition partners after victory, and even less likely to "be reasonable" with an external mediator, during or after regime overthrow.

> **P3.** In the second pattern, a Long Track produces a breakdown of insurgent unity and its breakup into segments based on local, regional, or sectarian identity and on the Tactical Question, as the solidarity of rebellion dissolves and creates additional impediments for effectuate negotiations for a New Order, until either some side's victory or a stalemate painful to both sides occurs.

POST-INSURGENCY COALITION AND FORMULATION

But this is just the beginning. The search for a formula for governance is not likely to be linear, arriving efficiently at a common unshakable position, as the simple model would have it. Instead it is a gradual ad hoc journey arriving at its goal through salami tactics or "on the installment plan" (Rustow 1970, 363). Issues under negotiation include procedural matters: Who should write the new constitution—a commission, a constituent assembly, a national dialogue, or a parliamentary body? How should the drafters be chosen? When should elections be held for what, and with what electoral system? Who could run, what parties should be recognized by what criteria, how should previous parties and elites be treated? What type of system is to be provided in the new constitution—presidential, parliamentary, hybrid, federal, and so forth? And overarching all these specific issues is the larger formulaic question, still hanging: Who forms common cause with whom, what legitimizes the choice, and what is their vision for the New Order?

In the post-overthrow period, these questions are now framed by the type of transitional dynamic that the overthrow has produced. Transitions have appeared in five types: *competing*, *pacting*, *fragmenting*, *adapting*, and *repressing*, each with its own type of negotiations and requirements. These types are not permanent and may evolve into each other. The *competing system* that emerged from a Short Track *intifada* involving a number of parties where no party has enough seats in parliament to rule alone, as in Tunisia, provides a dynamic stability. While negotiating their own cohesion, the parties and coalitions also take care not to push their rivals and voters too far away lest they lose allies and votes in the next elections. Larger parties tend to reach out, smaller parties to pull in, troubled by sharpened disputes over how seemingly anodyne religious references could be applied in practice and balanced again by rising public pressures on all sides to maintain a functioning system and a moderate lowest-common-denominator sense of identity and government program. The more the constituent assembly bargains, the more the voters become alienated over the absence of effective and unaccountable governance, which in turn causes the government to delay the electoral day of accounting (Rowsell and ben Yahia 2012). Efforts to "constitutionalize" identity issues, rather than to provide broadly accepted ways of handling them and associated questions of detail, introduce distributive exclusivist attempts (Weiner 2011, 13; Lerner 2011). "An alternative approach to constitution-making—one that portends a much less successful future for societies in transition—is one which seeks to entrench its particular set of interests and aspirations as constitutional rights that are not subject to the kind of discussions, negotiations and compromises that build political relationships that would allow for a viable model of diversity" (Weiner 2011, 10).

In Tunisia the result is an elite system run by older leaders including some who have had experience in political maneuvering and negotiation and others who have not, analyzed in the chapter by ben Hafaiedh and Zartman. Stability can be upset by fringe groups, such as Salafists, with votes that would be useful to al-Nahdha in future elections. More important strains come from hardliners within parties, holding sharper policy images and restive under older moderate leadership; more radical leaders in al-Nahdha with followers to back them, and more integral modernists and secularists on the other side, became locked in hostile visions of each other and suspicious negotiations for the shape of the New Order. The issue is whether constitutional legitimacy and provisions come from transcendental doctrine and belief, excluding nonbelievers, or from liberal practice and precedent, including believers, and whether zero-sum distributive concessions or positive-sum integrative consensus define the New Order. But the final challenge lies in waiting: the mass of dissatisfied *muntafadin* who made the uprising, who made up much of the 50 percent of the eligible voters who did not participate in the 2011 elections and still stayed home in the 2014 elections, who have been conducting vigorous tacit negotiations as civil society demonstrators but who disdain parties and formal politics in their still unsatisfied quest for dignity, liberty, and citizenship.

P4a. The first, *competing* pattern involves a multiparty system (even though with some larger members) that negotiates coalitions and constitutions with one eye on implications for the New Order and the other on electoral politics. A large ideological party stimulates the creation of a large heterogeneous countercoalition; other smaller parties keep the system multiparty and not bipolar.

The *pacting system* as evolved in Egypt and Yemen provides a potentially durable but unstable dynamic between two or three parties as in a seesaw. Continual although often tacit negotiation characterizes the system, in which each party tries to gain an advantage but is not able to muster enough to upset the seesaw. As long as both parties recognize the strengths and limits of the other and agree to keep their place on the seesaw, the pattern works. Since one of the parties is descended from the Old Order and the other was a contending player in it, they are experienced in negotiation and system maintenance, the one committed to remain part of the system and the other committed to become part of it. This sort of tacit pacting can obtain for a long time, durable and stable in its base but up and down as the weight of one side or the other shifts at any given moment. As seen in a larger context, a bipolar system can be quite stable, leading the sides to negotiate conflict management and even cooperative agreements (Kanet and Kolodziej 1991), all the while trumpeting how inimical the other side is and probing to make a final strategic move that will finally give it the edge. Stability is maintained as long as both sides prefer the dynamic balancing to a costly stab at dominance.

Even more than in the competitive system, outsiders and specifically the *muntafadin* are excluded. In both Egypt and Yemen those who made the uprising are not able to organize enough to be a player in the game in their own right, only an adjunct to the tacit bargaining between the two organizations. In both cases there are liberal and leftist parties lying around to form a third side, but they cannot get organized, and many of the youth are simply opposed to organization, negotiation, and partisan engagement; the most they can do is to go back to the streets and squares to provide bargaining power behind one of the two protagonists' demands (Trager 2011).

However, like any seesaw, pacting is inherently unstable. If one party gains a real advantage, the equilibrium is destroyed, and the game of seeking momentary advantage inherently drives the parties to look for an opportunity to seek permanent advantage. There is always the chance that one side on the seesaw will drop talking and go for broke, seeking to take over the system and stop negotiating temporary agreements with the other side, and the dynamics of the relationship drive or tempt each party to try for a final advantage. A single challenge too sharply posed by one side can lead the other to jump off the seesaw and let the opponent crash or to push the fulcrum of the seesaw in its favor by changing the rules or redefining the system. Ironically, an election pitting parties for a winning edge can upset the balance by according one side decisive legitimacy. Even when the balance is in jeopardy, negotiation continues, but with existential overtones, no longer for balance but for life. This drives the system from wary cooperation to a security dilemma.

In the Egyptian case, an unusual triangular relationship emerged involving the military (SCAF) backed by the courts, the Brotherhood's Freedom and Justice Party (FJP), and the uprisers (street, left, and liberals) (Trager 2011; Arjomand 2013), neither able to eliminate the other, as in a similar face-off in the 1950s (Alexander

2011). The remaining forces of the Old Order incarnated in the military and judiciary were initially not interested in restoration, in part because they did not have the strength to accomplish it and reverse the *intifada*, and in part because their interest was in containing the Brotherhood and preserving their position, political but above all economic, but not in governing. "The SCAF wants to manage and not rule," noted an Egyptian commentator (Kirkpatrick 2012b). The Islamist movement with its Freedom and Justice Party (FJP), the strongest (nonmilitary) organization of the transition, despite its tidal wave strength was initially not strong enough to wipe away the military but pursued a vigorous rivalry, interspersed with common cause to preserve its own position when it suited. The heterogeneous clump of youth that Raouf and El-Raggal in their chapter identify as a rhizome or an energy, plus labor and liberals that all made the revolution, was strong enough to wield demonstrative violence, but only in support of one side or another, not organized enough to be a negotiating partner of its own.

The pacting negotiations went on and off in Egypt through 2011–2012, with the Brotherhood repeatedly pushing the military into concessions—in election timing, military powers, parliamentary duties, among others—through the threat and use of the uprisers' violence, frightening the military lest it run out of control (Trager 2011). The military and the National Democratic Party, still in charge of the government, made common cause with the Muslim Brethren in early March 2011 to write eight constitutional amendments that provided for accelerated elections in September and ran the amendments through a national referendum on 19 March 2011. The liberal uprisers demanded a new constitution first but then negotiated with the Brotherhood to gain its support in exchange for its participation in renewed demonstrations in July to press for broader substantive demands—"Revolution First"—and a longer electoral preparation period. When the protesters dropped their "constitution first" demand, the Brotherhood supported their 8 July Day of Persistence demonstrations for later elections. The SCAF then in October pulled back under liberal pressure to establish a more spaced schedule culminating in presidential elections in 2013. The Brethren's trade-off was not to run candidates in more than a third of the districts—which it then broke—and not to run for president—which it also broke—in exchange for September elections while the opposing parties were still unorganized (Kirkpatrick 2011a).

The Brotherhood-SCAF pact was then renewed in late November by the negotiation—boycotted by the liberal parties—of a more detailed and accelerated schedule for a constitution and a presidential election in June 2012 in exchange for a truce in demonstrations, although the agreement appeared less to be negotiated horizontally at the meeting between the two sides than vertically by the military in confrontation with the prospect of increased street protests, much like the Nahdha and street negotiations in Tunisia. "They did not offer anything new; they are just bargaining with the people," commented an excluded dissident (Kirkpatrick 2011a).

As the parliamentary elections proceeded between November 2011 and January 2012, the Brotherhood's FJP withdrew in mid-December from the advisory council that, with the SCAF, was to appoint the constituent assembly (Kirkpatrick 2011b). The party then returned to nominate a slate containing, illegally, a large number of parliamentarians who were FJP members, which the SCAF then disallowed, leaving the constituent council in limbo. The FJP won an overwhelming majority with its Salafist allies, the Nour party, in parliament (43 percent and 24 percent, respectively), which the Supreme Constitutional Court dissolved in June. It also won the presidency on 23–24 May and 16–17 June 2012 with 52 percent of the 52 percent of eligible voters who voted, right after the parliamentary dissolution. Newly elected president Mohamed Morsi then struck from his new position of authority to cancel the parliamentary dissolution in the constitutional declaration of 12 August and took over the SCAF's full executive powers for the duration of the transition. "It's a chessboard," declared a Brotherhood spokesman: "They [the SCAF] made a move and we made a move" (Kirkpatrick 2012a), but the SCAF responded with martial law, which the courts then suspended. "All of that was a result of negotiations between the military and the Muslim Brotherhood in the last 24 hours," explained an Egyptian lawyer. "The military are giving a few things to the Muslim Brotherhood and keeping what is essential" (Kirkpatrick 2012b).

But then Morsi declared full and unreviewable powers for himself on 22 November and pushed a constitution to his liking through the constituent assembly and then a referendum a month later, without negotiating with the opposition, now organized as the National Salvation Front. The constitution received 64 percent of the 33 percent of eligible voters who turned out. Morsi also removed the aged leadership of the army and put in his own appointees, headed by Gen. Abdel Fatah al-Sisi. Incensed by the authoritarian turn of the president, huge demonstrations broke out on 30 June 2013, and both national and international figures urged Morsi to negotiate a consensual formula. "He just did not see the need to compromise," said an EU diplomat (ICG 2013). He refused, so General al-Sisi arrested him on 3 July, dissolved parliament, cancelled the constitution, banned the Brotherhood, and put in his own government in early August, reversing the *intifada* (ICG 2013). Al-Sisi then resigned as general and was elected president on 26–28 May with 97 percent of the 48 percent of the eligible voters who voted, after his constitution was approved on 14–15 January by 98 percent of the 37 percent of eligible voters who voted. The pacting was over, and the repression began.

Yemen's Long Track version of the seesaw took sustained negotiations, accelerated by violence, to evict the autocrat, leaving half-ousted, half-incoming elements to make a pact, as the chapter by Abdullah Hamidaddin describes (ICG 2012, 13; Kasinof 2011). A year of complex negotiations over the single demand for President Saleh's resignation, mediated by the Gulf Cooperation Council, the U.S. embassy, and the UN special envoy, Jamal Ben Omar, produced a proposal close to the finally adopted solution, for the transfer of powers to the vice president, Abdo Robo Mansour al-Hadi, rapidly followed by elections. Violence broke out between Saleh's family and army and his General People's Congress (GPC), on one side, and the opposing pieces of the army of Gen. Ali Mohsen al-Ahmar and the al-Ahmar brothers (no relation) and their Joint Meeting Parties (JMP), culminating in Saleh's hospitalization in Saudi Arabia with serious wounds, while his vice president was in effect a transitional president. A UN Security Council threat of sanctions brought agreement for Saleh to step down (but not out) in exchange for amnesty on 23 November 2011; Hadi was elected president in February 2012. The result was a tacit pact between the two forces, with the original liberal and leftist protesters and regional rebels looking in from the outside, resentful. The agreement also created an all-encompassing National Dialogue to contain the pact and work out a New Order and a constitution. The Dialogue continued the negotiation process within a larger and open venue, culminating in January 2014 guidelines for the new, federal constitution.

However, new forces entered the bargaining, and the old forces continued their maneuvers on the pacting seesaw, reviving the tribal rivalries and adding a broader sectarian dimension and additional foreign involvement. A lingering dissident movement from the north with ties to Iran, the Zaidi (Shiʿi) Huthis, reemerged in April to inject the sectarian issue and claim to speak for the poor. It destroyed the base of the al-Ahmar faction and with it the position of the Muslim Brotherhood and pro-Saudi party, Islah, and its broader coalition, the JMP (Schmitz 2014). Saleh, restive in unemployment, encouraged the Huthis, who had arrived at the gates of the capitol by the autumn of 2014, in order to undercut the position of the JMP and also of his successor, Hadi, and particularly his ineffective government (Greenfield and Milbert 2014). These developments in turn encouraged the Hirak movement seeking independence of the south (former Aden) to press its issue. Yemen's pacting sought to rise above the traditional tribal maneuvering that, in its way, had held the country together, but the religious issue and sectarian divide brought the country close to civil war again.

> **P4b.** In the *pacting* pattern, a bipolar system develops when neither side is likely to fall or push the other off the seesaw. The inherent outbidding characteristic of the system makes it durable but unstable, awaiting the time when one side moves to unseat the other or new sides appear to complicate the bipolarity.

The *fragmented system* is the most unstable and the most diverse in its negotiations, although its very instability makes it long lasting and impervious to evolution. The parties themselves are inward looking and are wary about negotiating for coalition and formulation with each other, which requires pressure and mediation from the outside. As already noted, warriors don't negotiate; they leave that to diplomats and politicians, whom they regard as selling out their hard-won victories. They become even more wary of any negotiated move that would weaken their position and tip the stalemate against them. The necessary de-escalation is difficult for the warriors, raising again the Tactical Question with increased ferocity. They tend to remain in a military mode, retreating to sectarian identities and territorial controls, hostile to any attempt to establish a central authority that is not theirs. The situation of the militias in Libya and Syria, but also Yemen, is the result.

As the war continues and when the war is over, unlike the other two systems, there are no rules of the game; indeed, there is no game. Interests, cohesion, and leadership devolve to the component fragments, and those who would aspire to lead a national coalition with a national vision are not yet in the dominant course. In the absence of large encompassing organizations, organization for bargaining power is found in small parties and militias, where negotiation focuses inward within these groups to assure identity and cohesion. They develop territorially limited and identity-centered interests, which they protect with central representation but not central rulership.

Negotiations for formulation in a fragmented system are entirely dependent on distributive negotiations for coalition, not the expected reverse. Work on multilateral negotiation suggests three patterns of building issue coalitions (Singh 2008; Narlikar 2003; Zartman 1987b, 2012; Dupont 1994; Hampson 1995; Ives 2003; Odell, 2000, 2006): a *concentrating* process around a central core where other parties are brought in, often by an exchange of favors under an ideological umbrella; an *aggregating* process where many pieces trade support without much concern for their coherence, producing a spotty and largely procedural agreement on how to deal with substantive issues later; and a *coagulating* process in which a few blocking coalitions consolidate internally and negotiate temporary agreements by shifting pairs (potentially producing a pacting pattern).

The first implies some kind of organization, an idea, and elements of power in the central core. The second lacks leadership and direction, except through mediators or regime builders whose purpose is simply to achieve an agreement, producing a result that is often procedural only and leaving orientation or direction to subsequent maneuvering. The third involves competing, narrowly focused leaders, at best dedicated to maintaining the system rather than providing societal vision. (Other patterns may also develop). The first is characterized by vision and can be integrative, the second and third by distributive bargaining over interests. Interests are the coalescing material of the demand-bearing groups that develop as great coalitions break apart and the groups look inside themselves. But fragmented systems never had a great coalition, and the more prolonged the war the greater the difficulty in cobbling one together. Interests are necessary to the working of a pluralistic society, but together they can also produce indirection and deadlock.

In the absence of the elements of an aggregating negotiation process, the other two appear most likely. Examples are seen in the competitive and pacted systems respectively, but the choice remains open for the Long Track fractured systems.

It might be thought that an authoritarian regime would prove the *casus foederis* for opposition parties to aggregate against a common enemy. Perhaps counterintuitively, the reverse is true. The authoritarian regime used its *mukhabarat* to divide and demoralize the opposition, and trained them so well that they remained under effects even after they were freed from the *mukhabarat*, as the cases have shown. The necessary secrecy and inward-focused attentions of the fragmented parties, fixated on identity and sectarian beliefs, makes them fight for their interests to prevail. The end comes only with general fatigue or domination; fatigue is rarely generalized at the same time, and domination requires huge force and inspiration.

But societies can stand pluralistic disorder only so long until they either feel a need for an aggregating process that mobilizes them behind a banner, aided by a little coercion, or are simply wearied by the ongoing violence and "accept any authority that can restore a semblance of normal life" (Hubbard and Anonymous 2014). Caught between the shattered Old Order and the elusive New, they seek simply order. The concentrating party gathers followers as True Believers, but also dissatisfied protesters and alienated populations, and it surges against weaker rebels and invalid governments alike. Islamist extremism lends itself well to the opportunity. Taking advantage of the disorder and infighting of the FSA and rebel groups in Syria, al-Nusra and the ISIS, with the initial approbation of al-Qaeda, arose over 2013 as the most effective fighting force, drawing volunteers from other groups that did not have the means to feed and arm them. Neither Libya, after the overthrow, nor Syria, still awaiting the overthrow, show a clear direction for climbing out of fragmenting. The Libyan pattern, at least, developed an NTC early on in the rebellion, but it fell apart after the 2012 election, as Mezran and Alunni's chapter shows. Syria started fragmented from the beginning, as Aita's chapter shows.

> P4c. The *fragmenting* pattern is produced by a Long Track lost in violence, where small, suspicious groups born of the conflict have difficulty in negotiating either coalitions or formulas. Any negotiations are highly distributive, resisting integration. Absent a strong party, the pattern is one of instability and a succession of temporary relationships.

Two other patterns occur when the Old Order is able to resist the *intifada*. *Adapting* occurs when the Old Order is strong enough to resist the challenge of the *intifada* but only by adopting milder versions of its demands and only when the demands are themselves moderate. Negotiations occur explicitly but secretly within the corridors of the Old Order and tacitly between sides but are denied. The *intifada* is too absolutely and relatively weak to enter into a pact or a responsible coalition, as in Morocco described by Hamblin and Algeria described by Roberts.

In Morocco, the monarchy, already preparing a constitution, undercut the demands of the 20 February Movement and its mobilizing possibilities faded away as its leaders and their demands were co-opted by the *makhzen*. But with the pressure gone, the real challenge to the Old (or Revived) Order is to implement its project and become a truly Renewed Order. The same obtains in the very different neighbor, Algeria, where the holder of order is not a monarch but a junta. Mini-*intifadat* in 2008 and 2011 were undercut by government largesse, co-opting negotiations and security crackdowns, and the uprisings lost their mobilizing potential against the background of a population rendered gun-shy by the memory of the bitter campaign against terrorism in the 1990s. After the 2014 presidential elections, the comatose political system awaited overdue succession and uprisings.

> **P4d.** An *adapting* pattern occurs when the uprising is strong enough to pose a challenge but weak enough to be undercut by a solid Old Order. The challenge remains in terms of the implementation of adopted provisions.

Repression occurs when the Old Order is so strong that it can quash the *intifada*, without adopting any of its demands as in adaptive patterns. Repression is rarely a definitive response, and so the uprising can be expected to appear again, probably with lessons learned, participants wisened, and radicalism accentuated. Complex internal negotiations on proper courses tear apart both sides, to the profit of the hardliners and preventing solid negotiations between the sides. Bahrain is the example presented by Meijer and Danckaert, and Syria by Aita, against all expectations (except Asad's).

> **P4e.** A *repressing* pattern occurs when the Old Order feels strong enough to crush the uprising without paying attention to any of its demands, hardening itself as a result. A worse reiteration of the challenge is the likely result.

THE ENDGAME: ELECTIONS, CONSTITUTIONS, FORMULAS, AND OUTCOMES

There are rare times when resistance and rebellion against the established order are not costly because of dwindling payoffs for loyalty and relaxed policing of exit, and the people can rise up and raise their voices against the Order and the rebellion becomes overt. If then the Old Order breaks, order is up for grabs (Hirschman 1070; Tilly 1991). The goal of the *intifada* in the overthrow of the Old Order is its replacement by a New one. In a few cases, this means rebuilding a collapsed state, where the conflict has destroyed state institutions and capacities, notably in the case of fragmented transitions, in Libya, Yemen, and Syria. More frequently, it is a matter of reforming state structures, deciding what to retain as compatible with formulations of a New Order and what to revise.

The path to institutionalization is one of constitution making, the culmination of the various negotiation processes. Constitutions are the ultimate field of negotiations for formulation, as they establish the shape of the New Order. But they also open the field of negotiations for coalition, as parties seek to know with whom to cooperate, during constitution building and government thereafter. A constitution should be a consensual document, a sociopolitical contract among the governed (through their representatives) about the way that governance should be exercised, the result of integrative negotiations that bridge differing visions. Consensus on the document and consensus building in the process of its creation do not mean that the parties cannot have positions, interests, and values, but only that they will use them to create a broadly unifying and workable contract. At the beginning and the end of this process, negotiation cedes its primacy to the vote, although it still remains an underlying and preparatory decision-making process. Elections are the result of more specific negotiations for formulation, in the type of polling regime chosen, and they are the scene for negotiations for coalition, in the congregations and alliances made for the campaign and then for governing afterward.

There has been a widespread debate in the countries and among commentators as to whether elections should precede or succeed the new constitution, but the debate begs the question of who has the legitimacy to do the drafting. That legitimacy can only come from a truly revolutionary movement or from an expression of public will. In the absence of the former in any of the Arab Spring countries, the appointing body has to be elected. But another consideration enters, in the matter of consensus that the constitution for a New Order requires. Election is one thing, testing the strength of political parties, but the drafting of a broadly accepted sociopolitical contract requires participation of other walkers of life than merely political parties, as encompassed in civil society and then also legal expertise. Thus the appointing body needs to proceed from elections but then to create a more inclusive agency for drafting the provisions of the new structure of governance to meet the double criteria of legitimacy.

Half the eligible Tunisian voters voted for the Constituent Assembly in 2011 and 68 percent for the National Assembly in 2014 (there was no constitutional referendum), a third of Egyptian voters voted in the constitutional referenda in 2012 and 2014, and 60 percent of the eligible Libyans voted for the General National Congress (GNC) in July 2012 but only 18 percent in the House of Representatives HR election two years later (that the GNC understandably declared invalid, to which the House returned the favor). The rest feel unconsulted and unrepresented. Negotiations did indeed take place, but they were less widespread than necessary to establish a consensus on the New Order, were often restricted in participation, were distributive in process, were characteristically tacit in nature, and were often replaced by heated declarations of positions rather than constructive exchanges of purposes. It is becoming apparent that consensus is an approach too little practiced, as parties shied from the need to share a goal and talk their way to it. Of the disputes leading to Egypt's constitutional referendum, Justice Minister Ahmed Mekki said, "I blame all of Egypt, because they do not know how to talk to each other" (Kirkpatrick and Fahim 2012).

In Tunisia, a National Constituent Assembly was also tasked with serving as a governing body until the constitution could be established to create a legitimate parliament; it did little as a government but spent twice the allotted one year squabbling over the regime's structure, thereby wasting its legitimacy. In addition, Tunisia's government was a heterogeneous troika, inhibiting any agreement of deductive principles, so that in the end the nation rose in demonstrations to demand a broadly representative drafting process. In the process the constitutional negotiations were conducted directly between the Islamist party and civil society, in the absence of a strong opposition party. Again and again, Al-Nahdha launched extreme positions but then pulled back when faced with a strong reaction from civil society and the street, a continuation of the negotiations between the uprising and the interim government in 2011 (Chakroune 2013). The negotiations brought in a new opposition party, Nida Tunis, from outside parliament, and then an overarching National Dialogue led by the labor union UGTT and business, civil rights, and bar associations, to produce the broader agency that the process required. The Troika negotiated actively among themselves but less with the opposition, whose votes they needed to pass the constitution, until they were forced by public outcry to negotiate in the dialogue forum and then to resign.

In Egypt and Libya, the newly elected Peoples Assembly and General National Congress, respectively, were to elect a constitutional committee. Egypt's was supposed to be constituted of nonparliamentarians to assure pluralistic civil society representation, but this was set aside in practice by an elected, essentially single-party parliament that appointed its own members to the committee and forced out the opposition. The liberal-leftist parties in Egypt with less than a quarter of the Assembly seats either boycotted or were excluded from membership in the Constituent Commission, leaving the Islamist FJP and the ultra-Islamist Nour party a free hand. As in Tunisia, the opposition called on the street to increase their bargaining power; in Tunisia the Islamist party heard and retreated, whereas in Egypt the government called on its own streets and plunged ahead on its own draft, over the abyss and into the face of the army. After the military coup, the 2013 constitution was redrafted by a restored military-approved constitutional committee. Libya's constitutional committee was finally, incompletely, directly elected by 30 percent of the eligible voters (or 40 percent of the eligible voters in the districts that voted) in February 2014, still looking for acceptance in the current anarchy, as the country turned its back on the issue and fought it out between Islamist Tripolitanian GNC militia and secular HR Cyrenaican armies. Yemen's National Dialogue laid out some constitutional ideas and then passed on the drafting to a committee that was lost in the emerging tribal and sectarian war. Morocco's constitutional committee met the criterion of broad representation but was appointed by the king without any element of electoral legitimacy.

Elections that have taken place in Arab Spring countries have been tinkered with a bit but are relatively free and fair, with widely varying participation. Participation rose in Tunisia after the constitution was adopted and fell in Libya as anarchy set in, as might be expected. Electoral regimes address a range of formulas that help shape the New Order: first past the post (FPTP) or winner take all (WTA) single-member districts to assure constituency contact, proportional representation (PR) to assure minority representation, list systems to assure party control, at-large seats to assure national identification, allocated seats to assure minority representation, runoff elections to assure majority winners, and so on (Reynolds and Reilly 1997; Brynen et al. 2012, ch. 7; Brownlee, Masoud, and Reynolds 2014). The Tunisian regime was a closed list PR system, the same as for the majority of the seats under the previous Order, favoring party organization and many parties; independents had to form lists of their own. Had the High Authority adopted a different voting system that favors larger parties, al-Nahdha would have won 70 percent of the seats in the NCA. The Libyan regime was the subject of repeated negotiations and several versions, ending as a hybrid with 80 of the seats chosen by PR from among national party lists and the remaining 120 from FPTP single-seat districts; in the 2014 elections, there were no parties, only individual candidates. In Egypt two-thirds of the seats were filled by a PR list system, and a third were reserved for party candidates running FPTP as independents in large districts with, as under the Old Order, half the seats reserved for labor/farm candidates.

Electoral regimes can favor or impede negotiating for coalition. The Tunisian regime did little to push the parties into coalitions, but the appearance of a dominant party impelled the opposition to coalesce. In Egypt, on the other hand, seventeen parties negotiated alliances and many of the independents also negotiated pairing with a worker or *fellah* or with the FJP (Hassan 2011), and in Libya the National Forces Alliance that won the largest number (39!) of the GNC 200 seats was itself a composite of sixty parties (Barfi 2012; *Libya Herald*, 19 July 2012). In the 2012 Egyptian Peoples Assembly of 498 members, the FJP won 235 seats and the Salafist Light (Nour) party 123, giving almost a majority to the FJP and 75 percent to the combined Islamists (when they stayed combined), the rest going mainly to ten liberal and leftist parties organized into three blocs forming a bandwagon around a leading party. In the next Egyptian Peoples Assembly of 567 members, the FLP was banned from participating and the election was still pending in mid-2015. The FJP won a third (10.5 million) of the votes in the 2011–2012 legislative elections but their candidate Mohamed Morsi received a quarter (5.7 million) of the votes in the first round of the May 2012 presidential elections and won in the runoff by only 882,000 votes with 52 percent of the electorate voting; in May 2014, ex-general Abdel Fatah al-Sisi won 98 percent of the 47 percent of the eligible voters who voted. In sum, the Tunisian and Egyptian electoral regimes favored the development of a few larger organized parties, and the Libyan regime worked in the opposite direction; the Egyptian results favored little negotiations with other, minority parties, and the Tunisian and Libyan results made active post-election negotiations necessary.

A resting point—scarcely an end—in the transition and in the present analysis is the new constitution itself, a stage attained in Morocco, Tunisia, and Egypt (and then annulled and reissued), and was in the works but suspended for the moment by the civil wars in Libya and Yemen. The constitution gives an institutionalized form to the New Order and sets the rules for its evolution (Brown 2008, 64). Constitutions have two faces, establishing the powers of government for its citizens and protecting the rights of citizens from the government. Optimally, they work together, but the extreme of either is antithetical to the other (Arjomand 1992; Cameron 2013). The fact that the two stand both in opposition and in cooperation with each other sets the stage for negotiation. It is the mix of the two that is salutary and delicate. These two questions have dominated the constitutional debates in various forms over the governmental structure and the place of religion (shariʿa).

The major structural question has concerned the choice between a presidential or a parliamentary system, the subject of much back-and-forth negotiating and eventual compromises that can also affect decisions made on other provisions. A presidential regime can be protective or repressive, and a parliamentary regime can be purposive or stalemated (Elster 2000). As a result of this debate, the basic nature of the government system has floated during negotiations. Large Islamic parties, in Egypt and Tunisia, have favored a parliamentary system, confident of their success at the polls for the legislatures, while liberal and leftist parties have tended to favor a presidential or mixed system, confident of their success at the polls for president, despite the fact that it was a presidential system against which the uprising occurred and a mixed system of cohabitation frequently provides incoherence and stalemate. However, a curious shift happened on the way to the referendum: in Egypt, the final drafts approved in the December 2012 and January 2014 referenda gave a strong role to the president, as assumed both by the FJP president Morsi even before the constitution was adopted but also by his toppled authoritarian predecessor, Mubarak, and his successor, Sisi. In fact, in Egypt the constitution established a "tricephalic" system, a "semi-presidential" regime with the armed forces' autonomy protected, for its own sake and as an overarching institution of government. Negotiations within the Tunisian constitutional committees deadlocked over the two models of government until the ruling Troika came to a minimum agreement on a bicephalic system with substantial presidential powers. Another form of the same issue then appeared before the Independent Election Committee on the election schedule; al-Nahdha wanted parliamentary elections first, the opposition wanted presidential elections first. The obvious compromise of simultaneous elections was adopted by the commission, then reversed in favor of October 2014 parliamentary elections and November presidential elections with a runoff in December. Mohammed Ghannouchi then proposed a single consensus candidate for president, in a transparent move to avoid an avowedly anti-Nahdha president. In the end, in the December runoff, the election showed a deeply and evenly divided electorate with 56 percent of the vote for Qaid es-Sebsi of Nida Tunis and 44 percent for Mohammed Marzouki, the proposed "consensual" candidate. In Morocco, the answer to the structural question was provided by the monarchy, under pressure from the 20 February Movement, to give greater participation in governance to the elected parliament; the 2014 constitution moved in that direction ever so slightly, with consummation awaiting the test of practice.

On the place of religion in the constitution, regimes vary. Shariʿa has been the "primary source" of legislation in past and present Egyptian constitutions and has been absent from both the 1959 and 2014 Tunisian constitution, where it is not even clear whether Islam is the religion of the state or of the nation. These two dispositions frame rather well the debate on the surface, but the real debate is over the implications of the constitutional article(s) and whether they can be turned to support a religious interpretation by a later government. The second level of the debate on religion involves the whole area of civil rights—whether there is freedom of worship or freedom of beliefs, whether human rights are "universal" (hence based on the human-made Human Rights Declaration) or come from God (hence subject to *fatwa*), whether women are fully equal or "have their place," whether minority communities are protected in the constitutional system or are folded into a single community (*ummah*), whether the freedom of the press and expression is protected or whether it is circumscribed by respect for religion and state security, among others. A solid bill of rights implemented by government protects the citizens, but the "right" of a minority to assume for all the proper way to implement its religion or of an ethnic militia to defend its people against perceived threats is tyranny and anarchy. In between, negotiations fill the grey area, and the Tunisian and Egyptian constitutions now stand for their test. On a whole series of provisions—the shariʿa issue in March 2012, the women's rights issue in August, the blasphemy issue in October, the universality of human rights in April 2013, Islam and the state in September, and control of the government in January 2014—al-Nahdha gave way to more liberal formulations. In the 2014 constitution in Egypt, human rights were generally freed of the restraints related to religion in the 2012 document but were still subject to legislative and judicial restrictions (Rashwan 2013; Al-Tawy 2013). Beyond the constitution, the government—legislature and courts—adopted its own more restrictive rules. With the Libyan and Yemeni constitutions still to come, the new constitutions of the Arab Spring have been generally liberal in protecting citizens and coherent in providing government powers, with religious impositions kept at bay.

Given the importance of the constitution as a step, if not full closure, in the transition, it is remarkable that there has been so little negotiation over the broad principles—the true formula—governing the New Order, as was done in the governance transition in South Africa, as described in the Anstey chapter. Commentators have noted that the inductive process of composing the constitution could have been avoided and greater coherence imposed if the parties had first established a declaration of intent or a common sense of governing principles (Pickard 2012, 5). As far as they have come, constitutions in the Arab Spring tend to be procedural rules of the game rather than substantive visions for a New Order, making symbolic nods in various directions that can either remain general pronouncements (as in many constitutions) or be interpreted by successive governments to drive extreme measures (Duverger 1968; Ashour 2012). In both Egypt and Tunisia, even though they mark public involvement in the constitutional negotiations, the negotiated compromises are indeed concessions, the mark of distributive bargaining. They do not represent integrative agreement on a *projet de société*, a consensus on a sociopolitical contract. They continue to be dogged by the liberals' "Trojan Horse" or "camel's nose" fear, that ambiguous wording used to cover over differences could be interpreted later by Islamic authorities to facilitate an Islamist takeover in substance, and the reverse fear of the Islamists that the secularists want to remove them from the political process, as the post-coup treatment of the Brotherhood in Egypt evidences. Both countries still remain very divided societies. Hence the two visions of a New Order can make distributive concessions but not integrated constructions of a consensual vision. In Tunisia the division is manifest on the political level, in Egypt on the level of violence and repression.

If material progress fails, people turn to ideology—a solid coherent formula—to provide an explanation for present failure and a promise for a glorious future instead. Populations who previously have been through unsatisfactory encounters with ideology often tend to be prone to repeat the search for ideological fixes later rather than giving them up for greater pragmatism. But stagnation and a return to dissatisfaction and alienation also tend to be accompanied by a return to an authoritarian regime, impelled by a need to overcome the breakdown in order that the dissatisfaction brings. In some cases, these events may also require an external enemy, and even external aggression, to support the authoritarian order and focus discontent outside; radical Islam is skilled in finding external enemies. An uprising is a huge amount of political energy and activity, beyond what people are used to, and they become tired. Revolutions peter out, and *intifadat* water down, leaving political activity to the few people committed to seeking and using power.

One ready group waiting in the wings is composed of members of the Old Order. Restoration is an alternative left over from the French Revolution, more recently endorsed by attempts at Russian and Eastern European and African democratization; accompanying chapters by Siniša Vuković and Mark Anstey show how this has worked in Serbia and South Africa. Members of the Old Order know how to run a state, win elections, restore security, and repress radicals, including religious devotees. In Egypt, the regime of Mubarak returned in force, even to the point of lifting charges against the former authoritarian ruler; in Syria, Asad never left; in Yemen, Saleh plotted a return, to more complicated tribal maneuvering; in Morocco, the king and his *makhzen* remained in control; in Algeria, both the ruler and the state persevered despite advanced sclerosis. Even in Tunisia, Qaid es-Sebsi led the restoration of the Destourians, doubtless to the betterment of the country but formalizing a deep cleavage in the body politic. Recuperation of the better, experienced elements of the Old Order is not incompatible within pursuit of the dreams and demands of the *intifada*, but it must be done through the conscious negotiation of consensus over a new synthesis to be effective.

Particularly after an intense effort such as an *intifada*, people become eager to find order, often any order, including even a nostalgic hankering for the Old Order that was at least orderly. "We got rid of a dictatorship, now we have anarchy," said a disgruntled Tunisian as early as May 2011 (Minoui 2011). Roving gangs, settling accounts, indecisive policy, resurgent identities and their hostilities, unsatisfied demands, lingering crises, and above all the need for jobs that was the background for the uprising in the first place all feed the human desire for a modicum of order and direction toward a normal situation. People cry for a return to order, and alienation, characteristic of the Old Order, returns when order is not restored. A continued downturn following the initial uprising in the middle run can provide an opening for local ideological forms and authoritarian order, taking the form in the Middle East of a commander on a white horse or a guru under a green banner or just remnants of the Old Order trying to put their house together again after the hurricane. By the fifth year of the *intifada*, the white horseman is ahead thus far, in Egypt and Syria, although the guru might be gaining in Syria; the guru tried at the wrong time in Egypt and failed to provide either order or jobs. When a guru fails, his cause fails with him and is discredited; when a new authoritarian fails, he merely clamps down harder. Hovering over such dramatic failures is the disembodied ghost of the ancien régime. If at all, the occasion for a radical Islamist takeover is only later when enforced order again fails. It must be remembered that all the Islamist takeovers that have taken place to date are not because of a rise in religious fervor but are a popular protest against corrupt, inefficient government, as in Iran in 1979, Sudan in 1989, Algeria in 1991, Afghanistan in 1996, Somalia in 2000, Gaza in 2006, Egypt, Syria, and Iraq in 2012, Iraq again and Yemen in 2014, among others.

P5a. If the negotiated transitions restore order, make progress toward providing economic growth, and "build political relationships based on their commitment to a vision of a mutually bearable future . . . as a kind of inter-communal peace-treaty," the process will result in a dynamic stability among moderate programmatic differences (Weiner 2011, 10, 11; Morrow 2005);

P5b. If not, the process will return to a search for order and will open to ideological absolutism or authoritarian regression, or simply to a return to the Old Order in new clothes.

P5c. These alternatives may meet in a single option.

The *intifadat* of the Arab Spring provide an exciting opportunity for their countries that carries the possibility of creating a New Order of participatory politics and accountable governance where they have rarely if ever been known before, with responsive decision making conducted through negotiation and voting. They also opened the door to a collapse of hope and a return to the same type of authoritarian or ideological regimes that the country has known so well, with decision making exclusively an executive exercise, backed by the use of force. The choice lies with the groups of the population who have been invigorated by the uprising. The most important element in bringing a positive outcome is the development of solid organizing and negotiating skills, so that decisions are made in the public interest and obscurantist forces are not allowed to turn fatigue, disorder, and leaderlessness to their advantage. Such skills include the ability to press to a decision, the concern for keeping a broad coalition together, the formulation of a creative and realistic vision, the willingness to make trade-offs and coherent packages, and the understanding of moments of opportunity and timing. Otherwise, the uprisings will end in a downfall of opportunity.

The resulting challenge for the uprisers is to build a new state on the ruins of the hard state, collapsed or reformed, more of a liberation than a revolution (Arendt 1963; Dawisha 2013). As a liberation, the events recall the nationalist movement itself in the first wave of democratization that brought government back into the hands of the nation, over a half century ago, but then left the people out of its exercise. Later, another precedent, generally ignored, is the Sovereign National Conference movement two decades ago, when West and Central African civil society retook sovereignty in their hands in a dozen countries, overthrew the dictators, and installed the second wave of democratization (Zartman 1997a). Twenty years later, two of the twelve remain in democracy's hands. Eight Arab countries underwent an Arab Spring experience, and four have ousted their authoritarian ruler. As the African experience shows, the event does not guarantee results. The *intifada* still has to negotiate meaningful change to prove its impact.

Notes

1. It may be objected that this study ignores the economic factor, which some claim was the single decisive cause. Jobs and development do indeed come into play in the negotiations, but the focus here is on the process; a politico-economic study would be a welcome complement.

2. In the following discussion of sides, the terms *intifada* (pl. *intifadat*), *uprising*, *movement*, *insurgency*, and *protest* are used generically and synonymously, with no particular distinction

among them, since the individual countries are not agreed on the proper characterization; the same goes for *muntafad* (pl. *muntafadin*), *rebel*, *uprisers*, and *insurgents*, with *tahriris* and *street* referring specifically to those who took part in the demonstrations in the Cairo Liberation Square (*Midan al-tahrir)*, the Tunis Kasba, the Bahrain Pearl Roundabout, and elsewhere. The term *revolution* is also frequently used in the countries concerned, although the connotation to date is a political, not a social, revolution (Zartman 2014).

3. For similar categorizations see Haddad and Schwedler 2013, 212; and Kamrava 2013.

4. "The problem is that it's impossible to predict when a spark . . . will set off a mass incident," Shan Guangnai, Institute of Sociology of the Chinese Academy of Social Sciences, advising the Chinese government on mass incidents; *Science* 323: 574–575 (30 January 2009).

5. Significantly, the reverse causal relation—Short Track negotiations whose failure then produces warfare—does not seem to obtain.

6. When asked about the effect of his decade in exile in England, Ghannouchi said it convinced him of the value of democracy (conversation with the author, 1 December 2011).

7. Arjomand 2013 overdoes the distinction in saying that some transitions are negotiated, whereas revolutionary ones are not.

References

Alexander, Anne. 2011. "Brothers-in-Arms? The Egyptian military, the Ikhwan, and the Revolutions of 1952 and 2011." *Journal of North African Studies* 16, no. 4: 533–554.

Arendt, Hannah. 1963. *On Revolution*. New York: Viking.

Arjomand, Said Amir. 1992. "Constitutions and the Struggle for Political Order." *Archives européens de sociologie* 33, no. 1: 39–82.

———. 2013. "Revolution and Constitution in the Arab World." In *Beyond the Arab Spring*, edited by Mehran Kamrava. New York: Oxford University Press.

Arrow, Kenneth. 1974. *The Limits of Organization*. New York: W. W. Norton.

Ashour, Omar. 2012. "Egypt's Draft Constitution." *Brookings Opinions*, 21 December.

Badrawi, Hossam. 2011. "Revolution Viewed from Inside the Regime." *Cairo Review* 1, no. 1: 79–87.

Barfi, Barak. 2012. "Libya's Uncertain Post-Electoral Direction." *PolicyWatch* 1965. Washington, D.C.: Washington Institute of Near East Policy.

Barrouhi, Abdelazziz. 2011a. "La Grande Muette a dit 'non.'" *Jeune Afrique* 2611 (23 January): 32.

———. 2011b. "L'Homme qui a dit non." *Jeune Afrique* 2612 (30 January): 44–48.

Beinen, Joel, et al. 2010. *Justice for All: The Struggle for Worker Rights in Egypt*. Washington, D.C.: Solidarity Center.

Beinen, Joel, and Vairel Frederic, eds. 2011. *Social Movements Mobilization and Contestation in the Middle East and North Africa*. Stanford, Calif.: Stanford University Press.

Bellin, Eva, 2004. "The Robustness of Authoritarianism in the Middle East." *Comparative Politics* 36, no. 2: 139–157.

Bettaieb, Mohammed Salah. 2011. *Dégage*. Dhaka, Bangladesh: Alif.

Binnendijk, Anika, and Van Marovic. 2006. "Power and Persuasion." *Communist and Post-Communist Studies* 39, no. 3: 411–429.

Blidi, Amel. 2012. "C'est l'injustice et l'humiliation de tous les jours: La ogra, un mal algerien." *El Watan*, 7 June.

Brahimi, Alia. 2011. "Libya's Revolution." *Journal of North African Studies* 16, no. 4: 603–624.

Brinton, Crane. 1965. *Anatomy of Revolution*. New York: Vintage.

Broom, Leonard, and Philip Selznick. 1958. *Sociology: A Text with Adaptive Readings*. 2nd ed. Evanston, Ill.: Row, Peterson.

Brown, Nathan J. 2008. "Bargaining and Imposing Constitutions: Private and Public Interests in the Iranian, Afghani and Iraqi Constitutional Experiments." In *Constitutional Politics in the Middle East*, edited by Said Amir Arjomand, 63–76. Oxford: Hart.

Brownlee, Jason, Tarek Masoud, and Andrew Reynolds. 2014. *The Arab Spring: Pathways of Repression and Reform*. New York: Oxford University Press.

Brynen, Rex, Pete Moore, Bassel Salloukh, and Marie-Joelle Zahar. 2012. *Beyond the Arab Spring*. Boulder, Colo.: Lynne Rienner.

Cameron, Maxwell A. 2013. *Strong Constitutions: Social-Cognitive Origins of the Separation of Powers*. Oxford: Oxford University Press.

Carr, Edward Hallett. 1949. *The Twenty Years' Crisis, 1919–1939: An Introduction to the Study of International Relations*. London: Macmillan.

Casper, Gretchen, and Michelle M. Taylor-Robinson. 1996. *Negotiating Democracy: Transitions from Authoritarian Rule*. Pittsburgh: University of Pittsburgh Press.

Chakroune, Bouchra. 2013. "Bargaining for Peace." MAIA thesis, Johns Hopkins University, Bologna Center.

Chomiak, Laryssa, and John P. Entelis. 2011. "The Making of North Africa's Intifadas." *Middle East Report* 259: 8–15.

Clark, Janine. 2004. "Social Movement Theory and Patron Clientelism: Islamic Social Institutions." *Comparative Political Studies* 37 (October): 941–968.

———. 2012. "Islamist Movements and Democratic Politics." In *Beyond the Arab Spring*, edited by Rex Brynen, Pete Moore, Bassel Salloukh, and Marie-Joelle Zahar. Boulder, Colo.: Lynne Rienner.

Coddington, Alan. 1968. *Theories of the Bargaining Process*. Chicago: Aldine.

Cook, Steven A. 2007. *Ruling but Not Governing: The Military and Political Development in Egypt, Algeria, and Turkey*. Baltimore: Johns Hopkins University Press.

Coser, Lewis A. 2000. *Continuities in the Study of Social Conflict*. New York: Macmillan.

Dahl, Robert A. 1955. "Hierarchy, Democracy, and Bargaining in Politics and Economics." In *Research Frontiers in Politics and Government*, by Stephen K. Bailey et al. Washington, D.C.: Brookings Institution.

———. 1957. "A Rejoinder." *American Political Science Review* 51, no. 4 (December): 1053–1061.

Dawisha, Adeed. 2013. *The Second Arab Awakening: Revolution, Democracy, and the Islamist Challenge from Tunis to Damascus*. New York: W. W. Norton.

Dawisha, Adeed, and I. William Zartman, eds. 1988. *Beyond Coercion: The Durability of the Arab State*. London: Croom Helm.

Elster, John. 2000. *Ulysses Unbound*. Cambridge: Cambridge University Press.

della Porta, Donatella, and Sidney Tarrow, eds. 2005. *Transitional Protest and Global Activism: People, Passions, and Power*. Lanham, Md.: Rowman and Littlefield.

Denoeux, Guilan. 2001. "Challenges of Transition in Tunisia." Unpublished manuscript.

DiJohn, J. and J. Putzel, J. 2009. *Building the State and Securing Peace*. London: Department for International Development (DFID).

Donohue, William, and Moty Cristal. 2011. " Growing Out in Organization." In Zartman 2011.

Dorsey, James M. 2011. "Role of Arab Militaries in Popular Uprisings." *Middle East Studies* 3, no. 6: 473–476. http://www.middle-east-studies.net/archives/22784.

Druckman, Daniel. 1977. "Boundary Role Conflict." *Journal of Conflict Resolution* 21, no. 4: 87–111.

———. 1986. "Stages, Turning Points, and Crises." *Journal of Conflict Resolution* 30, no. 2: 327–360.

Dupont, Christophe. 1994. "Coalition Theory." In *International Multilateral Negotiations: Approaches to the Management of Complexity*, edited by I. William Zartman. San Francisco: Jossey-Bass.

Duverger, Maurice. 1968. *Institutions politiques et droit constitutionnel.* Paris: PUF.

Eckstein, Susan. 2001. *Power and Popular Protest: Latin American Social Movements*. Berkeley: University of California Press.

Fahmy, Nabil. 2011. "Arab Foreign Policy Shift." *Cairo Review of Global Affairs* 1, no. 1:101–111.

Follett, Mary. 2012. "Constructive Conflict." In *Sociology of Organizations: Structured and Relationships*, edited by Mary Godwyn and Jody Hoffer Gittell, 417–426. Thousand Oaks, Calif.: Sage.

Frank, Ruediger. 2011. "The Party as the Kingmaker: The Death of Kim Jong Il and Its Consequences for North Korea." *38 North*, 21 December. http://38north.org/2011/12/rfrank122111/.

Gelvin, James L. 2012. *The Arab Uprisings: What Everyone Needs to Know*. New York: Oxford University Press.

Ghali, Amine. 2011. "Tunisia's Constitutional Process: The Road Ahead." *Sada*, 9 December. http://carnegieendowment.org/sada/2011/12/09/tunisia-s-constitutional-process-road-ahead.

Greenfield, Danya, and Svetlana Milbert. 2014. "Protests in Yemen Expose Weak Governance and Poor Economic Planning." Atlantic Council, 2 September.

Guirguis, Dina. 2011. "Egyptian Liberals Compromise for the Sake of Dubious Unity." *PolicyWatch* 1830 (8 July). Washington, D.C.: Washington Institute for Near East Policy.

Gurr, Ted Robert. 1970. *Why Men Rebel.* Princeton, N.J.: Princeton University Press.

Habeeb, Mark. 1988. *Power and Tactics in International Negotiation: How Weak Nations Bargain with Strong Nations*. Baltimore: Johns Hopkins University Press.

Haddad, Bassam. 2012. "Syria's Stalemate: The Limits of Regime Resilience." *Middle East Policy* 19, no. 1:85–96.

Haddad, Bassam, and Jillian Schwedler. 2013. "Editors' Introduction to Teaching about the Middle East Since the Arab Uprisings." *PS: Political Science and Politics* 46, no. 2: 211–215.

El-Hamalawy, Hossam. 2011. "English Translation of Interview with Hossam El-Hamalawy on the Role of Labor/Unions in the Egyptian Revolution." Translated by Bassam Haddad. *Jadaliyya*, 30 April. http://www.jadaliyya.com/pages/index1387/english-translation-of-interview-with-hossam-el-ha (accessed 7 January 2013).

Hampson, Fen Osler. 1995. *Multilateral Negotiations: Lessons from Arms Control, Trade, and the Environment.* Baltimore: Johns Hopkins University Press.

Hamzawy, Amr. 2011. "Challenge of Transition." *Cairo Review* 1, no. 1: 112–118.

Hassan, Mazen. 2011. "The Effects of Egypt's Electoral Law." *Foreign Policy*, 1 November.

Hess, David, and Brian Martin. 2006. "Repression, Backfire, and the Theory of Transformative Events." *Mobilization* 11, no. 2: 249–267.

Heydeman, Steven. 2007. *Upgrading Authoritarianism in the Arab World.* Washington, D.C.: Saban Center for Middle East Policy, Brookings Institution.

Hinnebusch, Raymond A. 1990. *Authoritarian Power and State Formation in Ba'thist Syria: Army, Party, and Peasant*. Boulder, Colo.: Westview Press.

Hirschman, A. O. 1970. *Exist, Voice and Loyalty*. Cambridge, Mass.: Harvard University Press.

Hof, Frederic C. 2014. "Syrian Peace Talks." Atlantic Council, 13 January. http://www.atlanticcouncil.org/.

Hogra en Algerie. N.d. Hogra Centerblog. http://www.hogra.centerblog.net.

Homans, Charles. 1960. *Social Change.* New York: Harcourt, Brace and World.

Hopmann, P. Terrence. 1996. *The Negotiation Process and the Resolution of International Conflicts.* Columbia: University of South Carolina Press.

Hostrup Haugbølle, Rikke, and Francesco Cavatorta. 2011. "Will the Real Tunisian Opposition Please Stand Up? Opposition Coordination Failures under Authoritarian Constraints." *British Journal of Middle Eastern Studies* 38, no. 3: 323–341.

Hubbard, Ben, and Anonymous. 2014. "Life in a Jihadist Capital: Order with a Darker Side." *New York Times*, A1, 29 July.

Humbaraci, Arslan. 1966. *Algeria: A Revolution That Failed; A Political History since 1954*. New York: Praeger.

Huntington, Samuel P. 1969. *Political Order in Changing Societies*. New Haven, Conn.: Yale University Press.

Indigo. 2011. "Epilogue: Why Ben Ali Fled the Country." *Maghreb Confidential* 956 (20 January): 1.

International Crisis Group (ICG). 2012. "Yemen: Enduring Conflicts, Threatened Transition." Sanaa, Yemen: International Crisis Group. Middle East Report 125 (3 July).

———. 2013. "Marching in Circles: Egypt's Dangerous Second Transition." Brussels: International Crisis Group. Middle East and North Africa Briefing Paper, no. 35 (7 August).

Ives, Paula Murphy. 2003. "Negotiating Global Change." *International Negotiation* 8, no. 1: 43–78.

Jebnoun, Noureddine, Mahrdad Kia, and Mimi Kirk, eds. 2013. *Modern Middle East Authoritarianism*. New York: Routledge.

Joffé, Geroge. 2011. "The Arab Spring in North Africa." *Journal of North African Studies* 16, no. 4: 507–533.

Jönsson, Christer. 1981. "Bargaining Power." *Cooperation and Conflict* 16, no. 2: 249–257.

Kamrava, Mehran. 2013. "The Rise and Fall of the Ruling Bargains in the Middle East." *Beyond the Arab Spring: The Evolving Ruling Bargain in the Middle East*. London: C. Hurst.

Kanet, Roger E., and Edward A. Kolodziej, eds. 1991. *The Cold War as Cooperation: Superpower Cooperation in Regional Conflict Management*. Houndmills, Basingstoke, UK: Palgrave Macmillan.

Kasinof, Laura. 2011. "Yemenis Organize Shadow Government." *New York Times*, 18 July, A5.

Kirkpatrick, David. 2011a. "Deal to Hasten Transition Jeered at Cairo Protests." *New York Times*, 23 November.

———. 2011b. "Islamist Quit Egypt Council." *New York Times*, 9 December.

———. 2011c. "New Clashes in Cairo." *New York Times*, 17 December.

———. 2012a. "After Victory." *New York Times*, 19 June, A4.

———. 2012b. "Egypt's Military Shapes Its Longterm Political Role." *New York Times* 4 July, 4.

Kirkpatrick, David, and Kareem Fahim. 2012. "Over Decree, a New Rift." *New York Times*, 26 November, A1, A8.

Kolb, Deborah, and Judith Williams. 2000. *Everyday Negotiation: Navigating the Hidden Agendas in Bargaining*. San Francisco: Jossey-Bass.

Lamen, Fadel. 2011. "Inside the Rebel Endgame." *Daily Beast*, 22 August. http://www.thedailybeast.com/articles/2011/08/22/libya-news-inside-the-rebels-secret-endgame.html.

Landis, Joshua. 2012. "The Syrian Uprising of 2011." *Middle East Policy* 19, no. 1: 72–84.

Larémont, Ricardo René. 2013. *Revolution, Revolt, and Reform in North Africa: The Arab Spring and Beyond*. New York: Routledge.

Lax, David, and James Sebenius. 1986. *The Manager as Negotiator*. New York: Free Press.

Lasswell, Harold, and Abraham Kaplan. 1953. *Power and Society: A Framework for Political Inquiry*. New Haven: Conn.: Yale University Press.

Lerner, Hanna. 2011. *Making Constitutions in Deeply Divided Societies*. Cambridge: Cambridge University Press.

Luciani, Giacomo, ed. 1990. *The Arab State*. Berkeley: University of California Press.

Lynch, Marc. 2012. *The Arab Uprising: The Unfinished Revolutions of the New Middle East*. New York: Public Affairs.

McAdam, Douglas, Sidney Tarrow, and Charles Tilly. 2001. *Dynamics of Contention*. Cambridge: Cambridge University Press.

McIntyre, Angus, ed. 1988. *Aging and Political Leadership*. Albany: State University of New York Press.

El-Menawy, Abdel Latif. 2012. *Tahrir: The Last 18 Days of Mubarak*. UK: Gilgamesh.

El Messaoudi, Amina. 2010(?). "Constitutional Reform in the Arab World." Unpublished manuscript.

Mezran, Karim K. 2007. *Negotiation and the Construction of National Identities*. Boston: Nijhoff.

Micaud, Charles, with L. Carl Brown and Clement Henry Moore. 1964. *Tunisia: The Politics of Modernization*. New York: Praeger.

Minoui, Delphine. 2011. "Le grand malaise des provinces tunisiennes." *Le Figaro*, 30 May, 2.

Morrow, Jonathan. 2005. *Iraq's Constitution Process II: An Opportunity Lost*. Washington, D.C.: United States Institute of Peace (USIP).

Nahdha. 2011. "Ennahda Movement Programme: For Freedom, Justice and Development in Tunisia." Al-Nahdha Party.

Narlikar, Amrita. 2003. *International Trade and Developing Countries: Bargaining and Coalitions in the GATT and WTO*. London: Routledge.

Nash, John. 1950. "The Bargaining Problem." *Econometrica* 18, no. 1: 155–162.

Nieburg, H. L. 1969. *Political Violence: The Behavioral Process*. New York: St. Martin's Press.

North, Douglass C. 1990. *Institutions, Institutional Change, and Economic Performance*. Cambridge: Cambridge University Press.

Noueihed, Lin, and Alex Warren. 2012. *The Battle for the Arab Spring: Revolution Counterrevolution and the Making of a New Era*. New Haven, Conn.: Yale University Press.

Odell, John S. 2000. *Negotiating the World Economy*. Ithaca, N.Y.: Cornell University Press.

———, ed. 2006. *Negotiating Trade: Developing Countries in the WTO and NAFTA*. Cambridge: Cambridge University Press.

O'Donnell, Guillermo, and Philippe Schmitter. 1986. *Transitions from Authoritarian Rule: Tentative Conclusions about Uncertain Democracies*. Baltimore: Johns Hopkins University Press.

Organisation for Economic Co-operation and Development (OECD). 2011. *From Power Struggles to Sustainable Peace: Understanding Political Settlements*. Paris: Organisation for Economic Co-operation and Development.

Ottaway, Marina. 2012. "Who Will Write the Egyptian Constitution?" *Carnegie Endowment Commentary* 13 March. Washington, D.C.: Carnegie Endowment for International Peace (CEIP).

Payne, James L. 1965. *Labor and Politics in Peru: The System of Political Bargaining*. New Haven, Conn.: Yale University Press.

Pew Research Center. 2013. "The World's Muslims: Religion, Politics and Society." Pew Research Center, 30 April. http://www.pewforum.org/2013/04/30/the-worlds-muslims-religion-politics-society-exec/ (accessed 26 Jan. 2015).

Pickard, Duncan. 2012. "The Current Status of Constitution Making in Tunisia." Washington, D.C.: Carnegie Endowment for International Peace, 19 April. http://carnegieendowment.org/2012/04/19/current-status-of-constitution-making-in-Tunisia.

Puchot, Pierre. 2011. *Tunisie: Une revolution arabe*. Paris: Galaade Éditions.

Quandt, William B. 1969. *Revolution and Political Leadership: Algeria, 1954–1968*. Cambridge, Mass.: MIT Press.

Raiffa, Howard. 1982. *The Art and Science of Negotiation*. Cambridge, Mass.: Belknap Press of Harvard University Press.

Raiffa, Howard, with John Richardson and David Metcalfe. 2002. *Negotiation Analysis: The Science and Art of Collaborative Decision Making*. Cambridge, Mass.: Belknap Press of Harvard University Press.

Rappoport, Anatol. 1960. *Fights, Games and Debates*. Ann Arbor: University of Michigan Press.

Rashwan, Nada Hussein. 2013. "Inside Egypt's Draft Constitution: Role of Sharia Redefined." Al-Ahram, Ahram Online, 12 December. http://english.ahram.org.eg/NewsContent/1/0/88632/Egypt/0/Inside-Egypts-draft-constitution-Role-of-sharia-re.aspx (accessed 26 Jan. 2015).

Reynolds, Andrew, and Ben Reilly. 1997. *The International IDEA Handbook of Electoral System Design*. Stockholm: International IDEA.

Roberts, Hugh. 2011. "Algeria's National 'Protesta.'" *FP: Foreign Policy*, 10 January. http://foreignpolicy.com/2011/01/10/algerias-national-protesta/.

Rowsell, Nicole, and Asma ben Yahia. 2012. *Confidence Gap: Citizen Priorities on the One-Year Anniversary of the National Constituent Assembly Elections*. Washington, D.C.: National Democratic Institute for International Affairs.

Rubenstein, Ariel. 1982. "Perfect Equilibrium in a Bargaining Problem." *Econometrica* 50, no. 1: 97–110.

Russell, Bertrand. 1938. *Power: A New Social Analysis*. London: Unwin.

Rustow, Dankwart. 1970. "Transitions to Democracy: Towards a Dynamic Model." *Comparative Politics* 2, no. 3 (April): 337–363.

Salamé, Ghassan. 1994. *Democracy without Democrats? The Renewal of Politics in the Muslim World*. London: I. B. Taurus.

Sallam, Hesham. 2013. "The Egyptian Revolution and the Politics of Histories." *PS: Political Science & Politics* 46, no. 2 (April): 248–258.

Sanderson, Stephen K. 2010. *Revolutions: A Worldwide Introduction to Social and Political Contention*. 2nd ed. Boulder, Colo.: Paradigm.

Schelling, Thomas C. 1960. *The Strategy of Conflict*. Cambridge, Mass.: Harvard University Press.

Schlumberger, Oliver, ed. 2007. *Debating Arab Authoritarianism: Dynamics and Durability in Nondemocratic Regimes*. Stanford, Calif.: Stanford University Press.

Schmitz, Charles. 2014. "The Fall of Amran and the Future of the Islah Party in Yemen." American Institute for Yemeni Studies, 25 August.

Schopenhauer, Arthur. 1896. *The Art of Controversy*. London: S. Sonnenschein.

Seif el-Dawla, Aida. 2011. "Seeking Justice." *Cairo Review of Global Affairs* 1: 119–125.

al-Shabbi, Abulqasim. 1954. "Ser al-Nawhud" [Secret of Awakening]. In *Anthologie de la nouvelle maghrébine: Paroles d'auteurs*, by Centre Pédagogique Maghrébine, 63. Paris: Libraine Hachette, 1954. [translation by the editor]

Shahid, Anthony. 2011. "Qaddafi's Death Stirs New Opposition, and New Hope, in Syria." *New York Times*, 22 October, A6.

Singh, J. P. 2008. *Negotiation and the Global Information Economy*. Cambridge: Cambridge University Press.

Sisk, Timothy D. 1995. *Democratization in South Africa: The Elusive Social Contract*. Princeton, N.J.: Princeton University Press.

Skocpol, Theda. 1979. *States and Social Revolutions*. Cambridge: Cambridge University Press.

———. 1994. *Social Revolutions in the Modern World*. Cambridge: Cambridge University Press.

Tanir, Ilhan. 2012. "Inside the Free Syrian Army." *Fikra Forum*, 2 February. http://fikraforum.org/?p=1908.

Tarrow, Sidney. 1998. *Power in Movement: Social Movements and Contentious Politics*. Cambridge: Cambridge University Press.

Tarrow, Sidney, and Doug McAdam. 2005. "Scale Shift in Transnational Contention." In della Porta and Tarrow 2005.

Al-Tawy, Ayat. 2013. "Inside Egypt's Draft Constitution: Progress on Key Freedoms." *Al-Ahram*, 12 December. http://english.ahram.org.eg/NewsContent/1/155/88716/Egypt/Constitution-/A-closer-look-at-Egypts-constitution.aspx.

Thiess, Johannes. 2012. "Negotiating with NATO over Libya." Thesis, Bruges Collège d'Europe, Bruges, Belgium.

Tilly, Charles. 1978. *From Mobilization to Revolution*. New York: McGraw-Hill.

———. 1991. "Domination, Resistance, Compliance . . . Discourse." *Sociological Forum* 6, no. 3: 593-602.

———. 2003. *The Politics of Collective Violence*. Cambridge: Cambridge University Press.

———. 2008. *Contentious Performances*. Cambridge: Cambridge University Press.

Tilly, Charles, and Sidney Tarrow. 2007. *Contentious Politics*. Boulder, Colo.: Paradigm.

Trager, Eric. 2011. "Egypt's Triangular Power Struggle." *PolicyWatch* no. 1834 (22 July). Washington, D.C.: Washington Institute for Near East Policy.

Walton, Richard, and Robert McKersie. 1965. *A Behavioral Theory of Labor Negotiations*. New York: McGraw Hill.

Weiner, Alan S. 2011. "Constitutions as Peace Treaties: A Cautionary Tale for the Arab Spring." *Stanford Law Review* 66, no. 8: 8–15.

Weslati, Slah 2011. *Démocratie ou guerre civile?* Tunis: Nirvana.

Wiktorowicz, Quintan, ed. 2004. *Islamic Activism: A Social Movement Approach*. Bloomington: Indiana University Press.

Zartman, I. William, ed. 1970. *Political Elites in the Middle East*. New York: Praeger.

———. 1978. "Negotiation as a Joint Decision-Making Process." *The Negotiation Process: Theories and Applications*. Beverly Hills, Calif.: Sage.

———. 1980. "A Theory of Elite Circulation." In *Elites in the Middle East*, edited by I. William Zartman. New York: Praeger.

———. 1982. *Ripe for Resolution: Conflict and Intervention in Africa*. New York: Oxford University Press.

———. 1987a. *International Relations of the New Africa*. Englewood Cliffs: Prentice-Hall, 1966. Reprint, Lanham, Md.: University Press of America.

———, ed. 1987b. *Positive Sum: Improving North-South Negotiations*. New Brunswick, N.J.: Transaction Books.

———, ed. 1995. *Elusive Peace: Negotiating an End to Civil War*. Washington, D.C.: Brookings Institution Press.

———, ed. 1997a. *Governance as Conflict Management: Politics and Violence in West Africa*. Washington, D.C.: Brookings Institution Press.

———. 1997b. "Justice in Negotiation." *International Political Science Review* 18, no. 2: 121–138.

———. 2000. "Ripeness: The Hurting Stalemate and Beyond." In *International Conflict Resolution after the Cold War*, edited by Paul Stern and Daniel Druckman. Washington DC: National Academy Press

———. 2005. "Analyzing Intractability." In *Grasping the Nettle: Analyzing Cases of Intractable Conflict*, edited by Chester A. Crocker, Fen Osler Hampson, and Pamela Aall. Washington, D.C.: United States Institute of Peace Press (USIP).

———. "Ripeness Revisited: The Push and Pull of Conflict Management." In *Deeskalation von Gewaltkonflikten seit 1945*, edited by Corinna Hauswedell. Essen: Klartext.

———. 2009. "Negotiation as a Choice of Parties." *PINPoints* 33: 13–16.

———. 2012. "La multilatéralité internationale; essai de modélisation." *Négociations* 1:39–50.

———. 2014. "Waiting for the Arab Spring." *Middle East Journal* 68, 3 (Summer): 465-468.

———. 2015. "Mediation in the Middle East: When to Get Involved and Stay Involved." *International Negotiation* (forthcoming).

Zartman, I. William, and Tanya Alfredson. 2010. "Negotiating with Terrorists and the Tactical Question." In *Coping with Terrorism*, edited by Rafael Reuveny and William Thompson. Albany: State University of New York Press.

Zartman, I. William, and Maureen Berman. 1982. *The Practical Negotiator*. New Haven, Conn.: Yale University Press.

Zartman, I. William, Daniel Druckman, Lloyd Jensen, Dean G. Pruitt, and H. Peyton Young. 1996. "Negotiation as a Search for Justice." *International Negotiation* 1, no. 1: 79–98.

Zartman, I. William, and Guy Olivier Faure, eds. 2011. *Engaging Extremists: Trade-Offs, Timing, and Diplomacy*. Washington, D.C.: USIP.

Zartman, I. William, and Jeffrey Z. Rubin, eds. 2000. *Power and Negotiation*. Ann Arbor: University of Michigan Press.

Zoepf, Katherine. 2011. "Long Repressed in Syria, an Internal Opposition Takes Shape." *New York Times*, 28 April.

Al-Zubaidi, Layla. 2011–2012. *Syria's Revolution: Statehood and Participation; Society, Power, Ideology*. Berlin: Heinrich Böll Stiftung.

Tunisia

Beyond the Ideological Cleavage: Something Else

ABDELWAHAB BEN HAFAIEDH AND I. WILLIAM ZARTMAN

AJMI LOURIMI (2012), a member of the Political Bureau of al-Nahdha, described the revolution in Tunisia as "a secular revolution. Not a secularist revolution, but secular in the sense that it was neither Islamist nor secularist." This statement suggests that the democratic transition in Tunisia has scrambled the secularist-Islamist divide. Parties and movements are creating and operating in spaces defined by "something else." Whether they succeed or not, this "something else" is already articulated around an effort of adaptation and compromise that came to a head in Tunisia around the negotiations on the new constitution (Hurd 2012). Adaptation is crucial to survival, as compromise is to consensus. As businesses chase customers and animals go where the water is, politicians chase voters and public opinion. This public opinion is an area in social life where political actors come together to identify and discuss societal problems and, through that discussion, influence political action. Unlike the anomic ideological discourse previously characteristic of the "Arab street," communication with public opinion requires a certain political marketing and a pragmatic discourse for better selling political platforms and programs.

In this sense, which is essential, the process of political adaptation to democracy in a transitional context is the choice to make concessions and compromises to reach potential voters inside the emerging political market, but also to seek consensus that reaches over partisan bargains to make a new social contract for the body politic. In this process, in which classical political identification is still inchoate, compromises are necessary if any progress is to be made. Even outside the context of new democracies, politicians have to be able to adjust their principles and work with their opponents if they are to govern at all. This tension is one of the great challenges of contemporary democracy and has become more difficult in the era of the permanent campaign (Guttmann and Thompson 2012, 145). In *Éloge du compromis*, Mohamed Nachi (Nachi and Nanteuil 2006) shows how Arab societies are well suited to the culture of compromise, and that the pragmatic approach to power is nearly universal. To compromise (in Arabic *tawafuq*, from the root meaning "to be right") or make concessions is to make a distributive deal between different parties where each party gives up part of its demand.[1] In arguments, compromise is a concept of finding agreement through communication, through a mutual acceptance of terms—often involving pulling back from an original goal or desire. Compromise is often considered as an antonym of extremism, associated with concepts of balance, adaptation, and negotiation. In this sense adaptive capacity refers to the ability of a political elite or actor to adjust, via changes in their characteristics or behavior, so as to cope better with continuing contextual variability.

In a transitional context and in new democracies, the need for compromise seems to be more vital and imperative independent of culture. But compromise and concession as pulling back is a zero-sum action, in which each side gives in a bit. When a society is confronted with the need to create a new social contract, something beyond compromise is required to formulate a shared meaning for the basis of governance. Such construction or reframing in terms of a common basis on which details can be determined is the heart of consensus in creating a New Order.

In a transitional context characterized by unpredictability, this adaptive capacity and need for consensus are imperative, especially where the dynamic of change is not determined by any charismatic role or by any militant ideology. Paradoxically perhaps, the absence of a charismatic figure and ideological reference in the early stage of the Tunisian *intifada*, carried out in the name of Dignity (*karama*), played a positive and constructive role. Three decades before its political transition, Tunisia started a demographic transition, comprising the growth of the middle class, the spread of urbanization, the consolidation of women's rights, the expansion of literacy, the neutrality of the military elites, and the moderation of political party discourses that became the key ingredients of the relative success of the Tunisian experience (Courbage and Todd 2007; Cincotta 2011; Larémont 2014). Even if major issues, such as civic and religious identity, social policy, privatization, social protection, and public service, among others, were long in being resolved and continued to reproduce some classical cleavages, the Tunisian experience moved toward a constitutional denouement through concessions, if not consensus. Both left and right, and religious and secular opinions, accepted some form of Civil State (*dawla madania*)[2] and an expanded public economy, the Keynesian welfare state. Both liberals and conservatives, and Islamists and laicists, have tried to be positioned in the center and in the middle range of the political scene (*ahzab al-wasat*), even though the two pairs operate on different bases of legitimization.

There is a special feature in the negotiations of the Tunisian *intifada* and transition. To be sure, the visible bargaining was carried out horizontally, between the *muntafadin* and the incumbent elites as they decided to leave, then among the parties at the National Constituent Assembly (NCA) and National Dialogue as they decided on governance and constitution. But in the absence of a strong organized opposition to the dominant but not majoritarian Nahdha, there rose from the beginning a vigorous vertical dimension to negotiation, between the transitioning government and civil society. The latter involved a congeries of actors, organized and disorganized—the labor union, the media, the civil rights groups, the *muntafadin*, simply the street, reacting to government proposals and pressing for a liberal compromise. Civil society felt itself liberated by the *intifada* and jumped in to play an active role, abetted by popular frustration in the work of the political parties. More than any other Arab Spring, even mob-struck Egypt or faction-roiled Yemen, Tunisia continued the bargaining behavior of the initial *intifada* and engaged public participation directly in integrative attempts at decision making.

But how is the Tunisian political garden being landscaped and what are the new political breeds? What is the underlying source of legitimacy on which the emerging formulation and nascent coalition of the New Order rest, to serve as a reference for popular approval and textual interpretation? And what are the real issues that divide the political scene and organize the political competition? Who talks and should talk to whom? If all the parties talk on behalf of the center, who is left on the left and who is right on the right side of the political scene? If each of the parties hides in its self-made corner, where is the national consensus? What is the meaning of conservative and liberal in this setting? How can we explain the discourse of a leftist activist who criticizes secularism in order to expand his audience in popular circles, and the discourse of a conservative religious figure who rethinks secularism from a positive perspective in order to gain the confidence of the elites and the assurance of the international community? How can we explain such interference of values in which the ideas of progress (*taqaddum*) seem to be less and less defended by leftist elites and the idea of dignity less and less defended by religious elites, who have more and more difficulty in communicating their messages?

BUILDING LEGITIMACY FROM ABOVE AND BELOW

On the way to independence, in 1951 the Neo-Destourian nationalist movement established a committee to work for constitutional guarantees for a number of national organizations. The founding meeting called for the establishment of a universally elected parliament and representative government in the cities and villages to ensure citizens' rights and their direct participation in management and collective action. At the end of its work, the committee declared that these principles were the only guarantee for human and civil rights, and thus it announced a new working charter. In 1955, just before independence, the Bey issued an order calling for a constituent assembly, the National Assembly was elected in 1956, and the Personal Status Code (CSP)[3] was enacted in August 1956. But the constitution of 1959, under the leadership of Habib Bourguiba, provided for a centralized party-state. Negotiation, compromise, and coalition were directed at the previous occupying forces and not to the emerging or future society. The idea of progress could be social or cultural but not political.

Most forms of subsequent coalitions between the ruling Neo-Destour—and then Socialist Destour (PSD)—Party and social actors such as the General Union of Tunisian Workers (UGTT) came to confirm this path. The political contract could be summarized and also translated into practice to the end of the 1970s in two fundamental directions: government recognition of economic and social pluralism, and rejection of any form of political pluralism. The coup d'état of Zine el-Abadine Ben Ali against Bourguiba in November 1987 brought the National Charter two years later, established for the approval of all political parties to fix rules for a pluralist political society. One of its clauses was to guarantee that "all parties will respect the character of the Republican State in accordance with the principle of sovereignty of the people and preserve the gains of the previous regime, including the Personal Status Code, the prohibition of any party based on religion or race, and the renunciation of violence in all its forms." But the good intentions of political openness turned into tyranny. Negotiation was conducted within the political elite of the Democratic Constitutional (Destourian) Rally (RCD) at the center and not with the social base of the margins or the local entities that the independent state had cast off. In 2005 when the repression was at its height, the opponents of the regime of Ben Ali, belonging to different political families—liberals, nationalists, leftists, and Islamists—came to an agreement to respect the civilian character of the state, the rights of women, and human rights. This coalition experience, seen as the result of four years of negotiations, paved the way for future compromises to take place after the revolution of 14 January 2011.

The Arab Spring broke out in Tunisia, but it was a creeping outbreak. Muted and repressed political opposition was centered in Tunis, as in the hunger strike of 18 October 2005 preceding the World Information Summit (Geisier and Gobe 2006), but the geographic focus of protest in its violent form was further away from the capital, in the impoverished south around the mining town of Gafsa. Occasional protests occurred after the Gafsa high school demonstrations in 1999, but the first labor protest came in nearby Redeyef on 5 January 2008 over a rigged employment offer by the Gafsa Phosphate Company; it soon spread to Gafsa, where the UGTT local called a general strike within the city. For the first time a labor demonstrator was killed, at Redeyef on 6 June, and for the first time the events drew public attention in the capital; the government announced that it would take measures to resolve the social problems and satisfy the employment demands (Puchot 2011, 65–67). The spark that set the country aflame, however, was the self-immolation of Mohammed Bouazizi in Sidi Bouzid, a bit further north in the same region, on 17 December 2010, posted on YouTube and picked up by Al Jazeera the same day. He died on 4 January, followed by a number of similar protest suicides.

"The Tunisian revolution is a revolution carried out in parallel by mostly educated, partly modernized Tunisians from the big cities and by the ordinary Tunisians of the towns and villages of the interior, [with] an ally of high quality and more fearsome efficacy than oppression and censure: Facebook, everyone politically and socially conscious of the situation that had become unbearable for them and for their country. Hence the urgency to eradicate all the sources and symbols of harm, . . . exorcise the demons of absolute power, corruption, illegal enrichment, traffic of influence etc, [and] to make their 'national society' free, democratic, pluralist and respectful of universal values" (Weslati 2011, 63).[4] The *muntafadin* of 2011–2012 were singularly without organization, benefiting from a sociopolitical wave of protest rather than a carefully coordinated movement (Angrist 2013). A coincidental opportunity was provided by the scheduling of university entrance exams in Sidi Bouzid at the very moment of the immolation, bringing thousands of students to town (Sghiri 2011). An online group, Takriz ("dissemination") then rushed to Sidi Bouzid to spread information and videos before the roads and Internet access were cut by the government (Pollock 2011).

Another source of major importance was the local workers, notably the schoolteachers and miners, the UGTT's largest sectors, who personified the parallel currents mentioned above. These various groups, and many others, negotiated lateral ties that produced the Caravan of Liberty (eventually Kasba 1, where the protest landed in Tunis on 23 January) and also constituted the force that negotiated for the support of the UGTT Central Committee behind the uprising. The best the local unions could obtain was permission on 11 January for "regional labor structures to observe the protests" and a succession of general strikes in principal cities, beginning with Sfax on 10 January and arriving at Tunis on 14 January, the day Ben Ali left (Puchot 2011; Piot 2011; Weslati 2011; ICG 2011). The massive demonstration at Sfax was a turning point in its focus of regime change rather than on day-to-day grievances. Three days later a YouTube video circulated, showing the army refusing to fire on the forming crowd and preventing the police from doing so, another turning point that changed the risk calculations of many who had previously hesitated to engage for fear of repression (Bellin 2011). "The barrier of fear that supported Ben Ali's dictatorship finally had been broken" (Hamblin 2012).

The history of the leadership of the UGTT was a story of interest and maneuvering, from its advocacy of social welfare reform to its support for Ben Ali's candidacy in the elections of 2004 and 2009, from the implementation of neoliberal economic measures to the betrayal of the Gafsa UGTT activists jailed during the 2008 uprising when the union limited itself to a simple request for the release of the prisoners, and eventually from its support of Ben Ali before his departure to its crucial role as mediator in the final formation of a government that could pass a constitution in 2014. The key to UGTT action, both before and after the uprising, has been a focused concern over its members' welfare, which dictated cooperation with the government before the uprising and engagement during the uprising, under new labor leadership. Surprised by the uprisings in the countryside leading up to the *intifada*, the labor leadership permitted only strikes at the local or regional level and called for democratic reforms once the rebel movement had spread throughout the country and many local unions had become directly involved. Two days before the general strike in Tunis, Abdessalem Jerad, then secretary-general of the UGTT, was among those who joined in Ben Ali's last talks, looking for negotiated solutions to the situation. While people were fighting Mohammed Ghannouchi's RCD government on the streets, the leadership of the UGTT in an attempt to please everyone recorded the president's "high consideration" and called for a "government of national salvation," without clarifying what it was to be or how it was to be made up. For most of the UGTT leaders the election for a constitutional assembly was not on the table.[5] Wildcat strikes and protests continued to occur throughout 2011 and into 2012, without a political agenda and regardless of social stability.

Negotiations for Coalition

With the departure of Ben Ali on 14 January 2011, Tunisians rediscovered their diversity and differences, negotiating their way out of the Old Order to provide a gradual Short Track transition. With Ben Ali gone, the remaining members of the Old Order negotiated among themselves to follow the constitutional provisions for filling the vacancy while negotiating tacitly with the uprising to complete their own momentary withdrawal from the transition institutions. As a result, the transition never experienced an institutional vacuum or a state collapse and moved within eight months to elections and then rapid negotiations on a coalition to form a government. But then came four months of stalling to make the coalition work and another six months to produce the first draft of a constitution, after which further negotiations on a final draft took another year and a half, and new elections were postponed two more years to the anniversary date of October 2014. The transitional institutions—National Constituent Assembly and its government, then doubled by the National Dialogue and popular activism—filled the institutional vacuum, under pressure from serious criticism for illegitimacy and deadlock.

The first step in the succession to Ben Ali on 14–15 January 2011 followed constitutional procedures: first the prime minister Mohammed Ghannouchi, under article 56 for temporary incapacity, and then Fuad Mebazza, speaker of parliament, under article 57 for permanent incapacity, became president and produced a motley caretaker government under the continuing prime minister. The government immediately set up commissions on political reform, corruption, and repression, negotiating with opposition forces in an effort to keep the uprising under control and the transition within the constitutional framework. Continuing protests demanded that ministers, including Ghannouchi, resign from the RCD; further protests demanded the removal of all other former RCD members, which Ghannouchi did (except for himself) two weeks later (27 January), and the disbanding of the party, which was achieved only on 9 March (Weslati 2011). These first steps established a pattern of relations that was to continue throughout the transition and well into the newly elected government. It consisted of government actions or statements, a public response, and then an accommodating government reaction—tacit negotiations in the public space without direct meetings, in a sort of direct, informal "democracy." Continuing exchange and negotiations between these bodies and civil society continued in strength until the elections of 2014, a special feature of the Tunisian Spring.

Leaders from the UGTT and the Bar Association brought together over two dozen political and civil society groups to form an organization to maintain the momentum of the uprising, press their demands, and negotiate with the government. The resulting National Council for the Protection of the Revolution (CNPR), formed on 11 February, organized further Caravans of Liberty to bring in protesters from the countryside. By 20 February, thousands of young people from all over the country, policed by a twenty-member "organization committee" and by "revolutionary safeguard committees," participated in continual ranging discussions in a sit-in in the Kasba to fill out the *intifada*'s galvanizing slogan of "Dignity, Liberty, Citizenship, Bread" with specific demands: replacement of the government, election of a parliament and constituent assembly, rejection of a presidential regime, protection of free speech and press, among others. These issues would continue to dominate the search for a formula for a New Order throughout the subsequent years of constitutional debate (Weslati 2011; Elloumi 2011).

The pressure of Kasba II brought the resignation of Ghannouchi—and also the leaders of opposition parties termed "dissident" under the old regime—after a month in office, and his replacement by the Political Reform Commission by eighty-four-year-old Beji Qaid es-Sebsi, a former minister under both Ben Ali and before him Bourguiba. After two weeks of the Kasba II sit-in, President Mebazza responded to the call to begin institutionalization of the New Order with the election of a National Constituent Assembly (ANC) in four months "in order to preserve the continuity of the State and in fidelity to the memory of the martyrs and to concretize the principles of the Revolution," and at the same time suspended the 1959 constitution. The sit-in in the Kasba ended, culminating "a long process of negotiations between the government, the president and the political groups and trade unions," according to Political Reform Commission chair Yadh Ben Achour (2011a); "We are working on a republican pact that will determine the principles and roles of a democratic competition," (Ben Achour 2011b).

As the CNPR came into being to organize the civil society pressure into negotiations to turn the *intifada* into a transition, it then demanded to become an institution of the transition itself. Qaid es-Sebsi proposed a compromise whereby the Council would join the Political Reform Commission to form a High Authority for the Realization of the Objectives the Revolution, Political Reform and the Democratic Transition (*sic*), understandably known as the Ben Achour Commission, an important extraconstitutional body that was authorized to draft decree-laws for presidential promulgation, prepare the elections, and monitor the government (Pickard 2011, 638). Under continuing criticism for lack of legitimacy, however, it expanded its central Council to 171 members from all walks of life (including regional youth councils), organized and unorganized (ICG 2011). Most importantly, it negotiated among its diverse membership and submitted for presidential decree a closed-list proportional representation electoral system that worked to prevent single-party dominance, with elections for a one-year ANC scheduled for 24 July. A preconstitution or Law on the Interim Organization of the Public Powers for the post-election government, similar to the previous regime but with presidential powers transferred to the prime minister chosen from the largest party, was also issued.

The High Authority also brought the twelve political parties in its membership to negotiate an important declaration on 14 September on the shape of the transition process.[6] The consensus was that the current interim government would continue in office to deal with day-to-day matters until the election of the ANC and its election of a new president and the installation of a new government; the ANC would negotiate a constitution within a period "not to exceed a year," although "they will carry out their missions until the setting up of durable institutions." Elections were delayed four more months to 23 October because of simple inability to organize them in time and were to be carried out in harmony and respect among the parties. This consensus was shattered in the aftermath of the elections.

Two important characteristics marked the work of the Ben Achour Commission: its emphasis on maintaining continuity of state structures and its active negotiations among the members to arrive at a consensus on significant pieces of legislation. In the process, the events established a crucial principle in the Tunisian transition: the role of popular pressure in negotiation with the authorities, whose legitimacy depended on their relations with the activated mass. In this span of negotiations, the government gave in to the Kasbah bit by bit but continued to insist on the continuity of the state framework, in order to prevent state collapse and revolutionary disorder (even though the term *Revolution* soon became standard currency). Not the Old Order or the 1989 constitutional order but constitutional order itself had to be maintained, into which a New Order would find its place. "We are in the middle of a process which should lead us to democratic governance, a transition from a hyperauthoritarian state to a state of liberty," declared Qaid es-Sebsi.[7]

Negotiation then shifted to the establishment of workable party coalitions in preparation for the elections for the ANC. The old parties were in shambles, between those that constituted the tolerated opposition in parliament (the "dissident" parties) and those outside, banned, or quiescent. The largest of the latter was al-Nahdha (The Renaissance) Party;[8] the others included the Progressive Democratic Party (PDP; "dissident") and Tunisian Workers' Communist Party (PCOT) (illegal), founded before Ben Ali's coup, and the Democratic Forum for Labor and Liberties or Ettakatol ("dissident") and the Congress for the Republic (CPR) (banned) formed against Ben Ali. After the uprising, new parties sprang up—112 more in all—to contest the elections, in order either to reach for a significant coalition of voters in a few cases or to establish themselves as legitimate players (often just individuals) for a later coalition of parties. Some of the new parties had a specific constituency, such as al-Watan (the Nation) and al-Mubadara (the Initiative) and later Afek Tunis (Horizons of Tunisia), who sought to represent the RCD constituency, or the Tunisian Labor Party (PTT), which sought to represent the UGTT. Others negotiated electoral alliances without losing their separate identities, such as the Modernist (or Socialist) Democratic Pole (al-Massar) (PDM) made of the Communist Attajdid (Renewal) and the PTT.

But negotiations for united coalitions to face the dominant (but not majoritarian) Nahdha Party were not for this round, as the first elections were viewed above all as an occasion to test individual parties' or candidates' strengths. And so in the October elections the secular parties and coalitions lost before al-Nahdha, which won more votes that the next three, giving it 41 percent of the seats.[9] It immediately set to replace the interim government and president and to take up the dual charge of both governing and drafting a constitution. By making religious identity the thrust of the campaign, al-Nahdha split the nation.

The constitution of a governing coalition then revived negotiations, which took seven weeks to produce a heterogeneous Troika composed of the first, second, and fourth largest parties—al-Nahdha, CPR, and Ettakatol.[10] "Coalition-building requires . . . a common problem and the decision to take joint action . . . with no commitment to a durable relationship" (Pierre 2002, 2–3). Negotiations were based on three parties' desire to take part in the formulation and, for the two lesser parties, on the desire to keep al-Nahdha in check; al-Nahdha needed partners to make a majority, and the partners needed al-Nahdha to participate in government, a fine tradeoff of convenience. Al-Nahdha held the prime ministry (Secretary-General Hamadi Jebali, later replaced by Ali Laarayedh) and thirteen other ministries, CPR the presidency (President Moncef Marzouki) and three other (unimportant) ministries, and Ettakatol the presidency of the ANC (President Mustafa ben Jaafar) and five other ministries, in proportion to their ANC seats. The coalition was durable for two years but not stable. Ettakatol temporarily dropped out of the early negotiations, both CPR and Ettakatol lost party members when the coalition was formed, and the CPR temporarily left the coalition in a crisis of February–March 2013 (Shirayanagi 2011; Ltifi 2012).

Through all this, al-Nahdha kept its discipline and even sought to negotiate an enlargement of the coalition, attempting to break off pieces from the PDP to bring them into the coalition in July 2012, but their secular membership objected; other attempts were mildly successful among the splintering parties in March 2013 (*Journal* 2012). Al-Nahdha's governing structure is semidemocratic, with most of the 120-member ruling Consultative (*shura*) Council elected from the local units, augmented by members appointed to fill in unrepresented constituencies. Its members negotiate among themselves, sometimes overridden by their leader Rachid Ghannouchi and sometimes the reverse. They are ideologically diverse within their general view, with a larger doctrinaire (and sometimes extremist wing) and a smaller pragmatic part, but follow a sense of party discipline once decisions are made. The more rigid wing has felt that the party won the 2011 elections and should aim to take over governance, while the moderate wing felt the party's aim out of exile was participation in governance and its electoral results marked its future as a coalition leader (Dahmani 2012; Wolf 2012). Once the Troika coalition was formed, negotiations on formulation began.

Negotiations for Formulation

The 2011 election of the ANC established both a basic notion of Tunisian identity and a debate over its meaning. Negotiations on the formulation of a New Order started on 13 February when the ANC took up its named task of drafting a constitution, after an animated debate among political parties, civil society, and citizens on the charge of the Assembly. At the same time pursuing its assumed task of supervising government (Ghali 2011). To write the constitution, the Assembly created six constitutional committees of twenty-two members each, allocated according to the votes each party received in the elections (nine Nahdha, three each CPR and PDM, two each to Ettakatol and the Republican coalition, and one to an independent). Although a number of NGOs and parties submitted draft proposals, the ANC decided that the work would not be just a revision of 1959 but would start from a clean slate. It assigned proposed articles according to subject to the relevant committees, which were to negotiate over constitutional articles until consensus was reached; consensus and compromise were considered the essential means in the drafting process. Results then went to the ANC Coordinating Committee and ultimately to the Troika's monitoring committee. Avoiding a vote meant that many issues remained long in negotiation. Seven months of negotiations produced a first constitutional draft with many brackets, released in mid-August 2012.

But when the mandated one-year deadline for a constitution produced nothing more than a second draft with more than eighteen of its most crucial articles still under tight negotiation, and no new deadline stuck out or could be agreed on, questions rose throughout Tunisian society concerning the continued legitimacy of the ANC (Rowsell and Ben Yahia 2012). Although the atmosphere and relations for dialogue in the small committees were good and frank and moved the parties to join in constructive drafting away from publicity, debates within the Assembly and larger committees, carried directly on TV, tended to be convulsive and tense, reflecting the difference between communications addressed in camera and those addressed on camera where electoral agitation and propaganda dominated. More than ever the question of legitimacy became a subject of political interaction in order to put pressure on the governmental coalition.

Legitimacy of any kind "is derived from shared beliefs, that is, from a consensus as to what constitutes proper allegiance" (Lipset 1967, 19). It has been perceived in different ways in the search for formulation, following Max Weber's three types—traditional (emerging from societal custom and habit based on cultural symbols and identity), rational (derived from the institutional procedure, providing law and order through a negotiated consensual contract), and charismatic (resting on the character of the political leaders). The body politic was inoculated by the Bourguiba experience against the third type, at least until the contest between the other two would prove irresolvable, but the negotiations on formulation were hung between the first and second. The uprising had focused above all on the elimination of vestiges of the Old Order. When it looked beyond at substance, it contained a desire for a New Order of "Liberty, Citizenship, and Dignity" as the slogan proclaimed (along with "Work"), pursuing rational sources of legitimacy based on the institutionalized protection of human security and rights and civil liberties. The emergence of al-Nahdha in the 2011 elections suddenly expanded the political palette to include religion and identity and turned the search for a formula for the New Order into a debate over the place of Islam, reverting to traditional legitimacy in an uncertain way and with indeterminate implications.

During Bourguiba's rule, Islam was a point of reference but personal freedoms were protected in law and equal rights guaranteed for men and women. Between the constitution of 1959 and the Constituent Assembly of 2012, the stakes changed. The ascendancy of al-Nahdha as the predominant player in the new political system raised the specter in more liberal minds of Tunisia's becoming a theocratic state similar to Iran. Morsi's year in Egypt made a sharp impact by moving the threatening possibility closer to home. However, the party, with a repeated reference to the Turkish experience, distanced itself from this idea, pointing to the results of its negotiated coalition with secular parties and its frequent compromises on important constitutional issues, and also to the unenviable fate of Morsi's experiment. While some perceived this as an ideological adaptation to the changed political environment, others saw it as a tactical compromise for political ends with a hidden agenda. In this transition process, for some, Islam must defend freedom of religion, especially freedom of conscience, and this means the possibility for a citizen to have no religion (atheism) or to convert (Ben Achour 2011b). For others, Islam is a doctrine to be followed to the letter, to be pursued even through temporary compromises, and to be imposed if not followed, as seen in the increasing use of violence by Salafi groups. Had the Islamic party really turned its back on its Wahabi dogma? It is very difficult to confirm, because many Nahdha leaders believe they would lose a part of their soul and maybe a part of their audience and their electorate if they did.

Despite al-Nahdha's oft-proclaimed stance of moderation, a different message was sent by the nonresponsiveness of the government before the violence of the repeatedly emboldened Salafi movement, the increasingly vocal and militant minority of ultraconservative Muslims who were demanding the application of strict Islamic law in a country long known for its progressive traditions. Salafi groups represent the attempted Terror phase of the "Tunisian Revolution," as imperfect an imitation as the "Revolution" itself. With the stomping of a female student for replacing a Salafi flag with the Tunisian flag at Menouba University in January 2012 without immediate government response,[11] the attack organized by these groups against the U.S. embassy under the passive eye of the police on 11 September, the revelations by WikiLeaks of the relationship between Abu Iyadh (founder of Ansar el-Shariʿa in April 2011) and the Ministry of the Interior under Ben Ali, and the assassination of ANC members Chokri Belaid of the Democratic Patriots' Movement on 6 February 2013 and Mohammed Brahmi on 25 July, a wide part of the opinion began to take seriously a conspiracy theory in order to explain government passivity toward the Salafi violence. The assassination of Brahmi opened a season of Salafi incidents that incensed public opinion and roused fears that the normally peaceful Tunisian scene that had never known political assassinations was under terrorist attack—attacks on Tunisian soldiers at Mount Chaambi on the Algerian border in August, assassination of police in villages in the center of the country in October, and botched suicide missions on the coast at the end of the month. By mid-2013 public anger had exploded against the government.

According to Rachid Ghannouchi (2012b), founder and president of the Nahdha party, al-Nahdha's negotiations with the Salafist groups "were unsuccessful and it is urgent to impose law and order to prevent any Somalization of this country." When he called the Salafists "a danger to public freedom" and vowed that the authorities would crack down on them after they caused serious violence at the U.S. embassy, he angered and irritated Salafi leaders (Ghannouchi 2012a). Was then the video posted in December 2012 on negotiations between Ghannouchi and Salafist groups about the necessity to abandon the principle of shariʿa temporarily a kind of cover or a serious indicator of the rupture between the two pretenders of religious legitimacy? In May 2013 the Nahdha government finally cracked down on the Salafis and banned their party congress, and in August the government declared Ansar a terrorist group. The measures convinced some doubters that the government had finally drawn a line in the sand, but to others it was too late: the impression had been set.

In an open debate with leading scholars, activists, civil society leaders, and politicians from across the full spectrum, Ghannouchi (2012a) argued that "secularism does not conflict with the principles of Islam. . . . Secularism appears to be a philosophy that contradicts religious perceptions, but things are not as has been posed. . . . Secularism is only procedural and not an atheist philosophy. . . . It's a kind of procedural arrangement designed to safeguard the freedom of belief and thought as Abd al-Wahab al-Masiri distinguished, in his writings, between partial and total secularisms."[12] As the situation evolved into 2013, he minimized the government's tolerance, not for secularism but for the extremist violence in the name of Islamic rigor, and declared, with all directness and possibilities of interpretation, "this country does not belong to one party or another but rather to all of its citizens regardless of their religion, sex, or any other consideration. Islam has bestowed on them the right to be citizens enjoying equal rights, and to believe in whatever they desire within the framework of mutual respect and observance of the law which is legislate by their representatives in parliament" (Ghannouchi 2013).

On the constitutional question of shariʿa as the source of Tunisian law, a 2012 opinion survey (ASSForum 2012a) indicated that 90 percent of Tunisians preferred to keep the first article of the 1959 constitution, which states only that "Tunisia is a free, sovereign and independent state. Its religion is Islam, its language is Arabic and its form of government is a republic," without reference to shariʿa and its place in legislation; 51 percent preferred that shariʿa be considered as one source among others, 21 percent favored shariʿa as the exclusive source for Tunisian law, 19 percent preferred that it not be considered as a source, and 10 percent said they knew nothing about the debate. The results indicate a public opinion both split and inconsistent on the subject. About 30 percent of the people said they would vote again for al-Nahdha (18 percent would still keep shariʿa as the sole source of legislation, but 12 percent favored maintaining the first article). Broken down by category, those most favorable to shariʿa as the sole source were, by age 15–35 (60 percent), male (78 percent) with only primary education (80 percent), including those who are illiterate (20 percent).

The first signs of the controversy over the issue of shariʿa appeared before the beginning of negotiations on the constitution. During the electoral campaigns, Ghannouchi emphasized that the party would not seek the implementation of shariʿa law and would instead advocate a reaffirmation of Article 1 from the 1959 constitution. However, other Nahdha leaders sought to incorporate shariʿa into the party platform. Through its Facebook account, al-Nahda leaked its draft of the constitution, which explicitly included the adoption of shariʿa as the main source of legislation. In response, ANC president Ben Jaafar (Ettakatol) announced that his party would withdraw from the ruling coalition should this policy be implemented. An internal Nahdha party draft in February 2012 referred to shariʿa as "a source among sources." As a result, the president of al-Nahdha engaged in a process of concession in two stages: first, in a lecture defending his understanding of the concept of procedural secularism or pragmatism, Ghannouchi (2012c) said: "We do not want Tunisian society to be divided into two ideologically opposed camps, one pro-shariʿa and one anti-shariʿa. We want above all a constitution that is for all Tunisians, whatever their convictions." But the next day, Sahbi Atig, the president of the Nahdha parliamentary group, shouted at a protest meeting that shariʿa would serve as the main source for legislation. Ten days later, at a press conference, Ghannouchi stressed that his movement would limit itself to the first article of the 1959 constitution.

The decision not to push for a reference to shariʿa law was the result of internal negotiations within the Nahdha party following a strong civil society reaction, notably at an Independence Day demonstration on 20 March. It marked a break for the moment between al-Nahdha and the Salafis. Only twelve of the eighty Shura participants voted in favor of retaining the 1959 language on shariʿa, although a straw poll of Nahdha members in parliament showed a slight majority favoring the reference (Pickard 2012). In its public declaration on 26 March, Nahdha spokespeople stated that the party's official policy on the shariʿa question reaffirmed the party's commitment to consensus politics and its desire not to alienate the secular parties in the ruling coalition, also noting that an explicit reference to shariʿa is not a prerequisite for a democracy to be compatible with Islamic principles (Ghannouchi 1993). As negotiations moved toward a final text a year later, al-Nahdha under heightening pressure dropped the constitutional reference (art. 141) to "Islam, the religion of the state."[13]

Throughout the constitution-building process, two dimensions of active negotiation interacted with each other. Horizontally, the various levels of committees and consultations in the ANC debated the issues and negotiated the provisions of the constitutional formula. Vertically, as a continuation of the Kasba events, political parties and government figures negotiated in the public space with civil society, sometimes tacitly and sometimes in direct confrontation. As the process dragged on toward the end of 2013, the vertical dimension more and more imposed itself on the horizontal. The question of judicial sanctions for blasphemy was another issue on which al-Nahdha pulled back under severe public pressure. After a Salafi attack in June on an art exhibit as blasphemous, al-Nahdha introduced a constitutional provision criminalizing "attacks on the sacred," followed by a statement of the Troika leaders in the same sense. As an issue no one dared oppose, the article was incorporated in the first constitutional draft. But after vigorous public demonstrations, including journalists' strikes and a hunger strike, the government announced in October that al-Nahdha had withdrawn the blasphemy article and would implement two press freedom decrees that it had blocked for nearly a year.

Other issues have been handled in a similar way, sometimes with similar ambiguous reactions. More fervent than the negotiations over the place of religion were those over the nature of the governmental system—presidential or parliamentary—where the negotiating positions were curiously arrayed. Traditional legitimacy, expressed in the principle of consultation, led the Nahdha party to argue for a parliamentary system, which they also saw themselves as best able to dominate with their organized party, but they also saw the likely parliament-based governing coalitions as best situated to spread responsibility over the difficult upcoming economic and political challenges (Ghannouchi 1993). Despite the stigma of the preceding presidential regimes, liberal parties opted for a presidential or semipresidential system, which they saw as incarnating rational legitimacy and gathering consensual support to hold al-Nahdha in check (Pickard 2013b). Public opinion rejected a parliamentary system (fewer than 20 percent in favor) but also a presidential system during the first half of 2012 (25 percent) in favor of a mixed system (50 percent), but suddenly in mid-2012 it shifted to give heavy support to a presidential system (50 percent) (Williams and Associates 2013). The result was a stalemate in the committee on executive and legislative powers, expressed in two alternative articles in the first (August 2012) draft, and the issue was kicked upstairs to the monitoring committee of the Troika. There a partial agreement was reached in time for the October announcement, providing for a directly elected president with extended powers but still no definitive structure. However, the parties moved closer to each other, with an increased role for the prime minister responsible to parliament; questions of presidential power on specific issues such as interim decrees, legislative initiatives, and internal security, remained as final points of contention. The issue went back to the executive-legislative committee, and details were fleshed out in further negotiations after a Nahdha Shura Council compromise in April. The result, representing a series of mutual concessions rather than a working consensus, was a bicephalic system, despite a record often marked by stalemate and rivalry in other countries where the system exists.

Another matter concerned the women's rights article, also discussed extensively and subject to active external pressure. The committee on rights and liberties, headed by Nahdha member Farida Labidi, drafted article 28 to read: "The government guarantees the protection of women's rights and supports their achievements; it also considers woman a true partner to man in building the nation. Their roles complement each other within the family." The fact that women were defined by their relationship to men and located within the family upset many Tunisian citizens, who had expected that in the new constitution women would be considered fully equal to men, not just as a partner or complement. After the annual vacation and a month's further negotiation under public pressure, notably through a demonstration by women on 13 August that drew wide support, the committee in its new session found a common ground in the principle of equality (*musawat*). Again, the pattern was repeated: an initial Nahdha draft, a public reaction, and a compromise, this time consensual.

An additional matter for debate and delay was the source of human rights, a seemingly uncontentious detail with little disagreement on the nature of the rights. However, the Ministry of Transitional Justice and Human Rights and the Human Rights League were locked in a negotiation over content. In addition, Ghannouchi held that the source of human rights was God, whereas there was a broad feeling that the Universal Declaration of Human Rights—thus, a human source—was the founding basis. In April 2013 al-Nahdha pulled back after strong civil society pressure. The issue on the liberal side was not only that the universality of the rights needed recognition but the concern that if human rights depended on an Islamic source, Islamic interpreters could later circumscribe rights by religious interpretation. Al-Nahdha launched a more extreme position and then pulled back when faced with a strong reaction from civil society and the street (Chakroune 2013).

As the drafting process moved toward closure in mid-2013, the same pattern was repeated. Confronted with parties' outcry and repeated mass demonstrations, al-Nahdha withdrew support for a bill on "political immunization" (or "isolation," as termed in Libya), that barred members of the Old Order (including Qaid Es-Sebsi) from competing in upcoming elections. In July, in conference the party withdrew its frequent and categoric objections to a national unity or technocratic government to replace its Troika coalition, its refusal to accept the suspension of the ANC in the culminating constitutional crisis, and its insistence that Islam is the state religion. The pattern was evidence of the weight of the party hardliners in proposing articles that tested public acceptability, and of the prevailing counterweight of moderates in opting for compromise.

Other issues beyond the constitutional text made up the agenda to complete the institutionalization of the New Order. There was need to reach consensus over the formation of the Independent High Authority for the Elections, the Independent Information Authority, the Transitional Justice Committee, the Fact-Finding Committee on Corruption and Embezzlement, the Commission on the Seizure of Illegally Acquired Property, and transitional justice. There was also a need to negotiate a consensus over appointments in the civil service that al-Nahdha had been packing with ill-qualified followers, over rapid reform and restructuring of the security system staffed mainly with holdovers from the Old Order who were uncertain about their role, over the neutrality of government services also staffed by the old regime, and over reforms of financial and banking systems that were Old Order corruption circuits. In a winner-take-all approach that undermined its coalescing reputation, al-Nahdha appointed its own candidates to 19 of the 24 regional executive positions and 229 of the 264 regional commissions by 2013. All were replaced in 2014 by the Jomaa government to assure free and fair elections.

Although the constitution-drafting process provided limited opportunities for direct civic input, civil society was an unusual and active participant in indirect or tacit negotiations with the drafters. Some civil society organizations were invited to present their opinions to the drafters, largely in an ad hoc manner, and the agreed timetable included a one-month period for members of parliament to discuss the draft constitution with their constituents. Public meetings throughout the country discussed constitutional provisions and carried the results back to Tunis, although the meetings were often seeded with vocal Nahdha claques that made sure the message went in the right direction. At least as notable was the general public reaction to constitutional drafts from *al-Maghreb* and other press outlets that caused a notable moderation in the original Nahdha version of August 2011 and continued to weigh in on subsequent ANC and government negotiations, in a shift of the balance of power from the state to the street. On significant issues, as noted, tacit negotiations between proposals and the ensuing public reactions brought Nahdha concessions as a result. Indeed, this activity represented an unusual continuation of the original public outburst that constituted the 2011 *intifada* and that stayed on as a part of Tunisian political life.

Yet the informal process of tacit negotiations with the public was not enough to produce a consensual draft and to consummate the process. In order to find a negotiated consensus to overcome a fractious debate, civil society organizations attempted an organized dialogue outside the official constitutional process while conducting their tacit negotiations with the government over specific issues. The UGTT called for the establishment of a National Dialogue Council gathering political parties and civil society to establish encompassing negotiations and formulate a consensus over the major issues and more broadly for an integrating *projet de société*. "The aim of this initiative is to reinforce national unity, preserve the democratic transition, and secure collective management of the transitional period," said UGTT secretary-general Houcine Abassi (2012). In mid-2012 the labor union again proposed a National Dialogue over a dozen major issues, including the revolution, the martyrs and wounded, transparency in employment, and a schedule for the drafting of the constitution. It reaffirmed its commitment to a civilian state and a democratic republican regime while stressing the need to secure the protection of human rights and individual liberties, the rejection of violence and terrorism, and the respect of others' opinions and worship. The refusal of two of the Troika parties, al-Nahdha and CPR, to attend the National Dialogue conference on 16 October 2012 underscored the failure of the initiative as a source of consensus, but the pressure generated brought forth from the ANC a second constitutional draft a week later.

Many observers were skeptical about the dialogue initiative and the ability of the UGTT to play a mediating role above the electoral legitimacy of the Constituent Assembly; the Union openly sided with the secularists, skewing its own mediation efforts. Yet forces, primarily secularist, were organizing outside the ANC, knocking at the door for inclusion in the constitutional process, and going so far as to question the legitimacy of the ANC itself for outrunning its mandated term. The union's deputy secretary-general, Mohamed Mseimi, declared in mid-October 2012 that the new constitutional drafts failed to grant adequate economic and social rights to workers in keeping with the pivotal role that union members played in the *intifada*, and the UGTT, with help from the EU, conducted negotiations to harmonize workers' concerns and articulate them to the six commissions of the ANC

(Presse 2012). The EU, the International Financial Institutions (IFIs), and other international actors were also instrumental in using their economic weight to push the constitutional negotiations forward (ICG 2014).

In the beginning of 2013, the union threatened a major strike to back wide-ranging demands for a revamped cabinet replacing inept political appointment ministers. Typically, the matter simmered in negotiations among the Troika and with the UGTT and ended in no strike but a change of prime ministers in March, with Ali Laarayedh replacing Jebali. Despite such efforts, workers directly protested some of the provisions in the draft constitution, and their continuing strikes presented an ongoing challenge to government legitimacy. Municipal workers organized a four-day strike at the national level in February 2012 to protest low wages, and hundreds of job seekers temporarily occupied the headquarters of the large phosphate mine in Gafsa in May to protest economic conditions within the country. Unemployment levels rose from 23 percent in 2009 to 33 percent in 2012 (INS 2013), and GDP contracted as more than 170 foreign companies closed down operations in Tunisia, precipitating an exodus of tens of thousands of Tunisian job seekers to Europe (Wynne 2012). Failure to address these grievances created a class of spoilers who sought to derail broader institution-building processes in the belief that these processes detracted from needed economic reforms.

Increasingly, drafting the constitution was seen as a ragged process, where controversial issues long lay lost on the table without finding a solution, so that by mid-2013 the whole political system rose in revolt over its delays and directions. While some believed that the body's mission had to end by its anniversary as originally prescribed, others believed the Assembly's legitimacy to be dependent on the progress it made on the constitution. The vocal, if uncoordinated, liberal opposition issued increasingly shrill attacks on the ANC and the entire process, raising the tone and lowering the level of debate. Faced with popular disillusion, the ANC set the next election date for 23 June 2013, giving itself a new deadline; by March it was clear that June was impossible, since there was still no constitution or electoral commission and code, and elections would take six months to prepare, so the anniversary month of October was the next target, which also was missed. Further compromises on basic issues, such as the nature of the governmental system and the powers of the head of state, freedom of the press, and the place of religion, were taken outside at the monitoring committee meetings of the Troika, not inside the Assembly, to produce the third draft in June.

The political structure flailed around, looking for procedural fixes to overcome the substantive delays in the midst of mounting security fears. The idea of dialogue was taken over by President Marzouki as part of the March agreement on changes in the Troika government, convening in mid-April a session of representatives of the seven leading parties. But the council did not go beyond the ANC framework, its negotiations were unproductive, and its membership fell. The UGTT then called a National Conference on Dialogue as a prolongation of its October initiative and combined it with the Dar Dhiafa Dialogue of the president, but frequent meetings until mid-May were limited to setting timetables rather than attacking substantive constitutional issues. The third (June 2013) draft of the constitution opened the full plenary consideration at the same time as the draft was referred to the president's Compromise Commission that he added to the commission structure of the Assembly. These negotiations produced new changes, strengthening the presidential powers, moving the center of gravity of elusive consensus toward the liberal parties, with the acceptance of the Nahdha Shura Council. But there were still twenty bracketed passages on the most controversial issues.

Following the July assassination of Brahmi, a strike by seventy ANC members and the sit-in/protest at the Bardo (the ANC meeting hall) revived the 2011 Kasba experience and fundamentally changed the terms of negotiations among parties and also between the government and the public. With the increasingly tense security situation and the indecisive culmination of the Assembly's final committee consideration of the constitutional draft, the Troika government lost its legitimacy, and the president suspended the ANC on 7 August (Collins 2013) until a full National Dialogue could take hold. Five weeks later on 17 September, the National Dialogue issued a Roadmap "for the Resolution of the Political Crisis." Now with presidential blessings, the UGTT, the Tunisian Union of Industry and Handicrafts (UTICA), the Tunisian Human Rights League (LTDH), and the bar association, launched the National Dialogue, with a member from each major civil society organization and political party. It provided a venue for broad negotiations as the parties reached desperately for a consensus to bridge the crisis atmosphere that they had created. The Roadmap was a negotiated document, containing most of the demands of the opposition (of which the UGTT gradually became a part) in exchange for dropping their call for the dissolution of the ANC.

The Quartet set up a draconian calendar for the completion of the constitution, the creation of an Independent High Authority on Elections and the electoral law, and the installation of a neutral independent government to complete the preceding tasks. Another four months of multipolar negotiations—between the Troika government and the major opposition party Nida Tunis outside the ANC, between the official institutions and the Quartet of the National Dialogue, between the ANC and the popular sit-in outside their offices in the Bardo, and peppered by individual proposals for constitutional articles—were required for the final passage of the constitution on 20 January 2014 (Gaddes 2014).

The active political forces of the country, including al-Nahdha's coalition partners, called for a nonpartisan, inclusive government to complete the drafting of the constitution and the formation of the Electoral Commission. The call had already been launched by the outgoing Nahdha premier Jebali in March 2013, but it took six more months of intense negotiations under the imposition of the National Dialogue and backed by insistent demonstrations by civil society groups and opposition parties, to bring about an agreement for the Nahdha government to resign in favor of a government of technocrats once the constitution had been finalized. Al-Nahdha insisted that the constitution be finished first, to be able to claim credit for the accomplishment when elections came, whereas the opposition wanted the government out immediately. Under threat of a UGTT general strike, Laarayedh agreed to resign along with his government upon the selection of a successor, and in exchange the leader of the neutral technocratic government, Mehdi Jomaa, a nonpartisan minister in the Nahda government, was to install his government only after the constitution was passed. The National Dialogue then turned to pushing the Electoral Commission and schedule through the ANC.

Although, from the very beginning, the National Council for the Protection of the Revolution had agreed to maintain unicameralism, in fact Tunisia in the most creative period of constitution making adopted a unique bicameral system. Instead of a lower and upper house, Tunisia had a lower and "much lower" house, the latter in the form of the National Dialogue, with some 150 members unelected but consensual in its formation and in its operations. The dialogue continued to function through the October 2014 National Assembly elections, issuing a "charter" for the elections, providing more effective negotiations for formulation, and undergirding the work of the NCA and Jomaa government to the end (Redissi 2014).

How much these compromises and the entire document represent zero-sum concessions rather than a national consensus that engages all sides is still uncertain. The bicephalic system of government is a telling example of a matching compromise that creates a difficult working system if the prime minister and the president come from different parties (Blondel and Müller-Rommel 1993; Diamond, Plattner, and Costopoulos 2010; Elgie 2007). The results do represent many retreats by al-Nahdha in an effort to find positions agreeable to both sides, but for these compromises al-Nahdha has received few concessions from the other side, only more and more strident demands; al-Nahdha felt unrequited.[14] Do these compromises constitute an integrative consensus on a sociopolitical contract or simply a distributive splitting the difference to avoid stalemate? They continue to be dogged by the "Trojan horse" or "camel's nose" fear on the part of many liberals that ambiguous wording used to cover over differences could be used later by the other side to facilitate an Islamist takeover in substance. The same fear is felt by al-Nahdha in reverse, especially when the mid-2013 events in Egypt ("Egypt's revenge" on Tunisia for starting it all) showed a neighboring society that seized the opportunity to eliminate its Islamists (after the Islamic party had clung to winner-take-all policies). Tunisia still remains a very divided society; a poll in mid-2013 showed that 56 percent of the population favored making shari'a "the official law of the land" (Pew 2013), to which Ghannouchi replied that al-Nahdha seeks cooperation and coalition, not takeover, and that its Islamist view is encompassing and tolerant (Ghannouchi 1993).

The Tunisian process of negotiation for formulation presents strongly contrasting images. On one hand, the job of constitutional drafting proceeded apace, marked by regular and significant concessions by the largest Islamist force. The process took twice as long as expected (and mandated), but that should not be surprising given the contentious context, and it was not an unusual length of time compared to other countries' experience (Egypt's was much shorter but failed as a result). The first (1959) constitution took three years, but it involved a regime change from the monarchy and was accompanied by major legislative innovations, such as the Personal Status and education reforms. On the other hand, the atmosphere began in existential hostility and rose to panic level. Nahdha members were driven by a "higher" legitimacy and affirmed a timetable of patience and inevitability; their concessions were suspected as being "one step back to make two steps forward," and the suspicion was often confirmed, verbally even if not in realization; their language, according to various spokespeople and sometimes by a single spokesperson, was contradictory and duplicitous; the electoral politics and shared ends if not means rendered them fellow travelers with the Salafists despite tactical differences. As a result, when incidents of violence occurred—storming of the American embassy, assassination of Chokri Belaid and Mohammed Brahmi, ambushes on the Algerian border and in Tunisian villages, among others—people felt fear and intimidation; by looking for a stronger government response and seeing too little too late, they felt confirmed in their suspicions and fears. The escalating cycle was vicious and self-feeding, and it undermined the initial positive progress to the point where that progress stopped in mid-August 2013, and a new, encompassing venue of National Dialogue was called upon. The same complex arrangement of multinegotiations then turned to finish the constitutional job—the interim government, the electoral code and commission, and the electoral schedule—under the charge of a caretaker government of technicians, from the passage of the constitution at the beginning of the year to the elections at the end, but under the careful guidance of the National Dialogue.

The goal of negotiation for formulation is the eventual consensual construction of a constitutional New Order (Rawls 1987). The constitutional process was one of vigorous negotiations along two dimensions, a long-fought process with extended delays. As horizontal negotiations over specific constitutional provisions bogged down, committee deadlocks were sent to the coordinating committee chaired by the Assembly president and then to the Troika monitoring committee and finally to the bodies created by the National Dialogue for final negotiations. Vertically, tacit or indirect negotiations continued between the Assembly and the organs of civil society—both organized such as the UGTT and the other Quartet organizations, and also public groups (Compass, Vigilance) and anomic groups such as street protests. The negotiations for formulation took only two years, beginning in February 2012, to produce a rather coherent, liberal constitution under the watchful eye of a public and civil society that has found again its interest in politics and self-government, after decades of elite monopolization and repression. But to the public that was too long, twice the allotted time, and the last steps dissolved in a bitter distributive battle between the Nahdha government and the liberal secularists that undermined any consensus and brought out fears and differences, in an atmosphere of growing popular impatience, indecisive attention to the other ANC charge of governance, party distraction by electoral reasoning, and government irresponsibility toward daily civil rights issues and subversive violence.

CONFLICT, COALITION, AND CHARISMA: WILL THE PAST DICTATE THE FUTURE?

When the Assembly turned to the constitution, negotiation for coalition returned to the scene, if it had ever left. Groups and small parties sought to make a force to counterbalance the large Nahdha bloc and to lead it, while at the same time being true to their divided ideologies and clienteles. The negotiations produced many attempts to overcome the party divisions but no lasting agreement over the membership of the coalition and its leader as long as each putative leader thought he had a chance, a return to the October 2011 situation. There was little negotiation among the parties in the effort to find a common formulation for coalescence but rather a constant reassertion of positions that at best produced competing ideologically oriented alliances.

Mid-2012 was a veritable *souq* for coalition formation. In early April, a number of established liberal parties—including PDP and Afek Tunis—negotiated a Republican alliance against the Troika, but the whole was no larger than the sum of its parts. Further to the right, the Initiative (*al-Mubadara*) gathered a number of splinters from the RCD of Ben Ali, lying in wait for the collapse of attempts at a New Order but without any new leadership of their own. Negotiations on the left produced a number of groupings, typically coalescing on programmatic orientations but divided by ideological purity. After the 2011 elections, *muntafadin* leaders, with the addition of other left tendencies and floating individuals, negotiated their own alliance of five small parties into a Popular Front (*jebha sha'biya*), "a political front and not essentially electoral [that] will work for the realization of the objectives of the revolution and constitutes a third pole of opposition," according to Hamma Hammami (2012), the historic leader of the Communist Party of Tunisian Workers (PCOT). The founding agreement signaled the need for local organization against forces hostile to the revolution and the working class, and opposition to diplomatic normalization (*tatbii*) with Israel, to foreign financing of associations, and to negotiations with the European Union, a negative and narrow platform (Belaid 2012). In midsummer another leftist party coalition was negotiated under the label of the Democratic and Socialist Way, including Tajdid, the Democratic Modernist Pole

(Massar) (itself a coalition), and the PTT; it then sought to negotiate a merger with the Republicans, but they could not agree on a common formula.

In politics, a big tent party (also known as a Great Coalition, a catch-all party, or Uncle Sasha's Store) is a political party seeking to attract people with diverse viewpoints, with little concern for a unifying vision other than winning or defeating a common opponent, much like the *intifada* movement itself that had toppled the dictator, the nationalist movement that brought independence, or the approach identified as aggregating in the introduction. The party does not require adherence to a particular ideology as a criterion for membership, and new joining groups do not influence policy or major party decisions measurably at first: it is a coalition with little formulation. Such was the Call for Tunisia (Nida Tunis), a provocative new initiative announced in mid-June 2012 by Qaid es-Sebsi with the aim of uniting Tunisia's "non-Islamist" parties under a big tent to counterbalance the Troika. Nida Tunis was a new coalition of five parties with some former and controversial leaders, leftists, and many conservatives (ex-RCD militants). The former regime officials or RCDists excluded from running in the previous elections saw in the new initiative a chance to revive their political prospects; the leftists who joined the movement saw Nida Tunis as the only possible way to regain control of the country; and the two factions sparred with each other within Nida Tunis, impelling Qaid es-Sebsi to recruit from formerly neutral circles. Early on, the movement undercut its own appeal by calling into question the legality of the entire Assembly and constitution-making process and by leaning on a single octogenarian leader. But as the crisis of mid-2013 through 2014 heightened, Nida Tunis was able to mobilize huge demonstrations behind its attacks on the evolving constitution and finally on 7 August 2013 force a total breakdown of negotiations and a suspension of the process.

The emergence of two conservative parties (al-Nahdha and Nida Tunis), Islamist and secular, and a divided gaggle of other leftist and liberal parties was to be expected in the new Tunisian political scene after the uprising. Whereas political Islam lends itself to a centralized internal organization, despite factional differences, the liberal and leftist opposition is by nature pluralist, so it takes some effort to cobble together a party to serve as a counterweight. One party derives its legitimacy from religious sources, the other from rational sources. At the same time, in this conservative society it is hardly surprising that the debate is over the kind of conservatism Tunisians would choose.

HOPE IN UNCERTAINTY

As a few dictatorships began to fall in the Arab region and disorder began to rise, some voices have been raised to express the risk that the Arab Spring could turn into an Islamic spring or simply a return of the cold weather of the Old Order. Such fears imposed the legitimacy question with force. Do those societies whose religion is Islam have nothing but this obsession of assuring their "religiosity" independent of any other need? (Al-Qarawee 2012). In other terms, will this "Islam" be soluble in democracy? And will Tunisia move toward "normal politics" that address public welfare demands, or will it remain stuck in a bipolar disorder over identity? Or will it reduce these questions into an equation of Islamism and extremism and seek refuge for stability in a return to the Old Order? The Tunisian experience will falter over these questions, if the negotiation process between political groups were to continue to be dominated by electoral politics and if the two formulations of the state were to continue to tear apart consensus on the social and economic demands, to the destruction of social and political stabilization. Only institutionalization and therefore the legal-rational legitimacy can save the outcome of the transition.

Thus the challenge of political coalition has evolved. The Troika coalition was launched after the 2011 elections and renegotiated in March 2013 for the primary purpose of finding a governing majority, even if temporary, and not on specific programs. With a clear majority and a diverse range of views, the coalition began with considerable legitimacy to address the two tasks of drafting a new constitution and running a caretaker administration. It was in the situational interest of the political parties to form the coalition, because no one wanted nor could have the sole responsibility for either task. However, the brief experience of power demonstrated the limited capacity of the Troika to mobilize its bases or to develop new consensual alternatives. It early made the mistake of excluding the likes of Kamal Jendoubi, Siham Ben Sedrine, and Yadh Ben Achour, basically the very secularists who took part in midwifing Tunisia's democratic birth. The two junior partners were wiped out in the October 2014 elections, yet President Marzouki gathered broad support (much more than his own party) just six points shy of Qaid es-Sebsi in the first presidential round and ten points in the second.

Despite its effective organization, publicity, and better financial resources than other parties, al-Nahdha began its governance with little confidence, internal splits, poor skills, and no experience. Throughout its life in a coalition it formulated no vision about what the political and civic partners could do or what the political New Order should be; it was more interested in social norms than in programmatic governance or economic measures. More important, the population felt that it squandered its initial legitimacy and showed itself to be weak and coddling toward the security problems of the country, especially those posed by the Salafists. As a result, it lost significant support in the October 2014 elections, ending with less than a third of the seats. But al-Nahdha did keep a coherent bloc of voters concentrated in the poorer south and did establish a place for itself in Tunisian politics—Ghannouchi's goal.

On the other side, the opposition was clumsy and suffered from an out-of-power complex, instilled by the lasting effect of Ben Ali's *mukhabarat*. It pursued little constructive initiative, acted as if it were still in the opposition, and focused on delegitimizing diatribes against the Troika coalition. Its character assassination of those in power was partly responsible, along with Salafist provocations, for the state of heightened tension and violence in the country. Yet Nida Tunis, under the helm of Qaid es-Sebsi, gathered together the diverse array of secularists and more—leftists, Destourians, traditional elites from the Sahel and from Tunis, among others, particularly in the north of the country and the Sahel (the northeast coast). It was no more of a coherent programmatic coalition than the Troika itself, and it had to seek other diverse partners to make a governing coalition. Yet it rode on popular dissatisfaction with the programmatic performance of the Troika to take over al-Nahdha's former dominant position of 40% of the Assembly seats and win the presidency to give to the past, once again, a future. In between the two largest coalitions, others more narrowly focused, such as the business-oriented Free Patriotic Union (UPL) and Afek Tunis and the socialist Popular Front (PCOT), carved out a part of public opinion, primarily also in the north of the country.

Barely half the eligible voters participated in 2011; on the social side, in spring 2013, 40 percent of the unemployed youth had given up looking for a job and 94 percent saw no point in registering with the local employment office (National Youth Observatory 2013). But in the middle of the following year, nearly a million new voters registered, half of whom were women and nearly half young people, for a total of over five million out of an eligible population of seven million (IRI 2014). When election day came in 2014, participation rose to two-thirds of the eligible voters in October for parliament and in November and the runoff in December for the presidency. These figures, unusually high for the region, constituted the strongest endorsement of the results of the negotiations for formulation of the constitution and for coalition for the elections and a heavy charge of expectations for rapid government action in the New (or Renewed) Order.

The upcoming challenge was about the process of legislative reform in order to ensure that all legislation be in conformity with the constitution and international law (which a draft article of the constitution declared to be subordinate to the constitution but was reversed) and about rationalizing the government structures. But the heaviest challenge of all was to be found in the need to revive Tunisia's economy, to provide the fourth element of the *intifada*'s slogan—work—for the educated as well as the meanly educated, who were the ones who made the *intifada*. That meant liberating business from its political and bureaucratic constraints, attracting foreign and domestic investment in productive enterprises, recruiting competent and uncorrupt civil servants, and restoring Tunisia's attractiveness as a tourist haven. More than anything, the Troika's failure at the economic task cost its three parties the election. More deeply, it was the transitional government's inability to set the socioeconomic machinery functioning again that caused the debilitating and demoralizing security challenge from rogue Salafists. Disillusioned *muntafadin* with no prospect for the present found revenge for an absence of a future in millennial nihilism that in turn sapped the optimism of the common citizen needed to push the new government to meet its more important positive challenges.

This account ends with the approval of the new constitution and the new elections of 2014 and the new government in 2015. The path from the initial uprising to the formulation of a New Order in elections and a constitution has been characterized as an example of Short Track transition because of the rapid overthrow of the authoritarian order and the assiduous negotiation processes that pulled Tunisia out of the Old Order. Tunisia was never a collapsed state, and the commitment of its new and old political figures to maintaining the state while negotiating hard to overhaul its contents was crucial to a smooth transition. This absence of collapse and the continuity of the state helped shape the negotiations for formulation along the path of legal-rational legitimacy. At the same time, despite the disorder of the political forces except for al-Nahdha and the inability of these forces to focus on appropriate organizations rather than narrow personal and party fortunes, negotiations for coalition provided the dynamic elements for transition politics, beginning with the willingness of the incumbents of the Old Order to negotiate themselves at least temporarily out of office, to negotiate the first steps of transition, and then to negotiate themselves back into the New Order.

It is also a Short Track transition for its relatively short constitution-making process, despite the nervous popular impatience. The spirit and function of National Dialogue was employed to handle rules of the game underlying the constitutional compact, such as reciprocal acceptance of winners and losers, rejection of winner-take-all policies and political corruption, and adoption of political tolerance and rejection of violent militancy (ICG 2014). In the end, the parties got what they wanted, which—as in negotiation—was a reduced version of what they originally really wanted: acceptance as a normal political party for al-Nahdha, against acceptance of a rational, verifiable sense of legitimacy and a return of politics to the politicians. This is the ultimate test to demonstrate whether the pragmatism of a new majority is just a political tactic or a strategic option, and whether the constitution will remain a moderated agglomeration of articles or a coherent, consensual declaration of the New Order. The result was a transition—uprising to constitution and elections—of four years and a constitution in 2014 somewhat more liberal than its predecessor. Every human activity has its warts, but Tunisia stands as a credible example for its Arab Spring compatriots of overcoming distributive bargaining to arrive at an integrative solution.

Notes

1. From Middle French *compromis*, from Medieval Latin, Late Latin *compromissum* ("a compromise, originally a mutual promise to refer to arbitration"), prop. neuter of Latin *compromissus*, past participle of *compromittere* ("to make a mutual promise to abide by the decision of an arbiter"), from *com-* ("together") + *promittere* ("to promise").

2. The term refers to a state were all would be equal as citizens, as opposed to an Islamic state (*dawla islamia*), where personal status depends on religion.

3. The Code of Personal Status (CPS) (Arabic مجلة الأحوال الشخصية) is a series of progressive laws aimed at the institution of equality between women and men in a number of areas. It was promulgated by *beylical* decree on 13 August 1956 and came into effect on 1 January 1957.

4. Material obtained through interviews in Tunisia is not sourced; printed sources are cited as possible.

5. Several of its leaders (without generalizing) benefited from the generosity and donations of the old regime. The labor leader Belgacem Ben Salem is accused of corruption under the former regime, after having acquired land near Carthage almost for free.

6. CPR was absent although it contributed to the drafting; al-Nahdha was present despite their resignation from the commission in disagreement over its work.

7. Qaid es-Sebsi, quoted in *Jeune Afrique* no. 2669 (4 March 2012), 36. Scattered other issues of the magazine have been consulted.

8. The party is variously referred to al-Nahdha, Nahdha, Ennahda, and Ennahdha (the transliterated pronunciation); the first version is used here; where the term is used as an adjective, the second version is used.

9. Nahdha hardliners felt they "wuz robbed" because a different electoral system would have given them 69 percent of the seats (Pickard 2013b; Carey 2013).

10. The process of negotiation for coalition in another Arab country—Iraq—is revealing. "[The] fundamental flaw towards government formation lies in its fixation on the country's identity politics, rather than the bargaining process. . . . Indeed, there is an extensive and intricate bargaining process that precedes the formation of the government. The Iraqis do not enter a power-sharing arrangement unless their interests are negotiated down to the last tee. This has not happened yet, and various parties have struck no significant bargains. If a unity government were formed without sufficient compromises that help glue the coalition together, it will most likely crash and burn, creating another cycle of political crises. . . . In Iraq, the usual case is that nothing happens until everything happens. The Iraqis will not start the clock until the politics have been settled on how the next government will be formed. Indeed, 99 percent of the government formation process takes place behind closed doors, while only 1 percent is open to the public and simply ceremonial" (Mardini 2014).

11. Manouba Dean Habib Kazdaghli was acquitted in May 2013 of charges of forcibly evicting Salafist students ransacking his office during the incident; the students were suspended from the university for six months but received no judicial sanctions.

12. CISD conference, 2 March 2012. Although secularism seems as if it was a philosophy and the fruit of philosophical reflections and meditations that came to fight idealist and religious outlooks, he said it is not so. Secularism appeared, evolved, and crystallized in the West as procedural solutions. "This leads us to ask the following question: are we in need of secularism in its procedural aspect? Perhaps the most important idea in the ensemble of these procedures is the idea of the state's neutrality i.e. towards religions and its abstention from interfering with people's consciences." Whereas the state's scope or jurisdiction is limited to the "Public Domain," religion's scope extends to the "Private." This stance on the role of religion in government had a huge impact on the constitution that finally emerged and has the potential to defuse growing political polarization between Islamists and secularists.

13. Some secularists were concerned, however, that the article stating "Tunis is a . . . state [rather that "a people"] whose religion is Islam" could be interpreted to mean that the state was to be Islamic.

14. When Ghannouchi, on 29 September 2014, was asked what he and the party got in exchange for the many concessions, he replied, surprised, "Why, we got a constitution. That is more important than any party."

References

Abassi, Houcine. 2012. *El-Chourouk*, 19 September.

Amdouni, Murad. 2012. *El-Hassad*, 12 September.

Angrist, Michele Penner. 2013. "Understanding the Success of Mass Civic Protest in Tunisia." *Middle East Journal* 67, no. 4 (Autumn): 547–564.

ASSForum. 2012a. *The 4th Wave of the Political Barometer*. January. www.assforum.org.

———. 2012b. *The 5th Wave of the Political Barometer*. October. www.assforum.org.

Belaid, Chokri. 2012. *El-Chourouk*. 21 September.

Bellin, Eva. 2011. "Lessons from the Jasmine and Nile Revolutions." *Middle East Brief* 50, May.

Ben Achour, Yadh. 2011a. Crisis Group interview, 10 March 2011. Qtd. in *Popular Protest in North Africa (IV): Tunisia's Way*. Middle East/North Africa (MENA) Report no. 106 (28 April): 19.

———. 2011b. *Democracy and Islam*. Conference, La Cité des Sciences, Tunis, 2 March.

Ben Hafaiedh, Abdelouahab. 1994. "Legality and Constitutional Legitimacy in the Maghreb." PhD dissertation, Faculté des Sciences Juridiques et Politiques (FSJP), University of Tunis, Ariana.

Biddle, F. 1957. "Necessity of Compromise." In *Integrity and Compromise: Problems of Public and Private Conscience*, edited by Robert M. MacIver. New York: Harper and Brothers.

Blondel, Jean, and Ferdinand Müller-Rommel, eds. 1993. *Governing Together: The Extent and Limits of Joint Decision-Making in Western Europe*. New York: St Martin's Press.

Carey, John M. 2013. "Electoral Formula and the Tunisian Constituent Assembly." Dartmouth College, 9 May. http://sites.dartmouth.edu/carey/files/2013/02/Tunisia-Electoral-Formula-Carey-May-2013-reduced.pdf.

Cincotta, Richard. 2011. "Tunisia's Shot at Democracy: What Demographics and Recent History Tell Us." *New Security Beat*, 25 January. http://www.newsecuritybeat.org/2011/01/tunisias-shot-at-democracy-what-demographics-and-recent-history-tell-us/.

Collins, Nicholas. 2013. "Actions." NDI Tunis Office, 7 August.

Courbage, Y. 2009. Interview in *Awrak Al-Awsat* 2:65–69.

Courbage, Youssef, and Emmanuel Todd. 2007. *Le rendez-vous des civilisations*. Paris: PUF.

Chakroune, Bouchra. 2013. "Bargaining for Peace." MAIA thesis, School of Advanced International Studies (SAIS) Bologna Center, Johns Hopkins University.

Dahmani, Frida. 2012. "Ennahdha, blocage à tous les étages." *Jeune Afrique* 2667 (1 February): 47–49.

Diamond, Larry Jay, Marc F. Plattner, and Philip J. Costopoulos, eds. 2010. *Debates on Democratization*. Baltimore: Johns Hopkins University Press.

Elgie, Robert. 2007. "Varieties of Semi-Presidentialism and Their Impact on Nascent Democracies." *Taiwan Journal of Democracy* 3, no. 2 (December): 67.

Elloumi, M. 2011. "Les gouvernements provisoires en Tunisie du janvier au octobre." Master's thesis, University of Tunis, el-Manar.

Emrhod. 2013. "Le baromètre politique d'Emrhod." Tunis: Emrhod Consulting (October–November).

Gaddes, Chawki. 2014. *Constitution of the Tunisian Republic. Jasmine Foundation for Research and Communication*. http://www.jasmine-foundation.org/en/.

Geisier, Vincent, and Eric Gobe. 2006. "Des fissures dans la 'Maison Tunisienne.'" *L'Année du Maghreb 2005*, 353–414.

Ghali, Amine. 2011. "Tunisia's Constitutional Process." Al-Kawakibi Democracy Transition Center, 9 December.

Ghannouchi, Rachid. 1993. "Participation of Islamists in a non-Islamic Government." In *Power-Sharing Islam?*, edited by Azzam Tamimi. London: Liberty for Muslim World Publications.

———. 2012a. Interview with AFP. *Agence France Presse*, 18 September.

——— 2012b. "Secularism and Relation between Religion and the State from the Perspective of the Nahdha Party." Lecture at Center for Study of Islam and Democracy (CSID), Tunisia, 2 March.

———. 2012c. Statement in lecture, 15 March.

———. 2013. "Secularism and the Relation to the State from the Perspective of the al-Nahdha Movement." CSID conference, 2 March, Tunis.

Goldner, S. N. 2006. "Pre-Electoral Coalition Formation in Parliamentary Democracies." *Brown Journal of Political Science* 36: 193–212.

Gutmann, Amy, and Dennis Thompson. 2012. *The Spirit of Compromise*. Princeton, N.J.: Princeton University Press.

Hamblin, Amy. 2012. "Evaluating the Impact of New Media on the Tunisian and Egyptian Uprisings." Conflict Management Program, SAIS, Johns Hopkins University.

Hammami, Hamma. 2012. Interview with radio station Oasis FM, Gabès, Tunisia, 11 September.

Henneberg, Sabina. 2013. "Governing Uncertainty: The First Provisional Government." Paper presented at the annual meeting of the African Studies Association, 21 November, Minneapolis.

Hurd, Elizabeth Shakman. 2012. "Tunisia: Democracy after Secularism." Al Jazeera, 11 April. http://www.aljazeera.com/indepth/opinion/2012/04/20124795440442662.html.

International Crisis Group (ICG). 2011. "Popular Protest in North Africa and the Middle East (IV): Tunisia's Way. Middle East/North Africa (MENA) Report 106 (28 April).

———. 2014. "L'exception tunisienne: Succès et limites du consensus." Briefing Moyen-Orient et Afrique du Nord no. 37 (5 June).

INS. 2013. Institut National de Statistiques, cited by Dean Lotfi Machichi, "The Economic Demands of the Tunisian Revolution," presentation, Johns Hopkins University, Washington, 20 March.

International Republican Institute (IRI). 2014. "Tunisian Elections Dispatch No. 1: Voter Registration." 29 July.

Journal Tunisie. 2012. "Rached Ghannouchi: Des négociations sont en cours pour élargir la coalition au pouvoir." 14 July. https://www.tunisia-sat.com/vb/archive/index.php/t-2313113.html.

Larémont, Ricardo René, ed. 2014. *Revolution, Revolt and Reform in North Africa: The Arab Spring and Beyond*. New York: Routledge.

Lipset, Seymour Martin. 1967. *The First New Nation*. New York: Anchor Doubleday.

Lourimi, Lajmi. 2011. Interview with Ettounisia TV, 12 April.

———. 2012. Interview with Ettounisia TV, June.

Ltifi, Afifa. 2012. "Tunisia's Second Largest Democratic Party Divides." *North Africa United*, 18 May. http://www.lemag.ma/english/Tunisia-s-Second-Largest-Democratic-Party-Divides_a1490.html.

Mardini, Ramzy. 2014. "Iraqis Spinning Their Wheels." Atlantic Council, 7 July. http://www.atlanticcouncil.org/blogs/menasource/iraqis-spinning-their-wheels.

Margalit, Avishai. 2009. *On Compromises and Rotten Compromises*. Princeton, N.J.: Princeton University Press.

Nachi, Mohamed, and Matthieu de Nanteuil, eds. 2006. *Éloge du compromis: Pour une Nouvelle pratique démocratique*. Louvain-la-Neuve: Academia Bruylant.

National Youth Observatory. 2013. *The Youth and Their Participation in General Life*. Tunis: National Youth Observatory.

Pew Research Center. 2013. Chpt. 1, "Beliefs about Sharia," in "The World's Muslims: Religion, Politics and Society." 30 April. http://www.pewforum.org/2013/04/30/the-worlds-muslims-religion-politics-society-beliefs-about-sharia/ (accessed 16 February 2015).

Pickard, Duncan. 2011. "Challenges to Legitimate Governance in Post-Revolution Tunisia." *Journal of North African Studies* 16, no. 4: 637–652.

———. 2012. "Lessons from Constitution-Making in Tunisia." *Issue Brief*, Atlantic Council, 13 December.

———. 2013a. "Electoral Politics under Tunisia's New Constitution." *Issue Brief*, Atlantic Council, 11 July.

———. 2013b. "The Politics of Tunisia's Final Draft Constitution." I-CONnect (blog of the International Journal of Constitutional Law and ConstitutionMaking.org), 16 May.

Pierre, Andrew. 2002. *Coalitions Building and Maintenance: The Gulf War, Kosovo, Afghanistan, and the War on Terrorism*. Washington, D.C.: Institute for the Study of Diplomacy, Georgetown University.

Piot, Olivier. 2011. *La Révolution Tunisienne*. Monts: Les Petits Matins.

Pollock, John. 2011. "Streetbook: How the Egyptian and Tunisian Youth Hacked the Arab Spring." *MIT Technology Review*, September–October. http://www.technologyreview.com/web/38379/.

Presse de Tunisie. 2012. "L'avant projet de la constitution ne répond pas aux aspirations des travailleurs." 19 October. http://www.lapresse.tn/19102012/57025/lavant-projet-de-la-constitution-ne-repond-pas-aux-aspirations-des-travailleurs.html (accessed 4 January 2013).

Puchot, Pierre. 2011. *Tunisie: Une révolution arabe*. Lonrai: Galaade.

Al-Qarawee, Harith. 2012. "The Outset of Post-Islamist Age." Reset DOC, 31 March. http://www.resetdoc.org/story/00000021543.

Rawls, John. 1987. "The Idea of Overlapping Consensus." *Oxford Journal of Legal Studies* 7, no. 1: 1–25.

Redissi, Hamadi. 2014. "What Role for Tunisia's National Dialog under the Interim Unity Government?" Arab Reform Initiative, July.

Rowsell, Nicole, and Adsma Ben Yahia. 2012. *Confidence Gap: Citizen Priorities on the One-Year Anniversary of the National Constituent Assembly Elections*. Washington, D.C.: National Democratic Institute (NDI), 12 December.

Sghiri, Malek. 2011. "Heroic Resolve in the Face of the Omnipresent Machine of Oppression." Testimony, Heinrich Böll Foundation.

Shirayanagi, Kouichi. 2011. "Ettakatol Suspends Coalition Building Talks." *Tunisialive*, 10 February. http://allafrica.com/stories/201111281780.html.

Strøm, Kaare, and Wolfgang C. Müller 2000. "The Keys to Togetherness: Coalition Agreements in Parliamentary Democracies." In *The Uneasy Relationship between Parliamentary Members and Leaders*, edited by Lawrence D. Longley and Reuven Y. Hazen, 255–282. London: Frank Cass.

Thompson, Leigh, and R. Hastie. 1990. "Social Perception in Negotiation." *Organizational Behavior and Human Decision Processes* 47: 98–123.

Weslati, Slah. 2011. *Démocratie ou guerre civile*. Tunis: Nirvana.

Williams and Associates. 2013. *Survey of Tunisian Public Opinion: October 1–12, 2013*. Salem, Mass.: Williams and Associates.

Wolf, Anne. 2012. "Divided and Looking Where to Stand." *Sada*, Carnegie Endowment for International Peace, 20 December.

Wynne, Ted. 2012. "Labor Strikes Plague New Islamist Governments." United States Institute of Peace, 7 May. http://www.usip.org/publications/labor-strikes-plague-new-islamist-governments (accessed 27 December 2012).

Zartman, I. William. 1995. *Collapsed States: Disintegration and Restoration of Legitimate Authority*. Boulder, Colo.: Lynne Reinner.

Zghal, Abdelqader. 1989. "L'islam, la constitution et les janissaires." *El-Mostaqbel El-Arabi*. Markiz Dirassat El-Wihda Al-Arabia, Beiruth.

Egypt

Can a Revolution Be Negotiated?

ALY EL RAGGAL AND HEBA RAOUF EZZAT

THIS CHAPTER EXPLORES the reasons for the failure of political negotiations in the different phases of the Egyptian revolution since 25 January 2011. This failure is rooted in the relational and structural map of the scene, as well as the discrepancy in the process of negotiation, as there is always one dominant party in a given scene and an absence of a vision, agenda, and strategy by the other parties engaged. The first party was the Supreme Council of the Armed Forces (SCAF), represented by the minister of defense, whose full control was challenged by the presidential elections of June 2012; the other parties are the political forces—movements, groups, political parties, and circles of activists. In fact, it could be argued that the authority in power is the actor that initiates, leads, and manages any round of negotiations without allowing other partners to decide the results while repeatedly asking them to commit to the outcome even though they lack the same degree of commitment. At some point two actors—the elected president and the minister of defense—assumed at the same time that they were in the seat of power, which resulted eventually in a conflict between them and led to the ouster of the president by a military takeover backed by the opposition and the old regime supporters.

The process of negotiation in the Egyptian revolution could be analyzed through different approaches. It could be studied in terms of the status of representation of the parties, their performance and their discourse during the process, the strategies employed, the tactics adopted, the subjects discussed, the objectives and goals set, the efficiency in managing the transitional process, and finally the outcome (Kremenyuk 2002). Another approach is to study the reasons behind the discrepancies of the process in relation to the asymmetry inherent in the dynamics of the revolution. This approach shifts the focus of researchers from the elements composing an effective and successful type of negotiation to studying the contradictory factors in the nature of the Egyptian revolution and their forms and dynamics, an approach that might be in deep tensions with the current approach to negotiation and representation itself. In this approach the task and the tools of the research on the subject are drastically changed in comparison to the classical approaches to study negotiations. It is therefore the task of this chapter to unveil the patterns of interactions and dynamics in the unfolding of the Egyptian revolution and at the same time to test the components of what we would call classical approaches to political negotiation. If political studies use the notion of a failing state, one can also talk in this case of a failing negotiation.

At the heart of any process of negotiations are the relational levels and the way they control and set the frames of interaction and the exercise of power. What are the main entities of representation and who leads the negotiations on their behalf are the main questions to ask in a political struggle that calls for liberation, revolution, or reform. In other words, we should search for the conditions and the factors of transformation needed to reach the point of negotiation before analyzing the course and the process of negotiation itself.

The difficulty in understanding the Egyptian scene is that the negotiation process is distorted and asymmetric. At the outset the Egyptian people wanted the government out. After only eighteen days President Hosni Mubarak had to step down. Yet the transition proved to be disorderly. Different groups started rounds of dialogues (assumed to be collective public negotiations). The process was monitored and formed by public speeches by "attendees" rather than being deliberative and based on points that were initiated by "participants." It was a multi-ring circus with negotiations within and among the rings/sides. The link between all the circles is missing, because the parties in such negotiations kept shifting positions; their actions and reactions lacked consistency and thus were challenging to predict and difficult to document. Secret meetings also took place between the SCAF and some groups, but the groups that did meet were not announced, SCAF's purpose for meeting was not clear, and the groups' standing in a negotiation process was off balance.

THE DIFFICULT TASK OF BUILDING AN ARGUMENT

Engaging with the main argument of this project, and being both political theorists and activists at the same time, the two authors of this text depart from the dominant approach of different negotiation theories that assume that the process is rational and orderly, based on rationality in its modernist definition as a dominant notion, and requiring a degree of orderly change or actions and clear relations between actors to be present even if such relations are not institutionalized. Unilinear and progressive theories are imbedded in the assumption too. The "revolutions" of the Arab Spring cannot be simply described as socially integrated secular mass uprisings against characteristically corrupt, arrogant, and inefficient governments. Their nationalist and religious components were obvious, even though the uprisings cannot be identified as religious (compared to the Iranian revolution).

Ideology, class conflicts, and religious revolts that are an integral part of the scene are often missed in the popular and apparently spontaneous disorderly democratic outbursts of 2011. The events are the culmination of dissent that took different forms and lasted for decades, resulting in confrontations of different degrees between the opposition groups and the regimes. There is no way this history can be overlooked as the old players are part of the scene after the fall of the Mubarak regime with its established legacy, while new actors who brought about the change in its last step still need to establish their legitimacy and build their own support structures. This is a problem of size as well as vision, and it is becoming rooted outside the big squares of main cities. Hence the urban setting of the negotiation process is a crucial factor, bearing in mind that urbanity does not necessarily mean rationality. But critique of a totally rational approach to the negotiation process does not mean other factors are irrational. Religion, passion, ideology, and memory play an important role in the distorted and fragmented process of negotiation.

In a world of social analysis there should be new approaches, as these events are substantially distinct from a previously well-analyzed transition. The parties and even the sides that characterized transitional pacts are absent or incapable of performing in the current revolts. Newly emerging groups with no prior political history play roles for which they have no experience in negotiation. This negotiation is done by big elephants that managed to survive over decades: lobbies of businessmen hiding behind a facade of new parties or holding big events, or members of the parties of the old regime building coalitions outside the party system. The challenge remains that patterns of the current political interactions need to be understood while they are still unfolding and transforming, making the task very difficult for theorists and analysts who want to explain the events and foresee the future.

THE FAILURE OF THE CLASSICAL NEGOTIATIONS

Negotiations in general require primary elements in order to take place. These elements could be summed up as parties, goals, strategies, process, and outcomes (Kremenyuk 2002). It is essential in any effective negotiations to negotiate with the right actors. If a negotiation process is to take place during a political struggle, the first questions are who are the political forces to be engaged in the process, are they able to control supporters, do the latter have to acknowledge the process and later be committed to the results, are negotiators delegated by their respective bodies or the society at large, and are they held accountable for the results? The question of who is selected to represent the group or the force has to be settled before embarking on the process; otherwise negotiations break down in terms of misrepresentation or inefficiency of participants (Zartman 1989, 2009). The forces included in such a process are supposed to be influential and aware of their power and weight as well as their limitations; otherwise it would turn into an active rhetorical process between the powerful sides, rather than a process of negotiation. As the different parties proceed forward in the negotiations, their intentions and strategies are unveiled, and each party seems to be closer to or far from the goals they initially sought. These essentials are found in any process of negotiations, and through analysis the type and form of negotiation can be mapped and discussed.

In the Egyptian case the roles and weights of parties are not clear on the map of power and negotiation, and the basis of representation and the foundations of trust are ambiguous. The liberal parties, for example, agreed to join against the Muslim Brotherhood (MB), yet with the rise of the Salafis some joined a democratic coalition with the Muslim Brothers and then split again, and only the Wafd Party kept its commitment with the MB when a new coalition of liberal parties was established. Many parties that were just formed at the time faced a problem in order to come up with five thousand members as required by law. The big elephants were more able to balance their weight. Not only must any transition be effective, but optimally it should be without long gaps between the breakdown of an order and the emergence of another. This might require not only negotiations but also mediation by neutral parties, who were missing in the Egyptian case. The fear of chaos or radical takeover from either side yields a situation where negotiation is a manifestation of conflict, not a process of resolution. Ultimate goals are not clear, competition over spaces and demonstration of power are tools of dominance, and new waves of revolt end up in more splits. The debates have negative effects, and events are organized to improve the chances of overcoming the other party as well as the ability to mobilize supporters, all of which does not end in a sense of mutual need to negotiate transition.

This study takes the Carl Von Clausewitz famous statement that "war is the continuation of politics by other means" and focuses on its inversion: the logic of negotiations is based on the capacity of politics to reach the goals of war without having to go through it. Drawing on Foucault we use this principle to spotlight the different important negotiations during the Egyptian revolution (Foucault 2003, 43). We argue that the revolutionary act of January 2011 manifested in occupying squares, deactivating governmental institutions, breaking into important buildings, confronting and battling with the security forces, and taking direct actions that go beyond simple vocal demands—all these are similar to "war actions" that attempt to drastically change the society and construct a New Order in Egypt. On the contrary, negotiations, elections, and reforms are mere political actions. These two forms create two levels of interaction in the dynamics of the revolution that influence any process of negotiations and set its structure, limits, efficiency, accountability, and effect on the dynamics of the street. This juxtaposition is used to combine the politics of war and its patterns with the form of the classical political negotiations and its success or failure.

Each milestone of the course of political change since 25 January 2011 can teach us something about the following dimensions:

- The importance—and limitations—of small numbers and big numbers (mapping the different parties and emerging groups)
- The role of religion and ideology and the danger of absence of a clear political agenda
- The dynamics of creating circles of fragile coalitions and the selective approach to negotiation partners (negotiation for coalition)
- The shifting ground of negotiation and the rise and fall of ideological coalitions

We can examine these dimensions through the following cases:

- The negotiations over a constitution: referendum and afterward
- The absence of trust and mediation in the case of the al-Azhar document
- The negotiation beyond parties and a revisit to party politics
- The politics of confrontation in the media
- The army and the incomplete negotiation process for power transfer.

In order to grasp the underlying rationale of events and the pattern behind political interactions—if there is any—that clarifies and helps develop the main argument of the research, the problematic with the political negotiations lies in the weight of the idea of negotiation itself and its incompatibility with the asymmetric form of the Egyptian transition after 25 January. But before exploring the process of failed negotiations, we provide an explanatory and descriptive paradigm for the nature of this revolution.

ON THE NATURE OF THE EGYPTIAN REVOLUTION: *THE RHIZOME AND MULTITUDE*

Everyone is heading to the city squares; chants vary according to the size of the grievances of groups of people who long remained under the weight of injustice and intransigence. A spark ignites a revolution affecting all parts of the country after 25 January 2011, and the political regime undertakes a widespread campaign of arrests. Security forces stationed in vital parts and roads of the country feel a relative success due to their ability to disperse the demonstrators after their success in occupying the Tahrir (Liberation) Square, the most symbolic place in the history of modern Egypt.[1] Continuous battles rage in the city of Suez, a number of wounded and martyrs fall in Suez and Sinai. Mass demonstrations start on 28 January in several governorates such as Alexandria, Suez, Cairo, Ismailia, Port Said, and Sinai, and some cities in Albehera. Crowds from the streets and inside mosques and houses come out to announce their determination to bring down a regime and witness the birth of a New Order. Repressive forces desperately try to suppress a public revolution and start clashing with the crowd. On the evening of 28 January the security forces are defeated and start retreating in several governorates such as Suez, Alexandria, and Cairo after a courageous struggle characterized by its steadfastness.

According to many mobilization theorists, "mobilizing people for collective action revolves around building organizations, such as unions, revolutionary parties, and grass-roots movement organizations" (McCarthy and Zald 1977; Tilly 1978). Such "social movement organizations" have been held to be at the heart of sustained collective actions (Goldstone 2001,15). But there was no mass-defined leadership, nor was there a single identity dominating and ruling the flow of the Egyptian revolution. Hardt and Negri (2011) take a more global perspective, saying that "the organization of the revolts resembles what we have seen for more than a decade in other parts of the world, from Seattle to Buenos Aires and Genoa and Cochabamba, Bolivia: a horizontal network that has no single, central leader. Traditional opposition bodies can participate in this network but cannot direct it."

Contrary to what many have expected, the revolution did not come out of the womb of any of the historically recognized political forces in Egypt such as the Islamists, or even new parties such as the Democratic Front Party and al-Ghad Party. One also cannot relate the outburst to certain unions or a specific labor movement. "An insight from mobilization theory has been the recognition that without prior leadership and planning, and without access to mass communication and free speech, challengers, under some circumstances, are capable of engaging in spontaneous mass demonstrations by using shared symbols and protest repertoires embedded in their culture" (Oberschall 2000, 30). There was no organization, no political or intellectual movement behind the revolution. This revolution has surpassed them all and did not have a real centrally organized leadership by new youth with a new language that will challenge the old generation and its language and dominance. It is important to link the absence of recognized and well-established political force to the wide distrust among most of the young people, their incapability to confront the Mubarak regime in a revolutionary way for decades, the failure of their reformist approaches, and the regime's successful mechanisms to either contain or uproot them if necessary. This problem has been extended even after the revolution broke out, and it is the cornerstone in the repeated failure of most of the negotiation processes on different levels and in different situations. A great gap was growing daily between different political parties and movements that failed to absorb the anger of the youth, who were laden with hope for a future much different from that of their parents and ancestors. The speed and dynamics of the movements ran in a stronger and more aggressive rhythm than could be understood by the repressive and corrupted structures of the Old Order.

The roles of leadership and the restructuring of the state have been two crucial issues for many of the theories. Although the third generation of revolution theories has excluded the role of charismatic leaders in favor of understanding the structural dimension and situational contexts, most of the revolution theories put a great focus on the role of organization and the capability of the different institutions, parties, and political and social movements to represent the demands and aims of the revolution, and mainly to pick up the spark of the struggle and to organize and institutionalize it (Goldstone 2001, 20). Most of these well-known revolutions were backed by a hegemonic bloc. The Egyptian revolution, on the contrary, is marked by the absence of both elements, leaving analysts to "assess whether this characteristic is a strength or a weakness" (Badiou 2011).

But after more than a year of revolution, both its grandeur and weakness appear clearly, particularly in relation to negotiations. Fluidity, decentralization, leaderlessness, and apparently spontaneity have been the main characteristics of the Egyptian revolution, and in Tunisia as well. Many theorists argue the great potential and capabilities of spontaneous movements. Rosa Luxemburg showed that organization of labor forces is not a must, and thus her argument was that spontaneity can be the main process of unification in a revolution (Laclau and Mouffe 2001, 8–12). Franz Fanon (2004) showed both sides of spontaneity, declaring its important role accompanied by violence to break down the social and political structure set up by the colonizer and, of course, preferring its velocity and capability to vigorously attack the enemy; however, Fanon also points to the importance of organizing the rebellion movements in different forms from those of the colonizer and the national elites created by the colonization. Oberschall (2000, 30) argues that "a spontaneous mass protest cannot be stopped by the authorities because neither they nor the protesters know that it is going to take place." But was the Egyptian revolution really spontaneous? We discuss this point in detail and link it to negotiation and organization. But "recent studies of recruitment and of the experience of movement participants [have] shown that formal organization is neither necessary nor sufficient to create the sense of commitment and energy needed for risky collective action to occur" (Goldstone 2001, 15).

In order to elaborate on the nature of the Egyptian revolution, its dynamics, and the impact on the different process of negotiations, three notions can provide a descriptive and explanatory paradigm: horizontalism, rhizomes, and the multitude. This paradigm helps bring out the new forms of "non-organization" adopted by the Egyptian revolution, to answer the question of spontaneity, and to explore misrepresentation in the different negotiations process and even the nonrepresentation tendency in the Egyptian revolution. Ostensibly the three concepts seem to be the same; all three tend to explain change in terms of networks and emergence. However, horizontalism explains things on a structural and organizational level; it is a more static and descriptive paradigm. It is featured as "the decentralized or networked form of organizing; the leaderless protest movements; the eschewal of top-down command; the deliberative, rather than representative, democracy; the emphasis on participation, creativity and consensus; the opposition to dogma and sectarianism, often associated with older generations; and new links, respectful of diversity and often youth-inspired, between formerly sharply opposed political currents" (Chalcraft 2012, 6).

The multitude is composed of innumerable internal differences that can never be reduced to simple factors or a single criteria. The multitude is an "internally different, multiple social subject whose constitution and action is based not on identity or unity (or much less, indifference) but on what it has in common" (Hardt and Negri 2005, 100) To explain and distinguish the multitude, Hardt and Negri differentiate between three notions of social subjects: the people, the masses, and the working class. "The people has traditionally been a unitary conception. . . . The masses certainly are composed of all types and sorts, but really one should not say that different social subjects make up the masses. The essence of the masses is indifference: all differences are submerged and drowned in the masses. All the colors of the population fade to gray. . . . Insofar as the multitude is neither an identity (like the people) nor a uniform (like the masses), the internal differences of the multitude must discover the *common* that allows them to communicate and act together. The common we share, in fact, is not so much to discover, as it is produced" (xiv, xv).

The difference between the multitude and the working class is not only important for understanding the multitude but crucial to the focal point of the negotiations. Egypt did not have strong labor unions before the revolution, the main bulk of them representing the interests of a class, and although it had witnessed many factional revolts, none of them succeeded in institutionalizing themselves in society, and none of the many social movements were independent and influential. This situation left civil society too weak to negotiate its demands with the authorities and put labor, for example, in an either/or choice; to confront in a strong strike and endure high risks or street wars in the whole urban space, as in Ghazel El Mahalla in 2008, or to submit to the authorities as in many other places. It is true that the absence of any popular organization has limited the capacity of the working classes and the masses to negotiate change.

But how could a revolution take place in these different sectors of the masses and the working class without any real negotiations and representation for their demands? It became possible when they succeeded in moving from being a working class to a multitude, and from being a separated archipelago to being and acting as rhizome. According to Oxford dictionary, a *rhizome* is "a continuously growing horizontal underground stem which puts out lateral shoots and adventitious roots at intervals." *Rhizome* is an agricultural term used to describe plants such as potatoes, bamboo, aspen, ginger, or grass. However, this term not only describes these plants but also explains them as systems and structure. "A rhizome as subterranean stem is absolutely different from roots and radicals. . . . Rats are rhizomes. Burrows are too, in all of their functions of shelter, supply, movement, evasion, and breakout. The rhizome itself assumes very diverse forms, from ramified surface extension in all directions to concretion into bulbs and tubers" (Deleuze and Guattari 2009, 6, 7). This term has been taken from the agricultural arena to the political and philosophical arena to explain and analyze structures and systems.

The term *rhizome* explains the dynamics, bonds, flow, and asymmetry; it explores the form and the movement, the idea and the manifestation; it explores them without putting them in a binary opposition. Rhizomes are against dualism; they do not separate form from content, dynamics from system. Rhizomes are about lines of interactions and not centers and pivots and not even nodes in networks; they are multiple, plural, and different, and they are fluid and nomadic. But they are not chaotic; organization and leadership are not transcendental and hierarchal but are dissolved and immanent in the dynamics of movements. They do not mobilize through a hierarchal institution or well-established organizations; rather, they arrange in mobility; they initiate and do not wait for external orders; they do not delegate to represent—actually, rhizomes are antirepresentation. In Deleuze and Guattari's (2009) philosophical words, they dissolve the boundaries between thinking and living.

According to Deleuze and Guattari (2009), a rhizome ceaselessly "establishes connections between semiotic chains, organizations of power, and circumstances relative to the arts, sciences, and social struggles." The rhizome likewise resists structures of domination, such as the notion of "the mother tongue" in linguistics, though it does admit to ongoing cycles of what they refer to as "deterritorializing" and "reterritorializing" moments (7). Through these movements of deterritorialization and reterritorialization one can understand the dynamics of the war going on between the system and the revolution. The rhizome is not limited to one spot, and if it is under siege in one, it transforms itself and increases its territory by deterritorializing itself (12). The rhizome has undefined features so as to disable anyone from catching up and following its traces. In case it has been beaten on a certain site, it reproduces itself from its "old or new lines once again" (10). One could not get rid of the rhizome without the full disarmament of the land and drying all its sources, which means killing huge numbers of Egyptian masses. "In other words, the rhizome is a robust structure because it cannot be decapitated; its chain of command cannot be disrupted, because it does not have one. Its communication cannot be easily censored or interrupted as it travels along too many interwoven lines" (Chalcraft 2012, 7). A rhizome cannot be traced or contained; its self-transformation cannot be prevented. Trees are "genealogical, where by contrast, the rhizome is an anti-genealogy. . . . The tree comes to symbolize the distinction between subject and object, . . . encompassing the whole of dualistic logic through its branching patterns, through its definitions of set pathways between root and branch" (21, 23). On the contrary, the rhizome deconstructs and demolishes all these dualities and binary oppositions.

Moreover, the concept is used to inspire new forms of political, social, military, and economic structures and systems and can also be used for different sorts of struggles. Even natural sciences such as pharmacology and the fields of technology are very much inspired by this concept. Rhizomatic connections and struggles create a strong resistance to the political system but at the same time work on drastic change on the social and cultural level. This is what we have been witnessing in Egypt before and during the eighteen days of revolution and until the time when every day the revolutionary project proves not to be only on the political level, and other faces of the many revolutions are unveiling daily.

The rhizome is in permanent movement and war against the state system; it is incompatible with the state and its system. In a rhizome, power relations are spread horizontally, where every point is on the same level as another. The rhizome is characterized by extreme flexibility, high speed of movement, ability to disguise itself, and tremendous capabilities for maneuvering. However, the rhizome is not random, despite the lack of clear leadership, with no center, head, or focal points. It works through coordination during the movement itself and uses its own system in diversity, expansion, multiplication, and multiplicity, which enables a spontaneous control over the revolution. Incidents of violence, confusion, and demagoguery in the revolutionary rhizome in Egypt have not executed any riot or panic actions; on the contrary, fingers have always pointed at the remnants of the former regime, the police in particular.

The rhizome moves in all directions with no fixed starting or focal point or pivot, where every point in the "rhizome is connected to the other" (Deleuze and Guattari 2009, 7), and thus all points form a number of lines that meet horizontally, distinguishing it from the "tree" model, which has a focal point with a constant reference. Literally speaking, mass groups of youth have coordinated with each other, forming a harmonious movement many times despite the presence of far leftists groups such as the Revolutionary Socialists, far right groups including the Muslim Brotherhood and their political party Freedom and Justice PJD, and other nonideological movements such as the Popular Movement for the Support of El-Baradei, the Demands for Change, and the 6th of April Movement. That is precisely what we have witnessed in the Egyptian revolution through the use of social media and networks such as Facebook and Twitter. Egyptian youth managed to organize and coordinate demonstrations and revolutionary events, where all details of gatherings, movements, or revolutionary events were well known to all at the same moment, thus enabling the youth to create the model of the rhizome virtually and de facto in the land of movements and battles. Even demonstrations from 25 to 28 January had this feature.

The demonstrations were not mass movements from famous squares, for the uprising began from side streets, not central squares, all happening concurrently and in many governorates, with no starting point, making it practically impossible for security forces to control. Although the moves were peaceful and the demonstrators free of weapons, they succeeded in besieging and defeating the security forces. Communication was achieved through cell phones, social networking, and web pages, as well as on the battleground. Seeing that it allows a wide range of differences and diversities, the *rhizome* has this very special feature matching the aspirations and spirit of youth. Straying away from it does not necessarily mean dispersion or fragmentation, but it infers the increase in the uprising of other different groups due to its high potential for networking. The model sees this as a kind of plurality, not disintegration or decomposition; if one strays away from one group, unit, or movement, one still keeps coordinating and communicating with it. This feature, which is characterized by its constructive disintegration that increases space, gives the rhizome great ability for quick horizontal expansion and thus explains the high prevalence in the city or within the same governorate.

After 25 January, the spark of revolution swept through Egyptian cities. The rhizome inflated and doubled combinations and variations while preserving harmony and homogeneity. There was no need to be reduced in a tree structure and organized control; any combination is allowed to lie horizontally (Deleuze and Guattari 2009, 6). In fact, all attempts embarked upon by the propaganda machine of the Old Order, through its media channels and armies of hypocrites, failed to halt the revolution. Even the series of negotiations carried out by the president's deputy, Omar Soleiman, failed to halt the momentum, for the revolution had no spokesperson.

CONTAINING THE REVOLUTION: BETWEEN VIOLENT CONFRONTATIONS AND FAILED NEGOTIATIONS

Before 25 January 2011, the call for the revolution on Facebook was widely spread among the Egyptians, even those who are illiterate and never sat in front of a computer. The authorities' counteraction for these fluid and liquid interactions among Egyptians, the young people and political activists in particular, was threatening and fearmongering. Through different media outlets controlled by the regime, talks and reports about conspiracies and targeting Egypt, assertions of attempts to break down the state and divide Egypt into four parts, and talks about the invisible Zionistic hands beyond this call on Facebook were widely spread in an effort to produce a strong campaign of fear and terror to counter this new social network, which turned out to be the strongest political campaign the Egyptian political regime and its security apparatuses had ever confronted. During this period most political parties, opposition groups, and the Muslim Brotherhood received several threatening messages.

When 25 January turned out to be a massive event and a historic day, the regime launched a wide campaign of arrests, in addition to its militarized actions to suppress the demonstrations through its central security forces. The squares and the important streets in many provinces such as Cairo, Alexandria, Suez, and Ismailia were occupied by central security forces and the police. Suez turned into a battlefield between these forces and the masses from 25 to 28 January; political negotiation disappeared, and harsh securitization prevailed. By 28 January a full state of revolution had taken hold, and the masses succeeded in defeating the central security forces in a military sense, but with peaceful means, in five provinces. Thus one of the most important arms of the system was broken by the revolutionaries. In military terms, the regime lost one of the most important battles in its war against the masses, and it seemed that continuing the war with the same response was leading nowhere. Thus a shift in the regime strategy took place: it was time to negotiate.

Omar Soleiman, who was director of the general intelligence apparatus and one of the most powerful men in the regime, and who became vice president after 28 January, launched the first negotiation process ever between the regime and the political forces. The regime was the one that called and initiated negotiations and that chose and invited the different parties: Muslim Brotherhood, Wafd, Tagmoa, and some political activists from Tahrir Square, such as Mostfa El-Najjar and Abd El-Rahaman Youssef. The negotiations witnessed the absence of any trade or labor union or any civil organizations in general. Thus the opposition did not set any items in the agenda of the talks. In addition to these negotiations, a council of wise men was formed. The regime and the council attempted to convince the masses in the squares, in particular Tahrir Square, to step aside and let political negotiations take place. However, the negotiations broke down, and the people did not leave the squares until Mubarak stepped down.

The problem was not the intentions of the parties, nor the tactics and strategies of the negotiators, and not even the process itself. The negotiations reflected a deep crisis of political representation. The core of the crisis was this: What interests and segments of society do these parties represent and in whose name are they negotiating? Only the Muslim Brotherhood could claim representation. As the revolution was not founded on strategic alliances between different forces, the Mubarak system succeeded in breaking down any possibilities of organizing the masses in political terms, and the negotiation process turned out to be a tool for dividing revolutionary forces instead of being a tool for managing their differences. Even the social movements that Egypt witnessed from 2006 until early 2009 were not a main part of the revolution through a clear participation by the main figures of these movements.

The negotiations led by Omar Soleiman included political activists from Tahrir Square, but they could not provide a clear representation for the revolution. On the contrary, very soon after the negotiations started, the Muslim Brotherhood and other activists returned to the course of action until Mubarak was ousted. Yet the Mubarak regime did not fall; the regime manifested its continuation through the

Supreme Council of Armed Forces (SCAF) that took over governing the country in the name of the revolution, a change of course that repeated itself after the 30 June 2013 massive demonstrations by the opposition of the elected president Mohamed Morsi, analyzed later in this chapter. The authorities militarized and securitized governance as they had not acknowledged the new forms of interactions showing the emerging "multitude." They needed a structure to deal with the multitude, to deconstruct it and then destroy it. The revolution was a very new challenge to the system and its heavy and well-prepared security apparatuses, and one of the main questions was, Who mobilized the masses and the resources? The system quickly resorted to what it knows very well: the use of force.

On 3 February 2011 and in the middle of the massive mobilization in Tahrir Square, the camels and the thugs openly attacked the protestors. "The Battle of the Camels" looked like a medieval scene, and the second day the thugs were defeated. The Egyptian revolution showed its high potential for confronting and fighting. The multitude proved to be genuine; the rhizome could not be defeated through war because it never ceased to expand. Whenever it is attacked on one of its lines, it grows from other lines; whenever some parts of it are destroyed, others are born. The multitude, once unleashed, becomes uncontrollable. Someone might start the war, as in most cases when the security forces attack the protestors, but there is no force that can force the multitude to retreat. This was proved through a pattern of interactions ranging from the very first day to the clashes in Alexandria and Suez in summer 2011, to Mohamed Mahmoud Street and beside the cabinet building in November 2011 in the area of the Ministry of Interior. All the parallel attempts at negotiation failed.[2]

THE MULTITUDE AND THE RHIZOME

Michael Hardt and Antonio Negri argue that we live in the age of empire, and the multitude is the other face of this empire. "There are two faces of globalization: network of hierarchies and divisions that maintain order through new mechanisms of control and constant conflict" (Hardt and Negri 2005, xiii). The other face is what is at stake here, as we believe it reflects and tells us a lot about the nature of this revolution. Hardt and Negri point to "the creation of new circuits of cooperation and collaboration that stretch across nations and continents and allow an unlimited number of counters. . . . it is not a matter of everyone in the world becoming the same; rather it provides the possibility that, while remaining different, we discover the commonality that enables us to communicate and act together" (xiii; Žižek 2007). It is not a matter of concrete and big allies negotiating political interests together to share occasional mutual benefits such as negotiating elections coalitions. The multitude is not just about searching and sharing the common; it is rather about the "production" of the common. This is a crucial point regarding negotiations for coalitions and formulation. The production of the common allowed the young people, before the outburst and during the revolution, to facilitate and accelerate any process of negotiations and hardships. It is very difficult to trace such negotiations, as their velocity is faster than can be caught or traced. But through our study of the youth movements and initiatives and their networks of friendships and allies before the revolution and to date, we can identify some characteristics we believe mark most of the internal negotiation process among the multitude.

After the revolution the issue with the National Dialogue platforms was that different networks and circuits created by the youth and formed within the multitude were organized horizontally. These forms of horizontal organization allowed more spaces for expression and reduction of hierarchies and antagonisms. Hardt and Negri (2005, xiv) argue that the multitude can be "conceived as a network: an open and expansive network in which all differences can be expressed freely and equally, a network that provides the means of encounter so that we can work and live in common." The tendency of postideology among the younger generation prevented these negotiations from being split and broken on ideological lines. As Aly El-Raggal puts it, "before 2005 they [the older generation] operated along lines of rigid ideological frames. After 2005 . . . [w]e [the youth] started to dissolve these boundaries. This generation is more into ethics than morals. We broke down all these binaries and dichotomies. Remember something: During the revolution, the youth who went to the streets on January 25 and 28 didn't call for an Islamic state or a secular state. During the 18 days you wouldn't find demands [for a specific political platform]. Our demand was, 'I don't want this kind of power to be practiced on me. I want my body and soul to be respected. I want to be who I am. I want my dignity'" (Herrera 2011).

But these types of negotiations before the revolution and to certain extent to the present were marked by the negative, by what the people do not want, but not by what they want and how they are going to establish it. As Ernsto Laclau and Chantal Mouffe (2001, 189) argue: "if the demands of a subordinated group are presented purely as negative demands subversive of a certain order, without being linked to any viable project for the reconstruction of specific areas of society, their capacity to act hegemonically will be excluded from the outset." As seen, what the young people in particular seek and negotiate for is to act in harmony, not fight over hegemony. Yet the old guards of the shaking regime counteracted.

There are many counterarguments on this approach. First, many scholars and activists alike argue that the revolution has already succeeded in formulating a map and an orientation. To be sure, this map is formed through the negative approach, but it draws the features of the required and desired system, which is mainly opening more horizons and democratic spaces for the multitude to work, freed from state domination and oppression, and to implement policies of social justice and dignity. This argument is immanent in the revolutionary dynamics, chants, and slogans, namely the famous triple mantra: *Aish* (bread), *Horia* (freedom) and *A'daila Egatma'ia* (social justice). Counterarguments see a conceptual distinction between horizontalism and the idea of moving from an agenda to a road map. "There remains a need to enable this logic to establish itself as the new hegemony, in other words, to be genuinely liberatory" (Chalcraft 2012, 10). There is a difference between a "strategy of opposition" and a "strategy of construction of a new order" (Laclau and Mouffe 2001, 189). The Constitutional Declaration, which was subject to public vote in March 2011, and the Constitutional Committee, which was supposed to write the postrevolution constitution and which was a platform of disagreement, failed to reach a consensus.

However, the crisis of negotiations in the Egyptian revolution, we argue, is important for an understanding of its dynamics and the imagination gap and cultural rupture between generations. It is a crisis of perception, and of the mechanisms of control and domination imposed by the well-established political forces when they jumped back to the game after the fall of Mubarak. The old binary oppositions and ideas, such as secularism versus Islamism, organization versus chaos, and the harsh mechanisms of delegation and representation are enforced in analysis though they are losing relevance. As Chalcraft (2012, 7) indicates, "The conventional idea is that discipline and doctrinal rectitude create a powerful and unified collective actor; the idea of the rhizome or network implies that participatory and creative energies are unleashed by the struggle itself to underpin a new kind of potent social force."

Immediately after the "resignation" of Mubarak, the scene moved backward to the 1990s, with the harsh confrontation between the Islamists and the Secularists. The older and formal political leaders and intellectuals could not comprehend the new dynamics. They thought curbing a spontaneous revolt of the masses capitalizing on it would go unchallenged. Thus two main approaches were developed. The first was to reduce the complexities of the revolutionary movement and outburst and transform it into a reform movement. This approach was adopted by some Islamists, such as the Muslim Brotherhood and Salafis. The second approach, an old Leninist one adopted by leftist groups, targets the creation and establishment of a strong organization and a vanguard to lead the revolutionary battles, speak on behalf of the masses, create a centralized point of reference, and represent, negotiate, and realize the demands and aims of the revolution. This approach did not take into consideration the huge historical transformations in the forms of political action, resistance, and war and how they moved from symmetric forms to asymmetric forms, from a restricted chain of commands to fluid and flexible networks, from trees to rhizomes, from seeking democracy through oligarchies' organizations to organizations and movements that resist authoritarianism on the micro level before the macro.

This approach has been criticized as being "unidimensional" insofar as it considered the political process and the revolutionary struggle as revolving around a single point: the seizure of power. Power was conceived of as a substance, having a source and a specific location within social relations—in the extreme case, as a building: the Winter Palace or the Abdeen Palace (Laclau and Mouffe 1981, 20). Multitude is not only about nonhierarchical relationships, but about "the striving for consensus, processes in which everyone is heard and new relationships are created," in a word, informal negotiations for formulation (Chalcraft 2012, 7). Rational representation, unification, universalism, progress, the glorification of the state, and building consensus were all challenged as underpinnings of the modern scene. "The idea of horizontalism has much in common with the idea of 'direct democracy,' where democracy is defined less by standard liberal mechanisms of representation, like parliaments, and more by collective self-rule, and where 'direct' implies an absence of mediation" (7). The narrative is produced through the struggle and the search for the common and not enforced by representative authorities of the society's institutions. "The people is one—a singular, a unity by definition and etymologically. The population of course is composed [of] numerous different individuals and classes, but the people synthesizes or reduces these social differences into one identity" (Hardt and Negri 2005, 99). But in the multitude, social differences remain different (xv). What are the people? This has been a question to raise antagonism and polarization in many negotiations that included Secularists and Islamists after the eighteen days of revolution.

CONSTITUTING A CONSTITUTION: FROM WAR AND RHIZOME BACK TO POLITICS AND ELEPHANTS

In March 2011 the Egyptian revolution was put on a road that ended up with the abortion of the transformation that was taking place. The revolution was set back from the multitude to a discourse of representation of the "people" and from war and revolution to politics. Two days after the resignation of Mubarak, on 13 February 2011, the SCAF announced a Constitutional Declaration, stating its commitment to lead the country through a transition period, which was not to exceed six months, when the SCAF would hand over power to an elected president and parliament. This declaration was not negotiated nor was it subject to a public referendum. The declaration suspended the 1971 Constitution and the 2010 parliament. It also stated the SCAF commitment to all the international agreements and treaties that Egypt had signed before the revolution, gave the SCAF the right to issue whatever laws are needed during the transitional period, and stated that the SCAF would form a Constitutional Committee that would be responsible for constitutional amendments, subject to a public referendum. This declaration was not contested except on one issue, the continuation of Ahmed Shafiq in his office as prime minster. The revolutionary forces objected to this article in the declaration, and after a big demonstration on Tuesday, 22 February, Shafiq's government resigned.

Some days later, in accordance with the article calling for the formation of the Constitutional Committee, the SCAF chose a few constitutional law experts to draft another constitutional declaration by which the SCAF would rule and lead the country in the transition period. This declaration was subject to a public referendum on 19 March 2011. The two declarations were designed to fill the constitutional vacuum. The choice was to accept these amendments and rule the transition period or to start writing a new constitution immediately in case the amendments were rejected by the voters. However, 77 percent of the voters approved the amendments. And on 30 March 2011 the SCAF announced the second Constitutional Declaration, yet it added articles that were not included in the text announced before the referendum.

The revolutionary forces opposed the referendum, arguing the need for a new constitution that would meet the revolutionaries' expectations, passions, and demands, not just some modifications on the old 1971 Constitution, considered by some groups to be authoritarian. At the beginning of discussions and negotiations, these forces did not argue along the lines of dualism. Later on, when the polarization became stronger, they moved back to binary opposition, mainly revolution versus reform, and their discourse started to be highly polarized as well; many of their statements, blueprints, and manifestos proclaimed that "those who are going to vote 'yes' are betraying the blood of the martyrs." This sentence was stated by many in different ways and was highly manifest in the Revolutionary Socialists' discourse through their different media platforms.

The Coptic Church and the secularists opposed the referendum, arguing that it was threatening the "Civil State." For many secularists, particularly those in political parties or aiming to establish new ones, the referendum was pushing the country too fast toward parliamentary elections for which the "civil forces" were not yet ready, and this would mean a sweeping victory in the elections for the Islamists, particularly the Muslim Brotherhood, leading the country to a "theocratic state."

The Islamists' arguments, in the different negotiations and discussions that took place, revolved around three main lines. The first line argued the importance of ending the transitional period as soon as possible and limiting the time of the SCAF in power by all possible means. This line was adopted mainly by radical revolutionary Islamists who later formed the Salafi Front, the Hazmoon Movement supporting Hazem Abo Ismail for president, and other independent Islamists. The second argument for stability and security was adopted mainly by the Muslim Brotherhood and the Alexandrian School of Salafism and al-Noor Party. This line was highly criticized by many revolutionaries arguing its irrelevance and its similarity to the discourse of Mubarak's era. The counterargument for this criticism was that Egypt cannot live without a constitutional framework and a temporary social contract, and that exposing the country to a constitutional vacuum is definitely threatening the security and stability of the country on all levels, as it leads to a chaotic situation where the relations of power and political actions are not governed by any law. However, when the scene turned to be highly polarized, the third line was to defend the Islamic identity of the Egyptian people on the level of the state and the society. This line of argument dominated the scene and turned the referendum into an identity conflict and a struggle over hegemony and representation in the society. On the day of the public vote, the polarization was extreme. Circles to be ticked on the voting card were colored in black and green. Some Coptic bishops told their followers to tick the black spot (the "No" sign on the voting card) as it represented the bishop's dress, whereas green represented the color of Islamic flags. When the results were announced, a famous Islamic Salafi Sheikh, Mohammed Hussein Yacoub, declared the victory of Islam in "The Battle of Electoral Boxes."

The Muslim Brotherhood and al-Noor tried to paint the people's identity with the Islamic color, claiming that the people are longing to apply the shariʿa. On the other hand, formally organized secularists' parties such as the liberal party of El-Maserioun al-Ahrar (Free Egyptians), the leftist party al-Tagmoaʿ, the democratic party al-Gabha al-Democratia (Democratic Front), and others argued instead that Egyptians are moderate by nature and that the people would not accept nor tolerate an Afghani or Iranian state or society. This was not just a heated intellectual debate. Many attempts and negotiations were made to reach a legal solution for this dispute. In June 2011, al-Azhar, the main religious governmental institution in Egypt and one of the most respected and well-known religious institutions in the Islamic world, initiated the draft of what has been called the al-Azhar Document. Using its respected reputation as the main official religious Islamic institution very much grounded in Egyptian and Islamic history, al-Azhar tried to play a mediation role to help ending the Islamist-secularist polarization. Al-Azhar represents a main Islamic point of reference, a pivot and center, which can claim the right representation of real moderate Islam and not any other religious group or movement. This perception is highly challenged by different Islamic groups, and secular and young people as well, because of al-Azhar's affiliation with the state and with all the political regimes that Egypt has known in its modern history. For them al-Azhar represents nothing more than a religious discourse of the state and the regime when a religious cover for the authoritative practices and wishes is needed. Being a state institution is a two-sided weapon.

One of the main problems of the al-Azhar Document that was finally issued on August 2011 was the unsatisfactory representation. The meeting on the document included many elites who are considered by revolutionary forces and Islamic groups to be part of the Old Order. However, the results were satisfactory to a certain extent. The document emphasized the role of Islam in the constitution and thus satisfied the Islamists; it emphasized the minority rights and freedom and thus satisfied the Copts; and it stressed personal freedom and democracy and thus satisfied many revolutionaries. The main task of the document was to build up a consensus in the public sphere regarding the role of religion in society and its relation with the state. It also had a strategic and tactical dimension, regaining the effective role of al-Azhar and establishing and grounding the challenged institution, which had been considered a tool in the hands of Mubarak, in the New Order of Egypt. The document included many articles aiming to build national consensus about the democratic system and the role of al-Azhar, but foremost it stressed the need for a constitution based on national consensus and wagered upon by all national forces. This was and remained for quite some time the main concern and fear: a constitution written by Islamists to "change the direction of the country" as the secular forces phrased it on many occasions.

A parallel effort took place in July 2011, as there was a major attempt to reestablish the public sphere on new bases represented by the National Council Document. The National Council was created by the SCAF, which then chose El Ghazaly Harb, the leader of the Democratic Front Party, to draft the High Constitutional Principles. The heated negotiations on the Constitutional Principles began in July 2011 and culminated in its denunciation in a large demonstration in November 2011. The introduction of a notion of High Constitutional Principles above the constitution raised a very controversial debate in a variety of public spaces. It was rejected by many people who argued that the idea of so-called Supra Constitutional Principles does not exist anywhere, and such principles are contradictory by definition to the constitution, which is supposed to be the supreme law of the country, with nothing above it. Others argued that the principles did not bring anything new and were just a collection of common rights recognized everywhere; they did not address any important issue in detail and were of no help to the transition period.

The main purpose of the document was not to allow one party or movement to write the constitution separately and independently from other political and social forces. According to Harb, the purpose was to establish the main guidelines for writing the constitution and to avoid the dictatorship of any electoral majority. However, it is clear that the split and the whole controversy were about the mutual fear between the Islamists and the secularists, both from the old organized forces and from newly shaped old forces in newly established parties. The youth of the 25 January Revolution were surprised by the people chosen to lead the negotiations. For the youth it was unacceptable to negotiate with those whom they consider to be the counterrevolution. Pillars of Mubarak's regime from different professions and backgrounds, such as Ismail Serag El-Din, director of Bibliotheca Alexandrina and the right arm of Susan Mubarak, Mofid Fawazy, one of Mubarak's media men, and other intellectuals and writers like Gaber Asfour, Mustafa El-Faky, Said Yassin, and others, were the leading negotiators. The meeting was an effort at reconciliation, but it failed in its attempt. The different Islamist groups, apart from the Muslim Brotherhood, also refused the outcomes of the National Council Document and declared their agreement on the al-Azhar Document few weeks later. Whenever a political crisis surfaced, all parties would state that the documents signed were not binding but only carried symbolic significance.

The Constitutional Declaration was modified twice after March, once by successful political negotiations and once by the courts. In the first case, the SCAF wanted the electoral system modified so that half the parliament was to be elected by a proportional representation list system and half from single member districts. The parties wanted the entire electoral system to be organized by proportional party lists. The SCAF argued that an entire proportional system would be against independents' freedom to run. The political parties argued that an entire proportional system is the right path to a democratic political life based on parties' participation and plurality. They also argued that an individual system would allow the former members of the National Democratic Party (NDP), which was dissolved after the revolution, to enter the parliament again. However, after a round of negotiations with the SCAF, represented by General Sami Anan, the parties and the SCAF agreed that two-thirds of the representation would be elected by a proportional representation list system and one-third as independents. The Constitutional Declaration was modified in consequence by the SCAF on 25 September 2011. The second amendment of the declaration was done on 19 November 2011 by the Supreme Constitutional Court, which approved the right to vote for Egyptian residents abroad.

In the midst of this continuous polarization a document was negotiated between SCAF and the political parties on 1 October 2011 that stated some principles for establishing a democratic system and other articles about the transitional period. The two most striking points were that all parties signed the document, while there was no signature on behalf of the SCAF, and that when opposition arose regarding the document's content, the political parties again stated it was a document of good intentions and not an binding document, with the Freedom and Justice Party and al-Noor announcing that their leaders were "representing themselves." When the parliamentarian elections took place over several weeks in different Egyptian governorates from November 2011 to January 2012, the Islamic parties together won over two-thirds of the seats.

The controversy then moved to the composition of the assembly to draft the constitution that was selected on 24 March 2012 by the parties in parliament from a list of suggested names of parliamentarians, experts, and public figures; it was dissolved by the administrative court in April 201 for containing too narrow a list of candidates dominated by parliamentarians, and a new assembly was chosen on 13 June 2012, still facing objections by the minority parties.

The political conflict then turned to the presidency, filled in the May–June 2012 election by Dr. Mohamed Morsi of the Muslim Brotherhood but seen by a slim majority as preferable to former prime minister Ahmed Shafiq, one of the figures of the old regime. A group of public figures meeting at the Fermont Hotel in Cairo declared their support for Morsi after the voting ended and before the results were declared. One main item in the meeting to support the goals of the revolution and pursue the struggle in case Shafiq won was that Morsi declare his commitment to change the constitutional assembly. When he won with 51 percent of the vote, he did not fulfill this promise, but negotiations continued with the Fermont front. A compromise was to assign a committee of ten legal experts and public figures to act as an advisory entity for the constitutional assembly. They also worked for only four weeks on the draft, but soon the voting over the articles started and their suggestions and recommendations were ignored. Eight out of ten (including the second author of this chapter) resigned from the advisory committee, which coincided with the withdrawal of the other non-Islamist forces as well. The draft constitution was shortly announced on 1 December, and the referendum took place on 15 December and was endorsed by 63.8 percent of the voters.

The scene of the revolution moved from the lines of pluralism and multitude to the pragmatic spheres of politics, to polarization and the creation of ideological blocs, and to the absence of youth and a lack of their representation. The divide was both vertical between competing political groups and horizontal between generations.

The constitutional court dissolved the parliament in June 2012, just a few weeks before Morsi took office as president, leaving him no option except to give his oath in front of the constitutional court. The court had become a cornerstone in the deep state system for challenging any outcome of barely successful political negotiations or democratic procedures. The first Egyptian parliament after the revolution elected by tens of millions was annulled for legal reasons related to the division of the electoral map. After assuming the presidency, Morsi attempted to call upon the parliament to resume its work, yet again this decree was annulled by the court.

One can track and analyze the rise in contestation and conflict between the different authorities and powers of the state and the emerging new system, but what was at stake was the constitution that became the battlefield of different forces, and the continuous challenge of the representative bodies by the judiciary. The second chamber of parliament (Sura Council), which was still functioning, took over the legislative power in the absence of the people's assembly but was also dissolved in June 2013. The president was left to face the hurricane of ultimatums given by the army to force him to accept early presidential elections or a referendum on the completion of his term. The escalation of the situation after the demonstrations of 30 June 2013 by the opposition to Morsi and the eventual ousting of the president declared by the minister of defense on 3 July 2013 brought an end to this episode of the revolution and the beginning of a new chapter where negotiations were a matter of media statements, not a political and deliberative process. Though the statement of al-Sisi urged the president to solve the crisis by negotiating with the opposition and different parties, this negotiation process had been in deep crisis since Morsi took office. Several calls to have a dialogue were rejected, and the last call after the armed forces' ultimatum also failed to bring parties to the negotiation table.

One can claim that the main problem revolves around the lack of rules for the political game. Presence and representation measures are absent, a long-term commitment to reach outcomes is not a tradition, and a lack of trust between different parties is dominant. Once the balance of power is in favor of one side, it considers earlier agreements void. The different landmarks mentioned above indicate this clearly, and the outcome was expected to be a rising use of force, either by the state apparatus against the emerging rhizome on the ground, such as the Mohamed Mahmoud Street confrontations that started in November 2011 and continued in different waves against the police force in the area of the Ministry of Interior close to Tahrir Square, or the sporadic violence that spread in different governorates. The peak was the ousting of president Morsi by the army (with support of the al-Noor Party, the Coptic Church, al-Azhar, and some public figures). The move from politics to the "war on terror" declared by al-Sisi on 26 July 2013, with supporting demonstrations authorizing him to use force, was a moment when war emerged again on the surface, creating a new rhizome of opposing background. The revolution became fragmented, and the forces on the ground divided, with Islamists being subject to excessive use of force by the army and police and with thousands of civilians losing their lives in clashes and demonstrations.

After 30 June and 3 July—the ousting of President Morsi—the constitution became again the heart of political conflict. A new committee of ten constitutional law experts suggested amendments to the 2012 constitution that was no longer in effect according to the statements of ousted president Morsi and following the presidential declarations by the head of the constitutional court, who took office as a temporary president. An assembly of fifty was formed to reverse the same debates on identity and division of power between different authorities. The armed forces negotiated even more power in the new constitution, including the approval of the appointment of the minister of defense by the Supreme Council of Armed Forces, taking the ceiling of any future negotiation to its lowest level possible. The officers' republic in Egypt is back, and the scene in Egypt is dramatically shifting (Sayigh 2012).

MOHAMED MAHMOUD STREET: MINIATURE OF AN URBAN CONSTRUCTIVE CHAOS

The other side of the story of negotiation's failing to build a revolutionary legitimacy did not take place in courts or meeting halls or cabinet and chamber halls. It is the story that took place on the street, where there was no room for negotiating by words but a battle to occupy space. Several years after the 3 July ousting of the elected president there is still a battle over spaces and places, symbolizing the presence and empowerment of the people on the street, even if in the course of the revolution the street became divided. After a revolution, one of the biggest challenges is to replace the Old Order with a New one.

The rhizome and the multitude grow in urban settings, hence it is important to look at the manifestations of conflicts not only in the battle over the constitution but also on the ground. The same scenario is repeated between Mohamed Mahmoud Street and Rabʿa (the square where the MB had their sit-in for almost eight weeks, which was dismantled by excessive force with a high death toll). The area lies between Tahrir Square and the streets of all governorates, between the state apparatus that stood against the revolutionary transition and the protests that never gave in to the opposing power, with their martyrs from diverse backgrounds who kept the struggle on the street vivid and vibrant.

In his seminal article "Urbanism as a Way of Life", Louis Wirth (1938, 49) defined urbanism as "that complex of traits that makes up the characteristic mode of life in the city," thereby linking the definition of urbanism to the definition of what constitutes the city. Accordingly, Wirth's sociological definition of the city is "a relatively large, dense and permanent settlement of socially heterogeneous individuals" (49). In his groundbreaking work *The Culture of Cities*, Lewis Mumford (1935, 480) defined the city as "a geographic plexus, an economic organisation, an institutional process, a theatre of social action, and an aesthetic symbol of collective unity."

According to both Wirth and Mumford, the city, as a composite physical, economic, social, and cultural entity, generates a specific form of social interaction different from that which prevails in rural settings, with additional "social drama," as Mumford calls it, that comes from the focusing and intensification of group activity. Zygmunt Bauman (1999) goes a step further, introducing an eye-opening understanding of urban spaces that challenges this sequence of conflict. He sees the chaos in the city as constructive and empowering versus the order that is destructive. The difference in rationale of groups might be an obstacle against Felstiner's logic (Felstiner, Abel, and Sarat 1981). The premodern chaotic and bewildering diversity of maps was to be replaced therefore not so much with one universally shared image of the world as with a strict hierarchy of images. In order to collect taxes and recruit soldiers, premodern powers, incapable of reading out the realities fully legible for their subjects, had to behave like alien, hostile forces: to resort to armed invasions and punitive expeditions. There was little to distinguish the practice of tax collection from robbery and looting and the practice of enlisting from that of taking prisoners; the armed hirelings of barons and princes persuaded "the natives" to part with their produce or their sons by using the arguments of swords and whips; they got away with as much as the display of brutal force allowed them to squeeze. Ernest Gellner gave the premodern system of rule the name "dentistry state": the rulers specialized, he wrote, in extraction through torture (Bauman 1994, 174–175).

The enquiry that follows from those definitions of urbanism and the city is one that seeks to identify the specific nature of social interaction that prevails in the city, which generates particular behavioral patterns. Violence and civility, struggle and conflict result in social cohesion or social instability, reaching the level of revolution.

This urban sociology approach along with the works of David Harvey (2009) and Frederic Jameson (2002) on the city and urban spaces allows us to add a highly important dimension to analysis: namely the spatial dimension. That dimension kept challenging any attempt by established and structured political forces to negotiate, and kept bringing the negotiation process to a halt or resulted in its failure in the end. This was the factor of urban chaos that was constructively used by revolutionaries and supported by the least advantaged segments of urban space right from the outset of the revolution. While political organized forces were willing to negotiate with SCAF, the urban poor were not. The most marginalized such as street vendors and street children were the most determined to challenge the remaining structures of the old regime, and this was the scene of the Mohamed Mahmoud battle of 2011.

Lucie Ryzova (2011) describes it as a battle where people were portrayed by the media not as revolutionaries but as vandals (*baltageyya*). Only after four days of clashes and the deaths of many activists did the state media admit the square was populated with "protesters" who might even have "legitimate demands." But explaining—and even more so, understanding—what has been going on in Mohamed Mahmoud Street and large parts of the Abdeen neighborhood is very important for understanding why negotiation failed to be an option to curb violence.

Clashes started when Egyptian police used numerous brutal methods to suppress the peaceful protesters who had been gathering in Tahrir Square since Friday, 18 November. In the early hours of Saturday morning, security forces cleared a small sit-in for those wounded in the January/February revolution and the martyrs' families. The tactical goal of such a brutal attack on a small number of protesters begs many questions. Revolutionaries rushed to their aid, and Twitter spread the news in seconds. For a few hours there were clashes, but on the afternoon of Sunday, 20 November, the military police once again "cleared" Tahrir Square. Videos of security forces throwing bodies on refuse piles shocked the world. But ever since that Sunday, the square itself and the Tal'at Harb area to the north of it have been a perfectly safe, "secured" zone.

And a battle it was. People went there knowing what they were striving for: liberation. They went there to fight. Police threw teargas canisters and used shotguns (occasionally also live ammunition); against the police was a line of young men mostly throwing stones, but also Molotov cocktails and small homemade bombs. The battle lines were drawn—on the first day of the Second Revolution—with a physical human barricade protecting the protesters in the square from the advance of police forces bent on clearing the area, but it then developed into a battle for its own sake. For the first five days of the battle, this fighting zone was constantly changing, consisting of advances and retreats closer and further from the Ministry of Interior, often penetrating deep into the Abdeen neighborhood. This moving battlefield was marked by smells, sounds, and collective body language.

Groups of young men on the front line were exposed to swathes of tear gas. Motorcycles carried the wounded and those exposed to the gas back to safety. Behind the front line, there were crowds of supporters and onlookers, escaping from the rain of tear gas and shotgun shells, and moving back and forth closer and further from the Ministry of Interior. It was a "Battle for the *dakhiliyya*" (the Ministry of Interior), but that does not mean that any of the young men facing the police necessarily wanted or intended to take over the ministry's building. It was a symbolic battle: the fight itself was the message.

Throughout the first week of the Second Revolution of October–November 2011, Tahrir Square and the battle zone to its east each had its own different crowd. Each can only be understood as a symbiosis—a specific social alliance—as both constructed and supported each other, and they increasingly overlapped. The square, the "safe" zone, contained a truly socially mixed crowd. People from all walks of life came there, often several times a day, in support of those who decided to camp out, to help "hold" the square and support its cause. The social mix was one rarely seen in Egypt (though it was famously present in the First Revolution of January and February): middle-class men and women, some of them activists but most of them not; young and old, in suits, *kefiyehs*, and jeans, alongside the *galabiyas* and long beards of the Salafis; bareheaded women as well as *munaqqabat* (fully veiled women). The city was represented by diverse faces, with the same message: challenging the force of the state represented by the Ministry of Interior.

On the front line, by contrast, the demographic was predominantly (though not exclusively) young male, the socially marginalized, street children, and members of the Ultras, a soccer fan group. For many of the men battling the police, it was less about politics and more about regaining personal dignity. This was a battle that is not articulated as being "for something," but as a visceral fight to settle accounts with the security forces. A battle of *karama* (dignity), but not of *karama* as a universal human honor. It is rather a historically and socially constituted honor that has a lot to do with how honor and masculinity were constructed locally. They were not fighting for any high-minded outcome such as democracy; in fact, most possibly they did not think anything "good" would come out of the fight. But the fight gave them back their dignity, even if temporarily. *Karama* for them means their bodies were not subject to torture, they were not mistreated at checkpoints and police stations, and they had the small change in their pockets to be extracted by each officer they passed so that they did not get thrown in the police station overnight—until they could produce more cash. They did not necessarily believe that any force (any political outcome that might come as result of this fight) would help them to recover their dignity.

The Ultras blurred the line between battle and sport early on; especially at night, the battlefield in Mohamed Mahmoud is often lit with *shamarikh*, the colored flare fireworks used during football matches. Provocateurs on the payroll of the secret service were also responsible for lighting on fire rubbish bins in the streets of Abdeen. Their purpose might again have been to create fear and chaos (and, of course, to feed the state media discourse portraying the events as acts of vandalism). But the real outcome was often the opposite. Small localized fires in the side streets of Abdeen helped the fighters. They lit up the streets whose public lights had been off for the whole week, and more importantly, they acted as morale boosters, adding to the dramatic battlefield mise-en-scène in which the line between what was a real fight and what was sport was increasingly blurred. Egyptian mainstream middle-class culture can hardly relate to most of the frontline fighters. Hence they could not build on it for negotiation, nor did the activists on the street care to join negotiations either.

Thursday, 24 November, the battlefront was demarcated by a wall built of concrete blocks, imposing a makeshift truce. The effort to stress the martyrdom of the not-so-middle-class youth was evident on banners across the Midan: *Rigala Bulaq al-Dakrur qadimuna li-shehada* (the men of Bulaq al-Dakrur coming for martyrdom). Bulaq al-Dakrur is one of the many informal but socially mixed neighborhoods on the periphery of the formal city of Cairo.

Two incidents changed that: the sniping of a sheikh from Al Azhar, Emad Effat, and the shooting of a Y5 medical school doctor who volunteered to help the injured, Alaa Abdel Hadi. For most of the week until that Thursday, the dynamics between the square and formal politicians had reached a standoff. Formal political forces and political alliances that emerged during the past nine months were null in Tahrir Square. From the square it seemed clear that the time for compromise has long since passed. Only radical solutions are acceptable: withdrawal of the army from politics, a complete restructuring of the police forces, and the imposition of a transitional government or presidential council with a clear time frame and full powers. From the position of formal politics, such solutions are not (yet) acceptable. One may question whether they ever will be. But the Square is determined to accept nothing less this time, as the comparison with the January revolution is on everybody's lips; indeed, people are here because they see themselves as having been naive back in the spring when they cleared the square, leaving the SCAF in charge of the revolution.

It is now a battle of wills: who will put conditions on whom, us or them? Who names the new government or transitional council: SCAF or the Square? Even if some do not express their positions in an articulate way, the general refusal to accept and trust the SCAF on the ground seems overwhelming. Just as the Square sees formal political channels (SCAF and parties alike) as illegitimate, the regime's tactic is to delegitimize the Square, to create a rift between it and the rest of the country, to pose the "Square" against the "street." Most of these youth come from neighborhoods that never experience constructive policing. The police for them constitute a repressive regime that extracts rents and performs its crude power on their bodies. They have never seen anything good come of it and cannot imagine that they ever will. The best that can happen for them is that the police stay away from their lives.

But while the momentous social alliance of the Square allows them, for the time being, to settle their accounts with the police "as men" (face to face, crude force against crude force), this is also a very momentous situation. Much of their determination comes from knowing that once the Mohamed Mahmoud Street Battle is done, the police are likely to continue their blood feud back in their neighborhoods, away from the scrutiny of the media, and far from the middle-class activists protected in the fight.

If we move to the scene of the street even before 30 June 2013, when the occupy action took place at al-Nahda and Rab'a, two places in Cairo that were closed by supporters of Morsi after the first statement of the minister of defense announcing intervention in the political process one week before the demonstrations at the end of June, we can find an increasing use of violence, more clashes. After 3 July, more force was used by the police and the military, and the death toll rose, in clashes from Bein El Sarayat near Cairo University to the republican guards' clashes in the Nasr City neighborhood, to the confrontations in front of the military platform near the Rab'a area and the tomb of Sadat, to the ultimate massacre at Rab'a and Nahda, to the increasing use of excessive force by the security apparatus in all hot spots of confrontation with protestors. The number of victims is horrific, and the situation can be described as a sporadic small-scale civil war where the opponents of the process of ousting the president (not all members of Muslim Brothers) are facing death every time they go to the street.

There is no opportunity to go into depth in comparing the nature of the multitude and the rhizome before and after the revolution, as the three months that passed since the army interfered in the scene and declared a war on terror need separate analysis. It is enough to mention that the strategies of using spaces, the diversity of tactics, the spread of the protests in different governorates, and the scale and degree of use of arms by the security forces (police and army) demonstrate a qualitative shift and a higher degree of conflict between the horizontal and the vertical rationales of the exercise of power and maneuvering with urban space. As well, the rise of nonpolitical actors using force against protestors side by side with the security forces in an unprecedented setting of relations between official forces and networks of thugs threatens the whole scene and can even distort the foundations of the rules of the game on the side of the security system, which can result in rising violence in return (indicators of such a shift are growing now in Egypt). The challenges facing the effort to keep the dissent actions civil and peaceful are increasing, and the risk/benefit calculations are becoming very complicated for the opposition in light of the current setting of power relations, the rising violence, and the skyrocketing number of victims and casualties. The factor of the existence of organized terrorist groups that were unleashed by the changes taking place will make the rhizome and the multitude face new challenges that need to be further explored and discussed.

FAULT LINES BETWEEN REVOLUTION, REFORM, AND COUP D'ÉTAT: OVERLAPPING APPROACHES AND INTERACTING GROUPS AND FORCES

Egypt faces a revolutionary process that interacts and mingles with a process of reform, and they both are surrounded by military coup (whether we call it soft or harsh), based on street support by some segments of society facing a strong, spreading, and continuous opposition and resistance. The overlap of these approaches is the main reason behind the complexity that exists in the current status quo. Each of the three parties (the revolutionaries, the reformists, and the military) has its own formula or perspective on the revolution, either as a totality that is going on or as something that is rejected altogether. Ideally and practically, revolution is "merely political" (or, rather, nonsystemic) in so far as it shakes off a political regime that is dysfunctional in relation to a fully fledged socioeconomic system. Political revolution "emancipates" the system from its political constraints.

None of these parties has reached anything tangible regarding its goal and purpose, and none of them managed to fully identify and draw down its scheme for managing the political conflict or its strategy for dealing with the others. Therefore, the scene is hazy and ambiguous. The military wanted only the beheading of the king—at least for the moment for later pardon—so as to calm the revolutionaries (or to suppress them). Getting Mubarak out of the equation allowed them to maintain the public order and preserve the structures and patterns of power in the military hand. This provided the military with full control of government, either directly or indirectly, and then started the reproduction of the old system to maintain the military leaders' economic and social gains that were subject to questioning after the revolution. The military may have supported the revolution at the beginning as part of the resistance against the "succession project" from Mubarak to his son Gamal, and also to preserve the apparatus of the Republic from collapsing, but the rationale and the vision of the army remain antirevolutionary.

However, one has to ask: What does "the Republic" mean for the military? The answer is simply that the Republic means nothing but a military dictatorship in the name of saving the sovereignty and protecting the country. The Free Officers that led the 1952 coup/revolution belonged to or were affected at one point by some authoritarian organization. Since the early days of the "blessed movement" of 1952 coup, which turned later in the memory of the nation into a revolution, extensive discussion occurred among the Free Officers regarding the formula for a New Order. The first proposal was to construct a military dictatorship, while the second was the establishment of democracy. Yet the vision was that it was not time to establish a democracy. Hence, one can understand this level of heterogeneity of opinions and the different contrasting visions between the military junta (SCAF) and the revolutionary movements in the Egyptian street.

The revolutionaries of all backgrounds and with the unfolding multitude wanted to restore the Republic of the people in contrast with the "state apparatus–centered" notion of the Republic adopted by SCAF. To be more precise, the revolution aimed "to build a new republic," not just establish a democratic system, based on the rules and principles of the revolution and in pace with the ambition of young people. "Revolutions seek to overturn a society's social, economic and political structures, and recast its international relations, all within a relatively short time-frame" (Lawson 2005, 479). The real conflict is over the system of power and its manifestations in the form of different practices. The revolutionary rebels unanimously voiced their rejection to the mere police authoritarian state that is returning to revenge (Eskandar 2013). Those who went to the streets to bring down the regime of Mubarak did not carry out the revolution to bring about a new dictatorship led by the military, and they remain very hostile to and critical of the patterns of militarized power in general. The revolution erupted against the different structures of repression and oppression; it came to stand against and defy "the patriarchal authority" and "the dominance of security policies and mind set" invading the various aspects of society. Both the patriarchal authority and the dominance of security policies are genuine features for the authoritarian militarized power structure.

The revolutionary project was moving toward the dismantling of that authority—in civilian areas—at an accelerated pace, which could also be with a high cost of disorder at some points. Though the coup had a high degree of interoperability with the revolution, the military soldiers now in power believed that they can subdue the masses again, and thus this coup has actually overtaken the revolutionary situation. The coup here does not necessarily mean the continuity of the military in direct ruling position as the head of the state. The changes at the global social, economic, and political levels as well as in the Egyptian arena make such an explicit military ruling presence very difficult and highly criticized, even with the media war now in action to rule out any other option under the slogan of War on Terror. The evolution of systems of governance and the patterns of economic production has made the real power not based only in the state apparatus, but rather in the interests of various networks at the internal and global levels in the way that exceeds and surpasses the states. The military coups in the 1950s and 1960s have been associated with military elites' occupation of the state and their adhesion to its institutions, thus building what is called "state capitalism." But now the matter has become more complex, since the state apparatus is still an important and effective possibility, yet it has also been transformed and evolved to become a node in a complex network, which did not remain the same as in the previous decades. Therefore, one can understand the concern by the military junta (SCAF) to keep and defend a government such as that of Prime Minister Kamal Ganzouri, which is entrenched deeply in the Old Kingdom of Mubarak, and to maintain the same elites and leaders of the former regime, especially in the second and third lines of command in various state institutions. A glance at the faces leading the government and the constitutional assembly of fifty people is a good proof of that—old faces restoring old power networks.

At the same time, one can understand why SCAF did not entirely take over power in the same manner of the military coups of the 1950s and 1960s, neither after 25 January nor after 3 July 2013, when it moved definitely more into the forefront than before. It is because the interests of the military junta are linked to the state and go beyond it as well. And at the same time, the military junta has no political project that requires SCAF to chair the state institutions directly. Just a war on terror and the promise of security can build a fair support by the masses. Still, there are huge economic and social interests that require the incursion and spread of the military in the state and the maintaining of a strong military existence above and beyond the state (and not only as the head of it). As the systems and patterns of governance—as well as the patterns of the revolutions—have evolved, one must take into account the evolutions that took place regarding the patterns of the military and quasi-military coups in the world.

It is the revolutionary side, which involves large sectors of the society, that continues to raise the slogan of toppling all of the Old Order altogether (*Isqat al-Nizam*) and to bring about a radical change in the system of power that runs extensively at all levels. It aspires to change the form and structure of power in the system and the regime, such as changing the structure of the state itself and thus the dismantling of the masculine power and the patriarchal society. The forces of this side were disenchanted by the one-year rule of the Muslim Brothers, yet they are now facing a serious challenge of the corrosion of public space and civil liberties and are witnessing a rise of a street-based opposition that exceeds the organization of the Muslim Brotherhood and is creating a new multitude. As mentioned earlier, the revolution was trying to change the relationship between the different institutions in society—that is, the state and the individuals—and to restructure the various functions in control of the political process as well as the cultural and social development. It was also seeking—from the first moment—to change the practices of power, which had been marked by subjugation and control through violence and repression coupled with corruption. The revolutionary multitude does not recognize the mechanisms of reform that are based on gradual change and step-by-step reformation. The revolution means to them a huge extended process of transformation that is not limited to the eighteen days (25 January to 11 February) or to removing the body of the ousted president from the palace to the hospital.

The revolution took the reformists by surprise, and they joined it to be part of a wave of change and paid high prices during its unfolding. The idea of the revolution was absent from the literature of the reformists, and they never showed a willingness to make a radical change in the heart of social and economic structures, or in the patterns of politics and power, because they actually do not have a major problem with structure, but rather with its asymmetry. Their vision is focused on making some reforms as well as reducing the severity and intensity of violence and oppression and creating a relative improvement in the economic conditions (but not in the correlations or mode of production). They participated in the revolution as a political opportunity to get rid of the oppressing members of the Old Order, who represented a major obstacle to the arrival of these reformist forces to the seats of governance through democratic mechanisms. "This differentiates revolutions from reformist change that is comprehensive but takes place over the long-term, reform programs that take place in the short-term but do not engender fundamental change and transitions which see only a partial modification of a society's main institutions and organizations and take place over a medium-term time-frame" (Lawson 2005, 479). This frame of analysis can explain the course of action of the Islamist parties and organizations through the two and half years until 30 June, a position that was subject to revision under the fire of the security apparatus and might result in the growth of more radical voices that will opt for revolutionary strategies.

The revolution for those reformists had ended with the end of the rule of the former president. The reformist process is not inconsistent with and it is not against the line of the revolutionary or the coup processes. The coup wants to preserve the institutions of the state as they are, and acts to save the intrusive and pervasive interests of the military in this state, while the reformists and their reformist processes want to keep the state institutions and introduce only some minor modifications to them. And the revolution—for the reformists—was good and helpful in vigorously and quickly removing some of the obstacles in the way of the reform process, while the reformists are not readily welcoming a drastic full-scale reform. The revolution aims to turn, shift, and change the state institutions and power structures in the most intensive and expanded possible way. Therefore, the revolutionaries are not communicating or negotiating with the coup and its people, as they side with the reformists, only against the fear of a possible overall militarized coup. "Revolutions are distinguished sometimes by outcomes, sometimes by actors. . . . Revolutions that transform economic and social structures as well as political institutions, such as the French Revolution of 1789, are called great revolutions; those that change only state institutions are called political revolutions. . . . Revolutions that fail to secure power after temporary victories or large-scale mobilization are often called failed or abortive revolutions; oppositional movements that either do not aim to take power (such as peasant or worker protests) or focus on a particular region or subpopulation are usually called rebellions (if violent) or protests (if predominantly peaceful)" (Goldstone 2009, 321). Due to the cloudy surroundings that enclose the Egyptian revolution, its relationship with the state, and its inability to offset the ruling class at lower levels, some academicians such as Asef Bayat (2011) describe the revolution as a process for reformation (refo-lution). What he means by this definition is that the masses were in dire need for abolishing certain forms and parts of the Old Order, headed by the deposed president, since they were major obstacles that impeded the reformation path and hindered the process of democratization.

There is no doubt that the chances for Egypt's improvement depend on the superiority of one of these approaches over the others, or on a possible conducive combination of political and social adjustments. If the reformists and revolutionaries fail in curbing the military incursions and allow the return of the military officers to their military barracks, then a dramatic shift can take place.

THE EMERGING AMBIGUITY AND THE LIMITS OF FORCE

The two authors of this chapter might disagree on the framing and categorization of the demonstrations of 30 June 2013 that led to the ouster of President Mohamed Morsi, the declaration of the minister of defense for an intermediate period, and the appointment of the head of the high constitutional court as a temporary president until the minister of defense, Abdul Fatah al-Sisi, was declared president after elections in June 2014 that witnessed poor turnout by voters.

During that year the political conflict turned into a clash of truths between the supporters of General Sisi and the supporters of Morsi, splitting the country into two camps and leading to the demonstrations of 26 July 2013 when Sisi asked the public to give him authorization for a war on terrorism that launched cycles of state violence against any opposition. The Muslim Brothers were the main target, which resulted not only in the massacre at Rabʿa and al-Nahda but also in the confiscation of the personal property of MB leaders, massive arrests including women and child demonstrators, as well as violent clashes on university campuses, which for the whole 2013–2014 academic year, especially at al-Azhar University, resulted in the loss of many lives and the detention of more than forty thousand people.

The second round of confrontation and the expansion of the state of emergency and the harsh fist was with the revolutionary forces on the ground, some of which supported openly the 30 June 2011 demonstration and the subsequent control of the military. On 8 July a law that criminalized demonstration without permission was issued by Adly Mansour, the transitional president, and initiated a wave of protests challenging it, leading to the imprisonment of many figures of the revolutionary groups, including Alaa Abdel Fattah, leaders of the 6 April Movement, Mahinour El Massry, a leading woman figure of the 25 January 2011 revolution in Alexandria, and many of her comrades. The regime went wild in assuming control and raising fear through the media, systematically distorting the 25 June revolution. The leaders of the Mubarak regime were given access to the media, and the voice of opposition was completely muted.

At the same time, explosions took place in different parts of the capital, including the attack on the national security building in Cairo and Qalubeya, and were claimed to be conducted by terrorist groups. A war broke out between different armed groups in Sinai and the army, which announced it would completely end terrorism in Sinai within weeks but failed to do so during the year 2014. On the side of the Muslim Brothers and the substantial number of supporters of the legitimacy of Morsi, demonstrations did not stop for a single day, shifting the ground from cities to towns and sometimes to villages. They soon developed a tactic of swift demonstrations of ten to twenty minutes to avoid casualties by the bullets of police forces and the arrest of their participants. On the other hand, the labor movement staged many strikes, but unfortunately these were overlooked due to the wider coverage of the political clashes.

The scene was tainted by regional alliances, with Qatar and Turkey siding officially with the MB, and Saudi Arabia and the United Arab Emirates supporting financially Sisi's military dominance and his political takeover via elections.

With the military control over politics, one might assume that the rhizome theoretical frame might no longer be relevant for the understanding of the situation in Egypt. Yet actions of dissent and contestations, whether civil or armed, did not cease to take place on the ground over the year 2014. Whether the rhizome emerges within a context of civil disobedience or more armed dissent, it did not vanish in the face of the fierce state security policy nor the attempt to claim control over the revolutionary street, and despite the rising accusations that the 25 January revolution was a conspiracy or a betrayal by groups of youth sponsored by the United States or backed by Hamas agents in Tahrir Square, the revolution succeeded in paralyzing the security system by burning police stations, attacking prisons, and freeing the detainees and prisoners 25–28 January 2011. The vibrant rhizome so far indicates that the full harsh power of the state did not achieve its goals despite the massive state violence.

On the political negotiation level, the Fermont agreement between civil forces and the 2012 campaign of Morsi failed to continue and collapsed soon after the Islamist monopoly over the constitutional assembly of 2012. The reluctance to pursue security system reform and investigation into the use of armed force against civilians since 25 January led to open polarization and lack of trust between different parties. It is noteworthy is that in the year after the ouster of Morsi, the 30 June movement also collapsed. The Salvation Front (*Gabhet Al Inqaz*) and their youth with their liberal perspectives had no issue with the dominance of the military forces, embracing an ultra-nationalist discourse, while the more revolutionary leftist forces wanted a limited intervention by the army and a stronger social justice stance from the state, as well as interior security system reform policies.

Some analysts tend to describe the scene as the end of politics, since under that expanded hegemony of the army over the political and economic sphere any democratic arrangement would be void of any content or legitimacy as the strategy of annihilation of any opposition is escalating. Under such circumstances the resistance and flourishing of the rhizome continues, and negotiation is no longer a preferred option by all actors. With challenges to national security on the western borders with Libya and on the eastern border with Gaza, and the presence of Egyptian troops at the Saudi-Iraqi borders following the deterioration of the situation with the rise of ISIS, more challenges threaten a governmental system that is stretching itself thin on the hot surface of a crucial economic situation and more unstable social implications of the end of gas subsidies. Not only is the system under stress, but it might face a sudden collapse or a high degree of instability in the short and medium term.

Notes

1. Midan al-Tahrir was formerly the site of the British army barracks, and is now an open traffic hub flanked by the Egyptian Museum and the Government Building.

2. It is not only the regime, but even the academicians before the revolution of 25 January who were searching for the political actor to analyze and predict what kind of role it could play in any process of change. The main arguments were that there is no political alternative, there are no actors who can play a counterhegemonic role against the system, and the communal organizations either do not exist or are very weak and unpoliticized.

References

Badiou, Alain. 2011. "Tunisia, Egypt: The Universal Reach of Popular Uprisings." *Lacan.com*. http://www.lacan.com/thesymptom/?page_id=1031 (accessed 2 May 2012).

El Basheri, Tarek. 2011. "Miser Wa Maza Yorado Bahia" [What is wanted of Egypt]. *Shorouk*, 12 November. http://shorouknews.com/columns/view.aspx?cdate=12112011&id=c0c6d13b-d586-4f11-92c7-ad005ca1f7af (accessed 2 May 2012).

Bauman, Zygmunt. 1994. "A Revolution in the Theory of Revolutions?" *International Political Science Review* 15, no. 1 (January): 15–24. www.jstor.org/stable/1601228 (accessed 2 May 2012).

———. 1999. "Urban Space Wars: On Destructive Order and Creative Chaos." *Citizenship Studies* 3, no. 2: 173–185.

Bayat, Asef. 2011. "Paradoxes of Arab Refo-lutions." *Jadaliyya*. http://www.jadaliyya.com/pages/index/786/paradoxes-of-arab-refo-lutions (accessed 2 May 2012).

Brown, Nathan J. 2011. "Landmines in Egypt's Constitutional Roadmap." *Carnegie Endowment*, 7 December. http://carnegieendowment.org/2011/12/07/landmines-in-egypt-s-constitutional-roadmap/838q (accessed 2 May 2012).

Chalcraft, John. 2012. "Horizontalism in the Egyptian Revolutionary Process." *Middle East Report* 262 (Spring): 6-11.

Deleuze, Gilles, and Felix Guattari. 2009. *A Thousand Plateaus: Capitalism and Schizophrenia*. London: Continuum.

Dunne, Michele. 2011. "Egypt: Elections or Constitution First?" Carnegie Endowment for International Peace, 21 June. http://carnegieendowment.org/2011/06/21/egypt-elections-or-constitution-first/qq (accessed 2 May 2012).

Eskandar, Wael. 2013. "The Revenge of the Police State." *Jadaliyya*, 17 August. http://www.jadaliyya.com/pages/index/13658/the-revenge-of-the-police-state.

Fanon, Franz. 2004. *The Wretched of the Earth*. New York: Grove Press.

Felstiner, William L. F., Richard L. Abel, and Austin Sarat. 1980–1981. "The Emergence and Transformation of Disputes: Naming, Blaming, Claiming . . ." *Law and Society Review* 15, no. 3/4: 631–654.

Foucault, Michel. 1980. *Power/Knowledge: Selected Interviews and Other Writings*. Edited by Colin Gordon. Brighton, Sussex: Harvester Press.

———. 2003. *Society Must Be Defended: Lectures at the Collège de France, 1975-76*. Edited by Michel Senellart. New York: Picador.

Goldstone, Jack A. 2001. "Toward a Fourth Generation of Revolutionary Theory." *Annual Review of Political Science* 4: 139–187.

———. 2009. "Revolution." In *The SAGE Handbook of Comparative Politics*, edited by Todd Landman and Neil Robinson, 319–347. Thousand Oaks Calif.: SAGE.

El Gundy, Zeinab. 2012. "MPs Inch Closer to Vote of No-Confidence in El-Ganzouri Government." Al-Ahram Online, 29 March. http://english.ahram.org.eg/NewsContent/1/64/38042/Egypt/Politics-/MPs-inch-closer-to-vote-of-noconfidence-in-ElGanzo.aspx (accessed 2 May 2012).

Hardt, Michael, and Antonio Negri. 2005. *Multitude: War and Democracy in the Age of Empire*. New York: Penguin Books.

———. 2011. "Arabs Are Democracy's New Pioneers: The Leaderless Middle East Uprisings Can Inspire Freedom Movements as Latin America Did Before. *Guardian*, 24 February. http://www.guardian.co.uk/commentisfree/2011/feb/24/arabs-democracy-latin-america (accessed 2 May 2012).

Harvey, David. 2009. *Social Justice and the City*. Rev. ed. Athens: University of Georgia Press.

Herrera, Linda. 2011. "Generation Rev and the Struggle for Democracy: Interview with Aly El-Raggal." *Jadaliyya*, 15 October. http://www.jadaliyya.com/pages/index/2869/generation-rev-and-the-struggle-for-democracy_inte (accessed 2 May 2012).

Jameson, Fredric. 2009. *Political Unconscious: Narrative as a Socially Symbolic Act*. London: Routledge.

Kremenyuk, Victor A., ed. 2002. *International Negotiation: Analysis, Approaches, Issues*. 2nd ed. San Francisco: Jossey-Bass.

Laclau, Ernesto, and Chantal Mouffe. 1981. "Socialist Strategy; Where Next?" Translated by Mike Mullan. *Marxism Today*, January.

———. 2001. *Hegemony and Socialist Strategy: Toward a Radical Democratic Politics*. London: Verso.

Lawson, George. 2005. "Negotiated Revolutions: The Prospects for Radical Change in Contemporary World." *Review of International Studies* 31, no. 3 (July): 473–493, http://www.jstor.org/stable/40072085 (accessed 2 May 2012).

McCarthy, John D., and Mayer N. Zald. 1977. "Resource Mobilization and Social Movements: A Partial Theory." *American Journal of Sociology* 82, no. 6: 1212–1241.

MENA. 2012. "People's Assembly Special Committee Slams El-Ganzouri Government." Al-Ahram Online, 28 March. http://english.ahram.org.eg/NewsContent/1/64/37952/Egypt/Politics-/Peoples-Assembly-special-committee-slams-ElGanzour.aspx (accessed 2 May 2012).

Mumford, Lewis. 1938. *The Culture of Cities*. New York: Harcourt, Brace.

Oberschall, Anthony. 2000. "Social Movements and the Transition to Democracy. *Democratization* 7, no. 3: 25–45. http://dx.doi.org/10.1080/13510340008403670 (accessed 2 May 2012).

Ottaway, Marina. 2011. "Transitional Failure in Egypt and Tunisia." Carnegie Endowment for International Peace, 10 August. http://carnegieendowment.org/2011/08/10/transitional-failure-in-egypt-and-tunisia/4ma4 (accessed 2 May 2012).

———. 2012. "Who Will Write the Egyptian Constitution?" Carnegie Endowment for International Peace, 13 March. http://carnegieendowment.org/2012/03/13/who-will-write-egyptian-constitution/a2sg (accessed 2 May 2012).

Ryzova, Lucie. 2011. "The Battle of Cairo's Muhammad Mahmoud Street." Al Jazeera, 29 November, Opinion section. http://www.aljazeera.com/indepth/opinion/2011/11/201111288494638419.html.

Said, Islam. 2011. "El-Baradeai: Watheqat El-Selmi Moshaaha wa Al-Qowat Al-Mosalaha laysat dawla fawq Al-Dawla" [Baradei: Selmi Document is disfigured and the armed forces are not above the state.] Shorouk, 2 November. http://www.shorouknews.com/news/view.aspx?id=90d91d49-b475–404a-9d19–1d4afd1392aa (accessed 2 May 2012).

Sayigh, Yezid. 2012. "Above the State: The Officers' Republic in Egypt. Carnegie Endowment for International Peace, 1 August. http://carnegie-mec.org/2012/08/01/above-state-officers-republic-in-egypt/d4sx.

Savage, Michael, Alan Warde, and Kevin Ward. 1993. *Urban Sociology, Capitalism and Modernity*. London: Macmillan.

Sharp, Jeremy M. 2011. "Egypt in Transition." Congressional Research Service, 23 August. http://fpc.state.gov/documents/organization/168035.pdf (accessed 24 October 2014).

Tilly, Charles. 1978. *From Mobilization to Revolution*. Reading, Mass.: Addison-Wesley.

Wirth, Louis. 1938. "Urbanism as a Way of Life." *American Journal of Sociology* 44, no. 1: 1–24.

Zartman, I. William. 1989. "Prenegotiations: Phases and Functions." In *Getting to the Table: The Processes of International Prenegotiation,* edited by Janice Gross Stein. Baltimore: Johns Hopkins University Press.

———. 2009. "Negotiation as a Choice of Partners." *PINPoints* 33: 13–16.

Žižek, Slavoj. 2007. "Tolerance as an Ideological Category." *Critical Inquiry*, Autumn. http://www.lacan.com/zizek-inquiry.html (accessed 2 May 2012).

Yemen

Negotiations with Tribes, States, and Memories

ABDULLAH HAMIDADDIN

BETWEEN 2004 AND 2012 Yemen witnessed six wars in its upper northern regions and in the civil uprising of the Arab Spring. During this time there were multiple negotiations and mediations that attempted to reach resolutions in order to save the country from further destruction. All those efforts failed, despite the fact that the parties involved seemed to have reached a mutual hurting stalemate (MHS), one of the ingredients of a ripe moment for negotiation, and that there had been external mediators who had enough credibility to elicit a lasting resolution on both sides. In 2014, a seventh war, more serious than the preceding six, resurfaced, and the two conflicts came together to destroy any progress made so far. In both the war in the north and the civil uprising of the Arab Spring, the reasons leading to a suspension of military activities were external to the events themselves. Both cases can provide some qualifications to the ripeness theory to allow it to accommodate more situations, in particular those of an internal nature. The following account lays out the structure and actors of Yemen as a setting for both the six wars and the events leading to the ousting of President Ali Abdullah Saleh, with the purpose of highlighting the various negotiation efforts and their ultimate failure.

To speak of negotiations is to describe the flow of a waterfall. In any given moment there are many processes with different starting points, multiple trajectories, and various outcomes taking place between competing political actors. Negotiation is indeed a fluid process splashing all over, and it is barely possible to describe it by taking a fast snapshot, zooming in to one specific current, and then trying to understand how it came to be and where it may head. Another way is to make snapshots of the water as it rushes against a large rock in an attempt to understand its effect. This chapter is written in the spirit of the second effort. Yemen is a fast-moving target. Negotiations there have been endless, and the processes that surfaced in the past two years were a continuation of previous politics by other means. Nevertheless those processes were taking place within a political structure that has been around for some time in the past and will continue to exist for some time in the future. The reason for choosing this second approach is to present some thoughts that can still be very useful after the phase of negotiations covered by it is long over.

As in the other chapters in this volume, this analysis shows how the attitudes of the parties in Yemen influenced their approach to negotiations with competing parties. But it also highlights the peculiarity of Yemen and the way that peculiarity influenced the ways each party maneuvered. Moreover, unlike the other cases, Yemen's negotiations were not the outcome of an outburst of popular emotions. They were an elite guided process. Negotiations in Yemen did not start from the bottom; rather, they started at the top, and when they failed, the elites leveraged the populace as cards with which to play. When the situation became too unpredictable, the elites negotiated. In this Yemen's pacted course is similar to Egypt's, without the double authoritarian denouement; in other ways, it is similar to the fragmented evolution of Libya (which lost its authoritarian ruler) and Syria (which did not).

This chapter concludes with the signing of the Gulf Initiative. After the signing, other processes of negotiations were initiated, namely the National Dialogue, which started on 18 March 2013 and formally ended on 25 January 2014. This round of negotiations was not just an elite process; it included many segments of society, as well as the active participation of the UN special adviser Jamal Benomar. Yet the political structure discussed in this chapter remained intact all through the negotiations of the National Dialogue. No one expected fundamental change in a short time, but the massive changes on the surface led many analysts to overlook the stability of the underlying political structure. So though the National Dialogue negotiation processes were fundamentally different from the processes of the negotiations that led to the signing of the Gulf Initiative, yet they were structurally constrained by the same factors that shaped negotiations before.

After the end of the Dialogue negotiations there were important changes to the balance of power within the same political structure. The Huthis expanded their control in Yemen over 2014 through a series of battles against the Ahmar family and its allies in which they came out victorious. Their reach extended to the city of Sanaa, putting Aden within their reach. More importantly this extension drove through Hashed, the Ahmar family home. The Huthis even temporarily ousted the Ahmar family, who were then unable to return to their Hashed homes, and supported a movement within Hashed to restructure the process of selecting a sheikh, a portent of dramatic change that complicated the future of reconciliation in Yemen. In the south, the Hirak (movement) continued to militate for autonomy or separation, further upsetting the National Dialogue process.

Thus the following discussion is written in the expectation that it will still be relevant some years after the Arab Spring, even though, hopefully, it may become just a moment in history. Yemen has suffered too much because of its political structure, and without a fundamental shift it will suffer more.

THE CONTEXT: TRIBES, STATES, AND MEMORIES

To understand the major political events in Yemen, three concepts need to be discussed: tribalism, the nature of the state of Yemen, and historical memory. While one may relate the failure of negotiations to Saleh's style of rule, or to the political immaturity or uncompromising idealism of the Huthis, it is more useful to look into the structural reasons, which give a better explanation of the failures. Questions need to be asked about the various players and their capacity of agency, and about the memories and the perceptions the warring sides had of each other. Understanding the first set of issues helps in understanding the complexities of reaching an MHS, while understanding the latter helps in understanding the hurdles of seeing a viable way out. And without both, it is not possible to envisage a successful negotiation.

Tribalism

Tribalism is a very elusive concept, and considering the amount of misunderstanding and confusion over the concept of tribalism in the case of Yemen, it is important to understand it clearly. Yemen is a tribal country, but tribalism doesn't explain the politics of Yemen at the level of the power structure. Tribalism is a very complicated reality, but as far as power politics is concerned, tribal politics is similar to politics in other societies. The way the people of Yemen respond to their problems is fundamentally similar to the way all societies do. Societies respond to anarchy by forming social structures that interact through a set of agreed-upon norms that serve to limit the ambiguity of the various agents within those structures, creating a limited sense of security through predictability. Some societies have a long tradition of social structures and well-established norms, thus diminishing the evils of anarchy. Other societies establish those structures in times of anarchy, which does not give them time to establish norms.

Apply this to Yemen, and one sees how similar it is to everywhere else. With the effective absence of a state, the population is functioning through a social structure that happens to be called the tribe. Tribal structures are old, stable, and familiar, and so the norms governing them have gained legitimacy and acceptance as effective means of avoiding a Hobbesian world. In effect, they have developed a state of "enlightened survivalism"; that is, "All against all but with rules." The matter is as simple as that, though in a complicated way. Many of the qualities associated with tribalism—such as "shunning central authorities," or "focusing on local and narrow priorities," or "opportunistic," or "self-centered," or "believe in their legitimate right to use violence"—are all part of the rules, qualities of any social unit living in a state of anarchy or in a state of an illegitimate central power. Those qualities are products of and contingent on a specific political and economic structure in which there is no monopoly of violence, which cannot protect those living within it, which is predatory, and which has strong powers that sustain themselves through divide and rule. This situation was amplified in Saleh's Yemen due to his specific policies. In other words, those qualities are not essential to the tribe, as the research sometimes tries to depict; rather, they are essential to that sociopolitical (tribal) structure.

There are many tribes in Yemen. The most significant ones are grouped under the two confederations of Hashed and Bakil in the upper north. Each tribe has a sheikh, who should be considered more a speaker for the tribe and less its leader. His authority is not vertical but rather is horizontal; that is, he needs to negotiate his authority and has little ability to impose it by force. Some sheikhs have strong and assertive characters and are able to exhort more obedience from their tribes. This is not due to their being sheikhs but rather to their characters, as well as the circumstances that surround them. The Hashed confederation includes the al-ʿusaymat tribe of the al-Ahmar family. It also includes the president's tribe of Sanhan. Hashed also has a paramount sheik; that is, one whose authority extends to all the tribes within the confederation, and the al-Ahmar family has had that role for three centuries now. This gives Hashed more influence in national politics. Bakil is a larger confederation, but it never had such a paramount sheikh, and this undermines the power of its other prominent sheikhs. The Saudis have tried more than once to develop such a position in Bakil but never succeeded.

Traditionally the tribe would protect its members, as it was the only means of ensuring mutual protection when needed. But this is not a consistent behavior, in particular when the state attacks. In those cases the internal politics of the tribe would become a more important factor. It is never acceptable to tolerate the aggression of another tribe because that would permanently undermine the position of the tribe vis-à-vis other tribes, but it is acceptable to look the other way when it was the state that was the aggressor. Though the state was treated as a "tribe" in terms of its legitimacy to govern other tribes, it was still considered a nontribal actor, whose actions have no long-term consequences on the position of the tribe. This double attitude toward aggression and the two ways of seeing the state are factors that complicated the Saadah wars, but it also came into play during the protests of the Arab Spring.

Statehood

Statehood does not fit the situation. It may seem an exaggeration to say that one must first suspend analyzing Yemen in Westphalian or Weberian terms, but that is what the situation calls for. Yemen is not, technically speaking, a sovereign state. It cannot and has not exerted control over its territories for decades. There is no sense of genuine legitimacy that the central government can leverage on most of the real powers in Yemen. And there is absolutely no monopoly of power. This has been the case since the coup d'état of 1962. Prior to 1962 the imams had successfully limited the powers of the tribes in much the same way as the Saudi monarchy did with its own tribes. Tribal challenge to the state was not tolerated, and since the 1930s most tribes had succumbed to that reality. Tribes are as powerful as the army to some degree, or at least able to resist its force. The Huthi wars have demonstrated the often superior fighting ability of tribes relative to the state, but there are many other examples in which the army has been defeated or has been unable to coerce a tribe.

The idea of national sovereignty has not been practiced either by the government or by local powers. Many elites in Yemen have special relationships with Saudi Arabia without hiding it; actually Saleh encouraged some of them. Tribal leaders believed they were entitled to financial support from the Saudis and many actually have monthly stipends. This sense of entitlement for support from a foreign country contradicted the sense of Yemeni sovereignty. Before the end of the fifth war the Saudis sent a senior official who met with hundreds of sheikhs and coordinated an effort to serve Saudi interests. This was done openly. In the end of 2010 the Saudis were seeking to create a tribal coalition in Yemen. This was also done openly. It is important to keep this in mind when looking at the various players. They were not acting as agents in a state to which they all belonged; rather, they were acting as agents within a nation, where one of the powers had control of the state. The state was simply one power among many. Negotiations were not considered to occur between a legitimate state and other parties, or even between a state and others. Yemen is a constellation of powers, and competition and negotiations are between the elements in the constellation.

Historical Memories

Historical memories need to be understood. History is useful in this regard, though one must be careful as there is a false sense of continuity regarding the history of some of the actors in this war. For example, when it comes to the Zaydis or the Hashemis it is commonly held that their behavior one hundred years ago is an indicator of how they would behave or act now. But there have been fundamental changes that have altered the way Zaydis and Hashemis see themselves and also altered the way others see them. It would also be useful to look at memory as a constructed effect that may or not fit experiential events. For example, many of those who detest the class structure prior to 1962 may not have experienced it but acquired that hate from the media and other socialization mechanisms employed by the revolutionary state. As an observer of Yemen, I have more access to the history and less to the constructed memory, while the participants in the events in Yemen have access to both. Thus I may draw assumptions on the memory each side has of each other based on the history, and not on the way memory was constructed.

Many of the events happening in Yemen now are not continuities of the past; the memories of today are not based on the perceptions and experiences in the past.

The most important shapers of the perceptions that were involved in this war were Zaydism and Hashemiism. They were the lenses through which both sides saw each other's intentions. From a sectarian perspective Yemen was mainly divided between Zaydis and Shafiʿi Sufis. Now there is also a Salafi component. But sectarianism was never a significant factor—at least in the contemporary history of Yemen. Sects were more social categories of people who had particular ways of religiosity, and less social identities that shaped or significantly influenced the ways people would create their alliances. Yet since the revolution in Iran the region became a hotbed of sectarian politics, and it wasn't difficult for a sectarian way of talking to enter the discussions in Yemen.

This was more the case when the Salafis entered Yemen in the 1970s with their agenda of purifying Yemen from all impure theologies, whether they be Shiʿi Zaydis or Sunni Sufis. The Salafis first focused on the tribal areas of what was then North Yemen, which were also the Zaydi areas. With Saudi resources and support they were able to disturb Zaydi existence, and within a few years Zaydis began to consider themselves a persecuted group. Given the close relationship that the Salafis had with President Saleh, Zaydis would accuse the Yemeni government of being the main source of that persecution, or at least as sanctioning it. While it may be true that the culture of Zaydis had been marginalized by the new Yemen after 1962, President Saleh cared less about issues of sect and religion. His interest was in retaining power, and during the Iran-Iraq war it was important for him as a supporter of Iraq and beneficiary of Saudi Arabia to uphold a discourse critical of Shiʿism. The stage was then set to transform a critical discourse focused on the Twelver Shiʿism of Iran into a hostile discourse targeting Zaydi Shiʿism in Yemen, despite the marked differences between the Iranian Twelver Shiʿa and the Zaydi form of Shiʿism.

Many years later the Huthis would interpret all the activity of the government and others with it through the memory of this earlier period in the 1980s. They were concerned that they were being restricted in their right to practice their religion freely, or even that they were being eradicated altogether. They were keen, however, to insist that they were fighting in self-defense and not to regain their religious rights, rights that should be defended using peaceful methods. In an interview with Mohammad al-Huthi, Husayn's brother, he was keen to distance the fighting from the restrictions of their rights. He probably was accurate in that, but those perceptions and memories caused the Huthis to consider the war an existential one, and this alone made it difficult for them to perceive the moment as ripe for negotiation. And at another time, when they were ready to see the MHS, they wouldn't be able to see a way out. On the government's side, this memory would make the Huthis an extension of Iranian influence, and thus they considered the war not just against a small group in the upper northern mountains of Yemen but rather a war with Iranian expansionism. This also made MHS further from sight, or made their willingness to tolerate the hurt much stronger. There were other structural factors, of course, which are mentioned later. But the memory also played a role in their capacity to see a way out. As long as they saw the Huthis as an extension of Iran, they were not able to accept any halfway deal, as that meant allowing a future role for Iran in Yemen through the Huthis.

It did not matter as far as perceptions and memories were concerned that Yemen was not a sectarian country in which the Sunni-Shiʿi split was not expressive of the realities on the ground. People did not align themselves with the Huthis because they were all Zaydis fighting for Zaydis or for the rights of Zaydis. The leadership of the Huthi movement is of the Zaydi sect, but it is not a Zaydi movement. The wide support they have is not by virtue of being Zaydi, nor for the cause of supporting Zaydism.

More important than Zaydism as a lens for MHS and a way out was the issue of the Hashemi. The Huthis are also from the Hashemi clan. Here the perceptions of persecution run much deeper and have enough events to sustain it. Though there were many Hashemis in the republican government, the official discourse was that Hashemis have enslaved the people of Yemen for 1100 years, and now that they have been put back into their rightful place; one should be wary of their activities that aim toward regaining their old status. What was said of Zaydism applies here more intensely. The Huthis believed that the war has strengthened the grip of the Hashemis. The government considered the growth of a Hashemi power a defeat for the republican project.

THE SIX WARS

In 2004 what started as an attempt to make an arrest became a full-scale war between the Yemeni Army and the followers of Husayn al-Huthi. In fact, this became the beginning of a six-year conflict with devastating consequences for the far north of Yemen and for the country at large. Six years and six wars in the northern region of Saadah claimed thousands of lives, displaced more than a hundred thousand civilians, virtually destroyed the economy of the region, and severely strained the economy of the whole state. The main actors in this conflict were President Ali Saleh, Ali Muhsen al-Ahmar, the Ahmar brothers, and the Saudis. There were other significant powers in the north and also in the south, and they played various important roles, but Ali Saleh, Ali Muhsen al-Ahmar, the Ahmar brothers, and the Saudis were the major players. The effect of the other powers was mediated by the interests and needs of these main players. In fact, the politics of the country as a whole in the past twenty years has been mainly determined by the competition among these four main powers.

The President

President Saleh had been in power from 1978 until 2012, when, as a result of the Gulf Coordination Council (GCC) deal, he was forced from office. His accession to power was facilitated by the Saudis and had been supported by them ever since, despite the times when they considered him an enemy. He turned out to be one of the shrewdest men in the history of Yemen. He understood that to stay in power he needed to keep people busy with each other, something he became very good at. Intertribal wars in the country increased during his time because he supported both sides against each other. Saleh comes from a small tribe called Sanhan, which itself belongs to the tribal federation of Hashed. Sanhan was his trusted source of power. The main leaders in the army are from Sanhan, and the most prominent of them was General Ali Muhsen al-Ahmar, who was at times so powerful that he was considered the shadow ruler of Yemen. The source of Saleh's power was mixed between his presidency that gave him access to resources and the military power that he built to serve him.

Ali Muhsen al-Ahmar

Ali Muhsen's power was from the army divisions that reported to him. He was able to build his division and the loyalty of its members through the foreign financial support he had. Some said it was Iraq at one point, then the Saudis and the Qataris. Whatever the case may be, he was the strongest man in Yemen after Saleh. He was also considered a religious person and a supporter of Sunni militants in Yemen. Most of the Yemen Afghans were brought into his divisions when they came back from Afghanistan, and he mobilized Salafi militias to fight in Saadah and encouraged the use of religious language in those wars.

The Ahmar Brothers

The Ahmar brothers are the third power in Yemen. They are the sons of the late sheikh Abdullah al-Ahmar, who passed away in 2007 and who was the paramount sheikh of the Hashed federation. The current prominent brothers are Sadeq, who is the formal sheikh of Hashed, Hamid, who is a very wealthy businessman, and Husayn, a well-funded person who was very active during the wars in mobilizing tribal militias to fight the Huthis. Hashed is a collection of tribes; in all they are a minority group, but because of the leadership of Sheikh Abdullah and the heavy Saudi financing, they were able to act as if they were the most powerful group of tribes in Yemen. After the death of the father, the brothers disagreed among themselves and were unable to rally the same support as their father.

In addition to their leadership position in Hashed, the Ahmars' power also came from the Islah Party, the Islamic brotherhood movement in Yemen that they led and influenced since its creation in 1990. The relationship between the Islah and the Ahmars has been one of convenience. The Islah needed a tribal base, and the Ahmars needed a religious banner. This also secured more financial funds from the Saudi government and citizens who had an interest in supporting political Islam. Though the party's formal leadership after the death of Abdullah al-Ahmar was not attained by any of his sons, the brothers still play a major and vital role in the party. The Islah Party allied with Saleh between 1990 and the 1994 war that sealed unification with the south, and the Ahmars were the main support for Saleh for almost thirty years, until relations soured over the issue of presidential succession and competition over power. Then Saleh started pushing them away from power in what could be considered the beginnings of the Saleh-Ahmar rivalry. The rise of the Huthis was particularly damaging to the Ahmars, as it undermined the authority their tribe had over the Saadah areas. It also made the Saudis reconsider their reliance on the Ahmars as their main partner in Yemen and led them to seek other coalitions in their stead.

Saleh focused on building his personal army after he became president. In time it became a strong force that was significant enough to reduce his need for the support of the Hashed tribal coalition. The 1990 unification of Yemen brought Saleh and the Ahmars very close to each other. The presence of socialist power in the south (Aden) pushed both of these northern powers to align. It was only a matter of time before his power and the power of the Ahmars' would collide. After the 1994 war, with the Socialists out of the picture, Saleh started his attack on his allies, the Ahmars and Ali Muhsen, to the extent that the politics of the country since then and until he left office was almost entirely about eliminating his rival powers. He first targeted the Ahmars' political arm, the Islah Party. In the 1997 elections he effectively forced them out of the ruling coalition in parliament. The matter became more complicated when the issue of leadership succession entered the equation, as that accelerated the strife between him and his allies from Sanhan. In 1999 Muhammad Ismail al-Ahmar was assassinated. One of the main allies of Ali Muhsen, he openly rejected the idea of Saleh's son becoming president and even rejected his appointment to senior army positions. By then a cold war had started between Saleh, the Ahmars, and Ali Muhsen, which would last until the Arab Spring, when their rivalry escalated into open conflict.

Saudi Arabia

As much as people discuss the Saudi role in Yemen's politics, it is still not given enough emphasis. The Saudis have been in the heart of everything significant in Yemen since the mid-1960s. After the failure of the Egyptian army to defeat the

Royalists, the Saudis turned to a strategy of co-opting tribal powers. By now tens of thousands of Yemenis depend on stipends from the Saudi government either directly or indirectly. Saudi Arabia played a major role in shaping the political identity of post-1962 Yemen. At one point much of this identity had been defined by "being on the other side" of the Saudi border. Thus being Yemeni had no independent content from "not-being Saudi." However, Saudi power has been considerably undermined by the Huthi wars, as their main ally inside Yemen was the Hashed confederation, which, as mentioned earlier, has lost most of its leverage. Currently the Saudis are attempting to build a new coalition that can perform the role that Hashed played previously.

"People of the Slogan"

Husayn al-Huthi, a local activist and member of the Yemeni parliament, started protesting against American interventionism in the early 2000s. After the invasions of Afghanistan and Iraq he believed Yemen was going to be next, and he believed it was his duty to warn against American intervention and to prepare for the defense of Yemen. As part of his preparations, he became active in promoting his own understanding of what he considered to be authentic Zaydism. Zaydism is a Shiʿi school of thought that is followed by most of those in the upper north of Yemen, and Husayn believed that Zaydis today were not practicing the authentic version, which was practiced by the early "imams" between the ninth and thirteenth centuries.

He quickly gained an audience in an area that was economically stricken, socially frustrated, and waiting for a legitimate way to vent its political antagonisms against the government. His ideas were simple and based on the eternal struggle between good and evil. He was on the side of the good, and so was his audience. America was the evil, which everyone should reject and resist. His solution was also simple: chant a slogan that will instill fear in the enemy and at the same time raise awareness among the population and inoculate them from American influence. The slogan was "death to America, death to Israel, victory to Islam." This was almost all that he required his followers to do for the purpose of resisting the United States. Soon he was attracting the very young, most of whom were under eighteen years of age. Many of them would stand after the Friday prayers ended and loudly chant the slogan. Its simplicity was appealing. He was also clear on the matter of authentic Zaydism. He thought the Quran had been sidelined and must come back to the forefront of the understanding of what God wills of us. The Quran was sidelined by complex scholarship that was advanced as a prerequisite to its understanding. All this must go, and the people must go back to the authentic practice of the imams, which was to depend on the spiritual leadership of a divinely inspired person. People must follow and give allegiance to this person, ensuring a simple and correct understanding of the Quran. In his particular case, it was clear that he considered himself to be that inspired person.

Very quickly those young men would be called the "people of the slogan," and they became a phenomenon in Yemen's capital, Sanaa. The slogan would soon draw much negative attention and various political interpretations. Because it was the same slogan used by radical Shiʿites in Iran and Lebanon, the Huthis were accused of affiliation with Iran and Hezbollah. This was not new, but it was more serious, as it had wider implications considering the overall situation in the region. As far as the "people of the slogan" were concerned, this was a statement that had become a public statement, to which no one had special monopoly, and they didn't see themselves at all affiliated with Iran or any other international group. Husayn actually reported to one his friends his deep frustration with the Iranians as he had expected more support from them. He didn't seem to realize that the Iranians had other calculations and were keen on avoiding any activity in Yemen that would push Yemen closer to the Saudis or the Americans. An alliance with or support from a group that aggravated the government would not serve its purpose, and they had invested much effort in building a strong relationship with Yemen, in the hope that they competed with the Saudis for influence in Yemen.

Saleh's Response

For Saleh these were sensitive times. He was anxious about Yemen's relations with the United States. He was clever enough to give the American administration absolute alignment in the fight against terrorism, "shoulder to shoulder" as he would say. When Saleh felt threatened, his usual approach was to amplify a fear of some enemy among the Americans or the Saudis. One of his responses to his fear of being the next American target was to create a sense of alarmism about Iranian influence. Soon accusations that the Huthis were an extension of Iran would become the consistent government line.

But the Huthis represented other fears that for Saleh may have seemed more imminent. The family of Husayn al-Huthi is from the Hashemi clan in Yemen, who were considered the political and social elites of Yemen until the 1962 republican coup. For eleven hundred years this group had produced leaders of the upper north, and some of them were able to extend their authority across all that is now known as the modern state of Yemen. Moreover, the Hashemis consider themselves the only legitimate rulers of Muslims. Saleh started accusing the Huthis of wanting to turn back the wheel of history to the times when the rulers of Yemen were of the Hashemi clan. And though the Huthis at the time were an insignificant power, they were quite strong in terms of the symbolism they were capable of mobilizing. So as the slogan chanters increased in numbers, the government started making wide arrests. Soon hundreds of young men were in detention, and the president demanded that Husayn stop his activities and come to Sanaa to meet the president. Husayn was afraid of being detained in Sanaa, so he refused to go there. Husayn also believed that the president's response was proof of the effectiveness of his approach. He thought the Americans were actually worried, and this was behind the crackdown on his people. So despite assurances from the president, Husayn refused to visit him, though he did at one point almost accept the invitation on the condition that he come there under the protection of one of the very prominent sheikhs, Mujahid Abu Shawareb, who did his very best to stop the matter from escalating into a military conflict.

To place matters in context, it is crucial to understand that up to this point what Husayn was doing was very common: a local leader who was wanted by the central government and who decides not to submit was the norm in Yemen. Usually such disobedience would be followed by arrest attempts, which in many cases would mean skirmishes between the arresting troops and the guards or followers of that leader. Then mediators would intervene to solve the problem. Thus, as far as Husayn was concerned, he was still within accepted norms, even though he had gone somewhat too far, in that his acts of civil disobedience were not limited to his dominions; rather, they extended to other cities and regions in the country. When the matter reached a deadlock, General Ali Muhsen told the president that he would have Husayn brought in before the end of the afternoon's qat-chew. Ali Muhsen was the military commander of the region where Husayn was located, but there were also other motivations for him being involved, as normally such issues are resolved by senior officers, not by the second man in command in Yemen. Saleh approved, and the matter lasted more than a qat-chew.

On 19 June 2004, Ali Muhsen's forces were sent to Marran to arrest Husayn. Husayn's followers were ready for such a day, and the matter escalated to a very deadly war. This first war ended in three months with the death of Husayn al-Huthi. A few months later following an attempt to arrest Badruddin al-Huthi, the eighty-year-old father of Husayn, a second war started that covered more regions in the Saadah area. This second round of fighting lasted only twenty-five days and was abruptly stopped by the president. A third war started on 12 July 2005. This time the fighting started to overshadow the coming 2006 elections and continued until Saleh sent Yahya al-Shami to head a mediation committee. On 16 January 2006, this committee started its work, and on 28 February the third war ended. Yahya al-Shami was also appointed governor of the region, until 17 April 2007, when he was replaced after being accused of being too lenient and supportive of the Huthi cause. Al-Shami also belonged to the Hashemi clan, and it was natural to accuse members of this clan of disloyalty to the republican regime (Omari 2010a).

Each round of wars would start with an assassination of a significant person or the arrest of a member of the Huthi group. But those weren't the reasons for the fighting; rather, it was the unresolved issues still on the ground despite the cease-fire. With each war the Huthis got stronger. The fourth war started at the end of January 2007 and witnessed a major expansion of Huthi influence. At that stage the Qataris offered to mediate, and as result a truce was signed in the middle of June 2007. Based on the agreement, the government would release the Huthi detainees, give information on those who were missing, and compensate those whose property was destroyed. The Huthis, for their part, were to abandon their positions in the mountains of Saadah, surrender their medium and heavy arms, and return to normal life. Months passed without any progress until February 2008, when both sides signed the agreement again with an addendum on how to implement it. Representing the Yemeni side was previous prime minister and adviser to the president Abdulkarim al-Iryani. Ali Muhsen was present. On the Huthi side was Saleh Habrah and Sheikh Ali Naser Qersha. Al-Iryani would later be accused by some media outlets of betraying the country for signing such a deal, and Qersha would later be arrested. Many committees were set up to implement the deal, but they all failed (Sabri 2011).

During the three wars there was virtually no media coverage in the Saadah area. The government banned journalists from going there or warned them that they would have no protection. Barely anyone mentioned it. The Arab media seemed to be unanimously silent. I recall a senior editor telling me that it seems that due to the sensitivity of the situation the prominent newspapers did not want to aggravate the government in Yemen. People in Yemen complained about the media blackout. Being in Sanaa did not mean easy access to information about what was happening in Saadah. But the Qatari involvement changed that. With Qatar came the media; with Qatar came international recognition of the Huthis as a player in the power of Yemen.

By the fourth war it was clear that the Huthis were a formidable force. They received wide support from local inhabitants in the north. Three major powers in Yemen were most keen to destroy this new Huthi power. The first was Ali Muhsen whose forces suffered a loss of reputation in the fighting. Second were the Ahmars of Hashed whose loss of Saadah to the Huthi forces was a double blow. On one hand it was the loss of what they considered their backyard. But this was made worse by the loss coming at the hand of a Hashemi led group. The third were the Saudis who were worried because the Huthis weakened the Saudis main allies in Yemen, the Ahmars of Hashed, and because the Saudis saw the Huthis as allies of Iran. On the other hand, the president saw in the Huthis a power that needed to be eliminated, but one that served some of his plans. The growth of Huthi power and the multiplicity of those threatened by them would become a major reason for failures of mediations and negotiations.

The fifth war started in May 2008 and ended on 17 July. It expanded to the suburbs of Sanaa, where pro-Huthi tribes fought against the army. The war was abruptly stopped by the president just days after actively mobilizing against the Huthis. Then, without any preparation and during one of his speeches, Saleh announced the end of the war. The reasons for this sudden decision had to do with the growing Saudi role in the war. At that point they were coordinating efforts to set up and finance a militia of radicals to participate in the war efforts. On 15 July, just two days before the president's decision, fifteen hundred tribal leaders and figures met under the banner of the newly created "Order of Good and Forbidding of Evil." This was a committee similar to the Saudi committees that regulate religious behavior. But instead of discussing vice and decadence in Yemen, their sole focus was the war in Saadah. They insisted in that meeting on the necessity of the war and the need for government people and parliament to collaborate. One of the Ahmar brothers, Husayn, had been assigned as a mediator in the beginning of the fifth war, but he was in full support of continuing the war. Two days after that meeting the president ordered a cease-fire and declared that the war would never begin again. Many considered the president's action as treason, including Husayn al-Ahmar. It was clear that Saleh saw that the war was becoming an opportunity for Islamic radicals to mobilize and create a new force that he would need to face very soon (Amin 2008; Al Nomani 2008).

Though the fifth war supposedly ended, skirmishes never did. The sixth and most aggressive war started on 11 August 2009 and lasted until 12 February 2010. In this war the fighting was widespread and included the use of the air force and the Republican Guards. The Huthis emerged from this war stronger than ever, and the reputations of Ali Muhsen and the Ahmar brothers were both severely damaged. It was during this war that the conflict spilled into neighboring Saudi Arabia. On 4 November 2009 the Huthis took control of a mountainous section inside Saudi Arabia, in the border region of Jabal al-Dukhan. The Saudis then launched air strikes on the Huthi-controlled areas and sent troops into Yemen. The situation lasted until 25 January 2010, when the Huthis withdrew from positions they held in Saudi territory.

Mediation Efforts

Since the first war there had been many attempts at mediation and many rounds of negotiation in efforts to reach a peaceful resolution to the conflict. But they all failed. Even those that did get signed by both sides never got implemented. Trust was absolutely absent, even before the wars began. But the way the deals were made and broken did not help either. One of the first mediation attempts was a confidence killer and may have shaped the perception of trust between the warring parties during the next six years. Forty prominent scholars and social leaders were allowed by the government to go to the village of Marran, where Husayn al-Huthi was located. Many of his followers were waiting in reception. The government calculated that Husayn would be among those waiting and sent helicopters to attack the reception, killing thirty people ("Habra" 2009).

Mediators were also given a hard time by the government. A member of one of the peace committees of July 2007 and member of parliament, Aidaroos al-Naqib, says that his committee was surprised by a sudden suspension of their activity and by the creation of a new presidential peace committee that was to do what they were commissioned to do. He also complained about lack of information to which the committee had access. They had no idea what impact they had, if they failed or succeeded. Nor did they understand the reasons behind the war. Actually up until 2008 the war was not covered by any neutral news source. Other times members of peace committees would be arrested or accused by government-sponsored media of siding and sympathizing with the Huthis ("Habra" 2009). Probably the most important mediation was that of Qatar, but even that failed dramatically. One of the reasons for the failure of this deal was the ambiguity and multiple meanings of the terms of the agreement, such as the return of life to its natural state. A second deal signed in Qatar was more explicit. And had it not been for the Arab Spring protests, there may have been a seventh war.

Failure of Negotiations

There was indeed a lack of will on the part of all the parties involved. Peace didn't serve anyone despite the losses on all sides. Lack of will was clearer on the government's side, maybe because of the multiple competing sides and interests in the government. Erratic decisions, contradictions of statements, and multiple committees all point to multiple wills as much as to one undecided will. But more importantly, the way the war was run made MHS a distant reality. To start with, the hurt was actually divided among the three powers, each with its own calculations, and with its own cost/benefit analysis, making MHS difficult to reach. Most of the time the hurt was beneficial to some as much as it was damaging to others. Saleh was indeed benefiting. From the second war one would hear about the losses on Ali Muhsen's side. The fourth war was a clear gain for Saleh. His foes were losing much more than he was. They were in a dire situation, and when in the fifth war they tried to balance their losses he stopped the war, and in the sixth war he was involved directly in the conflict. He wanted to end the sixth war with his forces, though he failed.

Ali Muhsen needed the war to continue. His real battle was with Saleh, and the ongoing losses on his side were not helping him. Losing against the Huthis meant for him losing against Saleh. He needed to continue despite the losses for fear of losing more. The Ahmars had similar reasons. They were losing their leverage and control over a whole region in northern Yemen, one that borders Saudi Arabia.

They needed the war to go on in order to regain that land. The Saudis could not see the region out of the Ahmars' control and potentially moving into the Iranian sphere of influence; the Saudis had the least to lose from the war or to hurt them. But by injecting resources into the pockets of all three parties to this side of the conflict they were able to minimize the pain that the president, Ali Muhsen, and the Ahmars were experiencing. So in effect there were gains and losses for Saleh, but he was gaining more than he was losing. There were also losses for Ali Muhsen and the Ahmars, but they were facing an existential threat, making the pain seem less important compared to an end to their political power. MHS in such a situation is unlikely.

One can also say the same of the Huthis. They had a lot to gain from the ongoing fighting. Their power was growing. They were gaining credibility and building fear. So in a way the pain was creating gains for each party pushing the line of MHS forward. This explains the way the wars ended and started. It was not due to pain, or to a resolution; rather it was due to the president's management of the gains and losses. This is particularly clear with the last three wars. The third ended to give the elections a clear space, the fourth as a gesture to the Qataris, the fifth to limit the capacity and degree of Saudi involvement and more importantly to cut short the development of the religious militia, and the sixth due to competition between the president and his rival allies. An arrangement of powers working together but also against each other, with an external actor continuously present to alleviate the pain, was one main reason the negotiations always failed.

Because of the limited external spillover there was no incentive for an external mediator to step in. Even when the Qataris did, they were doing it for the purpose of managing their politics with Saudi Arabia, which made the solution contingent on Saudi-Qatari relations. All that the Qataris had was money. Their intentions were not trusted in particular by the government side, and they did not have coercive power, soft or hard. Some would have thought that terrorism and the spread of al-Qaeda in the Arabian Peninsula (AQAP) in Yemen during those years would have also led to a fear of spillover, particularly since many of those who fought with the government were radical Islamists who considered this as a jihad. But those who were threatened from AQAP did not see it this way. The Saudis considered the Huthis a bigger threat in the long run than AQAP. The Americans didn't consider the Huthis as a direct threat, nor as a reason for the growth of AQAP. Their strategy to dealing with AQAP was direct hits, and not a comprehensive solution to Yemen's major problems. So neither the Americans nor the Saudis had a genuine interest in getting involved to stop the wars. But equally as important, neither of them was trusted by the Huthis. The Huthis saw the Saudis as the main force behind the situation of the Zaydis, and they always considered them as financiers to the war, even before the Saudis went to war against them. And their animosity toward the Americans was the main reason for the conflict in the first place.

So multiplicity of interests within one camp of actors made it nearly impossible for the situation to reach a threshold of hurt, and this also made the perception of a way out very limited. Each side saw the other as a threat, and each considered the war to be existential. The Huthis in particular found it difficult to compromise. Their legitimacy depended on their perceived puritanism and strong stands against their aggressors. If they had played the game pragmatically, they would have lost their popular support. The other sides couldn't accept a new reality where a new power was recognized, in particular one that was once considered a historical enemy or that would be a Trojan horse for Iranian power.

After the sixth war, President Saleh focused on his political rivals. And though the reasons for a seventh war were there, the Arab Spring eventually came to create a new political reality, postponing the seventh war for a few years.

YEMEN SPRING: REVOLUTION OR EXCHANGE OF POWER?

The events in Yemen that followed the uprisings in Tunis and Egypt can hardly be considered a revolution. In the first few weeks of the protests there was too much optimism to accept anything but revolution, but it became clearer as the months passed by that there was no transformation of the political—and even less, the social—system. Today almost no one believes that this was revolution, but rather that it was an uprising that was hijacked by the opposition to the president, namely the Joint Meeting of Parties (JMP) (Al Nomani 2012).

What actually happened was that power was reshuffled between the main actors in Yemen, with consequences that may lead to a complete exit of some and an entrance by other new actors. The events of 2011 that were effective in making the change happen were a continuation of the competition between the major powers of Yemen, but this time the conflict was in a different language and using the legitimacy of a globally inspiring event. What seemed at the start to be a youth revolt against a corrupt and authoritarian order would turn out to be a war of attrition between Saleh, the Ahmars, and Ali Muhsen. The same powers that were together fighting the Huthis were now turning against each other. As the protests spread, Hamid al-Ahmar mobilized the Muslim Brotherhood and encouraged its members to join the protestors. Soon Saleh's rivals, who were acting through the coalition of the JMP, were the ones talking with him, and the protestors were sidelined. It helped that the main demands of the protestors were the same demands that the JMP had before the protests, namely that Saleh and his family step down from power. The protestors simply gave a fresh legitimacy to this demand and encouraged the JMP to be more vocal. Thus there was nothing new in terms of the structure of power before and after the protests started. At the peak of the protests Ali Saleh's circles of power were the same. Those in the forefront of the opposition were the same contenders as before. When the deal for his resignation was signed in 2012, it was the old foes that divided power. Yemen was indeed not Tunis, as Saleh had said.

The origins of the JMP go back to 1999 when a coalition known as the Coordination Council for the Opposition was created to challenge Saleh. The Islah Party was not a member in that coalition, and the main force in it was the Socialist Party, but in 2003 the Islah joined, and the coalition was named the JMP. There were now seven parties: the Islah Party; the Yemeni Socialist Party; the Nasserite Unionist People's Organization; the National Arab Socialist Baath Party; the Haq Party; the September Congregation Party; and the Popular Forces Union Party. In 2006 the JMP went against President Saleh in the elections that gave him 77 percent of the vote in what was considered a fair election. In February 2009 the JMP and the president tried to reach a political agreement that would decrease the political tension between both sides. It didn't work. A dialogue was initiated between the JMP and the government in July 2010, but talks broke down, and the JMP went into confrontation with the president in September 2010. In December the JMP boycotted the parliament after the ruling party, the General People's Congress (GPC), announced that it would make constitutional amendments to allow the president to rule for life (Omari 2010b; Mansour 2010; "JMP" n.d.).

When the protests started at the end of January 2011, the JMP joined to further their demands against President Saleh. At first, it seemed as if the negotiations were between the president and the youth, when they were in fact between the president and the JMP. From the beginning the president had two goals: to discredit the JMP in front of the youth in the streets and to get a better political deal for himself, his family, and his party, the GPC. There was new momentum for the escalation of confrontation. The situation was full of emotion. Events were moving fast. What follows is a brief outline of the main milestones focusing on the messages that were being relayed back and forth over a very brief period of massive political upheaval. Also important were the events that were effective in convincing parties, local or international, that there needed to be intervention. I also mention those that were supposed to give an objective sense of a mutual sense of hurt. Then I examine the role played by the mediator, and the reasons the mediations succeeded.

In the end of January the government announced intentions for political reforms. This was in answer to the events in Tunis and Egypt and to the thousands of protesters demanding that Saleh step down. But even at this early stage in the events, one Yemeni journalist recognized that "these were not spontaneous or popular protests like in Egypt, but rather mass-rallies organized by the opposition who are using events in Tunisia to test Saleh's regime. This is only the start of a fierce political battle in the run-up to Yemen's parliamentary elections in April" (Finn 2011).

A War of Attrition

The journalist was right. A war of attrition had begun between the president and his opponents, and the protestors and their aspirations for a better Yemen were the battlefield. The language of the conflict was now one that the world understood and listened to. As would become clear later, the main driver of those protests was the Islah Party, in particular politician Hamid al-Ahmar. The protestors would be in the street, and Saleh would reject their demands, or sometimes call for dialogue, or, as happened most often, would confront them with bloody violence. The parties opposing Saleh would stand in their support of the protestors and align themselves with the demands of the street. Occasionally Saleh and the opposition would reach an understanding, but then it would quickly fail because no one believed that they had gotten enough. But negotiations also failed because of the differences between the needs of the various actors in the JMP. Hamid wanted Saleh completely out of power immediately, and he refused to compromise. He used the street to back his demands. Other members in the JMP, even in the Islah Party, were willing to accept a more gradual exit of Saleh. The protests continued, and Saleh resisted with security forces. In the end of February Saleh was still insisting that only defeat at the ballot box would make him quit. He also made proposals for a unity government, which the opposition dismissed. International pressure mounted when the European Union (EU) issued a statement strongly condemning the use of violence against peaceful protesters and urged Saleh to respond to the aspirations of the Yemeni people (Qahdi 2011; "Yemen Leader" 2011).

Various solutions for a way out were now being proposed, and events were moving fast. A solution would be put forward, quickly be rejected or amended, then maybe accepted, only to be rejected again. It was chaos. No one party had the capacity to push any initiative forward. Any one actor was only able to suggest solutions but not to move any step beyond that. Inertia was stronger. Trust was absolutely nonexistent, and the multiple sources of messages were confusing to anyone following the situation, but also to the players who lost capacity to talk directly or even through mediators. Coalitions offering solutions acted spontaneously without the effort to align their effort with the relevant stakeholders. An example was a coalition of opposition groups and religious scholars who proposed that Saleh make a gradual transition of power by the end of the year. Both Saleh and the protestors in the street rejected the idea ("Yemeni Army" 2011).

Defections

Friday, 18 March, was a milestone in the escalation of events. At least forty-five antigovernment protesters died and more than two hundred were injured as unidentified gunmen opened fire on them in Sanaa. Saleh said that his security forces did not open fire and were even unarmed at the time. He declared a state of emergency across the country. U.S. president Barack Obama, U.S. secretary of state Hillary Clinton, and French president Nicholas Sarkozy condemned the attack ("Yemen MPs Quit" 2011; "Yemen Unrest" 2011; Almasmari 2011; Love 2011).

The week that followed witnessed a number of defections and resignations by ministers and ambassadors. The most important one was that of Sadeq al-Ahmar,

Hashed's sheikh. On 20 March he issued a statement asking the president to respond to the people's demands and leave peacefully. It was cosigned by several religious leaders. Some saw this as the beginning of the end of Saleh and that the "tribe had spoken." But it was simply stating what was already obvious. Sadeq's defection was mostly symbolic because Hashed is known to be divided, and Sadeq has no central control over it. That same day Ali Muhsen announced that he would support the protestors, and a number of top army commanders defected as well, stating that they would protect the protestors from the government. This was a more serious message, but it did not really alter the balance of power because those who defected were loyal to Ali Muhsen and were not considered part of the power Saleh had. Yet now the army was divided into opposing camps, and this was a serious escalation. People thought the country was coming to a civil war. After this many analysts thought it signaled the downfall of the regime, and some believed that Yemen was breaking up. A senior EU official predicted that the president "won't last long." "I don't see how the president can hold on much longer, given the fact that part of the army, part of the tribal chiefs and part of his political allies have distanced themselves from him," he said.

Saleh submitted to the pressure and agreed to step down at the end of the year and transfer power, but he also warned that the protest movement constituted a coup and that the situation could escalate to a civil war. "Those who want to climb up to power through coups should know that this is out of the question. The homeland will not be stable, there will be a civil war, a bloody war," he said. The opposition rejected Saleh's proposal, confident that they had the political upper hand, and now they wanted no less than immediate exit. "Any offer that does not include the president's immediate resignation is rejected," JMP spokesman Mohammed Qahtan said ("Top Army" 2011; "Yemen President" 2011). Saleh responded by suspending the constitution, banning protests, and allowing tougher powers of arrest, all of which was approved by the pro-Saleh parliament ("Yemen MPs Pass" 2011).

As a response to the open defection of Ali Muhsen, the Presidential Guard led by Saleh's nephew clashed in the southern town of Mukalla with army units backing opposition groups that demanded Saleh's removal. This was a message to the various actors about the readiness to go into a full confrontation if needed ("Yemeni Presidential" 2011). That same day the Yemeni army repelled an attack on a military position by al-Qaeda in the Arabian Peninsula (AQAP). This also came as another message, directed now toward the West, and the United States in particular, telling them that the chaos that would ensue if Saleh stepped down would only serve AQAP. With such escalation Secretary of State Clinton called for political dialogue in Yemen involving all players to find a peaceful solution, and Defense Secretary Robert Gates stated that the United States was "obviously concerned about the instability in Yemen. We consider al-Qaeda in the Arabian Peninsula, which is largely located in Yemen, to be perhaps the most dangerous of all the franchises of al-Qaeda right now." Saleh's message was getting through (Jamjoon 2011).

As important as they may have seemed at the time, the defections did not have a positive impact on the situation in Yemen. Nothing changed in terms of either the power structure or the tactics in the ongoing war of attrition. The defections were a step toward more foreign pressure, and they did send signals about the direction of the events, but nothing more. Had Saleh decided at the time to make a stand, defections would have had no strategic value. But had a civil war broken out, a new dynamic would have been created, counterdefections would have happened on both sides, and new fronts would be created. Saleh knew that. So did his rivals. The rivals also knew that—as in many other *intifadat* in the region—they were united only by hatred of Saleh and that once he left they would turn against each other. In a way they needed Saleh to sustain their coalition. During this time the street rallies continued, with each party bringing people. The opposition would rally and the president would counter-rally.

Now the clear message coming out of Saleh's camp was that he was not leaving immediately but rather through a process of a power transition. On the other hand the street wanted his immediate exit with no immunity. The JMP was struggling within itself to determine what it should demand. In the open they were in alignment with the street, but in fact they were cutting a deal with Saleh. "We are on the path to completing a deal," an opposition figure said at the end of March. "The president is trying to improve the negotiating conditions, especially relating to the situation of his sons and relatives." There was also discussion that all competing powers leave. Saleh wanted Ali Muhsen to resign as well. The Gulf States sent a message that they would respect the choices of the Yemeni people so long as the Yemeni people supported security and stability.

Another message was sent to the West and to the Saudis on 28 March. News came out that the government had lost control of six out of eighteen of the country's provinces to radical Islamists. At the same time it was now becoming clear that the JMP and the defectors did not reflect the will of the youth or the neutral groups. As a response a coalition of opposition groups issued a statement saying that they would not leave the Taghyir Square until Saleh left. They also called for putting Saleh and his corrupt cronies on trial for the crimes they committed against the people of Yemen. Those demands went unheard, and the independent youth had no influence on the course of events whatsoever.

The president made a new offer. He would stay in office until elections were held, but he would immediately transfer his power to a caretaker government. It was reported that this deal was reached with Mohammed al-Yadomi, the head of the Islah Party. It was quickly announced that this was not the case, and that no agreement had been reached. A person close to the circles of Saleh stated that this was due to a disagreement within the Islah itself. Al-Yadomi represented a faction that considered the growth of the protests undermining its authority on the ground, and it wanted to secure a deal with Saleh that preserved its authority. Hamid al-Ahmar was opposed to any such deal ("Yemen's Saleh" 2011).

The GCC Deal

Deals were moving back and forth with no effect because too many actors were making them. The JMP was not united enough to cut a deal. Both parties could not talk with each other. The pressure on Saleh reached a new point when the United States openly called for him to step down. The Americans were now worried about the power vacuum and the way AQAP would benefit from it, but they were still calling for a transition and not an immediate stepping down ("U.S. Ratchets Up" 2011). After the American demand the Gulf Coordination Council (GCC) offered to suggest a plan for Saleh's stepping down. Sources in Yemen indicated that the GCC plan was essentially an American plan but given to the GCC to suggest; in any case, the U.S. ambassador was consistently involved in the negotiations. Saleh rejected the offer on 8 April, but two weeks later he accepted it. The plan allowed him to transfer power, in exchange for immunity, to a deputy within thirty days and for elections to be held sixty days after that. The Joint Meeting of Parties also agreed to the GCC plan. But the protestors rejected the plan. "It is the desire of the people, it is the will of the people, for Ali Abdullah Saleh to step down immediately," as one of the leaders of the protests said (Hatem and Carey 2011; "Rival Camps" 2011).

Just three days before the plan was to be signed, on 29 April, Saleh threatened to pull out of the GCC plan because of Qatar's planned presence at the signing event. The opposition also threatened to pull out of the plan because of ongoing protester deaths. The next day Saleh refused to sign the deal, and on the 5 May he once more agreed to sign ("Reports"). But on 22 May Saleh once more refused to sign the deal, and the GCC pulled out.

Confrontation

The following day, in what can be considered a response to Saleh's games, fighting erupted between Sadiq's followers and the Presidential Guard in Sanaa. A fierce street battle claimed many bystanders' lives and put the country on the edge of a civil war. Sadiq expected that this confrontation would bring Hashed in support of its sheikh. But that did not happen. Hashed was divided. The president was close to demolishing the Ahmar homes in Sanaa, had it not been for the personal intervention of King Abdullah. At the same time, in the south Islamic militants captured Zinjibar, the capital of Abyan Governorate ("Suspected al Qaeda" 2011). Both the battle in Sanaa and the takeover of Zinjibar were basically pushing each side to the extreme. On 25 May, Saleh's forces fired rockets at the Suhail TV channel building, the satellite channel of Hamid al-Ahmar that had been a main outlet for news against Saleh. The step itself was a message to Hamid that his economic interests would be targeted now ("Demanded" 2011). That same day a rocket blasted into the house of Sadeq al-Ahmar while a mediation committee was meeting. The target was Sadeq, but he survived (Al Qadhi 2001).

By now the situation was reaching its peak. A week later, on 3 June, Ali Saleh was almost killed while attending Friday prayer sermons. Many of his senior officials were injured and a number were killed. The following day he was flown to Riyadh, where he received extensive treatment. Rumors about his death followed; people thought this was the end of the Saleh regime. Saleh formally was said to hand over power to his deputy, but the effective power was in the hands of his son Ahmad. A few days later Ahmad rejected an offer by the JMP to talk. This signaled a confidence from his side, and his maneuvers thereafter were all to assert authority and control after the absence of his father. The Americans, Saudis, and British are said to have put on more pressure to end the standoff. They assumed that the absence of Saleh would facilitate an agreement, but Saleh's camp insisted that nothing would be discussed until Saleh returned.

Revival of the GCC Deal

After the attempt on Saleh's life, the mood was quiet. Saleh's camp gained more momentum because of his survival. The possibility of his absence brought to the forefront the fears that the Ahmars might take power. This was something even their allies rejected, and Saleh's camp used that fear to draw support. Ahmad Saleh was able to hold on to power, and was firm and immediate in his response to protests in particular from tribes or military. And despite the many battles that followed, it became clear that no side in the conflict had the power to take the other down (Haj 2011; "Yemen Rivals" 2011). In the meantime the Americans were stepping up their targeting of AQAP. Absence of power in Yemen was not what the Americans wanted at this time (Mazzetti 2011).

While Ali Saleh's camp was insisting that the president was coming back to Yemen after his treatment, there were messages being sent otherwise. "The Yemeni president will not return to Yemen," a Saudi official said. Those messages were supposed to ease the tension in Yemen and allow various parties to talk to each other. At the end of June Saleh reportedly suggested that a dialogue should begin with the opposition and that he was willing to consider a GCC-brokered transition of power. Then Saleh broke his silence and delivered a speech on 7 July reasserting his authority. It had become clear that not only were the various parties equally powerful, but that the Saleh camp did not depend on his presence to continue. A last attempt to break that camp would happen on 30 July, when an alliance of tribes was created under the leadership of Sadeq al-Ahmar. Clashes ensued between the Republican Guard and various tribesmen in different regions of Yemen, in particular in the tribe of Arhab and Hashed. There were also clashes between them and the 1st Army division. But Saleh's camp stood solid. A new change was then introduced into the GCC deal. The first version demanded that the army be restructured before the election of the new president. Then the army announced the restructuring would come after the elections. What this meant for Saleh was that the power that his son held would not be dissolved immediately, buying him important time in the future. The opposition tried to resist, but Saleh insisted and got his way (Al Sharq Al Awsat 2011).

Saleh returned to Yemen on 23 September to the disappointment of many of his rivals and the protestors, but also to the happiness of his supporters and those who feared the Ahmars. In October he tried to change the terms of the GCC deal again, in a way that would allow him to stay on until early elections, but the GCC rejected the change (Al Arabiya News 2011). On 21 October the UN Security Council voted unanimously for a resolution condemning the violence and calling on Saleh to transfer power immediately under the GCC plan, which would secure amnesty for him and his family. Now Saleh and his rivals had no choice but to sign. A month later, on 23 November, Saleh arrived in Saudi Arabia to attend the signing of the GCC agreement.

The Need for External Coercion

One can see from this brief overview that both sides were not willing to give in to each other. They were willing to destroy each other rather than compromise. Even after the battles in Sanaa where the Ahmars faced extinction and the attempt on Saleh's life, both sides were still resisting a compromise. Was it because they never perceived an MHS? Or was it because they did perceive it, but they couldn't see a way out?

As in the case of the Huthi wars, there was lack of trust between the relevant actors and a sense of an existential threat, and the escalation of the violence only heightened the perception of existential threat, rather than developing a perception of an MHS. Moreover, as in the Huthi case, the pain seemed to offer a chance to one of the sides. Ali Muhsen saw in the confrontation between Saleh and the Ahmars an opportunity to improve his standing. Though he was allied with the Ahmars, he still considered them eventual contenders, and he welcomed any action that would weaken them. The same goes for the Ahmars regarding Ali Muhsen. The same, too, goes for Saleh in the seventh Huthi war.

But what was different here was the strong incentive for external mediation or involvement. Fear of AQAP was genuine. The situation was one that would actually strengthen AQAP, which was now in control of some parts of Yemen and fiercely opposed the Huthis. There was serious fear of Iran's taking advantage and improving its standing in Yemen, in a way that would threaten the Saudis. There was also fear that an outright civil war would threaten Gulf security at a time when the Gulf countries felt vulnerable and exposed to an Arab Spring at home. So external mediators, instead of the actors in Yemen, imposed a deal. They dictated it, and though they did agree to change some of its terms, its essence was preserved: Saleh leaves, but he gets immunity. The deal was not made to serve the interests of the protestors but rather the more general security of Yemen. So it was essential that Saleh leave through a process, and that the balance of power not be detrimentally shaken. No one power should be able to take immediate control of the country, thus the restructuring of the army would happen through a long process as well.

Saleh and his rivals evaded signing, but they knew that they would eventually have to accept. The deal was being imposed, and in conditions that did not leave them much room to maneuver. Since there was no sense of an MHS, the other option was to hurt the players directly. Saleh witnessed what was happening to others around him and was clever enough to want to avoid that. His rivals were also being threatened with legal consequences. Corrupt and with interests in other countries, they too needed immunity. So in the end they all signed, not as an outcome of their own negotiation, but rather as an outcome of coercion that created their MHS and imposed its consequences (Stedman 1991). What happened in Yemen was a jump to an intrusive role of the mediator, made possible because of the MHS in which they were placed and because of the way out provided by the mediator, which the Yemeni parties were unable to provide for themselves. This worked because the various parties had more to lose on a personal level. But it also worked because all that was required was that they sign. As far as they were concerned, the GCC deal created a different way of confrontation rather than ending the confrontations. The years that followed the signing to the deal were now a witness to the transition of the conflict to a different arena.

In both cases, the Huthi wars and the events of the Arab Spring, all the parties seemed to have reached a mutual hurting stalemate but were either never able to conceive it as hurting, or were in a frame of existential resistance and thus could not see a viable way out of the conflict. In the Huthi wars, the infighting among the various factions on the government side meant that the hurt was not equally experienced. The pain on Ali Muhsen did not translate into pain for President Saleh. On the contrary, it may even have been considered a benefit for Saleh. The Huthis' sense of MHS was high and focused on them, but they saw no way out, except a return to a situation that they could not tolerate. So they continued despite everything. On the other hand, the only way out that the Huthis would accept was not in the interest of either Hamid al-Ahmar or Ali Muhsen al-Ahmar, even if Saleh considered it satisfactory. External mediators had little interest in getting involved, and those who did were not capable of more than bringing warring parties to the table. They thought this would be enough. But they miscalculated, or were misled, with regard to the sustainability of any deal that was reached.

In the Yemeni Spring the same situation was repeated with different actors. While all sides were in an MHS, they were also in an existential situation where it was "to be or not to be." This blinded all perceptions of a way out. The difference was that there was an interest for external mediators to be involved. And when they did get involved, they also realized that merely putting the various actors at the table to sign a deal was not enough. It was clear that the mediator had to intervene with coercion, which is what happened. The deal never would have gone through had not the UN Security Council—with American support and drive—threatened the personal interests and well-being of the leaders of the rival parties. But with Saleh removed by the deal, there was no string-pulling center to keep the rivalries in dynamic balance. What this may say about Yemen is that in the absence of an internal state actor that has legitimacy, and indeed in the absence of a state, the only way rivalry can cease is by annihilation of one side, or by coercive intervention of an external actor. Yemen was lucky that escalation to a civil war was considered a serious threat to the United States. Had that not been the case, it may have become another Somalia, a situation whose possibility reemerged when the seventh Huthi war began in April 2014.

References

Alley, April Longley. 2011. "Yemen on the Brink." *Foreign Affairs*, 4 April. http://www.foreignaffairs.com/articles/67699/april-longley-alley/yemen-on-the-brink (accessed 27 September 2012).

Almasmari, Hakim. 2011. "Yemen Imposes State of Emergency after Deadly Attack on Protesters." *Washington Post*, 18 March. http://www.washingtonpost.com/world/protesters-killed-in-yemens-capital-by/2011/03/18/ABFd2hp_story.html (accessed 2 September 2014).

Amin, Adel. 2008. "Al-Yemen and the fifth round of the Sa'ada war" [in Arabic]. *Mareb Press*, July. http://marebpress.net/articles.php?lng=arabic&id=3972 (accessed 2 September 2014).

Al Arabiya News. "GCC Rejects Saleh's Request for Amendment of Initiative to Resolve Yemeni Crisis." Al Arabiya News, 14 October 2011. http://www.alarabiya.net/articles/2011/10/14/171797.html (accessed 8 December 2014).

Bernin, Pierre. 2009. "Yemen's Hidden War." *Le Monde Diplomatique*, October. http://mondediplo.com/2009/10/06yemen (accessed 27 Sept. 2012).

Bonnefoy, Laurent. 2012. "Foreign Policy Magazine." *Foreign Policy*, 9 February. http://mideast.foreignpolicy.com/posts/2012/02/09/yemens_islamists_and_the_revolution (accessed 27 Sept. 2012).

Al-Dawsari, Nadwa. 2012. "Tribal Governance and Stability in Yemen." *Carnegie Endowment for International Peace*, 24 April. http://carnegieendowment.org/2012/04/24/tribal-governance-and-stability-in-yemen (accessed 27 September 2012).

"Demanded an investigation into the attack on the reporter and United Press International of U.S." [in Arabic]. 2011. *Alwahdwi.net*, 27 May. http://www.alwahdawi.net/news_details.php?lng=arabic&sid=7633 (accessed 2 September 2014).

Dresch, Paul. 2000. *A History of Modern Yemen*. Cambridge: Cambridge University Press.

Finn, Tom. 2011. "Yemenis Take to the Streets Calling for President Saleh to Step Down." *Guardian*, 27 January. http://www.guardian.co.uk/world/2011/jan/27/yemen-protests-president-saleh (accessed 2 September 2014).

"Habra: mediation committee reached an agreement for a cease-fire in the immersion" [in Arabic]. 2009. *Mareb Press*, 4 April. http://marebpress.net/news_details.php?lng=arabic&sid=15933 (accessed 2 September 2014).

Al-Haj, Ahmed. 2011. "Taiz, Yemen City, Partially Controlled by Tribesmen: Officials." *World Post*, 8 June. http://www.huffingtonpost.com/2011/06/08/taiz-yemen-tribesmen-_n_872992.html (accessed 2 September 2014).

Hatem, Mohammed, and Glen Carey. 2011. "Yemen's Saleh Agrees to Step Down in Exchange for Immunity, Official Says." *Bloomberg News*, 23 April. http://www.bloomberg.com/news/articles/2011-04-23/yemen-s-saleh-agrees-to-step-down-in-exchange-for-immunity-official-says (accessed 2 February 2015).

Haykel, Bernard. 2011. "Saudi Arabia's Yemen Dilemma." *Foreign Affairs*, 14 June. http://www.foreignaffairs.com/articles/67892/bernard-haykel/saudi-arabias-yemen-dilemma (accessed 27 September 2012).

Hiltermann, Joost R. 2009. "Disorder on the Border." *Foreign Affairs*, 16 December. http://www.foreignaffairs.com/articles/65730/joost-r-hiltermann/disorder-on-the-border (accessed 27 September 2012).

International Crisis Group (ICG). 2003. "Yemen: Coping with Terrorism and Violence in a Fragile State." Middle East Report no. 8, Amman/Brussels, 8 January. http://www.crisisgroup.org/en/regions/middle-east-north-africa/iraq-iran-gulf/yemen/008-yemen-coping-with-terrorism-and-violence-in-a-fragile-state.aspx (accessed 27 September 2012).

———. 2009. "Yemen: Defusing the Saada Time Bomb." 2009. Middle East Report no. 86, 27 May. http://www.crisisgroup.org/en/regions/middle-east-north-africa/iraq-iran-gulf/yemen/086-yemen-defusing-the-saada-time-bomb.aspx (accessed 27 September 2012).

Jamjoon, Mohammed. 2011. "Yemen's Leader Says He Will Accept Transition Plan." CNN, 24 March. http://edition.cnn.com/2011/WORLD/meast/03/23/yemen.protests/index.html (accessed 2 September 2014).

"JMP in Yemen" [in Arabic]. N.d. Al Jazeera. http://www.aljazeera.net/news/pages/ca048a5c-1f54-4e32-b4ce-ebc7d627ba12 (accessed 2 September 2014).

Johnsen, Gregory D. 2010. "Ignoring Yemen at Our Peril." *Foreign Policy*, 31 October. http://www.foreignpolicy.com/articles/2010/10/31/ignoring_yemen_at_our_peril (accessed 27 September 2012).

Love, Brian. 2011. "France Strongly Condemns Yemen Attack on Protesters." Reuters, 18 March. http://www.reuters.com/article/2011/03/18/yemen-france-idUSPISIEE78520110318 (accessed 2 September 2014).

Mansour, Anis. 2010. "Joint and the imminent risk" [in Arabic]. *Mareb Press*, 21 July. http://marebpress.net/articles.php?id=7569&lng=arabic (accessed 2 September 2014).

Mazzetti, Mark. 2011. "U.S. Is Intensifying a Secret Campaign of Yemen Airstrikes." *New York Times*, 8 June. http://www.nytimes.com/2011/06/09/world/middleeast/09intel.html?_r=1 (accessed 2 September 2014).

Al Nomani, Mohammad. 2008. "Fifth war enters its third month and the five provinces on the line Naralris Saleh announced completion in Saada and other provinces and varied reactions to the announcement of surprise" [in Arabic]. *Ahewar.org*, 24 July. http://www.ahewar.org/debat/show.art.asp?aid=141889 (accessed 2 September 2014).

———. 2012. "Revolutions of the Arab Spring between Containment, Circumvention, and Hijacking." *Modern Discussion*, 2 October. http://www.ahewar.org/debat/show.art.asp?aid=326547 (accessed 2 September 2014).

Omari, Aref Ali. 2010a. "Sa'ada war . . . a leadership crisis or a crisis of confidence" [in Arabic]. *Ahewar.org*, 6 February. http://www.ahewar.org/debat/show.art.asp?aid=202603 (accessed 2 September 2014).

———. 2010b. "Yemen Said a history of conflict and chaos" [in Arabic]. *Ahewar.org*, 10 November. http://www.ahewar.org/debat/show.art.asp?aid=234767 (accessed 2 September 2014).

Al Qadhi, Mohammad. 2001. "Yemen: Increase in the Ferocity of Confrontations and Security Forces Bomb with Rockets the House of Al Ahmar." *Al Riyadh*, 25 May 2001. http://www.alriyadh.com/635564 (accessed 9 December 2014).

———. 2011. "Saleh Tells Yemen Protesters He Will Only Go 'through Ballot Box Defeat.'" *National* (Abu Dhabi), 22 February. http://www.thenational.ae/news/world/middle-east/saleh-tells-yemen-protesters-he-will-only-go-through-ballot-box-defeat (accessed 2 September 2014).

"Reports: Saleh Refuses to Sign Exit Deal." 2011. Al Jazeera, 30 April. http://www.aljazeera.com/news/middleeast/2011/04/201143094747158908.html (accessed 2 September 2014).

"Rival Camps Hold Protests in Yemen." 2011. Al Jazeera, 22 April. http://www.aljazeera.com/news/middleeast/2011/04/20114229839290858.html (accessed 2 September 2014).

Sabri, Abdullah Ali. 2011. "Qatari role in the war in Saada fourth" [in Arabic]. *Islam Times*, 9 January. http://www.islamtimes.org/vdccp4qo.2bqop8aca2.html (accessed 2 September 2014).

Salmoni, Barak A., Bryce Loidolt, and Madeleine Wells. 2010. *Regime and Periphery in Northern Yemen: The Huthi Phenomenon*. Santa Monica, Calif.: Rand.

Schmitz, Charles. 2011. "Yemen's Tribal Showdown." *Foreign Affairs*, 3 June. http://www.foreignaffairs.com/articles/67877/charles-schmitz/yemens-tribal-showdown (accessed 27 September 2012).

Al Sharq Al Awsat. "Yemeni Opposition Reject Giving President Time for Negotiations." *Al Sharq Al Awsat*, 30 October 2011. http://classic.aawsat.com/details.asp?section=4&issueno=12024&article=647485&feature=#.VIa2_TGUeSo (accessed 8 December 2014).

Spencer, James. 2011. "A False Dawn for Yemen's Militants." *Foreign Affairs*, 8 June. http://www.foreignaffairs.com/articles/67883/james-spencer/a-false-dawn-for-yemens-militants (accessed 27 September 2012).

Stedman, Stephen John. 1991. *Peacemaking in Civil War: International Mediation in Zimbabwe, 1974–1980*. Boulder, Colo.: Lynn Rienner.

"Suspected al Qaeda Militants Seize Yemeni Town." 2011. *France 24*, 29 May. http://www.france24.com/en/20110529-suspected-al-qaeda-militants-seize-yemeni-town-zinjibar (accessed 2 September 2014).

Tayler, Letta. 2011. "Yemen's Hijacked Revolution." *Foreign Affairs*, 26 September. http://www.foreignaffairs.com/articles/68298/letta-tayler/yemens-hijacked-revolution (accessed 27 September 2012).

"Top Army Commanders Defect in Yemen." 2011. Al Jazeera, 21 March. http://www.aljazeera.com/news/middleeast/2011/03/2011320180579476.html (accessed 2 September 2014).

"U.S. Ratchets Up Pressure on Yemen's President." 2011. ABC News, 5 April. http://www.abc.net.au/news/2011-04-05/us-ratchets-up-pressure-on-yemens-president/2629086?section=world (accessed 2 September 2014).

Von Bruck, Gabriele. 2005. *Islam, Memory, and Morality in Yemen: Ruling Families in Transition*. New York: Palgrave Macmillan.

Weir, Shelagh. 2007. *A Tribal Order: Politics and Law in the Mountains of Yemen*. Austin: University of Texas Press.

Wells, Madeleine. 2012. "Yemen's Houthi Movement and the Revolution." *Foreign Policy*, 27 February. http://mideast.foreignpolicy.com/posts/2012/02/27/yemen_s_houthi_movement_and_the_revolution (accessed 27 September 2012).

"Yemeni Army 'Fires on Protesters.'" 2011. Al Jazeera, 4 March. http://www.aljazeera.com/news/middleeast/2011/03/20113494623209124.html (accessed 2 September 2014).

"Yemeni Presidential Guards Clash with Army." 2011. *Guardian*, 24 March. http://www.guardian.co.uk/world/2011/mar/24/yemeni-presidential-guards-clash-army (accessed 2 September 2014).

"Yemen Leader Blames Protests on U.S." 2011. Al Jazeera, 1 March. http://www.aljazeera.com/news/middleeast/2011/03/20113191141211328.html (accessed 2 September 2014).

"Yemen MPs Pass Emergency Laws to Quash Uprising." 2011. *Guardian*, 23 March. http://www.guardian.co.uk/world/2011/mar/23/yemen-approves-emergency-laws (accessed 2 September 2014).
"Yemen MPs Quit Ruling Party." 2011. Al Jazeera, 5 March. http://www.aljazeera.com/news/middleeast/2011/03/20113514455840795.html (accessed 2 September 2014).
"Yemen President Ali Abdullah Saleh Warns of Coup." 2011. BBC Mobile, 22 March. http://www.webcitation.org/5xO6WJZA6 (accessed 2 September 2014).
"Yemen Rivals Stage Mass Demonstrations." 2011. Al Jazeera, 10 June. http://www.aljazeera.com/news/middleeast/2011/06/201169235253459255.html (accessed 2 September 2014).
"Yemen Unrest: 'Dozens Killed' as Gunmen Target Rally." 2011. BBC News, 18 March. http://www.bbc.co.uk/news/mobile/world-middle-east-12783585?SthisFB (accessed 2 September 2014).
"Yemen's Saleh 'Makes New Offer to Protesters.'" 2011. Al Jazeera, 30 March. http://www.aljazeera.com/news/middleeast/2011/03/201133014584368624.html (accessed 2 September 2014).

Algeria

The Negotiations That Aren't

HUGH ROBERTS

ALGERIA SINCE INDEPENDENCE in 1962 has been an awkward state to classify. The product of the most profound revolution in the region, its form of government has often been cited as an instance of single-party rule (to 1988) when, in fact, it is the army, not the party, that has been the source of political power. Resembling in this respect the Free Officers' State in Egypt, it abruptly broke with this model in 1989 by introducing an apparently far-reaching form of political pluralism that included the legalizing of Islamist parties. Widely touted as "the next Iran" following the sensational electoral victories of the Islamic Salvation Front (Front Islamique du Salut, FIS) in 1990 and 1991, it turned out to be nothing of the kind and while it descended into nightmarish violence between 1992 and 1999, the state not only survived but managed to sustain the system of formal pluralism as modified—to rule out any sequel to the FIS's victories—by the regime's decision makers in 1997. The restablization of the state since 1999 did not involve any real resolution of the issues that led to the earlier upheavals, however, and since 2001, popular unrest, expressed in frequent if mainly localized disturbances, has been a constant feature of public life. But the expectation of many observers that Algeria would prove vulnerable to the contagion of the Arab Spring has not been vindicated. Instead, despite unusually impressive unrest early on, Algeria has been an unequivocal exception to the regional "norm" since 2011 (Arieff 2013; Boundaoui 2011; Daoud 2012; Darbouche and Dennison 2011). Why is this?

In January 2011, while the national revolt in Tunisia against President Zine El Abidine Ben Ali was nearing its climax and the massive demonstrations against Egypt's President Hosni Mubarak were yet to begin, Algeria was suddenly wracked by the first nationwide rioting since October 1988. A year later, Tunisians were celebrating the first anniversary of their revolution while Egyptians were digesting the results of the parliamentary elections that gave over 70 percent of the seats to Islamist parties, an outcome that appeared to vindicate the claim that Egypt, too, had had a genuine revolution. Algerians, on the other hand, had a very different reality to contemplate. On 12 January 2012, six new laws voted by the Popular National Assembly and the Council of the Nation in November and December

2011 were promulgated, putting the seal on what the government had claimed was a major program of political reform. Hardly any informed observers—and few Algerians—endorsed this judgment.

This program had consisted of a new electoral law (Loi organique No. 12-01, 2012), a law concerning cases of incompatibility with parliamentary mandates (Loi organique No. 12-02, 2012), a law promoting women's participation in elections (Loi organique No. 12-03, 2012), a new law on political parties (Loi organique No. 12-04, 2012), a new information law (Loi organique No. 12-05, 2012), and a new law on associations (Loi organique No. 12-06, 2012). Even in Algeria itself, much press commentary was extremely critical of the legislation and described it as marking, not progress toward democracy or the rule of law, but a serious regression. The perception that Algeria was in some sense or another an exception to the trend and had "failed to have its Arab Spring" was already a feature of international media coverage of the country. It was reinforced by the government's legislation, which, apart from a gesture toward improving women's participation, unquestionably amounted to a tightening up rather than opening up of the political system.

This dismal outcome to the debates, agitation, and general effervescence that had marked Algerian public life in 2011 reflected, among other things, the absence of anything that could accurately be described as a serious negotiation between the regime and its numerous domestic critics. The understanding of the other cases explored in this book is broadly informed by the general thesis that the *intifadat* that have occurred in the Arab world have required—and in at least some cases led to—a process of political negotiation in their aftermath, as attempts have been made to establish new understandings and ground rules in place of the discredited routines of the Old Order. But Algeria is clearly not an instance of this norm. The reality of the matter, already patent by May 2012 in the results of the legislative elections (which bucked the regional trend of Islamist victories), received additional emphatic confirmation in April 2014 in Abdelaziz Bouteflika's success in securing an unprecedented fourth presidential term. There has been no ejection of an autocrat, no transition to a new regime, and no negotiations to speak of.

The immediate reason for this is that Algeria did not have a genuine *intifada* in 2011 and that, in consequence, the regime was under no serious pressure to renegotiate the terms of the state-society relationship. But the absence of a genuine *intifada* is itself to be explained. Part of the explanation is that the various social forces that managed to combine in a unified uprising in other cases (Tunisia, Egypt), namely the desperate unemployed, organized labor, the liberal intelligentsia, and the main opposition parties, simply did not combine in the Algerian case. But this is itself to be explained.

The explanation offered here is grounded in an analysis of the particular character of the state-society relationship as this has evolved, without radical modification, since it was first established by the National Liberation Front (Front de

Libération Nationale, FLN) in 1962. Three aspects of this relationship receive particular emphasis: the oligarchical nature of the regime and the salience of the factional competition within it; its exceptional capacity for co-optation and its resulting control over associational life; and the character—and congenital weakness—of the opposition parties.

THE *INTIFADA* THAT WASN'T

Between 4 and 10 January 2011, Algeria was rocked by a wave of disturbances that expressed widespread anger at socioeconomic distress and the government's mismanagement of the economy but also a protest against the regime itself and its high-handed attitude to the Algerian public (Brown 2011; Roberts 2011). While parallels with Tunisia were mostly drawn by outside observers, Algerian commentators were concerned with a domestic and sinister precedent. In contrast to the locally circumscribed disturbances that had become a familiar feature of the political landscape since 2001, the way the disorder extended across the country recalled the traumatic riots of October 1988, which inaugurated the crisis of the Algerian state and led to the appalling violence of the 1990s. In the event, neither parallel proved a reliable guide to the outcome. Having been sustained for five or six days, the Algerian protests petered out everywhere fairly quickly following the government's announcement of measures to counter the startling rises in the prices of sugar, olive oil, flour, and also fruit and vegetables, which were widely, although not wholly convincingly, identified as the main trigger of the unrest.[1] These price rises were themselves explained primarily as the reaction of traders, especially wholesalers (*grossistes*), to new legislation requiring them to record all transactions of AD (Algerian dinar) 500,000 or more with invoices and to pay them by checks, a measure intended, in principle, to subject the informal sector of the economy to a necessary minimum of regulation and accounting. It was only after the government, on 8 January, announced a package of temporary measures to rein back price increases that the rioting stopped spreading and then stopped altogether.

The unrest in Algeria differed from the Tunisian case in both the social character of the protests and their political dynamics. Instead of beginning in a relatively deprived region and then moving from the periphery to the center, gaining support and coherence on the way, it did the opposite. The disturbances began in Algiers and Oran and then spread across the country; the movement exhibited a centrifugal, not a centripetal, dynamic, becoming more diffuse instead of more focused over time. In addition, the principal actors in the unrest were unemployed youths from the poorest districts of the big cities and of the other towns across the country, and their protest exhibited two striking characteristics: the absence of any intelligible statement of demands, and the destructive and violently antisocial nature of the actions in which many of the rioters engaged. As a result, their revolt repelled rather than attracted the sympathy of much of the middle class, while the trade unions made no offer of solidarity or guidance. Lacking coherent perspectives, the rioting died out once the fury that had initially animated it was spent.

Were the Riots a Manipulation?

Contrary to widespread media coverage, which suggested that the riots began in the western city of Oran on 5 January and were prompted by steep increases in the price of staple foodstuffs, the disturbances actually began in Algiers on 4 January (*El Watan*, 6 January 2011) and were then echoed by rioting in Oran the following day and in both cases had nothing to do with food prices. In Algiers, they originated in the popular neighborhood of Bab El Oued, where an exchange of insults between fans of rival football teams developed into a riot when policemen were attacked, and the disturbances seem then to have spread to neighboring districts (Brown 2011). The next day youths from peripheral districts of Oran—Ibn Sina and El Hamri—started throwing stones at policemen and passing motorists (*Le Quotidien d'Oran*, 6 January 2011). That evening, fresh rioting broke out in Bab El Oued, where hundreds of youths attacked the local police headquarters, and also in several other districts to the west of Algiers and in nearby Tipasa governorate (*Liberté*, 6 January 2011). It is not clear that much more than this had happened by the end of the day on 5 January, yet it was followed by a rash of riots in imitation across much of the rest of the country over the next two days, with disturbances erupting on 7 January at Tizi Ouzou in Kabylia and as far afield as Annaba and M'Sila (*El Watan*, 7 January 2011).

It was at this point that a link appeared between the unrest and factional rivalries within the regime. From the morning of 6 January onward, the Algerian media reports were insistently linking the unrest to the startling rises that had occurred in the price of various staple foodstuffs, while press commentary was speaking of "food riots" (*Washington Post*, 6 January 2011; *Financial Times*, 6 January 2011) or "hunger riots" and evoking the specter of a rerun of October 1988 (Grim 2011). *El Watan* seemed especially disposed to play up the unrest, whereas newspapers closer to the presidency, notably *L'Expression*, took a different line, suggesting that the riots were being exploited by particular interests, threatened to destabilize the country, and were the fruit of a manipulation of some kind.[2] The hypothesis of a manipulation was subsequently aired in other press commentary and invoked by the minister for youth and sport, Hachemi Djiar, in the course of his appeals for calm and by Seddik Chihab, a leading member of the Democratic National Rally (*Rassemblement National Démocratique*, RND), the second party in the governing coalition (Nadjib 2011a; Tadjer 2011). It seemed to be taken for granted by many ordinary Algerians and received some support from the testimony of rioters at

Blida (sixty kilometers south of Algiers), where "certain youths declared that they had been 'pushed' into rioting by 'persons unknown'" (*El Watan*, 7 January 2011).[3] It also received support from the way the riots spread so rapidly across the country, unlike any of the numerous disturbances at any point since the 1988 riots.[4]

The hypothesis is double-edged as well as controversial, and there are rival versions of it. One version is that the youthful rioters had been manipulated by the *grossistes* (wholesalers) in the informal sector of the economy as a way of pressuring the government to withdraw the legislation imposing new rules on traders. The popularity of this version testifies to the widespread perception that the informal sector of the Algerian economy has grown to huge and threatening dimensions, in part as a result of badly misconceived economic policies, while the formal sector is in crisis and with it the state as whole. As Algerian historian Omar Lardjane (interview, 25 June 2011) put it,

> the institutions no longer function—the popular communal assemblies, the customs, the ministries, except for the ministries of sovereignty. It is the big lobbies that pose a problem. A lot of commerce is conducted informally; the Islamists are involved, and there are very powerful networks. It is the informal sector that got the youth to go out into the streets.[5]

This notion also seemed to be favored by government spokesmen (Nadjib 2011a, 2011b; *El Watan*, 6 January 2011) and, while tending to delegitimate the rioters' grievances, drew some support from the behavior of the rioters themselves. The extreme violence this exhibited could not be assimilated to the patterns of direct action that had become a regular feature of Algerian public life over the previous decade, and independent observers as well as the press reported rioters being armed with fearsome weapons, including Molotov cocktails, knives, iron bars, pickaxes, and even sabres (Mohamed Lakhdar Maougal interview, 1 May 2011; *Liberté*, 6 January 2011; and *El Watan*, 7 January 2011). Two other features of their behavior stood out: the fact that they not only repeatedly threw stones at the police but equally pelted passing motorists and, second, that they not only indiscriminately attacked and looted public property, including establishments of service to the community such as schools and clinics (Nadjib 2011a), but also private property, an aspect that sharply distinguished them from the rioters of October 1988 (Khadda and Gadant 1990). In some places they even held up and robbed passing motorists (*El Watan*, 8 January 2011; *L'Expression*, 9 January 2011).

The thesis that informal sector interests were behind the riots amounted to a more sophisticated version of the government's initial claim that the unrest was due to price increases. As one observer noted, youths do not do the family shopping and so were unlikely to be mobilized by the prices of olive oil or sugar on their own (Mostefa Bouchachi interview, 24 April 2011; Korso 2011). But the same young men had plenty of other bitter grievances, notably the prospect of permanent unemployment and the difficulty of obtaining decent housing, and as such were disposed to riot on any one of a range of pretexts. So the thesis that the price hikes were engineered by the *grossistes* as a riposte to the government's legislation and that the same *grossistes* then instigated or at least encouraged the riots as a supplementary pressure tactic is plausible. But this leaves out of account the fact that the remarkably steep rises in the prices of staple consumption goods at the beginning of January 2011 were not unexpected. Newspaper reports since the middle of November 2010 had warned that these increases were imminent (*Liberté*, 15 November, 1 December 2010; *El Watan*, 20, 30, and 31 December). This is hard to square with the later official thesis that the rises were a cynical ploy by wholesalers, since these would scarcely have arranged for their intentions to be reported in advance. Clearly the *grossistes* could not have been the source of these stories; elements of the regime must have been.

The Factional Conflict as Political Context

Following President Bouteflika's success in securing a second term in 2004 and then forcing the chief of the general staff, Lt. General Mohammed Lamari, who had backed the rival candidacy of Ali Benflis, into retirement (Roberts 2007), the factional lineup was essentially a two-handed game between the Bouteflika presidency and Lt. General Mohamed Mediène's Département du Renseignement et de la Sécurité (DRS), which controls all the military intelligence services.[6] The power and omnipresence of the DRS had become a byword among all Algerian observers and analysts, and the department was widely assumed to have infiltrated its agents into all aspects of Algerian public life—opposition parties, voluntary associations, and the media as well as the government itself (Abdennour Ali Yahia interview, 27 June 2011; Rachid Tlemçani interview, 29 June 2011). Its role in the power game was a complex one. The DRS and the presidency cooperated for much of the time: Mediène's support was crucial to Bouteflika's success in 2004 and also to his securing a third term in 2009. But they had different and sometimes competing priorities, and so conflict between them tended to break out at intervals. This is what seems to have happened in the run-up to the riots, with the two factions at odds in the context of the jockeying for position with the 2014 presidential election in prospect.

In the course of 2010, Mediène's DRS acted to weaken the presidency in several ways. The first move was to secure the dismissal of Bouteflika's energy minister, Chakib Khelil, over the corruption scandal in the state hydrocarbons company, Sonatrach (El Kadi 2010), which swept away its top management team (*El Watan*, 14 January 2010; *Le Quotidien d'Oran*, 16 January 2010). Khelil's fall ended the presidency's control over Algeria's hydrocarbons industry and thus its control of the most important source of state revenue. A second defeat for Bouteflika's faction occurred in the wake of the mysterious assassination on 25 February 2010 of Ali Tounsi, the head of the national police force (Direction Générale de la Sûreté Nationale, DGSN). The interior minister, Noureddine Zerhouni, a powerful Bouteflika ally, was prevented from getting Tounsi's successor appointed from within the DGSN, the post going eventually to a senior army officer, Major General Abdelghani Hamel, instead. This represented a compromise between the two factions,[7] but it was the end of the road for Zerhouni, who was sidelined into a purely honorary post as deputy prime minister and replaced in the interior ministry by his deputy, Daho Ould Kablia.

At this point the factional conflict shifted to new terrain, that of the senior party in the majority coalition supporting the government in the National Assembly, the FLN. The immediate stake was control of the party at local and regional levels as well as the national level with a view to the selection of candidates for the upcoming 2012 legislative elections, but the long-term objective had to do with the next presidential election.

The FLN's active support has always been indispensable to the regime's candidate for election to the presidency (Djabi 2010). Accordingly, jockeying for position with the 2014 presidential election in mind was a prominent feature of factional activism within the party as in other apparatuses of the power structure since Bouteflika's reelection in 2009. The FLN was the first party to support Bouteflika's candidacy in 1999, and when its general secretary, Ali Benflis, a former Bouteflika ally,[8] unexpectedly chose to run for the presidency against him in 2004, Bouteflika's supporters organized a nationwide rebellion within the FLN to oust Benflis and recover control of the party. The rebels called themselves *les redresseurs* (the rectifiers), and one of their leaders, Abdelaziz Belkhadem, replaced Benflis as general secretary and retained the post until 2013. From late 2009, however, Belkhadem's position was under attack within the party (*L'Expression*, 5 September 2010; *El Watan*, 19 October and 7 November 2010; *Liberté*, 26 October 2010) from a current of opinion, dubbed *les néo-redresseurs*, that was rumored to have Lt. General Mediène's discreet support (Maougal interview, 26 June 2011).

The unrest in the party concerned the competition for control of party apparatuses at *kasma* (municipal branch) and *mouhafadha* (regional federation) levels, with Belkhadem's efforts to replace some functionaries with others of his choosing being resisted in many places (*L'Expression*, 5 September 2010). The conflict frequently assumed violent forms, as rival followings at the grassroots level came to blows, and local offices were taken by storm by one faction or another (*El Watan*, 19 Octobre 2010, 7 November 2010). Initially Belkhadem and his supporters managed to carry through the "renewal" of party structures they had decided upon; by the end of November 2010 the revolt appeared to have been quelled, and Belkhadem's (and thus the presidency's) grip on the party seemed safe. But no sooner had they achieved this success than they suffered a startling reverse, with the "neo-rectifiers" not only taking over the *mouhafadha* of Annaba in the east but also making dramatic gains in western Algeria, taking control of the party in Oran and securing a declaration demanding Belkhadem's resignation signed by all seven *kasmas* of the *mouhafadha* of the wilaya (governorate) of Tlemcen (the native wilaya of numerous leading Bouteflika appointees and supporters), including the *kasma* of Bouteflika's hometown, Nedroma (*L'Expression*, 18 December 2010).[9] Two days later, the factional conflict shifted to new terrain, that of the government itself.

On 20 December 2010, during a debate in the presence of the prime minister, Ahmed Ouyahia, the vice president of the Council of the Nation (the upper house of the Algerian parliament), Zohra Drif-Bitat,[10] queried the government's overall policy and directed extremely pointed questions at Ouyahia himself (*Liberté*, 21 December 2010; Zohra Drif-Bitat 2010; *Le Soir d'Algérie*, 21 December 2010):

> I do not understand why the statistics indicating the country's good health do not have positive implications regarding the situation of Algerian citizens. Why despite these figures are the Algerians not happy and enjoying tranquil lives? Over and above these figures, we must ask ourselves about the poor quality of life of the Algerians and the problems they live with each day. . . . One should not evade these problems by saying one has done this and done that, but rather take charge of this question of the miserable life people lead and do so very seriously. (*El Watan*, 21 December 2010 [my translation])

This is precisely what many ordinary Algerians have been saying for several years past. Drif-Bitat went on to raise the issue of the *harraga*, the desperate young Algerians who leave the country—often in unseaworthy boats, with many drowning in the attempt—in order to get to Europe as illegal immigrants: "Among the *harraga* there are young unemployed, young graduates, women with their children. This is not normal! The phenomenon must be dealt with at its root, by eradicating its causes and, to begin with, by giving back to the young people the hope they have lost" (*El Watan*, 21 December 2010 [my translation]).[11]

Drif-Bitat was close to President Bouteflika, and her speech, widely reported as a damning attack on Ouyahia, a long-time protégé of the DRS, was interpreted as a move in the factional conflict (interviews with Algerian intellectuals, 1 and 26 May and 27 June 2011). An indictment of Ouyahia's policies and stewardship, Drif-Bitat's speech also signaled, by citing the *harraga* and the distress of the younger generation, that competition for the political allegiance of youth was a stake in the factional game. At the same time, she opened up a second front in questioning the regime's policy and handling of the problem of al-Qaeda in the Islamic Maghreb in the far south of the country and the neighboring Sahel states, an extremely sensitive issue that has throughout been the policy preserve of Mediène's DRS.[12] In this way, Drif-Bitat tacitly put in question Ouyahia's principal sponsors as well as Ouyahia himself.[13]

At this juncture the countdown to the riots began.

A Remake of October 1988?

The way events unfolded in the run-up to the riots of 4–10 January, 2011, as well as the way these spread across the country, most certainly recalled the events of 4–10 October 1988, as did, of course, the striking similarity of the dates. But it was the contrast with October 1988 that was significant.

In 1988, the police were conspicuous for their absence during the riots, and it was the army commanders who took charge, declaring a state of siege and rushing troops into all the major towns, where they proceeded to fire at will, killing hundreds of rioters, while many hundreds more were arrested and then savagely tortured. The government fell and other senior heads rolled, including those of the FLN boss and the head of the intelligence services, followed by a raft of senior army commanders who were forced into retirement. Finally, the Islamists emerged as the leading force with authority over the street and able to contain and harness the anger of Algerian youth and the unemployed. None of this happened in 2011. The army did not move a muscle but stayed well away from the rioting; the state of emergency in force since 1992 was not upgraded; the police were on the front line everywhere but behaved with remarkable restraint; there were only five deaths and no reports of torture, and eight hundred of the reported thousand people who sustained injuries were in fact policemen (Mandraud 2011b); the Ouyahia government did not fall, no senior party or intelligence or military figures lost their posts, and Islamists played no visible role at all (*El Watan*, 9 January 2011).

These striking features of the drama do not invalidate the thesis of a manipulation. Rather, they are evidence of at least two things. First, both the regular army commanders and the president's supporters had anticipated the riots and had prepared their positions, the former determined not to be implicated and the latter determined not to be saddled with responsibility for a bloodbath (hence the impressive discipline and restraint under pressure that Bouteflika's appointee, police chief Abdelghani Hamel, managed to maintain in police ranks). Second, the faction that instigated and manipulated the riots was not seeking solely to weaken the president but had another and larger purpose.

Scarcely any of the Algerian observers interviewed doubted that the factional conflict had been a key element behind the unrest,[14] but most were of the opinion that it was not the whole story,[15] and that a full understanding of the logic of the drama required the regional context to be taken into account, above all the reaction of the regime to the events unfolding in Tunisia (analyzed in the ben Hafaiedh–Zartman chapter). As Mostefa Bouchachi observed, "regarding the January riots, there are people who think that they were deliberately provoked by *le Pouvoir* in order to abort a real uprising."[16]

If such an intention was indeed part of the story in January 2011, it has to be said that it worked. While uprisings have been in progress across the region, no really threatening, politically focused uprising has taken place in Algeria, and no serious reform has taken place either. This is connected to the fact that, whatever politically purposeful forces had purchase on the riots and influenced their course and character, neither the democratic current in Algeria nor the independent associations of Algeria's fledgling civil society nor any of the opposition parties were among them. As a result, as Rachid Tlemçani observed, "instead of advancing demands in a peaceful way, which would have put the regime on the spot, the demonstrations in the streets were transformed into 'descents' for the purpose of looting and smashing both collective and private property" (R. Tlemçani 2011a), and so "elicited no sympathy" (Bouchachi interview, 24 April 2011).

The Crucial Absence of Political Leadership

The riots of January 2011 dramatically illustrated several of the major features of the state-society relationship in Algeria today: the alienation and despair of Algeria's unemployed youth, the dangerously large dimensions of the informal sector of the economy, and the weakness of government policies and actions in the face of powerful informal lobbies and networks of influence. But they also laid bare the weakness of associative life in Algeria, the inability of Algeria's notionally independent associations to cater for and canalize socioeconomic grievances and discontent. Above all, they made clear the extreme weakness of Algeria's political parties.

Whether or not the riots were the product of deliberate manipulations, a premise of the explosion of violent unrest was the irrelevance of the political parties to a large section of society and thus their inability to act effectively as intermediaries between the government and the population as a whole. This is as true of the pro-government parties as of those in opposition. But the irrelevance of the opposition parties to the unrest, their evident failure to have any purchase or exercise any influence on the rioters, had important implications for the future.

Once the riots had come to an end, the diverse fractions of Algeria's political elite were bound to engage in vigorous competition to harness the grievances of the rioters and, in retrospect, the explosion as a whole to their respective rival agendas. In the political competition that got under way from mid-January 2011 onward, the parties of opposition and those other political and social forces that have aspired to promote substantive democratic reform in Algeria were badly placed to determine the subsequent direction of change. The overall upshot of the riots, therefore, was to confirm and illustrate both the dangerously unsatisfactory quality of the state-society relationship in Algeria today and the near impotence of those forces seeking to transcend this situation by radical reforms.

THE NEGOTIATIONS THAT AREN'T

The aftermath of the January 2011 riots in Algeria fell into four distinct phases. There was first of all a brief and ineffectual agitation (from 9 January to March 2011) conducted by elements of the liberal intelligentsia led by a human rights group. This was followed by a far more effective series of mobilizations by professional groups and sectional interests confronting the government with exclusively socioeconomic demands, most of which were conceded. The third phase was initiated by President Bouteflika when he promised major reforms and arranged for protracted consultations to be held from April to July. Phase four was the program of legislation in the national Parliament from October 2011 onward, culminating as already mentioned in the promulgation of six new laws on 12 January 2012.

The agitation of January–March was led by a new organization, the National Coordination for Change and Democracy (Coordination Nationale pour le Changement et la Démocratie, CNCD), which announced its existence on 21 January. This was founded on the initiative of the Algerian League for the Defense of Human Rights (Ligue Algérienne pour la Défense des Droits de l'Homme, LADDH) led by its president, Mostefa Bouchachi.[17] The CNCD grouped several independent trade unions and associations, including youth and student organizations, and three political parties, including Dr. Saïd Sadi's RCD, a mainly Kabylia-based party noted for its Berberist and secularist agenda. The RCD's arch rival in Kabylia, Hocine Aït Ahmed's Socialist Forces Front (Front des Forces Socialistes, FFS), did not affiliate with the CNCD, but the latter's agenda bore traces of the FFS's influence. Although the CNCD's leaders later claimed that their campaign had sought "to provide a framework for" the young people who had rioted in January (Bouchachi interview, 24 April 2011), in fact its sole explicit political demand from the outset was the lifting of the state of emergency, a demand that expressed the concerns of the dissident wing of the political class and intelligentsia but arguably meant nothing to the rioters.

The CNCD held unauthorized demonstrations in support of this demand on 12 February, the day after Mubarak's fall in Cairo, and on 19 February, by which time the rebellion against the Qadhafi regime in Libya was under way. The CNCD's demonstrations mobilized about two thousand supporters, but they were surrounded by some thirty thousand riot police, and while the demonstrators were allowed to stay where they were for hours, they were prevented from marching. By this time the authorities were reported to be alarmed by the developments in Tunis, Cairo, and Libya, and on 23 February the state of emergency in force since 9 February 1992 was finally lifted, although marches in Algiers remained banned, and extremely important emergency provisions giving the army wide powers to combat not only terrorism but also "subversion" remained in force since they were enshrined in separate legislation, a matter the CNCD entirely neglected. In announcing the end of the state of emergency, the regime took all the wind out of the CNCD's sails, and the CNCD promptly split into the CNCD–Parti politiques and the CNCD-Barakat. The first was spearheaded by the RCD and concentrated on defying the continuing ban on marches and demonstrations in Algiers by holding—in the event, pathetically small—demonstrations every Saturday. The second, led by Bouchachi's LADDH, opted for a more modest strategy of holding authorized meetings in halls but found the authorities unwilling to license such meetings in case after case. By April 2011, Bouchachi was acknowledging that "the lifting of the State of Emergency has entailed no change at all" (Bouchachi interview, 24 April 2011).

While the would-be democratic movement was getting nowhere, large swathes of Algerian society began engaging in sustained confrontations with the state. No fewer than seventy distinct movements of social protest took place during March 2011 (*El Watan*, 31 March 2011). These movements were quite unlike the January riots and the democracy demonstrations. They were nonviolent and mostly orderly because organized movements of particular occupational groups, including the clerks of court, communal guards, contract teachers, doctors and other health workers, ex-soldiers and temporary armed services staff, families that had been victims of terrorism, lawyers, magistrates, mayors, municipal workers, the "patriot" militias, university students, and workers in the hydrocarbons sector. These movements were all demanding that the state address their grievances, and their substantive demands concerned pay, conditions of employment, and related matters (e.g., pension rights) rather than political (procedural) objectives. While they placed the government under pressure, they did not challenge the nature of the state but called on it to perform its distributive role more equitably. They thereby afforded the regime an opportunity, by "taking charge of" their concerns, to reassert its hegemony over Algerian society.

This "tsunami of claims," as one observer called it (*L'Expression*, 15 March 2011), was triggered by two developments. First, in a context of a rising cost of living and static wages and salaries, the government's widely publicized decision to throw money at the problems of Algeria's youth stimulated other social interests to assert their needs. Second, the news that Algeria's police had been granted a 50 percent pay raise in effect from 1 January 2011, backdated to January 2008 (*Le Soir d'Algérie*, 28 December 2010), provoked other occupational groups to demand comparable treatment.

At the beginning of March the government had announced a package of measures addressing the problem of unemployed youth. Costing over AD 180 billion (about $15 billion) in the first instance (*L'Expression*, 3 March 2011), (a figure expected to rise), the main items in the package were easier credit terms to encourage young people to set up their own small businesses (*L'Expression*, 2 March 2011).[18] These measures followed from the government's declared ambition to sponsor the creation of between four hundred thousand and five hundred thousand small businesses per year as the way to "reabsorb" youth unemployment. Their announcement went almost entirely unremarked on by the Algerian political class, with the exception of the newly formed National Committee for the Defense of the Rights of the Unemployed (Comité Nationale de Défense des Droits des Chômeurs, CNDDC),[19] which bitterly criticized the government's policy of trying to get young people to become entrepreneurs. As its spokesman exclaimed, "The regime is throwing money around but this serves no good purpose. We don't want to become bosses, we want work!" (quoted in Mandraud 2011a).

In other cases, throwing money around was exactly what was wanted, in that demands for major pay increases were being made very emphatically. Moreover, the huge pay raise accorded to the police in December 2010 was taken by other occupational groups as the new norm. Accordingly, as the journalist Daikha Dridi noted: "All the banners demand the pay raises be backdated to 2008. People want to have really significant pay raises; the minimum they are accepting is 30 percent and back-dated to 2008" (Dridi interview, 29 June 2011).

But pay was not the only matter at stake. Many mobilizations targeted controversial and high-handed decisions taken without proper consultation by the ministries concerned, and on these and related issues the regime could not simply buy off trouble and was far less inclined to yield. Cases of this kind included lawyers protesting against the intimidatory articles in the draft law regulating their profession (*El Watan*, 29 March 2011), health professionals and their unions denouncing the dispositions of a draft health law announced on 27 January 2011, university students protesting against new government regulations concerning their degrees and against the authoritarian way the universities were run by government-appointed rectors (Mandraud 2011a; *Liberté*, 15 March 2011), the communal guards mobilizing against the interior ministry's decision to disband them by 10 March 2011, and supply teachers calling for the regularization of their position and an end to their precarious status.[20]

These confrontations cannot be said to have involved genuine negotiations. In some cases, the government could pick and choose, as when the ministry conceded the students' point about the degree regulations but nothing else (*Liberté*, 2 March 2011). The health professionals also won their point, while the minister covered his concession by denying that the draft law in question existed (*Liberté*, 2 March 2011). The quasi-military communal guards, who may well have benefited from moral support in the military hierarchy, were able to flout the ban on demonstrations by marching in serried ranks and then occupying the Place des Martyres for an entire week (*Liberté*, 7 April 2011), and they succeeded in securing President Bouteflika's intervention to induce the interior ministry to defer the disbanding of the corps until the end of the year. The ministry rationalized its failure to stop these marches by distinguishing between political and social (and supposedly nonpolitical) demonstrations (Mandraud 2011b), but this implied no general relaxation of the ban; it did not spare the weakly organized contract teachers, whom the authorities refused to receive, from being badly beaten (*El Watan*, 23 March 2011).

Algerian commentary on these events stressed the particular character of the regime's response, imputing varying degrees of panic to the authorities (Ali Yahia interview, 27 June 2011), widely seen as "buying social peace in order to survive" (Bouchachi interview, 24 April 2011). But the character of the social movements and the implications of the mobilizations that took place gave rise to contrasted evaluations, with some observers seeing the movements as an important development, others deploring the way they were limited to particular interests, and with no force calling for change in the general interest of the society (Belkacem Benamar, FFS mayor of Naciria, interview, 21 April 2011; Abdelmoumène Khelil, LADDH activist, interview, 26 June 2011; Dridi interview, 29 June 2011; Dr. Saïd Khelil, prominent activist, interview, 1 July 2011).

The main reason for this state of affairs is the failure of the political parties. This is a point on which there is near unanimity in democratic circles in Algeria (as in Morocco and the rest of the Maghrib), with the same emphatic disenchantment to be heard in provincial towns as one hears in Algiers. Saïd Chemakh, a university teacher in Tizi Ouzou, commented: "the parties do not fulfill their function; they can no longer contain all this protest" (Chemakh interview, 1 July 2011),[21] and Daikha Dridi spoke for many interviewees when she exclaimed: "It's almost unbelievable to what extent the parties are a letdown. It has become caricatural, it makes you despair!" (Dridi interview, 29 June 2011).

Thus the extreme weakness of Algeria's political parties was repeatedly demonstrated in early 2011, in their total irrelevance to the violent riots of 4–10 January, in their failure to provide effective support to the fledgling CNCD, and in their irrelevance to the waves of organized social demands in the months that followed. In the process, they offered not the slightest resistance to the regime's efforts to recover its position by selectively accommodating social demands. A key aspect of this situation was the regime's ability to co-opt influential social actors. As one analyst explained,

> Bouteflika is also buying social peace by buying off the elites. His minister of culture has played a fantastic role. The regime has all the artistic and cultural elites in its pocket. She's done a great job, they've all been co-opted. They have also been trying to buy the leaders of NGOs or people who can make trouble: local leaders, neighborhood notables—all bought and paid for. Of course the regime is living from day to day and storing up trouble for the future. It doesn't care! (R. Tlemçani interview, 29 June 2011).

On 19 March 2011, President Bouteflika announced his intention to introduce "profound political reforms" (*Liberté*, 20 March 2011), and anonymous sources suggested that the presidency envisaged "a profound reform of the constitution"

(*L'Expression*, 15 March 2011) and reforms that would strengthen the elected assemblies at every level (*Le Soir d'Algérie*, 23 March 2011), a suggestion that was promptly belied by Ahmed Ouyahia when he declared on 30 March that since there was no political crisis in Algeria, there would be no political change there either (*El Watan*, 2 April 2011). On 15 April 2011, President Bouteflika made his first full-length speech to the nation in over a year and announced his intention to undertake a "programme of political reforms aimed at deepening the democratic process" (*Liberté*, 16 April 2011), the main element of which would be a revision "of the whole of the arsenal of legislation on which the rules of the exercise of democracy are based" in Algeria, followed by "the revisions that are necessary to the country's constitution" (*Liberté*, 16 April 2011). It subsequently emerged that whereas the "reforms" would be enacted before the holding of the 2012 legislative elections, the constitutional revisions would be made after the elections had taken place (El Kadi 2011)—and it was still being promised in 2015, a year after the presidential reelections.

Since President Bouteflika proceeded to itemize most of the legislation to be revised, his speech gave a reliable preview of the eventual outcome of the "process" it served to set in motion. As such, it was badly received by the democratic wing of the Algerian political class. For one opposition party, the speech was simply "a non-event" (FFS officials interview 21 April 2011). A widely articulated criticism was that the political problem in Algeria was not one to be resolved by modifying legal texts (Rabia 2011). As the veteran nationalist and elder statesman Abdelhamid Mehri put it, "the failure of the system of power and its shortcomings lie more in the practices of the regime and in its occult rules of functioning than in the texts of either the constitution or the laws" (quoted in Rabia 2011).

What was especially significant is that none of the parties and organizations that claimed to be democratic challenged the basis of Bouteflika's vision. For the clearly stated premise of what he proposed was that *Algeria is already a democracy* and has been this for some time (*Liberté*, 16 April 2011), that the introduction of formal pluralism had been sufficient to establish this and the existence in 2011 of thirty-odd legal political parties was proof of it (*Liberté*, 16 April 2011), and that what was accordingly required was not a radical constitutional change to transform an authoritarian state into a democracy but merely a "deepening" of the democracy that already existed (*Liberté*, 16 April 2011; *Maghreb Émergent*, 28 August 2011).

Being themselves the beneficiaries and exemplars of the formal pluralism that exists, the parties could hardly contest Bouteflika's premise; the pro-government parties, the FLN and RND, had no interest in doing so, but the supposedly "opposition" parties—the Islamist parties: the Movement of Society for Peace (Mouvement de la Société pour la Paix, MSP), Ennahda, and Islah; the leftwing Workers' Party (Parti des Travailleurs, PT) and the Kabyle-based FFS and RCD—also behaved as if they had no interest in doing so. They accordingly responded in one of two ways:

either tacitly accepting the very limiting conception of the "reforms" envisaged and participating in the "reform process" in a correspondingly modest fashion, or dismissing the putative "reforms" from the outset and boycotting the "reform process."

The latter was framed as a process of consultation, to which all and sundry—parties, associations, and prominent individuals—were invited, and was managed by a commission consisting of Abdelkader Bensalah, the Speaker of the Council of the Nation; Mohamed-Ali Benzaghou, a presidential adviser; and Major-General (retired) Mohammed Touati, also a presidential adviser, seen as the army's guarantor in the proceedings (*El Watan*, 3 and 17 May 2011). The commission began sitting on 21 May 2011 and received a succession of personalities, some of whom also submitted memoranda. They included the leaders of the FLN and RND and eight smaller parties; former defense minister Major-General (retired) Khaled Nezzar; human rights lawyer Miloud Brahimi; former prime minister Smaïl Hamdani; notables representing the Tuareg of southern Algeria; the president of the National Union of Algerian Women (Union Nationale de Femmes Algériennes, UNFA); war heroine Meriem Benmihoub Zerdani; veteran human rights and democracy campaigner Hocine Zehouane; Zohra Drif-Bitat; representatives of the Sufi orders; former general secretary of the FLN Abdelhamid Mehri; representatives of the teachers unions, representatives of the employers' organizations, and a number of university professors and researchers. In addition, former member of the High State Committee Ali Haroun and former prime minister Belaïd Abdesselam submitted their ideas in written memoranda (*El Watan*, 20 May and 7, 13, 19, and 20 June 2011; *Le Quotidien d'Oran*, 25, 28, and 29 May and 1, 4, 5, 11, 19, and 22 June 2011; *Liberté*, 16 June 2011).

The commission and its consultation process were boycotted by the FFS, the RCD, Mostefa Bouchachi's LADDH, former head of state Ali Kafi, former prime ministers Mouloud Hamrouche, Mokdad Sifi (who nonetheless published his recommendations for reform), and Ali Benflis, Islamist leader Abdallah Djaballah, and the secondary schoolteachers' union Cnapest (*El Watan*, 26 May and 4, 7, 12, and 14 June 2011; *Le Quotidien d'Oran*, 2 June 2011; *Liberté*, 8 and 12 June 2011).

The boycott tactic expressed the refusal to legitimate the outcome by participating in the process. So the preoccupation with legitimacy and the strategy of denying legitimation to the regime or at least to the Bouteflika presidency seems to have been the uppermost consideration and prevented the boycotters, especially the FFS and the CNCD, from seizing the opportunity to state their own reform agendas clearly, agitate for them, and so inform and develop public opinion. This policy of the empty chair had costs, since public opinion remained exactly where it was, angry but entirely unable to develop its political outlook, so no consensus on a genuine reform agenda was able to form. Thus the tendencies of the political class claiming democratic credentials took no part in the elaboration of the legislation supposedly intended to "deepen" democracy in Algeria. The upshot, when this legislation was finally voted in November–December 2011, was a set of changes that had been almost entirely shaped by the executive branch of the state and by the interior ministry in particular (*Liberté*, 7 August 2011; *El Watan*, 9, 17, and 21 August and 8 October 2011), and had no genuine democratic content.

POLITICS WITHOUT NEGOTIATION

The radical absence of anything that could properly be called negotiations between the governors and the governed over major political issues is a significant and arguably defining feature of the Algerian political landscape. This fact is linked to two ways in which the Algerian case differs from what many analysts present as the norm.

First, the thesis that in the "contentious politics of social movements" there is typically movement "from demonstrations to violence" (Tilly 2003, 204) does not apply to the most striking events in Algeria, where the movement has typically been the other way. In October 1988, the violent upheaval was not preceded by peaceful demonstrations; the demonstrations were violent from the start—that is, riots—and extremely destructive. They eventually gave way, on 10 October, to a peaceful demonstration, led by the Islamists, after Islamist leaders had been received by the presidency and almost certainly encouraged to help end the rioting by guiding the rioters into peaceful channels (Charef 1989). Although this demonstration was fired on by a section of the security forces (for reasons that remain a mystery), the tactic seemed to work, since the rioting stopped everywhere that evening. Similarly, the upheaval in Kabylia in the "Black Spring" of 2001 began with violence: the violent provocations of the gendarmerie, the furious rioting these provoked, and the repeated shoot-to-kill tactics of the gendarmes in response. The violence then gave way to the massive and entirely peaceful demonstrations organized by the Kabyle political parties (the FFS and the RCD) and above all the new social movement called the Coordination des ʿarchs, daïras et communes (CADC),[22] also known as the Mouvement citoyen, which set out to stop the young rioters from getting themselves killed by providing a nonviolent channel for their anger (ICG 2003). This pattern was repeated in 2011: rioting across the country in January gave way to successive peaceful demonstrations by first a small democratic alliance, the CNCD, demanding the end of the state of emergency (which was formally conceded) and then by bigger and more sustained demonstrations by numerous professional and other sectoral groups demanding government attention (e.g., pay raises), which were also mostly conceded, since they occasioned no political cost—merely a financial one—to the regime.

Second, the expectation (that may well be vindicated in most other cases) that even violent conflict will eventually give way to negotiation—within the regime, within the opposition (in the broadest sense), and eventually between the two—also fails to apply effectively to the Algerian case. We can certainly see several competing viewpoints and outlooks within antiregime opinion as a whole: (1) the *hittistes*—unemployed urban youth who are liable to turn into violent rioters; (2) democratic or at least constitutional opposition parties and human rights activists; and (3) violent jihadi Islamists. But these do not really engage with each other or negotiate with each other to arrive at a common position. Instead they tend relentlessly to act independently of one another and often maneuver to exclude one another, even allying tactically with the regime or elements of it in the process. As for the regime, the various coteries within the power structure also mainly jockey for position against one another; the different currents of opinion (as distinct from group-vested interests) within the regime tend to reach a consensus of some sort only on short-term measures and usually on the most conservative basis available, and when bitter and polarizing factional conflict develops at critical moments it often happens that these conflicts dovetail with conflicts within the opposition forces or the revolt.[23] As a result, negotiation properly so-called between regime and revolt does not and arguably cannot really take place, both because no one has the authority to speak effectively for the opposition or revolt as a whole and because the regime invariably chooses its own interlocutors (these two facts are intimately linked in a complex dialectic). But there is another, and arguably more fundamental, reason for this.

It would be mistaken to suppose that an inclination to negotiate—and an aptitude for doing so—are entirely absent from the Algerian political landscape. The problem is that they are, as a rule, absent specifically from the state-society relationship. The Algerian state certainly negotiates with other states, usually with considerable skill, and Algerian companies, of both the state and the private sector, freely and vigorously negotiate with international partners. In internal political life, just as the importance of the factions within the regime is an open secret and the object of continuous commentary among ordinary citizens, it is also widely understood that the disagreements between factions give rise not only to trials of strength and all sorts of maneuvers and occasional score settling but also, at least eventually, to hard bargaining—what Algerians call "*les tractations en coulisse*." The point to understand here is that in all these cases the recourse to negotiation presupposes mutual respect. The unwritten rule is that you negotiate (only) with your peers. In a state founded by a protracted armed struggle and dominated since independence by the military, the precondition of respect is the possession of force of some kind. Every major faction in the power structure has among its most important members a number of senior military officers, and mutual respect, and so the disposition to negotiate, are present. But this rule does not apply to the state's relations with civilian interests and movements, as the repeated popular complaint about the contempt (*la hogra*) with which ordinary Algerians consider they are treated clearly articulates. The operation of this crucial unwritten rule was vividly illustrated in 1997, when the army commanders agreed to negotiate with the main armed organization in the Islamist rebellion, the Islamic Salvation Army (Armée Islamique du Salut, AIS), the military wing of the banned FIS, but at the same time absolutely refused to negotiate with the civilian leaders of the FIS itself. Thus in Algeria, the disposition to negotiate is fundamentally circumscribed by the continuing fact of military hegemony over the state, and this long-standing limitation has shaped and limited the political outlook and repertoire of opposition or dissident movements within the society.

THE SYNDROME THAT IS

The Algerian pattern, the eruption of violence happening first, without any prior demonstrations over a clear demand to orient the rioters' behavior, followed by attempts by opposition or dissident groups to harness and channel the rioters' grievances (if only rhetorically) to some political purpose, has two very important implications. The first is that, following the initial rioting, the subsequent attempts to capitalize politically on the outbreak through demonstrations cannot easily lead to a renewed but this time politicized *intifada* because the anger of the mobilizable mass (unemployed youths) has been already expressed and their energies spent. The second is that there is reason to believe that this pattern owes a great deal to the deliberate choices of the state, and that it is the state, through one particular apparatus or another, that acts to ensure events unfold in this sequence by deliberately precipitating the initial rioting. It is an open secret that the riots in Kabylia in 2001 were deliberately provoked by the gendarmerie.[24] It is also widely believed that the October 1988 riots were instigated by a faction of the regime (Semiane 1998, 65–96, 127–134, 267–271),[25] and as we have seen many Algerians believe that the January 2011 riots were a comparable manipulation. It is the state—not any of the opposition movements—that has effective purchase on the reflexes of the most alienated element of the population, desperate unemployed youth, and for as long as this remains the case a genuine *intifada* in Alger cannot happen.

Outbursts of unrest, including open revolt, riots, and so on, that go beyond the local level and express real alienation from the state (rather than simply impatience with the local authorities) are accordingly handled in Algeria in a manner that exhibits certain fairly regular features and normally go through a relatively constant series of stages in what clearly amounts to a syndrome. This syndrome can be described schematically as follows:

Phase 1: Riot

This sees an eruption of violent protests, often involving attacks on or seizure of government buildings, and thus a breakdown of order, a rupture of the implicit pact with the state, an announcement of revolt. The key message in these events is the following: "we are ignored, not answered for, victims of *la hogra* (contempt), *ergo* . . .": in short, a reciprocal withdrawal or canceling of recognition: "you (the state) do not recognise us, our problems, our *rights* (or even our existence) so we don't recognize your rights (authority, property)." But either there is no explicit positive political message (such as a demand for a change of government or new elections or a different economic policy or this or that) or the message is localized, as in many local-level riots ("stop neglecting us, pay attention, do something about our road/school/gas supply/electricity supply/housing problem"). In cases of the latter type, the degree of alienation is less, the resort to direct action is instrumental rather than expressive, and it often brings results as the authorities hasten to restore calm by addressing the grievance.

Phase 2: Political Competition

This sees intense maneuvering between the various organized political actors: between the factions within the regime, between rival opposition parties seeking to co-opt or surf on the protests, and in some cases between actors who are new entrants into the political field and who challenge both the authorities and the established opposition forces: for example, the Mouvement citoyen in Kabylia, 2001–2004, and, if rather ineffectually, the CNCD in 2011. In this, Algeria shares the experience of other *intifadat*. At stake in this political competition are two issues: *how* the rioters are to be answered (i.e., by what specific measures) and *by whom* they are to be answered for (i.e., which force or forces get to do the honors and profit politically in the ceaseless competition with their rivals). In 2011 the government acted promptly to answer for the rioters by throwing money at unemployed youth. Neither the CNCD nor the opposition parties had anything beyond rhetoric and platitudes to offer. The sole organization that entered into competition with the regime was the newly formed movement of the unemployed, the CNDDC. The regime acted vigorously to neutralize this movement, relentlessly harassing it, victimizing its leading activists, and thereby making clear its determination to monopolize the business of dealing with the problems of Algerian youth.

Phase 3: Maneuvering

The regime maneuvers to delegitimate prospective interlocutors it does not want to recognise and so empower and legitimize those it wishes to recognize because they pose no (or the least) threat. Factions within the regime similarly maneuver against one another, the tacit messages being, for external consumption: "we—our people or our policies—are not responsible for this mess, the other lot are" and, for internal consumption within the corridors of power: "our man (and/or our policy and/or our methods) can handle this, yours can't." Political parties maneuver to co-opt the protest or at least gloss and spin it as ammunition for their preestablished rhetorical critiques of the regime or one another. Where the protest movement is sufficiently developed (as was the case with the Islamist movement taken as a whole in the early 1990s and with the Mouvement citoyen in Kabylia), rival elements of it maneuver for recognition by the authorities and to delegitimate competitors.

Phase 4: Dialogue

Face à la protesta, le pouvoir dialogue avec lui-même (Confronting protest, the regime dialogues with itself). In October 1988, as already mentioned, the regime invited certain Islamist leaders to talks, and it was they who then organized the demonstration (peaceful and entirely orderly until suddenly fired on) on 10 October 1988. The man the Chadli presidency chose to talk to and thereby recognized as the Islamists' leading spokesman was Abassi Madani, who had some credentials as an Islamist but, crucially, prior credentials as a founder-member of the FLN qua man of 1 November 1954 (and so morally and spiritually "one of us"). It was this dialogue that inaugurated the process of co-opting the anger of the mass of unemployed youth (the *hittistes*) that climaxed in the FIS and its sensational election victories in 1990–1991. In 2001–2003, facing the Mouvement citoyen in Kabylia in the wake of the "Black Spring," the authorities systematically sought to secure congenial interlocutors, using notables with local connections to bypass the formal instances of the Citizens' Movement in the process. The result was what the rest of the movement denounced as *les délégués Taiwan* (made in Taiwan, i.e., prefabricated if not "imported" delegates). As one observer commented at the time, what this meant in practice is that "the regime dialogues with itself" (ICG 2003, 29–31).

The way the regime responds to challenges by choosing its own interlocutors should not be put down purely to the conservatism or cynicism of the authorities, although these are certainly in play. The point is that there is a tradition in play also, and one that is derived from the distant past: namely the tradition of representation of Algerian village and tribal society centered on the institution of the *jemaʿa*, the village or tribal assembly, composed primarily of men who "speak for" and "answer for" their respective lineages. In Kabylia, these are known as the *temman* (singular: *tamen*). They are not elected by their lineages but are selected by the *amin*, the man who presides over the *jemaʿa*, who thus chooses his interlocutors (Roberts 2001, 26, 29).

In other words, underlying the regime's behavior in this regard is an unresolved—and, in fact, long-standing—problem of political representation. This problem can be observed in the behavior of the regime's opponents and critics as well.

THE REFUSAL OF REPRESENTATION FOR REFORM

The absence of genuine negotiation over the issues that arise in the frequent spasms of unrest that reflect the troubled state-society relationship in Algeria should not be put down solely to the regime's attitudes, for the attitudes of opposition movements and protesters often preclude negotiation as well. In addition to the particular case of the jihadi movements, which explicitly refuse negotiation as a matter of course, these attitudes also inform the behavior of nonviolent opposition actors. In 1989–1991, the radical rhetoric of the Islamic Salvation Front delegitimated the state as "impious" and the Party of the FLN as "thieves," instead of emphasizing the legitimacy of its own particular proposals and demands as an argument for the regime to take at least some of them seriously and negotiate over them. In 2001, the Mouvement citoyen in Kabylia insisted that that its platform of demands was *scellé et non-négociable* (sealed and nonnegotiable) (ICG 2003, 21).

Thus both political and social opposition movements can be seen to be in key respects mirror images of the regime. In all cases, they appear to act on the fundamental assumption that legitimacy is something you monopolize and that possessing legitimacy or securing it by contesting others' title to it is the crucial aspect of every strategy, offensive and defensive: that is, you *dictate to* your adversary (the other side) and you *eliminate* your rival.

It can be seen that neither for the regime nor for the various types of protest or opposition that it arouses at frequent intervals is there really any question of respect for public opinion as the moral arbiter of the disagreement. Public opinion is called to witness in an essentially theatrical manner and spirit or dragooned if not coerced or terrorized. It is not respected, let alone empowered. This reflects the fact that, whether or not all actors are conscious of it, the historic FLN has served as the main template of political action and popular mobilization. The relationship of the FLN and of its military wing, the National Liberation Army (Armée Nationale de Libération, ALN) to the Algerian people was a commandist one, calling on Algerians to support them and obey their instructions as a *duty*. The attitude and discourse of the FIS was clearly in this tradition, but the same can be said of the Mouvement citoyen in Kabylia as well, despite its very different outlook in other respects.

One corollary of this state of affairs is the tendency to utopianism, in the form of the raising of unrealizable demands, on the part of the opposition forces. Since they are disinclined to negotiate with the regime (and it is disinclined to negotiate with them), they peddle the radical daydream of replacing it altogether:

- The FIS's utopian vision of *dawla islamiyya* (1989–1992);
- The FFS's utopian demand for a Constituent Assembly, and its insistence on this as the precondition of everything (and its consequent refusal to raise realizable demands in

the meantime) when the balance of forces rules this out of the question for the foreseeable future;

- The Mouvement citoyen's maximalist (and in the short term wholly unrealistic) demand that "all the executive functions of the state as well as its security forces be placed under the effective authority of democratically elected instances" (ICG 2003, 20–21).

Evidently the refusal to negotiate and the disposition to oppose conservative positions with utopian ones and vice versa operate in a relentless vicious circle.

Another corollary of this state of affairs is that constitutional change usually occurs in the form of a coup or conjuring trick of some kind, such as the Chadli regime's introduction of the 1989 constitution without any prior debate or preparation of public opinion. An exception is President Liamine Zeroual's revision of the 1989 constitution in 1996. But this actually proves the rule since, despite the fact that Zeroual circulated a long memorandum six months in advance and invited all parties and points of view to debate the proposed changes and suggest amendments, many leading personalities with reforming credentials (such as Mouloud Hamrouche) and supposedly democratic parties (notably the FFS) simply denounced Zeroual's project and boycotted the entire discussion. They thereby demonstrated their disinclination to engage in political negotiation on the most fundamental matters on the assumption that to do so would be to lose out in a zero-sum game in which the only stake that mattered was the distribution of legitimacy (Roberts 2003, 185–190).

The widely touted thesis that Algeria is subject to dictatorial rule overlooks the fact that the Algerian state actually possesses and operates a system of political representation. There are two aspects to this: the informal aspect—the plethora of clienteles and coteries and "courants" and factions within or possessing access to *le Pouvoir*—which dates from the establishment of the FLN in 1954, and the formal aspect, which in its current version of formal political pluralism dates from 1989. The problem is thus not the absence of political representation as such but the peculiar and wholly inadequate nature of the system of representation that actually exists and that, by enlisting, harnessing, and channeling political energies, constitutes a major obstacle to the advent of an adequate system of representation.

The key institutions in the formal aspect of this system are the political parties. But these have in common the fact that they owe their existence to executive fiat, that is, to the arbitrary *bon vouloir* of the regime. Like the political parties set up by the regime itself to act as its relays (the FLN and RND), the other, notionally opposition, parties have been entirely unable to emancipate themselves from the constraining implications of their birth certificates by gaining independent influence through their role in the legislative branch of the state—the national parliament, the regional and municipal assemblies—because these are more or less powerless bodies that are wholly dependent upon and tightly controlled by the executive branch of the state. For these and other reasons, the parties have been unable to provide effective representation of the population and the diversity of social interest and political outlook that actually exists within this and wholly unable to hold the government to account. They have accordingly been losing their grip on the reflexes of the Algerian people, as diminishing turnouts in elections have shown. The inability of the parties to provide effective representation is a major reason for the widespread resort to direct action, including rioting, that has been such a salient feature of the Algerian landscape over the last decade.

A consequence of this state of affairs is that it is the informal aspect of the system of representation—the cliques, coteries, and clientèles—that has substance and efficacy, but only for those with a foot in *le Pouvoir*, while the formal aspect—the parties—lacks substance and cannot channel the frustration and anger of the vast majority with no privileged informal access to the decision makers in the power structure. For the same reason, the parties cannot be the agents of any project of qualitative political and constitutional reform and are accordingly part of the problem. That this is so was graphically illustrated by the results of the legislative elections of 10 May 2012.

BUCKING THE TREND I: THE LEGISLATIVE ELECTIONS OF 2012

The National Assembly elections on 10 May 2012 were widely expected by external commentators to exhibit an "Arab Spring effect" in two ways: a further decline in turnout and in the scores of the regime-sponsored parties, especially the FLN, reflecting supposed popular alienation from the regime, combined with a quantum leap in the scores of Algeria's Islamists reflecting the regional trend of Islamist electoral victories (in Morocco, Tunisia, and Egypt). In the event, the results showed an increase in turnout (43.14 percent as compared with 35.67 percent in 2007), a fall in the combined Islamist vote (from 15.42 percent in 2007 to 13.2 percent) and a sensational increase in the FLN's tally of seats, up from 136 (35 percent of the total) in 2007 to no fewer than 208 (45 percent of the total), making it massively dominant in the National Assembly.

In reality, it was always unrealistic to expect Algeria's Islamists, long compromised by participation in "the system" and with nothing new to offer, to emulate their counterparts elsewhere in North Africa (Parks 2012). Moreover, although the official figures were contested and the turnout figure in particular was probably inflated, these results actually did exhibit an "Arab Spring effect," but one contrary to what outsiders anticipated, for the wider geopolitical situation, especially the events in Libya and the turmoil in Mali, benefited the FLN. Although there was initially some sympathy in Algeria for the rebellion against the Qadhafi regime, as for the Tunisian and Egyptian uprisings, this began to wane from mid-March 2011. As Omar Lardjane (interview, 25 June 2011) observed, "There had long been hostility towards Qadhafi here but that changed with the British and French intervention. Now, as regards Libya and Syria, the Algerians are much more reserved and doubtful."

By the time the election campaign got under way in spring 2012, the evolution of the Libyan situation had been working in favor of the regime for some months, especially given the way the fallout from the overthrow of Qadhafi had aggravated the crisis in the Sahel and the security problem on Algeria's southern frontiers. As a retired woman teacher in Algiers remarked, "even the young people feel this: we don't want what happened to Libya to happen to us" (Djamila Mohammedi [pseudonym] interview, 8 July 2012). The FLN and President Bouteflika worked this issue for all it was worth; Bouteflika's striking suggestion in a speech at Arzew on 24 February 2012 that the stakes in the election were so high that polling day on 10 May could be compared to the launching of the war for independence on 1 November 1954, while clearly hyperbole, translated the regime's anxiety about its geopolitical situation and the concern to remobilize nationalist reflexes to the utmost (Benachour 2012). As Djamila Mohammedi remarked in a 2012 interview, "Libya was a theme of the campaign. Have people really felt the danger? It's an open question, but there seems to have been a "seeking safety vote" [*vote-refuge*] for the FLN, with people putting stability first."

But while the increase in the FLN's tally of seats was remarkable, it polled only very slightly more in 2012 (1,324,363 valid votes) than in 2007 (1,314,494). The increase in its number of deputies does not seem to have owed anything to electoral fraud in the sense of ballot stuffing. We can also largely rule out the hypothesis that a different kind of fraud occurred—the discounting of valid votes cast for rival parties. The regime was extremely concerned to be able to announce an appreciable improvement in turnout over the low 2007 figure and could not have done this had it tacitly authorized any significant reduction in the true totals of valid votes cast for other parties. The explanation is to be found elsewhere.

In the previous legislative election, in May 2007, the FLN suffered a net loss of 63 seats from its 2002 total of 199, ending with 136 out of the total of 389 seats in contention. In 2012, the FLN, with only a very slight increase in its popular vote, secured a net gain of 72 seats and an overall tally of 208, out of an increased total of 462 seats. But the key figures to be considered are the percentages that the 2007 and 2012 tallies of FLN votes represented of (1) the total electorate, (2) the total votes, and (3) the valid votes cast (total votes less spoiled ballots), respectively. These are shown in table 1.

Thus the FLN secured 45 percent of the seats in the Popular National Assembly with 14.18 percent of the total vote and the votes of merely 6.12 percent of the total electorate. This fact is enough to make clear that there is something very wrong with the Algerian's government rules and procedures for holding legislative elections. But in order to establish how this could have happened, two key questions

Table 1. Changes in the FLN's share of seats and the total valid vote, 2007–2012

	2007	2012
a. Total number of eligible voters	18,761,084	21,645,841
b. Total number of voters	6,692,891	9,339,026
c. Turnout (voters as percentage of eligible voters)	35.67%	43.14%
d. Spoiled ballots	966,060	1,704,047
e. Total number of valid votes	5,726,831	7,643,979
f. Valid votes as percentage of eligible voters	30.53%	35.27%
g. Number of seats won by FLN	136	208
h. Seats won as percentage of total	34.96%	45.02%
i. Absolute change in (h), 2007–2012	+10.06	
j. Percentage change in (h), 2007–2012	+28.78	
k. Total votes cast for FLN	1,313,977	1,324,363
l. FLN votes as percentage of eligible	7.00%	6.12%
m. FLN votes as percentage of total vote	19.63%	14.18%
n. FLN votes as percentage of valid votes	22.94%	17.35%
o. Absolute change in (n) 2007–2012	−5.59	
p. Percentage change in (n) from 2007 to 2012	−24.37	

should be answered. How did the FLN improve its percentage share of the APN seats by 10.06, representing a 28.78 percentage increase, when its shares of the total electorate, of the total number of votes cast, and of the total of valid votes all fell very appreciably in 2012? Specifically, how in 2012 could the FLN register a 28.78 percent improvement on its 2007 share of seats, when it registered a 24.37 percent fall in its share of valid votes?

The answer is that it was the extreme proliferation of parties, in combination with the provision of the new electoral law that all lists failing to reach the threshold of 5 percent of the total vote would be eliminated and their votes discounted from that point on, that enabled the FLN to increase its share of seats while its share of votes declined. Having refused to legalize any new parties since 1999, the regime suddenly legalized no fewer than twenty-three new parties prior to the elections. The result was an extraordinarily high number of lists contesting every constituency. In all, there were 2036 lists contesting the elections. Taking Algeria's forty-eight wilayat and the overseas constituencies together, the average number of lists per constituency was thirty-nine. A very high proportion of these lists will have been eliminated and their votes, while counted for total turnout, then discounted in the calculation of the quota of votes determining the allocation of seats to the successful lists.

That the regime should have resorted to such ingenious and unscrupulous procedures in order to contrive the result it sought is evidence of the latent crisis of the political system. But what is even more remarkable is that Algeria's opposition parties and democratic activists should have completely failed to campaign against the insidious provisions of the electoral law in 2011 and that, as of this writing, they should have made no issue of this subsequently.

BUCKING THE TREND II: ALGERIA'S PRESIDENT FOR LIFE AND BEYOND

Already plagued by health problems since late 2005, elderly (he was born in 1937), and visibly tired by 2012, President Bouteflika suffered a stroke in April 2013, and on 27 April he was flown to Paris, where he remained in the hospital for the next eighty-two days, returning to Algiers on 16 July. It was assumed that although he might complete his current term, there was no question of a fourth. Yet, despite public concern that he was not physically fit to continue in office, on 17 April 2014 he was declared the winner in the so-called presidential election. The implication was that Bouteflika was determined to remain president as long as he drew breath and that the Algerian oligarchy as a whole was willing to go along with this at a time when the phenomenon of "presidents for life" was being violently repudiated in the rest of the Arab world (Owen 2012).

The proceedings called "presidential elections" in Algeria are not elections. They are held to dignify what are in reality decisions of the top echelon of the Algerian regime taken some time beforehand. The role of other "candidates" is to boost turnout by giving other options to those electors disinclined to vote for the "candidate of the system" and thereby endow the proceedings with a pluralist aspect sufficient to secure the endorsement of Western governments intent on dealing with the victor in any case (Roberts 2009). The decision of the oligarchs to authorize Bouteflika to continue in office represented a choice between the two difficult options facing them, and the choice they made was the product of a fierce factional conflict and external pressure.

In a speech to the national war veterans organization (Organisation nationale des Moudjahidine, ONM) in December 2004, Bouteflika declared "the end of historical legitimacy," that is, the end of the principal source of entitlement to high political office since 1962, namely the fact of participation in the revolutionary war of independence (B. Mounir 2004). It would seem that he has seen himself as the last president of the revolutionary generation, but if so, he has not prepared the ground for a successor to be chosen from the postrevolutionary generation in a manner that would be consistent with the revolution's purpose of establishing a sovereign Algerian state. If a record of honorable participation in the FLN-ALN of 1954–1962 is no longer available as a source of legitimacy, there are only two main alternatives: democratic legitimation in genuine elections or external/internal legitimation, that is, endorsement by Western capitals and by Paris in the first instance and by the ALN junta. The evidence to date suggests that it is the second choice that is tacitly being made, in part because it is more congenial to the army command. Possession of historical legitimacy has been a necessary but by no means sufficient condition of accession to the presidency. The other indispensable condition has been the confidence of the generals, who have tended to treat the presidency as an annex of the army high command and its incumbent as someone they have entrusted with a mission and answerable to them above all. For Algeria's generals to accept the need for democratic legitimation through real elections would be to surrender their most important political prerogative, whereas to choose a president with whom Paris is happy to do business leaves this prerogative formally intact.

As it happens, the military decision makers had at least two alternatives to the visibly ailing Bouteflika in men who, while younger than he, also had their portion of historical legitimacy as *anciens moudjahidine*, namely former prime minister Mouloud Hamrouche (born in 1943) and ex-president (general) Liamine Zeroual (born in 1941), both of whom had their supporters. But to choose Hamrouche would have been to select a president expected to enact controversial reforms at a delicate juncture when national security concerns tended to mandate a cautious if not frankly conservative policy, and to bring back Zeroual would have been to choose a president with a pronounced nationalist outlook whom Paris had always disliked for that very reason. And either choice would have presented difficulties for the regular army, given its role in evicting Hamrouche from the premiership in June 1991 and in provoking Zeroual to stand down from the presidency in September 1998. Nonetheless, had the generals decided that Bouteflika's health ruled out a fourth term, either of these alternative scenarios could have been made to work. (A third scenario that might also have gained support would have been to opt for veteran diplomat and former foreign minister Lakhdar Brahimi, widely respected at home as well as abroad, who while older than Bouteflika—he was born in 1934—has enjoyed appreciably better health.)

But for any of these options to fly would have required the army's political arm—Lt. General Mediène's DRS—to organize the necessary paving of the way, and this was ruled out by a remarkable development in the autumn of 2013, namely a major restructuring of Algeria's intelligence services at Mediène's expense. The army security service (Direction Centrale de la Sécurité de l'Armée, DCSA) headed by Mediène's man, Major General Mehenna Djebbar, was detached from the DRS and taken under the wing of the General Staff headed by Lt. General Ahmed Gaïd Salah, and Djebbar was replaced and subsequently forced into retirement. The DRS's criminal investigation service (Service Central de la Police Judiciaire, SCPJ), which spearheaded the campaign against corruption that cost Bouteflika's energy minister, Chakib Khelil, his post, was also attached to the General Staff, before being dissolved altogether. The service that assured the DRS's control of the media, the Center for Communication and Broadcasting (Centre de Communication et Diffusion, CCD), whose head, Colonel Fawzi, had been unceremoniously sacked in July, within days of Bouteflika's return from Paris, was also initially reported to have been attached to the General Staff before it too was dissolved. Further changes followed, including the retirement of the head of the Internal Security Directorate (Direction de la Sécurité Intérieure, DSI), Major General Athmane Tartag, and of the external intelligence service (Direction de la Documentation et de la Sécurité Extérieure, DDSE), Major General Rachid Lallali (R. P. 2013; Allam 2013; *Maghreb Émergent*, 10 September 2013; Lyès 2013; Mounir 2013; Hamadi 2013; Hamadi 2014). These changes were unprecedented and occasioned much Algerian media comment; while they were subject to conflicting interpretations (Aziri 2013; Moali 2013; Hachemaoui 2013), there can be little doubt that Mediène's position was weakened and that the capacity of the DRS to act with authority to organize the mobilization of consent within the armed forces and the wider power structure to an alternative to Bouteflika's candidacy was nullified for the time being. At the same time, they gave the impression that a reinvigorated Bouteflika was back in charge and immediately made a fourth term seem plausible (Charef 2013a; Charef 2013b).

Underlying these moves was a clear alliance between the presidency and the army General Staff. Gaïd Salah had visited Bouteflika in Paris and met with him several times in early September (Makhedi 2013; Bouaricha 2013), and in a government reshuffle on 11 September, Bouteflika named him to the new post of deputy defense minister while allowing him to remain chief of staff as well, which meant that Gaïd Salah would be answerable to Bouteflika (as minister of defense) for the conduct of the intelligence services now under his authority (S. Tlemçani 2013; K. A. 2013). At the same time, the change can be seen to have been a product of the complex "Arab Spring effect" on Algerian politics and of Bouteflika's decision to adopt a policy of courting French favor as insurance against external destabilization. This policy was already manifest in his dispatching of foreign minister Mourad Medelci to report to the French National Assembly on Bouteflika's "reform" program on 7 December 2011, as if the Algerian government was answerable to the French legislature and needed its approval, a move that created unease and provoked criticism in Algeria (R. P. 2011; Bouzeghrane 2011; Alilat 2011; *Algeria-Watch*, 8 December 2011). It subsequently became even clearer in respect of Algeria's regional position.

Developments in the Sahel and on Algeria's eastern frontier following the overthrow of the Qadhafi regime in Libya had caused great problems for the DRS's handling of Algeria's security interests on these fronts. The uprising on 16–17 January 2012 of a new Tuareg separatist movement in Mali, the National Movement for the Liberation of Azawad (Mouvement National pour la Libération de l'Azawad, MNLA) formed in October 2011 following the return to northern Mali of hundreds of heavily armed Tuareg from Libya, raised the specter of an independent Tuareg state on Algeria's southern frontier, something Algiers, with a Tuareg population of its own, has always been determined to prevent. The MNLA's success, in alliance with Ansar Dine (an Islamist movement drawing some support as well as its leader from the Tuareg minority), in taking control of northern Mali, while the Malian regime went into crisis following the overthrow of President Amadou Toure in a military coup in Bamako on 21–22 March 2012, climaxed with the MNLA's proclamation of the independent state of Azawad on 6 April 2012. But even before this happened the MNLA–Ansar Dine alliance had begun to disintegrate, and Ansar Dine fighters soon took control of the northern region at the MNLA's expense, imposing Islamic government complete with shariʿa law as they did so. The specter of northern Mali becoming an Islamic state, in which other Islamist movements, notably al-Qaeda in the Islamic Maghreb (AQIM) and a splinter group, the Movement for Unicity and Jihad in West Africa (Mouvement pour l'Unicité et le Jihad en Afrique Occidentale, MUJAO) formed in mid-2011, were also involved, led Paris to advocate a military intervention, a proposal supported by the Economic Community of West African States. This was initially resisted by Algiers as the NATO intervention in Libya had been resisted. The DRS favored a policy of seeking a cease-fire and a negotiated settlement with Bamako, using its own contacts with Ansar Dine as its main card (Dennison 2012, 3). But this position received little outside support, and France went ahead with its intervention, code-named Opération Serval, on 11 January 2013, while Algiers, at Bouteflika's insistence, cooperated with this by giving permission for the French air force to overfly Algeria. Five days later, a force of some forty armed Islamists seized control of a major Algerian gas plant at Tiguentourine, sixty kilometers from In Amenas in the Algerian Sahara, near the Libyan frontier, taking some 800 workers hostage, including 132 foreign personnel. The attackers had apparently come from Mali via Niger and Libya, and their success was seen to imply a major security lapse on the part of the DRS. The way the eventual military intervention to free the hostages was apparently botched by a unit of the DRS commanded by DSI chief Major-General Athmane Tartag sealed the discredit of the DRS in this affair, as foreign governments vehemently complained about an intervention in which 39 of the foreign personnel were killed. There were reports that regular army officers were vehemently opposed to the way Tartag's unit conducted its intervention (Souaïdia 2013), and several Western governments subsequently put pressure on Algiers to allow closer consultation and coordination between their intelligence services and the DRS ("UK" 2013; Wintour 2013b; "PM" 2013; Wintour 2013a). The restructuring of the intelligence services and the dismissal of Tartag in particular can thus be seen as, among other things, a response to the concerns of both foreign governments and Algeria's regular army commanders.

Thus a number of factors entered into the decision of the Algerian oligarchy to persist with Bouteflika in the presidency. A crucial corollary of this decision is that the problem of the presidential succession remained to be resolved, without any clear indication about how. Moreover, a succession problem in the DRS and in the army high command remained; both Medième (born in 1939) and Gaïd Salah (born in 1940 according to his official biography but rumored to be much older) required replacement. Thus the Algerian oligarchy faced a triple succession problem that would play an important role in the fourth term of the ailing president.

REFORMING ALGERIA: A PARTICULAR PROBLEM IN A DIFFICULT CONTEXT

Western perspectives on what is usually called the problem of "authoritarianism" and its supposed antidote, "democratization," in the Middle East and North Africa almost invariably assume that something exists that must be swept away ("dictatorship," "tyranny," etc.) and that this act of destruction will more or less automatically found democracy by liberating repressed political energies, as summarized in the "model" presented in the introduction of this book. But proper attention to the Algerian case mandates a very different vision, and it is not alone, for its own reasons. The problem is not a presence but an absence, or rather a set of linked absences or weaknesses:

- the weakness of all the instances of the legislative branch (National Assembly, Council of the Nation, wilaya assemblies, communal assemblies), their lack of substantive decision-making prerogatives and thus of their ability to provide politically effective representation to the society or act as curbs on or checks to the executive branch at national, regional, and local level;
- the congenital inability of the pseudoparties existing by executive fiat to make an issue of this;
- the corresponding absence of an organized force with a nationwide presence capable of conducting a serious peaceful agitation for genuine constitutional reform.

In this light, the supposed failure of the Algerians to join in the so-called Arab Spring can be seen to have a positive aspect: the refusal of political adventures when conditions are not yet ripe for radical action. Effective treatment of Algeria's political problems requires the development of a coherent political vision that is firmly anchored in a lucid analysis of Algerian reality before these problems can be addressed effectively. The development of such a vision is bound to take time. The Algerians have not, however, been merely sitting on their hands and passively regarding the shows and fireworks elsewhere. They have been considering these developments but also, crucially, debating and reflecting on their own circumstances and predicament. And that is exactly what they should have been doing at this juncture, if they are to succeed in drawing the lessons of experience and getting the measure of their problems and devise at last the appropriate agenda for constructive reform.

But there is little prospect of such an agenda to emerge and make headway in the near future and a danger that the development of a lucid reformist vision may be disrupted by fresh instability. In addition to national security concerns and external pressures, which incline the regime to very conservative if not retrograde policies in respect to political and constitutional reform, the presence, in the short term, of a complex triple succession problem at the highest level of the oligarchy is at least as likely to constitute a constraint on progress toward reform as it is to stimulate effective recognition of the need for this.

APPENDIX 1

Definitive results of the National Assembly elections of 10 May 2012, as revised by the Constitutional Council

- Number of registered voters: 21,645,841
- Number of voters: 9,339,026
- Global turnout: 43.14 percent
- Number of valid votes: 7,634,979
- Number of spoiled ballots: 1,704,047

Party	Votes	% of total votes	Seats	% of total seats
Front de libération nationale (FLN)	1,324,363	17.3	208	45.0
Rassemblement national démocratique (RND)	524,057	6.9	68	14.7
Alliance de l'Algérie verte (AAV)	475,049	6.2	49	10.6
Front des forces socialistes (FFS)	188,275	2.5	27	5.8
Parti des travailleurs (PT)	283,585	3.7	24	5.2
Indépendants	671,190	8.8	18	3.9
Front national algérien (FNA)	198,509	2.6	9	1.9
Front pour la justice et le développement	232,676	3.0	8	1.7
Mouvement populaire algérien (MPA)	165,600	2.2	7	1.5
Parti El-Fedjr El-Jadid (PFJ)	132,492	1.7	5	1.1
Front du changement (FC)	173,491	2.3	4	0.9
Parti national pour la solidarité et le développement (PNSD)	114,372	1.5	4	0.9
Front national pour la justice sociale (FNJS)	140,223	1.8	3	0.6
Ahd 54	120,201	1.6	3	0.6
Union des forces démocratiques et sociales	114,481	1.5	3	0.6
Alliance nationale républicaine (ANR)	109,331	1.4	3	0.6
Front El Moustakbel (FM)	174,708	2.3	2	0.4
Parti El-Karama	129,427	1.7	2	0.4
Mouvement national de l'espérance (MNE)	119,253	1.6	2	0.4

Party	Votes	% of total votes	Seats	% of total seats
Rassemblement algérien (RA)	117,549	1.5	2	0.4
Rassemblement patriotique républicain (RPR)	114,651	1.5	2	0.4
Parti des jeunes	102,663	1.3	2	0.4
Parti Ennour El-Djazaïri	48,943	0.6	2	0.4
Mouvement El-Infitah (ME)	116,384	1.0	1	0.2
Mouvement des citoyens libres (MCL)	115,631	1.5	1	0.2
Parti du renouveau algérien (PRA)	111,218	1.5	1	0.2
Front national des indépendants pour la Concorde (FNIC)	107,833	1.4	1	0.2
Front national démocratique (FND)	101,643	1.3	1	0.2
Total	6,327,798	83.0	462	100.0

Source: European Union, *Élections législatives Algérie 2012*, final report of the Election Observation Mission, July 2012, p. 47.

Notes

1. A major rise in food prices exactly a year earlier did not generate any riots, let alone nationwide ones; see Lamriben (2009).

2. "L'augmentation des prix de l'huile et du sucre menace la paix sociale: Attention, ça flambe!" *L'Expression*, 6 January 2011; "Qui jette l'huile sur le feu?" *L'Expression*, 6 January 2011; both articles asked the same rhetorical question: "À qui profite le crime?" [Who benefits from the crime?].

3. For ordinary Algerian view, see readers' responses to the article "Le pouvoir face à la rue," *El Watan*, 8 January 2011.

4. See the interview with prominent political analyst Rachid Tlemçani in *El Watan*, 10 January 2011.

5. The term *ministries of sovereignty* refers to the ministries of defense, finance, foreign affairs, interior, and justice.

6. Under Lt. General Ahmed Gaïd Salah, the General Staff withdrew from the political role it played during Lamari's tenure (1993–2004) and ceased, for the time being, to function as the core of a distinct faction.

7. Hamel is from Tlemcen, Bouteflika's home region, and his last post before the DGSN was that of commander of the Republican Guard, which guards the presidency, an indication that he enjoyed Bouteflika's confidence and favor. See *El Watan*, 7 July 2010; *El Watan*, 8 July 2010, and *Liberté*, 30 June 2008.

8. Originally associated with the "Reformer" grouping headed by Mouloud Hamrouche and minister of justice in Hamrouche's government (1989–1991), Benflis was appointed in autumn 1998 as Bouteflika's campaign manager and owed his later appointments as general secretary of the FLN (2000–2004) and prime minister (2001–2003) in part to Bouteflika's backing.

9. The principal nursery of elites from western Algeria, Tlemcen is the hometown of Chakib Khelil, Abdelhamid Benachenhou, and Hamid Temmar, three high-profile ministerial appointees

of Bouteflika from 1999 onward, and his foreign minister Mourad Medelci; the new police chief, Abdelghani Hamel, and the president of the Council of the Nation, Abdelkader Bensalah, are both from the wilaya of Tlemcen. Nedroma is also the hometown of former interior minister Noureddine Zerhouni, whose family boasts several other senior personalities including an army general.

10. Born in 1934, Zohra Drif was one of the FLN's women fighters in the Battle of Algiers; arrested in September 1957, she spent the rest of the war in prison. After independence she was on the staff of the FLN's weekly organ Révolution Africaine but dropped out of politics following Colonel Boumediène's coup in June 1965. She returned to prominence when President Bouteflika appointed her to the Council of the Nation.

11. The French expression "Ce n'est pas normal" really means "This is outrageous."

12. Mme Drif-Bitat's remarks followed a report published the previous day ("Wikileaks: Selon le président malien, Bouteflika ne contrôle pas ses services de renseignement au Sahel," *El Watan*, 19 December 2010).

13. A sequel to Drif-Bitat's attack on Ouyahia occurred after the riots, when minister of culture, Khalida Toumi, also close to President Boutelika, twice signaled her opposition to Ouyahia's policies at meetings of the Council of Ministers; see *Le Quotidien d'Oran*, 6 March 2011.

14. According to Mostefa Bouchachi, "all the independent analysts thought it was provoked by the regime"; interview, Algiers, 24 April 2011.

15. One analyst, assessing the theses that the riots were "a revolt of the informal sector or a skirmish of the factions," concluded that they were "the two together"; interview with Rachid Tlemçani, Algiers, 29 June 2011.

16. Interview with Mostefa Bouchachi, Algiers, 24 April 2011. This thesis was subsequently stated publicly by Saïd Sadi, the leader of the Rally for Culture and Democracy (Rassemblement pour la Culture et la Démocratie, RCD) when he declared at a meeting of the RCD National Council that "they lit the fuse in order to explode the situation with a movement that had no political demands" ("Saïd Sadi au Conseil National du RCD: 'Le pouvoir est usé, divisé et discrédité,'" *El Watan*, 4 June 2011).

17. The LADDH split in 2007 into two organizations using the same name, headed respectively by Mostefa Bouchachi and Hocine Zehouane. The LADDH–Bouchachi secured control of most of the original League's apparatus, but the LADDH-Zehouane has also stayed in business, having a strong base in the Maison des Droits de l'Homme et du Citoyen in Tizi Ouzou and in Bejaia (interviews with Mostefa Bouchachi, Algiers, 24 April 2011; Arezki Abboute, a member of the LADDH-Zehouane, Tizi Ouzou, 11 July 2012; and Abdennour Boumghar, former LADDH activist, Tizi Ouzou, 12 July 2012).

18. Among other measures, the government also undertook to waive the requirement of performance of National Service (formerly a precondition of government aid) for those over thirty.

19. The CNDDC has been by far the most significant critic of the government's policy for dealing with youth unemployment and the regime has displayed a relentlessly repressive attitude toward it.

20. The communal guards were created in 1995 as an auxiliary force to assist the Gendarmerie Nationale in maintaining security in the countryside.

21. Interview with Saïd Chemakh, deputy head of the Department of Amazigh Studies, Mouloud Mammeri University, Tizi Ouzou, 1 July 2011.

22. The *daïra* is the Algerian counterpart of the French *sous-préfecture* and so the intermediate level of administration between the governorate (*wilaya*) and the commune; *arch* refers in Kabylia to the distinct political communities, each consisting of a number of villages sharing a common territory, into which the population has historically been divided.

23. Notably in the mid-1990s when the regime faction seeking a political solution to the violence through negotiation with the Islamists (the so-called conciliators) had their counterparts

within the ex-FIS and its armed wing, the AIS, while their factional adversaries, led by the army chief of staff and intent on a military solution (the so-called eradicators), had their counterpart among the Islamist insurgents in the form of the notorious Armed Islamic Group (Groupe Islamique Armé, GIA), which refused all negotiation. See Roberts (2003, 151–159).

24. See the unprecedentedly frank and revealing report of the National Commission of Inquiry chaired by the eminent lawyer Maître Mohand Issad, cited in ICG (2003, 9–10).

25. See the accounts of various witnesses and actors in these events in Semiane (1998).

References

Alilat, Yazid. 2011. "Medelci explique les réformes aux députés français." *Le Qotidien d'Oran*, 8 December.

Ali Yahia, Abdennour. 2011. Interviewed in Algiers, 27 June.

Allam, Samir. 2013. "Le service de presse et la sécurité de l'armée rattachés au chef d'état major." *Tout sur l'Algérie*, 9 September.

Arieff, Alexis. 2013. "Algeria: Current Issues." Washington D.C.: Congressional Research Service, 18 November.

Aziri, Mohand. 2013. "Le president réduit ses prérogatives: DRS, le début du démantèlement?" *El Watan*, 12 September.

B. Mounir. 2004. "Bouteflika exclut les anciens moudjahidine du serail: Le lobby de l'ALN, les parrains et l'armée." *Le Quotidien d'Oran*, 4 December.

———. 2013. "Changements au DRS et à l'ANP: la nouvelle stratégie de défense se met en place." *Liberté*, 23 September.

Benachour, Djamel. 2012. "L'enjeu de la participation au cœur du discours de Bouteflika: La peur de l'abstention." *El Watan*, 25 February.

Benamar, Belkacem. 2011. Interviewed in Algiers, 21 April.

Bouaricha, Nadjia. 2013. "Bouteflika a reçu trois fois Gaïd Salah et Sellal en une semaine: Des 'audiences' et des interrogations." *El Watan*, 11 September.

Boundaoui, Assia. 2011. "'Reform Not Revolt' in Algeria." Al Jazeera, 2 March. http://www.aljazeera.com/indepth/features/2011/03/201132131733827907.html.

Bouchachi, Mostefa, 2011. Interviewed in Algiers, 24 April.

Bouzeghrane, Nadjia. 2011. "Medelci à l'Assemblée nationale française." *El Watan*, 8 December.

Brown, Jack. 2011. "Algeria's Midwinter Uproar." *Middle East Report*, 20 January.

Charef, Abed. 1989. *Dossier Octobre*. Algiers: Laphomic.

———. 2013a. "Bouteflika déroule tranquillement sa feuille de route." *Le Quotidien d'Oran*, 19 September.

———. 2013b. "Le président Bouteflika reprend la main, le 4ème mandat n'est plus un tabou." *Maghreb Émergent*, 11 September.

Chemakh, Saïd. 2011. Interviewed in Tizi Ouzou, 1 July.

Daoud, Kamel. 2012. "Le printemps arabe: Et si l'Algérie avait raison?" *Jadaliyya*, 20 March. http://www.jadaliyya.com/pages/index/4741/le-printemps-arabe_-et-si-l'algérie-avait-raison-.

Darbouche, Hakim, and Susi Dennison. 2011. "*A 'Reset' with Algeria: The Russia to the EU's South.*" December. European Council on Foreign Relations, Policy Brief.

Dennison, Susi. 2012. "The EU, Algeria and the Northern Mali Question." December. European Council on Foreign Relations, Policy Memo.

Djabi, Nasser. 2010. "Le soutien du FLN reste demandé et nécessaire pour le candidat du système." *El Watan*, 7 November.

Dridi, Daikha. 2011. Interviewed in Algiers, 29 June.

Front des Forces Socialistes. 2011. Interview with FFS officials in Algiers, 21 April.

Grim, Rachid. 2011. Interview. *El Watan*, 6 January.

El Kadi, Ihsane. 2010. "2010: L'Annus Horribilis de Sonatrach." *Maghreb Émergent*, 28 December.

———. 2011. "Les présidentielles, chaînon manquant dans l'agenda de Bouteflika." *Maghreb Émergent*, 6 May.

Hachemaoui, Mohammed. 2013. "Le service de renseignement détient tous les leviers du pouvoir en Algérie," *La Croix*, 1 October.

Hamadi, Riyad. 2013. "Sept colonels de la DCSA mis à la retraite." *Tout sur l'Algérie*, 25 September.

———. 2014. "De hauts gradés du DRS mis à la retraite." *Tout sur l'Algérie*, 13 January.

ICG (International Crisis Group). 2003. "Algeria: Unrest and Impasse in Kabylia." ICG Middle East/North Africa Report no. 15, Cairo/Brussels, 10 June.

K. A. 2013. "Les attributions du vice-ministre de la defense nationale fixées par décret: les nombreuses 'précautions' de Bouteflika." *Le Soir d'Algérie*, 10 October.

Khadda, Naget, and Monique Gadant. 1990. "Mots et choses de la révolte." *Peuples Méditerranéens* 52–53 (July–December).

Khelil, Abdelmoumène. 2011. Interviewed in Algiers, 26 June 2011.

Khelil, Dr. Saïd. 2011. Interviewed in Tizi Ouzou, 1 July 2011.

Korso, Merouane. 2011. "Un jeune en colère: 'Je ne suis pas sorti pour l'huile et le sucre!'" *Maghreb Émergent*, 10 January.

Lamriben, Hocine. 2009. "Flambée des prix des fruits et légumes: Le gouvernement face à ses échecs." *El Watan*, 30 December.

Lardjane, Omar 2011. Interview, Algiers, June 25, 2011.

Loi organique No. 12-01 du 18 Safar 1433 correspondant au 12 janvier 2012 relative au régime electoral. 2012. *Journal Officiel de la République Algérienne Démocratique et Populaire*, 14 January, 8–31.

Loi organique No. 12-02 du 18 Safar 1433 correspondant au 12 janvier 2012 fixant les cas d'incompatibilité avec le mandat parlementaire. 2012. *Journal Officiel de la République Algérienne Démocratique et Populaire*, 14 January, 34–36.

Loi organique No. 12-03 du 18 Safar 1433 correspondant au 12 janvier 2012 fixant les modalités augmentant les chances d'accès de la femme à la représentation dans les assemblées élues. 2012. *Journal Officiel de la République Algérienne Démocratique et Populaire*, 14 January, 39.

Loi organique No. 12-04 du 18 Safar 1433 correspondant au 12 janvier 2012 relative aux partis politiques. 2012. *Journal Officiel de la République Algérienne Démocratique et Populaire*, 15 January, 9–15.

Loi organique No. 12-05 du 18 Safar 1433 correspondant au 12 janvier 2012 relative à l'information. 2012. *Journal Officiel de la République Algérienne Démocratique et Populaire*, 15 January, 18–27.

Loi organique No. 12-06 du 18 Safar 1433 correspondant au 12 janvier 2012 relative aux associations. 2012. *Journal Officiel de la République Algérienne Démocratique et Populaire*, 15 January, 28–34.

Lyès, Sonia. 2013. "Nouveau changement au sein du DRS." *Tout sur l'Algérie*, 12 September.

Makhedi, Madjid. 2013. "Il a reçu hier le chef d'état-major de l'ANP: Bouteflika réapparait à nouveau." *El Watan*, 4 September.

Mandraud, Isabelle. 2011a. "Le pouvoir algérien distribute sans compter la rente pétroliere pour désamorcer la contestation sociale." *Le Monde*, 10 March.

———. 2011b. "Le pouvoir algérien tente de canaliser la contestation sociale et politique." *Le Monde*, 13 March.

Maougal, Mohamed Lakdar. 2011a. Interviewed in Algiers, 1 May.

———. 2011b. Interviewed in Algiers, 26 June.

Moali, Hassan. 2013. "Exploitation politicienne de la restructuration de l'armée: Jeu dangereux du clan présidentiel." *El Watan*, 16 September.
Mohammedi, Djamila (pseudonym). 2012. Interviewed in Algiers, 8 July.
Nadjib, Oussama. 2011a. "Algérie—Émeutes, silence du pouvoir et théorie du complot." *Maghreb Émergent*, 8 January.
———. 2011b. "Pour Bouteflika, l'alternance par les urnes est possible en Algérie." *Maghreb Émergent*, 28 August.
Owen, Roger. 2012. *The Rise and Fall of Arab Presidents for Life*. Cambridge, Mass.: Harvard University Press.
Parks, Robert P. 2012. "Algeria's 10 May 2012 Elections: Preliminary Analysis." *Jadaliyya*, 14 May. http://www.jadaliyya.com/pages/index/5517/algerias-10-may-2012-elections_preliminary-analysis.
"PM Unveils UK-Algeria Security Deal." 2013. Press Association, 30 January.
R. P. 2011. "Mourad Medelci: 'L'audition n'est pas attentatoire à la souveainté nationale.'" *El Watan*, 6 December.
R. P. 2013. "Le colonel Fawzi mis à la retraite." *Liberté*, 22 July.
Rabia, Salim. 2011. "La réforme par les textes de Bouteflika suscite des réactions mitigées." *Maghreb Émergent*, 15 April.
Roberts, Hugh. 2001. "Co-opting Identity: The Manipulation of Berberism, the Frustration of Democratisation and the Generation of Violence in Algeria." London School of Economics, Development Research Centre, Crisis States Programme Working Paper no. 7, December.
———. 2003. *The Battlefield: Algeria 1988–2002. Studies in a Broken Polity*. London: Verso.
———. 2007. "Demilitarizing Algeria. Carnegia Endowment for International Peace, Middle East Program, Carnegie Papers no. 86. Washington, D.C.
———. 2009. *Algeria: The Subterranean Logics of a Non-election*. Madrid: Real Instituto Elcano, 22 April.
———. 2011. "Algeria's National 'Protesta.'" *Foreign Policy*, 10 January. http://mideast.foreignpolicy.com/posts/2011/01/09/algeria_s_national_protesta.
Semiane, Sid Ahmed, ed. 1998. *Octobre, Ils Parlent*. Algiers: Édition Le Matin.
Souaïdia, Habib. 2013. "Révélations sur le drame In-Amenas: Trente otages tués par l'armée algérienne, neufs militaires tués." *Algeria-Watch*, 11 February.
Tadjer, Rafik. 2011. "Hachemi Djiar évoque des 'manipulations.'" *Tout sur l'Algérie*, 7 January. http://www.tsa-algerie.com/-/_13620.html.
Tilly, Charles. 2003. *The Politics of Collective Violence*. Cambridge: Cambridge University Press.
Tlemçani, Rachid. 2011a. Interview in *El Watan*, 10 January.
———. 2011b. Interviewed in Algiers, 29 June.
Tlemçani, Salima. 2013. "De Abdelmalek Guenaïzia à Gaïd Salah: Un compromis entre Bouteflika et l'armée." *El Watan*, 19 September.
"UK 'Would Have Preferred' Notice before Algeria Rescue Bid." 2013. Reuters, 17 January.
Wintour, Patrick. 2013a. "Britain to Work with Algeria on Counter-terrorism, Says David Cameron." *Guardian*, 30 January.
———. 2013b. "David Cameron to Visit Algeria for Talks over In Amenas Siege." *Guardian*, 29 January.
"Zohra Drif-Bitat à Ouyahia: Quand allez vous rendre l'espoir aux algériens?" 2010. *Le Matin.dz*, 21 December. http://www.lematindz.net/news/3565-zohra-drif-bitat-a-ouyahia-quand-allez-vous-rendre-lespoir-aux-algeriens-.html.

Morocco

The Struggle for Political Legitimacy

AMY HAMBLIN

ON THE HEELS OF THE UPRISINGS in Tunisia and Egypt, peaceful demonstrations were staged in fifty-three cities across Morocco on 20 February 2011, drawing tens of thousands of Moroccans to the streets to echo calls heard across the region, with one striking difference. The long list of demands never included the removal of Morocco's political leader, King Mohammed VI, only a limit on his royal powers. Taking its name from the fateful day it began, the 20 February Movement for Change (F20) would galvanize tens of thousands of additional Moroccans to join marches in the spring, but the demonstrations never blossomed into a mass movement. By summer, momentum had dissipated, and the old network of power and privilege emerged unscathed, despite a litany of constitutional reforms.

The regime's response initially relied more on appeasement by adoption than repression, though negotiations were little part of the equation. After salary raises and increased food subsidies failed to preempt the first round of protests on 20 February, the king announced a package of seemingly significant political reforms before the second national day of protests scheduled for 20 March. Having seen events unfold in Tunisia and Egypt, the king chose a controlled process of political evolution over the turmoil of revolution or the violent repression of protests. He received international praise for his deft management of the situation, which was touted as a much-needed "third way" to handling demands for political change.

An analysis of Morocco's social indicators would have suggested that the country shared the same vulnerabilities to unrest as other Arab states experiencing uprisings. In addition to high rates of poverty, corruption, and income inequality,[1] the country also was grappling with the volatile mix of a large and idle youth population. The 30 percent of the population between the ages of fifteen and twenty-nine were experiencing greater degrees of social exclusion than older segments of the population; nearly half of Moroccan youth were neither in school nor in the workforce, according to a 2012 World Bank survey. Moreover, this population was scarcely represented in the country's political institutions. Yet, Morocco was not gripped by mass demonstrations and social upheaval seen in some of the other countries in the region. It proved to be a case of short-track adaptation where the regime was able to stem the tide early before the protest movement threatened its vital interests.

The objective of this chapter is to explain the case of short-track adaptation in Morocco, or in other words, why the F20 protest movement failed to spark a mass uprising and why the regime chose to respond with a reform package. The lens of political legitimacy provides the best analytical tool to understanding the particularities of the Moroccan case. The traditional and religious legitimacy of the throne constrained the demands and efficacy of the protest movement and enhanced the ability of the king to intervene effectively. Moreover, F20's lack of popular legitimacy allowed the king to appease the population without resorting to direct negotiations with the movement.

THE POLITICAL SYSTEM BEFORE 20 FEBRUARY

The Alawite dynasty to which King Mohammed VI belongs stretches back more than 350 years. The royal family's resilience in the face of shifting political winds derives in part from its alleged descent from the Prophet Mohammed and in part by its co-optation of democratic forces by adopting many of the modern structures of democracy, including a bicameral parliament. The appearance of democratic reform belies the fact that power in all its forms is concentrated in the hands of the king, who serves not only as the head of state but also as the commander-in-chief of the armed forces and the commander of the faithful. Under the constitution prior to 2012, the king was responsible for appointing the prime minister and cabinet members and could dissolve parliament at any point or intervene in government affairs to change policy.[2]

The king's absolute power has gone unchallenged in parliament. Of the thirty-four legally recognized parties, only four, known as the radical left, call for a change to the current distribution of power, and these parties have not performed well at the polls. Three of these parties support the establishment of a "parliamentary monarchy," in which the king is mostly stripped of his political power and serves a more symbolic role. Running a joint list under the banner of the Democratic Alliance of the Left, these three parties won only 1 percent of the seats in parliament in 2007. The fourth party comprising the radical left, Annahj Addimocrati, calls for the abolishment of the monarchy and refuses to participate in elections under the current political system.

The religious and traditional legitimacy derived from the throne, strengthened by the popular legitimacy of elections, has rendered the Moroccan political system more resilient to attack than republics. Because Morocco's heritage and national identity are inextricably linked to the Alawite family, changing political leadership carries far graver implications than in the region's republics. Royal power can be diminished, but the bloodline requirement and the divinely ordained nature of the throne means that the king generally cannot be replaced without sacking the monarchical system altogether, and thus forsaking a potent symbol of national identity and unity. This acts as a natural constraint on opposition forces in a country still largely in favor of retaining the monarchy. So although Morocco's monarchy may appear more brittle compared to secular authoritarian and democratic regimes in which the leader can be replaced without overthrowing the system, the reality is that the Moroccan system has proven to be more durable because of its large traditional population unwilling to aggressively attack the institution of monarchy.

The Moroccan monarchical system also enjoys a second advantage over other regime types: the unique role a king can play as political arbiter. The sacred and protected status of the king allows him to act in the role as arbiter of the political system, intervening to quell public anger when it threatens the system's stability. This is commonly achieved by dissolving parliament to signal that the government is responsive to public cries for change. The scapegoat tactic is effective to the extent that the public believes that parliament is the political center of gravity and that the king is above the political fray. It is unclear to what extent the public believes the king is mired in the corruption of the *makhzen*. The term, originally meaning "storehouse" or "magazine," refers to "the apparatus of power, constituted as a chain from the sovereign who receives his power from God and passing without interruption down through the ministers, governors, and local authorities down to the doorman" (Pascon and Bentahar 1969, 228). In other words, the *makhzen* is "the place where power is concentrated and the resources used to exercise it are concentrated" (Michaux-Bellaire and Gaillard 1909, 2).

The king is better positioned to act as arbiter because his legitimacy is protected from attack by both the legal ban on criticism and practical barriers, which other political actors do not enjoy in Morocco. Legal risks aside, it is politically unwise to attack the behavior of the king, or the special economic and political privileges he enjoys, because it invites accusations of being against Islam. As demonstrated by F20, even criticizing the political distribution of power is fraught with political landmines because it calls into question the judgment of the highest religious authority in the country.

King Mohammed VI came to power at the height of optimism about the country's political development. After the brutal thirty-eight-year reign of King Hassan II, many Moroccans were clamoring for change, and King Mohammed VI quickly sought to establish himself as the reformer that many hoped he would be. The year before, the royal succession the Socialist Movement of Popular Forces (USFP) won parliamentary elections, marking the first significant change in power. Just as the king disappointed many democratic reformists with the passage of time, so the USFP fell short of expectations. It became indistinguishable from the parties under the control of the *makhzen*, underscoring the systemic constraints that stymied reform. Political inertia in parliament eroded public confidence in the institution's ability to enact policies capable of achieving tangible improvements in people's daily lives. Voter apathy was reflected in the dismal turnout figures for the 2007 parliamentary elections, which plummeted to 37 percent from 52 percent in 2002 (International Institute 2012). Similarly, faith in the king's desire for reform also had deteriorated by the time of the Arab Spring. Although the king had ushered in reforms, most notably with the family status code, education, and decentralization, the pace had been slow, and there were occasional reversals in progress made on human rights issues. Unsurprisingly, the king did not appear willing to push for reforms that would diminish his power.

It is impossible to gauge the popularity of the king in the absence of polling data and given the legal constraints on criticism of the palace. However, he is believed to be widely popular, in part due to the legitimacy of the throne and in part due to his image as a reformer. He also has benefited from the contrast with his father, King Hassan II, who reigned during the bloody "Years of Lead" in which the government took a hard line with dissent.

Although King Mohammed VI appears to have retained his personal popularity, the largest opposition group in Morocco, Al Adl wal Ihsane (Justice and Charity [JC]), does not recognize the sacred status of the king. Founded by a Sufi spiritual leader, the JC is focused on Islamization of society with the end goal to peacefully establish an Islamist system of government based on shariʿa law, a goal more or less shared with the Salafi Jihadis. However, the Jihadis seek to achieve this goal through violent overthrow. The exact governance structure sought by the JC has never been clearly or consistently articulated, since its focus has been on Islamization. The JC also has been intentionally ambiguous as to whether it opposes the institution of monarchy in the interim, or only the religious claims and misrule of King Hassan II and his son. The group's founder and charismatic leader, Sheikh Abdessalam Yassine, rose to prominence for his public condemnation of King Hassan's despotic rule and was imprisoned and under house arrest for seventeen years for his open opposition to the king. Furthermore, the group's motto is, "No king in Islam," but official JC spokesperson Fathallah Arsalane declared in a December 2011 interview with *Maroc Hebdo* that the organization has "no problem with the King" ("Interview" 2011).

Banned from the political system, the JC has undergone periods of heightened repression, but it has frequently been allowed to pursue its program of Islamizing society through grassroots activities. Under Yassine's leadership, the JC refused to engage in any "political" activity that would associate it with the government. Since the death of Yassine in 2012, the new JC leadership has expressed interest in incorporating a political party, although no further steps have been taken as the palace's position does not appear to have changed (Morocco World News 2013). Unlike Nahdha in Tunisia and the Muslim Brotherhood in Egypt, which ran candidates under the cover of other parties before the uprisings, the JC has never competed in elections. It also must contend with the Islamist Party of Justice and Development (PJD). While Nahdha and the Muslim Brotherhood have monopolized Islamist support until the recent rise of Salafists, the Islamist community in Morocco is divided primarily between the PJD and the JC. The latter is thought to enjoy the most support. Figures on the size of the JC's membership range from a hundred thousand to five million, with the real number likely to be closer to the conservative estimate.[3] Some analysts believe the group's support has waned since 2006, the year that some supporters believed there would be an uprising, which never materialized (Benchemsi 2012).

THE RISE OF THE 20 FEBRUARY MOVEMENT

Within the context of a stalled political reform process and rising socioeconomic grievances among the youth, the regional unrest inspired a new generation in Morocco to build a movement that eschewed the structure and ideology that had weakened past political forces. F20 is a product of its time, including the digital space, adopting similar operating structures and strategies to protest movements in Tunisia and Egypt. F20's decentralized, participatory structure was reflective of the ethos of the Web. The structure also reflected the fear that a chain of command would make leaders targets for repression and co-option by the regime.

F20 began with a Facebook group called Moroccans Converse with the King, created in the midst of the upheaval of Tunisia as an outlet for frustrated Moroccans to express their own grievances. The start of the Egyptian uprising fueled the growth of the Moroccans Converse with the King Facebook group and emboldened Moroccans to make similar demands of their government. The group changed its name to Freedom and Democracy Now, reflecting its escalating demands and boldness toward the regime. The Facebook group sought to harness the momentum for reform revealed through online discussions by announcing 20 February as a day for offline demonstrations. When Freedom and Democracy Now issued the call to action, no planning had taken place, revealing the lack of the group coordination and the true grassroots origins of F20.

F20's internal negotiations for coalition and formulation of the protest platform were chaotic, the natural product of the sudden flowering of the movement online and later offline without any centralized planning. More Facebook groups were created with the aim of mobilizing local populations for 20 February. Surprisingly, these groups operated autonomously and only shared the original "Freedom and Democracy" platform and the 10 a.m. start time for demonstrations. A video posted on its website by one of the group's administrators, Oussama El-Khlifi, became a small sensation online and unintentionally served as the group's manifesto. In the video, Khlifi declared his demands for reform, while donning a beret and a Palestinian scarf, which earned the former member of the Socialist Party's youth wing the title of Che Guevara of Salé. Online fervor piqued with the release of a web video featuring thirteen young activists, each stating their personal reasons for protesting. The video was meant to display the diversity of reasons for protesting. The video quickly became the main publicity tool for the demonstrations, surpassing the popularity of the Khlifi video with more than half a million views on YouTube within ten days of its release (Benchemsi 2012).

The offline architecture of the group grew in the same spontaneous, sporadic, grassroots fashion as the online form of F20. Local chapters were organized independently in cities across the country, the composition of each chapter negotiated locally and determined by existing local political forces. In Tangiers, for example, labor groups played a more significant role, while in Casablanca the Unified Socialist Party (PSU) helped younger activists organize, whereas in Marrakech there was no prominent political group that got involved (Benchemsi 2012). Because coalitions were forged first at the local level, significant decisions such as whether to include the JC were based on local considerations but influenced the national image of the protest movement. Moreover, the lack of a national body to act as a gatekeeper for the coalition-building process undermined the emergence of a national strategic vision for the movement. For example, the decision by Casablanca activists to extend an invitation to attend a local planning meeting to JC youth leaders helped precipitate the endorsement of the national JC organization, even though not all chapters would have supported the move (Benchemsi 2012).

To the extent that there was national coordination within the official movement, it happened informally through conversations between organizers in various cities and via a contagion model in which the decision of one chapter would be voluntarily adopted by other chapters, without much negotiation. The most prominent example of the contagion model was the Casablanca chapter's rule to ban gender segregation and religious slogans, which was then adopted by all the other chapters (Benchemsi 2012). The Rabat chapter tended to exert the most influence of any local chapters, in part because it was located in the capital city, and activists there were behind the initial online movement. Several defining elements of F20 can be traced back to the decisions made at one of the founding meetings of the Rabat group in early February, including the rule that there would be no leader and the creation of a new Facebook page dedicated to upcoming protests (Rahman 2012).

Although moderate, secular youth helped propel F20 initially, leftist parties and Islamists filled out the ranks of the movement as it mushroomed, a tenuous alliance that only worked thanks to the Casablanca rule. Instead of negotiating a coalition with like-minded groups, the movement attracted a wide array of sympathizers and their diverse causes. The stated nonideological character of the group, however, created an identity crisis and brought the secular vanguard into conflict with the sizeable segment of Islamists.

Unable to negotiate a coherent coalition, the uprisers could not arrive at a single formula to guide their actions. The problem was compounded by the fact that decision making occurred at the local level. Each local "general assembly" maintained its own private Facebook group, which was used to communicate information and facilitate discussion (Chapouly 2011). However, decision making occurred primarily offline through boisterous, freewheeling weekly meetings during which anyone could speak for unlimited time. Decisions were made based on an assessment of the prevailing opinion. Members of F20 feared that voting would highlight divisions and alienate those with dissenting opinions. The value placed on group consensus led to general assemblies adopting vague and simplistic guidelines and messaging.

While no formal coordination took place on a national level within F20, activities were coordinated outside the official F20 structure by a coalition of forty civil society groups. The National Council for Support of the 20 February Movement was formed in Rabat two days after the initial protests and included Democratic Alliance of the Left parties, Annahj Addimocrati, the Moroccan Association of Human Rights (AMDH) and the JC. As its name suggests, the coalition sought to support the decisions and activities led by the F20 youth (Benchemsi 2012). Even if the coalition had aspired to play a more active role in shaping the protest movement, it would have been difficult given the ideological diversity of the member groups that divided the support council along the same political fault lines as the F20 itself, even though the JC claims to have accepted less representation on the council for reasons similar to the Muslim Brotherhood in Egypt's uprising. The group wanted to build bridges with secular groups that were wary of the JC and avoid the image of an Islamist-dominated uprising, which would invite a more draconian response from the government (Masbah 2014).

The process of negotiating the movement's demands was shaped by the same forces driving the coalition-building process, with the lack of a centralized hierarchy being the most important. The Facebook page for Freedom and Democracy Now (2011) published the first set of demands on 27 January: (1) Reform the constitution; (2) Dissolve the parliament, the government, and political parties that have contributed to political corruption, and appoint an interim government; (3) Take concrete and tangible steps to alleviate the suffering of the Moroccan people, and create an emergency fund to offset unemployment; and (4) Release all political prisoners.

Without the legitimacy of a formal drafting process, the initial set of demands was quickly revised as more formal offline structures were formed. A second, more expansive platform with twenty demands was negotiated among the Rabat activists and released on 6 February. The jump in the number of demands highlighted the rapid bandwagoning taking place as activists with diverse causes attached themselves to the budding movement. New demands included recognition of Tamazight (Berber) as an official language and an end to the privatization of "strategic sectors." The second platform also featured a significant shift in the stance toward the monarchy. The first demand was to "change the style of rule from absolute monarchy to a parliamentary monarchy where all the power and sovereignty belongs to the people." This platform was not widely publicized, although at least a paper copy of it was circulated with the official F20 logo.

Reflecting the internal power struggle between various factions on the contentious issue of the monarchy, the next version of the platform released on 17 February omitted the demand for a parliamentary monarchy. Annahj Addimocrati and the JC opposed the use of the term *parliamentary monarchy* as a demand because it implied the continuation of the monarchy (Chapouly 2011). The revised, pared-down platform also was formulated by Rabat activists and was announced at a press conference at the Moroccan Association of Human Rights on 17 February in Rabat. The public, offline nature of the declaration at the AMDH headquarters gave legitimacy and some permanence to the new set of demands. The demands were further entrenched when they were posted to the new F20 Facebook page created by the same Rabat activists. The demands were the same as the original list posted on the "Freedom and Democracy Now" page with the addition of two more demands: the recognition of the Berber language and the creation of an independent judiciary. After the list of demands, there was an additional section on the socioeconomic goals they hoped would be achieved with the implementation of political reforms. In other words, they believed that corrections to the political system would improve socioeconomic conditions. The stated socioeconomic goals called for the integration of unemployed graduates into the public sector through transparent and fair competition and a dignified life for all, achieved in part through higher wages and access for the poor to public services. The already long list of national demands was embellished with additional demands by local chapters. For example, the Marrakech chapter focused on such issues as the forced relocation of four thousand families, sex tourism, and inadequate local hospitals.

The chaotic process of negotiating the coalition and demands of F20 was shaped by two main and related factors: the Internet and youth leadership. Even after F20 developed into an offline movement, it still clearly bore the markings of its online origins. The strong digital component to F20 did not determine the structure and nature of the group, but it undoubtedly facilitated the adoption of a flat, decentralized structure. The Internet enabled youth operating outside of formal organizations to spontaneously come together and as low-resource actors to reach a wide audience via social media. Moreover, their online campaigns generated more momentum than established groups could achieve, forcing these groups to bandwagon and play a supporting role to the youth leaders of F20.

The mostly secular, youth leadership of F20 also contributed to the adoption of a decentralized, participatory structure, as well as the broad ideological nature of the coalition. These youth had grown up in the ethos of Internet culture, where hierarchies had fallen away. Youth also tend to be excluded from the hierarchies of power and naturally chafe at the rigidity of such structures. The pervasive desire to keep the movement free of ideology was based on a strategic calculation about the efficacy of a big-tent approach, as well as the principle of inclusion. Many of the youth in F20 had previously been involved in the youth arms of political organizations. About half of the attendees at the founding general assembly in Casablanca were from leftist parties and civil society organizations (Benchemsi 2012). However, these activists had seen the failure of the older generation to bring reform by working along narrow, ideological lines.

Although F20 incorporated existing political forces, it should be viewed as a spontaneous and isolated political phenomenon rather than the culmination of past political movements. There is little sign that the advocacy campaigns in the preceding decade increased social awareness of political problems, built public support for a reform agenda, or galvanized people to take action. The most successful protest movement in the past decade—the National Association of Unemployed Graduates for Morocco (ANDCM)—did not share F20's call for sweeping social and political change. Instead, the group consisted of unemployed graduates trying to increase employment opportunities in the already bloated public sector. Digital activism campaigns had generated controversy for pushing the boundaries of acceptable political speech but had not enjoyed significant support.

THE ARC OF THE MOVEMENT

The pattern of mobilization in Morocco was distinct from other cases during the Arab Spring in that the movement grew at a slower rate before peaking and never escalated to the use of violent tactics. Yet, there was significant enough energy around the protest movement to prompt the king to make seemingly bold political reforms. This particular arc can be characterized as a short-track adaptation, forged out of F20's constraints and the effective royal response. Protracted mobilization is not necessarily problematic so long as a movement does not idle. New tactics, strategies, coalition building, or political conditions can create opportunities for a movement to achieve its goals. An analysis of F20's growth, however, shows that its protracted mobilization was a consequence of its own failings and constraints. The first phase of mobilization revealed societal constraints, while the second and third phases showed the internal constraints within F20 that kept it from adapting to the onset of negative political conditions.

The first phase can be characterized by the emergence of F20 and the building of momentum behind the movement. There were already indications, however, during this phase of the limits of F20. What quietly transpired on 21 February 2011 was the clearest sign of the bumpy road ahead for F20, and for this reason, it deserves as much attention as the day before it. After the first round of major demonstrations on 20 February protest organizers decided to wait another month to regroup and strategize before the next major day of demonstrations on

20 March. Smaller pockets of protest could be found the next day, but they were snuffed out with police violence, according to Amnesty International (2011). This detail in the story of F20 is noteworthy for two reasons. First, the small protests on the second day could be easily dispersed with police violence because the number of participants had dwindled substantially. This suggests that people were not ready to pour into the streets to protest at the first sign of tolerance by the police. The other interesting aspect of the second day of protests was the police's response. The change in police tactics suggests that the regime was more alarmed than it might have seemed and that it was calculating the risks and costs of repression. The same strategic use of police violence occurred again on 13 March when smaller crowds protesting the king's speech were dispersed by police wielding batons. Many protesters were injured, and more than a hundred were arrested, to be released later that day according to Human Rights Watch (2011).

Although the immediate aftermath of 20 February foretold of the challenges and constraints that would hamper the movement, momentum appeared to be building until the king's television address on 9 March in which he offered a multitude of concessions (Moroccans 2011). His offer of partial reforms that did not directly address F20 was a bold attempt to regain initiative and thus control over the reform agenda. The king outlined a number of reforms including free parliamentary elections, the establishment of a commission to revise the constitution, increased independence of the judiciary, a rule that the prime minister be chosen from the party with the most seats in parliament, and recognition of the Berber identity. The speech did not mention the demonstrations. The king appointed a commission composed of pro-regime supporters to review the constitution and draft recommendations within the framework provided by him. Although F20 was not represented on the commission, members of F20 were invited to participate in the consultative process. All those invited refused to take part on the grounds that the process was undemocratic and beholden to the interests of the *makhzen* (Benchemsi 2012).

The king's speech, however, provided the first challenge to the unity of the group. It created hairline fissures within F20 that would widen as political conditions deteriorated and put stress on the group. In a magazine interview, Abdallah Aballagh, a founding member of F20, admitted: "Within the group, opinions differ. Some want to rely on the speech to [make new demands]. Others want to strictly stick to the demands of the movement, written by the founding members before the march on February 20 published on Facebook and other sites. The founding members do not want to rely on the speech. We want to continue to push for reforms" (Rachidi 2011). As would be expected, major political parties, such as Istiqlal, the Socialist Union of Popular Forces (USFP), and the PJD, with a stake in the existing political system, extolled the king's proposed reforms (Fakir 2011). Although these parties never endorsed F20, many of their members had participated in the movement.

Most of the nonestablishment F20 forces were not ready to concede so easily and crafted their response to continue applying pressure by calling for the election of a representative body to write the new constitution, rather than a royal commission.

The concessions produced two countervailing effects on public opinion: the protest victory won support from those who were initially doubtful about F20's impact, but the speech lost F20 support from people who wanted socioeconomic or political reforms but were deferent to the king's judgment. In the short term, it was not immediately clear that the king would regain the upper hand by offering a partial reform package as turnout appeared to increase for the two following national days of demonstrations on 20 March 20 and 24 April.[4] Some analysts have speculated that the king's speech had the opposite intended effect in the short term and boosted participation in the protest movement by signaling regime weakness (Errazzouki, interview, 17 July 2012). Jack A. Goldstone and Charles Tilly (2001, 188–189) have noted that leaders always risk this possibility: "Modest concessions can lead to increased demands for further change, either because of the de Tocqueville effect—minor changes made by the regime are an advertisement of its illegitimacy, but do not fully correct that illegitimacy, and thus lead to greater demands for elimination or transformation of the regime—or because the concessions attract other supporters who now feel that they too can extract more from the regime." However, it does not seem that the speech delegitimized the king or the *makhzen* over the long term.

In fact, the short-term narrative of growing F20 momentum was deceiving because the speech had capped the limit of the movement's growth, and the short-term growth allowed organizational issues to be ignored. The king won the battle against F20 from the moment he gave the speech and F20 could only counter with a call for an elected constitution writing body. Of the hitherto neutral or apathetic segment of the population, the reform package kept more people ambivalent or turned them against F20 than it converted people to the protest movement. The reforms showed the king to be reasonable and willing to respond to his people, while F20 appeared more intransigent, unwilling to acknowledge the significance of the king's reforms. The vast majority of Moroccans did not want to suffer from complete political upheaval and were willing to settle for what the king had offered. This was not as clear at the time because the protest movement was growing; it had maintained the majority of its original support base and then added more people following the speech.

The period of May to June marked a new phase for the opposition movement as adverse political conditions began to turn the tide against the burgeoning movement. The festivity of earlier protests vanished as crowds dwindled and the government implemented a zero tolerance policy with street protests. The national mood turned somber with the rising violence in other countries in the region and an unrelated terrorist attack on 28 April in Marrakech, which killed seventeen people. Although the attack has not been linked to F20, it still played into the fear that terrorist organizations would capitalize on the instability created by the protest movement. Calls for national unity cut into support for F20.

Amid pressure, fissures widened within the group, and protest fatigue set in among nonactivists. The movement began to shrink, shedding many of its moderate elements but retaining the core support of the Islamists and radical leftists, alongside the smaller contingent of founding youth. The government capitalized on the shrinking numbers and shifting composition of the movement by implementing its first national crackdown on protesters on 22 May. The government blamed JC, the leftist Democratic Approach party, and the Salafist Jihadi group for trying to instigate unrest. Communications minister Khalid Naciri told Reuters: "They don't want democratic reform. Authorities have to deal with people who use the February 20 Movement to serve the agenda of three different groups. Their goal is to kill democracy. The February 20 Movement needs to be cautious" (Karam 2011). Many life-threatening injuries were sustained during the clashes with police on 22 May, foreshadowing the death of the first protester, Kamel Ammari, who was beaten by the police on 30 May (Karam and Tanner 2011). His death produced countervailing reactions much as the king's speech, which initially aided the protesters, but the effect that would dominate favored the king. The regime crossed the threshold of blood, and this temporarily injected new life into the movement as more than sixty thousand people took to the streets on 5 June (Abdennebi and Nasr 2011). However, the internal pressure within F20 to take a strong stance was counterbalanced by public pressure to de-escalate the situation before more blood was spilled. The spike in protest activity also fizzled with the emergence of pro-government thugs harassing and attacking protesters and the unveiling of the new draft of the constitution on 17 July. At the same time, and since the beginning of the uprising, government agents contacted movement leaders to ascertain possibilities for negotiation and to co-opt members with jobs. While employment was occasionally available in the event, negotiations were not.

In the midst of escalating tensions, F20's decision to boycott the referendum dealt the final coup to F20 as a major political force. The referendum pitted F20 squarely against the king, who took to the airwaves to personally urge voters to approve the new constitution. Not only did F20's official position place the movement outside of the political mainstream, which was influenced by the king's strong endorsement and the flood of advertising in support of the "yes" vote, but it also led to a further splintering of the F20 membership. The constitution was approved by 98 percent of voters with a reported 73 percent turnout. The referendum also drove a wedge into the existing base of support for F20. As tensions were escalating in Libya, Bahrain, Yemen, and Syria, many saw the bloody conflicts as a sign of what would lie ahead for Morocco if they continued down the same path. From this perspective, the constitutional reform process sponsored by the king appeared more productive than the tumultuous path taken in other countries in the region.

The palace's resounding victory with the referendum on 1 July marked the beginning of the final, moribund phase of the movement. The movement had been declining since the start of the second phase, but its numbers collapsed after the referendum results as morale plummeted and the movement seemed lost. In the absence of a new strategy to regain momentum, F20 continued to stage weekly Sunday protests of dwindling magnitude. The decision to also boycott the 25 November parliamentary elections reinforced the image of F20 as an unproductive and ineffective political force. The sweeping victory that brought the Islamist but pro-*makhzen* Justice and Development Party (PJD) to power for the first time dominated headlines and completed the narrative of political change, which had started with the constitutional reform process. Already weakened, the withdrawal of the JC in mid-December led to the collapse of F20. The JC continued to support F20 but felt that it was no longer worth making themselves a target for the regime in order to benefit their main Islamist rival, while suppressing their religious rhetoric in order to participate in the coalition (Masbah 2014). JC spokesperson Fathallah Arsalane stated in the 23–29 December 2011 edition of *Maroc Hebdo* magazine: "Continuing to protest in the streets every Sunday with repetitive slogans and no thought toward evolving accomplishes nothing." According to the same spokesperson, F20 had stagnated "because it has been taken hostage by certain extremist groups that want to limit the boundaries of its actions and demands."

A STRUGGLE FOR LEGITIMACY

Unpopular dictatorships are maintained in part by immobilizing fear and collective action coordination problems. A common concept in contentious politics literature is the idea of "collective action dilemmas," which explain the continuation of authoritarianism even when a majority would support regime change. As sociologist Zeynep Tufekci (2011) explains:

> A society-level collective action problem arises under an autocracy when costs of dissent are high for individuals and the means of organizing to overcome the dilemma are stifled. Thus, under autocracies, torture and arbitrary and lengthy prison sentences are not just expressions of capricious cruelty, but key mechanisms which allow these regimes to survive. When even a whiff of dissent is met with disproportionate response, this creates a strong disincentive for any individual to be among the first.

Once the barrier of fear crumbled in Egypt and Tunisia, people poured into the streets to express their discontent. Fear of repression in Morocco, however, did not seem to present the most significant obstacle to mobilization. Even after the police showed clear restraint during the first round of national protests, there was no immediate explosion in participation in the days after F20.

The Moroccan system, rather, was maintained through political ambivalence; there was no clear and shared understanding of the problem and how to solve it due to the king's legitimacy and the divisiveness of his role in politics. If the interaction between a protest movement and a regime is framed as a political struggle for the legitimacy to represent the demands of the public, then any opposition movement in Morocco would have faced significant barriers in winning broad public support because of the royal juggernaut of religious and traditional legitimacy. The fact that no significant call to topple the Moroccan monarchy emerged during the heady early days of the Arab Spring suggests that royal legitimacy was not considered a strategic target. This conclusion is also supported by the JC's willingness to participate in F20, rather than lead its own protests calling for an overthrow of the monarchy.

If Morocco did not appear ripe for revolution, even the lesser goal of forced evolution toward a true constitutional monarchy remained difficult to achieve. Any group would have found it enormously challenging to delegitimize the system when the leader of it was seen as legitimate. The religious authority of the king created an ambivalence among a large segment of the population toward reforming the system without his leadership over the process. When challenged by new actors with unclear objectives, the king was more likely to receive the benefit of the doubt. The gap in trust between the king and new challengers was naturally compounded by his control over mass media and the dependency of half the population that is illiterate on broadcast media. The impact of these issues is explored further below.

Royal legitimacy also put F20 at a disadvantage in terms of its platform. By trying to avoid a personal attack on the sacred figure of the king by focusing on institutional reform, F20 adopted a platform that was contradictory and unable to stir popular enthusiasm with its nuance. Even though F20 officially supported the king, its demand for a constitutional monarchy—even though this was omitted from the final set of written demands—was still an implicit rebuke of the king, whose prerogative should not be questioned in the eyes of many Moroccans. One of the main chants adopted by protesters, "Down with absolutism!" showed that F20's position was equivalent to standing against tyranny but not the tyrant. While this slogan supported the F20 platform of constitutional monarchy, it was too nuanced a position for a popular movement.

In targeting institutions rather than personalities, organizers diluted the mobilizing potential of the movement. Focusing anger and efforts on the removal of one person as an initial step helps to unify and energize a diverse coalition of actors. In Morocco, there was no consensus culprit for all that ailed the country. When discussing the country's problems, Moroccans were more likely to reference the nebulous *makhzen* than the king or any other individual.

THE PARTICULAR TROUBLES OF F20

Any political opposition movement to emerge in Morocco during the spring of 2011 would have been constrained by the legitimacy of the monarchy. The specific character and decisions taken by F20, however, also contributed to the failure of the movement to garner broader public support and assert greater pressure on the king. In certain respects, F20 suffered the same problems that would plague the protest movements in Tunisia and Egypt. The accelerated timeline in the latter countries allowed for diverse actors to unite initially around a clear target of their frustration in Ben Ali and Mubarak, swept away by the euphoria and chaos of crowds. A critical analysis of the long-term objectives of these movements and efforts to negotiate a focus of demands and a formula for the future would come later and would occupy the long aftermath of the overthrow. The protracted nature of the Moroccan case exposed and exacerbated the inherent flaws of such spontaneous movements—the fragility of ideologically diverse coalitions, the lack of strategic and charismatic leadership, the ambiguous goals, and the lack of an ideology to help motivate supporters through difficult times.

The most significant reason why F20 failed to mass mobilize must be attributed to the movement's inability to define itself and present a coherent, compelling narrative. The movement's messaging problem arose from the semiclosed nature of the media environment and the leaderless, decentralized structure of the group. The state-run media portrayed F20 as a group of extreme Islamists and leftists bent on destabilizing the country. The Polisario Front, the armed rebel group fighting for independence of the Western Sahara, along with the government of Algeria, was reported to be behind F20, stirring fears that the country would be seized by violent conflict.

Even outside of state-run media, coverage of F20 and the king's response was hindered by the prevalent practice of self-censorship. Morocco ranked 135 out of 178 countries in terms of the freedom of its press in 2010 by Reporters without Borders. A 2009 report by the organization stated: "Although Morocco now tolerates more media criticism and more editorial freedom, the Palace still does not accept that the media have an important role to play. It allows some leeway to print media journalists because only 1 per cent of the population buys newspapers and magazines. And only a few newspapers such as *TelQuel* and *Le Journal hebdomadaire* are really independent." Despite increasing editorial freedom to discuss previously red-line issues such as the monarchy, government, Islam, and the Western Sahara, journalists still risked lawsuits if they tackled such sensitive topics.

The poor education system and high illiteracy rate made it easier for the government to sell their narrative of events and frame F20 in unfavorable terms. Nearly half the adult population in Morocco is illiterate, according to the UN Development Program. This segment is more dependent on tightly controlled broadcast news for its information and is unable to access alternative perspectives offered through written online media. By contrast, F20 was heavily reliant on online media and social media sites to disseminate its message; therefore, its reach was far more limited than that of the regime. F20 did fully exploit the opening online platforms offered by creating a citizen media site to serve as a hub for information on the protests. The site's mission statement indicates that "Mamfakinch.com does not pretend to be a newspaper but a citizen media that believes in the right to access to information. Information often ignored or distorted in other more or less official media." Mamfakinch, however, could not correct for the inaccessibility of online content to illiterates.

The challenging media environment aside, the cacophony of voices and demands made it difficult to decipher what the movement represented. Despite the movement's stated and agreed-upon demands, there was concern about a "hidden" agenda of participating groups, some of which had held positions in the past that contradicted the official platform of F20. The three political parties that form the Democratic Alliance of the Left called for a "parliamentary monarchy," while Annahj Addimocrati seeks to abolish the monarchy, and it is believed that the JC holds a similar position. Such concerns regarding the F20 platform were deepened by ideological rows within the movement, which were aired in public. A cofounder of the original Facebook group that issued the call for nationwide protests on 20 February announced the day beforehand that he and his group were withdrawing their support due to the involvement of the JC. "After announcing their intention to join the February 20 protest, it emerged in discussions with them that they don't want to make a firm commitment in terms of respect for the monarchy," Rachid Antid told Reuters in a 19 February article ("Morocco" 2011).

Beyond the troubles with messaging and branding, F20 was hurt by its flat, decentralized decision-making structure that made negotiations unmanageable. Similar problems manifested in Egypt and Tunisia but were partially mitigated by the leadership of the Muslim Brotherhood and Nahdha, even if many participants in those uprisings refuse to submit to their leadership. The lack of strong, centralized leadership was not a problem in the short run when the initial euphoria of collective action brought group cohesion and broad consensus on the direction of the movement. If the movement had one clear leader or organization that would signal an ideological preference, the diversity of F20's coalition would have narrowed, but it also may have been more manageable. The movement's flat leadership structure, however, was not durable because it did not support nimble decision making, as well as agenda and messaging development. At several critical moments, the movement was unable to adapt to the changing circumstances. When F20 required a new strategy to respond to the king's proposed reform measures, the organization became gridlocked and could only agree to criticize the undemocratic drafting process of the constitution, rather than offer a counter proposal. While a legitimate critique, an attack on the undemocratic drafting process—as traditionally conducted in Morocco—does not resonate with the majority of citizens. Without visionary leadership, the default response of taking to the streets prevailed, even after it had become counterproductive. As nonactivists began to drop out in May and June, the movement became increasingly insular. At the chaotic general assembly meetings where anyone could have unlimited floor time, the most uncompromising and vociferous voices generally won out and alienated more moderate supporters. Decision making by taking the "trend" also diluted the movement's messaging to the point of trite pro-democracy slogans. Of course, this would have been an issue with any coalition as ideologically diverse as F20; however, a smaller executive committee may have been able to make more progress, as suggested by Ahmed Benchemsi (2012).

By choosing a "big-tent" approach and adopting the organizational structure to support such a broad coalition, F20 made a trade-off about which its leaders seemed unaware. The organizational structure and style adopted by F20 broadened its base of support and facilitated mass mobilization. But it was a short-term bargain. The vagueness of the movement's agenda, a cumbersome decision-making process, and the absence of an inspiring leader or ideology to unify the ranks all decreased the ability of the movement to withstand challenges.

CONTAINING THE MOVEMENT

The regime's response also played a role in limiting the size of the protests and mitigating the impact to the existing political order. Protest movements inherently call into question the legitimacy of a regime, even if they do not directly call for overthrow. The fact that citizens are taking to the streets rather than addressing their concerns through normal political channels signals a failure in the political system (Zartman 1995). Therefore, regimes must renew their legitimacy using negative means (such as discrediting or quashing the protest movement) or positive means (such as enacting reforms). Regime response is conditioned by the regime type and the costs of various actions in a given situation. Goldstone and Tilly (2001, 179–194) have argued that liberal democratic regimes are more likely to respond with concessions while authoritarian regimes are likely to respond with repression to protest movements due to differing cost structures. The cost in terms of regime support is a product of the legitimacy of a response, which in turn is determined largely by the regime type. In other words, a liberal democratic regime will face higher costs for using violence than an authoritarian regime because it is not seen as a legitimate response. Regime type influences the overall direction of the response (e.g., violence or concessions) but the precise calibration of a nonviolent response depends on two additional factors: the popular legitimacy of the regime and the protesters, and the availability of actors both within the regime and within or external to the protest movement who are willing to pact.

King Mohammed VI cleverly chose a combination of positive and negative tactics to reassert the legitimacy of his regime in what some have touted as the "third way" for handling the unrest that swept the region. The regime's response could be characterized by three defining elements: the selective use of repression, the co-option of the protest movement's reform agenda, and the smear campaign against the movement. The king's decision to act unilaterally by appointing a constitution-drafting committee rather than engaging in negotiations with F20 also is noteworthy and is explored in more detail below. The decision-making process at the palace was as opaque and undemocratic as F20's was transparent and participatory. While decisions were taken—and often announced—in the name of the king, negotiations for coalition and response formulation went on among his advisers within the walls of the palace. For this reason, it is impossible to know precisely how the Moroccan regime arrived at its response. However, a number of factors appear to have shaped the response.

As far as the constraints of regime type, the Moroccan political system falls somewhere between brutal authoritarianism and liberal democracy. Although the regime remains primarily authoritarian in nature, King Mohammed VI has taken steps to distance himself from his father's record of egregious human rights abuses. Thus, the political character of the regime during King Mohammed VI's reign could be described as soft dictatorship. Not only does King Mohammed VI's record point to a pattern of behavior, but it also conditioned the public to accept nonviolent means of handling challenges to authority as the natural and most legitimate response. A sudden departure from past regime behavior could delegitimize the regime, as well as signal weakness. On a personal level, it was only logical for King Mohammed VI to want to craft a response that would protect his reputation in this regard and preserve his popularity.

Furthermore, Tunisia and Egypt showed the perils of attacking protesters and delaying the granting of concessions. The regime's initial measured response, paired with a movement premised on nonviolence, ensured that a threshold of blood was not crossed in the first few weeks. Had early provocation from security forces sparked unrest, it might have polarized the country and forced the population to take sides. Violence against a mainstream movement tends to aid in the vilification of the regime in the eyes of those who were previously neutral, but much of the Moroccan population is not receptive to disparagement of the palace. Such a process of escalation in terms of tactics, stakes, and images is often necessary in order to reach a level of social upheaval that begets deep reforms.

With sustained, overt repression an unlikely tool for King Mohammed VI, the primary subject of interest, then, becomes the formulation of the royal appeasement strategy. Earlier it was posited that the popular legitimacy of the regime and the protesters and the availability of actors both within the regime and within or external to the protest movement who are willing to pact are the two primary determinants of an appeasement strategy. The most basic decision of whether to negotiate and with whom to negotiate can be analyzed through this framework. The king could have concluded from the Tunisian and Egyptian cases that it was necessary to open negotiations with protest leaders early to stem the movement's growth. And yet, no direct negotiations took place between the palace and the protest movement. They simply were not necessary in the absence of a mutually hurting stalemate that would incentivize both parties to participate. F20 did not appear to pose the same immediate threat to the survival of the regime as the Tunisian and Egyptian uprisings. The demonstrations galvanized old and new forces alike to take to the streets in sizeable numbers, but it was clear that they did not represent the majority of Moroccans who misunderstood the movement's objectives or actively opposed changing the current political system. For its part, the regime attempted to highlight this point by engaging in smear campaigns to varying degrees of effectiveness. The youth minister, Moncef Belkhayat, posted this on his Facebook wall on 16 February:

> My personal position, as a Moroccan citizen who lives in Casablanca and not Paris or Barcelona, is that this march is now being manipulated by the Polisario whose objective is to exploit the situation to create conflict that weakens the position of our country in the United Nations on the issue of human rights in the Sahara. I understand the aspirations of the youth. I think however that there are many ways to discuss and solve the problems including through communication and discussion. (Belkhayat 2011)

The king's relative legitimacy and the availability of the PJD with whom to pact created an opportunity for the palace to regain initiative on the reform agenda and marginalize F20. The king's attempt to co-opt the reform process was achieved through the creation of a royally appointed committee to propose constitutional amendments, which later would be popularly endorsed through a referendum. This approach was particularly effective in the Moroccan situation because King Mohammed VI enjoyed two inherent advantages over Mubarak and Ben Ali. First, the king was able to capitalize on his personal popularity and legitimacy by taking ownership of the constitutional reform process. To stabilize the political situation and build faith in the constitutional reform process, he sought to remind Moroccans of the inviolable sanctity and tradition behind the institution of the monarchy in his 9 March speech:

> The sacred character of our immutable values, which are unanimously supported by the nation—namely Islam as the religion of a state which guarantees freedom of wor-

> ship; Imarat al-Muminin (Commandership of the faithful); the monarchy; national unity and territorial integrity; and commitment to democratic principles—provides solid guarantees for a historic consensual agreement and a new charter between the Throne and the People. Building on the above, unshakable frame of reference, I have decided to introduce a comprehensive package of constitutional amendments.

The credibility of the constitutional reform process also benefited from the king's image as a reformer. Promises of reform from Ben Ali and Mubarak would have rung hollow. Although King Mohammed VI had shown enthusiasm for reforms that did not disturb the political balance of power, he still maintained the general image of a reformer. This led to the impression that the grassroots pressure had accelerated the reform process, rather than initiating it. The clearest example was the plans for increased decentralization that had been in the pipeline for years. The spontaneity of the king's reaction barely two weeks after the F20 explosion is often remarked upon, and the speed with which the Consultative Committee on Constitutional Reform (CCCR) was created and then the issuance of its report four months later, on 17 June, have been criticized as precipitous actions. Relative to the other leaders in the region, the king responded in a more rapid and productive manner. However, the greater anomaly is that more leaders did not act with equal haste after the fall of Ben Ali and Mubarak, even though King Mohammed was better positioned than his peers in the region to reignite the process of constitutional reform. The matter of a constitutional revision had been in discussion for years, since the king's gradual initiative for regionalization in 2008 following Morocco's proposal to the UN for autonomy for the Western Sahara. As the culmination of these preparations, the king created a Consultative Commission of Regionalization (CCR) on 30 January 2010 and then, following its report, on the anniversary of his accession to the throne on 20 August called for a "Charter of Deconcentration." "Whatever may be the system of regionalization, . . . it is absolutely necessary to revise the constitution," proclaimed a newspaper editorial (*Le Matin*, 27 February 2011), and the president of the CCR stated, before 20 February, "The present constitution cannot provide for advanced regionalization, and to do so, the constitutional dispositions must be reformed" (*Le Matin*, 14 February 2011). Thus when the pressure for constitutional revision came to a head, the topic was already ripe for action, and in addition, most of the members of the CCR found themselves on the CCCR, including its president, Abdellatif el-Menouni. This is not to say that the palace foresaw the coming *intifada* by any means, but that the train of events fortuitously left the *makhzen* in a position to react positively. With its ducks already in line, the palace could conduct tacit negotiations with a protest movement without even addressing it directly.

Aside from the relative legitimacy of the king as compared to F20, direct negotiations with F20 were not the most strategic regime response due to the availability of the PJD as a pacting partner. The inclusion of the most significant opposition party, the PJD, in the political system had divided and weakened opposition even before F20. The co-opted PJD operated under a different incentive structure than the JC, making cooperation unlikely. This division among opposition forces, particularly the Islamist community, did not exist in Tunisia and Egypt. These political conditions in Morocco meant that appeasement could be achieved with partial reforms endorsed and legitimized by the PJD, thus marginalizing the protest movement and minimizing the costs commonly associated with concessions. When the king announced his reform package on 9 March, PJD secretary-general Abdelilah Benkirane (2011) mostly had words of praise: "This speech is a roadmap that allows Morocco to start another revolution with the King and people to renew the national pact that allows for effective consolidation of the rule of law in our country." Unlike the politically excluded Islamist opposition groups in Tunisia and Egypt, the PJD stood to benefit from managed reform of the current political system rather than revolution, which would empower the JC. Moreover, the PJD's support of the king's reforms carried weight because it had not been delegitimized to the extent of sanctioned opposition parties in Tunisia and Egypt. The PJD's praise of the king's reform package and the party's victory in the November parliamentary elections sent a strong signal that the Moroccan political system was indeed changing.

THE VIABILITY OF THE THIRD WAY

Four years after the process of managed reform was initiated, however, the fundamental imbalance in power between the parliament and the palace remains, with little to no progress in addressing the other grievances of protesters—unemployment, corruption, and the high cost of living. The two key elements of the palace's appeasement plan—the constitutional reforms supposedly diminishing royal power and the election of the PJD—have proven hollow and confirmed the cynics' view that "managed" reform is just a euphemism for a time-buying strategy that robbed the protest movement of momentum while providing the regime space to strategize about how to pacify people without relinquishing power. Absent sustained and organized pressure, the palace had little incentive to reform, and it has not, nor has it changed its playbook for handling dissatisfaction by blaming the ruling party and jailing critics.[5] Without further adaptation or economic improvement, the regime is inviting stronger challenges to it and is equipped with fewer tools to handle them, having already played its hand in 2011.

The PJD, whose victory at the polls in 2011 signaled a new political era, was unsuccessful at exploiting the new powers and independence supposedly granted to the prime minister and parliament, perhaps because they were a chimera. The king held veto power over major decisions, and the political reality of coalition building forced the PJD to ally with parties close to the palace to form a new government. Cognizant of these constraints, the PJD consulted the palace on its appointments to different government posts (Zaaitar 2012), despite this being legally unnecessary, and it also has eased up its war against corruption.[6] Some attributed the party's impotence and reliance on the palace to its inexperience at governing. Regardless how veteran and adept the political operative, it would have been impossible for a party to radically break from its ruling coalition partners without triggering a no-confidence vote. The PJD's problems extended beyond having to moderate its reform agenda to general intransigence of its main coalition partner Istiqlal, which ultimately withdrew in July 2013, the first time in Morocco's history that a party has left the ruling coalition. Istiqlal's timing allowed for it to escape blame for unpopular austerity measures that the PJD adopted under pressure from international lenders in response to growing deficits tied in part to the king's package of subsidies to quell protests. With the tide shifting against the PJD, the king also began publicly questioning the abilities of the ruling party, even pinning flaws in the education system on them when the problems extend far beyond the tenure of the PJD (Sakthivel 2013b). Istiqlal's withdrawal nearly caused a government collapse, but eventually the PJD reached a deal with another royalist party, the National Rally of Independents (RNI). The weakened PJD was forced to accept the appointment of RNI head Salah al-Dine Mezouar as foreign minister, after outcry that the notoriously corrupt politician would be appointed to the post of finance minister (Sakthivel 2013a). The PJD for now has been rendered politically ineffectual.

Meanwhile, the JC appears to be reinvigorated after the 2011 protests brought it out of a period of dormancy and now under a new leader who is looking for the group to assert itself more in the political realm. The JC poses the most serious threat to the palace as it does not operate under the same set of constraints as the PJD. In October 2014, the JC joined a coalition of labor unions and secular parties calling for a general strike against austerity measures (Masbah 2014).

The king has emerged from the process of managed reform in relatively good standing, having stymied reform while scapegoating the PJD for this and the lack of economic progress. But he has weakened his long-term prospects of successfully countering another such challenge. He may have temporarily diverted blame for the stalled reform process, but the failure of yet another outside party (similar to the dashed hopes with the USFP) to implement meaningful reforms risks undermining the king's standing and jeopardizing the entire system. If even slow, gradual political reforms are not possible and the economy does not drastically improve, then pressure will build until it cannot be contained by the regime. The regime has weathered high unemployment rates and austerity measures in the three years since the emergence of F20 in part because the external environment has been favorable to the regime, with regional violent conflict increasing the value of stability and the Muslim Brotherhood's ignoble end to its rule in Egypt tainting the reputation of Islamists. If circumstances shift against the palace, however, it will find itself without a significant partner with whom to negotiate and form a compact, and who has "outsider" status but doesn't threaten the monarchy's position.

LESSONS FROM F20 AND THE REGIME'S RESPONSE

The case of Morocco during the Arab Spring raises a number of questions for future protest movements and the regimes they challenge. First is the issue of whether Morocco's "third way" of adopted and managed reform can be exported to other countries with equal success in stabilizing the political situation. After all, concessions can backfire by signaling weakness that protest movements can then exploit. When trying to generalize the lessons from the Moroccan Arab Spring, it is important to recall the factors identified earlier that enhanced the efficacy of the king's appeasement strategy: the weaknesses of F20; the unique role and legitimacy of a sacred monarch; the willingness of the PJD to support the reform package; and regional events that increased people's propensity to prefer the king's reform package over continued protests.

Besides the question of the effectiveness of the "third way" in other contexts, there is, of course, the issue of the desirability of the trade-off it implies. The "third way" suggests a short-term, compromise solution that mitigates violent escalation by placating protesters with limited reforms and ensuring regime survival. Managed reform processes create space for regimes to adapt and at least partially address grievances, but if they do not seize this opportunity, the same fault lines can trigger another mass movement that is harder to control. As the case of Morocco has illustrated thus far, a leader is unlikely to act beyond its myopic interests. Once the immediate threat is removed, there is little will to engage in a genuine political opening until the next round of unrest forces it to do so.

Finally, the trajectory of F20 offers lessons for other protest movements. The flat, decentralized organizational structure of F20 hindered the movement's ability to strategically respond to changing circumstances and formulate a clear and resonant message. At the same time, F20's flat structure limited the ability of the regime to weaken the movement by targeting its leaders. The participatory nature of F20 also contributed to the movement's initial vibrancy and its ability to attract Moroccans who had never been politically active. The flat, participatory structure of F20 should not be altogether scrapped in favor of a rigid hierarchy. Rather it should retain its democratic nature but also combine it with some degree of leadership and organization to streamline and improve decision making on complicated issues and messaging. One possible hybrid model would involve creating an executive committee—possibly elected—that coordinates the grand strategy that existing councils localize; this approach would force negotiations on the representation of various component movements and a means for their selection. The mere creation of a consolidated decision-making body is not sufficient to ensure better outcomes, but it could facilitate them. Whatever the structure, opposition groups must be willing to compromise with each other in meaningful ways in order to present a more detailed and strategic agenda for the protest movement.

Whatever its failings, F20 was able to breathe new life into the reform agenda in Morocco, mobilize new segments of the population, and begin a national dialogue on the country's political and economic order. F20 was a reaction against the failure of political parties and movements in the region to bring change, and it succeeded in invigorating the opposition movement. While F20 revealed the demand for a new form of opposition in Morocco, it also highlighted the numerous challenges associated with such an endeavor. Most crucially, future movements will need to find a new approach to handling the issue of royal legitimacy, which has divided existing opposition groups and hampered their ability to attract new support. Meanwhile, the challenge comes back again to the palace, to maintain the initiative and nurture its legitimacy by faithfully implementing the reforms it adopted from Morocco's shadow *intifada*.

Notes

1. Morocco ranked 130 out of 187 countries in the 2011 United Nations Human Development Index. In 2010, Transparency International ranks Morocco as the 85th most corrupt nation in the world, below Saudi Arabia (50) and Tunisia (59).

2. For further discussion of royal (sherifian) legitimacy in Morocco, see Hammoudi (1999); Leveau (1993); and Eickelman (1986).

3. A December 2007 U.S. government cable provided both figures, attributing the five million estimate to a JC spokesman and the hundred thousand estimate to the government of Morocco. Analyst Ahmed Benchemsi has used the 100,000 figure.

4. A Moroccan government official told Reuters that the 20 March demonstrations were at least as large as those of 20 February. Benchemsi (2012) stated that turnout on 20 March was widely believed to be significantly larger than the demonstrations the month before. See also Karam (2011).

5. As just one example, the rapper El-Haqed, who is considered by some to be the face of F20, has been jailed three times since the 2011 protests. Several other F20 leaders have been arrested. The Association for the Defense of Human Rights in Morocco in fact has reported an increase in the number of political prisoners from March to July 2014, from 288 to 338 prisoners.

6. The PJD performed well in the 2011 parliamentary elections in large part due to its strong rhetoric of reform and stated commitment to tackle corruption. Indeed, Prime Minister Abdelilah Benkirane promised to put "symbols of corruption" on trial, but now, as prime minister, he has reneged on this promise. The party has implemented some reforms such as listing government officials who are benefiting from contracts they have awarded. However, party officials have alluded to their inability to eliminate corruption without support from other political forces. Habib Choubani, the PJD minister for relations with parliament and civil society, has said, "Even a government of prophets can't end corruption in five years, if there was no collective consciousness to engage in the fight against this phenomenon" (qtd. in Allilou 2014).

References

Abdennebi, Zakia, and Joseph Nasr. 2011. "Morocco Softens Line against Pro-democracy Protests." Reuters. 6 June. http://uk.reuters.com/article/2011/06/05/morocco-protests-idUKLDE7540MR20110605, retrieved on September 25, 2012.

Allilou, Aziz. 2014. "Even a Government of Prophets Can't End Corruption in Five Years: PJD Minister." *Morocco World News*, 22 June. http://www.moroccoworldnews.com/2014/06/133275/even-a-government-of-prophets-cant-end-corruption-in-five-years-pjd-minister (accessed on 15 July 2014).

Amnesty International 2011. "Etouffement des manifestations," March 28. http://www.amnesty.ch/fr/pays/moyen-orient-afrique-du-nord/maroc-sahara-occidental%20/documents/2011/maroc-etouffement-manifestations (accessed 27 August 2012).

Belkhayat, Moncef. 2011. "A propos de la marche du 20 février" [Regarding the February 20 March]. Facebook, 16 February. http://www.facebook.com/notes/moncef-belkhayat/a-propos-de-la-marche-du-20-fevrier/183712778330952 (accessed 24 August 2012).

Benchemsi, Ahmed. 2012. "Feb 20's Rise and Fall: A Moroccan Story." *The Blog of Ahmed Benchemsi*, 17 July. http://ahmedbenchemsi.com (accessed 13 August 2012).

Benkirane, Abdelilah. 2011, Interview. *L'Economiste* 3487, 16 March. http://www.leconomiste.com/article/reforme-constitutionnellebr-le-roi-doit-conserver-son-role-d-arbitre-brientretien-avec-abdel (accessed 25 September 2012.

Chapouly, Romain. 2011. "Le 'mouvement du 20 février' au Maroc: Une étude de cas de la coordination locale de Rabat." Institut d'Etudes Politiques de Lyon. http://www.memoireonline.com/03/12/5508/Le-mouvement-du-20-fevrier-au-Maroc-une-etude-de-cas-de-la-coordination-locale-de-Rabat.html (accessed 28 August 2012).

Eickelman, Dale. 1986. "Royal Authority and Religious Legitimacy: Morocco's Elections, 1960–1984" In *The Frailty of Authority*, edited by Myron J. Aronoff. New Brunswick, N.J.: Transaction Books.

Fakir, Intissar. 2011. "Will Morocco's King Deliver on Reforms?" *Sada*. Carnegie Endowment for International Peace, 16 March. http://carnegieendowment.org/2011/03/16/will-morocco-s-king-deliver-on-reforms/6bj8 (accessed 12 September 2012).

February 20th Movement Platform. 2011. "The Demands of the Moroccan People—20 Urgent Points." 6 February.

Freedom and Democracy Now. 2011. Facebook group. Founding statement, 27 January. http://www.facebook.com/groups/MLEDM/doc/182441525128321 (accessed 24 September 2012).

Goldstone, Jack A., and Charles Tilly. 2001. "Threat (and Opportunity): Popular Action and State Response in the Dynamics of Contentious Action." In *Silence and Voice in the Study of Contentious Politics*, by Ronald R. Aminzade et al., 179-194. Cambridge: Cambridge University Press.

Hammoudi, Abdellah. 1999. "The Reinvention of Dar al-mulk: The Moroccan Political System and Its Legitimation." In *In the Shadow of the Sultan: Culture, Power and Politics in Morocco*, edited by Rahma Bourqia and Susan Gilson Miller, 129–175. Cambridge, Mass.: Harvard University Press.

Human Rights Watch. 2011. "Morocco: Thousands Demonstrate Peacefully." 21 March. http://www.hrw.org/news/2011/03/21/morocco-thousands-demonstrate-peacefully (accessed 27 August 2012).

International Institute for Democracy and Electoral Assistance. 2012. "Voter Turnout Data for Morocco." http://www.idea.int/vt/countryview.cfm?CountryCode=MA (accessed 2 September 2012).

"An Interview with JC Spokesman Fathallah Arsalane." 2011. *Maroc Hebdo* 959 (23–29 December): 20–21. http://www.maroc-hebdo.press.ma/Site-Maroc-hebdo/archive/Archives_959/pdf_959/mhi_959.pdf (accessed 26 August 2012).

Karam, Souhail 2011. "Thousands in Morocco March for Rights, End to Graft." Reuters, 20 March. http://www.reuters.com/article/2011/03/20/us-morocco-protests-idUSTRE72J2GT20110320 (accessed on 29 August 2012).

Leveau, Remy. 1993. *Le sabre et le turban*. Paris: François Bourin.

Mamfakinch. https://www.mamfakinch.com/a-propos/ (accessed 17 September 2012).

Michaux-Bellaire, Edmond, and Henri Gaillard. 1909. *L'administration au Maroc, le Makhzen, étendue et limites de son pouvoir*. Tangier.

Masbah, Mohammed. 2014. "Islamist and Secular Forces in Morocco: Not a Zero-Sum Game." Stiftung Wissenschaft und Politik, Comments 51. November. http://www.swp-berlin.org/en/publications/swp-comments-en/swp-aktuelle-details/article/morocco_islamist_and_secular_forces.html (accessed 4 December 2014).

Moroccans for Change. "King Mohamed VI Speech 3/9/11 (full text)." http://moroccansforchange.com/2011/03/09/king-mohamed-vi-speech-3911-full-text-feb20-khitab (accessed 28 August 2012).

"Morocco Feb. 20 Protest Leaders Quit after Row." 2011. Reuters, 19 February. http://www.reuters.com/article/2011/02/19/us-morocco-protest-idUSTRE71I3K220110219, retrieved on August 22, 2012.

Morocco World News. 2013. "Banned Morocco Islamist Group 'Ready to Form Party.'" 7 January. http://www.moroccoworldnews.com/2013/01/73024/banned-morocco-islamist-group-ready-to-form-party (accessed 6 December 2014).

Mouvement 20 Février. Facebook group. http://www.facebook.com/mouvement20fevrier (accessed 13 August 2012).

Ottaway, Marina. 2011. "The New Moroccan Constitution: Real Change or More of the Same?" Carnegie Endowment for International Peace. 20 June. http://www.carnegieendowment.org/2011/06/20/new-moroccan-constitution-real-change-or-more-of-same/6g (accessed 10 September 2012).

Pascon, Paul, and Mekki Bentahar. 1969. *Ce que disent 296 jeunes ruraux: Enquête sociologique*. Société d'études économiques, sociales et statistiques du Matoc. 112-113.

Rachidi, Ilhem. 2011. "Maroc: 'Le discours royal n'a pas répondu à nos attentes." *Rue 89*, 19 March. http://www.rue89.com/2011/03/19/maroc-le-discours-royal-na-pas-repondu-a-nos-attentes-195965 (accessed 10 September 2012).

Rahman, Zahir. 2012. "Online Political Activism in Morocco: Facebook and the Birth of the February 20th Movement." *Journal of New Media Studies in* MENA 1 (Winter): 5. http://jnmstudies.com/index.php/current/85-articles/102-onlineactivism-zahir (accessed 10 August 2012).

Reporters without Borders. 2010. Index. http://en.rsf.org/spip.php?page=classement&id_rubrique=1034.

Sakthivel, Vish. 2013a. "Assessing Morocco's New Cabinet." Washington Institute for Near East Policy, 16 October. http://www.washingtoninstitute.org/policy-analysis/view/assessing-moroccos-new-cabinet (accessed 15 July 2014).

———. 2013b. "Morocco's Governing Islamists Remain Vulnerable." Washington Institute for Near East Policy, 10 September. http://www.washingtoninstitute.org/policy-analysis/view/moroccos-governing-islamists-remain-vulnerable (accessed 15 July 2014).

Tanner, Adam, and Souhail Karam. 2011. "Many Wounded as Moroccan Police Beat Protestors." Reuters, 22 May. http://www.reuters.com/article/2011/05/22/us-morocco-protests-idUSTRE74L2YK20110522 (accessed 29 August 2012).

Transparency International. 2010. "Corruption Perceptions Index 2010." http://www.transparency.org/cpi2010/results/#CountryResults(accessed 1 September 2012).

Tufekci, Zeynep. 2011. "New Media and the People-Powered Uprisings." *MIT Technology Review*, 30 August. http://www.technologyreview.com/view/425280/new-media-and-the-people-powered-uprisings (accessed 23 September 2012).

United Nations Development Program. 2011. Morocco Country Profile: Human Development Indicators. http://hdrstats.undp.org/en/countries/profiles/MAR.html, retrieved on September 25, 2012.

World Bank. 2012. "The Challenge of Youth Inclusion in Morocco." 14 May. http://www.worldbank.org/en/news/2012/05/14/challenge-of-youth-inclusion-in-morocco. (accessed 22 August 2012).

Zaaiter, Haifa. 2012. "Morocco Still Waiting for Islamists to Deliver on Reform Promises." *Al Monitor*, 4 September. http://www.al-monitor.com/pulse/ar/politics/2012/09/morocco-stands-still-as-islamists-and-king-decide-what-to-do-next.html#ixzz39AnqnS2W (accessed 15 July 2014).

Zartman, I. William, ed. 1997. *Governance as Conflict Management: Politics and Violence in West Africa*. Washington, D.C.: Brookings Institution Press.

Bahrain

The Dynamics of a Conflict

ROEL MEIJER AND MAARTEN DANCKAERT

> We will stay. It will not end until the government listens to the people. We will not give up until the government collapses.
>
> Shiʿite demonstrator at the Pearl Roundabout, February 2011

> Citizens of Bahrain, let us work together with all political blocs to help return the security situation to normal so we can announce a day of mourning for those we have lost.
>
> Crown Prince Salman, HRW, 28 February 2012

> Any national demand cannot be ratified or answered without ratification of all communities.
>
> Leader of the Sunni National Unity Gathering, Abd al-Latif al-Mahmoud, *Gulf Daily News*, 22 February 2012

> No to negotiation, no to concessions until the comedy ends.
>
> Sunni Youth Awakening of al-Fatih, *al-Wasat*, 17 March 2012

HUNDREDS OF BAHRAINI SHIʿITE youth marched to the Pearl Roundabout on 14 February 2011, bringing the Arab Spring to the Gulf. After severe skirmishes on the morning of the 17 March, they returned the next day and reoccupied the roundabout for the next three weeks, as the Egyptians had done before them at Tahrir Square. The joyous and sometimes carnivalesque atmosphere attracted the world's attention, but more serious were the negotiations that took place behind the scenes between the crown prince and the major forces of the opposition. When they reached a deadlock at the beginning of March, the protestors at the Pearl Roundabout tried other means of contention, such as blocking the main highways, burning tires, and especially organizing marches to the palace of the king, the Ministry of Interior, and the Financial Harbor, the business center of Bahrain. The escalation of protest was the signal for the Gulf Cooperation Council (GCC) to intervene. On 14 March troops were brought over the causeway linking Bahrain to its powerful neighbor Saudi Arabia. A backlash followed; the hardliners in the ruling family used the coercive instruments they controlled—the military, police, security forces, and the judiciary—to repress the uprising. During the following months the opposition leaders and ordinary demonstrators were fired from their jobs, arrested, tortured, and sometimes killed. Their organizations were banned. In total thirty-four people died between the beginning of the uprising and the end of 2011. Bahrain was back to square one; many of the reforms initiated in 2000–2002 seemed to have been erased.

This chapter on the manner in which the Arab Spring has affected Bahrain uses theories on citizenship rights in combination with social movement and negotiation theory to analyze the uprising of February–March 2011 in Bahrain and show how it fits in a wider struggle for citizenship in the Arab world. It also situates these events in a longer historical perspective to show the depth of the movement's grievances and the extent of its experience. Despite the clampdown, it is unlikely that in the long run the regime can block significant reforms. Negotiating for citizenship rights is the key to understanding the problem and the solution.

This chapter investigates the political struggle between the regime and the opposition. The chapter is also situated within the debate on the Arab spring and the critique of the theories of authoritarian regimes and their assumed stability and flexibility. The most famous version is Steven Heydemann's report "Upgrading Authoritarianism in the Arab World." In it he argues that authoritarian regimes in the Middle East have over the past two decades succeeded in devising "top-down and controlled strategies for managing political contestation" (Heydemann 2007, 12). According to him, they have been able to "manage and control" (21) the major challenges of the past decades: neoliberal economic reform and liberalization, new political, civil society, and human rights claims, and the explosive growth of the Internet and access to new information and models. Since the massive revolts of the Arab Spring the authoritarian upgrading paradigm has been criticized for its "over-emphasis on the state, state elites, and traditional political and civil society actors" (Pace and Cavatorta 2012, 127). As a correction, Michelle Pace and Francesco Cavatorta suggest to look at "unintended consequences" of authoritarian upgrading. Others have made stronger arguments for not just looking at the state or unintended consequences. They point out that the impact of neoliberalism on employment, investment opportunities, and growing inequality has been hugely underestimated. Hazem Kandil (2012), for example, analyzes how the Egyptian bourgeoisie in all its forms—except for the small upper elite—became alienated from the Mubarak regime; Joel Beinin (2012) shows how working-class mobilization has dramatically increased since the privatization of companies, and he has "upgraded" the role of the workers during the uprising. The Egyptian bourgeoisie demand equal access to economic rights, while the workers defend their civil and social rights as citizens. Those willing to put their ear to the ground could have heard the rumblings two decades ago as youth movements started to protest against unemployment, marginalization, and alienation and demonstrated in favor of "recognition" and "dignity" (Bennani-Chraïbi 2000)—exactly those terms that denote a new civil awareness that has made the Arab Spring famous. Recent analyses only confirm that long-term demographic and cultural trends of the individualization of youth will undermine the existing patronage-client systems, paternalism, and existing political ideologies. Increasingly this will lead to a more modern attitude toward power, politics, and citizenship rights (Murphy 2012).

Indeed, our central argument is that the Arab Spring is largely the reflection of the third wave of citizen rights in the Arab world. The study of citizenship in the Middle East has been mainly limited to its aspect of status (who is a member of the political community) and, with few exceptions (Butenschon, Davis, and Hassassian 2000; Meijer and Wagemakers 2012; Meijer 2014), not to its relationship between citizen and state. In contrast, in the West citizenship studies has become an academic discipline (Isin and Turner 2002). Since T. H. Marshall's seminal study in 1949 (1964), and his historical sequence of citizenship rights in England from civil rights in the eighteenth century (equal access to the legal system, fair trials), political rights in the nineteenth century (expansion of the franchise through workers' struggle) and social rights after World War II (benefits of the welfare state, such as free education, social security, pension) have taken flight and others have constantly elaborated on his theme, by historicizing it (Mann 1987), deepening it (Turner 1990), and broadening the concept to include group rights, sexual rights, and so forth (Isin and Wood 1999).

So what do we mean when we talk about citizenship rights? Citizenship is defined by Keith Faulks as "a membership status (of a nation-state), which contains a package of rights, duties and obligations, and which implies equality, justice, and autonomy. Its development and nature at any given time can be understood through a consideration of the interconnected dimensions of its *content*, *extent* and *depth*" (Faulks 2000). In this definition, *extent* refers to criteria for citizenship (who is included or excluded); *content* refers to the level and form of *participation* of the citizen in the polity and his or her rights, duties, and obligations; and *depth* or *thickness* refers to the identities of citizens, in the sense of demands that citizenship makes on members of the communities (Faulks 2000, 7). The precise *combination* of rights differs from one state to another and determines to a large extent the political character of a state (Isin and Turner 2002, 3).

Citizenship is closely related to politics. Some state that citizenship can only exist in a democracy because it assumes equal rights and duties. Richard Bellamy and Antonino Palumbo (2010, xvi) in their important edited volume *Citizenship* define citizenship as "the right to have rights." They argue that "citizenship implies the capacity to participate in both the political and the socioeconomic life of the community." They believe it can only function when there is a common language for political debate, a common sense of belonging and identity. This is what distinguishes the citizen from the subject, who has no rights and does not take part in the political process (xviii).

Social movement theory also makes links between citizenship, politics, and democracy but connects it with contestation and struggle. Charles Tilly defines democracy as "broad, equal, protected, binding consultation of citizens with respect to states' actions." The terms *broad*, *equal*, and *binding* are the equivalent of political rights, while the term *protection* refers to civil rights and the freedom of organization, expression, and equal access to courts (Tilly 2007, 45). Although all social movement theorists are aware of the role of contestation and distrust in politics as part of political contestation, Tilly is careful to point out the importance of trust in a democracy. It is exactly the delicate balance between trust and distrust that makes a democracy work and that is required of the active citizen to internalize. Both are essential for the process of democratization, for on the one hand the citizen must trust his government, while on the other hand, the citizen must be alert and critical and must hold power holders accountable. Tilly calls this the *democratic dilemma of trust*, or *contingent trust* (93).

Thus, "trust networks" must be included in the political process. Civic organizations and networks (religious, social, professional) must trust the state enough to put their organizations under its control. If they remain outside state power, as is the case with the Muslim Brotherhood and the military in Egypt, or the ruling elite in the Gulf states, democratic control by citizens remains limited, but if they come under unaccountable state control, the functions of citizenship are curtailed. This dilemma is mirrored in the relation of the state to its citizens. Thus, a certain degree of state "capacity" is necessary.[1] Only a strong state can guarantee enough security and provide the necessary services for citizens to fulfill their duties and focus their claims on the state. The downside capacity can also be translated as repression of civil and political rights.

Another important issue is the sociological makeup of a certain country. Many theorists assume a certain level of modernization as a precondition for democratization. Bryan S. Turner argues, for instance, that citizenship can only arise when kinship relations have been eroded and the "triumph" of *gesellschaft* over *gemeinschaft* has taken place (Turner 2000, 31). This is certainly true when we look at such prevalent political relations as the patronage and patron-client system that are often kinship based and strongly related to neopatriarchy and its political form of neopatrimonialism (Sharabi 1988). The vertical relations of dependency of the client to the patron run contrary to those of equality and autonomy of the citizen. But Tilly also shows that patronage systems helped to incorporate ethnic minorities in the United States in the nineteenth century. Everything depends on context. Patronage can be useful in nineteenth-century America but can hamper citizenship rights and democratization in twenty-first-century Bahrain. The advantage of

Tilly's method is to historicize democratization, the development of politics, and the related concepts and practices of citizenship as a *process* that moves forward but also can be reversed. He and others have shown that the process moves in cycles (Tarrow 1998, 141–160). As a general rule, Tilly upholds the principle that all movement toward democracy, politicization, and citizenship rights is the result of struggle for rights and claims, while all movement toward de-democratization and the limitation of "broad, equal, protected, binding consultation of citizens with respect to states actions" is the result of actions of the elites who fear for their interests (Tilly 2007, 12, 33, 40).

Although Bahrain as a Gulf state has a somewhat different history of cycles, the Arab Spring was so vehement because the external Middle Eastern cycle reinforced the internal Bahraini cycle of contention. The next section addresses the struggle for full citizenship rights in Bahrain and the problems this struggle has encountered, dealing first with five issues that have hampered this struggle and then two elements that have worked in favor of citizenship rights and democratization. The next section deals with the history of social movements in the trend of the "mobilization-repression-bargaining" cycles in Bahrain. The chapter then returns to the main protagonists of the struggle and analyzes their perception of the conflict. This is followed by an analysis of the backlash and the phase of depoliticization, de-democratization, and decline of citizenship rights, returning subsequently to the protagonists and their views on the phase of bargaining that inevitably will come. Although at present the phase of repression is unabatedly in force, it is unlikely that it can continue indefinitely, given the widespread general mobilization and increasing awareness of citizenship rights.

CITIZENSHIP RIGHTS AND THEIR ENEMIES

One of the major hindrances to the expansion of citizenship rights in Bahrain is the neopatrimonial state. The relations between the ruler and the population are based on loyalty, and the legitimacy of ministers and other functionaries derive from their personal relations with the ruler (Schmidmayr 2011, 35). The premodern principle of the "benevolence of the ruler" (*makrama*),[2] patronage and clientalism, means that politics is arbitrary despite the installation of modern institutions such as the constitution.

The second factor that hampers a further expansion of citizenship rights is the oil/rentier nature of the state.[3] This means that income from oil flows directly to the state, and a large percentage is used by the ruling family for its personal use. This has enhanced the vertical relations of inequality and runs counter to equality, which is the basis of citizenship. It has also enabled the ruling family to expand the "capacity" of the modern state by distributing material gratuities, such as a one-month salary raise to all government employees, free electricity for poor families, or reduced education fees (Wright 2010, 2–3; Khalaf 2006, 36–39), or for political matters, such as granting amnesty to political prisoners, implementing political reforms, or even promulgating a constitution (Quilliam 2008, 84). In 1972, for instance, Prime Minister Khalifa bin Salman Al Khalifa remarked that "the people don't dictate the constitution; it's given to them by His Majesty the Amir" (Nakhleh 1976, 74). The coexistence of premodern and modern forms of government has led to a deep ambiguity of politics and has increased the distrust of the opposition.

The third major obstacle to further democratization is that the ruling Al Khalifa family rules as a collective and that most of the ministers are members of the royal family. This makes it very difficult to dismiss ministers or fundamentally reform the political system (Herb 1999; Gause 2011). In a sense, the state is the family. The uprising severely challenged this arrangement when it demanded not only a "government responsible to the people" but a constitutional monarchy where the monarch reigns instead of rules.

Fourth, the "capacity" or "infrastructural power" of the state in Bahrain is augmented by the fact that the Bahraini Defense Force and the country's security and police force consist in large part of foreigners (granted citizenship rights), who are willing to shoot at demonstrators (Bellin 2012). Thus, while the government derives its benevolent premodern capacity from *makrama* and neopatrimonialism, its coercive modern capacity is based on the unquestioned obedience of its security forces.

The fifth major hindrance to democratization is the "categorical inequality" that exists between Sunnis and Shiʿites. The ruling family is Sunni, and the majority (between 52 and 70 percent) of the population is Shiʿite. The sectarian divide is not so much a religious divide as such but a coincidence of class and religious divisions and systematic discrimination of the majority by the ruling family, which plays on this divide (al-Jamri 1998). Sectarian consciousness had increased with the emergence of the Islamist trend in the 1990s,[4] and one of the major challenges of the Bahraini social movements is to overcome this divide.

The presence of its powerful neighbor, Saudi Arabia, on which Bahrain is dependent, is the sixth factor that hampers any change for the better. As a tiny island with a small population of 1.2 million people (half of whom are expats), based on rentier income, with weak, exclusionary relations with the majority, being crushed between antagonistic neighbors Iran and Saudi Arabia makes it heavily dependent on Saudi support that also carries with it the Salafi anti-Shiʿite rhetoric to attack the opposition.

Against these six structural impediments, two elements have worked in favor of an extension of citizenship rights. The first is Bahrain's long history of social movements that has been reflected in a succession of cycles. The February–March uprising of 2011 should be analyzed as a cycle within a cycle (Tarrow 1998: 141–160). In Tilly's terms, Bahrain has been subject to "mobilization-repression-bargaining cycles" (Tilly 2007, 144) since the 1970s or even earlier (Nakhleh 1976, 75–84), and the February–March uprising was just the latest sustained campaign of "a powerful assertion of popular sovereignty" (Tilly and Wood 2009, 13).

The first broad mass-based cycle began just after Bahrain became independent from Great Britain in 1971. The ruling family decided to organize the election of a Constituent Assembly, established in 1973 by decree of the emir and providing for the "equality of all citizens" (Parolin 2006, 60–61). In 1975 this experiment was ended. The oil boom had massively shifted power toward the ruling family, which was able to expand state "capacity" and build an authoritarian state based on rentier income (Khalaf 2000).

The next uprising occurred in the form of the *intifada* of 1994–1998 in the wake of the U.S.-led liberation of Kuwait. It was caused by many of the same reasons as the February–March 2011 uprising: steadily rising unemployment, increasing gap between the upper middle class and the suburban lower middle classes and rural poor, expansion of exclusive housing, and systematic discrimination of Shiʿites in government employment, especially in the army and security forces, which recruited almost exclusively among foreign Sunnis (from Jordan, Pakistan, etc.) (Lawson 2004, 90). Protests started by the traditional repertoire of contention in the Gulf: the petition (Zartman 2008, 175).[5] The first petition handed to the emir in November 1992, the Elite Petition, signed by three hundred notables, demanded the reinstatement of parliament, release of political prisoners, and return of exiles. When nothing happened, a Popular Petition Committee was organized that basically voiced the same demands but was supported by a mass campaign that collected twenty thousand signatures (Lawson 2004, 96). After the arrest of one of its leaders, Sheikh Ali Salman, in December 1994, mass rallies and pro-constitution marches were organized in Shiʿite neighborhoods in Manama, along with electricity, water, and telephone boycotts. In 1995 the revolt escalated, and throughout 1995–1997 police stations and banks were sacked, and arson and car bombings took place against government buildings, luxury stores, and shopping malls. Meanwhile petitions and a hunger strike continuing to press for reform were drawn up by both Shiʿite and Sunni clerics. Most of the groups in the 1990s were both Islamist and left wing: the Islamic Front for the Liberation of Bahrain (IFLB) and the Bahrain Islamic Freedom Movement (BIFM), Bahraini National Liberation Front and the Popular Front for the Liberation of Bahrain (ICG 2011a, 5).

The repression of the *intifada*—as with the uprising in 2011—was "indiscriminate," and many of those arrested were never formally charged. Mosques were demolished as part of the clampdown, and dissidents' houses and clubs were set on fire. In 1998 the tactics became more coordinated and subtle. The cycle wound down with the death of the ruling emir, Isa bin Salman Al Khalifa, in 1999. The appointment of his son prince Hamad bin Isa Al Khalifa instead of his uncle Khalifa bin Salman Al Khalifa as his successor was a sign of reconciliation (Lawson 2004, 105).

The other element that has enhanced the power of social movements in Bahrain is the divisions within the royal family (conversation with Abdulhadi Khalaf, 8 July 2012). King Hamad and his son, Crown Prince Salman bin Hamad Al Khalifa, are usually seen as more moderate or aware that reform is necessary to preserve the monarchy, whereas his uncle, Khalifa, who was prime minister for forty years, is regarded as a hardliner.[6] This division has created access to the ruling family for the reform-minded Shiʿite opposition, and from their side, the reformist sections of the royal family have reached out to the opposition to counter the influence of the conservative branch. After Hamad became king in 1999, a period of reform inaugurated a new cycle of mobilization-repression-bargaining that in its repression phase was given a new mobilization impulse by the Arab Spring. What makes the latest phase more dangerous for the ruling family is that during the Arab Spring the awareness of rights has expanded tremendously and has reached the Sunni community, which has started to make its own political demands.

The basis of King Hamad's new regime was laid down in the National Action Charter drawn up by a group of experts in 2000. The reform envisioned a lower chamber that would "enact" legislation while members of the upper chamber would only "offer their advice and knowledge when needed."[7] This strategy was received enthusiastically (Nonneman 2008, 9–10), and on 14 February 2001 98 percent of the voters (89 percent turnout) supported the charter in a referendum. It seemed that King Hamad's position was secure and that his legitimacy would rest on the expansion of political rights, the limitation of the powers of the ruling family, and the end of what Tilly calls "categorical inequalities."

The limitations of his reform policy were, however, reflected in its unilateral character; he never entered the phase of "bargaining" with the opposition over the drafting of the constitution (Khalaf 2000). The new constitution became again a "granted constitution," giving the lower house fewer rights than under the National Action Charter and providing an upper chamber (Majlis al-Shura) narrowly selected from the ruling family, senior retired officers, and former ambassadors with a veto power over legislation (Parolin 2006, 65–70; Niethammer 2006). In addition, the king held the right to appoint all ministers, who alone had the right to initiate legislation. Parliament no longer had the power to monitor the ruling family's financial policy by means of a financial auditing agency (ICG, 2011a). The hope to dismantle the neopatrimonial state had been defeated. This new arrangement was not only regarded as a major step backward from the 1973 constitution, which prescribed one chamber of forty seats, thirty elected and only ten appointed; it was also seen as a betrayal of the trust the Shiʿites had put in the new king. They felt that their rights as citizens had been restricted by the ruling family, who regarded the constitution as a gift and an act of royal benevolence (*makrama*) instead of a right.

Three kinds of responses developed over the next few years, feeding the new cycle of contention in different ways. Although the elections of 2002 were boycotted by the major Shiʿite political grouping al-Wifaq (full name: Jamʿiyya al-Wifaq al-Watani al-Islamiyya, or National Islamic Covenant Society), and the liberal leftist al-Waʿd (Promise) grouping, they eventually accepted a gradual approach. In 2005 the king in a maneuver to co-opt and control the opposition typical of "façade democracy" initiated the Political Societies Act (Nonneman 2006). This step posed a dilemma: "political societies" (*jamaʿiyyat)* could choose either to be registered and participate in the formal political process that was heavily skewed to their disadvantage or to become illegal and go underground. Sheikh Ali Salman, the leader of al-Wifaq, decided to comply and take part in the upcoming elections (Wright 2010, 6).

Sheikh Ali Salman (2006) explained the strategy of the moderates: al-Wifaq's goal was a constitutional monarchy (*al-malakiyya al-dusturiyya*), based on a "contract" (*ʿaqd*), but that would take time. A constitutional monarchy could be brought about by gradually handing over crucial ministries to the opposition, and through participation (*musharaka*) the opposition would gradually become empowered. Al-Wifaq's focus on political reform and civil rights was captured by the slogan "the constitution first," under which it won seventeen of the forty lower house seats during the 2006 elections.

The alternative response was to continue the boycott of the political system. In protest against the process of co-optation, another part of al-Wifaq, led by former secretary-general Hasan Mushayma, decided to reject the offer to become legalized. He argued that the constitution must be changed *before* the opposition could participate in elections. Typically, he founded a "movement" (*haraka*) rather than a "political society": the Haqq Movement for Liberty and Democracy (Haraka Haqq: Haraka al-Hurriyyat wa-l-Dimuqratiyya). Mushayma and his supporters, ʿIsa al-Jawdar and ʿAbd al-Jalil Singace, called for increased grassroots activities and encouraged civil disobedience and more confrontational repertoires of contentious action. In 2007 the confrontation escalated when fighting broke out between police and youth in the poor Shiʿite villages around Manama, leading to a ban on demonstrations. However, Haqq, like al-Wifaq, during the coming years increasingly seemed to have lost control over the youth (al-Akhbar 2008).

A third response was led by the youth, who increasingly—as in Egypt and Tunisia—turned to new forms of protest that would manifest themselves in full force during the 2011 uprising. The political awareness of the Bahraini Shiʿites was raised by a new network around the Bahrain Center for Human Rights (BCHR), founded in 2004 and headed by ʿAbd al-Hadi al-Khawaja and Nabeel Rajab. Using the language of human rights, al-Khawaja and Rajab carved out influential political roles for themselves, inspiring younger Bahrainis to become involved in civic affairs and instructing them in how to build strong grassroots organizations. BCHR was more confrontational than al-Wifaq, concentrating on social justice, discrimination, and poverty. It introduced the innovative repertoire of contention of mass seminars (*nadwa jamahiriyya*) in which thousands participated (Niethammer 2006). Other active human rights organizations, such as Bahrain Youth Society for Human Rights, joined the escalating confrontation. At the same time, youth took advantage of the relative press freedom that was part of the reform program and founded weblogs such as BahrainOnline, Duraz.net, and al-Montadayat, opening discussion forums where local news and politics were freely discussed (Desmukh 2010). Facebook also became important, and by 2010 fourteen thousand Bahraini youth were on Facebook, extending the scope of potential participants in the new phase of contention (Seznec 2011). These more activist groups appealed to the Bahraini youth through their more impatient tone and modern media. Their concept of citizenship was broader, more inclusive, and more activist than that of al-Wifaq. In general, the youth movements took the side of Haqq in the competition with al-Wifaq. The London-based Bahrain Freedom Movement (BFM) and the BCHR launched campaigns against al-Wifaq leaders Ali Salman and Muhammad Jamil al-Jamri, the editor-in-chief of *al-Wasat*, the only Shiʿite oppositional newspaper, calling them "appeasers" (*al-Akhbar* 2008).

To counter these movements, and using his supreme power to manipulate the political field, King Hamad mobilized popular support among the conservative Sunni community as a counterweight to the opposition. The Sunni pro-government forces were represented by a coalition of two groups, the Salafi al-Asala (Authenticity) Islamic Society, which had won eight seats in parliament, and *al-Minbar* (Tribune) National Islamic Society, a group associated with the Muslim Brotherhood, holding seven seats in the 2006 parliament (Calderwood 2010). By promoting the Sunni parties behind the scenes, the king tried to present himself as standing above the sectarian fray, without much success (Niethammer 2012).

REPRESSION OF SUMMER 2010

But King Hamad was only one of the members of the Al Khalifa family that ruled. He pursued the internal power struggle with his uncle Prince Khalifa by developing parallel organizations that would take over functions Prince Khalifa had monopolized over the previous thirty years (Quilliam 2008, 82). By the end of the decade, however, King Hamad was losing the internal family feud (Kinninmont 2012). The hard-liners instigated a reign of repression against the activist groups that grew in popularity as the credibility of al-Wifaq through co-optation declined. In this period street protests in the form of tire burning on the highways, clashes with police in Shiʿite villages, arson of cars and houses, and attacks on policemen increased (Kinninmont 2006). In February 2010 Human Rights Watch released a report that showed that torture had returned as a means of repressing the opposition (HRW 2010). Civil and political rights had decreased instead of improved.

Government repression of the opposition started in the summer of 2010 and was directed against Haqq, seen as the main instigator of unrest. During this campaign twenty-three Shiʿite political leaders were arrested (Amiri 2011). They were charged with being members of a "terrorist network," "undermining national security," and organizing meetings inside and outside of Bahrain "to change the political regime by illegal means" (Al Jazeera 2010). The campaign was supported by Bahrain's neighbors, and in September the Gulf Cooperation Council (GCC) called for extraditing two leaders who were in exile in London. Blogger and human rights activist Ali Abdulemam was arrested for the second time in September 2010 (Free Blogger). Even al-Wifaq's website was shut down by the government during the election campaign. But not only Shiʿites were targeted—candidates of al-Waʿd also were harassed and limited in their campaigns and freedom.

Despite this governmental repression of the outsiders, the moderate wing was strong enough to allow the legal opposition to run for elections in October 2010. Al-Wifaq even won eighteen out of the forty seats of the Lower Chamber (Majlis al-Nuwwab), while the pro-governmental coalition of the Salafis and Sunnis collapsed (Calderwood 2010), losing ten of their fifteen seats. They were replaced by independent Sunni candidates who won seventeen seats and might have been willing to work together with al-Wifaq (Diwan 2010). However, the most important Sunni reformist politician, Ibrahim Sharif, the leader of the National Democratic Action Society al-Waʿd, was not elected.

THE UPRISING OF FEBRUARY/MARCH 2011

The occupation of the Pearl Roundabout from 15 February to 14 March should be regarded as a short cycle within a longer local cycle, instigated by a much larger regional cycle. As in the rest of the Arab Spring, it centered on the promotion of civil, political, and social rights (social justice) and the ending of growing inequality, repression, the patronage-client system, and its concomitant corruption. In the local setting of Bahrain, the uprising represented the clash of the previous six obstacles to reform (neopatrimonialism and *makrama*, collective family rule, rentierism, state repression, systematic discrimination, Saudi dependency, and anti-reformism) on the one hand, and the mobilization of different sections of the opposition as social movements, on the other hand. Crucial was whether the moderates on both sides would be able to strike a deal. The elements in favor of such a deal were the division of the ruling family and "access" of the Shiʿite to the moderate wing of the ruling family. In the end, the possibility of any concessions was blocked by royal family hard-liners, leading to the radicalization of the opposition, whose hard-line wing gained the upper hand.

The following points present the main developments in the escalation of the "mobilization-radicalization" cycle in February and March:

- *Participants.* The uprising started with the announcement of a "day of rage" on 14 February, the tenth anniversary of the publication of the National Action Charter, King

Hamad's original blueprint for reform. Encouraged by the Internet-savvy youth, tens of thousands of Bahrainis demonstrated in Manama and villages across the country. This was the 14 February Movement, which would occupy the Pearl Roundabout the following day.

- *Violence.* On the first day of demonstrations the government made the fatal mistake of shooting at demonstrators, killing one of them. The next day another demonstrator was killed. On 17 February, during what has since been called "Bloody Thursday," the police organized a 3 a.m. assault on the sleeping protesters at the Pearl Roundabout, killing 4 people and wounding another 250 by birdshot. The next day Bahraini Defense Force troops shot again at people at the roundabout, wounding 38. Ambulances that tried to reach the roundabout were ordered to turn back.
- *Contention.* At sunset on 15 February, the crowd registered several thousand members, swelling further as the evening progressed. Loudspeakers, a media tent, and food stalls appeared. A sit-in began. The next day seven legally registered Shiʿite and leftist political opposition groups called on their followers to take to the streets in support of the 14 February Movement. On 22 and 25 February and 1 March the opposition organized three other major demonstrations.
- *Demands.* At first, typical of the Arab Spring, the *intifada*—nonideological and nonsectarian—called for a constitutional monarchy and social justice. The slogan was "No Sunni, no Shiʿa, just Bahrain" (Seznec 2011). After security forces shot at demonstrators, they raised their stakes and demanded the fall of the prime minister. Later the fall of the government and even the regime were demanded.
- *Organization.* Not until 26 February did the Pearl Roundabout organize itself, and the National Coalition (al-Iʿtilaf al-Watani) was formed. It consisted of independent figures and members of political parties (*al-Wasat* 2011e). The coalition formulated six conditions for negotiation: resignation of the present government and its replacement by a temporary government of "committed national figures"; release of political prisoners; formation of an investigative committee into the police repression; withdrawal of the police and army; and reform of the national media (*al-Wasat* 2011c).
- *Mobilization.* The mobilization was massive and inclusive, attracting different layers of society, but mostly Shiʿites. Lawyers joined protesters at the square, and teachers left classes in support of the strike. In protest to the governmental crackdown, the eighteen parliamentarians of al-Wifaq resigned. As in Tahrir Square in Cairo, the people at Pearl Roundabout claimed to represent the whole of society.
- *Impasse in negotiations.* After the first week the movement on the Pearl Roundabout became more impatient as results of the negotiations remained unclear.
- *Raising demands.* As the stalemate continued, the demands of the National Coalition hardened into new demands: On 27 February it demanded a "new social contract" with the government, a "civil state" (*al-dawla al-madaniyya*) that would guarantee the "dignity of the citizens," and a division of powers between an executive, judiciary, and legislative (*al-Wasat* 2011a). On 1 March the National Coalition demanded the forma-

tion of a government and the installation of a committee that would draw up a new constitution within six months (*al-Wasat* 2011d). On 4 March nine hard-line groups, among them al-Wafa' and Haqq, held massive demonstrations during which they reiterated their demands: elections for a Constituent Assembly, a new government, followed by new general elections (*al-Wasat* 2011g).

- *Escalation and radicalization.* On 26 February the hard-line Shi'ite faction was reinforced by the return of the leader of the Haqq movement, Hasan Mushayma, from exile. It was supported by twenty-four civil society organizations (*al-Wasat* 2011f). In order to break the impasse, on 6 March another massive demonstration was staged in front of the office of Prime Minister Khalifa bin Salman, demanding his resignation. However, by far the most far-reaching move was the founding on 8 March of the Alliance for the Republic (Tahaluf min ajli al-Jumhuriyya) by *Haqq*, the 14 February Movement (*al-Wafa'*), and the Movement of Bahrain Liberals (Haraka Ahrar al-Bahrain). This constituted the ultimate insult to the ruling family (Alliance 2011a). These ideological steps were supported by actions. On 10 March strikes and demonstrations spread to schools. Clashes between Sunni and Shi'ite citizens started to take place. Trade union teachers demonstrated before the ministry of education demanding the resignation of the minister.
- *Emergence of the Sunni countermovement.* At an early stage of the uprising, on 21 February, a major counterdemonstration took place in favor of the government in which allegedly tens of thousands of Sunnis took part.[8] While they chanted some of the slogans of the Shi'ite opposition on the Pearl Roundabout, some of the slogans were also in support of King Hamad: "We love King Hamad and we hate chaos" (Slackman 2011). The movement called itself the National Unity Gathering (Tajammu' al-Wahda al-Wataniyya, TNUG) (Gengler 2012b). Although this movement is often regarded as manipulated by the regime, it also can be seen as representing for the first time the rights of Sunni citizens.
- *The turning point.* This came when youth groups called for a march on the royal palace and the American embassy on 11 March (ICG, 2011b). On 13 March youth groups decided to erect a barricade outside of the Bahrain Financial Harbor complex and blocked the major King Faisal Highway to the Financial Harbor. Many Sunnis started to fear for their personal safety, and in Sunni neighborhoods vigilante groups were formed. On 14 March GCC troops rumbled into Bahrain over the causeway connecting Bahrain with Saudi Arabia.

STRATEGIES OF THE MAIN CONTENDERS AFTER THE UPRISING

In contrast to Long Track—and even to Short Track—states, the Bahrain confrontation was brief. It also ended in a severe backlash. Despite the new round of repression, the tremendous mobilization and politicization cannot be that easily contained in the long run. The phase of bargaining will be reached sooner or later.

It is known that "behind-the-scenes discussion" (ICG 2011a) or "semi-secret talks" (ICG 2011b) took place after the initial violence and withdrawal of the troops from the Pearl Roundabout on 19 February, five days into the uprising (Diwan 2011d), but little is known about their content. Could they have led to an agreement? A closer look at the ideas and moves of the different players in relation to the concept of citizenship and rights can provide some insight.

The split within the ruling family has been one of the most discussed topics in the Bahrain uprising (Da Lage 2011). *The moderate wing of the ruling family* around King Hamad seemed prepared from the start of the Arab Spring to accept reforms and work within the constitution framework. The king was probably supported in this by the United States, which played a conciliatory role throughout the uprising. But how serious was he, and how far could he go? King Hamad himself responded to the crisis with traditional Gulf gratuities based on *makrama*. Ahead of the protests, and cognizant of the fates of autocrats in Tunisia and Egypt, King Hamad announced that every Bahraini family would receive a lump-sum payment of a thousand Bahraini dinars (approximately $2,650). He was also willing to take on the hard-liners in the ruling family in a number of actions. On the second day of the uprising, on 15 February, the king apologized on national TV for the police brutality and promised a swift internal investigation to punish the wrongdoers. Although few Bahrainis were convinced—he had done the same in 1999—his line of action was clearly directed against the hard-line faction within the family (Seznec 2011). The next step he made, on 18 February, was to order the security forces to withdraw and ask the crown prince to open negotiations with the opposition. On 23 February, after the massive demonstrations on the previous day at the Pearl Roundabout, he released twenty-three of the twenty-five defendants in a civilian trial accused of being part of the "terrorist network" in the 2010 trials (HRW 2012, 6). Exiles were also allowed to return. On 25 February, he sacked four ministers, of which two were members of the ruling family (BBC 2011).

Crown Prince Salman was bolder. In an interview with CNN on 19 February he allowed for peaceful demonstrations and gave permission for the crowd to remain on the Pearl Roundabout (HRW 2012). On 20 February he called for a National Dialogue, acknowledging that he received "clear messages from the Bahraini people . . . about the need for reforms" (Constatine 2011). The next day he announced: "citizens of Bahrain, let us work together with all political blocs to help return the security situation to normal so we can announce a day of mourning for those we have lost" (Wahab 2011). On the same day he canceled the Formula One races, a prestigious international event for Bahrain—also considered a major concession to the opposition. As late as 6 March he reaffirmed on Bahrain National TV that Bahrainis were allowed to hold peaceful demonstrations: "this is the right of Bahraini citizens, it is their right to gather and walk in peaceful marches. This is protected in the constitution and we have to support it" (HRW 2012).

The breakthrough from the side of the moderates finally occurred on 13 March, when the crown prince announced major concessions in a seven-point program. He promised: a parliament with full powers; a government that reflects the will of the people; just division of electoral districts; discussion of the issue of naturalization (especially police and security personnel); measures against corruption; scrutiny of the sale of state land; and ending of discrimination (*al-Wasat* 2011j). A day earlier, during a meeting with U.S. secretary of defense Robert Gates, who urged the royal family to implement real reforms and warned that taking "baby steps" would not suffice (ICG 2011a), he had stated that all issues agreed upon by a future National Dialogue would be confirmed by a national referendum (*al-Wasat* 2011i). These points constituted a major step in the direction of recognition of the civil and political rights of Bahraini citizens.

However, it is quite possible that these political concessions were a ploy. After all, the Bahrain Defense Forces (BDF), responsible for the killings, fell directly under the responsibility of the king, although the prime minister directed them (Da Lage 2011). Other disturbing signs were the Gulf Cooperation Council (GCC) meeting in Manama on 18 February and the visit King Hamad paid to King Abdallah of Saudi Arabia on 23 February, as well as the visit of Crown Prince Salman to Saudi Arabia on 3 March. His remarks that he believed the opposition was provocative and threatened the stability of the country did not help to assuage the misgivings of the opposition.

The major obstacle that hampered any serious opening of the phase of bargaining and negotiations was, however, the inability of the moderate wing of the ruling family to dislodge the prime minister, Khalifa bin Salman, who was regarded as the main obstacle for reform and responsible for the repression of 2010. This was a sign that they either were incapable or unwilling to find a solution.

The hard-line wing of the ruling family was completely opposed to any concessions and was afraid of investigations into corruption and control over finance and politics, which a more democratic structure would entail. Prime Minister Khalifa bin Salman was supported within the ruling family by the minister of defense and the royal court minister (Kinninmont 2012). The instruments and resources at the disposal of Khalifa bin Salman and his control over the state's modern "capacity" were considerable: he was the biggest economic player in Bahrain, owning the Bahraini financial markets. The police force took direct orders from him, and he was able to gain control over the BDF at crucial moments through the secretary of defense, also a hard-liner. By cracking down on protesters the conservative wing was able to impose emergency rule and force the moderates in the ruling family to follow suit (Seznec 2011).

Khalifa bin Salman also controlled the national television channels and could directly counter the conciliatory gestures of the moderate wing of the ruling family, often at the same time they were pronounced (*al-Wasat*, February 27, 2011a). By means of the media he could also play on the sectarian divisions by accusing Iran of meddling in Bahrain's internal affairs. This strategy was also meant to rein in the American preference for a negotiated solution. The major asset of the prime minister, however, was his relation with Saudi Arabia's ruling family, which also feared the Shiʿite influence in the region.

The moderate opposition of al-Wifaq and its coalition partners was put in an awkward position by the sudden uprising. During the previous years al-Wifaq had increasingly lost legitimacy, especially among the youth, and it only joined the uprising when it was already underway. What had further eroded its standing was the violence of the regime. Underlining the weakness of playing the game according to the rules of the regime, al-Wifaq's members resigned from the parliament and joined the larger movement at the Pearl Roundabout, demanding immediate investigation into the deaths of the seven protestors during the previous days, the release of all political prisoners arrested in 2010, the resignation of the government (and especially the prime minister), the appointment of an interim government, and the organization of new elections that would reflect the will of the people in order to draw up a new constitution to replace the one from 2002. At the same time, it tried to pursue its previous nonsectarian policy of reaching out to the Sunni minority by calling for a "civil state" (*al-dawla al-madaniyya*) and making demands for the whole nation (*al-Fajr* 2011). At every occasion its leader, Sheikh Ali Salman, repeated his pledge that the civil rights of the Sunnis would be guaranteed: "the safety and peace of every Sunni in Bahrain is my personal responsibility," "their blood is my blood" (*al-Wasat* 2011g). This partly worked to the extent that during the whole uprising al-Waʿd and other Sunni groups supported the demands of al-Wifaq. The spiritual leader of the Shiʿites, Sheikh Isa Qasim, as well stressed that the demonstrators spoke in name of the "legitimate rights of the people," "the national interest, national unity, and non-sectarianism" (al-Jamri 2011).

However, influenced by the intoxicating atmosphere of what was happening at the Pearl Roundabout and fed by the events in the rest of the Arab world, the demands of the moderates hardened during the next few weeks. Reflecting their distrust of the ruling family that had reneged on its previous promises in 2002, al-Wifaq asked for "guarantees that words will be backed by action" (Al-Shalchi and Surk 2011). In a statement on 25 February Sheikh Isa Qasim (2011), repeated the preconditions for negotiations: "We want a meaningful, viable and sustainable process with very clear deliverables and a time-table to check that all what would and could be agreed on is actually implemented on the ground." On 1 March, the spokesperson of the National Coalition said that a National Dialogue could only take place "under the aegis of a National Coalition government." In that way changes could be implemented "rapidly" (*al-Wasat* 2011d). As Kristin Smith Diwan (2011c) has pointed out, these guarantees undermined the bargaining position of the moderates, but in light of earlier experiences they were understandable. During the past decade the royal family had made no attempts to dismantle their own "trust networks" and subsume them under a neutral state that would enter into a new relationship with its citizens. Neither would the Shiʿite opposition do so if the ruling family was unresponsive to its demands.

The hard-line opposition's position was enhanced by the killings of the early morning of 17 February. The Shiʿite alliance consisted of unlicensed, illegal political groups with street credibility who rejected dialogue with the regime. Its militant leader Hasan Mushayma received a hero's welcome when he returned from exile in London to Bahrain on 26 February. It is important to look into his revolutionary, populist rhetoric, which to a large extent ran counter to the guarantees of civil and political rights that the moderates were trying to give the Sunni minority.

As an activist and a supporter of direct democracy, Mushayma's strategy was to let the Pearl Roundabout determine the demands of the uprising. Like al-Wifaq, he emphasized that it was a national and a political uprising, not a sectarian one (Mushayma 2011a). His discourse revolved around such terms as *unity* (*wahda*), the *community* (*al-jamiʿ*), *consensus* (*ijmaʿ*), the *people* (*al-shaʿb*). In an interview just after he returned on 26 February, Mushayma stated that "mobilized masses are the source [of legitimacy/power]" (*marjaʿiyya*). The "street" was now making the demands. From his rejection of "distinctions in national demands" (*taqsim al-matalib al-wataniyya*) it was clear that the ruling family and the Sunni minority could only save themselves if they joined the revolutionary momentum and subsumed their demands to the common good (Mushayma 2011b).

In his revolutionary fervor Mushayma at first only called for a constitutional monarchy along the "British model," where the monarch reigns but does not rule, but as the protests continued and concessions did not come forth, he called for the removal of the ruling family and the installation of a republic, as represented in the manifesto of the Alliance for the Republic. This document uses such phrases as the "unbreakable steel will of the people," "revolutionary resistance," "revolutionary peaceful means," and "legitimate revolutionary demands." These will bring down the "corrupt royal system" and end "oppression" (*zulm*) and "corruption" (*fasad*). The religious dimension of the thinking of its signees was reflected in their belief that the struggle would win "with the permission and help of God the highest" (Alliance 2011a). The same ambiguity is reflected in a term like *marjaʿiyya* (the religious source or guide), which is used here in a secular sense of the people as the source of power.[9]

The split with al-Wifaq occurred when the hardliners took the decision to expand contentious action to other repertoires than the sit-in at Pearl Roundabout (ICG 2011b). To break the impasse, Haqq, al-Wafaʾ, and the Bahrain Islamic Freedom Movement (BIFM) called for expanding the protests to the royal palace and the Financial Harbor a few days before the GCC intervention.

BACKLASH

Repression

The entrance of a thousand Saudi troops into Bahrain on 14 March, supported by five hundred United Arab Emirates police and a number of Qatari troops, signaled the victory of the hard-liners in the ruling family over the moderates who had seemed to support a negotiated settlement. The repression that was unleashed was, in contrast to the repression a year earlier, "indiscriminate," targeting all members of the opposition, whether moderate, hard-line, ordinary Shiʿite, or liberal Sunni. It was a massive revenge for the uprising and the deep fear it had instilled in the ruling family and Sunni community. In total, since February, forty-three (or many more) people were killed, fifteen hundred arrested and tortured, and nearly three thousand fired from their jobs. More than five hundred Bahraini employees were dismissed from their jobs, and two thousand workers were fired for participating in demonstrations. Since the demolition of the Pearl Roundabout monument in the week after the clampdown, resistance has moved to the Shiʿite villages, where clashes occurred almost every night (*Washington Post* 2011).

To demonstrate the unity of the royal family, most of the repression was executed under Royal Decree 18/2011, issued on 15 March 2011, starting a three-month "State of National Safety," akin to emergency laws. The decree granted wide-ranging authority to the commander-in-chief of the Bahrain Defense Force to issue sweeping regulations governing public order. The decree also established military courts, the so-called National Safety Courts, whose judges were appointed by the commander-in-chief of the Bahrain Defense Force (HRW 2012, 17). The charges against defendants were typical for their denial of basic civil and political rights (freedom of opinions and organization, and right to fair trial); they were reminiscent of the 2010 trials of the twenty-three protestors, who were convicted for calling for a "constitutional monarchy," "publicly inciting hatred and contempt for the governing regime," and engaging in "illegal assemblies." Fourteen defendants were convicted for "broadcasting false and tendentious news" and participating in "marches without notifying the competent body" (HRW 2012, 13).

Among the hundreds of people brought before National Safety Courts were many politicians. In early May Matar Ibrahim Matar, member of al-Wifaq, was arrested for resigning from parliament on 18 February (HRW 2012,3). No one was spared. An apolitical businessman, Ghazi Farhan, was ambushed in his office parking lot on 12 April and held incommunicado for fifty days before being sentenced to three years imprisonment (Shehabi 2011). On 22 June, twenty-one opposition leaders were sentenced to long prison terms, eight of them to life imprisonment. Sunni liberals especially were penalized for joining the opposition. Ibrahim Sharif and others were sentenced in the case of "the plot to overthrow the Bahraini monarchy and to conspire with a foreign nation" (*al-Wasat* 2011n). In April the regime handed down four death sentences. In addition, forty Shi'ite mosques and *husayniyyas* were demolished. Between forty and fifty doctors and medical personnel were accused of storing weapons and blocking Sunnis from receiving medical treatment. The only remaining independent newspaper, *al-Wasat,* was taken over, and its editor-in-chief Mansoor al-Jamri was interrogated and later accused of inventing news with the "intention of causing instability in Bahrain" (ICG 2011b, 7).

Not only were these measures a denial of civil rights; the backlash was a throwback to previous forms of political legitimacy based on subservience and loyalty. In government institutions, state-controlled companies, large private companies, and universities, staff were asked to sign loyalty oaths "in which they declared allegiance to king and country" (ICG 2011b, 7–8). A public campaign of naming and shaming was launched, demonstrators and their sympathizers were called "traitors," and detainees were forced to confess on state television (*Washington Post* 2011).

Restoration?

The regime, however, was not prepared to dismantle its traditional facade of benevolence and *makrama* completely. After the clampdown from March to May a series of measures was taken to enhance Bahrain's image abroad. The king lifted the State of National Safety on 1 June and Crown Prince Salman visited the White House on 7 June 2011, where he announced that "we are committed to reform in both political and economic spheres" (AFP 2011). Many workers and union activists who had been fired or suspended for taking part in demonstrations were reinstated. On the other hand, a teachers association was disbanded (Surk 2011).

The most conspicuous means of trying to control the damage of the backlash was appointment of the Bahrain Independent Commission of Inquiry (BICI) on 29 June 2011. The commission began its work on 20 July, and in his announcement speech King Hamad disingenuously stated: "We need to look back and to determine exactly what happened in February and March, and to consider the reactions to those events. There were victims of the violence that took place. They must not be forgotten. There have been accusations and counteraccusations about the origins of the violence. A lack of confidence has prevailed, and disagreements have led to conflicting beliefs about events, even if such beliefs are founded only on rumors" (Shehabi 2011).

The reason to install this commission has been heavily debated. The scholar Abdelhadi Khalaf had misgivings about its mandate (Shehabi 2011). He believed there are three reasons for BICI: overcoming divisions within the ruling family; improving the reputation of the regime; and erasing international tension (AFP 2011). Another conciliatory gesture was to initiate the National Dialogue on 9 July.

But out of the three hundred participants only fifteen were allocated to members of the licensed opposition, and the whole process was based on the idea of subjects asking for concessions from the government; al-Wifaq members resigned within two weeks (Diwan 2011d).

From the contradictory policies, it is clear that the ruling family is divided among itself. A good example is the response to the civil retrial of twenty medical personnel. While the moderates within the family wanted them to be acquitted and were glad that the public prosecutor at first dropped the charges against fifteen of the twenty accused, the hard-liners were glad that in the end the charges were upheld against all of the defendants (Carlstrom 2012a).

REBARGAINING

By the end of 2011 Bahrain had reached a stalemate. After being evicted from the Pearl Roundabout, the resistance had left the center and moved to the villages around Manama, where a constant resistance was organized by youth (Black 2011). Violence escalated. For instance, on 9 April 2012 a homemade bomb exploded, injuring—according to the Bahraini government—seven policemen (ICG 2012).

It is clear that the phase of bargaining still has not yet fully taken off, but given the dramatic increase of political awareness and mobilization during the February–March uprising, it is unlikely that another phase of depoliticization, dedemocratization, and demobilization will occur. Indeed, it seems that the awareness of civil, political, and social rights has deepened and expanded to previous apolitical Shiʿites, but, more importantly, also to Sunnis.

Al-Wifaq and its coalition partners continued to press for negotiations. Since the repression of the uprising, Sheikh Ali Salman (2011) repeatedly tried to explain the position of al-Wifaq. He denied the hard-line Sunni accusation that he wanted to implement *wilaya al-faqih* (rule of religious leaders) and repeated endlessly that al-Wifaq was loyal to Bahrain and its Arabness. He was also constantly at pains to include in the opposition (*al-muʿarada*) his Sunni coalition partners, al-Waʿd, al-Tajammuʿ al-Qawmi, al-Tajammuʿ al-Watani, al-Ikha. Despite the repression, they organized common demonstrations throughout this period—for instance, on 2 February 2012 a mass rally for the release of political prisoners, and on 15 April 2012 a rally to underscore the continuous struggle for democracy (*al-Wasat* 2011m).

The basis of the political claims of this coalition remained the Manama Document issued on 12 October 2011, which elaborates on the seven points the crown prince had issued as the basis of the National Dialogue on 13 March 2011. It demanded a new constitution that reflects the "will of the people"; a constitutional monarchy; a democratically chosen government; a parliament with only an elected chamber; reform of the electoral districts; and an independent judiciary. Its conciliatory tone is reflected in the slogan "the people want the reform of the system" (rather than the "fall of the system").[10] The points of the Manama Document have since been repeated in numerous interviews, sermons, and announcements (*al-Wasat*, 2011o).

There were also calls for negotiations with the Sunni organizations. On 9 July 2012, former MP Abd al-Jalil Khalil (2012) called upon all parties, including the Sunni hard-line TNUG (see below), to meet. He said that "we have no redlines and do not exclude any party." This solution, however, can only be based on "equality, justice and participation." He also rejected the idea that the problem is a sectarian one. The conflict has political roots that must be solved between the opposition and the ruling family, not between Shiʿites and Sunnis.

As for relations with the ruling family, Sheikh Ali Salman (2012) expressed his concern that since March 2011 all contacts with the government have been "cut" (*maqtuʿ*). He did not count the National Dialogue of July 2011 as relevant, because dialogue must be "open" and based on respect rather than "subservience" (*tabiʿ*). A dialogue must be based on "equality of voices." He further stated that it must be based on a chosen Constituent Assembly that "represents the will of the people." A month later, he announced that there had been contacts, "but they did not amount to a dialogue." Also Muhammad al-Qassab of al-Waʿd stated that "there is no solution for the crisis now except dialogue" (Carlstrom 2012b). The main conditions for negotiations are however the restoration of basic civil rights, such as the freedom of political prisoners, the ending of tear gas attacks on villages, the implementing of the BICI report recommendations, the release of 1200 prisoners, the reinstatement of workers and civil servants who were fired and the end of trials, media propaganda against opposition, and punishment of criminal offenses of security personnel (*al-Wasat* 2012j). In return the coalition would condemn violent resistance and promote peaceful resistance (*al-Wasat*, 2011q).

Haqq remained constant in its approach. The ideas of Hasan Mushayma, the militant leader of Haqq, who was jailed 17 March 2011, did not change either. The Alliance for the Republic (AFR) continued to exist and regularly issue pamphlets in which it opposed any negotiations with the regime, calling it "criminal" and "corrupt." It supported the open contestation, such as street fighting, and tried to prevent the negotiations from entering "closed rooms" where "pressure can be put on negotiators" (AFR 2012a). In other pamphlets, it rejects the invitation to the opposition to take part in the committee to implement the recommendations of the BICI Commission (AFR 2011d). It warned other political groups not to work together with the government (AFR 2011b). It combined the Ashura festival with revolutionary fervor (AFR 2011e), and supported all "activities [*faʿaliyyat*] of youth in all Arab countries that protest against the existing system (AFR 2011c).

Sunni self-defense groups were one of the most remarkable results of the uprising, as a social movement that defends its interests against *both* the Shiʿite opposition and the ruling family who it believes might sell them out (Gengler 2012b).

The movement started with a massive counter-rally organized by Sunnis in support of the ruling family on 21 February.[11] Demonstrators chanted "we want Khalifa bin Salman" (the prime minister). This event marked the birth of the National Unity Gathering (Tajammuʿ al-Wahda al-Wataniyya, TNUG). The TNUG was originally composed of three Islamist groups: the Muslim Brotherhood (al-Minbar al-Watani al-Islami), the Salafi trend (al-Asala al-Jamaʿiyya al-Islamiyya), and Jamiʿiyyat al-Shura al-Islamiyya, the charitable organization run by Sheikh Abd al-Latif al-Mahmoud, the leader of the initiative. Also, leftist secular Sunni leaders who had fallen out with the al-Waʿd group and who supported Bahrain's "Arabness" had joined (ICG 2011b, 8). Typically, it chose the square named after the conqueror of the ruling family of Bahrain two hundred years ago, the Ahmad Fatih (conqueror) Square, and its mosque as its place of mobilization. That in itself was a statement, as the gathering of the Fatih Mosque was opposed to the gathering of the Pearl Roundabout (Makki 2012).

The TNUG claimed to represent the silent majority of the Sunnis who had never properly organized (*al-Wasat* 2011h). But Sheikh Abd al-Latif al-Mahmoud was not a slavish follower of the ruling family. In 1992 he signed the so-called Elite Petition delivered to the ruler (Lawson 2004, 96). At the founding meeting of the TNUG on 21 February he demanded the release of the Shiʿite prisoners and the trial of culprits of killings. He opposed racial and sectarian discrimination and urged the government to continue its reform program and grant Bahrainis the citizen rights they were demanding (Mohammed 2011), recognizing that Shiʿites and Sunnis have common economic, social, and political grievances (*al-Wasat* 2011l). In later interviews Abd al-Latif al-Mahmoud always claimed that he was not opposed to reform until the opposition acquired a sectarian character (Hammond 2011). To underline his reformist credentials, he said that after the crisis the prime minister must resign. But he claimed circumstances had changed since he had joined the opposition in 1992: "then the regime was oppressive while today oppression comes from certain political groups who use force" (*al-Wasat* 2011h).

This ambiguity explains why Sheikh al-Mahmoud during the uprising had intensive contacts with the opposition, even engaging in long negotiating sessions. As late as 27 February 2011 the oppositional National Coalition formed at Pearl Roundabout announced that it did not know where he stood (*al-Wasat* 2011a). A few days later its spokesperson even proclaimed that negotiations with the TNUG had been "fruitful" (*al-Wasat* 2011d). However, on 2 March the TNUG finally made its position clear: it rejected the resignation of the government as a precondition for negotiations (Al Arabiya News 2011). Sheikh al-Mahmoud (2011a, 2011b, 2011c) later explained his position that the demands of the opposition were "cramped" (*al-mutashannuj*) and "inflexible" (*ʿadam al-lin*). He was not so much against al-Wifaq as against the "fanatical forces" of Haqq and its coalition partners, al-Wafaʾ, and Ahrar Bahrain (TNUG 2011–2012). He opposed the far-reaching demands "that wanted to monopolize power" and warned that the Pearl Roundabout was becoming a "state within a state," believing that "the opposition had prepared an agenda a long time ago with the sectarian media to undermine the country."

The basic dilemma of Abd al-Latif al-Mahmoud was that as a member of the Sunni minority he believes the ruling family is the only bulwark against a Shiʿite takeover (TNUG 2011–2012), while he distrusts the ruling family as capable of making deals with the Shiʿite opposition at the expense of Sunni minority interests. He expressed this distrust during the founding rally on 21 February when he warned that "any national demand cannot be ratified or answered without ratification by all communities" (Mohammed 2011). The only way out of this dilemma was massive Sunni mobilization for their rights, which was meant both as a warning to as well as a sign of support for the monarchy. This repositioning of the Sunni citizens and the ruling family was expressed in the statement that the nation (*watan*) and the ruling family (*hakim*) are one. Loyalty (*walaʿ*) to the one is loyalty to the other (*al-Wasat* 2011l). This did not mean that he rejected pluralism. He emphasized that adherence to different religions did not prevent attachment to the nation. But he asserted that only the existing system can prevent "division" and "chaos" (*al-Wasat* 2011f), and that reform can be achieved within the existing system: "if we can reform our house, why do we have to demolish it?" In fact, he believed that a "modern civil state" (*al-dawla al-madaniyya al-haditha*)—the centerpiece of Arab Spring citizenship rights discourse—that opposes discrimination and guarantees equality before the law can be built upon the 2002 constitution (*al-Wasat* 2011b).

Despite all his fears and clichés of Shiʿites as being driven by Iran and Iraq ("the Shiʿites, they have their ayatollahs, and whatever they say, they will run and do it. If they tell them to burn a house, they will. I think they have a clear intention to disrupt this country"), he has reiterated that negotiations with the opposition are welcome as soon as security returns. Basically, he remained in favor of an agreement and believed it attainable, under the condition that they stop violence and above all "accept the rights of the other" (*al-Wasat* 2012i). Negotiations with the Shiʿites, he stated, will resume when "their intoxications end and thought returns" (*al-Wasat* 2011l).

One and a half years after the uprising Sheikh al-Mahmoud seemed to have become vehemently opposed to Shiʿism. In a sermon given in April 2012, he still believed that Iran is a threat and that al-Wifaq intends to establish a "religious state" (*al-Wasat* 2012h). He became more intransigent and refused to take part in a National Dialogue (*al-Wasat* 2012f). From the speech he held during the second general conference of the TNUG as a political society, he made clear that the movement is as much directed against the ruling family as against the opposition. Building a strong party with committed members is a means to prevent the TNUG from being manipulated by the moderates and by the hard-liners of the royal family.

The Sahwa, not TNUG, however, appeared to constitute the major threat to negotiations. The Sunni Youth Awakening of al-Fatih (Sahwa Shabab al-Fatih) is much more contentious than TNUG. An alliance (*iʿtilaf*) of different youth groups, the Sahwa was founded on 16 December 2011 and modeled on the Tahrir movement (*al-Wasat* 2011p), intending to be democratically organized, with each group being represented in its executive organ (Sahwa 2011). It played on the generational gap between the older Sunni leaders such as Abd al-Latif al-Mahmoud and the aspiring youth of the Sahwa. It also adopted the same repertoire of contention as Tahrir, organizing weekly sit-ins at the al-Fatih Mosque. Its leaders, Khalid Musa al-Balushi and Ra'id al-Jawdar, were first members of TNUG, but they later criticized TNUG for not achieving enough during the previous year and not respecting the demands of the initial meeting in February (*Bahrain Mirror* 2012). They feel that TNUG has been co-opted by becoming a "[political] society."

Its critical attitude toward the government was even more pronounced than TNUG. In a speech al-Balushi (2012) said that the Khalifa family should be protected—"like any family in Bahrain"—but that it must rule "as a manager" with the rest of the Bahrainis. It clearly regarded the relationship between citizens and the ruler as a contract. Like TNUG it demands "transparency" (*shafafiyya*), "oversight" (*raqaba*) and "equality" (*masawa*). But it goes further, demanding "equal distribution of the Bahraini wealth" and the "curbing of corruption," referring to corruption in land distribution, housing, income from oil, "and other resources." In addition, it demanded the building of a productive economic policy (*al-Wasat* 2011p). During its Friday sit-in organized on 20 January 2012 it demanded the prosecution of "embezzlers of public funds" and stated that "justice is the basis of stability" (*al-Wasat* 2012b).

But, more than TNUG even, the Sahwa was deeply paranoid when it comes to the Shiʿite opposition. It is in favor of democracy, but not one that would lead to the victory of the Shiʿites or would be led by Shiʿite clerics (*al-Wasat* 2012g). Typically international bodies and countries favoring negotiated accommodation are attacked. For instance, on 27 January 2012 it organized a sit-in in front of the UN representative building (*al-Wasat* 2012c), repeated in February (*al-Wasat* 2012d), and on Friday, 16 March, it organized a sit-in against negotiations and U.S. interference in Bahrain's affairs. It threatened to organize a sit-in in front of the U.S. embassy if it did not stop its "manipulation" behind the scenes (*al-Wasat* 2012e).

Despite its basically reformist attitude that entails far-reaching citizenship, its deep fear of a Shiʿite takeover turned it into an antidemocratic, exclusive (communitarian) movement, rejecting any changes to the constitution as a "coup d'état" (*inqilab*) (Abna 2012). Its radicalism led to the establishment of Sunni vigilante groups that attack Shiʿites and commit acts of retaliation, and the Sahwa has warned that it intended to organize "people's committees" to protect the Sunni community (*al-Wasat* 2012c). Nevertheless, it is important to point out that since late 2012 not much has been heard from it. At the time of publication it was unclear whether it only temporarily has vanished from the political scene because it was marginalized by other actors, has been co-opted back into al-Minbar—of which it, according to some sources, had been a youth wing organization—or it simply has disappeared below the radar for more "tactical" reasons as at times it seemed to be lacking the required level of public support.

AFTER THE *INTIFADA*

The relentless crackdown on opposition activists and vocal human rights defenders did not bring a halt to the willingness of large parts of the Bahraini population to take part in protests and demonstrations. Small as well as mass protests, sometimes with as many as tens of thousands of participants, still took place in the following years (Matthiesen 2014). Influenced by events in Egypt, a Bahraini Tamarrod (rebellion) movement was set up to give new oxygen to the protests. It called upon the people of Bahrain to let their voices be heard on 14 August 2013, the date of the forty-second anniversary of the country's independence from the United Kingdom.

In its preparation to counter this potentially threatening situation, the Bahraini parliament convened an emergency meeting where it adopted twenty-two recommendations for new laws that would tighten the security situation. According to Emile Nakhleh (2013) these recommendations "aimed at giving the regime pseudo-legal tools to quash dissent and violate human and civil rights with impunity. All in the name of fighting terrorism." Examples are the prohibition of (unapproved) protests[12]—in the form of sit-ins, rallies, and gatherings—in the capital Manama, holding fathers criminally responsible for the actions committed by their underage children, and stripping those who get convicted of "terrorism" charges of their Bahraini citizenship. The recommendations were accepted by the king, who ordered the government to duly codify and implement them as decree–laws. The prime minister, furthermore, even threatened to fire those members of the government who would dare to hinder their implementation (Nakhleh 2013).

Meanwhile, in an effort to polish up Bahrain's image on the international stage, King Hamad bin Isa Al Khalifa in 2011 proposed to set up a pan-Arab Rights Tribunal, to be headquartered in his country, in order to promote the protection of human rights in the Arab world (Toumi 2013b). His proposal, to establish and host the permanent headquarters of an Arab Human Rights Court, immediately received approval from the Arab League Council (BNA 2013). Yet, if the Bahraini government were serious about respecting human rights and achieving real justice, a whole lot of other measures would urgently need to be taken. The UN Human Rights Council, in its third joint statement on Bahrain, during its twenty-sixth session on 10 June 2014, expressed serious concerns about lack of sufficient guarantees to a fair trial in Bahrain's criminal justice system, an increase in long-term prison convictions for exercising rights to freedom of peaceful assembly and association, continuing reports of ill-treatment and torture in detention facilities, and the arbitrary deprivation of nationality without due process (OHCHR 2014).

Marc Owen Jones (2014) has noted: "Over the past three years, the scale of killings and torture, coupled with the most limited veneer of police accountability, have underscored the Bahraini government's failure to address one of the most important elements of political reform: achieving justice. Without justice, the state remains unaccountable for violations of civil and human rights, and its progressive credentials, if any, are rendered laughable." Another example of the complicated situation is a "defamation campaign" by a pro-regime newspaper and three Human Rights GONGOs (government-organized nongovernmental organizations), who published "Wanted (for arrest)" posters of eighteen activists and human rights defenders, portraying them as "traitors" responsible for incitement to violence and human rights violations. This slander was meant as a reaction to the Bahrain Center for Human Rights' own "End Impunity in Bahrain" campaign, which in November 2013 published the names of government officials and state employees who they deemed responsible for, or involved in, the (ongoing) human rights violations. The BCHR campaign was intended to raise awareness at home and abroad. But it backfired when some activists subsequently were imprisoned, and others felt the need to leave the country in order not to jeopardize their own safety, as a result of the slander against them (BCHR 2013).

If moderate opposition leaders fail to achieve some sort of political settlement that would improve the socioeconomic living conditions of many Bahrainis and would get the Shiʿite community more involved with the governing of their state, there is a likely chance that more and more disenfranchised youth will resort to more violent ways to express their resistance toward the current situation. In order to break through the stalemate and achieve long-term stability it is therefore of the utmost importance that thirteen imprisoned leaders[13] of (unlicensed) opposition societies be released and be able to join the National Dialogue.

Continuation of National Dialogue talks. In early January 2014, the Bahraini government again officially suspended its efforts to hold national reconciliation talks that had been initiated a year earlier. According to the government, all dialogue attempts had stalled because of the refusal of Shiʿite opposition groups to participate. Nevertheless, in a surprising meeting on 15 January 2014 between the crown prince and the representatives of some of the opposition parties, including al-Wifaq's secretary-general Sheikh Ali Salman, renewed hope was raised that the negotiations would be rejuvenated when the opposition was invited to submit a list of detailed proposals, covering five major topics, to the Royal Court (Matthiesen 2014).[14] Since then, the minister of the Royal Court, Sheikh Khaled bin Ahmed Al Khalifa, sat down with representatives from the two political coalitions, namely the opposition political societies and the "pro-government" societies, and presumably some other civil society organizations as well (Toumi 2014b).

Earlier reconciliation initiatives came to a halt either because the regime was unwilling to make political concessions required by the opposition or because pro-government groups were not invited to the negotiation table. The first national dialogue attempt, for instance, ended in July 2011. While the second effort to start a new round of reconciliation talks, in March 2012, never took off because the TNUG and Sahwa objected (Gengler 2012a). A third national dialogue initiative, alluded to above, was started in February 2013 and was suspended by the government on 8 January 2014, even though five opposition groups already had decided to boycott the talks—after al-Wifaq's deputy secretary-general, Khalil Marzooq, was arrested on fabricated charges of inciting hatred, violence, and terrorism—in September 2013. Even secret talks held by the crown prince, between March and July 2013, which could have led to an agreement with the opposition, came to a halt after the explosion of a car bomb on 17 July at the parking lot near a Sunni mosque in Riffa, where many royal family members have their homes (Al Arabiya News 2013; Matthiesen 2014).

The involvement of the crown prince in the latest attempt to revive the reconciliation talks, only a week after they were suspended, was nevertheless very important—not only because the opposition groups previously had complained about the lack of involvement of high-ranking members of the royal family, but also because it signified, as Justin Gengler (2014) has pointed out, the crown prince's "long-awaited return to national relevance" after he was sidelined—by more conservative and security-oriented hard-line factions of his family—following the GCC intervention in March 2011. Moreover, the crown prince's appointment as first deputy prime minister in March 2013 also helped to re-empower his position in the Bahraini cabinet.

Apart from that, it might have been advantageous as well that the new reconciliation talks were to be held in the form of bilateral meetings between representatives of the political societies and members of the Bahraini government and parliament. This would not only have increased the likelihood that the demands and suggestions of the opposition groups—which otherwise might have gotten lost in the voices and opinions of the quantitatively often overrepresented pro-regime groups—really would have been heard. It would also have provided the government with the opportunity to prevent Shiʿite and Sunni actors from combining their strengths in an effort to achieve a common position in regard to their shared demands for political and socioeconomic reforms.

Nonetheless, mutual distrust remains, and the TNUG has expressed its unwillingness to take part in any new dialogue "unless there are the necessary guarantees for it to be a dialogue that represents all the components of this nation, fully engaging all, and on an equal footing" (TNUG 2014). In other words, they would not accept any agreements that might have been made outside of the dialogue table—to which they were not invited in 2012—between, for instance, al-Wifaq and the crown prince. Neither would they accept the government to act as supervisor, but only as an equal party at the negotiation table. As such, notwithstanding that the TNUG eventually decided to take part in the negotiations, the talks again stalled.

According to the prominent human rights defender Nabeel Rajab, who was released from jail on 24 May 2014, the Bahraini government lacks the incentive to hold serious dialogues: "Parliament is in its hands and so it can legislate repressive laws that turn the country into a dictatorship without headaches. Its PR machine has effectively normalized the situation so that it faces no threat of consequences from its main international allies. . . . Most importantly, the government is in control of the street now. Protests can be contained" (LeVine 2014).

Run-up to the *Parliamentary elections*. After the main (Shiʿite) opposition parties boycotted the Majlis al-Nuwwab by-elections in 2011—which needed to be organized in order to replace the MPs from al-Wifaq who had resigned from parliament in protest over the harsh crackdown on the Pearl Roundabout protesters—some members of the regime appeared eager to try to persuade al-Wifaq to take part in the elections, presumably to polish their image abroad and thereby giving some legitimacy to the soon-to-be-elected new parliament.

Yet, in July 2014, in an action that endangered the latest attempt to revive the national dialogue, the Ministry of Justice, Islamic Affairs and Endowments filed lawsuits against three opposition societies. The ministry asked the court for a three-month suspension of al-Wifaq, al-Waʿd, and the Justice and Development Movement, in order for them to rectify their (il)legal status in accordance with their statute. According to the Justice Ministry's Political Societies' Affairs Office, these three political societies did not respect the law and their own statuses by canceling general and elective assemblies (due to a lack of the required amount of delegates), violating regulations of transparency, or refusing to elect a new secretary-general (BNA 2014; Khalifa 2014a).

In an expression of solidarity, the three affected opposition societies stated that "the motive behind the Justice Ministry's lawsuit against Al Wefaq is to strangle political activism and refuse dialogue that could produce a political solution" (Al Wefaq 2014b). Even though the ministry claimed that it had notified the societies about their violations and had instructed them to take appropriate measures, the opposition groups claimed that they had never received any official notifications and that they always abided by the law and their statuses (Al Wefaq 2014a). It should appear to be no coincidence that the lawsuit against al-Wifaq came a little over a week after its secretary-general and deputy secretary-general were both charged with breaching a law—which amended a prior decision from the Justice Ministry on communications between local political societies and foreign officials. The law ordered political societies to notify the Ministry of Foreign Affairs in advance of any meetings with foreign diplomats or government representatives. Moreover, according to this amendment, which was announced in September 2013, a ministry official needs to be present at all times during these sorts of meetings

(Toumi 2013). The TNUG has welcomed this new law, which they believe will contribute to the preservation of the sovereignty of Bahrain and will counteract foreign interference in the state's domestic affairs. It is in this context that the U.S. assistant secretary of state for democracy human rights and labor, Tom Malinowski, was expelled from Bahrain in June 2014 after meeting the al-Wifaq leadership, in what thus apparently can be considered an "illegal" meeting, which most probably has been the real motive for the lawsuit against al-Wifaq.

A three-month suspension of the activities of al-Wifaq—as well as the other effected societies—still left them able to field candidates in time for the parliamentary elections in November 2014. Earlier, al-Wifaq's leadership declared that they again would boycott the upcoming elections unless "the opposition's demands for fair electoral districts, a parliament with full powers and an elected government" would be accepted (Al Wefaq 2014b).

Two months before the first round of the parliamentary elections, Crown Prince Salman announced that the aforementioned invitation to submit a list of detailed proposals, and the minister of the Royal Court's efforts, had resulted in a new five-point framework to resume the reconciliatory dialogue. This framework was composed of five core elements including commitments to redefine electoral districts (in order to ensure greater representation and enhance electoral oversight); revise the appointment process for members of the nonelected, upper chamber of parliament; give MPs new rights of approval on the appointment of the cabinet, on questioning the actions of ministers and on seeking amendment or rejection of the cabinet's annual budget; and further reform the judiciary (to strengthen its constitutional independence) as well as the police and security services (National Dialogue Media Center 2014).

Yet, the core elements of this new framework fell short of the major concessions that the crown prince had announced in his seven-point program in March 2011. As Jane Kinninmont and Omar Sirri have noted: "From the point of view of the crown prince and his supporters, this was a framework that should [have] provide[d] the opposition with incentives to re-enter parliament and thereby kick-start an ongoing process of gradual reforms. [Yet, for] the opposition, the offer was unconvincing" (Kinninmont and Sirri 2014, 12). Therefore, many of the opposition societies, including al-Wifaq, decided to keep boycotting the elections as was evidenced by a mass protest rally— witnessed by one of the authors—that came only one day after the crown prince's five-point framework announcement. Moreover, less than one month before the elections, the Ministry of Justice tried to ban al-Wifaq's activities again, for a three-month period, after having sought a court conviction which it eventually received but almost immediately suspended for three months (al-Akhbar 2014b; Henderson 2014).

Regardless of al-Wifaq's and other opposition societies' decision over participation in the elections, the Sunni political societies sought as many seats as possible.

Al-Minbar and al-Asala already announced that they once again had the intention to field candidates together (Singh Grewal 2014).[15] The TNUG would also take part in the elections, either in coalition with al-Minbar and al-Asala or alone. Such negotiations for coalition had previously failed because of internal rivalries back in 2012, when the TNUG and the Sunni political societies parted ways (Al Hasan 2012).

Parliamentary Elections were held on 22 and 29 November. In the end, perhaps in part due to the electoral districts that were indeed redrawn in line with the crown prince's five-point framework for dialogue and reform, al-Asala and al-Minbar decided not to collaborate with the TNUG. As a result, ten of the TNUG's members ran as independents; yet none of them were elected. Apart from the redrawn electoral districts, which with hindsight appear to have been detrimental to the established Sunni-loyalist political societies, another "innovation" of the first full parliamentary elections since the outbreak of the Arab Spring protests was the threat of penalties against persons who intentionally declined to participate in the elections. Rumors had started to circulate that civil servants, policemen, and personnel of the BDF would be pressured to vote, and that people who would decide not to take part in the elections would not be allowed to participate in future elections. Even though the minister of justice had announced in September that no penalties would be taken against nonvoters, the chief of the high election committee stated in the press, only two days before the first round of the elections, that the Bahraini cabinet was studying administrative measures, including the prevention of receiving a government job, against those who would abstain from voting (Al A'Ali 2014).

As a result, voter turnout appeared to be a test of the election's and new parliament's legitimacy. According to figures reported by the authorities, it would seem that around 51.5 percent of the approximately 350,000 eligible voters took part during the first round of elections on 22 November (al-Akhbar 2014a). When also taking into account the percentage of voters participating in the second round runoff elections on 29 November, in the thirty-four districts where no candidate won at least 51 percent of the ballots cast during the first round, the overall official turnout reached 52.6 percent (Khalifa 2014c). These official electoral turnout figures are contested by the opposition, mainly al-Wifaq and four other opposition societies, who decided to boycott the elections and put the estimate of the real voter turnout at around 30 percent (al-Akhbar 2014a; Khalifa 2014b).

Whatever might be the real case, considering the redrawn electoral districts and al-Wifaq's boycott, it is safe to say that Sunni Islamist and (mostly inexperienced) independents from the Sunni as well as Shiʿite communities have dominated the elections. Hence, it is therefore not surprising that pro-regime candidates ended up winning most of the parliamentary seats. Twenty-seven seats were won by Sunni candidates, while the remaining thirteen seats went to independent Shiʿite candidates (Khalifa 2014c). What is much more surprising is that only a very small number of candidates from established Sunni-loyalist political societies were able to win parliamentary seats, two of which went to al-Asala and only one to al-Minbar candidates (Citizens for Bahrain 2014), while none of the candidates of the TNUG was successful in winning a seat in the Majlis al-Nuwwab at all. On the other hand, one thing that has not changed is Sheikh Khalifa bin Salman's position within the government. He was instructed to form a new cabinet by his nephew, King Hamad, shortly after the elections (Henderson 2014).

CONTINUED REPRESSION

The conflict in Bahrain fit the general course of events in the rest of the Arab world during the Arab Spring. The new wave of citizenship rights cannot be easily contained. Claims of citizens on their governments and revolts against corruption, authoritarian arbitrariness, repression, neoliberal reform, and neopatrimonialism and in favor of jobs, rights, and political solutions and "dignity" (*karama*) and recognition were recognizable enough to spill over into Bahrain to give the movements that represented its long-standing grievances a new momentum, as expressed in the month-long occupation of the Pearl Roundabout. As in the other countries, the regime, despite the "authoritarian upgrading" and the "facade democracy" of the past decade, was unable to "control and manage" these new challenges. Indeed, while the opposition enthusiastically received the National Action Charter, it was not duped into accepting the new constitution of 2002, which led to even greater anger. That was expressed in new forms of contention, including new forms of protest (human rights organizations), mobilizing new groups (the youth), leading to new coalitions (al-Wifaq and al-Waʿd), mobilizing transnational connections (with London and Shiʿite relations in the Gulf) and finding new forms of expression (*al-Wasat* newspaper, Internet, bloggers, Facebook, etc.). These forms of contention were fed by long-term structural developments (a demographic youth "bulge," structural unemployment, and rapidly increasing levels of education and political awareness) and the systematic discrimination—"categorical discrimination"—of the majority of the population. The protests fundamentally challenged the central concept of the neopatrimonial state of royal benevolence and gratuities (*makrama*) that limited civil, political, and economic rights to the elite only via corruption, patronage, and cooptation. They also challenged the modern "capacity" of the state as expressed in either its repressive function or economic aspects (as the Financial Harbor). Protests erupted because the regime tried to limit *content*, *extent*, and *depth* of citizenship to the elite or the absolute minimum for the general public by not fulfilling one of the basic preconditions of democratization—inclusion of "trust networks" (royal family, its patronage system, the security apparatus) and putting them under the purview of the state. The room for politics as a separate field therefore remained restricted, and democratization defined by Tilly as "broad, equal, protected, binding consultation of citizens. Although al-Wifaq joined the limited political process in 2006 and participated again in 2010, its decline in support showed that its strategy was marred, despite its electoral victories. The 2010 clampdown, foreshadowing the March 2011 backlash, was an indication that the regime itself, or at least its hard-line wing, realized that the "facade democracy" had backfired and that the gloves were off.

The February–March 2011 uprising, as elsewhere in the Middle East, underlined the fact that authoritarian upgrading had failed. The difference in Bahrain, however, was that it led to a minicycle within a major cycle, accelerating a process of increasingly expanding mobilization for rights that now included the Sunni minority, which also demanded rights and made claims on the ruling family, demanding reform as a new basis of trust and loyalty.

The violent repression of the Pearl Roundabout further radicalized the resistance, undermining the "moderates" all around (in the ruling family, al-Wifaq, and the Sunni minority). The bargaining process between al-Wifaq and the crown prince, despite concessions, floundered on the rocks of distrust as a result of previous broken promises of reform and inclusion made since his father Hamad became emir—and later king—in 1999. The result was a polarization strengthening the position of the hard-liners on both sides. The opposition moved from a position demanding a constitutional monarchy to a republic, as expressed by the Alliance for the Republic. At the same time, contentious activism expanded to include the Financial Harbor, giving the GCC states the pretext to intervene. As a counterpoison to the demands for the expansion of citizenship rights, the right wing employed a discourse of sectarian exclusion and strife, diverting the distrust between citizens and the ruling family to distrust between the minority and majority religious communities.

Most attention goes to the current repression of the Shiʿite opposition. Characteristic of the situation is that Shiʿites are being punished by losing their citizenship rights. The major change, however, must come from the Sunni minority. Having become much more politically aware, organizations such as TNUG and the Sahwa have started to formulate their own programs and demands for reform based on citizenship rights. Although it is quite possible that the ruling family can play on their fears of a Shiʿite takeover, their ideas show many similarities with the Shiʿite opposition, and both could come to some common position in regard with their political reform program. A future solution could lie in an agreement to cooperate on the basis of equal civil, political, and social rights if the identity rights of the Sunni minority are guaranteed and remain so. In that respect, movements like Haqq will have to downplay their revolutionary rhetoric of what is in their eyes the "will of the people."

Notes

1. Tilly defines *capacity* as "a degree to which governmental actions affect distributions of populations, activities, and resources within government's jurisdiction, relative to some standard of quality and efficiency" (Tilly 2006, 21).

2. With this I am not implying that the Bahraini political system is traditional. It is authoritarian, but it uses traditional elements such as *makrama* to refrain from implementing political reform.

3. By definition more than 40 percent of its income derives from oil.

4. Growing sectarianism is noticed by numerous researchers: Lawson (2004, 91); Niethammer (2006, 3); Schmidmayr (2011).

5. The petition, or discrete "advise" (*nasiha*), is part of the traditional political culture of the Gulf. It is part of the culture of nonbinding consultation. In Bahrain the petition is not called an "advise" but a "public announcement" (*al-ʿarida*).

6. This had been known in the 1970s when the present king, then the crown prince, was not allowed to build a power base for himself by his uncle, the prime minister (Abdulhadi Khalaf, personal communication, 9 July 2012, The Hague). See also Da Lage (2011).

7. http://www.pogar.org/publications/other/constitutions/bahrain-charter-01e.pdf.

8. The government press claims three hundred thousand government supporters took part, but that number would be impossible. Most neutral observers list the number as around forty thousand. See Mohammed (2011).

9. The recent history of the term *marjaʿiyya* is fascinating. Originally a Shiʿite term used for a cleric whom believers follow and see as their "source," it has come to denote a founding political document or doctrine. Mushayma uses it here to denote in an activist, populist sense, as the "people."

10. For the Arabic version of the Manama Document see http://alwefaq.net/index.php?show=news&action=article&id=5933. For the English version, see http://alwefaq.net/index.php?show=news&action=article&id=5934.

11. The number of people attending the rally is in dispute, with estimates ranging from ten thousand to the unlikely figure of three hundred thousand (that many Sunnis do not even live on the island).

12. Human Rights Watch (2014) has reported that this "law on public gatherings, requiring organizers of all demonstrations in Manama to seek official permission," was further amended by parliament in November 2013, "effectively suspending the right to assembly."

13. Abdulhadi Al-Khawaja, Abdulhadi Al-Makhdour, Abduljalil Al-Muqdad, Abduljalil Al-Singace, Abdulwahab Husain, Hasan Mushaima, Ibrahim Sharif, Mohammed Hassan Jawad, Mohammed Ali Ismael, Mohammed Habib Al-Miqdad, Salah Al-Khawaja, Mirza Al-Mahroos, and Saeed Al-Noori are being called the "Bahrain 13." They all were arrested in March 2011 after calling for civil and political rights, social justice, and institutional reforms during the 14 February Uprising. The sentences for this group of leading opposition prisoners range from fifteen years up to life imprisonment.

14. *Gulf News*'s Habib Toumi (2014b) has reported that "the delegates were asked to detail their proposals for the future on the legislative, juridical and executive branches, the electoral constituencies and security for all."

15. In the 2002 and 2006 elections the two societies ran in the polls together. In 2010 they fielded candidates against each other, which caused both societies to lose seats to independent Sunni candidates.

References

Al A'Ali, Mohammed. 2014. "Penalties Plan for Not Voting." *Gulf Daily News*, 21 November. http://www.gulf-daily-news.com/NewsDetails.aspx?storyid=390418 (accessed on 21 November 2014).

Abna. 2012. 17 March. http://www.abna.ir/data.asp?lang=2&Id=303259.

AFP. 2011. "Obama Meets Bahrain Crown Prince at White House." *Middle East Times*, 8 June. http://www.mideast-times.com/home_news.php?newsid=3346 (accessed 11 November 2014).

al-Akhbar. 2008. "Rivals for Bahrain's Shi'a Street: Wifaq and Haq." 9 April. http://www.al-akhbar.com/node/9124.

———. 2014a. "Bahrain Opposition Slams 'Ridiculous' Official Voter Turnout Rate." 23 November. http://english.al-akhbar.com/content/bahrain-opposition-slams-ridiculous-official-voter-turnout-rate (accessed 23 November 2014).

———. 2014b. "Bahrain Suspends Main Opposition Movement for Three Months." 28 October. http://english.al-akhbar.com/content/bahrain-suspends-main-opposition-movement-three-months (accessed 29 October 2014).

Alliance for the Republic (AFR). 2010. "Bahrain Dissidents Charged." Al Jazeera, 8 September. http://www.aljazeera.com/news/middleeast/2010/09/201095201748804676.html.

———. 2011a. Manifesto, *al-Fajr*, March 7. http://www.fajrbh.com/vb/showthread.php?t=16886.

———. 2011b. Pamphlet. 15 April. https://www.fajrbh.com/vb/showthread.php?t=18614.

———. 2011c. Pamphlet. 13 September. https://www.fajrbh.com/vb/showthread.php?t=33713.

———. 2011d. Pamphlet. 28 November. https://www.fajrbh.com/vb/showthread.php?p=510788.

———. 2011e. Pamphlet. 1 December. https://www.fajrbh.com/vb/showthread.php?t=44828.

———. 2012a. February 1. http://www.abna.ir/data.asp?lang=2&Id=294106.

———. 2012b. N.d. https://bahrainrevolutionnews.com/bh32800.

Amiri, Rannie. 2011. "Days of Rage, Decades of Oppression." Antiwar.com, 21 February. http://original.antiwar.com/rannie-amiri/2011/02/20/bahrain-days-of-rage/.

Al Arabiya News. 2011. 2 March. http://www.alarabiya.net/articles/2011/03/02/139944.html.

———. 2013. "Iran-Linked Group Claims Responsibility for Bahrain Car Blast." 18 July. http://english.alarabiya.net/en/News/middle-east/2013/07/18/Iran-linked-group-claims-responsibility-for-Bahrain-car-blast.html.

Bahrain Center for Human Rights (BCHR). 2013. "Bahrain Judicial System Continues to Hammer Human Rights Defenders with Prison Orders." 26 November. http://www.bahrainrights.org/en/node/6625.

Bahrain Mirror. 2012. 23 January. http://www.bahrainmirror.com/article.php?id=2846&cid=73.

Bahrain News Agency (BNA). 2013. "HM King Hamad Congratulated on Arab Honour." 2 September. http://www.bna.bh/portal/en/news/577692.

———. 2014. "Justice Ministry Files Lawsuits against Two Societies." 24 July. http://www.bna.bh/portal/en/news/627174.

al-Balushi, Khalid Musa. 2012. *al-Wasat*, February 22. http://www.alwasatnews.com/3455/news/read/635034/1.html.

BBC. 2011. "Bahrain Unrest: Shia Dissident Hassan Mushaima Returns." BBC News, 26 February. http://www.bbc.co.uk/news/world-middle-east-12587902.

Beinin, Joel. 2012. "The Rise of Egypt's Workers," *Carnegie Papers*, June. Carnegie Endowment for International Peace. http://carnegieendowment.org/files/egypt_labor.pdf.

Bellamy, Richard, and Antonino Palumbo. 2010. Introduction. *Citizenship*, edited by Richard Bellamy and Antonino Palumbo, xi–xxv. Farnham: Ashgate.

Bellin, Eva. 2012. "Reconsidering the Robustness of Authoritarianism in the Middle East: Lessons from the Arab Spring." *Comparative Politics*, January, 127–149.

Bennani-Chraïbi, Mounia. 2000. "Youth in Morocco: An Indicator of a Changing Society." In *Alienation or Integration of Arab Youth: Between Family, State and Street*, edited by Roel Meijer, 143–160. London: Curzon.

Black, Ian. 2011. "Bahrain Protests: 'The Repression Is Getting Worse.'" *Guardian*, 8 August. http://www.guardian.co.uk/world/2011/aug/08/bahrain-protests-repression-getting-worse?intcmp=239.

Butenschon, Nils, A., Uri Davis, and Manuel Hassassian, eds. 2000. *Citizenship and the State in the Middle East: Approaches and Applications*. Syracuse: Syracuse University Press.

Calderwood, James. 2010."Divided Islamists Face Poll-Erosion in Bahrain." *National* (Abu Dhabi), 15 October. http://www.thenational.ae/news/world/middle-east/divided-islamists-face-poll-erosion-in-bahrain.

Carlstrom, Gregg. 2012a. "In the Kingdom of Tear Gas." *MERIP* (Middle East Research and Information Project), 13 April. http://www.merip.org/mero/mero041312.

———. 2012b. "Little Optimism as Bahrainis Talk about Talks." Al Jazeera, 27 March. http://www.aljazeera.com/indepth/features/2012/03/201232616533553623.html.

Citizens for Bahrain. 2014. "Winners of 2014 Parliamentary Elections." Citizens for Bahrain, 1 December. http://www.citizensforbahrain.com/index.php/entry/winners-of-2014-parliamentary-elections-capital-governorate (accessed on 5 December 2014).

Constatine, Zoi. 2011. "Bahrain Protestors Prepare Demands for Crown Prince." *National* (Abu Dhabi), 21 February. http://www.thenational.ae/news/world/middle-east/bahrain-protesters-prepare-demands-for-crown-prince.

Da Lage, Olivier. 2011. "Bahreïn: Dissensions chez les Al Khalifa?" *Le Blog d'Olivier Da Lage*, 20 February. http://wp.me/pHhNF-av.

Davidson, Christopher, and Kristian Coates Ulrichsen. 2010. "Bahrain on the Edge." *Open Democracy*, 18 October. http://www.opendemocracy.net/christopher-davidson-kristian-coates-ulrichsen/bahrain-on-edge.

Desmukh, Fahad. 2010. "The Internet in Bahrain: Breaking the Monopoly of Information." *Foreign Policy*, 21 September. http://mideast.foreignpolicy.com/posts/2010/09/21/bahrain_government_vs_the_internet.

Diwan, Kristin Smith. 2010. "Why the Bahraini Elections Matter." *Foreign Policy*, 1 December 2010. http://mideast.foreignpolicy.com/posts/2010/12/01/bahrain_elections.

———. 2011a. "Bahrain's Deceptive National Dialogue." CNN World, 1 July. http://globalpublicsquare.blogs.cnn.com/2011/07/01/bahrains-deceptive-national-dialogue/.

———. 2011b. "Bahrain Shia Question: What the United States Gets Wrong about Sectarianism." *Foreign Affairs*, 2 March. http://www.foreignaffairs.com/print/67484.

———. 2011c. Gulf/2000, 20 February.

———. 2011d. "Regarding the Possibility of Dialogue in Bahrain." Gulf/2000 entry, 19 February. http://www.alwasatnews.com/3602/news/read/688908/1/سلمان%20علي%20الشيخ.html.

al-Fajr. 2011. 4 March. http://www.fajrbh.com/index.php?show=news&action=article&id=3673.

Faulks, Keith. 2000. *Citizenship*, London: Routledge.

Free Blogger Ali Abdulmam. 2011. "Bahrain: Leading Blogger Ali Abdulemam Sentenced to 15 Years in Prison, along with Other Human Rights Defenders." Posted 17 July by leilanachawati. http://freeabdulemam.wordpress.com.

Gause, Gregory. 2011. "Why Reform in the Gulf Monarchy Is a Family Feud." *Foreign Policy*, 4 March. http://mideast.foreignpolicy.com/posts/2011/03/04/why_reform_in_the_gulf_monarchies_is_a_family_feud.

Gengler, Justin. 2012a. "Are Bahrain's Sunnis Still Awake?" *Sada* (Carnegie Endowment for International Peace), 25 June. http://carnegieendowment.org/2005/04/06/tortuous-path-of-arab-democracy/fdxu.

———. 2012b. "Bahrain's Sunni Awakening," *MERIP* (Middle East Research and Information Project), 17 January. http://www.merip.org/mero/mero011712.

———. 2012c. "The Other Side of Radicalization in Bahrain." *Foreign Policy*, 15 July. http://mideast.foreignpolicy.com/posts/2011/07/15/the_other_side_of_radicalization_in_bahrain.

———. 2014. "Bahrain's Crown Prince Makes His Move." *Foreign Policy*, 20 January. http://mideastafrica.foreignpolicy.com/posts/2014/01/20/bahrains_crown_prince_makes_his_move.

Hammond, Andrew. 2011. "Bahrain Sunni Opposition Says Opposition Must Change Leaders." Reuters, 28 May. http://www.reuters.com/article/2011/05/28/us-bahrain-cleric-interview-idUSTRE74R18Q20110528.

Al Hasan, Hasan Tariq. 2012. "'Too Big to Succeed': A Case of Sunni Politics in Bahrain." *openDemocracy*, 23 July. http://www.opendemocracy.net/hasan-tariq-al-hasan/%E2%80%98too-big-to-succeed%E2%80%99-case-of-sunni-politics-in-bahrain.

Henderson, Simon. 2014. "Between ISIS and Iran: Bahrain Tweek Washington." Washington Institute, 1 December. http://www.washingtoninstitute.org/policy-analysis/view/between-isis-and-iran-bahrain-tweaks-washington (accessed 2 December 2014).

Herb, Michael. 1999. *All in the Family: Absolutism, Revolution, and Democracy in the Middle Eastern Monarchies*. New York: State University of New York Press.

Heydemann, Steven. 2007. "Upgrading Authoritarianism in the Arab World." Saban Center for Middle East Policy Analysis Paper, no. 13, October. Washington, D.C.: Brookings Institution.

Human Rights Watch (HRW). 2010. *Torture Redux: The Revival of Physical Coercion during Interrogations in Bahrain*. 8 February. http://www.hrw.org/en/reports/2010/02/08/torture-redux-0.

———. 2012. *No Justice in Bahrain: Unfair Trials in Military and Civilian Courts*. February 28.

———. 2014. "Bahrain: Prospects of Reform Remain Dim: Government Arrests, Tortures Imprisons Activists." 21 January. http://www.hrw.org/news/2014/01/21/bahrain-prospects-reform-remain-dim.

International Crisis Group. 2011a. "Popular Protests in North Africa and the Middle East (III): The Bahrain Revolt." Middle East/North Africa Report no. 105, 6 April.

———. 2011b. "Popular Protests in North Africa and the Middle East (VIII): Bahrain's Rocky Road to Reform." Middle East/North Africa Report no. 111, 28 July.

———. 2012. "Conflict Risk Alert: Bahrain." 16 April. http://www.crisisgroup.org/en/publication-type/media-releases/2012/mena/bahrain-conflict-risk-alert.aspx.

Isin, Engin F., and Bryan S. Turner, eds. 2002. *Handbook of Citizenship Studies*. London: Sage.

Isin, Engin F., and Patricia K. Wood. 1999. *Citizenship and Identity*. London: Sage.

al-Jamri, Mansoor. 1998. "State and Civil Society in Bahrain." Paper presented at MESA 32nd annual meeting. Chicago, 6 December. http://bahrain.wikia.com/wiki/State_and_Civil_Society_in_Bahrain.

———. 2011. "Shaykh's Isa Qasim's Friday Sermon on 4 March." Gulf/2000, March.

Al Jazeera. 2010. "Bahrain Dissidents Charged," Al Jazeera, October 8. http://www.aljazeera.com/news/middleeast/2010/09/201095201748804676.html.

Jones, Marc Owen. 2014. "Bahrain's State Unaccountability." *Muftah*, 17 April. http://muftah.org/bahrains-state-unaccountability/#.U1B4z6Ioqy-.

Kandil, Hazem. 2012. "Why Did the Egyptian Middle Class March to Tahrir?" *Mediterranean Politics* 17, no. 2: 197–215.

Khalaf, Abdulhadi. 2000. "The New Amir of Bahrain: Marching Sideways." *Civil Society* 10, no. 9. http://bahrain.wikia.com/wiki/The_New_Amir_of_Bahrain:_Marching_Sideways.

———. 2006. "Rules of Succession and Political Participation in the GCC States." In *Constitutional Reform and Political Participation in the Gulf*, edited by Abdulhadi Khalaf and Giacomo Luciani, 33–50. Dubai: Gulf Research Center.

Khalifa, Reem. 2014a. "Bahrain Files Lawsuit to Suspend Opposition Group." ABC News, 20 July. http://abcnews.go.com/International/wireStory/bahrain-files-lawsuit-suspend-opposition-group-24639921.

———. 2014b. "Bahrain Opposition Blasts Electoral Turnout Figure." ABC News, 23 November. http://abcnews.go.com/International/wireStory/bahrain-opposition-blasts-electoral-turnout-figure-27115440 (accessed 24 November 2014).

———. 2014c. "Bahrain's Pro-Government Bloc Dominates Vote." ABC News, 30 November. http://abcnews.go.com/International/wireStory/bahrain-14-shiite-candidates-win-seats-27259029 (accessed 1 December 2014).

Khalil, Abd al-Jalil. 2012. *al-Wasat*, 9 July. http://www.alwasatnews.com/3593/news/read/686586/1/الشيخ%20علي%20سلمان.html.

Kinninmont, Jane. 2006. "Castles Built on Sand." *OpenDemocracy*, 22 August. http://www.opendemocracy.net/conflict-middle_east_politics/bahrain_3846.jsp.

———. 2012. "Bahrain: Beyond the Impasse." June. London: Chatham House (Royal Institute of International Affairs).

Kinninmont, Jane, and Omar Sirri. 2014. "Bahrain: Civil Society and Political Imagination." October. London: Chatham House (Royal Institute of International Affairs), October.

Lawson, Fred. 2004. "Repertoires of Contention in Bahrain." In *Islamic Activism: A Social Movement Theory Approach*, edited by Quentin Wiktorowicz, 89–111. Bloomington: Indiana University Press.

LeVine, Mark. 2014. "Nabeel Rajab: The Problematic Success of 'Human Rights' in the Arab World." Al Jazeera, 6 June. http://www.aljazeera.com/indepth/opinion/2014/06/nabeel-rajab-problematic-succes-201463141553579358.html.

al-Mahmoud, Abd al-Latif. 2011a. "Societies 'Respect National Unity Gathering Demands.'" *Gulf Daily News*, 9 March. http://www.gulf-daily-news.com/NewsDetails.aspx?storyid=301435.

———. 2011b. *al-Wasat*, 7 March. http://www.alwasatnews.com/3104/news/read/530924/1.html.

———. 2011c. *al-Wasat*, 20 March. http://www.alwasatnews.com/3602/news/read/688908/1/الشيخ%20علي%20سلمان.html.

Makki, Yusuf. 2012. *Bahrain Mirror*, 17 May. http://www.bahrainmirror.com/article.php?id=4332&cid=125.

Mann, Michael, 1987. "Ruling Class Strategies and Citizenship." *Sociology* 21, no. 3: 339–354. Reprinted in *Citizenship*, edited by Richard Bellamy and Antonino Palumbo, 27–42. Farnham: Ashgate, 2010.

Marshall, T. H. 1964 [1949]. "Citizenship and Social Class." Rept. in *Class, Citizenship and Social Development*. New York: Anchor.

Matthiesen, Toby. 2014. "(No) Dialogue in Bahrain." *Middle East Research and Information Project (MERIP)*, 13 February. http://www.merip.org/mero/mero021314.

Meijer, Roel. 2014. "Political Citizenship and Social Movements in the Arab World." In *Handbook of Political Citizenship and Social Movements*, edited by Hein Anton van der Heijden, 628-660. Northampton, Mass.: Edward Elgar.

Meijer, Roel, and Joas Wagemakers. 2012. "The Struggle for Citizenship of the Shiites in Saudi Arabia." In *The Dynamics of Sunni-Shia Relationships: Doctrine, Transnationalism, Intellectuals and the Media*, edited by Sami Zemni and Brigitte Maréchal, 117–138. London: Hurst.

Mohammed, Basma. 2011. "Massive Show of Support!" *Gulf Daily News*, 22 February. http://www.gulf-daily-news.com/NewsDetails.aspx?storyid=300173.

Murphy, Emma. 2012. "Problematizing Arab Youth: Generational Narratives of Systemic Failure." *Mediterranean Politics* 17, no. 1: 5–22.

Mushayma, Hasan. 2011a. *al-Wasat*, 27 February. http://www.alwasatnews.com/3096/news/read/529203/1/حسن%20مشيمع.html.

———. 2011b. *al-Wasat*, 28 February. http://www.alwasatnews.com/3097/news/read/529658/1/حسن%20مشيمع.html.

Nakhleh, Emile. 1976. *Bahrain: Political Development in a Modernizing Society*. Lanham, Md.: Lexington Books.

———. 2013. "Bahrain Declares War on the Opposition." Inter Press Service (IPS), 1 August. http://www.ipsnews.net/2013/08/op-ed-bahrain-declares-war-on-the-opposition/.

National Dialogue Media Center. 2014. "Crown Prince Delivers Dialogue Framework." *National Dialogue*, 18 September. http://www.nd.bh/en/index.php/media-center/dialogue-news/english/item/198-crown-prince-delivers-dialogue-framework (accessed 4 December 2014).

Niethammer, Katja. 2006. "Voices in Parliaments, Debates in *Majalis*, and Banners on the Streets: Avenues of Political Participation in Bahrain." European University Institute Working Papers, no. 27.

———. 2012. "Cycles of Conflict in Bahrain: The Limits of Monarchical Reforms." Paper presented at the internal workshop Rethinking the Monarchy-Republic Gap in the Middle East, University of Marburg, 20–21September.

Nonneman, Gerd. 2008. "Political Reform in the Gulf Monarchies: From Liberalization to Democratization? A Comparative Perspective." In *Reform in the Middle East Oil Monarchies*, edited by Anoushiravan Ehteshami and Steven M. Wright, 3–45. Reading, UK: Ithaca Press.

Oassab, Muhammed. 2011. *al-Wasat*, December 30, http://www.alwasatnews.com/3401/news/read/617824/1.html.

Office of the High Commissioner for Human Rights (OHCHR). 2014. "Joint Statement on the OHCHR and the Human Rights Situation in Bahrain." 26th Session of the Human Rights Council, Geneva, 10 June.

Pace, Michelle, and Francesco Cavatorta. 2012. "The Arab Uprisings in Theoretical Perspective: An Introduction." *Mediterranean Politics* 9, no. 2: 125–138.

Parker, Ned. 2011. "Police Let Protesters Take Square." *Los Angeles Times*, 19 February. http://articles.latimes.com/2011/feb/19/world/la-fgw-bahrain-square-20110220.

Parolin, Gianluca P. 2006. "Generations of Gulf Constitutions: Paths and Perspectives." In *Constitutional Reform and Political Participation in the Gulf*, edited by Abdulhadi Khalaf and Giacomo Luciani, 51–87. Dubai: Gulf Research Center.

———. 2009. *Citizenship in the Arab World: Kin, Religion and Nation-State*. Amsterdam: Amsterdam University Press.

Qasim, Sheikh Isa. 2011. *al-Wasat*, 27 February.

Quilliam, Neil. 2008. "Political Reform in Bahrain: The Turning Tide." In *Reform in the Middle East Oil Monarchies*, edited by Anoushiravan Ehteshami and Steven M. Wright, 81–102. Reading, UK: Ithaca Press.

Sahwa. 2011. Manifesto, 16 December. http://www.b4bh.com/vb/t245215.html.

Ali Salman, Sheikh. 2006. *al-Wasat*, 8 January. http://www.alwasatnews.com/3602/news/read/688913/1/الشيخ%20علي%20سلمان.html.

———. 2011. *al-Wasat*, 11 October. http://www.alwasatnews.com/3321/news/read/600325/1.html.

———. 2012. "Little Optimism as Bahrainis Talk about Talks." Al Jazeera, 27 March. Talkshttp://www.aljazeera.com/indepth/features/2012/03/201232616533553623.html.

Schmidmayr, Michael. 2011. *Politische Opposition in Bahrain: Stabiltät und Wandel in einem autoritären Regime*. Baden-Baden: Nomos Verlag.

Seznec, Jean-François. 2011. "Crackdown in Bahrain." *Foreign Policy*, 17 February. http://www.foreignpolicy.com/articles/2011/02/17/crackdown_in_bahrain?page=full.

Al-Shalchi, Hadeel, and Barbara Surk. 2011. "Bahraini Opposition Plots Strategy before Talks." Associated Press. ABC Action News, 20 February. http://abclocal.go.com/story?section=news/national_world&id=7970241.

Sharabi, Hisham. 1988. *Neopatriarchy: A Theory of Distorted Change in Arab Society*. New York: Oxford University Press.

Shehabi, Alaa. 2011. "Bahrains' Independent Commission of Inquiry: A Path to Justice or Political Shield." *Jadaliyya*, 22 November. http://www.jadaliyya.com/pages/index/3244/bahrains-independent-commission-of-inquiry_a-path-.

Singh Grewal, Sandeep. 2014. "Islamists Join Forces for Polls." *Gulf Daily News*, 31 July. http://www.gulf-daily-news.com/NewsDetails.aspx?storyid=382970.

Slackman, Michael. 2011. "Protests in Bahrain Become Tests of Wills." *New York Times*, 22 February. http://www.nytimes.com/2011/02/23/world/middleeast/23bahrain.html?_r=0.

Surk, Barbara. 2011. "Rights Group Pushes Bahrain to Investigate Firings." *Washington Post*, 16 July. http://www.washingtonpost.com/world/rights-group-pushes-bahrain-to-investigate-firings/2011/07/15/gIQAVi61GI_story.html.

Tarrow, Sidney. 1998. *Power in Movement: Social Movements and Contentious Politics*. 2nd ed. Cambridge: Cambridge University Press.

Tilly, Charles. 2006. *Regimes and Repertoires*. Chicago: University of Chicago Press.

———. 2007. *Democracy*. Cambridge: Cambridge University Press.

Tilly, Charles, and Lesley J. Wood. 2009. *Social Movements, 1768–2008*. Boulder: Paradigm, 2009.

TNUG, 2011–2012. *Second Annual Report*. http://altajam3.org/portal/arabic/files/2012/06/-التقرير-السياسي-المؤتمر-العام-الثاني.pdf.

———. 2014. "Statement from the Coalition of the National Political Associations (Al Fateh) Non Participation in the National Dialogue." 19 January. http://altajam3.org/portal/arabic/post/1922.

Toumi, Habib. 2013. "Bahrain to Set Up First Pan-Arab Rights Court." *Gulfnews.com*, 2 September. http://gulfnews.com/news/gulf/bahrain/bahrain-to-set-up-first-pan-arab-rights-court-1.1226580.

———. 2014a. "Bahrain Parliamentary Elections in November." *Gulfnews.com*, 2 June. http://gulfnews.com/news/gulf/bahrain/bahrain-parliamentary-elections-in-november-1.1341985.

———. 2014b. "Bahrain Political Parties Asked for Dialogue Ideas." *Gulfnews.com*, 23 January. http://gulfnews.com/news/gulf/bahrain/bahrain-political-parties-asked-for-dialogue-ideas-1.1280976#.UuGOzAQ9cxc.twitter.

Turner, Bryan S. 1990. "Outline of a Theory of Citizenship." *Sociology* 24: 189–217. Reprinted in *Citizenship*, edited by Richard Bellamy and Antonino Palumbo, 73–101. Farnham: Ashgate, 2010.

———. 2000. "Islam, Civil Society, and Citizenship: Reflections on the Sociology of Citizenship and Islamic Studies." In *Citizenship and the State in the Middle East: Approaches and Applications*, edited by Nils A. Butenschon, Uri Davis, and Manuel Hassassian, 28–48. Syracuse: Syracuse University Press.

Wahab, Siraj. 2011. "Bahraini Protests Not Sectarian, Says Muneera Fakhro," *Arab News*, 21 February. http://www.arabnews.com/node/368873.

al-Wasat. 2011a. 27 February. http://www.alwasatnews.com/3097/news/read/529658/1/%20حسن.مشيمع.html.

———. 2011b. 27 February. http://www.alwasatnews.com/3096/news/read/529211/1.html.

———. 2011c. February 28. http://www.alwasatnews.com/3097/news/read/529658/1/حسن%20مشيمع.html.

———. 2011d. 1 March. http://www.alwasatnews.com/3098/news/read/529842/1/حسن%20مشيمع.html.

———. 2011e. 3 March. http://www.alwasatnews.com/3100/news/read/530218/1/حسن%20مشيمع.html.

———. 2011f. 3 March. http://www.alwasatnews.com/3100/news/read/530195/1.html.

———. 2011g. 5 March. http://www.alwasatnews.com/3102/news/read/530574/1/حسن%20مشيمع.html.

———. 2011h. 7 March. http://www.alwasatnews.com/3104/news/read/530924/1.html.

———. 2011i. 13 March. http://www.alwasatnews.com/3110/news/read/532122/1.html.

———. 2011j. 14 March. http://www.alwasatnews.com/3111/news/read/532283/1.html.

———. 2011k. 17 March. http://www.alwasatnews.com/3479/news/read/643896/1.html.

———. 2011l. 20 March. http://www.alwasatnews.com/3602/news/read/688908/1/الشيخ%20علي%20سلمان.html.

———. 2011m. 16 April. http://www.alwasatnews.com/3509/news/read/656163/1/حسن%20مشيمع.html.

———. 2011n. 23 June. http://www.alwasatnews.com/3211/news/read/568944/1/حسن%20مشيمع.html.

———. 2011o. 11 October. http://www.alwasatnews.com/3321/news/read/600325/1.html.

———. 2011p. 17 December. http://www.alwasatnews.com/3388/news/read/615276/1.html.

———. 2011q. 30 December. http://www.alwasatnews.com/3401/news/read/617824/1.html.

———. 2012a. 12 January. http://www.alwasatnews.com/3414/news/read/621184/1.html.

———. 2012b. 21 January. http://www.alwasatnews.com/3423/news/read/623177/1.html.

———. 2012c. 28 January. http://www.alwasatnews.com/data/2012/3430/pdf/loc4.pdf.

———. 2012d. 14 February. http://www.alwasatnews.com/3447/news/read/628806/1.html.

———. 2012e. 22 February. http://www.alwasatnews.com/3455/news/read/635034/1.html.

———. 2012f. 8 March. http://www.alwasatnews.com/3480/news/read/644121/1.html.

———. 2012g. 17 March. http://www.alwasatnews.com/3479/news/read/643896/1.html.

———. 2012h. 14 April. http://www.alwasatnews.com/3507/news/read/655746/1/حسن%20مشيمع.html.

———. 2012i. 30 June. http://www.alwasatnews.com/3585/news/read/684559/1.html.

———. 2012j. 9 July. http://www.alwasatnews.com/3593/news/read/686586/1/الشيخ%20علي%20سلمان.html.

Washington Post. 2011. "Bahrain Needs U.S. Attention Now." Editorial, 10 September. http://www.washingtonpost.com/opinions/bahrain-needs-us-attention-now/2011/09/09/gIQAjoH9FK_story.html.

Al Wefaq. 2014a. "Al Wefaq: Claims Made by Justice Ministry Are Based on Wrong Explanation of the Law." 22 July. http://alwefaq.net/cms/2014/07/22/31502/.

———. 2014b. "Bahrain Opposition: Motive behind Suspending Al Wefaq Is Refusal to Dialogue." 22 July. http://alwefaq.net/cms/2014/07/22/31505/.

Wright, Steven. 2010. *Fixing the Kingdom: Political Evolution and Socio-Economic Challenges in Bahrain*. Occasional Paper no. 3. Doha, Qatar: Center for International and Regional Studies, Georgetown University.

Zartman, I. William. 2008. *Negotiation and Conflict Management: Essays on Theory and Practice*. London: Routledge.

Libya

Negotiations for Transition

KARIM MEZRAN AND ALICE ALUNNI

LIBYA WAS THE THIRD North African country, after Tunisia and Egypt, to oust a dictator, but it took a long and bloody eight months of civil war. The positions of the rebel forces and the position of the regime were irreconcilable. The former posed the departure of the dictator, Muammar Qadhafi, as a precondition to the end of hostilities. The latter was determined to lead the transition himself or to lead it through one of his sons. Given the impossibility of achieving an agreement between the two parties, negotiating a breakthrough proved even more difficult as the two sides never really reached a "zone of possible agreement" (ZOPA) or a point of "mutually hurting stalemate" (MHS) (Zartman 1985), both having a blind belief in their invincibility. Qadhafi lost.

The absence of negotiations between regime and rebels contrasted with the intense level of cooperation among the rebels themselves, who represented diverse groups and interests and negotiated in order to achieve their common goal: the end of the regime, obtained on 23 October 2011. How did these fragmented forces, which followed regional and municipal divides and, at times, tribal lines, manage to continue to work together? And how much unity were they able to maintain once the Long Track overthrow was accomplished? At the outbreak of the revolt, a political organ of the revolution, the National Transitional Council (NTC), was created to conduct the war and represent the opposition vis-à-vis the rest of the world in a unitary manner. The council assumed a guiding role during and after the armed conflict, a choice that proved to be successful in rallying support for the revolution abroad.

In order to guarantee military and political support from external actors in its effort against the regime, the NTC elaborated a vision of the new Libya. A constitutional declaration, issued on 10 August 2011, was anticipated by another document released on 29 March 2011, in which the idea of a democratic, liberal, and pluralist Libya was clearly sketched. According to the U.S. National Democratic Institute (NDI 2011), the NTC was busy drafting papers on constitution writing, systems of governance, and "democratic culture" since the very beginning of the uprising while demanding expert advice on election systems, formation of a constituent assembly, political party development, civic education, and other issues. There were very few negotiations over these two documents since the support of external actors depended on their content as much as the outcome of the Libyan revolution depended on external military intervention. If Libyans wanted the political and military support of the West, they had to provide a plan for the new Libya acceptable to their supporters, and so they did.

The NTC represented a return to an executive decision-making system. However, that system cannot be defined as authoritarian, since, according to the official narrative, the NTC was born out of the aspirations of the local councils that sprang up in the first days of the clashes between the rebels and the regime. The actions and inactions of the NTC were not determined by ideological considerations unless "anti-Qadhafism" is considered an ideology. In fact, the NTC, and the interim government appointed by it on 22 November 2011, were continuously under pressure from militias, civil society, tribes, and foreign countries. The interim institutions managed through negotiations to reconcile the positions of the various factions. Overall, the political organ of the revolution had a very pragmatic attitude during and after the conflict. But once the General National Congress, elected on 7 July 2012, replaced the authority of the NTC, the political system entered a stalemate among parties that had lost what initially appeared to be a common view of the future.

In fact, the Libyan revolutionaries did not share a common ideology nor a common vision of the future of the country; they only shared a common goal to be achieved by all means and at all costs: the overthrow of the regime. Once the goal was reached, the fictitious unity created by the NTC dissipated, and the civil war that characterized the 2011 uprising quickly reemerged three years later, this time fought by those same revolutionary forces who seemed so collaborative in 2011. This chapter retraces and analyzes the key events that led Libya from one civil war to the other.

PRE-INSURGENCY DIAGNOSIS

Libya is different from most other North African countries, not only because it was subject to international intervention during the 2011 revolution, but also, more deeply, because of its nature as rentier state (Beblawi 1990; Gurney 1996; Bellin 2004). The Old Order could count on external rent from natural resources, mainly oil, to boost a strong security apparatus and provide generous social benefits to the people, guaranteeing higher standards of living than other North African countries (Martinez 2007; Mezran 2011d). By redistributing oil revenues, the regime was able to keep the tax burden to the minimum while investing in welfare programs. Nevertheless, it could not manage to keep unemployment under control, estimated at the outbreak of the revolution at 30 percent (ILO 2011).

During his forty-year reign, Qadhafi had tried to suppress any kind of opposition to his rule (St. John 1983; Joffe 1988; Ronen 2002; Vandewalle 2011). The regime exerted strong control through a security apparatus of personal brigades, financed by oil revenues, while keeping the army weak in order to avoid a military coup and, through tight censorship of the national media, keeping not only the press, radio, and TV channels but also the Internet under strict control (Martinez 2007). This system prevented the development of civil society and a strong political opposition. By centralizing the security apparatus and also relying on tribal ties, Qadhafi tried to dominate the fragmented Libyan regional identities and the Islamist opposition particularly active in the eastern region of Cyrenaica.

Qadhafi loyalists were based principally in Sirte, Bani Walid, and Tripoli. The support for the colonel in Sirte, his hometown, was never questioned. Dominated by the leader's Qadhadhafa tribe, Sirte fell under the rebels' control only on 23 October 2011, after the capture and killing of Qadhafi. On the contrary, Bani Walid, a stronghold of Qadhafi's allied tribe, the Warfalla, was internally divided between supporters of the regime and opponents (ICG 2011b). As a former official said, "The long battle for Bani Walid was in part a struggle of Warfalla against Warfalla" (ICG 2011a). In Tripoli itself, the regime had favored certain neighborhoods—notably Hayy an-Nasr and Umm Durban in Abu Slim—that proved particularly resistant to liberation by the rebels. Other groups in the country supported the Old Order because in the past they were favored by it. Libyans of Saharan origin, for instance, resettled in the north and were awarded land as well as housing in Tripoli, Sirte, and other towns; they include in particular the Mashashiyya (located south and east of the Nafusa Mountains) and residents of Tuwergha, near Misrata (ICG 2011a).

By the early 2000s, presumably with the intention of solving the economic and social crisis, a reformist camp, led by Qadhafi's reformist son Saif al-Islam, had emerged. Its goal was to privatize the socialist-oriented economy following years of economic stagnation amid tight state control over industry. Through economic liberalization, privatization, modernization, and diversification, the reformists aimed at creating small- and medium-sized enterprises that could create new jobs and make the country less subject to the volatile price of oil and more attractive to foreign investors in sectors such as civil engineering and agriculture. However, the transition proved difficult, and only the banking sector and telecommunications witnessed significant liberalization (Varvelli 2010). The regime also tried to deal with the problem of unemployment through the so-called policy of Libyanization, which imposed the creation of an ambitious infrastructure project and the hiring of Libyan personnel on foreign firms. However, without improvements in the education system and the creation of a new working ethics, the reforms proved unsuccessful. Moreover, they were accompanied by cuts in subsidies and by an increase of tariffs on imports and the price of gasoline (up more than 30 percent) and electricity (which doubled) (Mezran 2011e).

Saif al-Islam and his camp also tried to open up Libyan society by creating new media and discussing the project of a new constitution in 2006. In doing so, they met determined opposition from hard-line conservatives opposed to any change that might move Libya away from a highly centralized, authoritarian political system (St. John 2010). Old Guard elements, led by another son, Mutassim al-Qadhafi, viewed the introduction of a private-sector economy and a more open political system as a threat to both their economic interests and the patronage networks underpinning the existing political framework (St. John 2010).

In the polarization within the regime that seemed to emerge between reformers and conservatives, led supposedly by brothers Saif al-Islam and Mutassim, respectively, Muammar Qadhafi acted as the "balancing force." While Mutassim had been appointed national security adviser and his mentor, Musa Kusa, had been nominated for foreign minister in 2007, an ally of Saif's progressive movement, Shukri Ghanem, had been reinstated in his position as president of Libya's National Oil Corporation (NOC), and Saif himself had been appointed to the People's Social Leadership Committees (St. John 2010). However, in the unpredictable and variable dynamics of Libyan politics, Saif appeared to be losing power throughout much of 2009, while Mutassim was emerging as heir apparent. This seemed to be confirmed when in mid-December 2010 the board of trustees of the Qadhafi International Charity and Development Foundation, the NGO chaired by Saif al-Islam, announced that the foundation would no longer promote human rights and political reforms in Libya (St. John 2011). But a few months before, in mid-2010, things had also turned bad for Mutassim, who was dismissed from his post for abusing a senior member of Qadhafi's inner circle, and the National Security Council was suspended (ICG 2011b).

The regime, actually, had rejected any political or social domestic competitors to its hegemonic political discourse and practice (Joffe 2011). The opposition between the two camps was de facto a farce dominated by Qadhafi and meant to maintain the power firmly in the hands of the family. In fact, at the outbreak of the revolution, the family coalesced around the colonel. Mutassim and Saif unconditionally took the side of their father. The notorious Thirty-Second Brigade, headed by another son, Khamis, previously in charge of the personal security of Qadhafi, became the military arm of the regime against the revolt, along with the Revolutionary Legion that was part of Qadhafi's secret police (ICG 2011a). Such a strong security apparatus, based on familial and tribal loyalties, allowed the regime to fight a civil war for eight months.

At the beginning of 2011, witnessing the revolts in Tunisia and Egypt, the regime tried to anticipate the outbreak of a revolt in Libya by passing emergency measures such as the reduction of the price of foodstuffs and electricity (and allowing the payment of electricity bills by installment), while lavishing contributions to new graduates in order for them to buy a house (Mezran 2011e). The days before the revolt, the regime had also legalized the arbitrary occupation by many homeless families of houses still under construction, in an attempt to face the mounting housing problem in the country. However, this was not enough to placate the malcontent among the population. The social contract that had guaranteed the survival of the regime for forty years seemed no longer to hold.

Nevertheless, it seemed that many Libyans, particularly in Tripolitania, accepted the trade-off between relatively high standards of living and lack of political and civil freedoms. Even if tensions had emerged in the past few years, particularly in those areas that were prevented from embarking on a path of serious economic development, the fact that the only real and organized political opposition lived abroad under the protection of Western powers rendered the opposition politically and economically weak. So it was against all the expectations that the revolution broke out in February 2011, leading to the killing of Qadhafi on 23 October 2011 (Chorin 2012; Mezran 2014; Pack 2013).

Local Activists

Although the uprising was supported by external actors and by the exiles, who played a significant role, operational leadership in the revolution was localized, necessitating negotiation for strategic coordination and coalitions among disparate bands. On the wave of the demonstrations in Tunisia and Egypt, people in Libya first took to the streets spontaneously on 15 and 16 February 2011. The demonstrations were repressed by the army, which shot at people in Benghazi and Bayda. The protesters were initially peaceful. They demanded freedom, human dignity, and a solution to economic deprivation (Brahimi 2011). Apparently, the trigger was the arrest in Benghazi of Fathi Terbil, a young lawyer and human rights activist who had represented the families of the twelve hundred detainees massacred by the regime at the Abu Salim prison in 1996. Terbil and Abdel Hafidh Ghoga were prominent representatives of a small group resident in Libya who supported the cause of human rights in the country. The early protests and demonstrations, which in the past had receded naturally or were repressed by the regime, left a training experience and continuing communications contacts that proved useful in 2011. These activists were responsible for initiating the uprising, but they did not have a prominent role in the phase immediately following its outbreak. Older forces more grounded on the social fabric, such as former regime members or the traditional Islamist opposition, took the lead. Social networks such as Facebook and Twitter were useful means of spreading the voice and bringing people to the streets on 17 February. When the Libyan regime decided to use violence to confront popular protests, a violent civil war erupted between regime supporters and opposition forces. Libyans fought against Libyans in an eight-month struggle characterized by defections, crimes against humanity, and military foreign intervention authorized by the UN Security Council, discussed in the subsequent chapter by Johannes Theiss. This civil war characteristic of the Libyan conflict in 2011 should be kept in mind when addressing the issues of transitional justice and reconciliation.

The Defectors

Since the very first days of the revolution, members of the regime from the army, the government, and the diplomatic corps defected. Among them were Mustafa Abdel Jalil, then minister of justice and later president of the NTC; Abdul Fattah Younis, then minister of the interior, who became commander in chief of the rebel army and whose assassination on 24 July 2011 signaled the high level of political infighting among the rebels; Mahmoud Jibril, former head of the National Economic Development Board, who became head of the NTC executive board until 24 October 2011, when he resigned following the killing of Qadhafi; and a few Libyan ambassadors including Abd al-Rahman Shalgam (UN), Ali Suleiman Aujali (U.S.), and Hafed Ghaddour (Italy). Later in May, Shukri Ghanem, chairman of the National Oil Corporation (NOC) and former prime minister, essential in running the NOC given his relationships with the oil and gas industry outside of Libya, joined the group of defectors. According to a leaked State Department cable from 2008, Ghanem had stated that "meaningful economic and political reform will not occur while al-Qadhafi is alive" (Birnbaum 2011).

The defections were justified by the violence committed by the regime against the demonstrators. However, a parallel narrative emerged later (Bechis 2011; Mezran 2011c; Canal+ 2013): the defectors were among the people who negotiated a coup d'état against Qadhafi, allegedly organized by the French Secret Services with the complicity of Nouri al-Mesmari, the general director of public protocol and ceremonies. Al-Mesmari was the first Libyan official to abruptly withdraw from Qadhafi's inner circle, in December 2010, before even the Tunisian uprising, suggesting the drawing in of the members of the regime mentioned above (*Asharq Al-Awsat* 2010). However, spontaneous demonstrations in Cyrenaica in mid-February forced the group to accelerate the plan. The existence of an underground network of people involved in the coup would explain the defections in a "leopard spots" pattern and would also explain the swift establishment of the National Transitional Council on 27 February 2011, the appearance of so many weapons since the very beginning of the revolt, and the intense French and British diplomatic activity in the first phase of the rebellion. Whether this narrative is accepted or not, former regime members including a few army officers became key leading personalities of the revolt and of the NTC.

The Army

At the outbreak of the revolt, the army opened fire on the demonstrators. Differently from Egypt and Tunisia, the army did not act as a neutral buffer between the protesters and the regime. The military in the Libyan conflict was neither a significant nor an independent actor. Its decisions did not constitute crucial turning points in the uprising. Even if key defections emerged immediately in Cyrenaica, in Tripolitania and Fezzan most of the army and the brigades took the side of the regime to the point where, without the external military intervention of Western powers, the rebellion would have probably been repressed as at other times in Libyan history.

Comprising an estimated twenty-five thousand ground troops, with an additional, estimated twenty-five thousand reserves, the army was kept weak and divided under Qadhafi's rule, bereft of a serious middle-ranking officer corps or well-trained rank-and-file troops in order to ensure that it was not strong enough to challenge the one and only colonel (ICG 2011b). Qadhafi's concerns proved correct when a few members of the Libyan Army started to defect on the very first days of the revolution, offering weapons and support to the rebels. In terms of military equipment, the army and the brigades loyal to Qadhafi were better off compared with the opposition forces. Defections among the Libyan Army and Air Force impelled Qadhafi to hire mercenaries from sub-Saharan Africa, Eastern Europe, and other Middle Eastern countries (D. Smith 2011), but the contractors could do nothing against the air strikes of Western forces and, later, against the trained forces of the rebels who advanced toward Tripoli and liberated the capital in August.

The gap between army defectors and brigades loyal to Qadhafi became more and more evident as time went by. Benghazi became the center around which army defectors in the east gathered in a secure area where they were able to regroup and organize, particularly after the NATO military intervention, a natural consequence of the way in which the regime confined the National Army to operations in the east, with security in the west being handled by the more loyal Thirty-Second Brigade (the Khamis Brigade) (ICG 2011a). The defectors in the east formed the rebel army whose authority, however, was limited to their region. Even if defections within the army later occurred also in the west, they were not responsible for the uprisings in this region, where local militias and councils were key in organizing the military opposition to Qadhafi's brigades. Army officers in Tripoli had either to flee to Tunisia and from there support or join the militias or stay inside to work covertly for NATO forces (ICG 2011a). Internal divisions and defections within the Libyan Army proved determinant in the development of subsequent events, but the role of the army in Libya was closer to the role of the Syrian army than to the Egyptian or Tunisian military forces in their respective uprisings.

Islamist Opposition

The rebellious eastern regions of Libya have traditionally represented the core of the Islamist opposition to the regime. From the Libyan branch of the Muslim Brotherhood to the militant cells that sprang up in the 1970s and 1980s, these groups have been focused primarily in and around the eastern cities of Benghazi, the second largest city in Libya, Derna, and Ajdabia, with some support outside these areas—some of the movements' leaders came from the capital (Pargeter 2009). The roots of this opposition are to be found in the strategy of differential development adopted by the regime. Since he took power in 1969, the colonel started to marginalize the local tribes in the east, considered guilty of being the backbone of the Sanusi monarchy (1951–1969). Later, following Islamist uprisings of the 1980s and mid-1990s, he punished the eastern regions by keeping them in a state of underdevelopment even if Cyrenaica possessed 80 percent of Libya's oil reserves (Menon 2012). Moreover, Islamic identity in the east, rooted in the nineteenth-century experience of the Sanusi order, goes hand in hand with social conformism, a feature that characterizes the region known for its insularity and conservatism—although the city of Benghazi may be an exception in such a scenario—in stark contrast to the revolutionary and socialist ideas of Colonel Qadhafi, especially around issues related to women. The combination of poverty, social conservatism, and marginalization, in some cases accompanied by long-standing historical antagonisms still vivid in the collective memory, proved and is likely to continue to prove a potent mix.

At the beginning of the century, thanks to a strong collaboration with the United States in the so-called War on Terror, the regime inflicted heavy losses on the Libyan Islamic Fighting Group (LIFG), the main anti-Qadhafi Islamist militant network allied with al-Qaeda (Blanchard and Zanotti 2011). The threat from the Islamists was diminished to the point that, in 2006, Saif al-Islam felt secure enough to conduct a mediation that led, in 2010, to the release from prison of more than two hundred Islamists, thirty-four of them members of the LIFG, as part of a program of rehabilitation of militant groups (BBC News 2010). At the outbreak of the revolt in 2011, it seemed—erroneously, as shown later—that this traditional Islamic opposition was not at the forefront of the rebellion. Indeed, through the years, while some of the old national militant groups had dissolved and members of others, including LIFG, were undergoing de-radicalization programs in prison, the moderate Islamist movements had taken the path of compromise, trying to strike deals with the regime. For example, the Libyan Muslim Brotherhood, which was based abroad, had been willing to open channels with the regime in Tripoli in recent years in the hope of negotiating an official presence in the country (Pargeter 2009).

The boundaries of the Islamist movements in Libya are quite nebulous. Many of the members do not declare their affiliation, and this makes the identification of the movement complicated. The Libyan Islamist elite is ideologically and culturally linked to the international Islamist movement led by the charismatic Sheikh Yusuf Qaradawi that includes the Muslim Brotherhood but does not necessarily identify with it (Sallabi 2012). During the years, the Libyan Muslim Brotherhood joined the National Front for the Salvation of Libya, a resistance movement to Qadhafi's regime established by Muhammad Yusuf al-Magarief in 1981. The group, whose activity has been based abroad, mainly in the United States, opposed military and dictatorial rule in Libya through media campaigns and political alliances with opposition forces, but its role in the 2011 conflict had been of minor importance until the 7 July 2012 elections and the appointment of Magarief as president of the General National Congress (Sawani 2012).

It was only with the liberation of Tripoli on 28 August that the militant Islamist troops emerged as the leading military force on the ground. One of the main Islamist militias was the one led by Abdel Hakim Belhaj, who later became the head of the Tripoli Military Council. Belhaj once headed the LIFG and was subjected to extraordinary rendition with his wife, in 2004, in an operation initiated by British intelligence officers. They were detained in Bangkok in a U.S.-run detention facility where they were tortured before being rendered to Libya (Cobain 2012). Along with Ali Sallabi, who calls Qatar home and commands broad respect as an Islamic scholar and populist orator and who was essential in leading the mass uprising (Nordland and Kirkpatrick 2011), Belhaj was instrumental in obtaining strong support from Doha, where a Libyan opposition base was set up. Moreover, Qatar dispatched Western-trained advisers, who helped finance, train, and arm Libyan rebels (Shadid 2011). In the aftermath of the uprising, the Islamists, both the militant and the political formations, quickly reorganized their networks around mosques and Islamic centers and, supported by Qatar and other Arab countries, became central actors in the revolts.

The Libyan Exiles

It is difficult to quantify the group of Libyan exiles and its presence in the country today. As Anna Baldinetti (2010) puts it, the term *exile* in the study of the Libyan diaspora is more appropriate than *refugee* since it is strictly connected to the historical concept of *hijra* (migration) and to the term *muhajirun* used by Libyans who left their country during the Italian occupation. In 2011, a large number of Libyans from the exile communities in Europe, North America, and the Gulf countries, who had left their country mainly for political reasons, arrived in Benghazi at the outbreak of the revolution (Tarkowski Tempelhof and Omar 2011). Some of them had held high-level positions abroad. Ali Tarhouni, for instance, exiled since 1974 for political activism, was a lecturer in economics at the University of Washington before returning to Libya in February 2011 to manage the rebel government's finances in the first phases of the revolution and to become the president of the Constituent Assembly in February 2014. Khalifa Hifter, who lived in exile in Virginia for two decades, was involved in coordinating the Libyan opposition in exile, and his collaboration with the CIA has been often suggested (Al Jazeera 2011c). His popularity among rebel fighters was due in great part to his participation in Qadhafi's Chad war in the late 1970s. He returned to Libya after the uprising started and began a public rivalry with General Younes by appointing himself field commander (*New York Times* 2011a). Following a failed "You Tube coup" in February 2014, General Hifter launched Operation Dignity in the east of the country in May 2014, claiming to rid Benghazi and other cities in the region of all Islamist groups.

More generally, the exiles are human rights activists, lawyers, judges, journalists, and businessmen and women who are well educated and able to provide technical expertise in the transitional phase. Some assisted the NTC as advisers, and others created media outlets or fought on the front lines, but above all they were extremely relevant as an external source of financial and operational support for the revolution (Tarkowski Tempelhof and Omar 2011). Nevertheless, their presence in the transitional institutions such as the NTC and the interim government had to be mediated in order to balance the role they played during the revolution and their absence from the country during Qadhafi's dictatorship.

Coalitions

What were the contacts between the opposition groups prior to the outbreak of the revolt? On the one hand, the defectors were militarily and politically supported by Western powers such as France, the United Kingdom, and the United States. On the other hand, the Islamist forces, militant and political, received money, weapons, and political support from Qatar, while other armed groups received support from the United Arab Emirates (UAE) since the very first days of the demonstrations (RUSI 2011). These external backers mediated between the two main local political actors, defectors and Islamists, particularly in the first phase of the insurgency, in order to coalesce and organize the opposition against the regime regardless of the groups' political agendas (Sallabi 2012). The Western powers supported the rebels in their demands by overlooking the fact that it was prevalently the militant Islamists who had become the armed wing of the revolt and needed to be trained and armed if the Qadhafi regime was to be toppled. Early in the conflict the coalition formed by former regime elements and Islamists demanded the end of the regime to be achieved through external military intervention short of the deployment of troops in the country. The NTC official founding statement of 5 March 2011 clearly expressed this position: "we request from the international community to fulfill its obligations to protect the Libyan people from any further genocide and crimes against humanity without any direct military intervention on Libya soil" (NTC 2011a). In March, facing the standoff between regime and opposition forces, the Western allies decided it was time to break the standoff, and they did so, as discussed in Theiss's chapter. The establishment of a joint mission in April 2011, with French, British, and Qatari special forces sent to Libya to assist with training as well as coordinating their command and NATO air strikes, followed visits from British and French military chiefs in Qatar, although special forces activities had been conducted on the ground since the end of February (RUSI 2011). The French went to the west and the British to the east, and by August 2011 some twenty men from D-squadron 22 SAS were operating in small teams in Brega and Misrata while a training base was set up in southern Libya (BBC 2012).

It should be emphasized that the revolt against Qadhafi was not based on tribalism. For this reason tribes are not addressed per se in this chapter. Tribalism was one of the factors occasionally at play during the revolution. Indeed, the NTC negotiated with tribal leaders for support, as demonstrated by the council's co-option of members of Qadhafi's tribe (Sawani 2012). In many cases, the defections of senior officers and politicians in the first weeks of the uprising reflected their tribes' decision to turn against Qadhafi (Lacher 2011). The significance of tribal considerations appeared again when the regime's security apparatus showed its tenacious resistance against revolutionary forces, given that recruitment into the apparatus had been based largely on tribes; it is not a coincidence that the remains of Qadhafi's brigades made their last stand in the strongholds of the Warfalla (Bani Walid), Magarha (Fezzan), and Qadhadfa (Sirte), tribes historically loyal to Qadhafi (Lacher 2011). Each side sought to use tribal loyalties to generate tribal consensus and support, with both the regime and the NTC organizing rival conferences with representatives of the country's leading tribes in order to affirm their legitimacy to rule (Cherstich 2011). Tribal politics did play a role in the hinterland while urban and ideologically based networks—for example, Islamist groups—dominated in the big coastal cities (Lacher 2013). Nevertheless, it would be wrong to state that tribes as such played a major role overall in the Libyan conflict. Membership in municipalities and localities had a much bigger role in sparking the revolution and determining its outcome.

From the analysis of the actors involved in the conflict a few main characteristics of the Libyan uprising emerge. Libya's eight-month civil war qualifies it as a Long Track case for the purpose of analysis. What determined the occurrence of a Long Track in the Libyan revolution was not the role of the army. The peaceful protests turned immediately into an armed insurgency that, however, would not have succeeded without the external military intervention and the prompt creation of the NTC.

INSURGENCY COALITION AND FORMULATION

The Libyan Long Track started on 15 February 2011 and officially ended on 23 October 2011 with the killing of Qadhafi and his son Mutassim and the capture of Saif al-Islam. The nature of the uprising in Libya was different from that of the uprisings in Tunisia and Egypt. After the first two days of peaceful protests in Benghazi and Bayda, on 15 and 16 February, a "day of rage" was organized on the third day by the National Conference for the Libyan Opposition, an organization based in London that brought together different political opposition groups (*Asharq Al-Awsat* 2011). Initially, the army responded by shooting at the demonstrators, causing fourteen casualties in Benghazi, ten in Bayda, and six in Derna (*USA Today* 2011). On the fourth day, protesters occupied a military base in Bayda, where the local police joined the demonstrators (Black and Bowcott 2011). The same happened in Derna, where the rebels set fire to a police station while the army joined the demonstrators (*New York Times* 2011b). According to regime sources, the peaceful demonstrators in Derna looked more like a well-trained and armed commando. They distributed weapons to the rebels, accounting for the appearance of so many weapons in their hands in the very first phase of the revolt (Mezran 2011b). Meanwhile, Justice Minister Abdel Jalil and Interior Minister Abdul Fattah Younis al-Obeidi, both originally from Cyrenaica, rapidly negotiated—together with tribal support—the National Transitional Council (NTC), a mixture of urban intellectuals, former Islamist guerrillas, secular professionals, and tribal leaders, to guide the "breakaway proto-state" that emerged in Cyrenaica from 27 February 2011 until 8 August 2012 (Joffe 2011).

The progress of the rebels on the ground, marching toward Tripolitania, seemed unstoppable, but after the initial astonishment, the loyalist forces looked determined to conduct a harsh repression against the insurgents. While Qadhafi called the demonstrators "cowards, traitors and cockroaches" who should be attacked (*Al-Ahram* 2011), Saif al-Islam in a speech on Al Jazeera on 20 February, issued at the threat of repression, stated, "We will fight to the last minute, until the last bullet" to safeguard the regime (Moss 2011). Later on 10 March he stated, "This is our country, we will never, ever give up and we will never, ever surrender. We fight here in Libya, we die here in Libya" (*Sidney Morning Herald* 2011). The government refused to acknowledge any hurting stalemate, seeing its situation in existential terms.

The determination of the regime to repress the insurgency forced the decision of Western powers to side with the rebels and advocate military intervention to protect civilians (Chivvis 2013). A week after the outbreak of the revolt, French president Nicolas Sarkozy demanded the departure of Qadhafi from Libya, denounced the repeated and systematic violence of the regime against the demonstrators, and called for an investigation by the International Criminal Court against the regime (All Voices 2011). British foreign minister William Hague echoed Sarkozy in his quest for Qadhafi's departure (BBC News 2011) while on 28 February 2011 the European Union announced a package of sanctions against Qadhafi's family and his closer collaborators. Such a strong position, probably based on the evidence reported by special forces active on the ground since February (RUSI 2011), was strengthened by the "media blitz" of satellite channels, at the forefront of which was

Qatar's Al Jazeera (Sawani 2012). From that moment it became politically very difficult for any other European country to offer political asylum to the Libyan leader, an action that, in retrospect, would probably have avoided military intervention.

Within the UN arena the Franco-British duo presented the draft of resolution 1973 demanding an immediate cease-fire and the imposition of a no-fly zone over Libya, as analyzed in the chapter by Theiss. The initiative succeeded in obtaining the support of the United States, having received a green light for a no-fly zone by the Gulf Cooperation Council (7 March), the Islamic Conference (8 March), and later the Arab League (12 March) (RUSI 2011). With renewed vigor and determination, the loyalist troops were marching toward Benghazi. The international community acted in a very quick and resolute way in order to avoid a massacre. The Security Council invoked the principle of "responsibility to protect" and, having obtained the abstention of China and Russia but the support of Lebanon, the Security Council adopted resolution 1973 on 17 March 2011. In the following two days, Qadhafi's loyalist forces approached Benghazi. On 19 March, after the Paris conference in which the possibility of a military intervention had been discussed, President Sarkozy unilaterally announced that French aircraft were already in action over Benghazi (RUSI 2011).

That night Operation Odyssey Dawn was initiated by France, the United Kingdom, and the United States, a mission that passed gradually under NATO command by 27 March. The United States was determined to maintain control of the operation, leading from behind, through NATO (Mezran 2012a). This brief history of the diplomatic activity, more fully developed in the Theiss chapter, is necessary to underline the decisiveness of the international community in supporting the Libyan opposition forces from the very beginning. This gave the Libyan rebels the impression that the support of the international community was strong enough for them not to accept any kind of mediation with the regime during the conflict, whether it was coming from the African Union, Turkey, Venezuelan president Hugo Chávez, or the UN. Before moving to the analysis of these attempts toward negotiation, it is crucial to analyze the formation of the National Transitional Council (NTC), as this was the body presumed to speak for the rebels in the negotiations with the regime.

The Creation of the National Transitional Council and Its Evolution

The formation of the NTC was announced on 27 February 2011. The council derived its legitimacy from the aspirations of the 17 February revolution that set up the local councils that in turn took the decision to create the NTC (NTC 2011a), hence the criterion of representation based on municipal constituencies. The efficiency and rapidity in forming the council is astonishing, coming only twelve days after the outbreak of the first demonstrations. In this respect the Libyan uprising differs from other Arab Spring uprisings. The rebels had no problems in getting themselves an organization at the very beginning. The support of external actors contributed to the success of the NTC as it established itself as the sole legitimate representative of all Libya on 5 March. In the same declaration, the council requested the international community to fulfill its obligations to protect the Libyan people from further genocide and crimes against humanity, although without any direct military intervention on Libyan soil, wanting to rely on the will of the Libyan people for a free and dignified existence. In so doing, the council relied on a self-founding legitimacy and on the legitimacy derived from an external source of power—current international representatives and members of Libyan delegations and embassies, encouraged to defect from the regime (Matthews 2012). Therefore, as Daniel Matthews (2012) points out, the NTC was born from a paradox: asserting its role as sole representative of the Libyan people while looking for legitimacy within organs of the previous regime that the NTC itself aimed at disrupting. The NTC became the "voice of the rebels," presenting the rebellion to the international community with one single face and silencing other voices in and outside the country. The council created a "ghostly unity" that did not actually exist and that dissipated once it handed over power to the elected General National Congress (Matthews 2012).

Opacities characterized the negotiation of the council. Since its inception it was accused of being non-inclusive and dominated at times by few powerful families, at other times by the Muslim Brotherhood or by the Libyan diaspora. Nevertheless, the council proved to be a catalyst that kept the country on track in the first phase of the political transition. Its action heavily relied on the brigades for security and defense as much as on local notables and family heads who convened reconciliation councils handling the burden of peacemaking, creating a sense of activity that was abruptly interrupted when the NTC handed over power to the elected General National Congress (GNC) (ICG 2012). Not always did the NTC manage to control violence and insecurity in the country; for example, Tebu and Arab tribes kept confronting each other in the south throughout much of 2012 while the Tripoli airport witnessed clashes between militias in June 2012 (Mezran 2012e). Nevertheless, this does not nullify the unifying role that the NTC had during the conflict and in its aftermath, even if questions of legitimacy and transparency tarnished at times its reputation (Wehry 2012).

The NTC offered its formulation for rebuilding the democratic state of Libya based on the rule of law on 29 March 2011, because, as stated in the document, "there is no alternative to building a free and democratic society and ensuring the supremacy of International Humanitarian Law and Human Rights Declaration" (NTC 2011c). Dialogue, tolerance, cooperation, national cohesiveness, and political and intellectual pluralism were outlined as the pillars of the new social contract. In its declaration, the NTC stated its determination to transfer power in a peaceful way through legal institutions and ballot boxes in accordance with a national constitution crafted by the people and endorsed in a referendum. The council recognized without reservation its obligation to draft a constitution based on the separation of legislative, executive, and judicial powers; form political organizations and civil institutions, such as political parties, unions, and civil associations; maintain a constitutional and pluralist civil state; recognize universal suffrage, freedom of expression, political democracy, and values of social justice, among which were respect for human rights and empowerment of minorities and women; and commit to international and regional cooperation and integration. Islam was not mentioned in the statement, except for a reference to a "State that draws strength from our strong religious beliefs in peace, truth, justice and equality" (NTC 2011c).

The NTC had a legislative body, an executive board, and an armed wing. In the initial stages of the revolution the group of former members of the regime, university professors, businessmen, intellectuals, and human rights activists, such as Abdel Hafidh Ghoga and Salwa Bughaighis, prevailed in the council. The president of the council, Mustafa Abdel Jalil, allegedly represented the instances of the Muslim Brotherhood in the country. The executive board was headed by Mahmoud Jibril until liberation was declared in October after the killing of Qadhafi. Jibril lived in the United States until 2007, when he was appointed head of the Libyan National Economic Development Board to promote liberalization and privatization policies; he was also involved in the "Libya Vision" project to bring democracy to Libya, but he left his position in 2010. Jibril then became the leader of the National Forces Alliance, which won the elections in July 2012. In order to maintain their objectivity, all NTC members pledged not to take part in future elections. However, very soon those representatives of more liberal and progressive forces within Libyan society were pushed aside by the Islamists who slowly gained control not only of the NTC but also of the military forces on the ground (Alunni 2014b).

The armed wing, the Free Libya Armed Forces, was composed of defectors from the army and air force as well as civilians who took up weapons against the regime. General Younis Obeidi, former commander of special forces and interior minister under the regime, defected on 22 February 2011 to join the opposition forces but was killed on 28 July by members of the Abu Obaida al-Jarrah Brigade, one of the most extreme Islamist militias loosely attached to the rebels, probably on suspicion that his family, of the Obeidi tribe in eastern Libya, had maintained links with Qadhafi (Bloomfield, McElroy, and Sherlock 2011). Ali Issawi, foreign minister in Jibril's NTC cabinet, called Younis back from the front lines to Benghazi to question him about rumors that he had remained in contact with regime members. Younis had agreed to return to Benghazi, and to show his good faith, he agreed to remove his personal bodyguard. The al-Jarrah Brigade was sent to pick him up. On the way to Benghazi the news arrived that the orders for the general's confinement had been countermanded by Abdel Jalil; three members of the militia, determined that the general should not escape punishment for his alleged treachery, took the law into their own hands and shot the general and his two aides. Although different narratives emerged accusing al-Qaeda or pro-regime forces (Shelton 2011; Stephen 2011), the NTC confirmed the role of the al-Jarrah Brigade, who had blamed Younis for the Abu Salim massacre in 1996 when he was Qadhafi's interior minister (Bloomfield, McElroy, and Sherlock 2011; Benotman 2011). His death paved the way for the rise of the Islamists in the liberation of Tripoli but also highlighted the divisions and rivalries within the opposition forces, just at the moment when thirty-two nations, including the United States and the UK, formally recognized the NTC as Libya's sole legitimate government (Joshi 2011; Mostyn 2011).

In sum, the negotiation of an NTC coalition helped create a common front against the regime and organize the rebels, giving form and direction to the uprising although a division developed within the NTC. On the one hand, the legislative body presided by Abdel Jalil, which slowly came to be dominated by the Islamist forces, faced, on the other, the executive branch headed by Jibril, who represented the country's nationalist forces (Alunni 2014b). The Islamists too, therefore, were involved in the organization of the revolt within the framework set out by the NTC.

The NTC did not have a monopoly over the threat and use of violence, which mainly rested in the hands of the militias. Military wings of the local councils, they exerted a significant control over the NTC's decision-making system, managing at times to influence it. The NTC did, however, claim legitimacy and organization as a basis for negotiation. Indeed, although they were not directly involved in the negotiations, the militias managed to transform their possession of weapons into a negotiating tool as well as a means of defense against rival groups, protection to the respective localities, and control over the transition (Kadlec 2012). They were determined to wait for the establishment of a strong central authority before relinquishing their military power. Nevertheless, the fact that militia leaders such as Belhaj created political parties in the aftermath of the conflict indicated that some of them understood that a party rather than a militia was needed if they were to be part of the political game. However, in the very fluid and unstable political scenario that materialized following the July 2012 elections, the militias remained key tools to control the political power and determine political outcomes through the threat of armed confrontation in a process that, in the course of 2014, saw the role of militias dominate the political landscape.

The rebel forces of various orientations coalesced around the NTC in order to guarantee for themselves the support of the external powers that had already proved essential in defending the revolution from the regime. This support was subordinate to the formulation of a democratic vision of Libya. The NTC managed to keep the many different forces within the opposition together in a continuous negotiating and balancing exercise among them. This was particularly true in the negotiation of the road map and constitutional declaration. During a meeting of the International Contact Group in Rome on 6 May 2011, Jibril reaffirmed a project for the new Libya and sketched the road map approved by the council on 3 August and publicly presented as the Interim Constitutional Declaration on 10 August 2011 (NTC 2011b).

The Constitutional Declaration was negotiated to be the basis of rule in the transitional stage until a permanent constitution was ratified in a referendum. The declaration set out the steps leading to democratic elections monitored by the United Nations within eighteen months from the "Declaration of Liberation." Libya was designed as a democratic, independent state with Tripoli as its capital, Islam as its religion, shariʿa as the main source of legislation, and Arabic as the official language. The rights of minority groups and all sections of society were guaranteed as well as nondiscrimination and equality before the law. Freedom of opinion and expression, as well as freedom of the press and peaceful protests, was to be guaranteed along with the right to form political parties, peaceful societies, and civil society organizations unless they were not complying with public order. A democratic political system based on political and party pluralism following a peaceful, democratic transition of power was to be established. The declaration designed the transition in three steps (NTC 2011b):

- *Step 1: The elections of a General National Congress (GNC).* The declaration established the NTC as the highest authority in the transition. Made up of representatives of local councils chosen on the basis of population density, the NTC appoints an Executive Office responsible for implementing NTC's policies and a transitional government; within 90 days, the NTC issues the electoral legislation to vote for a General National Congress (GNC); appoints an electoral commission; and organizes the election of a two-hundred-member GNC within 240 days. The NTC is dissolved at the first meeting of the GNC, while the transitional government maintains its role until the appointment of an interim government by the GNC.
- *Step 2: The making of the constitution.* The GNC appoints a Constituent Authority for drafting a constitution, which submits a draft constitution to the GNC within 60 days of its first meeting. The GNC approves the draft constitution and puts it to a referendum within 30 days. If approved by a two-thirds majority, it is ratified by the GNC; if rejected, the Constituent Authority re-drafts it and puts it to a referendum again within 30 days.
- *Step 3: The organization of general elections.* The GNC issues a general election law in line with the constitution within 30 days, and a general election is held within 180 days of the declaration of the law. A Supreme National Elections Commission, appointed by the GNC, is responsible for holding general elections under the supervision of the national judiciary and internationally monitored. When new legislature convenes, the GNC is dissolved, and the new legislature assumes its duties; the government becomes a caretaker until the appointment of a permanent government in accordance with the constitution.

Although with delays and amendments to the Constitutional Declaration, a Constituent Drafting Assembly (CDA) was elected in February 2014 at a time when the derailment of the transition process appeared more and more inevitable, as discussed later.

Mediation Attempts in the Early Stages of the Conflict

The NTC plan and vision for a new Libya were relatively detailed. One would have expected such a strong political actor to undertake negotiations with the regime in the attempt to find a political solution to the crisis. This was not the case, although there had been a few mediation attempts by different actors, particularly at the beginning of the conflict (Bartu 2014; Kuperman 2013). Al Jazeera news channel reported that Qadhafi and Arab League chairman Amr Moussa had agreed to Venezuelan president Hugo Chávez's plan to send representatives from Latin America, Europe, and the Middle East to Libya to broker negotiations between Qadhafi and the rebel leaders (Al Jazeera 2011b). The potential breakthrough came as Qadhafi's Libyan Army faced an increasingly organized and confident rebel force appealing for international support and looking to take its military successes westward toward Tripoli (*Telegraph* 2011). However, the proposal for mediation was brushed aside by the United States and France. The United States repeated its calls for Qadhafi to step down from power in the face of the three-week-old uprising. France followed the same line: "Any mediation that allows Colonel Qadhafi to succeed himself is obviously not welcome," said Alain Juppe, the French foreign minister, after talks with his British counterpart (Al Jazeera 2011a). Abdel Jalil, head of the NTC, declared that he totally rejected the concept of talks with Qadhafi and said that no one contacted him regarding the Venezuelan initiative. The rebels did not look favorably upon any kind of mediation unless it considered an exit strategy for Qadhafi, his family, and all his close aides. The rebels stated that there was no longer time for dialogue and no way to achieve any kind of settlement since there was a complete lack of trust (Al Jazeera 2011a).

This uncompromising stance was confirmed and reinforced a month later when, looking for a political solution to the Libyan crisis after the beginning of UN-authorized air strikes on 17 March 2011, the African Union (AU), which had rejected foreign military intervention in Libya, presented Qadhafi and the rebels with an African roadmap to end the conflict. An AU delegation of the presidents of South Africa, Congo-Brazzaville, Mali, and Mauritania and Uganda's foreign minister arrived in Libya on 10 April to meet with both parties. The plan, considerably more detailed than the Venezuelan proposal, included an immediate cease-fire, delivery of humanitarian aid, protection of foreign nationals in Libya, and dialogue between Libyan parties on the establishment of a transition period toward political reform reflecting the aspirations of the Libyan people (Sherwood and McGreal 2011). The plan, however, did not include the possibility of Qadhafi's relinquishing power. This was the main reason the regime accepted the roadmap and the opposition forces firmly rejected it, having already made clear that they would not consider any deal that involved Qadhafi or his family retaining power. The African Union was perceived by the rebel leaders and the people in Benghazi as a creation and tool of Qadhafi's ambitions and therefore was not considered as an honest broker (Murphy 2011). South Africa president Jacob Zuma met again with the Libyan leader on 29 May on behalf of the AU, but the visit merely seemed to allow the *qaʿid* (leader) to express his determination not to leave Libya. Qadhafi called for an end to the bombings to enable a Libyan dialogue, but this was clearly a prerequisite that he was not in the position to set (Bearak 2011).

Turkey also tried in early April to invest work and prestige into the effort to find a political solution. The use of soft power was expected to be more efficient than Western air strikes. The Turkish plan was designed in three steps: a cease-fire, a political dialogue between the government and the opposition, and the establishment of a democratically elected government. But behind the scenes, the Turkish foreign minister and his aides were confronted with the stubbornness of the two warring sides that deeply distrusted each other, shared no common ground, and were uninterested in yielding. As a senior Turkish diplomat stated: "One side, the opposition, is insisting that Qadhafi should go and [that] the presence of any member of the Qadhafi family in the new administration is not acceptable. The other side is saying Qadhafi should stay. So there is no breakthrough yet" (Seibert 2011).

The UN was also trying to mediate, but it found itself in a rather awkward position, attempting to play the double role of negotiator and law enforcer in the conflict (Piiparinen 2011). UN secretary general Ban Ki-moon appointed former Jordanian foreign minister Abdelilah Al-Khatib as his special envoy on 6 March. However, the prospects for UN mediation had already been complicated by the UN Security Council's decision a week earlier to authorize criminal enquiries against the Libyan leadership by the International Criminal Court. During the defensive phase of the civil war, Qadhafi's internationally isolated regime reportedly sought negotiations and a channel of communication with the National Transitional Council as well as with its closest, albeit few, allies on the international stage. These initiatives, however, either backfired or were rejected, leaving a peace mediation gap in the Libya crisis, which was particularly alarming and unflattering for the UN (Piiparinen 2011).

The regime put forward a few proposals that included Qadhafi or one of his sons overseeing political change in Libya, but these attempts were promptly rejected by the rebels. Later during the conflict, rumors were floating among the expatriate community of attempted "informal" negotiation efforts led by individuals from both sides and meant to find a political solution to the conflict (Mezran 2011a). Saif al-Islam, who had personally conducted a mediation effort in the past with the Islamists, tried to contact and win the Islamist wing of the opposition forces on the side of the regime, but the attempt was clearly unsuccessful (Kirkpatrick 2011). This indicates that during the conflict there was a lack of direct negotiation between the rebels and the regime. Facing Qadhafi's refusal to step down and having the political support of the West, the rebels demanded external military intervention and ruled out any possible mediation with the regime, not to speak of direct negotiations. In fact, the parties involved in the conflict were never really susceptible to their own or others' efforts to turn the conflict toward resolution through negotiation, but why was this the case?

The conflict in Libya never reached the mutually hurting stalemate (MHS). The regime and the opposition forces did not find themselves locked in a deadlock painful for both of them that could have pushed the parties to seek a way out of the conflict (Zartman 2000). On the contrary, as in Syria two years later, one party was always stronger than the other, and this was mainly due to the role of external actors. Indeed, if between 15 February and 6 March the advance of the opposition forces toward the west seemed unstoppable, leaving the regime in an initial disarray, on 6 March the regime forces led a counteroffensive that only the UN-authorized military mission, Odyssey Dawn, was able to stop. From that moment on, the primacy of the opposition over the loyalist forces was established. The superiority of the rebel forces became a constant, clearly determined by a foreign military intervention, and remained so until the end of the eight-month conflict. The rebels only needed to stay united in one common front whose protection was guaranteed by NATO air strikes. The unity among the rebels was based on a marriage of convenience: the Islamists organized forces on the ground and provided weapons necessary to win the battle, while the defectors had on their side Western political and military support. During the conflict, there had been no common formulation that brought together the political or armed forces of various orientations except the goal of overthrowing the regime. The situation in Syria as it evolved in 2013 was different only in details.

POST-INSURGENCY FORMULATION

After Qadhafi's death and the proclamation of national liberation, on 23 October 2011, the debate over substantive issues intensified within the coalition of the rebels. Indeed, even if, with the Constitutional Declaration and the Vision for Libya, the NTC had already determined in theory the skeleton of the New Order, only in the post-insurgency phase did a real discussion of substantive issues as well as rivalries within the coalition start to take place in the country. The liberation of Tripoli, on 28 August 2011, opened the way to the rise of new political and military figures among military commanders eager for leadership and power, among tribal leaders from the freed regions, and within the Tripolitanian elite. Skepticism on the future of the country and the strength of the NTC political leadership started to emerge. A Western diplomat attending the liberation ceremony declared: "Toppling Gaddafi was the unifying force. Now that he's gone, will they be able to hold it together?" (Sheridan 2011a).

Contrary to expectations, within a month the NTC managed to appoint a new prime minister, Abdurrahman al-Keib; as a professor and engineer who lived in the United States for more than twenty years, al-Keib was above suspicion (*Huffington Post* 2011). The selection of al-Keib was the result of a conglomerating process of negotiations that saw the parties involved in the big coalition responsible for toppling the regime come together to negotiate their positions within the new government to take Libya through its first democratic elections. The lack of a strong leadership may have favored the aggregation of the many factions involved in the conflict into a conglomerate movement, and agreement over an acceptable formula for future governance made this stage of negotiations relatively easy. Al-Keib's selection suggests that the country's interim rulers were seeking out a government leader palatable both to the West and to Libyans who distrusted anyone connected to the Old Order. He negotiated a cabinet coalition composed mainly of moderates, marginalizing prominent members of the Islamist groups (Stephen and Harding 2011). For instance, the appointment of Osama al-Juwali as defense minister was at the expense of Abdel Hakim Belhaj. Juwali, the commander of a militia from the small city of Zintan that played a central role in storming Tripoli in August and capturing Saif al-Islam, had previously had no national political profile. Al-Keib picked Hassan Ziglan, a technocrat, to replace Ali Tarhouni, former NTC minister of oil, gas, and finance. The cabinet won approval from Libya's western backers who were concerned about hard-line Islamists after President Abdel Jalil declared that shariʿa law would form the basis of a new constitution (Hounshell 2011).

The West, although reassured by the absence of religious hard-liners in the interim government, questioned what kind of stability or recognition a government like this would have without the moderate Islamists. But, in fact, both moderate and radical elements were standing by the government, when not part of it in lower posts, checking on its moves and preparing for the elections for the two-hundred-seat General National Congress. For instance, a key post like that of deputy defense minister went to Khalid al-Sharif, a former member of the Libyan Islamic Fighting Group (LIFG) who was subject to extraordinary rendition in 2003. The Islamist forces kept control of the territory through armed militias and therefore maintained a political control in the country (Alunni 2014b).

Moreover, it was during the al-Keib government that some militias were embedded within government structures and became official tools to safeguard and enhance influence and power of some political actors (Pack, Mezran, and Eljarh 2014). Osama al-Juwali, the Zintani minister of defense, was keen on embedding the militias from his hometown, which politically responded to Mahmoud Jibril.

He did so while Fawzi Abdel Aʿal, the Misratan minister of the interior, and Yousef Mangoush, the Misratan chief of staff, created the Supreme Security Council (SSC) and the Shields, respectively, embedding in the government and army structures those Islamist-leaning militias and militias from Misrata. This process jeopardized the effective integration of militias that those government actors should have sought and established a system of patronage in disguise of a compromise (Pack, Mezran, and Eljarh 2014, Alunni 2014b).

The post-insurgency phase in Libya proved particularly difficult as the intensification of the negotiations for formulation had a breakup effect on the opposition forces. A long, violent uprising characterized the Libyan case, and clashes occurred even immediately in the post-insurgency phase. The city of Bani Walid serves as an example. Bani Walid, 104 miles away from Tripoli and dominated by the Warfalla tribe, loyal to the regime until the very end, resisted the occupation, and in mid-January 2012 the tribe violently expelled pro-government forces, illustrating the power of tribal leaders over the fragile interim government. A few days after the city uprising, Salah al-Maayuf, a member of the Warfalla elders council in Bani Walid, said that the NTC defense minister had recognized the new local council appointed by his body. Bani Walid is an example of a rural area where clashes followed the lines of tribal affiliation. U.S. and European officials prodded the NTC to be more "inclusive" by broadening the body and reaching out to leaders of the western tribes, but signs of discontent emerged in this phase (Carpenter 2011).

Indeed, this was only one in a series of clashes between rival armed groups that occurred after the official liberation of Libya. Early in January, armed clashes between militias in the towns of Assabia and Gharyan left twelve people dead and about a hundred injured. NTC leader Abdel Jalil warned of the dangers of a civil war if the country's militias were not disarmed (BBC News 2011), but the problem of militias retaining control of arms is only one of the many issues that the interim government had to address in order to take Libya toward a more democratic path.

The country faced the risk of breaking down into many pieces because of divisions that go back in history and follow regional, religious, and tribal divides. However, what kept Libya together were the continuous negotiations over a formula for the New Order that were never suspended. On the contrary, these negotiations were instrumental—particularly after the overthrow—in maintaining territorial control and stability in order to proceed toward a New Order as mandated by the 2011 Constitutional Declaration. For instance, just two days before the National Congress election on 7 July, the NTC had amended article 30 of the Constitutional Declaration determining that the Constituent Assembly would be elected by public, direct, and free ballot rather than selected by the Congress (Updike Toler and Peyerl 2012). It was the second time that the article had been amended; on 13 March 2012 the NTC had specified that the Constituent Assembly should have sixty members "on the model/like the committee of sixty that was established to develop the constitution of the independence of Libya in 1951," none of whom could also be members of Congress (Updike Toler and Peyerl 2012). The 1951 "Committee of Sixty," assigned twenty members to each of the main Libyan regions—Tripolitania, Cyrenaica, and Fezzan—regardless of population distribution. Both amendments were explained by the NTC's desire to allow for greater regional representation in the transitional process in response to federalist movements that threatened to boycott the congressional elections and to disturb the security of the transitional process (Updike Toler and Peyerl 2012).

The announcement on 6 March 2012, by a conference, known as Barqa conference, of three thousand tribal and political leaders from eastern Libya that they intended to push for greater autonomy for Cyrenaica was greeted with surprise, confusion, and even dismay (Ahmed and Martin 2012). These leaders demanded enhanced financial contribution—given that 80 percent of the resources are located in the east—and a bigger piece of the political pie through redistribution of seats in the organ responsible for making the constitution and in the future Libyan Parliament (Lawrence 2012). The NTC's move appeased them and allowed for the 7 July elections to happen without major disruptions.

The NTC was not the only actor involved in the negotiations with the federalists. Mahmoud Jibril, no longer head of the NTC executive board but leader of the National Forces Alliance—a new political alliance formed by political organizations, NGOs, and independents—was handling "promising" discussions with federalists in eastern Libya well before the elections (*Libya Herald* 2012). Jibril showed a conciliatory and pragmatic stance toward the east. He aimed at decentralizing power within the framework of a strong central government (Lawrence 2012).

To sum up, the NTC set a coherent vision for the New Order and maintained its role of guardian of the revolution until 8 August 2012, when it handed power over to the elected General National Congress (GNC). In this process, which lasted eighteen months, negotiations, organization, armed intervention, and the threat or use of violence were used as carrot and stick by the NTC and the al-Keib government as well as by the other political and military forces on the ground, such as tribes and militias. The NTC lacked political and military clout, but its ability to negotiate with local and international actors was key to the success of its project, along with the recognition by the Libyan people that unity was a necessity. However, this is not to say that the Libyan transition in the post-insurgency phase lacked in tensions, conflicts, and divisions among the various factions composing the coalition that toppled the regime. The Long Track, indeed, strengthened rivalries, exacerbated leadership tensions, and reinforced regional identities.

At the beginning of 2012 order and security in the country were rapidly dissipating, putting many competing forces under the spotlight. Geography and localisms explain these divisions and the difficulty of reconciling them. The wedge of desert that divides Cyrenaica from Tripolitania creates a deep divide in the country and gives room for the empowerment of local communities and tribes who had been kept under strict control in the Old Order. The political geography of Libya determines the affiliation to a tribe or a city and creates a strong sense of membership to these local communities. In the conflict that saw forces from the east marching toward the west, the affiliation to local families, cities, and tribes was dominant, and this factor did not simply fade away with the liberation of Libya (Lacher 2011). In a way, factionalism was exacerbated by the uprising, although, as explained, factionalism was more the result of political geography rather than the result of deeply rooted identity issues.

Moreover, the Libyan people seemed more concerned with practical issues such as government's transparency, rather than with identity matters. Mohamed Omeish, member of the Libyan Muslim Brotherhood, raised the main concern of the Libyan people: "[They] don't know what the NTC is doing, who are the members and what is their number" (Al Jazeera 2011d). Azza al-Maghur, lawyer and activist, plied NTC representatives with questions on the voting system they used in order to make their official decisions, as well as with questions on the kind of issues that the council was discussing (Al Jazeera 2011d). On this the NTC might have done better, but one aspect about which the NTC felt comfortable was the exclusion of Qadhafi loyalists and pro-regime forces from any decision concerning the transitional period. Their position did not change: there cannot be negotiations with Old Regime loyalists.

FROM THE GNC ELECTIONS TO THE STALEMATE

Elections for the National Assembly took place on 7 July 2012. In the run to the elections, political parties sprang up in the country ranging from Islamist to more secularist formations, although in Libya no candidates have defined themselves as Islamist or secularist. Instead, everyone used the term *Muslim* for self-identification (Mezran 2012d). Among the Islamist parties it was possible to identify four main groups ahead of the GNC elections: the Justice and Construction Party (JCP) (representative of the Libyan Muslim Brotherhood) led by Mohammed Sowan; the National Gathering for Freedom, Justice and Development led by Ali al-Sallabi; the Reform and Development Party headed by Khaled al-Werchefani, a former member of the Libyan MB (Muslim Brotherhood); and Al-Watan chaired by Abdel Hakim Belhaj. Among the more "secular" parties are the National Forces Alliance (NFA) led by Mahmoud Jibril, the National Front for the Salvation of Libya (formation derived by the homonymous group of the Libyan diaspora), and the National Centrist Party headed by Ali Tarhouni.

The NFA emerged the strongest among the parties that contested the election by gaining 39 seats, followed by the JCP with 17 seats (*Libya Herald* 2012). "Nobody saw this coming," said Dirk Vandewalle, a U.S. academic and former adviser to the UN special envoy for Libya, Ian Martin (Stephen 2012). These results only concerned the portion of the assembly elected through party lists, which is limited to 80 seats out of 200. The other 120 seats were reserved for independent candidates.

As stated by NFA leader Jibril, the Alliance cannot be defined as either a secularist or a liberal party (Stephen 2012). It presented itself as a moderate Islamic movement that recognizes the importance of Islam in political life and favors shariʿa as the basis of the law (Grant 2012b). The coalition consisted of 58 parties, 200 civil society associations, and 281 independent national figures. Members of the coalition included representatives from the Amazigh, Tuareg, and Tabu tribes (Tunisia Live 2012c). The NFA considered Libya to be a pluralistic, civil democratic society, and it plans to protect the freedom of all its citizens, promising to guarantee gender equality and to protect minority rights. It supported decentralization but not federalism (Grant 2012b).

The JCP presented itself as a moderate and progressive religious party that uses Islam as the frame of reference in all areas of life. An advisory council (*shura*) of forty-five members determines the direction of the party and its executive decision-making system. The party believes that the parliamentary system will be most suited to Libya. It supports decentralization but strongly opposes the idea of federalism. It wants to see an institutional democracy in Libya with an independent judiciary and a powerful army. Additionally the party has advocated for upholding transparent political competition, establishing a durable legal and institutional framework for the country, and ensuring a place for women in politics (Tunisia Live 2012a). It promises to develop relations with international organizations to implement human rights covenants and to work on international relations on the basis of equality (Khan 2012).

Given the important role played by the Islamist forces in the revolution, many expected a landslide victory for this party in the 7 July election. On the contrary, their weak showing demonstrated that they were not grounded in the social fabric of the country. The fact that they had been repressed by the regime gained them popularity but only up to a certain point. During the revolution, what was exceptional about the Islamist forces was their organization and contacts with external powers needed to succeed in the uprising, but these external links did not translate into internal political superiority in the electoral competition.

Three issues were at the forefront of the 7 July electoral debate: the new system of government, the role of Islam in the state, and the role of women in society. These issues are discussed in depth below.

Federal versus Unitary State

In the aftermath of the declaration of liberation, centrifugal forces began to emerge from the coalition that toppled the regime. Some advocated the establishment of a federal state. In its sixty years of modern history, Libya has experienced both a centralized government and a federal system. After independence in 1951 and the establishment of a constitutional monarchy, Libya was governed through a federal system that left wide powers to the provinces (Vandewalle 2006, 44). That system only favored dysfunctional governance and corruption. Provincial legislators and bureaucrats protected their local interests, while in crucial areas such as taxation, electoral laws, and economic development, the federal government had to go through the provincial governments, rendering extremely difficult any sort of wide-scale planning (Pack 2012; Vandewalle 2006, 46). With the discovery of oil in 1959, as the country's oil industry increasingly necessitated a unified legislation, in 1963 the king had to abandon federalism in favor of a centralized form of government.

The revolt against Qadhafi's regime reinvigorated localisms and tribalism, especially in those regions or cities that figured prominently in the revolution. This was evident when on 6 March 2012 tribal figures and leaders announced the creation of the federal region of Barqa (Kane 2012). One fundamental idea was shared by the participants at the Barqa conference: Cyrenaica did not topple a dictator from Libya's western region to fall back under a new Tripolitanian hegemony (Sadiki 2012). The gathering in Barqa was only one of numerous tribal gatherings convened in the eastern province that rejected any form of unitary state and asked for Libya to be administered regionally. These events have been read as a strong indication of the predominance of a spirit of regionalism and tribalism coming from the region (Sawani 2012).

However, even in Cyrenaica, support for federalism, advocated by the self-appointed Interim Council of Barqa, was limited. Several thousand people gathered in Benghazi the same night to protest against the push for autonomy, carrying placards saying "No to federalism" (Fetouri 2012). A survey of public opinion in the east in October 2011 (IRI 2011) found that only 7 percent of respondents favored a federal system. The local councils in Benghazi, Derna, Bayda, and Tobruk did not recognize the Interim Barqa Council and issued a statement that the NTC remained the sole legitimate representative of the Libyan people (Lacher 2012). High-level criticism toward the Barqa declaration also came from almost every major political movement in Libya, both Islamist and more secular parties (Alunni 2013). Libyans seemed no longer willing to travel to Tripoli to conduct routine administrative business and access government services, but if a wide range of authorities including budgeting processes were delegated to municipal and provincial councils in charge of local government under a single national parliament and judicial system, it would cement the influence of those towns and tribes prominent during the civil war (Lacher 2012, Kane 2012). In an opinion survey (ORI 2012), 64 percent of those interviewed said they would like to see a semicentralized Libya with a government in Tripoli but ministries in cities across the country, while 21 percent said they want pure centralism, and 14 percent opted for federalism. The division of the country was not even an option (1 percent).

Islam and Its Political Role in the New Libya

An intense debate mounted on the role Islam should play in public life. NTC president Abdel Jalil gave prominence to the role of Islamic law when he declared in his liberation address, "We are an Islamic state," and he pledged to remove regulations that did not conform to shariʿa (Sheridan 2011a). "We strive for a state of the law, for a state of prosperity, for a state that will have Islamic sharia law the basis of legislation," Abdel Jalil stated (Al Jazeera 2011e). As pointed out by Younes Abouyoub, research scholar at Columbia University, Abdel Jalil "wanted to make sure that people understand that this revolution is not going to steer the state towards either a liberal, western-style state or an extremist-style like some people would like to have—which I believe is a minority" (Al Jazeera 2011e). After all, religion has remained a central component of the cultural composition and definition of Libyan identity, although Islam in Libya is of a tolerant and moderate nature (Sawani 2012). After the fall of the Old Order, ideological trends deriving from contrasting views of Islam, life, and politics emerged. None has rejected democracy, although each has a different interpretation of the concept and the means necessary to achieve a democratic state in the Libyan context.

The Libyan Muslim Brotherhood views democracy as an instrument or technique to be utilized in order to create a civil state that recognizes the primacy of shariʿa in legislation. They criticize and reject any call for secularism, proclaiming their adherence to the Islamic religion and its value system, therefore exploiting the hold Islam has on the minds of people (Sawani 2012). Saif al-Islam was aware of the power of the Islamist movements when he commented in February 2006 that democratic elections in any Arab country would have inevitably led the Islamists to power because "people trust them" (Pargeter 2008). Surprisingly, this was not the case in Libya. Within the Islamist trend there are a few groups with different orientations. The cleric Ali Sallabi, also leader of the National Gathering for Freedom, Justice and Development Party, considers the *shura* (advisory council) to be legally binding (Sallabi 2012).

The Salafi movement, the most extreme within the Islamist spectrum, underlines the contradiction between democracy and the historical course of the pious ancestors (*salaf*). Salafists stress the historical precedents of *shura* and the role of the *ahl al-hall wa al-ʿaqd* (those who bind and loosen; i.e., those with the authority to conclude and dissolve agreements) (Sawani 2012). The movement counts for some sympathizers within the al-Wafa bloc. As for the liberal, nationalist, and leftist groups, they formed political parties that advocated a civil state and criticized the use of religion to control the public, but they still referred to moderate Islam in their platforms.

In a recent survey asking if religion and politics should either be much the same thing or distinct, 49 percent of the respondents said "same thing," and 21 percent said "distinct," with the remaining 30 percent opting for more moderate answers (ORI 2012). This reflects a discrete polarization within Libyan society over the understanding of roles and duties of religious and political/state institutions, which will be a key issue in the process of constitution making.

Role of Women in Society

Women were the Libyan rebellion's "secret weapon" (Hammer 2012). The Libyan revolution was a huge event for women to participate in the life of their country in a much more active way. Women dominated a second front raising money for munitions, smuggling bullets past checkpoints, tending injured fighters in makeshifts hospitals, spying on government troops, and relaying their movements to the rebels. Although on paper during Qadhafi's era women enjoyed relatively greater rights than their counterparts in the Arab world, in practice they were denied a political voice in Libya's conservative and male-dominated society to a level unparalleled in neighboring Tunisia and Egypt. After the revolution, women who had an active role in it decided to transform their wartime activism into greater political clout (Sheridan 2011b).

Not many Libyans will argue against women's right to work and vote, and the same is true for political parties. The electoral law required them to field up to 50 percent female candidates (Grant 2012a). Six hundred women ran in the elections, but they won only thirty-three out of the two hundred available seats in the National Congress, or 16.5 percent of the transitional legislative body (Tunisia Live 2012b). Moreover, the fact that only 84 women were standing as individual candidates against 2,417 men and that only one of them was successful in the electoral bid demonstrated that Libya has some way to go before attaining full female equality (Grant 2012a).

Political participation of women, violence against women, and, more generally, women's rights are thorny issues in Libya today, and two main trends have emerged regarding these matters. On the one hand, people—mainly involved in NGOs activities—praise and encourage women's involvement in the life of the country. On the other hand, there is another group of Libyans who consider women's protests against their marginalization to be an attempt to tarnish the postrevolution spirit and to damage Libyan culture; they are considered as being anti-Islamic and portraying an inaccurate, negative picture of a woman's life in Libya (R. Smith 2012). It will be necessary to reconcile these two sides of the same coin in order to ensure that progress toward women empowerment proceeds steadily.

THE POLITICAL STALEMATE AND HEIGHTENED ARMED CONFRONTATIONS

When on 8 August 2012 the NTC turned over power to the newly elected General National Congress, the international community welcomed this step in the Libyan transition that technically opened the way to the formation of a constituent authority responsible for drafting the constitution. In fact, from that point the country entered a political stalemate and a period of renewed and heightened armed confrontations which some observers described as a renewed civil war.

In principle, the election of Mohammed Magarief on 10 August as president of Libya's GNC, following the timeline set by the NTC, was interpreted as a positive sign along the path toward democracy. Magarief, although a pious and respectful Muslim, had a quite pragmatic and secular vision of society and politics. Even more important, having defected from Qadhafi's regime in 1980, he had distanced himself from the Old Order early on. Moreover, hailing from eastern Libya, he was considered a political personality capable of compromising with the federalists in that region and overall as someone well positioned to guide a process of national reconciliation in the country. The car bombings by supporters of the former regime that occurred in Tripoli and Benghazi in August 2012 underscored the need for a process of national reconciliation, and Magarief seemed well placed to guide it.

Then came the attacks on the U.S., UK, and Tunisian foreign diplomatic missions in Benghazi, which along with the killings of former Qadhafi regime officials began in June 2012 and suggested the reemergence of terrorist activity and radical Islamist militants in eastern Libya. In particular, the attack in Benghazi on the U.S. consulate and the killing of Ambassador Christopher Stevens and three other American diplomats on 11 September 2012 served as a wake-up call for Libyan authorities and the international community.

Strong leadership was needed at that time of the transition, and on 13 September, following a month of hesitation, Mustafa Abushagur was appointed prime minister by the GNC. Abushagur embarked on the formation of a new cabinet with the intent of reconciling the different political forces represented in the National Congress. The consultations produced a list of ministers that, however, was not the list later presented to the Congress and the public at large. In that second list, indeed, the position of interior minister was given to Omar Aswad, closely associated with the former regime; members of the National Forces Alliance were left out, and there was only one female minister. According to key interlocutors in Tripoli, Abushagur, advised by members of his entourage, decided to replace those ministers who would have been more difficult to control with weaker personalities (Mezran 2012b). As a consequence, the GNC voted in favor of a no-confidence motion and the dismissal of Abushagur on 7 October.

The failure to establish a viable government pointed to the lack of capacity and experience at all levels of the political and administrative apparatus and to internal politicking, with serious implications for the transition timeline as well as for the precarious security in the country. Integrating the militias, restructuring the armed forces, and establishing the rule of law through a new constitution were tasks that only a government approved by the elected GNC could legitimately perform. The appointment a week later of Ali Zidan, a trained human rights lawyer and former diplomat who served in India before defecting in 1980 and joining the opposition National Front for Salvation, broke the impasse, although once again only momentarily.

Indeed, in the following months a battle emerged between the prime minister and GNC president Magarief over the definition of responsibilities and duties of the country's nascent institutions that resulted in institutional paralysis (Mezran and Knecht 2013). Magarief had been free to exercise power far outside the scope of his office, provoking the NFA boycott of the GNC on 6 January 2013 and resulting in a dangerous de facto stalemate. Magarief was also accused of monopolizing control over the GNC's agenda, overshadowing the work of GNC special committees, and delaying the election of the sixty-member constitutional committee. However, the fact that the same institutional paralysis was observed even when new actors took the lead in the GNC (Nouri Ali Abu Sahmein) and government (Abdullah al-Thinni) shows that the key problem in this political transition lies in the wrongly conceived and perceived division of duties and responsibilities among transitional institutions, first and foremost the executive and legislative organs. It would have been key to address this issue before the election of a new legislative assembly in June 2014, in order to avoid the same stalemate, but this did not happen (Alunni 2014a).

Overcoming the gridlock proved extremely difficult. The political groups crystallized into, on the one hand, the NFA and, on the other, the JCP and al-Wafa (the Martyrs' Loyalty Bloc)—organized by Abdel Wahab al-Qaid among the independent GNC members. A year after the election, the former still looked extremely fragmented while the latter gained strength. Indeed, the informal and instrumental alliance negotiated between these two Islamist formations succeeded in guaranteeing the passage in the GNC of the Political Isolation Law on 7 May 2013, banning from public activity anyone with links to the former regime. In this way, the Islamist formation opened new space for its candidates (Mezran and Lamen 2013). Following the passage of the law, Magarief resigned as GNC president and was succeeded by Abu Sahmein, a member of the al-Wafa bloc and the Amazigh community that had been repressed and isolated by the Qadhafi regime (Mezran 2013). Following this political maneuvering, the Islamist-leaning formations dominated the GNC.

The Political Isolation Law is among those measures that hampered attempts toward national reconciliation pursued by some key political and religious figures such as Ali Sallabi, a Muslim cleric who emerged as "the negotiator" in the Libyan scenario (Pack and Mezran 2013). Sallabi tried to reach out to the various political groups as well as to militia commanders and former regime members, both in Libya and outside the country, in order to mediate an agreement behind closed doors on their future and on the future of the country. In light of the political paralysis faced in 2013, this negotiated approach might be seen as a short-term solution rather than a longer-range attempt at national reconciliation, very much needed but probably very ambitious in the Libyan political scene. While the NFA and the JCP announced in the summer of 2013 their intent to limit their participation in the future activities of the GNC because of the inertia and delays that have characterized the activities of this body, the passage of the electoral law for the sixty-member constitution-drafting committee in mid-July 2013 was a positive and hopeful sign in this stalled situation (Collins 2013). At the end of February 2014, a Constitutional Drafting Assembly (CDA) was elected. The results showed a victory for non-Islamist forces, and Ali Tarhouni, a representative of the nationalist wing, was elected as president of the committee. The CDA became the transitional institution best positioned to design an exhaustive institutional framework. Indeed, the National Dialogue Initiative, endorsed in August 2013 by Zidan's government and promoted across Libya by a Preparatory Committee, was suddenly halted in the face of new clashes.

From mid-2013 onward, strikes and occupations of oil infrastructures occurred on and off in all corners of Libya. Ibrahim Jathran emerged as the commander of the oil facility guards that occupied the oil fields in Cyrenaica. They halted oil production in the east, creating a major economic crisis that pushed the government to tap into its foreign currency reserves (Toaldo 2014). Prime Minister Ali Zidan repeatedly threatened to use force to break the oil blockades in the east, but he never took action against the opponents, compromising the credibility of the government. He was also accused of lacking power to confront the militias. His brief kidnapping in October 2013 by the Libya Revolutionaries Operations Room (LROR)—a group of former militias under the Ministry of Defense created by GNC president Abu Sahmein and charged with providing for the security of Tripoli—is a case in point. In November 2013 the so-called Gharghour incident, in which forty-four protesting civilians were killed in Tripoli by militias from Misrata, highlighted once more the lack of government control, even in the capital, over the militias on the ground (Pack, Mezran, and Eljarh 2014). After repeated attempts by the GNC, Prime Minister Zidan was ousted from office in March 2014 after the *Morning Glory*, a tanker laden with oil from a rebel-held port, was said to have broken through a naval blockade. In his place Abdullah al-Thinni was appointed as caretaker prime minister while Zidan left the country.

The Political Isolation Law as well as the ousting of Zidan from office reflected a growing polarization in the Libyan political scene between, on the one hand, the government and the non-Islamist factions, and, on the other hand, the GNC and the Islamist-leaning groups. While on 23 December 2013 the GNC voted for a one-year extension of its mandate, anti-GNC protests erupted in February 2014 at a time when, according to the Constitutional Declaration, the tasks of transitional institutions should have been completed and power handed over to new permanent institutions. The GNC was considered by the protesters to be an illegitimate body that failed to lead the transition and did not intend to relinquish power, and therefore they demanded that the GNC resign.

In the wake of these popular protests General Khalifa Hifter, in a YouTube video posted on 14 February 2014, announced the suspension of the GNC and the government, leaving the Qaaqaa and al-Sawaiq brigades from the city of Zintan to militarily put into effect his claim in Tripoli; they never tried to seize power, although ultimatums were launched without any evident consequence. In May 2014, Hifter launched the military attack called Operation Karama (dignity) to eradicate Islamists from the east in response to the continuing wave of assassinations and attacks targeting army and police personnel in Benghazi. This time the attack was done in coordination with the militias from Zintan, which stormed the GNC in Tripoli on 18 May 2014 (El Gomati 2014). In the aftermath of the *intifada*, Hifter had found support against the Islamist militias in the area of the Green Mountain and had started to regroup disaffected army units. However, by no means all the former Libyan soldiers within Qadhafi's Libyan Army joined him. In fact, some of them entered the ranks of the Ministry of Defense or joined the Shields set up by the chief of staff, General Yussef al-Mangoush, himself a former member of the Libyan Army (Alunni 2014b). Therefore, it is not appropriate to refer to those army units led by Hifter as the Libyan Army.

Al-Thinni had resigned as interim prime minister on 13 April after an attack on his family, and the GNC, dominated by the Islamist faction, elected Ahmed Maiteeq as prime minister on 4 May in a highly contested election. Maiteeq's cabinet was approved by the GNC on 25 May, but in June the Supreme Court ruled the election unconstitutional, reinstating al-Thinni as interim prime minister (Reuters 2014).

Efforts were made to find a negotiated solution to the divisive polarization and the consequent paralysis, but all were unsuccessful. The UN attempts at establishing a framework for political dialogue were rejected in June 2014, this time by the non-Islamist factions, which felt strong in light of the poor performance of the Islamist-led GNC and the popular support for the military attacks against the Islamists in the east. From their perspective, a sound electoral victory had to be obtained before engaging in a political dialogue with the Islamists (Alunni 2014a). This came with elections for the new parliament, the House of Representatives (HoR), on 25 June, where the Islamists incurred a major defeat, winning around only thirty out of two hundred seats, although only 18 percent of the electorate participated, compared to 60 percent in 2012. An Egyptian-like scenario where the

Islamist forces were eliminated from the political arena appeared plausible in Libya also. Thus facing complete political marginalization, the Islamists decided to act and preempt this scenario. In mid-July, with the support of allied militias from the city of Misrata, the Islamists unleashed an offensive against the rival militias from Zintan by attacking Tripoli International Airport, which was under their control. Manifestly, this attack had two major objectives: to defeat Zintani forces for control of the airport and in congruence with a hold on the airport in Maitega, to control all air traffic in and out of the country. Meanwhile Khalifa Hifter continued shelling Islamist bases in the east. Despite numerous calls for help and the request for military support, the international community did not seem inclined to intervene in Libya above and beyond diplomatic means.

As of the end of 2014, two parliaments, two governments, and two armed factions dominated the scene in the country. One was led by the government of al-Thinni in Bayda as expression of the House of Representatives elected in June 2014 and seated in Tobruk. The armed forces behind Operation Karama were the military arm of this faction. A multiplicity of actors regrouped around Karama, its leader, General Hifter, and the HoR, including Mahmoud Jibril, head of the National Alliance Force; the federalists of the eastern region; the group of former state oil protection guards led by Ibrahim Jathran; eastern tribes and militias opposed to the Islamist militias gaining ground; the Zintan brigades; and disaffected army units and some local leaders from the south such as Tabu leaders from Kufra.

The other faction was led by Islamist militias based in the west and by powerful militias from the city of Misrata. These armed groups launched a military operation, Operation Fajr (dawn), in July 2014, in response to the campaign initiated by Hifter. They established their control over the capital and large parts of the country's western territory. The Justice and Construction Party, the political emanation of the Muslim Brotherhood in Libya, was part of this alliance, together with representatives of the Amazigh community and the powerful el-Nasser family from Sabha (Alunni 2014b). Their members within the General National Congress rejected the dismantling of the assembly following the June elections and appointed a new government in Tripoli in August 2014. The Fajr coalition distanced itself from Ansar al-Sharia, which is operating in the east, in particular in the city of Benghazi, and stressed its commitment to democracy and constitutional legality.

These two factions have promoted two radically divergent and conflicting narratives over their struggle for power. One propagated by the Tobruk assembly saw the struggle between Karama and Fajr as the struggle between a secularist, liberal, modernist, and internationally legitimized entity versus the terrorist, radical Islamist, and illegitimate alliance of Operation Fajr. The other narrative fostered by the Tripoli government and Fajr saw the struggle as one between the supporters and militants of the 17 February Revolution, who are trying to prevent the reestablishment of the former regime, and those who are making of the counterrevolution their main objective. The controversial pronouncement of the Supreme Court in November 2014 declaring the democratically elected House of Representatives illegal and unconstitutional further entrenched the polarization in the country while leaving the international community to wonder.

FROM CIVIL WAR TO CIVIL WAR?

The 2012 election vote reflected how a democratic and pluralistic order seemed to have been accepted by the majority of groups within Libyan society, whose stability depends on its resilience and responsiveness to popular demands, through electoral participation, party representation, and institutional pluralism. Pragmatism dominated the initial, NTC stages of the transition, and this was reaffirmed in the elections. The Libyan people did not want these elections to be about Islam and identity. Therefore, they rewarded a coalition like the NFA, whose main focus was on practical issues about the future and on opening to the world rather than on nebulous identity matters (Lawrence 2012). It did not take long for that pragmatism to disappear.

Initially, the negotiated transition restored order on the surface. Political relationships based on the commitment to a common vision of the future resulted in a dynamic stability among moderate ideological differences. In the aggregating process of negotiations, many pieces came together without much concern for their coherence, producing a procedural agreement on how to deal with substantive issues and partially defining the features of the New Order. This did not mean that substantive issues would not be further negotiated during the drafting of the constitution. Indeed, one can wonder whether the vision for the new Libya established by the NTC was fully embraced and interiorized by all the members of the coalition or whether they only accepted it in that phase in order to obtain the support of external actors with the idea of changing it later in the process. In fact, the substantive and procedural agreement among rebel forces left room for maneuver in the phase of constitutional negotiation.

The GNC was the only legitimate representative of the Libyan people until February 2014 when the Constitutional Drafting Assembly was elected. This legitimacy should have resulted in a new decision-making system capable of replacing the NTC's action/inaction of the former months. However, the momentum for political reform seemed to be rapidly lost once the GNC achieved full powers. The country became stuck in a severe political impasse that not only aggravated the already precarious situation in the eastern and southern regions but also jeopardized the overall transition. Negotiations for formulation were held hostage to negotiations for coalition, unfortunately for a country that in mid-2012 had seemed set on a path of extraordinarily rosy transition. The newly elected legislative assembly faced the vital task of inverting the situation and regaining lost legitimacy, giving room to the Constituent Assembly to draft the constitution, but the declaration of its unconstitutionality in November 2014 tarnished its legitimacy once and for all.

Following the predominant regional trend, political negotiations in Libya were quickly abandoned in favor of armed confrontations. Despite attempts from the moderates on both sides to foster a negotiated solution, the military wings of both factions moved to take the upper hand and slowly plunge the country into a full-fledged civil war. The UN special representative of the secretary general and head of the UN Support Mission in Libya (UNSML), Bernardino Leon, led the effort of the international community in trying to foster a negotiated solution by coalescing all international actors and to pressure both sides to understand that a military solution is no solution and requires a negotiated outcome for the crisis.

Moreover, the role of external actors reappeared as key in the Libyan transitional process and was not necessarily a positive factor. Indeed, particularly destabilizing for the success of the negotiations was the support that the United Arab Emirates and Egypt gave to the HoR and to the military campaign of General Hifter. The bombings presumably carried out by the air force of these two countries in the east and west were received with mixed feelings by the population. Moreover, the support of Qatar and Turkey to Operation Fajr fosters the narrative of the existence of a Muslim Brotherhood project in Libya, fueling the distrust of the non-Islamist actors toward the Islamist forces and their allies. This was particularly detrimental to any kind of political dialogue among the parties. More important, such external interventions prevent the parts in the conflict from achieving a mutually hurting stalemate (MHS), a deadlock painful to both factions that could compel both the political and military wings of these factions to opt for a negotiated solution rather than to pursue military victory on the ground. In a country awash with oil and weapons, a political and negotiated solution to the renewed conflict is the only feasible way Libya could pursue a democratic transition.

References

Ahmed, A., and F. Martin. 2012. "Understanding the Sanusi of Cyrenaica: How to Avoid a Civil War in Libya." Al Jazeera English, 26 March. http://www.aljazeera.com/indepth/opinion/2012/03/201232681712769133.html (accessed 30 July 2013).

Al-Ahram. 2011. "Keeping an Eye on Libya." Issue no. 1036, 24 February–2 March 2011. http://weekly.ahram.org.eg/2011/1036/re104.htm (accessed 30 July 2013).

All Voices. 2011. "France Claims the Departure of Muammar Gaddafi." 25 February. http://www.allvoices.com/contributed-news/8306074-france-claims-the-departure-of-muammar-gaddafi (accessed 30 July 2013).

Alunni, A. 2013. "Lo scontro politico tra nazionalisti e federalisti in Libia: (1951–2011): l'unione fa la forza?" *Afriche e Orienti* 15, no. 1–2.

———. 2014a. Author's confidential interviews with international officials, Tripoli, April and May.

2014b. Author's confidential interviews with Libyan politicians, Tunis, November.

Asharq Al-Awsat. 2010. "France Arrests Former Member of Gaddafi's Inner Circle." 1 December. http://www.aawsat.net/2010/12/article55248455 (accessed 30 July 2013).

———. 2011. "Gaddafi Ready for Libya's Day of Rage." 9 February. http://www.aawsat.net/2011/02/article55247591 *(accessed 30 July 2013)*.

Baldinetti, A. 2010. *The Origins of the Libyan Nation: Colonial Legacy, Exile and the Emergence of a New Nation-State*. New York: Routledge.

BBC. 2012. "Libya: Britain's Secret War." 19 January. http://www.youtube.com/watch?v=f3ztaPqIwiI (accessed 30 July 2013).

BBC News. 2010. "Libya Frees More Than 200 Islamist Prisoners." 23 March. http://news.bbc.co.uk/2/hi/africa/8583819.stm (accessed 30 July 2013).

———. 2011. "Hague: Gaddafi Must Go." 27 February. http://www.bbc.co.uk/news/uk-politics-12590167 (accessed 30 July 2013).

———. 2012. "Libyan Defence Minister in Restive Bani Walid for Talks." 25 January. http://www.bbc.co.uk/news/world-africa-16725653 (accessed 30 July 2013).

Bartu, Peter. 2014. *Libya's Political Transition: The Challenges of Mediation*. New York: International Peace Institute.

Bearak, B. 2011. "Zuma's Office Says Qaddafi Intent on Staying in Libya." *New York Times*, 31 May. http://www.nytimes.com/2011/06/01/world/africa/01zuma.html (accessed 30 July 2013).

Beblawi, H. 1990. "The Rentier State in the Arab World." In *The Arab State*, edited by G. Luciani. Berkeley: University of California Press.

Bechis, F. 2011. "Sarkò manovra la rivolta libica." *Libero*, 23 March.

Bellin, E. 2004. "The Robustness of Authoritarianism in the Middle East: Exceptionalism in Comparative Perspective." *Comparative Politics* 36, no. 2: 139-157.

Benotman, N. 2011. "Libya after General Younis's Murder: Q And A with Noman Benotman." *Eurasia Review*, 4 August. http://www.eurasiareview.com/04082011-libya-after-general-younis (accessed 30 July 2013).

Birnbaum, M. 2011. "Gaddafi Oil Minister Appears to Have Defected." *Washington Post*, 17 May. http://articles.washingtonpost.com/2011-05-17/world/35265125_1_musa-kusa-wave-of-libyan-diplomats-libyan-arab-league-representative (accessed 30 July 2013).

Black, I., and O. Bowcott. 2011. "Libya Protests: Massacres Reported as Gaddafi Imposes New Blackout." *Guardian*, 18 February. http://www.theguardian.com/world/2011/feb/18/libya-protests-massacres-reported (accessed 30 July 2013).

Blanchard, C. M., and J. Zanotti. 2011. "Libya: Background and U.S. Relations." *Congressional Research Service*, 18 February. http://fpc.state.gov/documents/organization/158525.pdf (accessed 30 July 2013).

Bloomfield, A., D. McElroy, and R. Sherlock. 2011. "Islamists Blamed for Killing General Abdel Fattah Younes as Libya's Rebels Face Up to Enemy Within." *Telegraph*, 30 July. http://www.telegraph.co.uk/news/worldnews/africaandindianocean/libya/8673021/Islamists-blamed-for-killing-General-Abdel-Fattah-Younes-as-Libyas-rebels-face-up-to-enemy-within.html.

Brahimi, A. 2011. "Libya's Revolution." *Journal of North African Studies* 16, no. 4: 605–624.

Canal+. 2013. "Special investigation—Gaz et pétrole guerres secrètes." http://www.canalplus.fr/c-infos-documentaires/pid3357-c-special-investigation.html?vid=760326 (accessed 30 July 2013).

Carpenter, T. D. 2011. "Libya's Deep Tribalism." *National Interest*, 25 January. http://nationalinterest.org/blog/the-skeptics/early-signs-libyan-civil-war-6403 (accessed 30 July 2013).

Cherstich, I. 2011. "Libya's Revolution: Tribe, Nation, Politics." *Open Democracy*, 3 October. http://www.opendemocracy.net/igor-cherstich/libyas-revolution-tribe-nation-politics (accessed 30 July 2013).

Chivvis, C. 2013. *Toppling Qaddafi: Libya and the Limits of Liberal Intervention*. New York: Cambridge University Press.

Chorin, E. 2012. *Exit the Colonel: The Hidden History of the Libyan Revolution*. New York: PublicAffairs.

Cobain, I. 2012. "Special Report: Rendition Ordeal That Raises New Questions about Secret Trials." *Guardian*, 8 April. http://www.theguardian.com/world/2012/apr/08/special-report-britain-rendition-libya (accessed 30 July 2013).

Collins, N. 2013. "An Update from NDI's Office in Tripoli." Email communication, 16 July.

El Gomati, A. 2014. "Khalifa Hifter: All Things to All Men?" Sadeq Institute, Policy Brief, 10 June.

Fetouri, I. 2012. "Libyan Leader Says Autonomy Call a Foreign Plot." Reuters, 6 March. http://uk.reuters.com/article/2012/03/06/uk-libya-east-federalism-idUKTRE8251J820120306 (accessed 30 July 2013).

Grant, G. 2012a. "Elections Analysis: So Who Are They and What Do They Actually Stand For?" *Libya Herald*, 30 June. http://www.libyaherald.com/2012/06/30/elections-analysis-so-who-are-they-and-what-do-they-stand-for/ (accessed 30 July 2013).

———. 2012b. "Party Profile: The National Forces Alliance." *Libya Herald*, 1 July. http://www.libyaherald.com/2012/07/01/party-profile-the-national-forces-alliance/ (accessed 30 July 2013).

Gurney, J. 1996. *Libya: The Political Economy of Oil*. Oxford: Oxford University Press.

Hammer, J. 2012. "Women: The Libyan Rebellion's Secret Weapon." *Smithsonian*, April. http://www.smithsonianmag.com/people-places/Women-The-Libyan-Rebellions-Secret-Weapon.html (accessed 30 July 2013).

Hounshell, B. 2011. "Libya's New Leader Declares an Islamic State." *Foreign Policy Blog Passport*, 23 October. http://blog.foreignpolicy.com/posts/2011/10/23/libyas_new_leader_declares_an_islamic_state (accessed 30 July 2013).

Huffington Post. 2011. "Abdurrahim el-Keib, New Libyan Prime Minister, Taught at University of Alabama." 1 November. http://www.huffingtonpost.com/2011/11/01/abdurrahim-el-keib-taught-alabama_n_1069693.html (accessed 30 July 2013).

ICG (International Crisis Group). 2011a. "Holding Libya Together: Security Challenges after Qadhafi." *Middle East/North Africa Report* no. 115, 14 December.

———. 2011b. "Making Sense of Libya." *Middle East/North Africa Report* no. 107, 6 June.

———. 2012. "Divided We Stand: Libya's Enduring Conflicts." Middle East/North Africa Report no. 130, 14 September.

ILO (International Labour Organization). 2011. *Libya: Overall View*. International Labor Organization North Africa Regional Office. http://www.ilo.org/public/english/region/afpro/cairo/countries/libya.htm (accessed 30 July 2013).

IRI (International Republican Institute). 2011. "Survey of Public Opinion in Eastern Libya, October 12–25, 2011." http://www.scribd.com/doc/76544715/IRI-2011-Dec-19-Survey-of-Eastern-Libya-Public-Opinion-October-12-25-2011 (accessed 30 July 2013).

Al Jazeera. 2011a. "Chavez Libya Talks Offer Rejected." 3 March. http://www.aljazeera.com/news/africa/2011/03/201133231925866727.html (accessed 30 July 2013).

———. 2011b. "Gaddafi Accepts Chavez Talks Offer." 3 March. http://www.aljazeera.com/news/africa/2011/03/20113365739369754.html (accessed 30 July 2013).

———. 2011c. "General's Death Puts Libyan Rebels in Turmoil." 28 July. http://www.aljazeera.com/indepth/features/2011/07/2011728215485843.html (accessed 30 July 2013).

———. 2011d. "Libya: When the Impossible Became Possible." *The Café*, 31 December. http://www.aljazeera.com/programmes/thecafe/2011/12/201112317379728638.html (accessed 30 July 2013).

———. 2011e. "Libya's New Leader Calls for Civil State." 13 September. http://www.aljazeera.com/news/africa/2011/09/2011912214219388500.html (accessed 30 July 2013).

Joffe, G. 1988. "Islamic Opposition in Libya." *Third World Quarterly* 10, no. 2 (Islam & Politics): 615–631.

———. 2011. "The Arab Spring in North Africa: Origins and Prospects." *Journal of North African Studies* 16, no. 4: 507–532.

Joshi, S. 2011. "Libya Conflict: Younes Death Betrays Rebel Divisions." BBC News, 30 July. http://www.bbc.co.uk/news/world-africa-14350915 (accessed 30 July 2013).

Kadlec, A. 2012. "Disarming Libya's Militias." *Sada Journal*, 16 February. http://carnegieendowment.org/2013/02/26/forced-confessions-non-crime-and-punishment-in-iran/flny (accessed 30 July 2013).

Kane, S. 2012. "Federalism and Fragmentation in Libya: Not So Fast . . ." *Foreign Policy: The Middle East Channel*, 20 March.

Khan, U. 2012. "Party Profile: Justice and Construction Party." *Libya Herald*, 30 June. http://www.libyaherald.com/2012/06/30/party-profile-justice-construction-party/ (accessed 30 July 2013).

Kirkpatrick, D. 2011. "Libya Allying with Islamists, Qaddafi Son Says." *New York Times*, 3 August. http://www.nytimes.com/2011/08/04/world/africa/04seif.html?pagewanted=all (accessed 30 July 2013).

Kuperman, Alan, 2013. "A Model Humanitarian Intervention." *International Security* 38, no. 1 (Summer): 105–136.

Lacher, W. 2011. "Families, Tribes and Cities in the Libyan Revolution." *Middle East Policy* 18, no. 4 (Winter).

———. 2012. "Federalism Is Unlikely in Libya, However, Decentralization Is Probable." *Daily Star*, 3 April.

———. 2013. "The Rise of Tribal Politics." In *The 2011 Libyan Uprisings and the Struggle for the Post-Qadhafi Future*, edited by J. Pack. New York: Palgrave Macmillan.

Lawrence, W. 2012. ICG interview. http://www.youtube.com/watch?v=UI5-pZxEYpo&feature=youtu.be (accessed 6 July 2012).

Libya Herald. 2012. "National Congress Party Results." 18 July. http://www.libyaherald.com/2012/07/18/party-results/ (accessed 30 July 2013).

Martinez, L. 2007. *The Libyan Paradox*. London: Hurst.

Matthews, D. 2012. "The Question of Political Responsibility and the Foundation of the National Transitional Council for Libya." *Law Critique* 23: 237–252.

Menon, R. 2012. "Libya in Chaos." *National Interest*, 27 June. http://nationalinterest.org/commentary/libya-in-chaos-7096 (accessed 30 July 2013).

Mezran, K. 2011a. Author's interviews with Libyan expatriates, February and March.

———. 2011b. Author's phone interviews with former regimes' security officials, February.

———. 2011c. "Come l'Italia ha perso la Libia: Il gioco della Francia e il fallito golpe anti Gheddafi." *Limes, Rivista Italioana di Geopolitica*, no. 2.

———. 2011d. "Libia: La fine di un'era?" In *L'Africa Mediterranea: Storia e futuro*, edited by K. Mezran, S. Colombo, and S. Van Genugten. Rome: Donzelli Editore.

———. 2011e. "Perché il colonnello si sentiva al sicuro." *Limes, Rivista Italiana di Geopolitica*, no. 1.

———. 2012a. Author's interview with Ali Sallabi and other eminent Islamist leaders, Tripoli, 29 May.

———. 2012b. "The Dismissal of Abushagur and Libya's Leadership Crisis." *Atlantic Council MENASource*, Viewpoint, 11 October. http://www.atlanticcouncil.org/blogs/menasource/the-dismissal-of-abushagur-and-libya-s-leadership-crisis (accessed 16 November 2014).

———. 2012c. "Libya: The Election of Magarief and National Reconciliation." *Atlantic Council MENASource*, 14 August. http://www.atlanticcouncil.org/blogs/menasource/libya-the-election-of-magarief-and-national-reconciliation (accessed 16 November 2014).

———. 2012d. "Libya Has Successful Elections but Not Yet Democracy." *New Atlanticist*, 10 July. http://www.atlanticcouncil.org/blogs/new-atlanticist/libya-has-successful-elections-but-not-yet-democracy (accessed 16 November 2014).

———. 2012e. "New Militia Clashes Endanger Transition in Libya." *New Atlanticist*, 4 June. http://www.atlanticcouncil.org/blogs/new-atlanticist/new-militia-clashes-endanger-transition-in-libya (accessed 16 November 2014).

———. 2013 "Rumors from Tripoli." *Atlantic Council MENSource*, 27 June. http://www.atlanticcouncil.org/blogs/new-atlanticist/new-militia-clashes-endanger-transition-in-libya (accessed 16 November 2014).

———. 2014. "Libya in Transition: From *Jamahiriya* to *Jumhuriyyah*." In *The New Middle East: Protest and Revolution in the Arab World*, edited by F. Gerges. New York: Cambridge University Press.

Mezran, K., and E. Knecht. 2013. "Libya's Fractious New Politics." *Atlantic Council MENASource*, 9 January. http://www.atlanticcouncil.org/blogs/menasource/libyas-fractious-new-politics (accessed 16 November 2014).

Mezran, K., and F. Lamen. 2013. "Frustration and Isolation in Libya." *Atlantic Council MENASource*, 7 May. http://www.atlanticcouncil.org/blogs/menasource/frustration-and-isolation-in-libya (accessed 16 November 2014).

Moss, D. 2011. "Libya in Crisis . . . What's Next?" *E-Notes*, Foreign Policy Research Institute, February. http://www.fpri.org/enotes/201102.moss.libya.html (accessed 30 July 2013).

Mostyn, T. 2011. "Gen Abdel Fatah Younis Obituary." *Guardian*, 31 July 31. http://www.theguardian.com/world/2011/jul/31/abdel-fatah-younis-obituary (accessed 30 July 2013).

Murphy, D. 2011. "Why the African Union Road Map for Libya Is Unlikely to Go Anywhere." *Christian Science Monitor*, 11 April. http://www.csmonitor.com/World/Backchannels/2011/0411/Why-the-African-Union-road-map-for-Libya-is-unlikely-to-go-anywhere (accessed 30 July 2013).

NDI (National Democratic Institute). 2011. "Notes from Benghazi: Libyans Hungry for Information and Help." 13 May. http://www.ndi.org/notes-from-Benghazi-Libya (accessed 30 July 2013).

New York Times. 2011a. "Leaders of the Libyan Rebellion." 22 August. http://www.nytimes.com/interactive/2011/08/21/world/africa/leaders-of-the-libyan-rebellion.html (accessed 30 July 2013).

———. 2011b. "Map of the Rebellion in Libya, Day by Day." 20 February. http://www.nytimes.com/interactive/2011/02/25/world/middleeast/map-of-how-the-protests-unfolded-in-libya.html (accessed 30 July 2013).

Nordland, R., and D. Kirkpatrick. 2011. "Islamists' Growing Sway Raises Questions for Libya." *New York Times*, 14 September. http://www.nytimes.com/2011/09/15/world/africa/in-libya-islamists-growing-sway-raises-questions.html?pagewanted=all&_r=0.

NTC (National Transitional Council). 2011a. "The Founding Statement." 5 March 5. http://www.ntclibya.org/english/founding-statement-of-the-interim-transitional-national-council/ (accessed 29 January 2013).

———. 2011b. "The Interim Constitutional Declaration." 10 August. http://www.mpil.de/en/pub/research/details/know_transfer/constitutional_reform_in_arab_/libyen.cfm (accessed 30 July 2013).

———. 2011c. "A Vision of a Democratic Libya." 29 March. http://www.theguardian.com/commentisfree/2011/mar/29/vision-democratic-libya-interim-national-council (accessed 30 July 2013).

ORI (Oxford Research International). 2012. "First National Survey of Libya, Executive Summary." February. http://www.ox.ac.uk/media/news_releases_for_journalists/120215.html (accessed 30 July 2013).

Pack, J. 2012. "Federalism in Libya: Tried and Failed." Al Jazeera, 20 April. http://www.aljazeera.com/indepth/opinion/2012/04/20124187135558488o.html (accessed 30 July 2013).

———. 2013. *The 2011 Libyan Uprisings and the Struggle for a Post-Qadhafi Future*. New York: Palgrave Macmillan.

Pack, J., and K. Mezran, K. 2013. "Libyan Stability at Risk." *New Atlanticist*, May 3. Accessed July 30, 2013. http://mideastafrica.foreignpolicy.com/posts/2013/05/02/libyan_stability_at_risk (accessed 16 November 2014).

Pack, J., K. Mezran, and M. Eljarh. 2014. "Libya's Faustian Bargains: Breaking the Appeasement Cycle." Atlantic Council Report, 5 May. http://www.atlanticcouncil.org/publications/reports/libya-s-faustian-bargains-breaking-the-appeasement-cycle (accessed 29 July 2014).

Pargeter, A. 2008. "Qadhafi and Political Islam in Libya." In *Libya since 1969: Qadhafi's Revolution Revisited*, edited by D. Vandewalle. New York: Palgrave MacMillan.

———. 2009. "Localism and Radicalization in North Africa: Local Factors and the Development of Political Islam in Morocco, Tunisia and Libya." *International Affairs* 85, no. 5: 1031–1044.

Piiparinen, T. 2011. "Law Enforcer or Mediator?" Finnish Institute of International Affairs, Comment, April. http://www.fiia.fi/en/publication/175/ (accessed 30 July 2013).

Reuters. 2014. "Libyan Court Says PM's Election Invalid, Raising Hopes of End to Stalemate." 9 June. http://uk.reuters.com/article/2014/06/09/uk-libya-politics-idUKKBNoEKoW320140609 (accessed 29 July 2014).

Ronen, Y. 2002. "Qadhafi and Militant Islamism: Unprecedented Conflict." *Middle Eastern Studies* 38, no. 4 (October): 1-16.

RUSI (Royal United Services Institute). 2011. "Accidental Heroes: Britain, France and the Libya Operation." September. http://www.rusi.org/news/ (accessed 30 July 2013).

Sadiki, L. 2012. "Libya's New 'Feds': The Call of Cyrenaica." Al Jazeera, March 7. Accessed July 30, 2013. http://www.aljazeera.com/indepth/opinion/2012/03/20123771523372117.html (accessed 30 July 2013).

Sawani, Y. M. 2012. "Post-Qadhafi Libya: Interactive Dynamics and the Political Future." *Contemporary Arab Affairs* 5, no. 1 (January–March): 1–26.

Seibert, T. 2011. "Turkey Pursues Its Libya Mediation Efforts despite Setbacks." *National* (Abu Dhabi), 7 April. http://www.thenational.ae/news/world/europe/turkey-pursues-its-libya-mediation-efforts-despite-setbacks (accessed 30 July 2013).

Shadid, A. 2011. "Qatar Wields an Outsize Influence in Arab Politics." *New York Times*, global ed., 14 November. http://www.nytimes.com/2011/11/15/world/middleeast/qatar-presses-decisive-shift-in-arab-politics.html?_r=0&adxnnl=1&pagewanted=all&adxnnlx=1375175128-zEQHUKf/5tWM+tVKQrXsXw (accessed 30 July 2013).

Shelton, T. 2011. "The Death of General Younis Makes Us Stronger, Libya Rebels Say." *National* (Abu Dhabi), 31 July. http://www.thenational.ae/news/world/middle-east/the-death-of-general-younis-makes-us-stronger-libya-rebels-say (accessed 30 July 2013).

Sheridan, M. B. 2011a. "Libya Declares Liberation with an Islamic Tone." *Washington Post*, 23 October. http://articles.washingtonpost.com/2011-10-23/world/35279134_1_gaddafi-officials-benghazi-anti-gaddafi-forces (accessed 30 July 2013).

———. 2011b. "Libyan Women Savor New Freedoms after Revolution." *Washington Post*, 4 November. http://articles.washingtonpost.com/2011-11-04/world/35284017_1_libyan-women-anti-gaddafi-gaddafi-security-forces (accessed 30 July 2013).

Sherwood, H., and C. McGreal. 2011. "Libya: Gaddafi Has Accepted Roadmap to Peace, Says Zuma." *Guardian*, 11 April. http://www.theguardian.com/world/2011/apr/10/libya-african-union-gaddafio-rebels-peace-talks (accessed 30 July 2013).

Sidney (Australia) Morning Herald. 2011. "We Will Never Surrender, Says Gaddafi's Son." 11 March. http://www.smh.com.au/world/we-will-never-surrender-says-gaddafis-son-20110311-1bq42.html (accessed 30 July 2013).

Smith, D. 2011. 2011. "Has Gaddafi Unleashed a Mercenary Force on Libya?" *Guardian*, 22 February. http://www.theguardian.com/world/2011/feb/22/gaddafi-mercenary-force-libya (accessed 30 July 2013).

Smith, R. 2012. "Are Libyans for or against Women's Rights?" *Libya Herald*, 9 March. http://www.libyaherald.com/2012/03/21/are-libyans-for-or-against-womens-rights/ (accessed 30 July 2013).

Stephen, C. 2011. "Abdul Fatah Younis Ambush Killing Blamed on Pro-Gaddafi Forces." *Guardian*, 29 July. http://www.theguardian.com/world/2011/jul/29/abdul-fatah-younis-killed-libya (accessed 30 July 2013).

———. 2012. "Mahmoud Jibril Seeks Coalition with Libya's Islamists after His Poll Win." *Guardian*, 14 July. http://www.theguardian.com/world/2012/jul/14/libya-jibril-coalition-election-victory (accessed 30 July 2013).

Stephen, C., and L. Harding. 2011. "Libyan PM Snubs Islamists with Cabinet to Please Western Backers." *Guardian*, 22 November.

St. John, R. B. 1983. "The Ideology of Muammar al Qadhafi: Theory and Practice." *International Journal of Middle East Studies* 15, no, 4: 471–490.

———. 2010. "The Slow Pace of Reform Clouds the Libyan Succession." Real Instituto Elcano, ARI 45/2010. 11 March. http://www.realinstitutoelcano.org/wps/portal/rielcano_eng/Content?WCM_GLOBAL_CONTEXT=/elcano/elcano_in/zonas_in/ari45-2010 (accessed 30 July 2013).

———. 2011. "Libya: Cracks in the Qadhafi Foundation." *Sada*, Carnegie Endowment for International Peace, January 17. http://carnegieendowment.org/2011/01/18/libya-cracks-in-qadhafi-foundation/6baj (accessed 30 July 2013).

Tarkowski Tempelhof, S., and M. Omar. 2011. "Stakeholders of Libya's February 17 Revolution." United States Institute of Peace Special Report, 12 December. http://www.usip.org/publications/stakeholders-libya-s-february-17-revolution (accessed 30 July 2013).

Telegraph. 2011. "Libya: Hugo Chavez Peace Plan under Consideration." 3 March. http://www.telegraph.co.uk/news/worldnews/africaandindianocean/libya/8358645/Libya-Hugo-Chavez-peace-plan-under-consideration.html.

Toaldo, M. 2014. "A European Agenda to Support Libya's Transition." European Council on Foreign Relations, Policy Brief, 19 May. http://www.ecfr.eu/publications/summary/a_european_agenda_to_support_libyas_transition308 (accessed 29 July 2014).

Tunisia Live. 2012a. "Justice and Construction Party." 12 July.

———. 2012b. "Marginal Victory for Women in Libya's GNC Elections." Gender Concerns International, 18 July. http://www.genderconcerns.org/article.php?id_nr=3406&id=Marginal%20Victory%20for%20Women%20in%20Libya's%20gnc%20Elections (accessed 30 July 2013).

———. 2012c. "The National Forces Alliance." 5 July.

Updike Toler, L., and T. Peyerl, T. 2012. "Selection or Election for the Constituent Assembly? Lessons from History." *Libya Herald*, 11 August. http://www.libyaherald.com/2012/08/11/selection-or-election-for-the-constituent-assembly-lessons-from-history/ (accessed 30 July 2013).

USA Today. 2011. "Anti-government Protesters Killed in Libyan Clash." 17 February. http://usatoday30.usatoday.com/news/world/2011-02-17-libya-protests_N.htm (accessed 30 July 2013).

Vandewalle, D., 2006. *A History of Modern Libya.* Cambridge: Cambridge University Press.

———. 2011. *Libya since 1969: Qadhafi's Revolution Revisited.* Basingstoke: Palgrave Macmillan.

Varvelli, A. 2010. "Libia: Vere riforme oltre la retorica?" *ISPI Analysis* no. 17 (July). http://www.ispionline.it/en/pubblicazione/libia-vere-riforme-oltre-la-retorica-0 (accessed 30 July 2013).

Wehry, F. 2012. "Electing a New Libya." Carnegie Endowment for International Peace, 2 July. http://carnegieendowment.org/2012/07/02/electing-new-libya/chk3 (accessed 30 July 2013).

Zartman, I. William. 1985. *Ripe for Resolution: Conflict and Intervention in Africa.* New York: Oxford University Press.

———. 2000. "Ripeness: The Hurting Stalemate and Beyond." In *International Conflict Resolution after the Cold War*, ed. P. Stern and D. Druckman. Washington, D.C.: National Academy Press.

Syria

Aspirations and Fragmentations

SAMIR AITA

THIS CHAPTER ADDRESSES the events of the Arab Spring in Syria from the perspective of negotiations as a process. It tries to set the background that led to a massive uprising that has turned into a deadly and lengthy civil war whose outcomes are still unclear.

For many reasons, Syria appears to constitute the turning point of the events of the Arab Spring, inevitable in many perspectives: its complex social fabric, with in particular the presence of a strong awakening Kurdish identity following the Iraq invasion and regime overthrow in 2003; its location as the junction between the "Shiʿi crescent" and the "Sunni axis";[1] its position on the Palestinian-Israeli issue and the other Levant countries' history (Lebanon, Jordan); its occupied Golan Heights and long-term conflicts with Turkey; but also and mainly its former intellectual role in defining the "Arab" identity of the region, and now the dilemma of framing the targets of what the young angry crowd of the region call "revolutions" or "civic democratic states" to be sought.

Over three years the events in Syria experienced different phases. Each phase could be described in terms of negotiation theories: negotiations for coalition; negotiations for formulation; within the two parties, "who's talking to whom about what?"; what is the ultimate goal and how does it change?; the means to resort to: political or violence; and how the "end game" could take place on what formulation, with what practical modalities? This chapter is a tentative approach to the Syrian conflict on those terms. It is dedicated to those who lost their lives or endured injuries, starvation, prison, or exile, and more generally to this young generation who lost fear, broke the old commonalities, and is shaping its future.

BACKGROUND AND ROOTS

Posing the issue of negotiations concerning the deep transformations occurring in the Arab states necessitates a thorough understanding of the roots and context of such transformations. The case of Syria is far from being an exception, especially as the uprising that started in early 2011 has been continuing ever since and has reached a level of violence that has no equivalent in all Arab Spring events. At different moments, the crisis reached stalemates, which did not lead to a real process of negotiation. On each occasion, the crisis deepened and widened, along with the level of violence, strongly implicating complex internal and foreign-regional dynamics.

As in other Arab countries, the "spring" of societies could be schematized as a "youth tsunami hitting a power body enthroned over states' institutions" (Aita 2007, 2011a). This image refers first to demographics: high population growth rates in the 1980s (around 3.5 percent yearly) have led a new generation of youth to come in the present years to the age of work and conscience (Goldstone 1991). The labor force is increasing at more than 6 percent yearly, while participation rates are still low (around only 20 percent for women) (Aita 2011b). The problem is aggravated by deep economic changes in agriculture that have led to the renewal of rural-urban migration, in particular to small- and medium-sized towns, and to the suburbs of major cities. These are precisely the towns and villages where the social uprising has emerged and developed.

The political system of Syria has also experienced fundamental changes since 2000, the year of accession of Bashar al-Asad to the presidency. Contrary to his father's rule, where "socialist"-minded state institutions were providing basic services while controlling the economy (i.e., "state capitalism"), the new president developed new policies which can be characterized as "crony capitalism" (Aita 2006): members of the president's direct family capturing rent-producing activities: oil revenues, mobile phones, real estate, and so on. The power body became more closed around the Asad family (and the cousins Makhlouf and Shalish) and more directly based on clienteles, including secret services (*mukhabarat*) that emerged more than ever as political and economic tools of this "power body." State institutions were weakened, especially as public services were gradually privatized: universities, schools, health services, and so on. Poverty increased, and migrant workers' remittances become the essential "social safety net." And for around three hundred thousand newcomers yearly to the labor market, only sixty-five thousand jobs are created, mostly informally. This is even with a yearly GDP growth rate of around 5 percent (Aita 2009).

This "youth tsunami" is a major factor of the Syrian uprising, as it would have caused major transformations to society and politics even if Syrian governance were democratic. One could compare it with a similar wave in Europe and the United States at the end of the 1960s, when the younger generation coming from the post–World War II baby boom completely changed the social and political perspectives. The difference is that the Arab tsunami comes in a period of economic difficulties and absence of democracy; the authoritarian crony capitalism and the lack of decent work opportunities mean that the youth uprising is asking for freedoms and dignity as well as the overthrow of the regime.

In Syria, a social movement has developed since the early 2000s, led by intellectuals and activists, under an umbrella called Committees for the Revival of the Civil Society (CRCS) (Landis and Pace, 2006–2007). These committees were the core phenomena of the so-called Damascus Spring; they spread new thoughts and paradigms, liberating minds for social and political activism. Most of the initial leaders of the uprising come from this background. They are the sons or admirers of the prisoners of conscience of the Damascus Spring; they were raised reading the books or watching the TV series written by those writers or scenarists.

A spirit of civil society has then spread in Syria, in a country constituted of a mosaic of religions (even within Islam and Christianity, with also significant roots of secularism), ethnic identities (Arab, Kurd, Cherkess, etc.), and tribal or regional behaviors (traditional society) more complex than in any other Arab country experiencing a "spring" (Gelvin 1998; George 2003; Kilo 2003; Al-Om 2011). The "power body" (the president himself, his family, or at least the high command of the army and the security services) has played on these divisions, while proposing itself as the—only—safeguard for their coexistence.

THE DEVELOPMENT OF THE SYRIAN UPRISING AS A FAILURE OF NEGOTIATIONS

The Deraa Uprising and the Speech of Denial

The Syrian uprising started in March 2011 with an event in the city of Deraa, south of Damascus.[2] Adolescents wrote antiregime slogans on a wall, influenced by what they saw on satellite TV channels during the uprising in Tunisia and Egypt. They were jailed and tortured (9 March) by the regional chief of the security services Atef Najib, a close cousin of the president. When the families demonstrated to ask for their children back home (17 March), many were jailed. The Friday prayer on the second day called for calm and time for negotiations (18 March); however, a demonstration followed, and the police fired on the crowd, killing four people. The Mosque Al Omari then became the site of a continuous sit-in, while several sporadic demonstrations were occurring daily in Deraa and with its surrounding villages. A famous chief of the security, Rustom Ghazala, was sent on 19 March to meet with local leaders, and a complaint was remitted to him, mainly asking for Najib to be punished. The vice president, Farouk Sharae, also originating from the region, arrived on 21 March and managed to bring some calm, promising to bring the complaints to the president and obtaining the revocation of the governor of the city.

But a military operation was conducted during the night of 22–23 March to end the sit-in at the mosque, killing twelve people and injuring hundreds. To cover up the issue, the secret services and special troops brought weapons and ammunition, and they were shown on TV as being gathered there by "terrorist" groups. This immediately ignited massive demonstrations from surrounding villages converging on the city. The slogans were "freedom . . . freedom," "peaceful . . . peaceful," and "end the siege of Deraa," but also "the people and the army, hand in hand," as some of the soldiers in the military camps on the way encouraged the demonstrators.[3] Tens more were killed at the entrance of the city, on this day named "the massacre of the villagers."

The country woke up shocked on the morning of 24 March. The general feeling was that Syria was at a turning point. In the afternoon, the spokeswoman of the president, Buthaina Shaaban, came on TV announcing an end to the shooting of demonstrators and reporting on a speech to the nation Bashar al-Asad planned for 30 March, where he would announce "significant reforms." But the next day, a Friday, saw even more impressive demonstrations ignited by some aspects of Shaaban's speech, that the uprising was due to hunger, and by the news of others being killed in the cities of Sanamein and Tafas (near Deraa) and also in Latakia. The security services shot and killed demonstrators, the Baath party's offices and the public services building were burned, and for the first time the slogan "the people want to put down the regime" was heard, while images of Asad the father and son were burned. The Deraa uprising went into continuous unrest: massive demonstrations every day, shooting on demonstrators, followed by crowds mourning the martyrs; a developing cycle leading to generalized uprising.

The government resigned on 29 March, but Asad's speech on 30 March was a disappointment. He accused the Deraa uprising as being a conspiracy, manipulated by "Salafi armed bands," and showed no respect for those killed.[4] He promised reforms, but after defeating the conspiracy. At no time did he suggest any action against those responsible for the killings. Thus Bashar al-Asad showed no willingness to negotiate; and Deraa had only to choose between backing down without any consolation or going further in its uprising.

Deraa and its region (named the Hauran) were put under siege, but the security services eased their control of the city, making it appear as a "free region." Several delegations came from the central government, with no solution for the stalemate. On 4 April, the head of the tribes of the Hauran, Nasser Hariri, called on Bashar al-Asad personally to stop the violent cycle. On 16 April, Sheikh Ahmad Sayasneh, the respected preacher at the Omari Mosque, met personally with the president, who promised him to answer all complaints. And the news emerged 19 April on lifting the state of emergency.[5] But on 23 April, following the arrest of leaders, Hariri quit his functions as parliamentary representative, and he, the other deputies from the region, Sayasneh, and other civil servants resigned. On 24 April, the High Council of the Syrian Revolution was formed, mainly of local tribal and religious leaders of the Hauran region. (Later, it sent representatives to various opposition meetings, did not join the Syrian National Council [SNC] when it was created, and slowly lost its importance a year later.) On 25 April, a major military operation by the armored fourth division of the Republican guards led by Maher Asad, brother of the president, was launched against Deraa and the Hauran. The fight, assisted by helicopters, reached the Omar Mosque on 30 April in the center of the old town and ended on 5 May with a military occupation of the city and the surrounding villages ("Syrian Troops"). But the uprising had already spread around the country in support to Deraa and the Hauran.

Why Deraa and Hauran Triggered the Syrian Revolution

Many observers have been surprised that the Syrian revolution started and developed from Deraa and the Hauran, a traditional base of the regime. In fact, many members of the Baath Party and security services leaders originate from this (supposedly) rural area: notably, Farouk Sharae, the former minister of foreign affairs and then first vice president; and General Rustum Ghazala, the former chief of Syrian military intelligence in Lebanon. The region is known for its aversion to the Muslim Brotherhood and political Islam, and the economic conditions of the population were better than in many other regions, even if it received its share of the internal migrations originating from the Jezireh.[6] The authorities had much leverage to break the developing cycle of unrest.

Not only were humanitarian and civic sentiments shocked by the torturing of children and the firing on demonstrators, but the outrage at a remark made by Atef Najib to a traditional leader also ignited tribal solidarity, still extremely strong in Hauran.[7] By doing so, the regime created a coalition between traditional society, which was not really in the mood of revolt, but on which those in authority trampled in trying to solve social issues, and the civil society activists around the country, who wanted to use the Arab Spring to bring major changes in governance.[8] It united the two slogans of the uprising: "dignity" with "freedom."

The president also failed to put himself as a guarantor of social peace in the early days and to profit from the example of the initial calming steps made by his Haurani deputy. Above all, he failed to measure the shock produced nationwide by the killings on 23 March. Not only did he not pay tribute to the martyrs and to the lost honor, but he also ignored major measures that were necessary at the national level, starting with the sacking of Atef Najib and going further to remove the hated figures of his own family, such as his brother Maher or his other cousin, Rami Makhlouf, who represented the image of cronyism and corruption. Asad's speech of 30 March sent a humiliating message that the only formula for negotiation with society is surrender and applause, shown by the reception made to his speech by the parliament: "Burying sedition is a national, moral, and religious duty; and all those who can contribute to burying it and do not are part of it. The Holy Quran says, 'Sedition is worse than killing,' so all those involved intentionally or unintentionally in it contribute to destroying their country. So there is no compromise or middle way in this." He acknowledged that "when there is blood it becomes more difficult to solve the problem"; but he put the blood spilling as the responsibility of a conspiracy, which is "highly organized": "There are support groups in more than one governorate linked to some countries abroad. There are media groups, forgery groups and groups of 'eye-witnesses.' . . . They started in the governorate of Deraa." The only way to deal with them is force, what had been later called the "security solution."

From Local Troubles to a Generalized Uprising

The uprising of Deraa and the Hauran came in Syria in an environment much influenced by the events of Tunisia, Egypt, and Libya. On 26 January, shortly after the death of Mohammed Bouazizi in Tunisia, Hassan Ali Akla immolated himself in the town of Hassakah, in Jezireh province. On 30 January, a small demonstration in support of the Egyptian revolution (25 January–11 February) was repressed by the security services. On 22 February, a similar demonstration occurred at the site of the Libyan embassy (following the fall of Benghazi and Beida to the Libyan uprising). These demonstrations, which continued afterward, were organized by civic activists, who were later to play a major role on the political scene.[9] More significant was the spontaneous demonstration in Damascus on 17 February after a policeman insulted a driver near the old "souk" of Damascus. More than five thousand people quickly gathered, chanting "the Syrian people cannot be humiliated." The interior minister walked to the scene, extracted the policeman from the angry demonstrators, and calmed the crowd. He was dismissed the next day.

On the other hand, a Facebook page was created on 18 January named "the Syrian revolution against Bashar al-Asad."[10] It called for the start of a revolution on 15 March, after an earlier call for revolt on 4 February met with little success. But this day's events were limited to small symbolic demonstrations, as they were the next day, when a few people gathered near the Ministry of Interior calling for the release of political prisoners. The demonstrations grew stronger on the next Friday, 18 March, echoing the events in Deraa, and in response to the repression in the city and its surroundings. But the real turning point was reached on Friday 25 March after the bloody massacre at the Omar Mosque in Deraa. The uprising spread in support of Deraa and the Hauran from Damascus to Latakia and eastward toward Deir Ez Zor. These events occurred when the bombing of Libya by an "international coalition" started, as analyzed in the chapter in this collection by Johannes Theiss, along with the civil war in the country.

The cycle of confrontation developed inexorably, gradually reaching most of the cities and villages in the country. The demonstrations gathered more and more people, mourning the killed martyrs and supporting the besieged or invaded cities. Most of the demonstrations were made on Fridays. The evolution of the names of the Fridays and the slogans reflected the evolution of the mobilization.[11] They started with morally unifying symbolic names: "Dignity," "Glory," "Martyrs," "Resisting," "Insisting," "Great Friday," "Anger" (following the massacre in Deraa), "Challenge," "the Free Women of Syria" (in a wording showing the first slip toward Islamic traditional names), "Azady" (seeking national union between Arabs and Kurds), "Home protectors" (calling the army to stand with the people), "the Children of freedom" (following the arrest, torture, and killing of the thirteen-year-old Hamza Al Khatib, who became a symbol of the civic uprising),[12] "the tribes" (in a second slip toward traditional society, calling the tribes to join the movement, after the army raided the tribal town of Tal Kalakh on the Northern border of Lebanon), "Saleh Al Ali" (following the name of the Alawite hero of Syrian independence, decrying sectarianism[13] and calling the Alawites[14] to join the uprising).

A more political shift was made in mid-June 2011: "Lost legitimacy" (with the first announcement of a National Council patterned after the image of the Libyan National Transition Council), "Departure," "No dialogue" (following the call of Vice President Sharae for a major national dialogue conference near Damascus), "your silence is killing us" (as a call for foreign intervention while the war in Libya was raging), "beginning of victory" (following the shift of Turkish policy and its threats for a military intervention, as well as the U.S. and EU statements that "Asad must resign"), "international protection" (in response to the Arab League mission to broker a solution), "Continuing until we bring down the regime," "Unification against the regime," "Victory for the Levant and Yemen" (McGreal and Chulov 2011; DPA 2011). And it quickly turned to be mixed with slogans with Islamic and religious background mid-July, simultaneously with the call for foreign intervention: "Khalid bin Walid grandsons" (in reference to the besieged city of Homs and its hero who headed the Muslim army that conquered Syria), "God is with us," "We won't kneel except for God," "Patience & steadfastness" (in reference to the month of Ramadan); then culminating in October 2011 with "the Syrian National Council is our representative."

Local Politics versus National Dialogue

One of the main characteristics of the Syrian uprising is the formation of hundreds of "coordination committees" in each village and city quarter ("Altenseekiat" 2014). These committees were led by young civic activists, belonging to the "youth tsunami" and claiming that "we want to change the regime, but not to talk politics." These committees were mostly made up of educated young people, communicating through the new medias (Internet, Facebook social networks), acting locally, with a main mission to bring the images and videos of the Syrian uprising to the outside world. Some of these activists were politicized through the classical political parties or the movement of the Damascus Spring in the early 2000s.[15]

Quickly, coalitions started to be created between these committees.[16] Hence, the Local Coordination Committees organization (LCC) was created as early as March, organized by young political, media, and human rights activists, such as Omar Idlebi and Razan Zeitoun.[17] It was mostly secular, politicized, aimed at "creating a civic and democratic state, based on equal citizenship," the Tunisian motto, and long opposed to foreign military intervention. In June, it emerged as "a pivotal force in Syria" (Shadid 2011a). The competing Syrian Committees Union (SYRCU) followed in the same month and then merged in August with the Syrian Revolution General Commission" (SRGC), which the LCC refused to join, as the SGRC launching in Istanbul was keener on political Islam and military activities.[18] Other coalitions also gradually appeared: the April 17 Movement for Democratic Change in Syria (in reference to the date of the national day), which is mostly made up of civic activists from the Hauran; the Pulse movement of the civic youth (Nabad), made up of multiconfessional activists sticking to pacifist uprising; and the Supreme Council of the Syrian Revolution, more Islamic and militarized ("Supreme Council" 2012). Most of these youth coalitions acted as news agencies;[19] some later joined the political coalitions or the militarized uprising but disintegrated in practice.

On the level of the political parties and prominent intellectuals, the move toward coalitions was slower, as they were more detectable by the security apparatus, and members experienced jail and penalties. However, two hundred intellectuals called for the first public conference of the opposition figures at the Semiramis Hotel on 27 June, under the slogan of "Syria for all in a democratic and civic state." On 30 June, several political parties and personalities among the participants announced the creation of the National Coordination Committee for Democratic Change in Syria (NCB).[20] Hassan Abdel Azim was nominated as its chairman, and Burhan Ghalioun as deputy and spokesperson abroad. It was formed from most of the political parties and personalities of the National Democratic Rally,[21] which had opposed Hafez Asad since the 1970s and experienced long years of imprisonment, and of Kurdish parties and personalities. From the latter, only the Democratic Union Party (PYD, linked to the Turkish Kurdistan Workers' Party [PKK] of Abdallah Ocalan) remained in the NCB. Long negotiations were made to bring in the Muslim Brotherhood movement, banned from Syria,[22] but they failed. This movement was negotiating directly its rehabilitation with the Syrian authorities, under the auspices of the Turkish government, led by the Justice and Development Party (AKP), and at that moment the Turkish government was reassessing its own policies.[23] The NCB held its own conference only on 17 September, in an extremely tense environment.

While the uprising was developing and spreading all over the country and the opposition groups were forming, the president started a long process of negotiations on the local level. For two months starting in April, he successively received delegations from the different cities and neighborhoods, almost two delegations per day. He also sent many of the pillars of the regime (the vice president, his friend General Manaf Tlass, governors of provinces) to the different localities to listen to their grievances, to negotiate calm, or to promise changes. The delegations of the revolting localities expressed a mixture of political complaints (against the brutality of the security forces and their deep involvement in public life) and local complaints (such as the confiscations of lands of villages or suburbs by his crony "power body" directly or by its clientele). These rounds of negotiations went on endlessly, with no significant results, and even with deceptions for unfulfilled promises, igniting more anger. This is when the security services infiltrated the delegations and forbid the most influential local personalities to participate. Many of the intermediate brokers also lost their credibility as they did not bring to reality the commitments of the president. In fact, the local claims were difficult to solve and would have necessitated complex bargains, such as in the case of disputed land ownership; they could also have opened the way to similar claims in many other areas.

In the end, these rounds of local negotiations failed for two reasons. On one hand, the uprising became widespread, so that solving a few local problems would not have a general impact on the country, giving a strong impression that some real "reforms" have been made. On the other hand, the new government appointed on 14 April also constituted a deception, as it contained no personalities acceptable to the population and was headed by a former minister of agriculture whom many held responsible for the massive rural-urban migration. The "power body" did not make any real concession, even concerning local disputes. Such concessions would have introduced cracks in its own clientele base. This was already the case for dealing with Atef Najib, the torturer of Deraa's children: his jailing would have given the signal that the president could divide the ruling family or sack heads of security services in case of "errors." The president and his "power body" needed total unity in his own camp, as they were working for the "security solution"; and they needed to mobilize the whole family group and "power body" as one man for the fight, as well as all of their clientele bases to constitute a militia: the Shabiha.[24]

The concessions made on the national level had ambiguous meanings.[25] The first appeared to be aimed at neutralizing part of the population and creating divisions within the uprising camp on a very sensitive issue: the rights of the Kurds. In fact, the president announced on 7 April a singular measure awaited for decades: finally giving Syrian citizenship to several hundred thousand Kurds who had been clamoring for it since 1962. Next, on 16 April, Asad issued a decree granting general amnesty on all crimes. But the confusion made between ordinary and political "crimes" and between pacifist activists and al-Qaeda members to be freed rendered this measure ineffective ("Bashar al-Asad" 2013). It was followed by two other amnesties on 1 and 22 June. On 19 April, another major longstanding demand of civil society was granted: the state of emergency in place since 1963 was abrogated, along with the state security tribunals. The right to peaceful demonstration was granted, but these measures came a few days before the bloody crushing of the Deraa uprising, with its massive campaign of imprisonment. The measures then lost their significance. It was only in August 2011 that a new party law was promulgated, with news in the press on the abrogation of Law 49 banning the Muslim Brotherhood.

As these last measures did not come from negotiations at the national level, they appeared to be cosmetic concessions to foreign pressures, more than successes of the uprising. It was only on 10 July that a "national dialogue" conference was hosted in Damascus and aired on TV. Vice President Farouk Sharae expressed the "hope that at the end of this comprehensive meeting to announce the transition of Syria to a pluralistic democratic nation where all citizens are guided by equality and participate in the modeling of the future of their country" ("Activists" 2011). The youth coordinating committees condemned the conference as useless, but intellectuals and political activists participated in its public debates, while many others, including the NCB members, called for ending the "security solution" and for the retreat of the army to its barracks as a precondition to participate and engage in a real negotiation. This "national dialogue" conference was set finally as a "consultative meeting," since Bashar al-Asad did not participate in it, contrary to earlier reports. It was a failure, despite some very courageous statements and the saving in extremis of its outcomes by the civil servant organizers through a final communiqué calling for "a state based on the rule of law, justice, equal citizenship, plurality and democracy where ballot boxes are the fundamentals of the political mandate" ("Final statement" 2014). In fact, this final communiqué recognized only the "patriotic" (*sic*) opposition as part of the "Syrian national fabric," although it put in front the necessity to preserve "the stature of the state." A mild recognition, with the state as an institution making its best efforts to save the country from an already written fate, while the "power body" denied the need to be engaged in the process. More importantly, this tame conference came a few days after the massive demonstrations of hundreds of thousands on 1 July in the city of Hama, symbol of the 1982 bloody repression, the most impressive since the beginning of the uprising, the "Friday of Departure" (of the president) and on 8 July, the "Friday of No Dialogue" (to which the U.S. ambassador to Syria paid a visit).

After June 2011, the paradigm of the Syrian uprising changed its nature at the national and local levels. The "national consultative dialogue" was a lost opportunity and a signal of a shift toward an open confrontation between the "power body" and the population, although still mainly pacifist, but with massive foreign implications. The only positive outcome was that it had somehow lowered the weekly death toll. This was while the Libyan civil war was raging.

NO TO FOREIGN INTERVENTION, NO TO SECTARIANISM, NO TO VIOLENCE

Protecting the Revolution or Arming It?

By June 2011, the uprising had reached most parts of Syria with massive demonstrations, but the uprising was still peaceful in most of its aspects, even if some sporadic violence occurred against government troops or Alawite figures. Excessive violence came from the regime. The first images of weapons appeared on 19 June, as government forces conducted major military operations using tanks and helicopters against demonstrators.[26] In addition, at the same time as he called for a national dialogue, Bashar al-Asad released extremist activists who were imprisoned for various reasons, some of whom quickly turned to violent organized actions. Zahran Alloush, a native of Douma (a neighborhood of Damascus, the main stronghold of the uprising) was freed on 22 June and created the Brigade of Islam.[27] Earlier, Abu Mohammad Al Golani (Al Fateh), an eminent member of al-Qaeda, was freed, went to Iraq, and returned to Syria to create Al Nusra Front (The Support Front for the Syrian People) initially in Deraa and the Hauran region (Hamidi 2013; *Al-Nusra* 2013). Others joined ISIS (the Islamic State of Iraq and the Levant).

Soldiers and officers began to defect, refusing to shoot on people and starting to conduct military operations against the military units invading the various cities. A group of Free Syrian Officers (FSO) was announced in early July, led by Lieutenant Colonel Hussein Harmoush. On 29 July, Colonel Riyad Assʿad created the Free Syrian Army (FSA), stating that it would work to protect the people and to bring down the regime; it called "all opposition forces to unite" (Landis 2011b). This army was composed of phalanges with names like "Freedom," "Hamza Al Khatib," "Al Qashoos," reflecting the moral values of the uprising.[28] Harmoush took part in spectacular military operations as early as 9 June, when 120 government soldiers and security men were reported killed near Jisr Ash Shoughour in the north (Tantawi 2011). Later he was forced to flee to Turkey while directing the operations of the FSO, and on 29 August, he disappeared during a meeting with Turkish intelligence in a Syrian refugee camp; later he reappeared in Syria and retracted his defection but was reported to have been executed by the regime forces ("Syria: report" 2011; "Syria Army" 2011). The role of the FSO declined afterward, and the FSA took the lead, at least as a media voice, especially following the establishment of Ass'ad headquarters in Alexandretta-Hatay province in Turkey at the end of July 2011.[29]

At this stage, the move to arm the revolution and military actions against the government forces was still extremely controversial ("Stages" 2011). The example of Libya with the acceleration of the rebel offensive toward Tripoli was tempting, while the images and casualties were making most of the Syrian population worried about the future. Thus, the big demonstrations in major towns like Damascus, Homs, or Hama refused in many cases to be "protected" by armed men (private Skype discussions with members of the "coordinations committees"). The FSA was merely a media operation, with no major influence on ground or armed phalanges and looking nothing like an "army." The FSO were more organized but started in local and limited contexts, such as in Jisr Ash Shoughour or in Rastan and Talbisseh. Jisr Ash Shoughour is a mountain area, near the Turkish border, one of the poorest and least developed parts of the country, a crossing place between the internal hinterland and the Alawite Mountains. Rastan is the hometown of General Mostapha Tlass, the former defense minister and close friend of Hafez Asad. It was he who forced the military to accept Bashar al-Asad as the inheritor of the throne. A large number of Syrian army's officers come from this town on the Orontes River, close to the Lebanese border, which the government forces invaded on 28 May after large demonstrations. A major battle between the FSA and the regular army occurred in Rastan between 27 September and 1 October.

Hence as conciliatory negotiations were stumbling and the "power body" was using extreme force to crush the uprising, armed struggle appeared to be developing inevitably, in a systemic way, with confused politics, mostly in border areas and towns where foreign powers could smuggle in weapons and money ("Arms" 2011).

The Division of the Opposition

The move from an uprising for "freedom and dignity" toward a "revolution" for "toppling the regime" with foreign assistance saw the creation of its first political coalition in Antalya, Turkey, on 1 June under the umbrella of the Syrian Conference for Change. It grouped the Muslim Brotherhood (MB), the Damascus Declaration, Kurdish and tribal figures, some representatives of local coordination committees, and Syrian businessmen living abroad, who had financed the event.[30] It called for the immediate resignation of Bashar al-Asad and stated that it did not target any particular group (Landis 2011a). But even at this stage, the battle was fierce among the participants to convince the MB to accept the separation of state and religion (Landis 2011c). This battle was mainly led by the young activists, as the Damascus Declaration members were already open to a more indulgent view on the issue of the "religion of the majority."[31] At this moment when all other opposition groups were looking to create the National Committee for Democratic Change (NCB), this meeting appeared as a first attempt of the MB and the Democratic People's Party (DPP), the main component of the Damascus Declaration body, to head out on a different path, even if they stated that they were participating only as observers in this conference. It is to be noted that this was the first conference of the opposition raising the "independence flag," taking the Libyan case as an example.[32]

Another opposition conference was held in Brussels two days later, organized mainly by the MB (Exclusive 2008), and on 4 July, a meeting in support of the Syrian opposition was organized in Paris and addressed by Bernard Henri Levy, in which some members of the Antalya conference follow-up committee participated, creating a significant polemic within the opposition.[33] On 16 July, a few days after the end of the government's failed "national dialogue" in Damascus, another "National Salvation" conference was convened in Istanbul by the Islamist lawyer Haytham Maleh, to create a National Salvation Council in the image of the Libyan National Transition Council and even a transitional government. Burhan Ghalioun, a writer and Paris university professor, participated in this conference, despite the opposition of his own constituency, the NCB. This conference was supposed to be Skype-linked between Istanbul and Damascus, but the security forces attacked the area where the meeting was to be held and managed to cancel it.

In the environment of tension that followed, the Doha Institute called opposition figures and intellectuals for a "scientific" (*sic*) conference in Doha, Qatar, on 30–31 July, under the theme of "Syria: Choices, Interests and the Possibilities of Change" ("Syria: Choices" 2011). This institute, led by Azmi Bishara and financed by the Qatari authorities, invited secular and Islamist intellectuals and historians, as well as representatives of the Coordination Committees; some were already calling for armed struggle.[34] The discussions, aired directly on TV, went into polemics on the notions of "majority, minority and equal citizenship" and whether the events in Syria were "an uprising or a revolution," but also whether "non-democratic Gulf countries stand supporting a revolution" (Manna 2011; Sadasyria12 2011). When some called for using the occasion of the conference to set commonly agreed targets for the change, Bishara stated: "no one [can] put conditions on a revolution." A second meeting in Doha on 4 September grouped mainly the NCB, the Damascus Declaration, and the MB. A week's negotiations led to an agreement between all these forces for the creation of a Syrian National Coalition ("Clarification"). The Doha meeting followed an announcement in Ankara on 30 August of the creation of a Syrian Transition Council of ninety-four members, to be headed by Burhan Ghalioun. It was a failure, but Ghalioun accepted the assignment and promised to form a National Council, although he was still deputy chair and foreign representative of the NCB. Several meetings followed in Cairo and Istanbul for this purpose. It was clear at this point that Qatar and Turkey had taken their own ways to gather the Syrian opposition.

The NCB held its first public meeting in Damascus on 17 September. Its slogan called for three no's: "No to violence, no to sectarianism, no to foreign intervention" ("Syrian Opposition Meet" 2011). It adopted a Charter of Dignity and Rights, the first formula for the future since the beginning of the uprising. It states in particular: "The Syrian State is founded on the principle of complete equality between its citizens, and of their rights and obligations. More specifically, there is complete equality between men and women, without any discrimination by race, color, gender, language, ethnicity, political opinion, religion or religious denomination. Specifically, this equality is inspired by the founding motto of the first republic: 'Religion is for God, the Fatherland is for everyone'; The Syrian State guarantees respect for civil liberties, including . . . freedom of conscience and religion and the freedom to peacefully demonstrate and strike. The State establishes rules to protect these freedoms against the hegemony of financial or political power" (National Coordination Body 2011). The final declaration called for the "toppling of the despotic and security services based regime," and asked for realization of the union of the opposition within two weeks under the terms convened in Doha as the Syrian National Coalition ("National Coordination Body" 2011).[35]

Immediately a polemic raged in the Gulf media, in particular Al Jazeerah, on how the authorities allowed such a meeting to be held inside Syria, on the slogan of three no's, and on a supposed ambiguity of the "toppling of the regime" sentence. The press campaign looked like a preparation for the announcement next 2 October in Istanbul of the creation of the Syrian National Council (SNC).[36] Actively prepared by a "team of experts," in particular Basma Kodmani and Obaida Nahas,[37] the SNC called for "breaking down the existing regime, including all of its operatives and symbols," for "uniting the efforts by the revolutionary movement and the political opposition," and for "working to secure international protection for civilians," while "maintaining a positive and flexible outlook towards all political opposition forces that are not part of the SNC, and working with them towards joining the SNC," aiming at "pursuing the official recognition of the SNC by Arab and foreign states." The mission of the SNC was, in fact, to "take responsibility, with the military apparatus, to manage the transitional period and guarantee the security and unity of the country once the regime falls. For that, it was to "form a transitional government to manage the affairs of the State."[38] The backbones of the SNC were the MB and the Damascus Declaration, as well as some of the newly created coalitions of committees (such as LCC and SRGC).

Revolution or Civil War?

The creation of the SNC marked a second major transformation of the Syrian uprising toward a civil war with foreign implications. The "power body" gathered all the forces it could mobilize for its war on terror, invading the cities and villages to crush armed groups. It was strongly backed in this by Russia and China, which on 4 October 2011 vetoed a UN Security Council resolution to sanction the Syrian regime, a singular move of the two countries cutting with their silent reaction to Libyan developments and foreign intervention.

On the other hand, it was clear that a number of countries were behind the creation of the SNC and the compromises that led to its composition: France and Qatar (as in the case of Libya), in addition to Turkey, strongly supported the council, which was also backed by Saudi Arabia (busy brokering the solution for the

Yemeni revolution) and the United States.[39] The first official recognition of the SNC was made on 19 October by the Libyan National Transition Council as "the sole legitimate government in Syria," similar to the way the NTC itself was recognized by France's Nicolas Sarkozy.[40] It promised to hand over the Syrian embassy to the SNC and to arm and finance the rebellion. This recognition was followed by France on 21 November, but as "legitimate interlocutor"; Spain on 23 November; the United States on 5 December; the UK on 24 February 2012; Egypt on 24 February (but only as an "opposition group"). Turkey did not make a similar formal recognition, but allowed the SNC to open legal offices in the country in December 2011.

Hence, the Syrian uprising was no longer a call for moral values. The naming of Fridays changed to "the SNC is our representative," "the Freemen of the Army," "No-Fly zone," "Freezing Syria's Arab League membership," "Expulsion of the Ambassadors," "the FSA is protecting me," "Syrian buffer zone." At the same time the conflict became increasingly armed and escalated with the battles of Rastan (27 September–1 October) and of Homs (starting in September and October), among others. Weapons started to flow, mainly through Turkey and northern Lebanon.

The political arena for discussions became the Arab and international media, in particular Al Jazeerah and Al Arabiyah TV channels, which started special twenty-four-hour information channels dedicated to Syria. The major political confrontation of the SNC was no longer against the regime, but against the other component of the opposition, the NCB, as it was necessary to obtain international legitimacy as "sole representative" in order to move to the UN Security Council to support foreign intervention. Yet this move showed later to be ineffective in an international environment that was strongly divided over what began to be called "the Syrian crisis" or "the Syrian civil war." The SNC obtained its recognition as "sole representative" from some countries and as only "a representative" from others, but no foreign intervention came to put it in power as in the Libyan case. More astonishingly, it kept its constituency and its recognitions, even after it became only a part of the larger "Syrian National Coalition," which obtained similar recognitions.

A MEANING OF THE SYRIAN REVOLUTION IN THE MIDDLE OF CIVIL WAR

Bringing Calm through Nonarmed Monitors

In an environment of political blockage between the different players ("the power body," the SNC, the NCB, the military insurgency, the foreign powers, etc.) and of military escalation, nothing seemed able to stop an inevitable drama, with the explosion of violence, sectarianism, and foreign interventions. The Arab League (LAS) took the initiative to broker a negotiated solution. Contrary to the initial drive of the LAS Ministerial Committee, led by the Qatari prime minister and minister of foreign affairs, to recognize the SNC and take the Syrian crisis to the

UN Security Council,[41] a plan was proposed in October 2011 to call for a cease-fire, the return of the army to its barracks, the sending of nonarmed monitors, the release of political prisoners, and a dialogue with the opposition within fifteen days. The Syrian authorities accepted the plan on 2 November, but it collapsed with the escalation of violence concentrated mainly on Homs, a besieged Sunni-Alawite crossroads city where large military operations were taking place (see Al Jazeera 2011 and Reuters 2011).[42] The Syrian opposition tried to make a united delegation to back the LAS initiative, but the SNC refused to join, and members of the NCB delegation were beaten up at the entrance of the LAS offices in Cairo (Spears 2011). The LAS secretariat and other Arab countries pushed for the plan that the Syrian authorities refused, while Qatar and the SNC were working for Security Council action. Finally, it was only after several delays for further negotiations, as the LAS suspended Syrian government membership and imposed sanctions, that the plan protocol was signed, on 19 December, and the first observers arrived in Syria three days later. They came from Saudi Arabia, Qatar, Egypt, Sudan, Bahrain, and the UAE, with many Arab NGO activists, and stayed for a month.

Their arrival in the besieged cities and areas constituted a light of hope, even for government soldiers. Despite the fact that some of the monitors were "not qualified, did not have prior experience and were not able to shoulder the responsibility" and others "declined fulfillment of their mission" or "used flimsy pretexts" or "had personal agendas," as stated in the final report, violence diminished on both sides, the forces practiced "self-control, and a noticeable calm prevailed" (Ahmed and Al-Dabbi). However, the SNC and the Gulf media quickly started a polemic on the integrity of the observers and later on the Sudanese chief of monitors' mission report. One of the monitors suddenly became a media superstar, accusing the mission of siding with the Syrian authorities ("Discord" 2012). The polemic succeeded in breaking this attempt to lower the violence and to start negotiations. On 22 January 2012, Saudi Arabia withdrew its observers, followed two days later by the other Gulf countries. On 28 January, the LAS suspended indefinitely its mission due to "the critical degradation of the situation" (Samir and Solomon 2012). Immediately, the death toll rose from fewer than two hundred weekly to more than four hundred; the uprising again changed in nature from massive demonstrations to military battles; and the polemic made its point to move the Syrian file from the LAS to the UN Security Council, hoping for foreign intervention to support military actions as in the Libyan case.

Would the Security Council Do Better Than the Arab League?

On 3 February, Russia and China vetoed a proposed Security Council Resolution that could have allowed a foreign intervention under the umbrella of the "right to protect" civilians (Harris et al. 2012; Charboneau 2012). Instead, international agreement turned on 23 February to commissioning former UN secretary general

Kofi Annan to be a joint UN-LAS special envoy. The six-point plan addressed the necessity of a cease-fire, the provision of humanitarian assistance, the release of prisoners, the freedom of movement for journalists, and the respect of freedom of association and peaceful demonstrations. But mainly, it focused on an "inclusive Syrian-led political process" ("Kofi Annan's" 2012). This was while the fighting in Homs was raging and was starting in the Aleppo surroundings, almost as regular wars ("Homs 'Massacre'" 2012). Neither side respected point 2 of the plan, which stated that "the Syrian government should immediately cease troops movements . . . and bring out a sustained cessation of armed violence," and the same for "the opposition and "relevant elements."

An incomplete cease-fire was finally obtained on 14 April; around two hundred international observers were deployed, and casualties again fell to two hundred weekly or fewer. But not for long. On 1 May, Hervé Ladsous, UN under-secretary-general for peacekeeping operations, stated that "the level of violence in Syria has been appalling. I think the violations that are observed come from both sides. I would not establish a ratio. Now is not the time. . . . The important fact is that violations do come from both sides." Finally, the Houla Massacre on 25 May signaled the end of the supposed cease-fire, and most of the UN mission was withdrawn ("Houla" 2012). At the same time, the FSA pushed the regular army out of the key city of Azzaz near Aleppo, paving the way for the beginning of the battle of Aleppo in August. At this stage, the FSA was no longer mainly made up of unorganized defectors and armed civilians acting in self-defense. It contained battalions like Al Tawhid Brigade, made up of several thousand fighters, armed with MB ideology, and equipped and trained through Turkey (Bolling 2012).

While the UN was declaring that "the Syrian conflict is a civil war" (Reuters 2012), Kofi Annan pushed for an Action Group meeting in Geneva involving the five permanent members of the Security Council (including the usually vetoing Russia and China), and neighboring countries (except Iran). The Action Group negotiated an agreement on "principles and guidelines for a Syrian-led transition" (the Geneva I Principles), including "the establishment of a transitional governing body which can establish a neutral environment in which the transition can take place. That means that the transitional governing body would exercise full executive powers. It could include members of the present government and the opposition and other groups and shall be formed on the basis of mutual consent" ("Action Group" 2012). "Mutual consent" replaced other wording that excluded "those whose continued presence and participation would undermine the credibility of the transition and jeopardize stability and reconciliation," which meant Bashar al-Asad and his power body. This concession to Russia and China was obtained in exchange for the cancellation of a paragraph where all parties committed not to smuggle weapons to Syria. The Geneva I Communiqué constituted the major achievement of the Annan mission, along with forcing the convening of an all-Syrian opposition conference to be held two days later.

But Annan resigned on 1 August after a Security Council resolution placing his plan under chapter VII was vetoed by Russia and China, rendering his action an "impossible mission" (Black 2012). "You have to understand," Annan stated, "as an envoy, I can't want peace more than the protagonists, more than the Security Council or the international community for that matter. My central concern from the start has been the welfare of the Syrian people. Syria can still be saved from the worst calamity—if the international community can show the courage and leadership necessary to compromise on their partial interests for the sake of the Syrian people." He also said that the focus remained on political transition, as President Bashar al-Asad "will have to leave sooner or later." But "political process is difficult, if not impossible, while all sides—within and without Syria—see an opportunity to advance their narrow agendas by military means. International division means support for proxy agendas and the fueling of violent competition on the ground" (Annan 2012). The FSA battle for Aleppo, the second major metropolis of Syria, had started. The death count after a year and a half of uprising and civil war stood at twenty thousand killed.

The Cairo All Opposition Agreement

The division between the opposition bodies, the SNC and the NCB, went deep on the issues of violent resistance, sectarianism, and foreign intervention, all basic matters for formulation in the negotiations. The sectarian divide became even more acute when SNC chairman Ghalioun (2011) answered a *Washington Post* interview question on 2 December 2011, whether shariʿa could be accommodated in Syria: "The source of legislation will be the parliament, and if the parliament is made up of a majority of Muslims, it will reflect their culture or propensities. In today's Syria shariʿa is one of many sources of legislation. This is one way of satisfying religious sentiment of the people. We want a true democratic system that represents the wills and aspirations of its citizens." This statement, complaisant to the Islamists while minimizing their role in the NSC and the armed insurgency, came as a shock in a period when the LAS was bargaining its plan for political negotiations with a monitored cease-fire.

Nonetheless, negotiations were held between the SNC and NCB under the auspices of the LAS, involving most of the key members of both coalitions and producing an agreement on 31 December in Cairo.[43] It stipulated the "rejection of any foreign intervention" and the "refusal and condemnation of sectarianism," and it based the transition phase, to begin with the "fall of the existing regime," on principles similar to the Charter of Dignity, including full equal citizenship and the "refusal of sanctity over political and civil life" (meaning, in other words, the refusal of shariʿa and the dominance of political Islam). A joint committee was to be formed from an all-opposition conference to be organized under the auspices of the LAS. A few hours later, the chairman of the SNC discovered on his arrival at the Paris airport that his own office had issued a declaration rejecting the agreement ("Ghalioun" 2013): only intervention by ground forces should be rejected, not the air force for imposing a no-fly zone, and recourse to the UN Security Council and full support for the FSA were necessary. The MB followed, stating that "this agreement contained many details [that are] controversial on the national level; it omitted many important patriotic positions and demands; and many of the verbal formulations have been made in a suspicious and blurry manner" ("Agreement with" 2011). Following this, Ghalioun and the other members of the SNC retracted their signatures.

These developments had a deep effect on the exceptional popularity that Ghalioun had benefited from since the beginning of the uprising, when he appeared as its symbol.[44] Thus divisions started to appear within the SNC, further sparked by the twice-repeated extension of Ghalioun's mandate as chairman contrary to the SNC's initial bylaws and by a statement he made on the Kurdish issue ("Extension" 2012; "Erbil" 2012). He finally resigned and was replaced on 10 June 2012 by the Kurdish intellectual Abdulbasset Sida, who in turn was replaced on 2 November by the Christian Georges Sabra.[45]

The first major split within the SNC had occurred in February, when a group led by Haytham Maleh took the name of the Patriotic Action Group.[46] Kofi Annan and his deputy, the Palestinian Nasser Al Kudwa, spent much effort on negotiating the reintegration of this group within the SNC, much more than for the unification of all opposition constituencies. At the same time, a new opposition body was created, the Syrian Democratic Forum (SDF, or SDP as Syrian Democratic Platform).[47] It was based on individual membership, contrary to the SNC and NCB, which were coalitions of political groups; and members of both had joined the SDF. It was both civic and political, gathered around liberal personalities such as Michel Kilo, Aref Dalila, Habib Issa, Faeq Huweijeh, Hazem Nahar, Fayez Sara, activists of the LCC and the SRGC, SYRCU, as well as the author (Hassan 2012). It held a major conference in Cairo later in April, which was deliberately ignored by the Gulf media despite its strong participation (Middle East Agency 2012). It aimed at uniting the opposition, mainly the SNC and the NCB, around a common program for ousting Bashar al-Asad.

It was only in early June 2012 in Istanbul that negotiations for a coalition of opposition bodies was able to group representatives of the SNC, the NCB, the SDF, and other components to agree on the election of a Preparatory Committee for an all-opposition conference to be held at the end of the month in Cairo, as proposed by the UN-LAS joint envoy's plan ("Syrian opposition agreement" 2012). The Preparatory Committee met continuously for almost three weeks and finally agreed on the selection of around three hundred participants and on two project formulation documents: a "Compelling National Charter, which forms the basis for a comprehensive historical settlement and for a new constitution," and a "project for the ousting of the present power body and for the transition phase, which constitutes the vision of the victory of the targets of the revolution."[48] It also recommended the creation of a commonly approved "follow up committee, which shall (as first step to unify efforts) coordinate the actions of all opposition components, and commit on the implementation of the two documents as they shall be opted for in the conference." All opposition delegates signed this project deposited at the LAS, including the MB and the FSA.

The all-opposition conference convened on 2 and 3 July in Cairo in an extremely tense environment. Confusion was created when nonapproved participants tried to generate polemics, but finally the two project documents were agreed on with very few modifications.[49] Four core issues were the main difficult points of these agreements:

- *The place of religion and equal citizenship*: the National Charter stated that "the Syrian people are one people, whose identity was established through history. It rests on full equality of citizenship (. . .) on the basis of a comprehensive national consensus. No one has the right or authority to impose a religion or a belief on anyone, or to prevent anyone of freely choosing his religion and his practice.[50] Women are equal to men, and it is unlawful to renege on any of their rights. Any citizen has the right to occupy any position in the state, including that of President of the Republic, regardless of his religion or political affiliation; and the head of state can be either a man or woman."
- *The rights of the Kurds*: The Charter stated that "Syria is part of the Arab Nation" and "the Syrian people are one." They "are free and sovereign in their country and land, which are two inseparable political units. Giving up any inch of Syrian territory, including the occupied Golan Heights, is strictly prohibited." At the same time, the "Syrian State recognizes the existence of a Kurdish nationality among its citizens, with its legitimate national identity and rights according to international conventions and protocols, within the framework of the unity of the Syrian nation. The Kurdish national identity in Syria is considered a genuine component of the Syrian people," and while in a new constitution the "State will adopt the principle of administrative decentralization, so that local administration is based on representative executive institutions, providing citizen services and development in provinces and regions, in order to achieve sustainable and balanced development."[51]
- *The removal of the "power body"* ("Cairo Documents" 2012): The final text insisted on phrasing implying the possibility of use of foreign intervention for the removal of Bashar al-Asad: "The desired change will not take place but through the will and sacrifices of the Syrians, and through Arab and international effective mobilization, in order to protect the unity, sovereignty and stability of Syria, and to set an abiding mechanism for the protection of the Syrian civilians and a timetable for the immediate and full implementation of the resolution of the relevant Arab League and Security Council

Resolutions, while requesting the Security Council to take the necessary measures to impose the immediate implementation of these resolutions." Also it insisted not to mention the Geneva I Communiqué or the UN-LAS special envoy, and on supporting the "FSA" in name.

- *The constitution of a common structure of all opposition bodies*: The toughest negotiations were held in closed meetings concerning the creation of a common structure of all opposition groups, even as a simple follow-up committee for the diffusion and implementation of the agreed documents. The SNC, backed by Turkey, France and Qatar, refused absolutely. The LAS later issued a communiqué asking for the creation of such a committee, and two meetings were conducted in August, with members of the Preparatory Committee (which was not dismantled officially) and others, forming such a follow-up committee, backed by the U.S. State Department. Its resolutions were deposited at the LAS on 28 August. However, these efforts were completely discouraged when the newly elected French president, François Hollande, received a delegation of the SNC alone on 21 August and stated that he would recognize a provisional government that they would form, breaking the hopes for the unification of the opposition (Associated Press 2012).[52]

While the battle of Aleppo was starting, formulating targets of the revolution could appear as useless, as the real partners had become the fighting battalions as well as the countries training and arming them. However, the Cairo Documents were the first formulation of humanitarianism and equal citizenship of the Arab Spring.

DIVIDING SYRIA?

The Fate of Syrian Kurds

As the Syrian crisis evolved, the Kurdish question began to emerge strongly as a core issue. Bashar al-Asad tried to neutralize the uprising within the Kurdish population as early as 7 April 2011 by granting Syrian nationality to those Kurds who had waited for the long-promised measure for decades. However, the implementation of the measure remained opaque, as the unrest led to the dysfunctioning of state institutions. But the authorities had played the Kurds with a policy similar to that used toward Christians and other minority groups, claiming that the "revolution" was made by extremist Sunni religious groups who would threat their existence.

Even if the Kurds are in the majority Sunni Muslims, they are sensitive to such claims, since they also include Shiʿa, Alawite, and Yezidi,[53] and are generally more secular than their Arab Sunni counterparts, mainly because of their active politicization in the last decades and the awakening of their sense of national identity (Lowe 2006). From the first weeks, Kurdish youth participated in the demonstrations, shocked like all Syrians by the bloody repression in Deraa and the Hauran. However, the security services and the military avoided shooting on their demonstrations, even when the Kurdish flag was raised, defying symbolically Syrian territorial integrity. The memory of the 2004 Kurdish revolt was too strong, and any bloody repression would have triggered an even stronger uprising than that of Deraa (ICG 2013).[54]

Restraint was exerted from both sides. The authorities even released from prison the Kurdish opposition figure Mish'al Temo in June 2011 in a gesture to ease the tension.[55] Temo led many of the demonstrations in Qamishli and participated in the meetings organizing the creation of the SNC, where he insisted on the unity of the Syrians, Kurds, and Arabs in the uprising. After a failed attempt on 8 September, he was assassinated on 7 October, a few days after the announcement of the SNC. The opposition blamed the regime for this assassination, while the regime mourned him and blamed the "armed groups," and the PYD and PKK accused the Turkish government ("Syria's Kurds" 2011). His funeral led to more important Kurdish demonstrations and the first use of fire by the security forces. Later, the demonstrations calmed as the Kurdish political parties took over the youth movement and the local Coordination Committees.

The assassination of Temo marked definitively the failure of the integration of the Kurdish movement within the SNC and the marginalization of the Kurdish youth groups (Kurd Watch 2013). Initially, many of the Turkish political parties had joined the NCB but then withdrew, mainly as the PYD dominated the scene inside, while the local Kurdish Coordination Committees were trying to group with other LCC's. Finally, eleven (later fifteen) Kurdish parties and Coordination Committees formed the Kurdish National Council (KNC) on 26 October ("Kurdish National Council" 2012), backed by Masʿoud Barzani, president of the government of the Kurdistan Region in Iraq (KRG). The attempt to merge the KNC and SNC later collapsed after a declaration of the SNC president suggesting a comparison between the Kurds in Syria and the migrants in Europe.[56]

As the situation began to turn into civil war in the other Syrian areas, this autonomization of the Kurdish question led their region to become a relative safe heaven. The KNC was freely active, while their leaders installed strong support centers in Sulaymaniah and Erbil in the KRG area, with the local coordination committees organizing weak demonstrations supporting the "Syrian revolution." At the same time, in Syria, the PYD tightly organized the area, putting in place the People's Council of Western Kurdistan (PCWK), the People's Local Committees (PLCs), and its militia, the People's Defense Corps (Yekîneyên Parastina Gel, YPG), taking charge of public, security, and military affairs. The Syrian security services' offices remained in place, avoiding intervening, and the army retreated to other areas.

The domination of the Kurdish question became measurable in all opposition meetings that followed; for example, as I observed, half of the four-day conference for the creation of the Syrian Democratic Forum was devoted to the Kurdish question, and the issue was predominant during the preparation for and meetings of Cairo's all-opposition conference of 2–3 July 2012. The KNC representatives insisted on defining the Kurds as "Kurdish people," while putting reservations on any proposed text in order to preserve further possibilities. They also left the conference proceedings following provocation, in order to assess the specificity of their demands. The issue became a regional playground between Damascus (the Syrian regime), Erbil (the KRG in Iraq), Ankara (the Turkish government), Sulaymaniah (hometown of Jalal Talabani, the president of Iraq, and the rival of Barzani) and Qandil (the stronghold of the PKK in Northern Iraq). Tension increased between the KNC, backed by Erbil, and Ankara,[57] and the PYD, backed by Qandil; the PYD remained a strong component of the NCB, while suspected, even within the NCB, to deal with the Syrian regime. What has led Barzani to intervene to broker a marriage of convenience forming the Supreme Kurdish Committee (SKC) uniting both Kurdish blocs. This marriage was negotiated in several steps: on 11 June, a few days before the Cairo conference, but it failed; on 11 July, just after the YPG took over most of the towns of the North and Northeast with a strong Kurdish presence, which led to the Erbil declaration[58] and, later in November, to the constitution of a joint security and military corps. However, the *peshmergas* (Kurdish fighters) trained in Northern Iraq were not allowed by the PYD to enter Syria, to avoid creating tensions with the other Syrian components.

The clashes soon started between the PYD and the government forces, even in the Sheikh Maqsoud district of Aleppo, which had long remained neutral. Clashes also developed with the FSA, mainly with Liwa al-Tawhid units in Aleppo, but culminated in the Ras-Al-'Ayn (Serekani) battle of November 2012–January 2013, where the fighting was mostly with Al-Nusra Front and Ghouraba' Al-Sham, both extremist Islamists groups. Such clashes had made the PYD emerge as the strongest military and political opposition group defending the Kurds (and maybe the only such coordinated political group in Syria), taking control one after the other of the different cities with a Kurdish majority and of the oil fields in the Northeastern region to obtain revenues, while leading the fighting with the Jihadist groups (Al-Nusra, the Islamic State of Iraq and the Levant [ISIS], and others) and with the other FSA bodies turning to extremism. The other KNC parties accepted de facto its leadership, while Saleh Muslim, the leader of the PYD, appeared alone and was officially received as a strong player in Erbil, Ankara, and Tehran. The Kurdish question had obtained a political structure, an army, and a territory, as well as an enemy: the Jihadist groups, even those associated with the FSA.

A Northern Free Syria?

During the Cairo all-opposition conference in July 2012, few among the participants were aware that the battles for Aleppo and Damascus were under preparation. The fighters of the FSA had been grouped in brigades, the strongest being

Al-Tawhid, initially with six to seven thousand fighters and many recruits from the small and medium-sized towns such as Azaz, Marae, Tel Rifaat, al-Bab, and Manbij. The push toward the two major cities started in mid-July, leading the regime to systematically use airpower and missile bombings to break up the offensives; the Red Cross declared that Syria had entered a civil war ("Syria in Civil War" 2012).

At the same time, most of the key officers of the government's "crisis cell" were killed in a bomb attack that may have put an end to a Track 2 negotiation initiated by the Community of Sant'Egidio to solve the conflict (McElroy 2012).[59] Kofi Annan resigned as the UN-LAS secretary-general's special envoy, to be replaced on 17 August by the Algerian diplomat Lakhdar Brahimi.

The main target of the war seemed to be Aleppo, and the fighting soon reached the center of the Old City, a World Heritage site that would be severely damaged. But the city did not fall completely, with a frontline stalemate separating west from east Aleppo. This stalemate led the battles elsewhere to become more ferocious, with the FSA starting systematically to take control of the border crossing points with Iraq and Turkey and then installing its headquarters in the "liberated areas" in Northern Syria. It seized successively several major military bases and cities: Maarat Al-Nuʿman (near Aleppo, 9 October); Douma (neighborhood of Damascus, 18 October); Saraqeb (near Aleppo, 2 November); Mayadeen (near Deir-Ez-Zor, 22 November); Yarmuk Palestinian camp (neighborhood of Damascus, late December); Harem (near Aleppo on the Turkish border, 24 December); Al Thawra (near Raqqa, 11 February); Raqqa itself (6 March, the first provincial capital to fall); and Muzeirib (and a twenty-five-kilometer strip land on the Jordanian border).

The regime forces seemed to be losing the war for a while, until April 2013 when major counterattacks started, in particular on Al-Qusayr (near Homs), a major supply point to the rebel forces from Lebanon. The Lebanese Hezbollah force claimed publicly for the first time to be participating in the Syrian war. SNC and FSA leaders had pointed out very early (2011) that the Hezbollah, Iranian forces, and Shi'ite militias from Iraq were participating in the fights in Syria in order to excite sectarian feelings and solidarities; long months before that such participation was significant. The Hezbollah had sent a few fighters to protect Shiʿa villages fearing attacks and sectarian slaughter. But the real involvement dated from 2013. Al-Qusayr fell back to government forces and allies in June 2013, marking the first major setback for the FSA in the "war of liberation." These military developments led to the division of the country into two zones, separated by a shifting front line: the regime-controlled area from the coastal region to Homs and Hama, south to Damascus, and the "liberated" areas—the main one in the north and northeast, supplied from Turkey; the second in the south, supplied from Jordan, pressuring on Damascus where most of the neighborhoods were in FSA hands; and the third near Homs, supplied from Lebanon. The regime's strategy seemed to concentrate on keeping strong ties between its strongholds, the coastal area and Damascus, while ruthlessly defending the control of Homs and Hama. Aleppo was abandoned as a "Leningrad" ("Aleppo" 2013). And while the opposition tried to seize and control a "liberated" and safe haven area, the regime entrenched its military bases in precisely these areas, making them unsafe.

In parallel, the need to create a political cover for the "liberation" (or at least the "liberated" safe haven) and to circumvent the loss of popularity of the SNC on the ground had led Qatar and its allies to broker the creation of a National Coalition for Syrian Revolutionary and Opposition Forces in November 2012, grouping mostly the opposition forces that had earlier defected from the SNC. The creation of the National Coalition was prepared by an initiative of Riad Seif, a moderate businessman taking refuge in Germany, through two meetings: one in Paris with opposition forces out of the SNC, and the second in Amman, organized by foreign security services. The United States obtained the nomination of a moderate engineer and religious scholar, Moaz Al-Khatib, while Qatar and Turkey kept their control through its secretary general, the Gulf-based businessman Mustapha Sabbagh. The invitation to join the National Coalition was based on the Cairo documents, but its members soon rejected them. The SNC was not dismantled but was kept as a structure within the structure, both structures being recognized by some countries as "legitimate representative of the Syrian people," quickly unique and sole for the GCC countries, France and Turkey ("Hollande" 2012).

But the National Coalition soon entered into turmoil. Its chief, Al-Khatib, proposed an initiative to negotiate with the regime with minimal conditions,[60] an initiative called a breakthrough by Brahimi. At the same time, the SNC/Sabbagh/MB camp pushed for the nomination of an interim government, leading to further divisions. Al-Khatib finally resigned in March 2013, citing interference by Qatar and Saudi Arabia: "I have become only a means to sign some papers while there are hands from different parties involved who want to decide on behalf of the Syrians . . . and there were ambiguous agreements that I think were not in the interest of the Syrian people" ("Moaz al-Khatib" 2013). His resignation shook the National Coalition, which was taken over by the SNC and saved only by its extension later in June to include a Democratic group created by Michel Kilo, which had quit the SDF with a few others.

The National Coalition soon entered a major crisis following significant change in the region's politics: Qatar's prince retired and gave the throne to his son, while the strongman of the Qatari regime, Prime Minister Hamad Bin Jassem who also controlled foreign affairs, was ousted. The powerful man who for two years led the operations for the removal of Bashar al-Asad disappeared suddenly from the Arab League and international scene. The Syrian file leadership passed to the hands of Saudi Arabia and to its strong security man, Bandar bin Sultan. Kilo appeared to manage the necessary Saudi reshuffling of the National Coalition, nominating as its head a tribal chief closely linked to the Saudis, Ahmad Assi Jarba, who had long been their weapons' dealer to the FSA. He also launched the Democratic Union (DU), a counterpart within the National Coalition to the still MB-, Qatari-, and Turkish-dominated SNC ("Syrian Democratic Union" 2013).

On the military side, a Supreme Military Council (SMC) was created, also mainly by the Saudis, in December 2012 to encourage the military victories of the opposition. This body was assumed to channel financing, ammunitions, and weapons to the FSA and to give it some structure. However, divisions soon appeared between the different armed groups, especially as the Al-Qaida-affiliated Al-Nusra Front and ISIS went their separate ways to establishing Islamic "Emirates" (O'Bagy 2013). These divisions exploded later, especially after the loss of Al-Qusayr to the government troops in May, and then with the change in the Syrian civil war's paradigm upon the appearance of the chemical weapons issue and the U.S.-Russian deal.

A Foreign Coalition for Syria?

In February 2012, just after the collapse of the Arab League monitors' mission and the Russian and Chinese vetoes of a second UNSC resolution, French president Sarkozy called for the creation of a "contact group on Syria to find a solution to its crisis, to help implement the Arab League plan." But the real idea was similar to that concerning Libya, where a roadmap was put up for the "After Qadhafi" period. The first meeting of the Group of Friends of the Syrian People (FSG) was held in Tunisia, opened by the foreign minister, who was the nephew of the chairman of Al Nahda, the MB-affiliated Islamic party. More than seventy countries participated to the event, intended to balance the blockage of the UN Security Council. The FSG met again in Rome a year later, on 28 February 2013, and in Istanbul on 20 April, but only eleven countries—Turkey, the United States, UK, Saudi Arabia, Jordan, Egypt, United Arab Emirates, Qatar, Italy, Germany, and France—participated in its proceedings.

Thus, the FSG failed to create a strong coalition behind the SNC and the National Coalition to face Russia and China. Despite the efforts of France, the positions of the different countries of the European Union remained diversified. When a call was made in August 2013 for an international strike on Syria, following the killing of hundreds in Damascus neighborhoods by chemical weapons, the prime minister of the UK, the strongest ally of France, chose to consult his Parliament, which rejected the war. Soon after, the French president and his allies in Turkey and Saudi Arabia found themselves undercut when the U.S. president stopped the U.S. involvement in such a strike at the last minute.

How could Syria avoid a military strike, a journalist asked the U.S. secretary of state. If Asad "could turn over every single bit of his chemical weapons to the international community," answered John Kerry ("Kerry" 2013). A few hours later, Russian minister of foreign affairs Sergey Lavrov proposed such a deal, which was immediately accepted by Syrian minister of foreign affairs Walid Al-Moallem, present in Moscow (Associated Press 2013). On 14 September, Russia and the United States reached an agreement on the destruction of Syria's chemical weapons arsenal. A few days later, a UN Security Council resolution on Syria was adopted for the first time since the beginning of the uprising and the war. The deal completely changed the paradigm of the Syrian civil war. The destruction of the chemical weapons arsenal and facilities became a priority for the international community, forcing a stalemate in military conquests for several months, making the Asad regime its partner in the chemical weapons agreement, and pushing strongly to convene a "Geneva II" conference for peace in Syria. Thus, by autumn 2013 the civil war became deadlocked with broad zones partially controlled by various factions—the Syrian regime, Islamists, Kurds, FSA—a situation preferable to a rival side's victory to all outside patrons—the United States, Russia, Iran, Qatar, Saudi Arabia—leaving only the Syrian people to suffer continued massacres within and between the zones.

COULD A GENEVA II CONFERENCE HAVE BROUGHT PEACE IN SYRIA? AND WHAT PEACE?

Who Should Negotiate with Whom?

The Geneva Communiqué foresaw negotiations between Syrians—the regime on one side and the opposition on the other—to form a commonly agreed-upon "governing body" for the transition. However, reaching the proper constituencies of each party and overcoming substantial difficulties jeopardized the formation of such a coalition:

- On one hand, the political "opposition" had to go into the bargaining without the minimal level of unification and into open ground where their divisions emerged. Three main groups were called to the table: the National Coalition, living with deep divisions between the Qatari-backed SNC and the Saudi-backed "Democratic" group; the NCB, which had managed with Russian support and with its historical legitimacy to break the monopoly of the coalition but which was not accepted by the FSG (the Friends of Syria Group of countries); and the Kurds, under the umbrella of the SKC, while the group of the KNC entered the National Coalition, and the other formed by the PYD, still part of NCB, announced that it would not go to Geneva without it.
- In the previous months, these three groups had lost much of the public support from their own constituencies, and many other groups and leaders still had a good deal of public support: Moaz Al-Khatib, the former leader of the National Coalition, the different movements of the youth and the civil society, the SDF, and so on. Their exclusion from the negotiation weakened any public acceptance of its outcomes.

- Otherwise, it was not clear how the military side of the opposition was to be represented at the conference, where a ceasefire constituted an essential element. The SMC had no control on the ground, and many fighting brigades recently refused its leadership, as well as the legitimacy of the National Coalition. ISIS refused to be part of any negotiation, but continued, in Syria and in Iraq, to push to create strongholds and facts on the ground, such as strong links to tribes and combating opposition groups, that helped ISIS later take full control of large parts of Syria and Iraq. This meant that violence could explode at any time during the negotiations, making them irrelevant.
- On the government side, it was also unclear how the military was to be represented, and how the cohesion between the military apparatus and the "power body" would be maintained with evolution of the negotiations on critical issues as the dealing with ISIS, the implementation of a ceasefire, and the authority over the army during the transition.

Moreover, Geneva II also involved regional and international negotiations, as most of the Syrian players had become heavily dependent on their supporting foreign countries, with strong divisions even within each camp. Here, also, the process and outcome of Geneva II was very much dependent on difficult topics:

- The fate of Syria had become a major issue for the role of Iran in the region and the impact of the negotiations on Iran's nuclear program. Iran was deeply involved, directly or indirectly through Hezbollah, in the Syrian war. There were questions whether Iran, in its absence from Geneva, could find a way to promote its interests and protect its allies in Lebanon and Iraq within the formulas of the Geneva Communiqué, with or without Bashar al-Asad and on what basis. This might typically depend on how the U.S.-Russian deal on Syria's chemical weapons could open a way for a deal on the Iranian nuclear program, which in the end was handled as a separate issue.
- Turkey had also been deeply involved in the Syrian war, at a level endangering its own national cohesion, as well as its emergence as an economic and regional power and appearance of the "Turkish model" of globalized political Islam (Amin 2012; Kuran 2013). Bashar al-Asad deliberately retreated very early from Northern Syria in order to leave the Turkish leaders to face ISIS, the exploding Kurdish issues, and the Sunni-Shiʿa divide. Thus the Turkish negotiations in Syria very much depended on its positioning toward the ISIS form of political Islam and its dealings with the Kurdish and Alevi/Alawite issues in its own territories.
- The Gulf countries were occupied with the Arab Spring that took all other populated Arab countries into a long and bumpy transition, as other chapters in this book describe. They used their financial power, strong media outlets, and co-optation of Arab intellectuals to influence the course of the transitions and to push the Arab Spring away from their borders. Qatar took the lead in the first years and used the vector of the Muslim Brotherhood; but the leading role turned to Saudi Arabia, which used a combination of Salafi Islamists and Sunni moderate leaders as vectors. The continu-

ation of war in Syria depended on the competition between Qatar and Saudi Arabia over the leadership and control of a Sunni Crescent facing a Shiʿite one, given Egypt's long isolation from the regional scene for the difficulties of its own transition.

- Also European countries such as France and the UK were deeply involved in the Syrian conflict, as they were in Libya. France considers that it has a "historical responsibility" for Syria, its mandate from 1920 to 1946, although it lost the support of the Syrian (and Lebanese) Christians for its positions in the crisis, to the profit of Russia.[61] On the other side, the alignment of China with the Russian positions vetoing UN Security Council resolutions on Syria is striking, since China has significant economic relations and energy dependence on Saudi Arabia and Qatar.
- Finally, Geneva II negotiations resulted from the U.S.-Russian deal on the issue of Syria's chemical weapons. Both countries enjoy excellent relations with Israel. Such a deal has meant direct U.S. implication and management of the outcome, while the dominant U.S. policy after the collapse of the Eastern bloc has been "leading from behind" (Rubin 2013). Russia is not the USSR, and its strong implication in the Syrian conflict cannot be understood as presented in the media as a new expression of the old Cold War. It can only be explained by vital competition with other old and emerging powers on the Middle East and beyond, and its fear of having an Islamic presence too close to its borders, against which it saw Asad as the best guarantee.

Thus in many aspects the regional and international negotiations around Geneva II and the fate of Syria had the potential for shaping a "new world order" (Sharma 2013).

What the Negotiations Are About

The situation in Syria had changed drastically compared to the moment when the Geneva Communiqué was agreed to, or the subsequent Cairo conference of the opposition that led to the National Charter was convened in June 2012, before the launching of the battles of Aleppo and Damascus. In the following years, Syria had fallen into pieces, de facto divided into several parts, with violent friction along their boundaries and borders with neighbor states. Each piece has its own militias, its own governing bodies, its own leaders, its own divided political scene, its own identities, its own legislations (shariʿa courts and so on), its own ways for financing, and its own internal and foreign trade: the Syria of the coastal area down to Damascus, which the "power body" and the regular army share with their Shabiha gangs and pro-Iranian militias; the Syria of the North, around Aleppo, that the National Coalition disputes with local FSA groups and some extremist militias such as the Al-Nusra Front linked to al-Qaeda; the Kurdish Syria of the PCWK and SKC; the Syria of ISIS, strongly linked to the Sunni areas of Iraq then proclaimed as an Islamic State (IS); the Syria of the "liberated" South, near the Jordanian border;

the Syria of the Eastern Ghouta suburbs of Damascus, and so on. Also, there has been a substantial transfer of population inside Syria and to the surrounding countries: Lebanon, Jordan, Turkey, Egypt, and Iraq. The city of Latakia, controlled by the regime, received hundreds of thousands of internally displaced persons (IDPs) from the Aleppo region; the Homs region population was spread wide internally, including in ISIS-controlled cities, and abroad; a third to a half of the total population was scattered.

The challenge is no longer one of reaching an agreement on a "governing body with full executive powers," but rather on how any single body could unite Syria again: its armies, its public services, its rules and regulations. . . . Weapons are everywhere; no elections are reasonably possible in the foreseeable future; hatred, sectarianism, and distrust are imbedded; famine and disease are rampant; and the humanitarian burden has become tremendous inside Syria as well as in neighboring countries. This is a monumental challenge that will need enormous imagination and political courage, and a long time.

Notes

1. The term "Shiite crescent" was coined in 2004 by King Abdallah of Jordan; see Wright and Baker (2004). This crescent links Iran, South Iraq, Eastern Saudi Arabia, Central Turkey, Syria, and South Lebanon, the homeland of Hezbollah. The "Sunni axis" emerged when Turkey came to be ruled by political Islam and established strong relations with the Gulf countries, especially Saudi Arabia. See Guzansky and Lindenstrauss (2013).

2. There is a controversy on the starting date of the Syrian revolution, and this controversy has a symbolic significance. Some place it 17 February, when a spontaneous demonstration erupted in Old City Damascus after an incident with a policeman, and claim that the "Syrian people cannot be humiliated." Others put it on 15 March, as Internet and Facebook activists had long called for an uprising on this date, but not much really happened. A third group place the starting date on 18 March, when Deraa and its Hauran region experienced a major uprising after the arrest and torture of the young adolescents.

3. See reports of eyewitness accounts such as "Eyewitness tells" (2011).

4. See the full text of Asad's speech at http://www.al-bab.com/arab/docs/syria/bashar_assad_speech_110330.htm (accessed 3 September 2014).

5. The state of emergency law (Legislative law no. 51 dated 22 December 1962) was issued a few months before the coup of 8 March 1963, which has permitted the Baath Party to rule Syria. It restricts personal and collective freedoms and allows authorities to put violators before military tribunals. It has been in place since then (over fifty years).

6. The Jezireh is the northeastern region of Syria, between the Euphrates and Tigris Rivers, which experienced in 2003–2004 massive internal migration outflow, exacerbated after the drought of 2008–2009; see Aita (2009).

7. Najib was reported to have told the traditional leader: "Forget your children. If you really want your children, you should make more children. If you don't know how to make more children, send your women, we'll make them for you."

8. The symbolism of this alliance was the core of a debate on why the demonstrations always start in mosques, the only place where people could gather with some immunity.

9. For example, the activists included Suheir Atassi, who entered the SNC as a leader of the Syrian Revolution General Commission (SRGC); and Mazen Darwish, a journalist and human rights activist who has been jailed since 2012.

10. The Facebook page is available at https://www.facebook.com/Syrian.Revolution/info (accessed 30 November 2014).

11. A polemic emerged on the naming of the Fridays. Normally the choice is made through voting on the Syrian Revolution Facebook page, but as the administrators of this page were hidden, the slip in the names of the days from moral to political and religious reflected the divisions within the youth and political movements. See, for example, Atassi and Wikstrom (2012); Friedman (2011); and http://www.kebreet.net/%D8%AF%D8%B1%D8%A7%D8%B3%D8%A9-%D8%B9%D9%86-%D8%A3%D8%B3%D9%85%D8%A7%D8%A1-%D8%AC%D9%85%D8%B9-%D8%A7%D9%84%D8%AB%D9%88%D8%B1%D8%A9-%D8%A7%D9%84%D8%B3%D9%88%D8%B1%D9%8A%D8%A9/.

12. A big demonstration occurred this day in Hama, leading to the killing of seventy people. The next Saturday saw equally big demonstrations in "support of Hama." On Khatib, see Macleod and Flamand (2011).

13. The Syrian population was shocked by the "leaked" videos of the takeover by security services of the Sunni village of Bayda, near Banyas, in the heart of the Alawi Mountains. With an Alawi accent, armed men were kicking demonstrators with their boots and yelling, "you want freedom, you (insult)" (see "Syrian Security" 2011). The images have ignited the sectarian feelings around the country.

14. The Alawites are an Islamic mystical religious group, living mainly in the coastal mountains and in Homs. Contrary to Ismaelis and Druzes, they follow the branch of Twelvers (twelve Imams after Mohammad, while only seven for the formers) of Shiʿa Islam (prominent in Iran, south of Iraq and Lebanon). This name of the group had been given in the early days of the French mandate, as the old name of the group, Nusayris, was considered degrading. The Alawis are also present in the Sandjak of Alexandretta (the present Turkish province of Hatay); they are historically and religiously linked to the Turkish Alevis (formerly named Kizilbas). The Assad family ruling Syria since 1970 belongs to this group, but Bashar al-Asad is married to a Sunni Muslim woman originally from Homs.

15. See George 2003. The Damascus Spring" was a civic and political movement in the early 2000s, following the accession of Bashar al-Asad to presidency, which asked for reforms and more freedom. The movement was also driven by committees: "the committees for the revival of the civil society," which used to hold discussion forums in homes and public spaces.

16. Some of the activists and committees received assistance, financing, and communication equipment from international organization such as Avaaz or Hivos and even directly from some foreign countries. This is what Bashar al-Asad calls the "foreign conspiracy inciting sedition."

17. The Local Coordination Committees' website is available at http://www.lccsyria.org/. For a statement from one of the founders, see Omar Idlebi, at http://www.maalouma.org/studies-awrak.php?table=dirasat&id=8.

18. The Syrian Revolution General Commission's website is available at http://www.srgcommission.org/.

19. See, for example, Sham press, http://www.champress.net/; Syrian Revolution News, http://www.syrrevnews.com/; Shahba Press, http://www.shahbapress.com/; Aleppo News, http://halabnews.com/; Sana of the Revolution, http://www.sana-revo.com/news/.

20. The National Coordination Committee for Democratic Change in Syria's website is available at http://syrianncb.org/.

21. Namely the Democratic Arab Socialist Union, a Nasserist party with large popular bases especially in Damascus and Aleppo; the Syrian Democratic People's Party (DPP, the former Communist Party political bureau, led by Riad Al Turk, who remained in prison for nineteen years and was called by some "the Syrian Mandela," but the DPP left the NCB because of personal rivalries with some members); the Communist Labor Party (a leftist party, strongly present among the Alawite intellectuals, which suffered the highest number of political prisoners during the repression of the 1980s); the Arab Socialists Movement; the Democratic Arab Socialist Baath party (the branch of the Baath Party that Hafez Assad had belonged to before making his 1970 coup d'état following the events of "black September." See Seale (1990) and the Arab Revolutionary Workers Party.

22. Following the Syrian uprising of 1979–1982, led by the Muslim Brotherhood, and supported and armed by Iraq's Saddam Hussein waging the war against the Iranian revolution, the movement had been severely repressed and its membership punished by death (Law no. 49 of 1980).

23. See, for example, Alfoneh (2013). Turkey was one of the last countries to break with Bashar al-Asad. During the development of the uprising, a delegation of forty Turkish security men and civil servants, led by the minister of foreign affairs, Ahmet Davutoglu, visited Syria in April and August 2011 to advise on reforms. Including the Muslim Brotherhood in a new government was thought to be part of these reforms. See Bakir (2011); Balci (2012).

24. Literally, the word comes from *shabah* (the ghost), which is a nickname given to Mercedes-Benz cars that some of the power system clientele use to show off.

25. http://www.mpil.de/en/pub/archive/projekte_2010_11/globaler_wissenstransfer/constitutional_reform_in_arab_/syrien.cfm.

26. Agence France Press, quoted in *Al Rakoba*, 19 June 2011, http://www.alrakoba.net/news.php?action=show&id=23342.

27. In October 2013 this became the Army of Islam, establishing distance from the Syrian Coalition and the Free Syrian Army.

28. Khatib is the thirteen-year-old boy tortured and killed by the security forces for whom Friday, 3 June 2011, has been named "Children of the Revolution"; see above note 11. Ibrahim Al Qashoosh was a thirty-five-year-old young man from Hama who invented slogans and songs for its massive demonstrations, calling for the "departure of Bashar." He was arrested during the massive demonstration of Hama on 1 July 2011 and was found the next day in the Orontes River with his throat cut. See Shadid (2011b).

29. The Sandjak of Alexandretta was part of Syria until 1936, when it was conceded by the French mandate to Turkey, to be named Hatay province. Syria did not officially recognize this annexation, especially as it ruled out a decision of the League of Nations, as its capital Antiochus is the seat of most regional Christian archdioceses, and as a large share of its population are Arab Alawites. However, following the Turkish-Syrian crisis of 1999 and the normalization of the relations between the countries after 2005, Syrian official maps started not to include Alexandretta.

30. The Damascus Declaration was a call launched in October 2005 for "peaceful and gradual reforms" against the "authoritarian, totalitarian and cliquish" regime, following the assassination of Rafiq Hariri in February 2005. It has gathered most of the activists of the Committee for the Revival of the Civil Society, as well as the political parties of the National Democratic Rally; also included for the first time since the 1980s is the Muslim Brotherhood, which soon quit establishing, with former vice president Abdel Halim Khaddam, the National Salvation Front. It has since become an umbrella organization for political opposition activists, mainly dominated by the DPP. See "Damascus Declaration" (2012).

In particular among businessmen financiers were Ghassan Abboud, who had fled Syria after a business dispute with Rami Makhlouf that involved control over Orient TV, which he created in 2009 in Damascus; Kamal Sankar, the former Mercedes Benz dealer in Syria, also in a dispute with Makhlouf; and Mouayyad Rashid, who made his fortune in Nigeria and who recently opened a private university in Syria.

31. The text of the Damascus Declaration, written by Michel Kilo and Abdel Razak Id, stated: "Islam—which is the religion and ideology of the majority, with its lofty intentions, higher values, and tolerant canon law—is the more prominent cultural component in the life of the nation and the people." See full text in "Damascus Declaration" (2005).

32. Until this moment, as in Egypt, Tunisia, and Libya, the Syrian demonstrations used to raise the national flag, sometimes with the word "freedom" written between its two stars. However, in Libya, the uprising adopted the old royal flag, after the creation of the National Council for Transition, to oppose the Muammar Qadhafi state.

33. Levy was the instigator of the creation of the Libyan NCT and supporter of military intervention in this country. He was known as pro-Israeli, and the meeting held at his initiative was seen by many as a tentative push of the Syrian revolution to the Libyan civil war fate. See "Rassemblement" (2011).

34. Bishara is an Israeli-Palestinian and former deputy of the Knesset, who was banned by the Israelis for having met with the enemy Bashar al-Asad.

35. This was the first time that the word *Coalition* was chosen to name an opposition body.

36. More information on the Syrian National Council is available from its website: http://www.syriannationalcouncil.com/AboutUsEN.html.

37. Basma Kodmani is a political scientist based in France, who previously was responsible for the Middle East desk at the Institut Français des Relations Internationales (IFRI) and at the Ford Foundation office. Formerly married to a PLO activist, she was involved in the Israeli-Palestinian negotiations. Obaida Nahas is a MB scholar based in the UK.

38. From the initial program of the Syrian National Council. "Political Programme for the Syrian National Council," posted 20 November 2011 on the website of the Local Coordinating Committees of Syria, http://www.lccsyria.org/2630 (accessed 25 February 2015). Also available as "SNC: Political Program," Syria in Crisis, Carnegie Endowment for International Peace, http://carnegieendowment.org/syriaincrisis/?fa=48407&reloadFlag=1 (accessed 25 February 2015).

39. On 9 October 2011 the French Ministry of Foreign Affairs exerted pressure to cancel a press conference organized for Michel Kilo and other activists visiting France. First announced at the Centre d'Accueil de la Presse Etrangere, the press conference finally took place at *Le Monde* newspaper premises. Such pressure had been applied twice in the past for foreign dictators, when Kilo was a former political prisoner and was granted a visa by the French authorities, officially for the health treatment of his son. Later on, Kilo stayed in France, with the French authorities pressing him to join the SNC. Most of the other known activists present in France had experienced similar pressures. Kilo finally joined the National Coalition when it was "expanded" at the end of May 2013. See "Prevents" (2011).

40. It is worth noting that the Libyan NTC and the Syrian SNC are very different in nature, even if the French and Qatari authorities were strongly involved in the formation of both. The NTC is mostly constituted of civil servants, while the SNC is organized as a coalition of political groups (MB, Damascus Declaration, LCC, etc.), which form its backbone, adding personalities and representatives of ethnic or religious groups. Many of the key players of the SNC had always lived abroad and had no experience with Syrian state institutions. This very much influences the trajectory and the discourse of the SNC. The NCB was also created mainly as a coalition of political groups, also with no civil servants.

41. The Arab League is organized in a General Secretariat, led during the Syrian crisis by the Egyptian Nabil Al Arabi, which has little executive power, and in a Ministerial Committee, composed of Arab ministers of foreign affairs, which is the decision maker. The chairmanship of the

Ministerial Committee changes by alphabetical order between Arab countries. Qatar managed to take this chairmanship for several rounds during the crisis. See the Arab League's website, http://www.arableagueonline.org/.

42. Homs is one of the oldest towns to include an important urbanized Alawite community. It is the major crossroad city between the line of internal cities from Damascus to Aleppo, the coastal region (Alawites stronghold), and the Jezireh. It is also the hometown of Burhan Ghalioun, the chairman of the SNC, Riad Al Turk, head of the DPP, and Razan Zeitoun, a leader activist of the LCC. The events in Homs started with clashes between the different city areas, leading to kidnappings and killings. Also, the FSA chose Homs as a bigger city for their military operations after the fall of Rastan, although Homs can be easily supplied by weapons from Northern Lebanon.

43. The signatories for the SNC were Burhan Ghalioun (chairman), Haytham Maleh, Walid Bunni, Catherine Al Talli; and for the NCB were Haytham Manna (now representative abroad), Mohammad Hijazi, Saleh Muslim Mouhammad (PYD). See "Agreement between" 2011.

44. It is worth noting that Ghalioun never resigned officially from the NCB, and that he threatened publicly to leave the SNC if his chairman mandate was not renewed; see http://www.zengil.net/dp/?p=1957.

45. Sida was a university professor in Libya in the early 1990s and has since taken refuge in Sweden. See "Kurd Moderate" (2012). Sabra is a member of the Central Committee of the DPP and of the Executive Committee of the Damascus Declaration. He went into exile in March 2012, after two arrests by the security services during the uprising. See "Syria Opposition Bloc" (2012).

46. Also joined by Kamal Al Labwani, Walid Al Bunni, Catherine Al Talli, Fawaz Tello, Ammar Qurabi, and his "Change current," etc. "Defection" (2014).

47. See the Syrian Democratic Forum (now named the Forum of the National Call) website at http://syriandemocraticforum.org/ (accessed 25 February 2015).

48. See http://syriandemocraticforum.org/?p=133 (accessed 25 February 2015).

49. See translation of final text in Eriksson (2012). The LAS and some foreign countries imposed the presence of participants not approved by the preparatory committee, such as the activist from Homs Khaled Abu Salah, a tribal representative and a Kurdish religious scholar. Most of the confusion was created by these participants.

50. The MB had succeeded during the conference in imposing that the historical slogan "Religion is for God, the Fatherland is for everyone" be taken out of the initial version by the Preparatory Committee; but the text is clear enough to specify that the state could not be based on shariʿa, and that it should guarantee freedom of conscience and religious choice.

51. In the Preparatory Committee, the term "Kurdish people," on which the Kurdish parties were insisting, was used instead of "Kurdish Nationality." Some troublemakers voiced complaints against both formulations, which led the Kurdish participants to leave the conference and to meet alone with other participants, the LAS secretary general, and the U.S. ambassador. Finally, they agreed to return if the Preparatory Committee wording was adopted, but the final declaration had already been finalized. The agreement of the Kurdish parties on the initial formulation was later adopted in the proceedings of the "Follow-up Committee" also deposited at the LAS.

52. See the photo at http://www.gettyimages.co.uk/detail/news-photo/french-president-francois-hollande-poses-with-leader-of-the-news-photo/150556950. It is worth noting that a meeting followed between Hollande and Qatar's prince, and that a U.S. State Department speaker announced a few hours later that such a measure is a "too early step."

53. Mabatli (Mabta in Kurdish) is a small town in the Afrin district, lying between Aleppo governorate and Alexandretta (Hatta), with a majority of Kurdish Alawites. See Ehmed (2010). The Yezidis are a small religious community living in Iraq, Syria, and Turkey. In Syria, they are mostly present in two locations: the Jezireh, in the historical Sinjar Mountains, and in the Kurdish Mountains (Kurd-Dagh) near Afrine, northwest of Aleppo. Many members of the more import-

ant Yezidi community of Iraq emigrated to Syria after the sectarian violence of 2006–2007. Their beliefs are a mixture of old Mesopotamian traditions, old Iranian and Greek religions, Christianity, and Islam. They venerate the Umayad Caliph Yezid, whom the Shiʿa blame for killing their martyr Hussein, grandson of the Prophet Mohammed. See *Encyclopedia of Islam*.

54. Following a soccer game on 12 March 2004 in Qamishli (Qamishlo for the Kurds), troubles occurred between Arabs and Kurds. The problem quickly spread all over the regions inhabited by the Kurds and transformed into a real uprising, with burning of police stations and the shutting down of public services. The unrest flared up again in May and June 2005 after the assassination of Sheikh Ma'shuq Khaznawi.

55. Mishʿal Temo is an activist and politician who in 2005 founded the Kurdish Future Movement after being part of the Committees for the Revival of the Civil Society (CRCS) of the Damascus Spring and his involvement in the 2004 Kurdish uprising. He was jailed by the secret services in 2008.

56. On Deutsche Welle TV, see "Kurds" (2011).

57. Erdogan's Turkey and Barzani's KRG had established a strategic partnership, and the latter has been received in Ankara as a head of state, which led to strong Iraqi-Turkish tensions. But the positions of the two could differ on the Syrian issue and evolve with time: for Erbil's functioning of internal politics and for Turkey's functioning of its negotiations with the PKK.

58. The text of the Erbil/Holeir agreement is not public, but see Pollock (2012).

59. The Community of Sant'Egidio had negotiated the peace process following the civil war in Algeria. It called for a meeting of opposition figures a few days after the Cairo conference, resulting in the Roma Declaration. The Sant'Egidio community members indicated that they were negotiating with the regime, and precisely with General Hasan Turkmani, the minister of defense, and General Assef Shawkat, the brother-in-law of Bashar al-Asad and head of security. Both were assassinated during the attack.

60. Such as the release of political prisoners and the granting of passports for the Syrian refugees. See Black (2013).

61. Syria was under the French mandate between 1920 and 1946. The UK helped the Syrians end the mandate. See "France" (2013).

References

"Action Group for Syria Final Communiqué." 2012. 30 June. http://www.un.org/News/dh/infocus/Syria/FinalCommuniqueActionGroupforSyria.pdf (accessed 4 September 2014).

"Activists at Syrian 'National Dialogue' Call for End to Violence." 2011. CNN, 11 July. http://edition.cnn.com/2011/WORLD/meast/07/10/syria.unrest/index.html (accessed 4 September 2014).

"Agreement between the National Coordination Body for Democratic Change (NCBNCB) and the Syrian National Council (SNCSNC), to be Submitted to the Secretariat of the Arab League as a Joint Political Document for the Congress of Syrian Opposition That Is Expected to Take Place under the Umbrella of the Arab League in January 2012." 2011. Cairo, 30 December. http://www.al-akhbar.com/system/files/Mannaa_English.pdf (accessed 4 September 2014).

"'An agreement' with the coordination draft! And internationalization is still required!" [in Arabic]. 2011. *Middle East Transparent*, 30 December. http://www.metransparent.com/spip.php?page=imprimer_article&id_article=17302&lang=ar (accessed 4 September 2014).

Ahmed, Mohammed, and Moustafa Al-Dabbi. 2012. "Report of the LAS Observers Mission to Syria, December 24, 2011–January 18, 2012-01-26." http://www.foreignpolicy.com/files/fp_uploaded_documents/120131_1306_001.pdf (accessed 4 September 2014).

Aita, Samir. 2006. *Syria: What Reforms While a Storm Is Building?* Arab Reform Initiative, April.

———. 2007. "Reform, State and Politics in Syria." In *The Changing Role of the State*, edited by Samir Radwan and Manuel Riesco. Cairo: Economic Research Forum (ERF).

———. 2009. *Labor Markets Policies and Institutions, with a Focus on Inclusion, Equal Opportunity and the Informal Economy: The Case of Syria*. Geneva: International Labor Office (ILO).

———. 2011a. "Follow the Money." *Le Monde diplomatique*, English ed., April.

———. 2011b. *Les travailleurs arabes hors-la-loi*. Paris: L'Harmattan.

"Aleppo like Leningrad under Siege—Syrian Dep. PM." 2013. *Voice of Russia*, 29 January. http://voiceofrussia.com/2013_01_29/Aleppo-like-Leningrad-under-siege-Syrian-Dep-PM/ (accessed 3 September 2014).

Alfoneh, Ali. 2013. "Turkey's Strategy in Syria." *Foundation for Defense of Democracies*, 19 September. http://www.defenddemocracy.org/media-hit/turkeys-strategy-in-syria/ (accessed 3 September 2014).

"Altenseekiet: Born from the Underground." 2014. *Al-Akhbar*, 3 September. http://www.al-akhbar.com/node/22408 (accessed 3 September 2014).

Amin, Samir 2012. "The Failed Emergence of Egypt, Turkey and Iran." *Pambazuka News*, issue 590, 21 June. http://pambazuka.org/en/category/features/83115 (accessed 16 November 2014).

Annan, Kofi. 2012. "My Departing Advice on How to Save Syria." *Financial Times*, 2 August. http://www.ft.com/intl/cms/s/2/b00b6ed4-dbc9-11e1-8d78-00144feab49a.html#axzz2hMOWCQze (accessed 4 September 2014).

"Arms Smuggling into Syria Flourishes." 2011. *Naharnet*, 16 October. http://www.naharnet.com/stories/en/17624 (accessed 4 September 2014).

Associated Press. 2012. "Hollande: France Would Recognize Syrian Opposition Government Once Formed." *Haaretz*, 27 August. http://www.haaretz.com/news/middle-east/hollande-france-would-recognize-syrian-opposition-government-once-formed-1.461028 (accessed 4 September 2014).

———. 2013. "Syria Accepts Russian Proposal to Surrender Chemical Weapons, Foreign Minister Says." *Huffington Post*, 10 November. http://www.huffingtonpost.com/2013/09/10/syria-accepts-proposal-to-surrender-chemical-weapons_n_3898941.html (accessed 3 September 2014).

Atassi, Basma, and Cajsa Wikstrom. 2012. "The Battle to Name Syria's Friday Protests." Al Jazeera, 14 April. http://www.aljazeera.com/indepth/features/2012/04/201241314026709762.html (accessed 3 September 2014).

Bakir, Ali Husain. 2011. "The Determinants of the Turkish Position towards the Syrian Crisis: The Immediate Dimensions and Future Repercussions." Doha: Arab Center for Research and Policy Studies. http://english.dohainstitute.org/file/get/610dc2f0-d4e7-41ff-a8ee-7a589c7ee8da.pdf (accessed 3 September 2014).

Balci, Bayram. 2012. "Turkey's Relations with the Syrian Opposition." *Carnegie Endowment for International Peace*, 13 April. http://carnegieendowment.org/2012/04/13/turkey-s-relations-with-syrian-opposition/a88u (accessed 3 September 2014).

"Bashar al-Asad Issues Amnesty Decree for Criminals." 2013. *Times of Israel*, 16 April. http://www.timesofisrael.com/bashar-assad-issues-amnesty-decree-for-criminals/ (accessed 4 September 2014).

Black, Ian. 2012. "Kofi Annan Resigns as Syria Envoy." *Guardian*, 2 August. http://www.theguardian.com/world/2012/aug/02/kofi-annan-resigns-syria-envoy (accessed 4 September 2014).

———. 2013. "Divided Syrian Opposition Ponders Leader's Offer of Talks with Assad." *Guardian*, 8 February. http://www.theguardian.com/world/2013/feb/08/syrian-opposition-rows-talks-assad (accessed 3 September 2014).

Bolling, Jeffrey. 2012. "Rebel Groups in Northern Aleppo Province." Institute for the Study of War, Backgrounder, 29 August. http://www.understandingwar.org/sites/default/files/Backgrounder_RebelGroupsNorthernAleppo.pdf.

"Cairo Documents: Joint Political Vision." 2012. Carnegie Middle East Center, 8 November. http://carnegie-mec.org/2012/11/08/cairo-documents-joint-political-vision/exg9 (accessed 4 September 2014).

Charbonneau, Louis. 2012. "Russia U.N. Veto on Syria Aimed at Crushing West's Crusade." Reuters, 8 February. http://www.reuters.com/article/2012/02/08/us-un-russia-idUSTRE8170BK20120208 (accessed 4 September 2014).

"Clarification from Hazem Nahar . . . the Doha meeting: the most serious tentative from the Syrian opposition" [in Arabic]. *Zaman Al Wasl*, 17 September 2011. http://www.zamanalwsl.net/news/21568.html (accessed 25 February 2015).

"The Damascus Declaration." 2012. Carnegie Middle East Center, 1 March. http://carnegie-mec.org/publications/?fa=48514 (accessed 4 September 2014).

"Damascus Declaration in English." 2005. *Syria Comment* (Joshua Landis's blog), 1 November. http://faculty-staff.ou.edu/L/Joshua.M.Landis-1/syriablog/2005/11/damascus-declaration-in-english.htm (accessed 4 September 2014).

"Defection of a prominent group for the Syrian National Council opposition" [in Arabic]. 2014. BBC News, 27 February. http://www.bbc.co.uk/arabic/middleeast/2012/02/120226_syria_opposition_splinter.shtml (accessed 4 September 2014).

"Discord among Arab Monitors as Russia Warns of Syria Intervention." 2012. *Al Akhbar*, 12 January. http://english.al-akhbar.com/node/3319 (accessed 4 September 2014).

DPA. 2011. "Arab League Chief Urges Stability in Syria during Assad Meet." *Haaretz*, 10 September. http://www.haaretz.com/news/middle-east/arab-league-chief-urges-stability-in-syria-during-assad-meet-1.383639 (accessed 3 September 2014).

Ehmed, Maya. 2010. "Alawite Kurds in Syria: Ethnic Discrimination and Dectarian Privileges." *Kurdnet*, 22 July. http://www.ekurd.net/mismas/articles/misc2010/7/syriakurd268.htm (accessed 4 September 2014).

"Erbil: Chairman of the Syrian National Council Comments on the Kurdish Question." 2012. From *Kurdwatch*, 23 April. Available at Joshua Landis, "Week's Round Up (4 May 2012)," *Syria Comment* (blog), 4 May 2012. http://www.joshualandis.com/blog/weeks-round-up-may-4-2012/ (accessed 4 September 2014).

Eriksson, Leif. 2012. "Syria: The Final Statement for the Syrian Opposition Conference." *Other Suns* (blog), 6 July. http://othersuns.wordpress.com/2012/07/06/syria-the-final-statement-for-the-syrian-opposition-conference/ (accessed 4 September 2014). See also http://syriandemocraticforum.org/?p=136 (accessed 25 February 2015).

"Exclusive: Syrian Opposition Conference Organized by Muslim Brotherhood Leader." 2008. *Global Muslim Brotherhood Daily Watch*, 25 April. http://globalmbreport.org/?p=4570 (accessed 4 September 2014).

"Extension of three months for proof pipe at the head of the Syrian National Council Opposition" [in Arabic]. 2012. *Alittihad*, 16 February. http://www.alittihad.ae/details.php?id=16288&y=2012&article=full (accessed 4 September 2014).

"An eyewitness tells the events of Daraa" [in Arabic]. 2011. Al Jazeera, 11 March. http://www.aljazeera.net/news/pages/14827695-c025-4bfb-9202-841a7cbc833f (accessed 3 September 2014).

"The final statement of the consultative meeting for national dialogue held in Damascus" [in Arabic]. 2014. *Middle East Watch*, July. http://www.middleeastwatch.net/%D8%A7%D9%84%D8%A8%D9%8A%D8%A7%D9%86-%D8%A7%D9%84%D8%AE%D8%AA%D8%A7%D9%85%D9%8A.html (accessed 4 September 2014).

"La France en Syrie: Une longue responsabilité." 2013. *France Culture*, 28 September. http://www.franceculture.fr/emission-concordance-des-temps-la-france-en-syrie-une-longue-responsabilite-2013-09-28 (accessed 3 September 2014).

Friedman, Uri. 2011. "How Syrian Activists Name Their Friday Protests." *Wire*, 16 September. http://www.theatlanticwire.com/global/2011/09/how-syrian-activists-name-their-friday-protests/42586/ (accessed 3 September 2014).

Gelvin, James L. 1998. *Divided Loyalties, Nationalism and Mass Politics in Syria at the Close of Empire*. Berkeley: University of California Press.

George, Alan. 2003. *Syria: Neither Bread Nor Freedom*. London: Zed Books.

"Ghalioun: The agreement with the NCB is only a draft" [in Arabic]. 2013. CNN, 7 February. http://arabic.cnn.com/2012/syria.2011/1/1/syria.opposition/index.html (accessed 4 September 2014).

Ghalioun, Barhan. 2011. "Syria Opposition Leader Interview Transcript: 'Stop the Killing Machine.'" *Wall Street Journal*, 2 December. http://online.wsj.com/article/SB10001424052970203833104577071960384240668.html.

Goldstone, Jack. 1991. *Revolution and Rebellion in the Early Modern World*. Berkeley: University of California Press.

Guzansky, Yoel, and Gallia Lindenstrauss. 2013. "The Emergence of a Sunni Axis in the Middle East." *Strategic Assessment* 16, no. 1 (April).

Hamidi, Ibrahim. 2013. "Brigades of Islamic Syria Unite in Anticipation of Regional Support for a Political Solution." *Al Hayat*, 5 October. http://alhayat.com/Details/558955 and the Israeli intelligence report (accessed 4 September 2014).

Harris, Paul, Martin Chulov, David Batty, and Damien Pearse. 2012. "Syria Resolution Vetoed by Russia and China at United Nations." *Guardian*, 4 February. http://www.theguardian.com/world/2012/feb/04/assad-obama-resign-un-resolution (accessed 4 September 2014).

Hassan, Sayyed Mahmoud. 2012. "Syrian opponents announce from Cairo the creation of the Syrian Democratic Forum" [in Arabic]. *Al Ahram*, 21 February. http://gate.ahram.org.eg/News/175258.aspx (accessed 25 February 2015).

"Hollande reconnaît la coalition nationale syrienne." 2012. *Europe1*, 13 November. http://www.europe1.fr/Politique/Hollande-reconnait-la-coalition-nationale-syrienne-1310361/ (accessed 3 September 2014).

"Homs 'Massacre' Leaves 260 Dead." 2012. *Telegraph*, 4 February. http://www.telegraph.co.uk/news/worldnews/middleeast/syria/9061181/Homs-massacre-leaves-260-dead.html (accessed 4 September 2014).

"Houla: How a Massacre Unfolded." 2012. BCC News, 8 June. http://www.bbc.co.uk/news/world-middle-east-18233934 (accessed 4 September 2014).

ICG (International Crisis Group). 2013. *Syria's Kurds : A Struggle within the Struggle*. Middle East Report no. 136, 22 January.

Al Jazeera. 2011. "Syria Enters in Civil War with Combat between Syrian Army Soldiers Defectors." YouTube, 11 November 2011. http://youtu.be/vRJ57US6x_c (accessed 25 February 2015).

"Kerry Says Syria Can Avoid Military Strikes If al-Assad Gives Up Chemical Weapons." 2013. Euronews, 9 September. http://www.euronews.com/2013/09/09/kerry-says-syria-can-avoid-military-strikes-if-al-assad-gives-up-chemical-/ (accessed 3 September 2014).

Kilo, Michel. 2011. "Syrian Activist: Regime Making Political Solutions Impossible." People's World, 28 July. http://peoplesworld.org/syrian-activist-regime-making-political-solutions-impossible/ (accessed 16 November 2014).

"Kofi Annan's Six-Point Plan for Syria." 2012. Al Jazeera, 27 March. http://www.aljazeera.com/news/middleeast/2012/03/201232715311767387.html (accessed 4 September 2014).

Kuran, Timur. 2013. "Political Islam's Loss of Democratic Legitimacy." Project Syndicate, 2 August. http://www.project-syndicate.org/commentary/political-islam-s-retreat-from-pluralism-and-legitimacy-by-timur-kuran.

"The Kurdish National Council in Syria." 2012. Carnegie Middle East Center, 15 February. http://carnegie-mec.org/publications/?fa=48502 (accessed 4 September 2014).

"Kurds Are Genuine Migrants/Kurden sind wie geborene Immigranten." 2011. *MESOP*, 29 October. http://www.mesop.de/2011/10/29/kurds-are-genuin-migrants-kurden-sind-wie-geborene-immigranten/ (accessed 3 September 2014).

Kurd Watch. 2013. "What Does the Syrian-Kurdish Opposition Want? Politics between Erbil, Sulaymaniah, Damascus and Qandil." Kurd Watch Report no. 9, September. European Center for Kurdish Studies, Berlin. http://www.kurdwatch.org/pdf/KurdWatch_A009_en_Parteien2.pdf.

Landis, Joshua. 2011a. "The Final Declaration of the Antalya Opposition Conference." *Syria Comment* (blog), 4 June. http://www.joshualandis.com/blog/the-final-declaration-of-the-antalya-opposition-conference/ (accessed 4 September 2014).

———. 2011b. "Free Syrian Army Founded by Seven Officers to Fight the Syrian Army." *Syria Comment* (blog), 29 July. http://www.joshualandis.com/blog/free-syrian-army-established-to-fight-the-syrian-army/ (accessed 4 September 2014).

———. 2011c. "Syrian Opposition Meeting in Antalya: Day Two." *Syria Comment* (blog), 2 June. http://www.joshualandis.com/blog/syrian-opposition-meeting-in-antalya-day-two/ (accessed 4 September 2014).

Landis, Joshua, and Joe Pace. 2006–2007. "The Syrian Opposition." *Washington Quarterly* 30, no. 1 (Winter): 45–68.

Lowe, Robert. 2006. "The Syrian Kurds: A People Discovered." Chatham House, Briefing Paper, January. http://www.chathamhouse.org/sites/default/files/public/Research/Middle%20East/bpsyriankurds.pdf.

Macleod, Hugh, and Annasofie Flamand. 2011. "Tortured and Killed: Hamza al-Khateeb, Age 13." Al Jazeera, 31 May. http://www.aljazeera.com/indepth/features/2011/05/201153185927813389.html (accessed 3 September 2014).

Manna, Haytham. 2011. "Intervention by Mr. Samir Aita" [in Arabic]. YouTube video, 4 August. http://www.youtube.com/watch?v=NL1h8aegRN4 (accessed 4 September 2014).

McElroy, Damien. 2012. "Assad's Brother-in-Law and Top Syrian Officials Killed in Damascus Suicide Bomb." *Telegraph*, 18 July. http://www.telegraph.co.uk/news/worldnews/middleeast/syria/9408321/Assads-brother-in-law-and-top-Syrian-officials-killed-in-Damascus-suicide-bomb.html (accessed 3 September 2014).

McGreal, Chris, and Martin Chulov. 2011. "Syria: Assad Must Resign, Says Obama." *Guardian*, 18 August. http://www.theguardian.com/world/2011/aug/18/syria-assad-must-resign-obama (accessed 3 September 2014).

Middle East Agency. 2012. "Al Arabi meets the delegation of the Syrian Democratic Forum" [in Arabic]. 11 April. http://www3.youm7.com/News.asp?NewsID=650842.

"Moaz al-Khatib: The Priority Is to Save Syria." 2013. Al Jazeera, 11 May. http://www.aljazeera.com/programmes/talktojazeera/2013/05/20135101411126813 80.html (accessed 3 September 2014).

National Coordination Body for Democratic Change in Syria. 2011. "Declaration of the Charter for Dignity and Rights." 17 September. http://syrianncb.org/2012/01/20/declaration-of-the-charter-for-dignity-and-rights/ (accessed 4 September 2014).

"National Coordination Body for Democratic Change in Syria: the final statement of the National Council expanded" [in Arabic]. 2011. *Levant News*, September. http://www.levantnews.com/archives/10117 (accessed 4 September 2014).

The Al-Nusra Front (Jabhat al-Nusra) Is an Al-Qaeda Salafistjihadi Network, Prominent in the Rebel Organizations in Syria. 2013. Meier Intelligence and Terrorism Information Center, 23 September. http://www.terrorism-info.org.il/Data/articles/Art_20573/E_076_13_1861409435.pdf (accessed 4 September 2014).

O'Bagy, Elizabeth. 2013. "The Free Syrian Army." Middle East Security Report no. 9, March. Washington, D.C.: Institute for the Study of War.

Al-Om, Tamara. 2011. "Empowering Syrian Civil Society." BRISMES conference, University of Exeter.

Pollock, David. 2012. "Syria's Kurds Unite against Assad, but Not with Opposition." *Policywatch 1967*, Washington Institute, 31 July. http://www.washingtoninstitute.org/policy-analysis/view/syrias-kurds-unite-against-assad-but-not-with-opposition (accessed 3 September 2014).

"Prevents a conference of the National Council for in Paris" [in Arabic]. 2011. *Al-Akhbar*, 11 October. http://www.al-akhbar.com/node/23354 (accessed 4 September 2014).

"Un rassemblement à Paris divise l'opposition syrienne." 2011. *Le Voix du Monde*, 5 July. http://www.rfi.fr/moyen-orient/20110705-rassemblement-paris-divise-opposition-syrienne (accessed 4 September 2014).

Reuters. 2011. "Tanks Come under Attack in Homs." YouTube, 18 November. http://youtu.be/492Bzz97DVo (accessed 25 February 2015).

———. 2012. "Syria Conflict Is Civil War, Says Herve Ladsous, U.N. Peacekeeping Chief." *Huffington Post*, 20 June. http://www.huffingtonpost.com/2012/06/12/syria-civil-war-herve-ladsous_n_1590271.html (accessed 4 September 2014).

Rubin, Jennifer. 2013. "The Gruesome Repudiation of 'Leading from Behind.'" *Washington Post*, 25 August. http://www.washingtonpost.com/blogs/right-turn/wp/2013/08/25/the-gruesome-repudiation-of-leading-from-behind/ (accessed 3 September 2014).

Sadasyria12. 2011. "Intervention by Mr. Samir Aita 2" [in Arabic]. YouTube video, 4 August. http://www.youtube.com/watch?v=kKIfo7HMSK8 (accessed 4 September 2014).

Samir, Ayman, and Erika Solomon. 2012. "Arab League Suspends Syria Mission as Violence Rages." Reuters, 28 January. http://www.reuters.com/article/2012/01/28/us-syria-idUSTRE8041A820120128 (accessed 4 September 2014).

Seale, Patrick. 1990. *Asad of Syria: The Struggle for the Middle East*. Berkeley: University of California Press.

Shadid, Anthony. 2011a. "Coalition of Factions from the Streets Fuels a New Opposition in Syria." *New York Times*, 30 June. http://www.nytimes.com/2011/07/01/world/middleeast/01syria.html?_r=3&pagewanted=all& (accessed 3 September 2014).

———. 2011b. "Lyrical Message for Syrian Leader: 'Come on Bashar, Leave.'" *New York Times*, 21 July. http://www.nytimes.com/2011/07/22/world/middleeast/22poet.html?_r=0 (accessed 4 September 2014).

Sharma, Rajeev. 2013. "Will Syria Crisis Create a New World Order That Favours Russia?" *Firstpost*, 10 September. http://www.firstpost.com/world/syria-now-will-the-crisis-be-averted-1096901.html (accessed 3 September 2014).

Spears, Mohammed. 2011. "Assault on the Opposition Blocked inside the Meeting with the Arab." *Al-Akhbar*, 10 November. http://www.al-akhbar.com/node/25395 (accessed 4 September 2014).

"Stages in the peaceful Syrian revolution (peaceful realism or undisciplined)—2" [in Arabic]. 2011. *Syrian*, 25 October. http://the-syrian.com/archives/48911 (accessed 4 September 2014).

"The Supreme Council for the Leadership of the Syrian Revolution." 2012. *Carnegie Middle East Center*, 20 December. http://carnegie-mec.org/2012/12/20/supreme-council-for-leadership-of-syrian-revolution/f056 (accessed 4 September 2014).

"Syria: Choices, Interests and the Possibilities of Change." 2011. *Arab Center for Research and Policy Studies*, 30 July. http://english.dohainstitute.org/event/5b0833a8-9520-4bbe-a851-5a4f68f2e5aa (accessed 4 September 2014).

"Syria: report 'dissident' Hussein Hermosh retract his statements" [in Arabic]. 2011. BBC Arabic, 16 September. http://www.bbc.co.uk/arabic/middleeast/2011/09/110910_syria_harmoush.shtml (accessed 4 September 2014).

"Syria Army Defector Hussein Harmoush in TV 'Confession.'" 2011. BBC News, 16 September. http://www.bbc.co.uk/news/world-middle-east-14945690 (accessed 4 September 2014).

"Syria in Civil War, Red Cross Says." 2012. BBC News, 15 July. http://www.bbc.co.uk/news/world-middle-east-18849362 (accessed 3 September 2014).

"Syrian Democratic Union Convenes Its Conference." 2013. *Zaman Alwasl*, 20 August. http://zamanalwsl.net/en/readNews.php?id=1147 (accessed 3 September 2014).

"Syrian opposition agreement to attend a conference of the Arab League during the current month" [in Arabic]. 2012. *Alaraby*, 17 June. http://www.masress.com/elfagr/1125795 (accessed 4 September 2014).

"Syrian Opposition Meet in Damascus to Support Protests." 2011. BBC News, 17 September. http://www.bbc.co.uk/news/world-middle-east-14958541 (accessed 4 September 2014).

"Syria Opposition Bloc Elects George Sabra as Leader." 2012. Al Arabiya News, 9 November. http://www.alarabiya.net/articles/2012/11/09/248645.html (accessed 4 September 2014).

"Syrian Security Forces Kill Demonstrators." 2011. YouTube, 12 April. http://www.youtube.com/watch?v=wGLMX-DicHY (accessed 3 September 2014).

"Syrian Troops Start Withdrawal from Daraa." 2011. Associated Press, 5 May. http://www.ynetnews.com/articles/0,7340,L-4064992,00.html (accessed 3 September 2014).

"Syria's Kurds: Are They about to Join the Uprising against Assad?" 2011. *Kurdish Globe*, 26 October. Reprinted from *Time*, 21 October 2011. http://www.kurdishglobe.net/article/B401BD71512EFC6525D69EA3048CD6F7/Syria-s-Kurds-are-they-about-to-join-the-uprising-against-Assad-.html (accessed 4 September 2014).

Tantawi, Mohammed. 2011. "Submitted Syrian dissident claimed responsibility for the killing of soldiers" [in Arabic]. *Suez Canal*, 10 June. http://www.youm7.com/News.asp?NewsID=432424 (accessed 4 September 2014).

Wright, Robin, and Peter Baker. 2004. "Iraq, Jordan See Threat to Election from Iran: Leaders Warn against Forming Religious State." *Washington Post*, 8 December. http://www.washingtonpost.com/wp-dyn/articles/A43980-2004Dec7.html (accessed 3 September 2014).

NATO

The Process of Negotiating Military Intervention in Libya

JOHANNES THEISS

WHEN LOOKING AT NEGOTIATIONS in transitions and especially the *intifadat* of the Arab Spring, Libya stands out not only as an example of a Long Track uprising but as the only one that led to a multilateral intervention involving the use of force. This provides an opportunity to take a look "at the other side" of negotiation processes ignited by the Arab Spring, moving away from internal rebels and dictators to focus on outside politicians and diplomats. The concepts of negotiation analysis, used to explain the evolution of the *intifadat*, are useful in providing insights into the process of negotiating a multilateral military intervention.

The subject is of particular relevance since entering a war is probably the most extreme decision a state or an organization can take. Like opposition groups, states must make tough decisions on the Tactical Question of whether to use political or violent means. Military intervention is often an unpopular step; it certainly causes the loss of lives and unfortunately often those of civilians. Beyond understanding how individual states decide to use force, it is even more relevant to explain multilateral compromise on military action. Against the backdrop of a global system of collective security, multilateral actions are more likely to curtail the spread of conflicts and prevent arbitrary action of individual countries that might only escalate an already tense situation. However, processes that lead to this decision take place in secrecy, with the public only being aware of information that has leaked to the media. Thus, the processes behind multilateral compromise on the use of force are even more complex to analyze.

By focusing on the case of NATO's intervention in Libya, this chapter seeks to provide insights into a subject on which public information is almost totally unavailable. It emphasizes the negotiation processes that led to the action termed Operation Unified Protector and captures the main dynamics of the process by comparing the perspectives of the United Kingdom, France, the United States, Germany, and Turkey.

The concepts used to explain negotiations under conditions of transition, such as the process of moving from diagnosis to formula and details and the dynamics behind coalition building and leadership, are also useful to shed light on negotiations regarding a multilateral military intervention. The chapter starts by describing the sequence of major events throughout the Libyan *intifada* before continuing with the application of concepts taken from the theoretical framework of negotiation analysis. Thus the process is divided into three stages, each of which is analyzed according to negotiation structure, strategy, and actors. With time, information, and communication, the analysis also accounts for interacting factors. After a brief outcome assessment, the chapter concludes with some lessons for the practical negotiator.

THE CASE OF LIBYA: SEQUENCE OF MAJOR EVENTS

One month after Zine El Abidine Ben Ali had fled from Tunisia and four days after Hosni Mubarak had resigned in Egypt, large-scale protests against the regime of Muammar al-Qadhafi in Libya started on 15 February (Clarke 2011, 3). The Libyan version of the Arab Spring turned out soon to be more violent than in Tunisia and Egypt. Already on 22 February, Qadhafi called the demonstrators "cockroaches" that should be eliminated (BBC 2011a). On the same day, the Arab League expressed its support for the protest movement (Rinke 2011, 45).

In order to evacuate citizens and to collect information about the rebels, international special forces entered the country allegedly between 23 and 25 February (Turnbull 2011, 10). On the latter day, NATO's North Atlantic Council (NAC) met for the first time to discuss the Libyan crisis (NATO 2011a). The ongoing violence in the country led the United Nations Security Council to unanimously adopt Resolution 1970 on 26 February, imposing an arms embargo on Libya as well as a travel ban and an asset freeze on major players of the regime, mainly the Qadhafi family (UNSC 2011a). The resolution also formed the basis for the International Criminal Court (ICC) to start investigations, which the court confirmed on 3 March (Clarke 2011, 3). Two days later, the rebels declared that only the newly established National Transitional Council (NTC) would represent Libya (Turnbull 2011, 2). Less than a week later, France was the first country to recognize the NTC as legitimate representative of the Libyan people (BBC 2011b).

However, from 6 March onward, Qadhafi regained terrain and started moving toward the city of the rebellion's origin, Benghazi, in the east (Interview 1 2012). On 7 and 8 March, the Gulf Cooperation Council (GCC) and the Organization of the Islamic Conference (OIC) expressed their support for a no-fly zone, while on 10 March, the African Union (AU) was reluctant to support any military operation by foreign forces. At the same time, NATO started preparing the evacuation of civilians (9 March) as well as the enforcement of the arms embargo and a possible no-fly zone (10 March). The latter issue divided member states of the European Union (EU) and was opposed by Russia and China. Nevertheless, France and the United Kingdom (UK) started drafting a UN resolution to implement a possible no-fly zone (Clarke 2011, 3). The measure received support by a vote of the Arab League on 12 March (BBC 2011c). Furthermore on that day, Ali Hassan al-Jaber, a Qatari journalist working for Al Jazeera, was shot by regime forces and became the first journalist who died in the Libyan conflict (Wells 2011).

Three days later, NATO approved a NAC Initiating Directive (NID) regarding the possible no-fly zone. This is the first political document in NATO's decision-making process, which marks the beginning of formal planning for an operation (NATO 2011g). On 17 March, a few hours before the UNSC voted on Libya for the second time, Qadhafi announced his intention to attack Benghazi and to show "no mercy" to the rebels (Black 2011). Later that day, the UNSC (2011b) adopted Resolution 1973, which enforced the previous measures but mainly imposed the no-fly zone and additionally authorized UN "Member States . . . , acting nationally or through regional organizations or arrangements . . . , to take all necessary measures . . . to protect civilians and civilian populated areas under attack . . . while excluding a foreign occupation force of any form on any part of Libyan territory." Russia, China, India, Brazil, and Germany abstained. The resolution was justified with the UN concept "Responsibility to Protect (R2P)," which allows foreign countries to intervene if "national authorities manifestly fail to protect their populations from genocide, war crimes, ethnic cleansing and crimes against humanity" (UNGA 2005; Daalder and Stavridis 2012).

During the following days, Qadhafi's forces were further approaching Benghazi and reached its outskirts on 19 March (Interview 1, 2012). On the same day, a conference was organized in Paris to discuss a possible intervention. After the summit, the French president Nicolas Sarkozy unilaterally announced military action of French aircraft over Benghazi (Clarke 2011, 4); the UK and the United States soon joined the operation. One day later, Qadhafi's forces had to retreat from Benghazi. Basing their actions on the UNSC Resolution 1973, France, the UK, and the United States ran a number of airborne and naval attacks on regime forces until the NAC decided on NATO's gradual takeover of the enforcement of the arms embargo (22 March), the no-fly zone (24 March), and the protection of civilians (27 March) within the Operation Unified Protector (OUP) (Clarke 2011; NATO 2011b, 2011c, 2011d). A compromise was reported on 24 March between the United States, France, and Turkey on NATO enforcement of the no-fly zone, while the coalition around France, the UK, and the United States would temporarily continue to enforce the protection of civilians (SF 2011).

A summit was organized on 29 March in London to gather support for NATO's military intervention, and two days later NATO finally took over all military activities in Libya (Interview 1 2012; Clarke 2011, 5). Under the strategic command of the Supreme Allied Commander Europe (SACEUR) at the Supreme Headquarters Allied Powers Europe (SHAPE), OUP was run from the Allied Joint Force Command (JFC) in Naples with its subordinate components Allied Maritime Command Naples (MC Naples) and Allied Air Command Izmir (AC Izmir) (NATO 2011e). The United States ended its direct participation in combat on 4 April but continued providing Intelligence, Surveillance, Target Acquisition, and Reconnaissance (ISTAR) assets as well as refueling capabilities (Clarke 2011, 5; Quintana 2011, 6).

After first successes, a standoff emerged between regime and opposition forces from 7 April onward (Turnbull 2011, 2). The foreign ministers of the countries contributing to OUP met in Berlin on 14 April and decided on three conditions to terminate the operation: end of "attacks and threats of attack against civilians and civilian-populated areas," withdrawal of forces loyal to the regime, and full access for humanitarian aid (NATO 2011f). In late May, France and the UK decided to deploy attack helicopters, which first struck on 4 June. Support for the rebels with weapons was officially confirmed by France at the end of June (Turnbull 2011, 2). It is to be underlined, however, that special forces activities on the ground by various allies had been continuing since the end of February and likely may have been involved in providing equipment, weapons, and training to rebel forces as well as keeping their leaders safe (Phillips 2011, 11–12; Joshi 2011, 11). To what extent this represented part of the "necessary measures to protect civilians" or a violation of the arms embargo is open to dispute. Nevertheless, it happened and contributed to the opposition's victory in Tripoli on 23 August.

The French president and the prime minister of the UK visited the Libyan capital on 15 September while fighting continued in Ban Walid and Sirte. On 27 October, a week after the fall of Sirte and Qadhafi's death (BBC 2011d), the UNSC (2011c) adopted Resolution 2016, which set 31 October as the date for terminating military operations in Libya related to the protection of civilians or the enforcement of the no-fly zone. At this date, Operation Unified Protector was concluded. Four non-NATO countries—Sweden, Jordan, Qatar, and the United Arab Emirates (UAE)—had participated in the operation and therefore also attended NAC meetings of relevance to them (Interview 1 2012). On the whole, eighteen countries had contributed to OUP. The operation caused comparably few civilian casualties and none within the alliance (Daalder and Stavridis 2012, 3; Quintana 2011, 5). These events can be grouped according to several stages, reflecting a process of negotiation (for a detailed timeline see figure 1).

STAGE ONE: TOWARD RESOLUTION 1973

Two crucial turning points appear from the interviews conducted for this study[1] and divide the process into three stages. The first stage is the adoption of UNSC Resolution 1973 on 17 March; the second is the compromise between the United

FIGURE 1 Detailed timeline of major events of the *intifadat* in Libya in 2011

15 February 2011:	• Start of large-scale protests in Libya
22 February 2011:	• Qadhafi calls protesters "cockroaches" • Arab League supports protesters
23–25 February 2011:	• International special forces enter Libya
25 February 2011:	• First NAC meeting on Libyan crisis
26 February 2011:	• UNSC Res. 1970 (arms embargo, travel ban, asset freeze)
27 February 2011:	• Replacement of French foreign minister Michèle Alliot-Marie by Alain Juppé
28 February 2011:	• Change of French Permanent Representative to NATO
2 March 2011:	• NAC meeting on Libyan crisis (UK presents "Leslie Principles")
3 March 2011:	• ICC confirms start of investigations
5 March 2011:	• NTC declares itself Libyan representative
6 March 2011:	• Start of Qadhafi's counteroffensive
7 March 2011:	• GCC supports no-fly zone
8 March 2011:	• OIC supports no-fly zone
9 March 2011:	• NATO starts preparation for evacuation of civilians
10 March 2011:	• AU objects to no-fly zone • France first country to recognize NTC • Regime forces start moving toward Benghazi • NATO starts preparing enforcement of arms embargo and no-fly zone • Letter by Cameron and Sarkozy to van Rompuy
12 March 2011:	• Arab League supports no-fly zone • Qatari Al Jazeera journalist killed
15 March 2011:	• NATO approves NID (no-fly zone) • United States changes position in favor of intervention
16 March 2011:	• Germany reaffirms anti-intervention position, but then becomes aware of changed U.S. position
17 March 2011:	• Qadhafi announces "no mercy" attack on Benghazi • UNSC Res. 1973 (protection of civilians, no-fly zone)

End of first stage

FIGURE 1 (continued)

18 March 2011:	• French veto in the NAC
19 March 2011:	• Regime forces reach Benghazi's outskirts • Paris conference • Beginning of military intervention by France with air strikes
20 March 2011:	• Regime forces retreat from Benghazi • Press conference convened by Rasmussen to demonstrate NATO's readiness
21 March 2011:	• Turkish veto in the NAC
22 March 2011:	• NAC decision (takeover of arms embargo enforcement) • Start of OUP
24 March 2011:	• Compromise between United States, France, and Turkey • NAC decision (takeover of no-fly zone enforcement) • Blitzer interviews Rasmussen (command question)

End of second stage

27 March 2011:	• NAC decision (takeover of protection of civilians)
29 March 2011:	• London conference (establishment of Libya Contact Group)
31 March 2011:	• NATO assumes overall command of military activities in Libya
1 April 2011:	• U.S. deadline to withdraw from direct combat participation
4 April 2011:	• United States ends direct combat participation
7 April 2011:	• Start of stalemate between regime and opposition forces
14 April 2011:	• Berlin foreign ministers' meeting
4 June 2011:	• First strike of attack helicopters
29 June 2011:	• France confirms weapons support for rebels
23 August 2011:	• Fall of Tripoli
15 September 2011:	• Sarkozy and Cameron visit Tripoli • Fights continue in Ban Walid and Sirte
20 October 2011:	• Fall of Sirte • Death of Qadhafi
21 October 2011:	• NAC preliminary decision (termination date for OUP)
27 October 2011:	• UNSC Res. 2016 (termination date for military operations in Libya)
31 October 2011:	• Conclusion of OUP

Source: compiled by the author.

States, France, and Turkey on 24 March. Negotiations for formulation and for coalition were the two interrelated tracks of the process. As it will be shown, the first and also largely the second stage were marked by contentious or distributive negotiation behavior while the emphasis in the third stage was on problem solving or integrative behavior. Although negotiators during both the first and third stages sat at the negotiation table, the two stages fulfilled the function of pre- and postnegotiation. A look at the different influencing factors shows that the overall process follows a pattern comprising diagnosis, a formula, and details, rather than concession/convergence through continuous exchange of mutual concessions.

Structure in the First Stage

Power is the conceptual basis of negotiation analysis. Analytically, power can be divided into two types, aggregate and issue-specific, the two constituting the basis of *bargaining power* for multilateral decision making. Not surprisingly, the bases of bargaining power in NATO are quite different from the bases within the countries of the *intifadat* discussed in the introduction to this book, although there are some correspondences. Conceptualized in terms of what a negotiating party owns, two aggregate power resources were important for the Libyan intervention decisions, both referring to matters of distribution and relation. The first one is military power (related to violence in the *intifadat*'s bargaining power in the introduction to this book), which is substantive as well as asymmetrical, and largely dominated by the United States (Interview 6, 2012). Even when the military operation in Libya was finally executed by NATO, the U.S. ISTAR and refueling capabilities were indispensible assets that could not be provided by other allies or at least not to the same extent. The second aggregate resource of bargaining power is veto power, a procedural element that evens the substantive asymmetry (related to a procedural form of legitimacy in the *intifadat*, as seen in the introduction to this book) (Interview 5, 2012). Inside the NATO institutional framework, in which decisions are taken only by consensus, each of the twenty-eight countries can equally block decisions. Both power resources have played an important role in the analyzed case. The opposite of the veto is the fait accompli, which carries back to asymmetrical power. While veto is a negative block on collective action, fait accompli is a positive one, as is seen later on in the events. However, power can also be issue specific, related to certain procedural as well as substantive actions in the negotiation process.

Leadership can be identified with initiative to deal with the multilateral complexity brought on by many parties and many issues and was the key to effective negotiations for formulation. In the case of the intervention in Libya, this role was adopted by the UK and France. The latter joined the former at the latest on 10 March, when France became the first country to recognize the NTC (Rinke 2011, 46–47). In the evening of the same day in a letter to EU president Herman van

Rompuy, Sarkozy and his UK colleague David Cameron (2011) pointed toward the possibility "of a no-fly zone or other options against air attacks."

Initiative was used for the purpose of setting the agenda for the military intervention in Libya. While awareness on the issue among allies and within the NATO apparatus actually was first raised through a letter circulated by the Italian military representative, describing concerns of a possible spillover effect from the events in the country's North African neighbors, it was the UK that developed three key principles to be fulfilled for any NATO role in Libya: demonstrable need, regional support, and a sound legal basis (Interviews 5 and 1, 2012). The identification of principles of a formula made the agenda-setting initiative work. Named after the UK permanent representative to NATO, Mariot Leslie, these three criteria became a touchstone for every possible NATO action in Libya and were soon referred to as "Leslie Principles" or even "Mariot Principles" (Interviews 3 and 4, 2012). After the emergency meeting of the NAC on 25 February, the UK convened the second NAC meeting on Libya on 2 March, at which it presented these criteria (Interview 1, 2012).

A look at the other four key actors supports the view that the UK drove the NATO agenda from the very beginning. The United States soon aligned with the UK's position, arguing that NATO should be prepared if it was called upon, without knowing at this point if this was actually going to happen (Interview 6, 2012). However, until the evening on 15 March the United States followed a very skeptical approach and questioned any military intervention in Libya (Rinke 2011, 48–49). Likewise on 2 March, France did not play a large role yet since it had just replaced its foreign minister Michèle Alliot-Marie for having too close contacts with the autocrats in North Africa (27 February) and had changed its permanent representative to NATO (28 February) (Rinke 2011, 46; Interview S1, 2012). Moreover, Germany and Turkey had a very critical stance toward any military intervention in Libya. Consequently, the UK was the primary agenda setter in the first stage of the negotiation process, and the Leslie Principles were ambiguous enough for the other allies to agree to (Interview S3, 2012). This formula for agreement in turn made possible a process of entrapment and "verbal safeguards," as is discussed below.

Other procedures were used to structure complexity. One is the single negotiation text (SNT), which is initially drafted by a mediating or leading party, distributed, and then successively redrafted until a final agreement is reached (Raiffa 1982, 211; Fisher and Ury 1999, 118–122). In the case of Libya, different SNTs existed for different issues and different steps of NATO's crisis management process. Consequently, the allies negotiated a NAC Initiating Directive, a Concept of Operations (CONOPS), an Operations Plan (OPLAN), and an NAC Execution Directive (NED), at first for humanitarian efforts, including the evacuation of civilians,[2] then for the enforcement of the arms embargo, afterward for the no-fly zone, and finally for the protection of civilians and civilian populated areas, also called "no-fly zone plus"

(Interviews 1 and 2, 20–12). Although these were several documents, they followed the SNT logic: as a neutral party, NATO's International Staff (IS) tried to gather the interests of the twenty-eight in advance, drafted one text—for example, the NID for the enforcement of the no-fly zone—which then was distributed electronically and could be modified by each delegation. As one negotiator put it: "They [the NATO IS] presented these documents and we messed them around, pulled them apart, added, subtracted, and tried our best" (Interview 1, 2012).

Coalition building has been the prime means used to manage complexity among the twenty-eight NATO member states. In the case of Libya, cross-cutting issue coalitions were the main attributes of negotiation for coalition. Instead of "band-wagoning" or rallying around one hegemon, negotiators built coalitions with like-minded partners, an aggregating process that partly changed depending on the issue. In the first stage, the five countries analyzed in this study formed coalitions concerning the issues of a military intervention in Libya in general and a NATO role therein. On the one hand, the UK and soon also France favored a solution including the use of force, while the United States, Turkey, and Germany were skeptical and preferred a diplomatic approach (Rinke 2011, 46, 48–49; Head 2011). On the other hand, the United States was in favor of pushing preparations inside NATO for a possible operation, which was opposed by France and Turkey, although for different reasons, as is shown when examining the interests at the respective domestic levels (Interview 6, 2012). The UK and Germany took a middle stance on this second issue without any clear indication toward one or the other side (Interview S2, 2012).

Another structural factor is the *number of negotiation levels,* reflecting the matter of interests (Putnam 1988; Sebenius 2002). Here, the first critical question concerns the motives that drove the positions of the respective national ratification levels. Since a thorough answer would require a study of its own, only some indications that appeared during the interviews are given here. UK prime minister Cameron may have favored a military intervention since the UK had had strong links to Libya and the Qadhafi regime (Interviews 1 and S2, 2012; Leithäuser 2011). Both enforcing the former and ridding itself of the latter determined the UK's position. After all, the North African country was under the UK's occupation during and after the Second World War, the UK under Tony Blair substantially prepared the comeback of Qadhafi's Libya to the international respected nations, one of Qadhafi's sons had studied at the renowned London School of Economics, BP had major investments in Libya, and there was a great number of Libyan expatriates living and working in the UK. On the issue of the framework in which a military intervention should be executed, the UK took a pragmatic stance of "whoever is best placed and has the resources and capabilities to do something, should do it." As a result, London had no specific interest in NATO, the EU, or a "coalition of the willing."

France also had strong ties to the Qadhafi regime, which did not match with Sarkozy's approach to realign French policy vis-à-vis the Middle East and North

Africa, for instance, through the Union for the Mediterranean. Influential French elites, such as Bernard-Henri Lévy, fueled internal pressures to intervene for humanitarian reasons; France's anti-NATO position could be explained by its concerns about estranging the Arab world (Interview S1, 2012). On the one hand, this argument was weakened when the Arab League started to support a Western intervention. On the other hand, Sarkozy may have also considered strengthening the EU's Common Security and Defense Policy (CSDP) through NATO's backdoor (Irondelle and Mérand 2010, 36–40).

Marked by the experiences of intervening in Afghanistan and Iraq, their costs, and decreasing public support, the U.S. national level did not support an operation in Libya in the first stage of the negotiation process (Interviews S2, 6, and 2, 2012). This position was characterized by the skeptical stance of Defense Minister Robert Gates. However, the U.S. concerns about a new involvement in an Islamic country and the questionable success of an operation that excluded ground troops were outweighed on the evening of 15 March in the Situation Room of the White House (Rinke 2011, 48–49). From this point onward, President Barack Obama followed his advisers Samantha Power and Susan Rice, who argued with the UN R2P concept. This swing toward an intervention was largely determined by two contextual factors (Interviews S2 and S3, 2012; Wells 2011). One was the rising support in the Arab World, expressed, for instance, by Al Jazeera's coverage after the death of its journalist and by the Arab League's call for intervention. The example shows that the media should not be underestimated when considering *actor types* that influence the process. More important with regard to the UN principle was the changing situation in Libya, where Qadhafi's counteroffensive was pushing the rebels back and started to threaten Benghazi. His strong language toward the rebels raised concerns of an impending massacre comparable to Ruanda (1994) or Bosnia and Herzegovina's Srebrenica (1995). However, a U.S. change of position regarding the question of a military intervention was linked to a condition for the second issue in question. Since Washington in principle was still not willing to wage another war, it pushed for NATO preparation, anticipating a takeover by the alliance that would allow limiting U.S. military participation without losing political influence.

The national ratification level in Turkey had different concerns. As a formal colonial power, the country had strong ties with Libya, including substantial financial investments. Especially in the beginning, Turkey could not accept any military intervention before evacuating approximately twenty-five thousand construction workers (Interview T1, 2011). At the same time, Ankara tried to negotiate with the Qadhafi regime about a peaceful solution to the conflict, as the Libyan chapter by Karim Mezran and Alice Alunni also notes (Interviews 2, 3, S1, 2012). Regarding itself as a model for the future Libya, Turkey was also concerned about its reputation in the Arab world and therefore initially opposed NATO action. This position was fuelled by Turkey's general suspicion of a possible EU role and its "reluctance to give a blank check to the EU for access to NATO intelligence and assets" (Aydin qtd. in Oğuz 2011). Given the skeptical stance of Germany, Turkey also doubted the effectiveness of a divided NATO and felt that its best allies in Washington and London did not play such a strong role as Paris, with which it had a fraught relationship since Sarkozy had taken office (Interview T1, 2011; Oğuz 2011).

Due to the time difference, the German government became first aware of the changed U.S. position on a military intervention in the afternoon of 16 March (Rinke 2011, 49). In the morning of that day, German foreign minister Guido Westerwelle had reaffirmed his position of opposing a no-fly zone. This measure had been pushed in the meantime by the UK and France in the UNSC in form of a new draft, which later became Resolution 1973. Furthermore, Chancellor Angela Merkel had already given an interview to the *Saarbrücker Zeitung* that was to be published on 17 March, in which she clearly rejected any military intervention in Libya. Against the backdrop of the upcoming regional elections in the Land Baden-Württemberg, she gave in to electoral pressure, trying to avoid another domestic political debate besides the discussions of the sovereign debt crisis and on her position regarding Germany's energy mix after the disaster at the Fukushima Daiichi Nuclear Power Plant (Rinke 2011, 51; Interview S1, 2012). Consequently, Germany abstained in the vote on Resolution 1973. Since it was not participating militarily from this point onward, it did not take a position on who would finally be in charge of the operation.

In this vein, the UNSC constituted a second ratification level for NATO negotiations besides the national levels, although actors in NATO did not directly "sit at the game board" in New York. Moreover, for many allies only a UNSC resolution provided a "sound legal basis" for NATO action (Interview 1, 2012). Therefore, three negotiation levels mattered for engaging in Libya: the national environment, the UNSC, and NATO itself. Besides these insights on structure, the first stage also sheds light on negotiation strategy.

Strategy in the First Stage

Strategy can be analyzed by looking at possible *game-theoretic moves* from the perspective of subjectively perceived outcome preferences (see figures 2 and 3). All five states wanted the violence of the Qadhafi regime to end, and especially to avoid a massacre in Benghazi. However, there were differences concerning the ways of achieving this goal (see Solution Issue in figure 3). In the beginning of the first stage, a military intervention by the UK and France to end the violence was the preferred outcome for both countries (4). The second best result was exerting influence in a diplomatic solution (3). The second worst outcome was a military intervention that was not coordinated with diplomatic efforts of others and that

FIGURE 2 Configuration of preferences in the basic Battle of the Sexes scenario

Battle of the Sexes

		Actor B	
		C	D
Actor A	C	1/1	3/4*
	D	4/3*	2/2

Source: based on Duncan J. Snidal (1985), "Coordination versus Prisoners' Dilemma: Implications for International Cooperation and Regimes," *American Political Science Review* 79, no. 4, 932. Rows and columns are renamed, and Nash equilibria are added by the author.

C: Cooperation, D: Defection, *: Nash equilibrium

would not have been able to end violence (2). However, the worst outcome was not to intervene while others did and still not prevent a massacre (1). Since, with the coordinated diplomatic solution at the top, the preferences of the United States, Germany, and Turkey exactly mirrored this distribution, the strategic situation equaled the game Battle of the Sexes (BotS) or coordination game, in which coordinated solutions, once they are found, mark Nash equilibria—that is, situations in which none of the actors can improve his or her position by unilaterally changing his or her strategy (see figs. 2 and 3; Snidal 1985; Sebenius 2002). The application of this game matrix rests on the assumption that only a coordinated solution leads to success, thus expanding the value of an agreement beyond the resistance points or Best Alternatives to a Negotiated Agreement (BATNA) of each negotiating party. Throughout the first stage, the United States changed the camp after altering its assessment of the situation (see Solution Issue in figure 3).

The BotS matrix also fits the different perceptions between the United States on one side and France as well as Turkey on the other side, concerning the choice of

FIGURE 3 Configuration of preferences in BotS scenarios applied to the case

Solution Issue

G/T (in the beginning, U.S.)

UK/F (later, U.S.)	Military Solution	Diplomatic Solution
Diplomatic Solution	1/1	3/4*
Military Solution	4/3*	2/2

Framework Issue

F/(T only in stage 1)

U.S./(T only from stage 2)	NATO	and U.S.-led Coalition
U.S.-led Coalition	1/1	3/4*
NATO	4/3*	2/2

Regime Change Issue

G/(U.S.)

UK/F/(T)	Almost outspoken	Not mentioned
Not mentioned	1/1	3/4*
Almost outspoken	4/3*	2/2

Operational Measures Issue

U.S.

UK/F	Surge	Sustainability
Sustainability	1/1	3/4*
Surge	4/3*	2/2

Operation Unified Protector Termination Issue

U.S.

UK/F	Extend	End
End	1/1	3/4*
Extend	4/3*	2/2

Source: based on Duncan J. Snidal (1985), "Coordination versus Prisoners' Dilemma: Implications for International Cooperation and Regimes," *American Political Science Review* 79, no. 4, 932. Rows and columns are renamed, and Nash equilibria are added by the author.

U.S.: United States, UK: United Kingdom, F: France, T: Turkey, G: Germany, *: Nash equilibrium

NATO to bring about a solution or some kind of coalition with the United States in the lead (see Framework Issue in figure 3). Throughout the first stage, the perceived payoffs in this game remained the same.

Although the end values are now outlined, the presentation cannot show how negotiators tried to achieve them. Analysis of *non-game-theoretic moves* provides more insights. A number of factors suggest that negotiators within NATO largely applied integrative bargaining. Regarding the two interacting factors, information and communication, all interview partners agreed that by and large information was available and shared and that communication was clear and coordinated. A largely positive working relationship between NATO negotiators also promotes integrative bargaining (Pruitt 2002). There is mutual dependence since NATO is a defense alliance; parties refrain from searching advantage over each other; they trust each other and had found in Qadhafi even a common enemy. As one negotiator put it: "It is actually a very collegiate and friendly group. We know each other very well, use first names, and we usually understand when one, two or three nations have a difficulty with a piece of text. Quite often we can have a little conversation in the margins and say: 'Ok, if I support you on this, will you support me on that?' We tend to try to give each other support" (Interview 1, 2012).

However, even mutual gains have to be distributed, or in game-theoretic terms: BotS requires choosing one coordination point to reach these gains. This was a problem since, as shown, the preferred coordinated solutions differed. Consequently, actors found themselves in the Negotiator's or Toughness Dilemma (Lax and Sebenius 1986; Zartman 2002). If all had been trying to impose their preferred coordination point, there would have been no coordination at all, and giving in early might have led only to the second best solution, or hypothetically, if the others had done the same, even to the worst solution. It is now interesting to see how the Dilemma is *reflected* in the *moves* of the five analyzed countries throughout the first stage and which *moves* they applied *to escape the Dilemma.*

By presenting the Leslie Principles, the UK found the right balance for an opener on the question of a military solution. Even though most allies referred to the UNSC to provide a "sound legal basis," it was not part of the principles. The criteria "demonstrable need" and "regional support" were even more ambiguous. While wanting a military outcome, the UK had not positioned itself on the framework issue yet. In applying this strategy of "firm flexibility" or "salami tactics," the UK managed to escape the Dilemma throughout the first stage (Pruitt and Kim 2004).

Moreover, the nations that favored a military solution tried to entrap the ones that opposed it (Meerts 2005). The United States and the UK but also France stressed the fact that NATO should be prepared if it was to be called upon (Interview S2, 2012). This was the first "slice of the salami," since next steps would involve concrete planning for NATO action and NIDs on less controversial issues, such as the arms embargo, until finally a NED for the use of force would have to be decided on, and prior investments would be too substantial to block this final compromise. Turkey and Germany tried to counter their entrapment by insisting on formulations that worked as "verbal safeguards" against the "short-circuiting" of NATO procedures. Examples include expressions such as "as appropriate," "on a case-by-case basis," "in accordance with existing procedures," or "a NAC decision to initiate planning does not prejudge any final NAC decision to launch an operation" (Interviews 1, 2, and 3, 2012).

Taking into account the issue of a role for NATO, the situation becomes more complex. For the skeptical and war-weary United States, it was internally soon very clear that only a military solution inside NATO could be supported (Interviews 1, 2, and 3, 2012). The United States therefore tried to entrap France on the NATO track. Recognizing this, but also not wanting to put the military solution at risk, France also attempted to rely on "verbal safeguards" in every official document that was negotiated. Instead of calling it "planning" (*planification* in French), France wanted NATO action to be termed "preparation" (*préparatifs* in French). In this vein, it would manage to ensure military readiness while keeping a backdoor open for NATO alternatives.

Believing that the United States was on its side, Germany decided to entrap itself. This process largely took part outside the NATO negotiation chamber. From an initial skepticism, Westerwelle and Merkel committed themselves more and more to a diplomatic solution as the only reasonable option. When Berlin discovered that Washington had changed sides at the end of this first process stage, it found itself in a situation in which leaving its position would have led to a loss of prior investments. Consequently, German leaders perceived an abstention in the UNSC as "the final slice of the salami," which they had to swallow in order to remain domestically credible. It becomes obvious that this is not the behavior of rational actors—in the sense of Weber's purposeful rationality (*Zweckrationalität*)—but of human beings who judge subjectively and can be influenced by psychological pressures, such as entrapment.

Turkey followed a similar trajectory but remained more flexible since it did not have to decide on Resolution 1973. Although all five countries appeared much more contentious in public than in the negotiation chamber, this gap was probably the highest for Turkey. In the first half of March, Prime Minister Recep Tayyip Erdoğan (in Head 2011) still called an intervention by NATO in Libya "absurd, unthinkable," "useless," "dangerous," and an option that "should not even be discussed." With the process of (self-)entrapment in mind, it might have been possible that Turkey would have blocked Resolution 1973 if it had been a member of the UNSC at that time. However, as shown in the next section, Ankara relinquished its skeptical stance in the second stage. Further moves became not particularly apparent at this stage. In the following section, the analysis focuses on the actors negotiating inside NATO.

Actors in the First Stage

Only two *actor types* were and are directly in charge of negotiating any NATO role. The highest political level is the NAC, in which permanent representatives of the twenty-eight member states sit at the negotiation table. One level below, the allies are represented in the Operations Policy Committee (OPC), which "seeks to enhance collaboration between the political and military sides of NATO Headquarters" and "aims to provide coherent and timely advice to the North Atlantic Council, to which it reports directly" (NATO 2010). Consequently, negotiations in NATO are executed by two types of agents whose powers are delegated by their principals and, as shown in the next section, whose autonomy differs depending on the country.

In the first stage of the negotiation process, almost all aspects of a possible NATO operation were discussed at the NAC level, so that the OPC even "felt a little bit upset that it was being neglected and everything was going straight to the NAC" (Interview 1, 2012). Actors can also be analyzed according to their *personality*, here measured by the Thomas-Kilmann Conflict Mode Instrument (TKI) (Thomas and Kilman 1977). Seven of the ten interview partners in this study are active negotiators, either in the NAC or the OPC. Six of them filled out the TKI questionnaire. The sample comprises four men and two women. Table 1 displays the results.

On the whole, NATO negotiators hardly differ from the updated TKI norm sample of 2007 (Schaubhut 2007). Comparing the means or raw score ranges of accommodation, avoidance, and collaboration with the interpretative ranges of the norm, NATO negotiators appear to be somewhat less cooperative but also slightly less assertive. The low standard deviations of avoidance and collaboration especially show that this result is not caused by extreme cases. Differences between men and women follow the expected patterns, with men tending to behave more competitively, less accommodatively, and less collaboratively than women. Exceptions are in the avoidance and compromise categories. While men scored lower on the former, they scored higher on the latter than women. Due to the small sample, these results are by no means representative of NATO negotiators and should therefore not be overstated. However, they indicate one suggestion, to be tested in a broader sample: if other NATO negotiators follow similar patterns of conflict behavior, reaching agreement within the alliance might be hampered, or at least not facilitated. Having said this, the analysis turns to possible changes of the mentioned factors in the second stage of the negotiation process.

STAGE TWO: GETTING TO COMPROMISE IN NATO

The second stage centers on negotiations inside the OPC and the NAC. Issues have now been defined, possible options assessed, and costs and benefits deliberated. Therefore, although the previous phase already included NATO negotiations, it can

Table 1. Personalities of NATO negotiators, according to the Thomas-Kilmann Conflict Mode Instrument

N=6 (Male=4, Female=2)	Competition	Accommodation	Avoidance	Collaboration	Compromise
Mean	5.00	4.33	7.17	5.67	7.83
Mean Male	*5.50*	*3.50*	*7.00*	*5.25*	*8.75*
Mean Female	*4.00*	*6.00*	*7.50*	*6.50*	*6.00*
Standard Deviation	2.45	3.14	1.94	1.75	2.56
Range	1–7	1–8	5–10	3–7	3–10
Norm Range*	3–6	4–6	5–7	5–8	6–9
Norm Percentile*	Middle 50%	Middle 50%	Middle 50%	Middle 50%	Middle 50%

Source: compiled by the author (except as indicated).

*Taken from Nancy A. Schaubhut (2007), "Technical Brief for the Thomas-Kilmann Conflict Mode Instrument: Description of the Updated Normative Sample and Implications for Use" (Mountain View, Calif.: Consulting Psychologists Press), https://www.cpp.com/pdfs/tki_Technical_Brief.pdf (accessed 12 April 2012), 4.

be described as a prestage, in which diagnosis and the initial search for an appropriate formula took place. Throughout that phase, parties showed constructive but also contentious behavior. The analysis now turns to factors that changed in order to reach the compromise of 24 March, the second turning point of the process.

Structure in the Second Stage

Power resources remained the same but were now used for the first time to create bargaining leverage. One day before the Paris conference on 19 March, France blocked progress for a no-fly zone in the NAC (Interview s3, 2012). Since NATO preparations were ready to be decided on, this came as a surprise for the other member states. The French argument, not to overshadow possible outcomes of the conference, was not comprehensible to them: "[Almost] everyone spoke, which is very rare here. Twenty-six of them said: 'We need to move forward.' One of them [France] said: 'No, we need to not move forward until this conference is concluded,' and one of them [Germany] did not say anything" (Interview 6, 2012). As the first nation to attack Qadhafi's forces shortly after the conference (fait accompli) but knowing that at least the UK and the United States would join soon, France managed to create a power asymmetry in its favor. Not coordinating the first strike with its allies was justified by the argument of imminent danger (Clarke 2011, 4; Interview s3, 2012). From the French perspective, the outcome of the Paris conference, which favored a military intervention, had increased the pressure on Qadhafi to attack Benghazi preemptively before having to face foreign forces (Interview S3, 2012). However, the Libyan dictator had already announced he would show no mercy in Benghazi shortly before Resolution 1973 was adopted. Consequently, it can be assumed that the combination of veto (in the NAC) and fait accompli (first air strikes) rather served France's main positions of intervening militarily but not within the NATO framework.

Although shortly after the Paris conference France agreed on further planning in the NAC, it caused Turkey to also use its veto power (Traynor 2011). The Turks had already felt ignored in NATO decision making and were upset about not having been invited to Paris as well as outraged about Sarkozy's unilateral approach (Interview T1, 2011). Their blockade brought in the United States. Knowing that any UK and French operation in Libya would sooner or later be depending on U.S. military assets, the United States used this power resource to reconcile French and Turkish positions, a point to be elaborated when strategy is examined.

The process of *coalition building* continued. Contrary to the first stage, a military intervention was no longer questioned. The United States had already changed its position and the largely critical reaction to Germany's abstention in the UNSC had caused rethinking in the Chancellery. While participation was no longer possible, Berlin wanted nonetheless to demonstrate solidarity with its allies. In addition, it did not have the opportunity to abstain again since NATO agrees only by consensus, thus reducing decision alternatives to "yes or no." Therefore, Germany continued to fund NATO, maintained personnel in its command structure, and supported the alliance's Airborne Warning and Control System (AWACS) mission in Afghanistan with additional forces as compensation (Interviews 5 and S2, 2012).

In the meantime, Turkey also changed its position after it had evacuated its citizens from Libya and negotiations with Qadhafi had not made much progress (Interview T1, 2011). Furthermore, the Arab League's support of an intervention and the adoption of Resolution 1973 had shaped Ankara's assessment of the situation. With regard to the issue of a role for NATO, Turkey also changed its position. Against the backdrop of Erdoğan's strong language regarding the use of force throughout the first stage and a French-led coalition of the willing, it regarded the NATO framework as the best way to remain influential (Interviews 2 and 4, 2012). Being the only nation that still opposed a role for the alliance, France was quite isolated during the days around the Paris conference (Interview 4, 2012).

In the run-up to the compromise, mostly French and Turkish positions had to be reconciled. In a nutshell, France did not want "to leave the driver's seat," whereas Turkey tried to put at least "one hand on the steering wheel." A number of disagreements on details followed this pattern, such as on robust Rules of Engagement (RoE) or the political guidance of the Libya Contact Group (later, Friends of Libya) (Interview 3, 2012). France's position largely prevailed as it received support from the UK, which did not favor a weaker mandate for NATO than for the "coalition of the willing" and which was among the main initiators of the Contact

Group, officially establishing it at the London conference on 29 March (Hague 2011; Interviews 1 and S3, 2012).

The United States seemed to be a good mediator for these detailed questions since its priority was getting things off the ground for NATO (Interviews 6 and S3, 2012). After its significant participation in combat soon after the Paris conference, it wanted to hand *leadership* over to the UK and France, where it was at the beginning. The United States was a natural leader in any "coalition of the willing," and only NATO's established institutional structures allowed Washington to reduce its involvement. During this intense negotiation period, some nations sought to change the use of procedures. However, attempts, such as merging the CONOPS and the OPLAN for the no-fly zone plus in order to bypass a NAC decision, were blocked, for example, by Germany (Interviews 2 and 3, 2012). Apart from ensuring that rules and procedures were followed, the German permanent representative was mainly a silent observer after the abstention of his compatriots in the UNSC.

Since the Security Council did not pass a new resolution on Libya, the *number of negotiation levels* in the second stage was reduced to a two-level game between capitals and Brussels. Messages from the principals have already largely been elaborated. In sum, the UK and France wanted to maintain the military flexibility of a coalition of the willing. France additionally tried to restrict a NATO role, whereas the United States and Turkey, supported by the UK, pushed for a takeover of the alliance. Germany observed these discussions, with its permanent representative only speaking on procedural matters, if any. Talks took place on a formal and an informal track: "What happened was that the Council [NAC] would sit, debate, negotiate, then break for some twenty to thirty minutes to allow nations to get on the phone to their authorities in capital, explaining where other nations were, . . . and then reconvene to continue negotiations" (Interview S3, 2012).

The compromise between the United States, France, and Turkey on a common NATO operation was not based on an objectively ripe moment (Interview 1, 2012). Although negotiators perceived a way out, the stalemate was not mutually hurting but mainly harmful from the U.S. and the Turkish perspective. Driven by past experiences in Afghanistan and Iraq, Washington did not want to get stuck in Libya but knew that the chances for success of the coalition would decrease without an established command and control structure. Since Turkey was not part of the coalition, it needed a NATO compromise to regain influence. However, France was not hurt by the deadlock but had achieved all its goals so far. A look at strategy provides further insights.

Strategy in the Second Stage

From the perspective of *game-theoretic moves*, the first BotS game on ending violence by the Qadhafi regime and particularly avoiding a massacre in Benghazi had arrived at an equilibrium point (see Solution Issue in figure 3). With their attacks on regime forces, France, the UK, and the United States had imposed their preferred solution. Although this was only the second best outcome for Turkey and Germany, they had no incentive to deviate since a massacre in Benghazi had been avoided while negotiations with Qadhafi had not succeeded. Quite on the contrary, it could be interpreted that from their point of view, the solution was not fully coordinated yet since they were not able to influence the coalition of the willing. This leads to the second game, concerning NATO's role (see Framework Issue in figure 3).

In contrast to the previous stage, Turkey had switched its camp after a coalition initiated by France had already been operating and was coordinated with Arab countries, which hypothetically could have formed a coalition with Turkey and the United States. While for both countries the best outcome was a coordinated solution within NATO (4), a U.S.-led coalition was still the second best one (3) according to the BotS payoffs. The second worst outcome was to participate in a NATO operation that was not coordinated with coalition actions running in parallel (2), and the worst one was a U.S.-led coalition with Turkey while France and others were acting through NATO at the same time (1). France's preferences mirrored this distribution with a U.S.-led coalition at the top.

In the world of pure game theory, the coordinated U.S.-led coalition represents a Nash equilibrium. However, the United States had the opportunity to manipulate French payoffs. A coalition of the willing with the United States in the lead was France's favored outcome, but this also represented its BATNA, its Best Alternative to a Negotiated Agreement within NATO. Without a NATO compromise, the United States preferred its BATNA to the coalition, which was simply withdrawing its forces and waiting. In doing so, the French BATNA would change to running the coalition without the United States, which might not be sustainable from the military point of view and was not supported by the UK (Interview S3, 2012). Consequently, an agreement within NATO would be more valuable to France than its BATNA.

When examining the *non-game-theoretic moves*, it becomes clear that this is exactly what happened. The tactic of "shaping perceptions of alternatives to agreement" is part of a distributive bargaining strategy (Sebenius 2002, 240). A look at the *moves that reflect* the Negotiators' Dilemma and the *ones to escape* it reveals that the United States had been trying to entrap France by pushing for NATO preparations already throughout the first stage. The French had recognized the trap and reacted with "verbal safeguards." Beside intending to avoid the word "planning," French delegates kept on mentioning a possible "support role" for NATO until mid-March, after the coalition of the willing had already started its operations (Interview 4, 2012). On 21 March, Turkey played its card and vetoed progress in the NAC (Spiegel Online International 2011). More specifically, it "blocked NATO planning on the no-fly zone and insisted that NATO be put in control of it" (Traynor 2011). This reads like a paradox, but it had the desired effect: the United States set a deadline to withdraw from combat activities by 1 April (which it finally did on the morning of 4 April) (Interview 3, 2012; Clarke 2011, 5). In lowering the value of France's BATNA, the United States made the stalemate "mutually hurting" and increased the pressure on Paris to find a "way out," in the sense of searching for a compromise on a common NATO operation with Turkey. Consequently, a ripe moment did not objectively exist but was created by the U.S. deadline. This example further shows how structure and strategy interact with time, information, and communication.[3]

So far, the French strategy had worked out. By agreeing on NATO preparations, it had promoted the process of entrapment toward a military intervention while delaying a final decision in order to prevent NATO involvement as long as possible. Thereby, it had linked the Solution Issue with the Framework Issue (see figure 3). Aiming at its favorite outcomes, France had used the mentioned verbal safeguards and its veto in the NAC shortly before the Paris conference. It could even be argued that it had not invited Turkey to Paris on purpose, anticipating that the then slighted ally would block a NATO consensus, which was actually the case on 21 March (Interview 6, 2012; Spiegel Online International 2011). A negotiator described the French contentious issue-linkage tactic as follows:

> Not certainly unique to Libya, France has a distinctive negotiating style within NATO, which is that it tends to link many issues together and it tends to obstruct progress in one area if progress in another area is perhaps not going in the direction that it wants. . . . France is very practiced in the art of NATO obstruction and will always find ways to slow things down or to block progress on various issues if it determines that it is in its interest to do so. (Interview 6, 2012)

However, France probably had not expected that a Turkish veto could promote a U.S. decision to time its combat engagement. Once this deadline was communicated, France had to agree on putting coalition operations related to the protection of civilians under NATO command, while Turkey only participated in NATO activities enforcing the arms embargo and the no-fly zone. Although it had to make some minor concessions regarding the degree of political guidance executed by the contact group, France managed to shape the package deal substantially while relying on the support of the UK (Interviews 1 and S3, 2012). Germany, still self-entrapped by its vote in the UNSC, could only make some "statement[s] for the record" ('verbal safeguards'), but did not block compromise on a NATO operation in which it would not have a role to play.

Actors in the Second Stage

Although this second stage appeared even more contentious than the first one, it took only seven days. Therefore, the standoff might not have been as dramatic as presented by the media. A second element supports this argument. Driven by personal enthusiasm, NATO's Secretary General Anders Fogh Rasmussen had convened a press conference for 20 March in order to demonstrate that the alliance was ready to act, although he had been approached by delegations to wait (Interview S3, 2012). Since there was no agreement yet on that date, the story about the deadlock was spun out for the next few days (Interview S1, 2012). This, as well as Al Jazeera's role during the first negotiation stage, is another example of the media being an exogenous actor that affects the context and, thus, influences the process of negotiation.

As in the first stage, the NAC continued to be the primary forum of negotiations at the beginning of the second stage, but it involved the technical level (OPC) as discussions became less controversial, mainly after more and more operational aspects were taken over by NATO. The second phase also showed how the five countries' principal-agent relationships differed, especially with regard to their respective negotiators' autonomy. Statements, such as "the French ambassador has his president at the phone all the time" or "they [Turkey] basically cannot decide on anything without Ankara," display that French and Turkish negotiators certainly were less autonomous than their colleagues from the UK and the United States (Interviews 4 and 1, 2012). Having abstained in the UNSC, Berlin had no further instructions for its delegation throughout this second stage (Interview S2, 2012). Since there were no replacements of negotiating personnel, the results for the factor *personality* remained unchanged.

STAGE THREE: OPERATION UNIFIED PROTECTOR

After the compromise on 24 March, NATO assumed overall command of military activities in Libya on 31 March under Operation Unified Protector, which lasted seven months. Although negotiations within the NATO apparatus on executing and terminating the operation were largely characterized by problem solving, there were some frictions over details. Since by far the allies met not as often as throughout the previous phase and mostly focused on compliance to what had been agreed on, this final period fulfilled the function of a postnegotiation stage. Again, the analysis starts with structural factors in comparison with the second phase.

Structure in the Third Stage

While the same *power* resources mattered for the third stage as for the ones before, they were not used to influence the negotiation process in this final phase. As in the previous stages, *coalitions* were built around issues of the Tactical Question that represented the points of friction during this period.

The first issue emerged during the foreign ministers' meeting in Berlin on 14 April. Germany's skepticism had not yet disappeared. It wanted clarity regarding the criteria for a fulfilled UN mandate, the future end state in Libya after defeating Qadhafi, and a possible exit strategy (Interviews 1 and 3, 2012). The discussion centered on the question of regime change as operational objective. Since this had not been mandated by the UNSC, NATO documents neither permitted targeting of individuals, such as the authoritarian leadership, nor mentioned any NATO position on the issue (Interviews 5 and 6, 2012). However, Cameron and Sarkozy (2011) had already clearly distanced themselves from Qadhafi on various occasions, for instance, in the letter to van Rompuy, by recognizing the NTC as legitimate representative of the Libyan people, or by supporting the rebels through activities of their national special forces on the ground. There are indications that Turkey also favored regime change, yet was less outspoken than the UK and France (Head 2011; Zalewski 2012). Rather aligned with the German position, the United States could principally envision a scenario in which Qadhafi would have no longer threatened civilians but introduced reforms (Interview 6, 2012).

Secondly, as the stalemate between Qadhafi and the rebels evolved throughout April and May, differences on how to react appeared between the UK and France on one side and the United States on the other side. In this debate over surge versus sustainability, the UK and France favored a more "flexible" approach, including the deployment of attack helicopters to undermine Qadhafi's strategy to disguise his forces as civilians, while the United States preferred a "tactic of attrition," which in its view contained less potential to "scare off" some already critical allies (Interview S3, 2012). The stalemate never reached a mutually hurting stage propitious for negotiations, as the Libyan chapter in this book describes.

The final point of friction disunited the same three allies. While the United States, after Tripoli had fallen at the end of August, sought to end OUP as soon as possible, the UK and France strove to continue the operation (Interview S3, 2012). From their perspective, the threat to civilians was persistent since Qadhafi forces still resisted, as in Sirte. This point of view was supported by members of the NTC who even shortly before the termination of OUP still lobbied for extending NATO's presence (BBC 2011e). The UK and France mostly managed to obtain their objectives on these issues, which indicates their *leadership* role in this operation. Contrary to the second stage, the United States had withdrawn from immediate participation in combat and was from the start of OUP merely "leading from behind" (e.g., by supporting the alliance with ISTAR and refueling capabilities) (Interview 1, 2012; Lizza 2011).

From a procedural perspective, the most controversial document was the statement of the foreign ministers' meeting in Berlin. Its preparation followed the logic of a single negotiation text with first drafts being negotiated at OPC and then at NAC level. However, the issues were so sensitive that at the end the foreign ministers themselves still fought about words, which "is rare" for NATO negotiations (Interview 6, 2012).

Domestic ratification levels again played an important role. When CNN journalist Wolf Blitzer (2011) interviewed Rasmussen on 24 March, asking him about the future commander of Operation Unified Protector, NATO's secretary general tried to avoid the answer by not naming specific candidates or even their nationalities. If the usual NATO chain of command had been followed, running OUP from JFC Naples would have implied that its head, the U.S. admiral Samuel Locklear, would have been in charge (Interviews S3 and 2, 2012). However, this degree of involvement could already not be ratified at the U.S. domestic level. As a result, Operation Unified Protector's operational command was only attached to the structures of JFC Naples but set up ad hoc, with the deputy commander of the Italian Allied Command at the top: the Canadian general Charles Bouchard. Although there is no information about German and Turkish ratification levels at this stage, it is possible that setting up the foreign ministers' meeting in Berlin, a conference to clarify exit options for the intervention, was a measure to please the German domestic level.

However, there is evidence that public pressures in the UK and France influenced their decision to deploy attack helicopters when the stalemate on the ground emerged and Qadhafi's regime forces were harder to distinguish from the rebels (Interviews 3, 5, and S3, 2012). With their constituencies' concerns about a long and bloody war in mind, the UK and France argued that a quick success in Libya would create more political sustainability than the attrition tactic of the United States. Again, the interacting factor of time becomes important as time pressure to successfully end the operation.

Strategy and Actors in the Third Stage

With OUP under way, the BotS game on a NATO role had arrived at a Nash equilibrium (see Framework Issue in figure 3). The combination of Turkish veto power and U.S. military power could impose the NATO solution against the will of France. Still, France had no incentive to unilaterally deviate from the outcome, which represented its second best result, and had no means to alter the payoff perceptions or BATNAS of the other two countries. Moreover, the end of the coalition of the willing enforced the equilibrium of the first BotS game concerning a coordinated military solution (see Solution Issue in figure 3). The disagreements on the mentioned details throughout the third stage could also be modeled as BotS games, since their central problem was coordination with various kinds of minor distribution conflicts (see Regime Change Issue, Operational Measures Issue, and Operation Unified Protector Termination Issue in figure 3). Instead of elaborating once again on *game-theoretic moves*, it appears more fruitful at this point to directly turn to the *non-game-theoretic ones*.

As already stated in the context of the first stage, negotiations inside NATO largely followed the pattern of integrative bargaining, although there were still a number of disagreements on "how to distribute the pie." Solutions, such as the creative compromise at the end of the second phase, showed nevertheless that the twenty-eight allies were interested in solving problems and creating a win-win situation. With regard to integrative bargaining, the main obstacle in the third stage was to agree on a "shared vision" of the end state in Libya (Sebenius 2002). The foreign ministers' statement in Berlin indicates that the concessions, a move that reflects the Negotiators' Dilemma, had been balanced. For instance, while already in the first paragraph of their letter to van Rompuy, Cameron and Sarkozy (2011) had underlined that it was "clear to [them] that the [Qadhafi] regime has lost any legitimacy it may have once had", the Berlin statement (NATO 2011f) pointed out: "Qadhafi and his regime have lost all legitimacy through their comprehensive and repeated refusal to abide by UNSC Resolutions 1970 and 1973." Although the UK and France managed to keep the core formulation, it was embedded into a UN frame and appeared only at the end of the second paragraph of the text to appease German interests, among others (Interview 1, 2012).

When the first discussions on terminating OUP were held in September, the UK and France managed to delay this decision for a few weeks (Interview S3, 2012). It is likely that this time was gained by the move to wait for a UNSC Resolution setting a clear date. However, on 21 October they agreed on a "preliminary decision to end Operation Unified Protector on the 31st of October" (NATO 2011h). Before NATO would make a final decision, Rasmussen would "consult closely with the United Nations." Four days after UNSC Resolution 2016 had been adopted on 27 October, OUP was formally concluded. In this vein, the Security Council could again be conceived as some kind of second-order ratification level.

The OPC, having already assumed more responsibility in the second stage, was interacting throughout the third stage with the NAC as procedurally previewed—for example, when predrafting the Berlin foreign minister's statement (Interviews 1 and 6, 2012). However, the discussion was so controversial that the document could not be finished before the summit, and ministers had to do the final editing.

So far, this study has focused on various independent factors and outlined some of their interactions with time, information, and communication, where appropriate. The following section sheds more light on these interacting factors.

INTERACTING FACTORS

Time pressure facilitated agreement, especially at the highest decision-making levels. No matter if it occurred in the form of an anticipated massacre in Benghazi or was induced by the lack of domestic support for an enduring operation, it forced negotiators to make decisions faster than without time pressure. The same holds for the manipulation of time, as the example of the deadline by the United States has shown. As time was short throughout the whole process, negotiators tried to win time—for example, shortly before the Paris conference or when OUP's conclusion was discussed in September.

Although *information* was largely available and shared, there were some shortcomings. For example, combat imagery that visualized, on the one hand, Qadhafi's war crimes and, on the other hand, NATO's thoughtful approach toward civilians was often rather exploited for national profiling than shared within the alliance (Interview 5, 2012). Bi- and plurilateral defense cooperation arrangements were also partly perceived as an impediment in terms of intelligence sharing (Interview 3, 2012). Additionally, some negotiators complained "that nations did not put all the cards on the table regarding their national motivations" (Interview 2, 2012).

Finally, it has proven essential what and how messages were *communicated*. Qadhafi's threats toward Benghazi, the disclosure of the U.S. deadline when NATO got stuck, the discussion on regime change, and the "word games" by various nations are some prominent examples for the impact of this interacting factor.

OUTCOME

Although there had been no codified *agreement* yet, the decision to start NATO preparations constituted what Arild Underdal calls a "meeting of minds" (2002, 112). Seeking to cover diverging positions in order to survive disagreement, the formulations in the first written texts were vague and ambiguous. Examples are the Leslie Principles and the decisive paragraphs of Resolution 1973. A more concrete but only partial agreement in form of the coalition of the willing proved not to be sustainable. Only the NATO compromise solution at the end of the second stage constituted a highly codified agreement, which was backed by all twenty-eight member states.

In game-theoretic terms, both interim and final outcomes were located at equilibrium points, which are Pareto *efficient* in the BotS game, meaning that no actor can improve his or her situation without worsening the situation of at least one of the other actors. However, a NATO agreement before the United States revealed its deadline had been only "weakly integrative" since its value did not exceed the French BATNA (Underdal 2002, 113). The same holds for the coalition of the willing from the U.S. perspective. When Washington communicated the deadline to withdraw from combat within a few days, the French BATNA changed, and the NATO solution became "strongly integrative." The study shows that the parties arrived at an efficient and satisfying consensus by an interactive process of moves and contextual evolution, under the pressure of time and domestic concerns. The more parties joined, the more equilibrium points were reached, and the less payoff perceptions could be manipulated, the more *stable* the outcomes were. Without incentives for defection, the successful cooperation might even promote closer relations. However, the case for dynamic stability can only be assessed when comparing this operation to future ones.

When evaluating *distribution*, it certainly can be stated that, for most countries, throughout the sequence of events the benefits of intervening gradually outweighed the costs of a continuing status quo. Since interviewed negotiators consistently believed that the final NATO outcome was quite close to their initial positions, it might be assumed that the solution was largely perceived as fair and just.

ELEVEN LESSONS FOR THE PRACTICAL NEGOTIATOR

Besides explaining the Libyan case and testing theoretical concepts against empirical evidence, the results of this study provide the basis for a number of practical lessons regarding future negotiations, especially within a consensus environment. First, negotiators should try to set the agenda, however, with ambiguous openers that include their preferred outcome, but that also seek consensus among the other parties. In doing so, they preempt—or at least begin—the formulation of a formula. The UK's Leslie Principles provide a good example how this might succeed. Second, negotiators should avoid strong initial positions and early self-entrapment. As the examples of the German abstention in the UNSC and the Turkish veto in the NAC show, conditions may change as time elapses, but the loss of flexibility is irreversible.

Even principally cooperative games contain distribution conflicts. Therefore, it is a reasonable advice, thirdly, to focus on core interests and try to entrap others, especially when knowing that a negotiator's position constitutes an equilibrium point whose payoffs cannot be manipulated by others. As in the case of the United States, the UK, and France, this could be done through initiating or trying to short-circuit procedures. The French negotiating behavior further provides lessons four and five. Lesson four is the use of self-entrapped others for one's own purposes. In this sense, upsetting Turkey by not inviting it to the Paris conference might have been a trigger for its subsequent veto in the NAC. Thus, progress in NATO was blocked, although France did not have to do the vetoing itself. A fifth lesson of French behavior is issue linkage in order to increase the overall benefit of the package.

There are also some pieces of advice to counter contentious behavior. Lesson six identifies communication in the form of "verbal safeguards," such as by France, Germany, and Turkey, as a useful anti-entrapment strategy. Seventh, disclosing critical information can be an asset to create time pressure. In reference to the example of the U.S. deadline for troop withdrawal, it can be alternatively said that it is possible and useful to create a ripe moment by making a stalemate mutually hurting through changing payoff perceptions, such as the BATNA. Eighth, time pressure can also be created by influencing exogenous events with reverberation potential. While Resolution 1973 and the outcome of the Paris conference probably increased the time pressure on Qadhafi to attack Benghazi, the French air strikes accelerated countermeasures by the international community.

In the ninth place, negotiators are advised to use procedures to win time, as it was done through the French veto shortly before the Paris conference or by the UK and France when delaying the termination of OUP. Tenth, principals should not forget to provide their negotiators with enough leeway to maneuver, especially on the details of an agreement. While the UK constitutes a positive example here, Turkey and France are rather negative ones. As an eleventh and final lesson, capitalizing on both aggregate and issue-specific power resources can be an effective means to create bargaining leverage, which can be used to, for instance, escape entrapment. Examples are the dependence of others on one's own military capabilities as the U.S. case has shown and, especially in a consensus environment, the use of both veto and fait accompli.

Overall, the Libyan case demonstrates that agreeing on a multilateral military intervention within NATO is not an easy task, however: "The decision to go to war is the most extreme decision an organization can take. . . . If an organization decides to go to war easily, there is something wrong with the organization" (Interview 5, 2012).

Abbreviations

AC	Allied Air Command
AU	African Union
AWACS	Airborne Warning and Control System
BATNA	Best Alternative to a Negotiated Agreement
BotS	Battle of the Sexes
BP	BP plc, formerly British Petroleum
CONOPS	Concept of Operations
CSDP	Common Security and Defense Policy
EU	European Union
GCC	Gulf Cooperation Council
ICC	International Criminal Court
IS	International Staff
ISTAR	Intelligence, Surveillance, Target Acquisition, and Reconnaissance
JFC	Allied Joint Force Command
MC	Allied Maritime Command
NAC	North Atlantic Council
NATO	North Atlantic Treaty Organization
NED	North Atlantic Council (NAC) Execution Directive
NID	North Atlantic Council (NAC) Initiating Directive
NTC	National Transitional Council
OIC	Organization of the Islamic Conference

OPC	Operations Policy Committee
OPLAN	Operations Plan
OUP	Operation Unified Protector
R2P	Responsibility to Protect
RoE	Rules of Engagement
SACEUR	Supreme Allied Commander Europe
SHAPE	Supreme Headquarters Allied Powers Europe
SNT	Single Negotiation Text
TKI	Thomas-Kilmann Conflict Mode Instrument
UAE	United Arab Emirates
UK	United Kingdom
UNHCR	United Nations High Commissioner for Refugees
UNOCHA	United Nations Office for the Coordination of Humanitarian Affairs
UNSC	United Nations Security Council
U.S.	United States

Notes

1. This study relies on eleven interviews with ten partners (one interviewed twice in different contexts), representing national, institutional, and academic perspectives. All interviews were conducted by the author unless stated otherwise.

2. Since this was a comparably simple operation, it did not comprise a CONOPS. However, humanitarian assistance was never executed by NATO since there was no request by the United Nations Office for the Coordination of Humanitarian Affairs (UNOCHA) or the United Nations High Commissioner for Refugees (UNHCR).

3. For a similar procedural course to ripeness, see Zartman (1997).

References

Aydin, Mustafa. 2012. Professor for International Relations and Rector of Kadir Has University (Istanbul), interviewed in Bruges, 21 February 2012.

BBC. 2011a. "Libya Protests: Defiant Gaddafi Refuses to Quit." 22 February. http://www.bbc.co.uk/news/world-middle-east-12544624 (accessed 16 April 2012).

———. 2011b. "France Recognises Rebels as Government." 10 March. http://www.bbc.co.uk/news/world-africa-12699183 (accessed 22 April 2012).

———. 2011c. "Arab League Backs Libya No-Fly Zone." 12 March. http://www.bbc.co.uk/news/world-africa-12723554 (accessed 16 April 2012).

———. 2011d. "Anti-Gaddafi Forces 'Seize Sirte.'" 20 October. http://www.bbc.co.uk/news/world-africa-15384335 (accessed 22 April 2012).

———. 2011e. "Libya's Mustafa Abdul Jalil Asks Nato to Stay Longer." 26 October 2. http://www.bbc.co.uk/news/world-africa-15459473 (accessed 30 April 2012).

Black, Ian. 2011. "Gaddafi Threatens Retaliation in Mediterranean as UN Passes Resolution: Gaddafi Vows to 'Get Crazy' in Event of Foreign Attack as UN Security Council in New York Passes Resolution." *Guardian*, 18 March. http://www.guardian.co.uk/world/2011/mar/17/gaddafi-retaliation-mediterrane an-libya-no-fly-zone (accessed 22 April 2012).

Blitzer, Wolf, and Anders Fogh Rasmussen. 2011. "NATO Secretary-General Anders Fogh Rasmussen on NATO Agreement." CNN, 24 March. http://cnnpress room.blogs.cnn.com/2011/03/24

/nato-secretary-general-anders-fogh-rasmussen-on-nato-agreement/ (accessed 30 April 2012).

Cameron, David, and Nicolas Sarkozy. 2011. "Letter from David Cameron and Nicolas Sarkozy to Herman van Rompuy." *Guardian*, 10 March. http://www.theguardian.com/world/2011/mar/10/libya-middleeast (accessed 1 December 2014).

Clarke, Michael. 2011. "The Road to War." In "Accidental Heroes: Britain, France and the Libya Operation," edited by Saqeb Mueen and Grant Turnbull, 3–5. Interim Campaign Report, Royal United Services Institute (RUSI), September. https://www.rusi.org/news/ref:N4E7B610E8D672/#.VH-rkdYtdTY (accessed 1 December 2014).

Daalder, Ivo H., and James G. Stavridis. 2012. "NATO's Victory in Libya: The Right Way to Run an Intervention." *Foreign Affairs* 81, no. 2: 2–7.

Fisher, Roger, and William Ury. 1999. *Getting to Yes: Negotiating an Agreement without Giving In*. 2nd ed. London: Random House.

Hague, William. 2011. "London Conference on Libya: Chair's Statement." 29 March. https://www.gov.uk/government/news/london-conference-on-libya-chairs-statement (accessed 1 December 2014).

Head, Jonathan. 2011. "Libya: Turkey's Troubles with NATO and No-Fly Zone." BBC, 25 March. http://www.bbc.co.uk/news/world-africa-12864742 (accessed 25 April 2012).

Interview 1. 2012. NATO Official 1, Brussels, 6 March.

Interview 2. 2012. NATO Official 2, Brussels, 6 March.

Interview 3. 2012. NATO Official 3, Brussels, 7 March.

Interview 4. 2012. NATO Official 4, Brussels, 7 March.

Interview 5. 2012. NATO Official 5, Brussels, 22 March.

Interview 6. 2012. NATO Official 6, Brussels, 26 March.

Interview S1. 2012. Senior NATO Official 1, Bruges, 16 January.

Interview S2. 2012. Senior NATO Official 2, Brussels, 7 March.

Interview S3. 2012. Senior NATO Official 3, Brussels, 22 March.

Interview T1. 2011. Conducted by Paul Meerts with a Turkish Foreign Ministry official, Ankara, 16 November.

Irondelle, Bastien, and Frédéric Mérand. 2010. "France's Return to NATO: The Death Knell for ESDP?" *European Security* 19, no. 1: 29–43.

Joshi, Shashank. 2011. "How the Rebels Became an Effective Fighting Force." In "Accidental Heroes: Britain, France and the Libya Operation," edited by Saqeb Mueen and Grant Turnbull, 11. Interim Campaign Report, Royal United Services Institute (RUSI), September 2011. https://www.rusi.org/news/ref:N4E7B610E8D672/#.VH-rkdYtdTY (accessed 1 December 2014).

Kremenyuk, Victor A., ed. 2002. In *International Negotiation: Analysis, Approaches, Issues*. 2nd ed. San Francisco: Jossey-Bass.

Lax, David A., and James K. Sebenius. 1986. *The Manager as Negotiator: Bargaining for Cooperation and Competitive Gain*. New York: Free Press.

Leithäuser, Johannes. 2011. "Großbritannien und Libyen: Heikle Interessen" [Great Britain and Libya: Delicate interests]. *Frankfurter Allgemeine Zeitung*, 22 February. http://www.faz.net/aktuell/politik/arabische-welt/gross britannien-und-libyen-heikle-interessen-1594472.html (accessed 26 April 2012).

Lizza, Ryan. 2011. "Leading from Behind." *New Yorker*, 26 April. http://www.newyorker.com/online/blogs/newsdesk/2011/04/leading-from-behind-obama-clinton.html#ixzz1Vg4u7yg4 (accessed 30 April 2012).

Meerts, Paul W. 2005. "Entrapment in International Negotiation." In *Escalation and Negotiation in International Conflicts*, edited by I. William Zartman and Guy-Olivier Faure, 103–130. Cambridge: Cambridge University Press.

NATO (North Atlantic Treaty Organization). 2010. "Operations Policy Committee." 14 December. http://www.nato.int/cps/en/natolive/topics_69312.htm (accessed 27 April 2012).

———. 2011a. "NATO Secretary General Convenes Emergency Meeting of the North Atlantic Council." 25 February. http://www.nato.int/cps/en/natolive/news_70800.htm (accessed 22 April 2012).

———. 2011b. "Statement by the NATO Secretary General on Libya Arms Embargo." 22 March. http://www.nato.int/cps/en/natolive/news_71689.htm (accessed 19 April 2012).

———. 2011c. "NATO Secretary General's Statement on Libya No-Fly Zone." 24 March. http://www.nato.int/cps/en/natolive/news_71763.htm (accessed 19 April 2012).

———. 2011d. "Statement by NATO Secretary General Anders Fogh Rasmussen on Libya." 27 March. http://www.nato.int/cps/en/natolive/news_71808.htm (accessed 19 April 2012).

———. 2011e. "Operation Unified Protector: Command and Control." 29 March. http://www.nato.int/nato_static/assets/pdf/pdf_2011_03/20110325_110325-unified-protector-command-control.pdf (accessed 19 April 2012).

———. 2011f. "Statement on Libya Following the Working Lunch of NATO Ministers of Foreign Affairs with Non-NATO Contributors to Operation Unified Protector." Press release, no. 045, 14 April. http://www.nato.int/cps/en/natolive/official_texts_72544.htm?mode=pressrelease (accessed 22 April 2012).

———. 2011g. "NATO's Assessment of a Crisis and Development of Response Strategies." 10 May (updated 16 June 2011). http://www.nato.int/cps/en/natolive/official_texts_75565.htm (accessed 1 December 2014).

———. 2011h. "Press Conference by NATO Secretary General on the Latest Developments in Libya and Operation Unified Protector." 21 October (updated 24 October 2011). http://www.nato.int/cps/en/natolive/opinions_79807.htm (accessed 1 May 2012).

Oğuz, Mustafa. 2011. "Turkey Ignoring NATO Allies for Its Neighbors." *Hürriyet Daily News*, 12 May. http://www.hurriyet.com.tr/english/domestic/10644905.asp?gid=244 (accessed 26 April 2012).

Phillips, Mark. 2011. "The Ground Offensive: The Role of Special Forces." In "Accidental Heroes: Britain, France and the Libya Operation, edited by Saqeb Mueen and Grant Turnbull, 10–12. Interim Campaign Report, Royal United Services Institute (RUSI), September. https://www.rusi.org/news/ref:N4E7B610E8D672/#.VH-rkdYtdTY (accessed 1 December 2014).

Pruitt, Dean G. 2002. "Strategy in Negotiation." In Kremenyuk, *International Negotiation*, 85–96.

Pruitt, Dean G., and Sung Hee Kim. 2004. *Social Conflict: Escalation, Stalemate, and Settlement*. 3rd ed. Boston: McGraw-Hill, 2004.

Putnam, Robert D. 1988. "Diplomacy and Domestic Politics: The Logic of Two-Level Games." *International Organization* 42, no. 3: 427–460.

Quintana, Elizabeth. 2011. "The Air Operation." In "Accidental Heroes: Britain, France and the Libya Operation," edited by Saqeb Mueen and Grant Turnbull, 5–7. Interim Campaign Report, Royal United Services Institute (RUSI), September. https://www.rusi.org/news/ref:N4E7B610E8D672/#.VH-rkdYtdTY (accessed 1 December 2014).

Raiffa, Howard. 1982. *The Art and Science of Negotiation*. Cambridge, Mass.: Belknap Press of Harvard University Press.

Rinke, Andreas. 2011. "Eingreifen oder nicht? Warum sich die Bundesregierung in der Libyen-Frage enthielt" [Intervening or not? Why the federal government abstained in the Libya question]. *Internationale Politik* [International politics] 4:44–52.

Schaubhut, Nancy A. 2007. "Technical Brief for the Thomas-Kilmann Conflict Mode Instrument: Description of the Updated Normative Sample and Implications for Use." Mountain View, Calif.: Consulting Psychologists Press. https://www.cpp.com/pdfs/tki_Technical_Brief.pdf (accessed 12 April 2012).

Sebenius, James K. 2002. “International Negotiation Analysis.” In Kremenyuk, *International Negotiation*, 229–255.

SF (Schweizer Fernsehen [Swiss Television]). 2011. “Nato übernimmt Ruder von UNO-Allianz in Libyen” [NATO takes over from the UN Alliance in Libya]. 24 March. http://www.tagesschau.sf.tv/Nachrichten/Archiv/2011/03/24/International/Machtwechsel-in-Libyen/Nato-uebernimmt-Ruder-von-UNO-Allianz-in-Libyen (accessed 25 April 2012).

Snidal, Duncan J. 1985. “Coordination versus Prisoners’ Dilemma: Implications for International Cooperation and Regimes.” *American Political Science Review* 79, no. 4: 923–942.

Spiegel Online International. 2011. “Command Conflict: Turkey Blocks NATO Mission in Libya.” 21 March. http://www.spiegel.de/international/world/0,1518,752222,00.html (accessed 3 May 2012).

Thomas, Kenneth W., and Ralph H. Kilmann. 1977. “Developing a Forced-Choice Measure of Conflict-Handling Behavior: The ‘Mode’ Instrument.” *Educational and Psychological Measurement* 37, no. 2: 309–325.

Traynor, Ian. 2011. “Libya No-Fly Zone Leadership Squabbles Continue within NATO.” *Guardian*, 23 March. http://www.guardian.co.uk/world/2011/mar/23/libya-no-fly-zone-leadership-squabbles (accessed 28 April 2012).

Turnbull, Grant, 2011. “Timeline.” In “Accidental Heroes: Britain, France and the Libya Operation,” edited by Saqeb Mueen and Grant Turnbull, 2. Interim Campaign Report, Royal United Services Institute (RUSI), September. https://www.rusi.org/news/ref:N4E7B610E8D672/#.VH-rkdYtdTY (accessed 1 December 2014).

Underdal, Arild. 2002. “The Outcomes of Negotiation.” In Kremenyuk, *International Negotiation*, 110–125.

UNGA (United Nations General Assembly). 2005. “Sixtieth Session: Items 48 and 121 of the Provisional Agenda: 2005 World Summit Outcome.” A/60/L. 1, New York, 15 September.

UNSC (United Nations Security Council) 2011a. “Resolution 1970 (2011): Adopted by the Security Council at its 6491st Meeting, on 26 February 2011.” S/RES/1970 (2011), New York, 26 February.

——— 2011b. “Resolution 1973 (2011): Adopted by the Security Council at Its 6498th Meeting, on 17 March 2011.” S/RES/1973 (2011), New York, 17 March.

——— 2011c. “Resolution 2016 (2011): Adopted by the Security Council in its 6640th Meeting, on 27 October 2011.” S/RES/2016 (2011), New York, 27 October.

Wells, Matt. 2011. “Al-Jazeera Cameraman Chased and Shot Dead by Gaddafi Regime Supporters.” *Guardian*, 14 March. http://www.guardian.co.uk/world/2011/mar/13/al-jazeera-cameraman-lured-into-trap-gaddafi-libya (accessed 23 April 2012).

Zalewski, Piotr. 2012. “Turkey’s Democratic Dilemma: Letter from Istanbul.” *Foreign Affairs*, 21 March. http://www.foreignaffairs.com/features/letters-from/turkeys-democratic-dilemma?page=show (accessed 30 April 2012).

Zartman, I. William. 1997. “Explaining Oslo.” In Lessons Learned from the Middle East Peace Process,” edited by Dean G. Pruitt. Special issue of *International Negotiation* 2, no. 2: 195–215.

———. 2002. “The Structure of Negotiation.” In Kremenyuk, *International Negotiation*, 71–84.

Serbia

Moderation as a Double-Edged Sword

SINIŠA VUKOVIĆ

ON 5 OCTOBER 2000, after a week of mass protests over electoral fraud, Democratic Opposition of Serbia (DOS) toppled Slobodan Milošević, ending his more-than-a-decade-long authoritarian rule. The actor responsible for the regime's downfall—DOS—was a conglomerate of eighteen parties, led by the Democratic Party of Serbia (DSS) and the Democratic Party (DS), and their respective leaders Vojislav Koštunica and Zoran Đinđić. Such a broad and diverse coalition was needed to overthrow Milošević, but it showed signs of internal (ideological) discord that would hamper the transition process from autocracy to democracy. According to Pešić (2009, 72), who directly participated in those events, "If one reads the DOS programs from today's perspective, one gets the impression that the promises of constitution, legal state, independent judiciary, strong democratic institutions, and transparent government were made with little thought: a memorized lesson, without assessing whether any agreement actually exists on the future value framework." In fact, the coalition had not negotiated a clear plan on how to realize these values as there was no shared formulation about the future state of affairs. As a result, post-Milošević Serbia was more characterized by Old Order continuity and cooperation in governance with members of the former regime than anything new.

This chapter argues that the reasons for such an outcome can be found in the way the opposition parties negotiated for coalition, which prevented them from negotiating a clear formula for the future. The common perception that only a broad coalition could defeat Milošević forced the opposition leaders to join forces with ideologically distant political actors. Their cooperation was driven by a shared agreement that Milošević's rule had to end. Perception of a common enemy became the foundation on which the coalition was negotiated. However, such an ideologically heterogeneous coalition was unable to strike an agreement on how the New Order should look. Rather, given the extent of the internal ideological discord, the coalition served as a catalyst to put aside doctrinal differences and focus on the negative demand of ousting Milošević. As a result it assumed a very moderate, if not ambiguous, policy orientation and showed signs of confusion already on the first day in office. Moderate policies abated the revolutionary drive of DOS, as they refused any activity that might destabilize the country. In such an environment most of the representatives of the structures of the right hand of the former regime—especially the security apparatus, such as the police, army, and intelligence—managed to find a way to be spared from any widespread lustration and were even treated as indispensable in the interim period. Similarly many mid-ranking and low-ranking officials of the former regime stayed in office. Not surprisingly, this produced direct consequences on the transition process, which was slow and incomplete for a long period of time.

CHALLENGES OF NEGOTIATED TRANSITION

Negotiations are unquestionably an essential part of every transition process, even though they generally receive marginal treatment by the media, especially compared to revolutionary dynamics. Just as in any conflict—violent or not—in revolutions and transitions the parties have two simple options to find a solution to their quarrel: to talk or to clash, known as the Tactical Question (Zartman and Alfredson 2010). But negotiations do not take place only in the midst of the revolutionary days; they represent an ongoing process, starting with the moment citizens have decided to challenge the current state of affairs. People first need to negotiate with others who share their intention to challenge the regime, and this negotiation is referred as *negotiating for coalition*. In the second step (or even parallel to previous one) political actors also discuss what kind of a state of affairs they have in mind for the future order, once the transition has occurred, referred to as *negotiating for formulation*.

But they do not negotiate only among themselves. The challengers also negotiate with representatives of the regime, or at least face the policy decision of whether to negotiate. This is especially the case in the first days of transition, when it is clear that the regime is about to fall and a New Order needs to be established. Willingness of the opposition to talk with their enemies depends on the level of trust and the extent of grievances that they have in regard to the regime. So while on one hand opposition forces would rather fight than talk (as in Libya), on numerous occasions the two sides managed to find a way to engage in negotiations (as in Tunisia, Egypt, and Yemen). It is usually the moderate forces within the opposition that are willing to talk to the representatives of the regime and are more inclined to come up with a compromise solution. Moderates generally chose "not to rock the boat," and in their quest to stabilize the situation they aim to find interlocutors among those who represent institutions most important for the internal stability of the system. In authoritarian regimes (which are mostly challenged by such revolutions) such institutions are usually the police, the army, the civil service, and the intelligence, but sometimes they include dissidents or doves in the core of the Old Order.

Negotiating for a Coalition

However, moderation might turn out to be a double-edge sword in the processes of negotiating a transition from one Order to another. Moderation is often promoted as a way to achieve a balanced view of the situation that evolves during these transition periods. It implies political inclusivity of various forces that might not even share a common ideology. As such, moderation allows for formation of a larger coalition of political actors. The presence of a multitude of political actors directly increases popular support and improves the chances that a coalition will have a larger following. Actors that form this coalition enter for various reasons that are molded according to their ideological outlook on the unfolding situation. Despite an apparent variety of motives to form a particular group, once formed this coalition needs to be grounded in a particular, commonly shared reason. Stability of this coalition is based on a dynamic that aims to establish an overlapping consensus (Rawls 1987).

Despite a potential mix of various ideologies, a coalition still allows opposition actors to rally around notions that are crucial for any political campaign, such as rule of law, equality, liberties, and justice. These, however, can be interpreted in various ways by the same political actors, depending on their ideological positions. While everyone in the opposition might agree that the country needs a constitution that promotes the rule of law and that citizens should enjoy their liberties, each actor might have a different idea how should this be put into practice. The only real motive that is shared across the coalition and that is not subject to different ideological interpretations is a common disagreement with the Old Order and an immediate goal of removing the authoritarian ruler. Having the regime as a common enemy also allows for the coalition to solidify its (potential) popular support, as it submerges those ideological differences that might discourage people from gathering around such a diverse coalition. At the same time, as the number of actors with ideological differences grows, in order to put those differences aside the coalition tends to converge around lowest common denominator policies.

Negotiating for Formulation

While providing internal stability to the coalition, overlapping consensus and moderate political standpoints can well abate its revolutionary drive. If we think of political revolutions as radical changes in political organization manifested through a removal from power of one political entity and its replacement with a new one, then those forces that aim to attain power are also faced with a challenge of formulating a clear idea of what they are going to do once in power. While the seizure of power might be a product of a revolutionary momentum, preservation of that power in order to remodel the system requires a more comprehensive strategy.

Therefore, when forming a coalition of opposition forces that aim to challenge the Old Order, actors who negotiate for a coalition also need to *negotiate for formulation* of an operational plan for the future, derived from a shared vision of the New Order.

In this negotiation process, the opposition is faced with a challenge to come up with a platform capable of appeasing various political ambitions that motivated opposition forces to form a coalition. In order to do so, it needs to find balance between what Pešić (2009) calls "synergy of unity," which reflects the general agreement on regime as a common enemy, and latent ideological incongruity within the coalition. While having a common enemy might be useful to rally popular support, a clear plan for the future helps the coalition to face the challenge of the first day in power. In case members of the coalition do not strike a clear accord on what the New Order should be like, their "synergy of unity" might disappear in the moment the old regime gets toppled, and they face a very difficult challenge of running the country without a clear plan.

In fact, processes of negotiating for coalition and for formulation are not just significant for the preliminary stages of the transition; they carry on into the post-revolutionary period. Moderation that is induced by the size of the coalition does not only accommodate ideologically diverse actors, but it allows for a more flexible or pragmatic treatment of those political opponents who did not join the coalition, notably the representatives of the regime. Moderate forces usually do not refuse the possibility of actually negotiating with political adversaries that were just toppled and engage in pacting in order to keep the New Order moderate. By doing this, former regime members regain a certain degree of legitimacy in the new circumstances. Thus, the result might be the overthrow of those members of the regime that impersonated the Old Order, while preserving the structures and personnel that provided stability for the entire system despite their involvement in the former regime. In such an environment the mid-ranking and low-ranking echelons might remain in office, because they are the people who know how things are done. By preserving a certain degree of legitimacy, in the long run members of the old regime might actually be given a second chance to get back to power using the mechanisms set up in the New Order, thus questioning the revolutionary rationale of the opposition coalition.

OPPOSITION AND CIVIL SOCIETY IN SERBIA UNDER MILOŠEVIĆ

Milošević's Regime and the Fragmented Opposition

Since the introduction of the multiparty elections in 1990 throughout the entire Milošević era, voters in Serbia participated in elections that were neither free nor fair. Milošević's regime as "a hybrid regime, while maintaining a democratic façade, was essentially authoritarian" (Bieber 2003, 74). The regime was characterized by limited civil liberties, harassment of opposition parties and nongovernmental organizations, strong control of the media, control of the electoral procedures and outcomes, and limitation of state institutions' independence through continuous centralization of power within his presidency (Bunce and Wolchik 2012, 89; Goati 2001). Pešić argues that Milošević was well aware how much Serbian nationalism—a fairy tale about "Serbian statehood"—could help him maintain power: "in the long run, authoritarian government could only remain in power by permanently inciting paranoid nationalism and through the perpetual expectation of statehood" (Pešić 2009, 83). Thus, throughout his rule, Serbian nationalism became part of the political culture, as even the opposition parties embraced nationalist rhetoric as an essential element of their political program.

Political opposition, even though it could not match the regime's resources, was still participating in the political life of the country and was able to challenge the regime by participating in the elections. As Bieber (2003, 74) points out, "The long delay of the democratic transition process alone can thus not be explained solely by the autocratic nature of the regime. Instead some aspects of the delay (and later success) of the transition to democracy have to be located within the opposition parties." The elections were both an obstacle and an opportunity for the opposition: an obstacle that induced intra-oppositional rivalry and fragmentation but an opportunity that provided a means of peaceful transition from authoritarianism to democracy.

From the first multiparty elections it was clear that the opposition scene would suffer from strong ideological divisions between liberals and extreme nationalists, which in turn only solidified the position of Milošević and his Socialist Party of Serbia (SPS), a direct successor of the former Communist Party. Even with the first electoral victory, in the local elections in 1996, opposition parties still lacked strong programmatic orientations and were rather characterized by their relationship with the regime and its policies, especially regarding the national question. From the start it was quite difficult to imagine a broad coalition consisting of extreme nationalists, democratic nationalists, and reform-oriented parties.[1] The situation recalls the condition of opposition parties in the countries of the Arab Spring in North Africa, notably Tunisia and Egypt before the uprising, and the effects of this situation afterward.

Bieber (2003) identified three groupings. The first consisted of parties radically opposed to any contact with the regime and rejecting its policies. In most instances these were the parties that managed to achieve the first electoral victory in 1996. While some members of this group still maintained some nationalistic rhetoric, by 1999 their priorities shifted toward economic and social issues. The strongest party of this coalition was the Democratic Party (Demokratska stranka, DS), led by Zoran Đinđić.

The second grouping was the moderate opposition that rejected the regime's policies but was open to cooperation with it. The most significant party of this group was the Serbian Reformation Movement (Srpski Pokret Obnove, SPO), which, despite its strong antiregime stands from the early 1990s, promoted an unequivocal nationalist rhetoric. In the mid-1990s SPO started developing ambiguous relations with the regime parties, which even resulted in SPO's participation in the Yugoslav government in 1999. However, the two attempts to assassinate its leader, Vuk Drašković, in September 1999 and June 2000 made it return to its radical antiregime stance (Bieber 2003, 78).

The erratic relationship between SPO and DS in the 1990s emblematized the intra-oppositional inability to form a strong alternative to Milošević's regime. Despite their programmatic differences, in the fall of 1996, SPO, DS, and GSS (Građanski Savez Srbije—Civic Alliance of Serbia—at that time led by Vesna Pešić) formed the coalition Zajedno (Together), which managed to achieve the first oppositional victory in multiparty elections in Serbia. Their victory in the local elections allowed them to rule several cities including Belgrade, making Đinđić its first oppositional mayor. Before their victory was official, the regime was caught in electoral fraud. The opposition organized mass protests, which lasted from fall 1996 until spring 1997, inducing the regime to eventually yield and accept electoral defeat. However, the regime, well aware of ideological differences and mutual distrust among the leaders, played the card of "divide and rule" by scheduling elections for the Serbian Parliament. Drašković, encouraged by Zajedno's victory on the local level, indicated his intention to participate. Đinđić, on the other hand, promoted the idea of boycott, especially in light of blatant electoral fraud committed by the regime on the local level. The idea of boycotting the elections greatly irritated Drašković, who withdrew his support for DS on the local level and, thanks to SPS, took over Belgrade from Đinđić. After this, prospects of another rapprochement between SPO and DS were virtually nonexistent. Drašković and Đinđić accused each other of backstabbing and collaboration with the regime, transforming the intra-opposition struggle into a personal rivalry (*Vreme,* 12 August 2008).

The third group consisted of parties that opposed any cooperation with the regime but did not object to its policies, especially regarding the national question. This nationalist line was most evident with the Democratic Party of Serbia (Demokratska Stranka Srbije, DSS) and its leader, Vojislav Koštunica. Even though it constantly maintained the status of an opposition party, DSS was very open in supporting the regime's nationalistic policies vis-à-vis Kosovo. For years DSS criticized the policies of the other opposition parties and avoided joining opposition coalitions (Bieber 2003, 78).

"Unlike other transitional countries, which usually saw a broad anti-Communist coalition in the first free election, the [Serbian] opposition with an extreme nationalist and a liberal wing could not mount a unified challenge to Milošević in the first elections" (Bieber 2003, 74).[2] Along with ideological differences, a big problem for the opposition was to overcome mutually incompatible leadership ambitions of the opposition leaders. "The Drašković-Đinđić rivalry had destroyed the *Zajedno* coalition in 1997 and in 1999–2000 threatened to prevent any strong sustained opposition alliance to Milošević regime" (Cohen 2001, 319). Both leaders had a political reputation that kept them from assuming a leadership role of a broad coalition. On one side, Drašković was seen as an "erratic figure" who abandoned the extreme nationalistic rhetoric only after it was obvious that Belgrade had lost all the wars of secession from Yugoslavia, and furthermore who compromised himself in the eyes of other opposition leaders by participating in the Yugoslav government in early 1999. On the other side, Đinđić was often prone to combine "moderate liberalism" with "credible nationalism" (319).

Despite their differences, they were united in their request that Milošević step down. They blamed Milošević for a dire socioeconomic situation in the country and its international isolation, and since Milošević maintained his power with a strong nationalistic platform, they made sure that their "patriotic credentials" were solid enough to challenge the regime. They unanimously criticized the NATO bombing campaign and supported the idea of Kosovo's formal constitutional status within Serbia. The sentiment was overwhelmingly shared not only among the opposition leaders but also throughout other important societal pillars such as the Serbian Orthodox Church and Serbian Academy of Arts and Sciences. As Bishop Atanasije, vicar of the patriarchy in Belgrade and a cleric close to Patriarch Pavle, pointed out, "We blame Milošević not for trying to defend the nation but for failing" (qtd. in Cohen 2001, 320).

FORMATION OF DOS: THE "PULL" FACTOR

"A revolution in a modern sense cannot take place unless both 'push' and 'pull' factors are present. In practice the 'pull' factor of ideology is usually represented by enlightened elites while the 'push' factor is embodied by disgruntled masses" (Nodia 2000, 165). When the push and pull are outweighed by the "stay factors," as in Serbia at the end of the twentieth century, revolution is unlikely. Milošević remained in power, and the basic pillars of his regime were still solid. The link between the masses and the opposition forces was still not solid enough to create the necessary momentum for a transition of power from the ruling elite, through either election or revolution (Cohen 2001, 355).

Yet popular dissatisfaction was slowly mounting. The loss of Kosovo and the country's overall international isolation in the aftermath of the NATO bombing and the subsequent military defeat of Milošević's regime in June 1999 severely weakened the position of the ruling elite. Popular support for the regime dropped from 29 percent before the NATO campaign to 22 percent right afterward. At the same time 69 percent believed that the authorities were "very responsible" (23 percent) or "mostly responsible for the country's deteriorated situation" (46 percent). However, 21 percent still remained strong supporters of the regime (Cohen 2001, 321). Both sides now had to cope with the highly disillusioned population that, despite frustration with their socioeconomic situation, was still not ready to enter active sustained antistate demonstrations.[3]

Founding Conference

On 10 January 2000, SPO, the strongest opposition party of that time despite its cooperation with the regime, invited interested opposition leaders to negotiate a coalition in an "anti-regime conference." The conference was attended by nearly all of the opposition leaders. Noticeable absentees were Zoran Đinđić and Goran Svilanović. Despite his absence, Đinđić immediately pointed out that the conference was "an important step in a good direction," and signaled his readiness to meet with Drašković and discuss future activities (Ninčić 2000). Those opposition leaders who attended the conference, while sharing a common aversion toward Milošević, were hardly friendly to each other. From the beginning of the conference, participants were more engaged in discrediting one another than proposing viable solutions for a joint course of action (Drašković 2010, 361). Despite the high level of suspicion about Drašković's credibility and legitimacy to chair the conference because of his past relations with the regime, the tense discussion between opposition leaders was in fact mediated by him. While evidently lacking the necessary leverage to impose anything on other participants, as a host he proposed a document that he had formulated earlier together with his colleagues from SPO, containing the basic principles and guidelines for future opposition activities.

The document, entitled *Sporazum o zajedničkoj strategiji borbe za vanredne izbore* [Agreement of a common strategy for early democratic elections], directly called on Milošević as the president of Yugoslavia, SPS, the presidents of Serbia and of the Serbian Parliament, and the prime minister of Serbia to accept an agreement on scheduling early democratic elections on *all* levels (both federal and republic). After more than five hours of bickering negotiations, the proposed document was amended on only two points. The formulation "potential compromises with the ruling parties" from Drašković's draft was taken out. The phrase was intended for the electoral rules, in the spirit of the opposition's readiness to make concessions, given the fact that they are calling for the regime to agree on holding the elections. The majority were against such a formulation, as they wanted to promote the idea of noncooperation (Ninčić 2000). Opposition leaders agreed to refrain from mutual attacks, to focus all their energy on discrediting the current regime, and, if their requests did not produce any reaction from the regime, to start protesting in early March in Belgrade and other Serbian cities until their demands were met. However, the opposition parties could not agree on the exact date of the first protest. In his draft, Drašković favored holding the rally on 9 March, the date that venerated the ninth anniversary of violent demonstrations against the regime, which consecrated him as "the king of the streets." As a sign that the intra-oppositional rivalries were still strong, other opposition leaders (especially those close to Đinđić's DS) feared that a rally on that day would be identified solely with Drašković and SPO (Cohen 2001, 358). The majority voted against a specific date, under the excuse that the entire action might lose credibility in case the date had to be postponed due to unexpected circumstances (Ninčić 2000).

These minor changes to the text show how most of the conference was frittered away in mutual accusations. Clearly the opposition leaders were left with a document that in reality represented a fait accompli, and despite latent noncommittal behavior from the past, they chose to sign the agreement instead of sending another signal to the public that they were unable to join forces. According to one of the participants, "it was not important what we proposed during the conference, what is important is that we accepted everything and that the document contains the word 'together' a lot" (Ninčić 2000). However, the signing of the document proved to be more difficult than what one would expect. Mutual distrust between opposition leaders was transposed into reluctance to even shake hands and put a signature on the same piece of paper. Drašković again stepped in as a mediator, proposing that they make three copies of the document, giving each leader freedom of choosing a copy on which they wanted to put their signature. The last one to sign was Koštunica, claiming the need to discuss the issue with his party organs before committing to anything. According to Drašković's accounts, for more than twenty minutes he "nearly begged" Koštunica to stay on board with the rest of the opposition, fearing that the nearly born opposition coalition was sentenced to fail even before it was formed (Drašković 2010, 362). Once Koštunica signed, Drašković proved to be quite inventive and used a stapler to put together all three copies of the document. A new opposition coalition called the Democratic Opposition of Serbia (DOS) was stapled together. For the first time since 1997, it was clear who stood in opposition to the regime (ICG 2000b, 6).

The 10 January conference was founded primarily on a general agreement that Milošević's rule had to end (Ninčić 2000; Pešić 2009). Other details in the document were of technical nature and did not prescribe what New Order the opposition leaders had in mind for Serbia. Soon after the conference, opposition leaders started emphasizing the significance of having a united opposition coalition and participating in the elections on a common list (Milošević 2000a). In the next two months hardly any progress was made in formulating a common platform for the elections, and opposition meetings were spent simply repeating what was already agreed to at the founding conference. In the meantime the ruling parties were not responding to any of the opposition's initiatives. The opinion polls still indicated a high level of distrust toward the opposition (more than 50 percent of respondents), which was still seen as "divided, corrupt and incompetent" (Bunce and Wolchik 2012, 96). More than two-thirds of those polled showed signs of political passivity, believing that political activity would not change anything. However, the polls also indicated that the respondents "overwhelmingly" also wanted change, and nearly 35 percent favored "quick and deep changes by force if needed" (Cohen 2001, 357).

The polls also recorded a steady decrease in Milošević's popularity, which was not coupled with any increase of popular confidence in the opposition's activities. In other words, the conventional wisdom that presumes an automatic transfer of popular support from the ruling parties to the opposition forces as soon as the masses become angry at the regime was not taking place in Serbia. Of primary importance is the condition that the "people must think that their voting is a meaningful way to signal this dissatisfaction, believe that their votes will count, and support the opposition when they vote" (Bunce and Wolchik 2012, 96). In order to challenge the regime, the opposition had to find a way to engage the wider audience and find support for its cause. Nebojša Popov from the Belgrade Center for Human Rights noted the apparent unity as a positive sign of opposition leaders seeking the support of the people,

> but one still doesn't know exactly for what, or how, or when they will acquire the confidence of the people and build forces of society . . . of course it is good that the opposition meets and agrees; it would be even better if the government would discuss matters normally with them; but how can one decisively set matters in motion about which there hasn't been serious discussion, still less agreement; and at protests and demonstrations there can't be real dialogue; conversations and agreements, of course, but they can only take place among actors who take responsibility for future events. (Popov 2000, 3)

Facing growing public cynicism about their performance, the opposition leaders were committed to show their serious intentions to launch a series of protests and rallies in order to put pressure on the regime to schedule early elections on all levels. On 22 March, the opposition leaders agreed that the first rally should be held in Belgrade on 14 April, and that in the meantime an expert team should be convened with the task of setting up criteria for the creation of a joint candidate list for the elections. The two-hour rally attracted more than a hundred thousand people and showed at least symbolic unity, with Drašković and Đinđić shaking hands in front of the masses (Cohen 2001, 359).

Sufficient incentive for a mass rally was given by the government on 1 April, with its formal rejection of the opposition's initiative to schedule the elections. According to the official statement, the initiative was refused on the grounds of "insufficient conditions" and because the primary prerequisite for early elections was disbanding of the Parliament (*Blic* 1 April 2000). Milošević's decision to tighten his authoritarian hold over Serbian politics led to the emergence of two new civil society organizations well situated to contest Milošević's hold over Serbian society and shifted politics on the ground to Milošević's removal from power (Bunce and Wolchik 2012, 97). The first organization was a student movement, Otpor (Resistance), and the other was the Center for Free Elections and Democracy (CeSID), an NGO of experts dealing with electoral rules and proceedings.

INVOLVEMENT OF THE CIVIL SOCIETY: THE "PUSH" FACTOR

Otpor

Disappointed by the opposition's performance and disillusioned by the effectiveness of party politics, the most active members of civil society started organizing themselves in different forms of NGOs and similar ad hoc movements. Students were most inventive in their methods of challenging the regime. At the April 2000 rally, the opposition leaders received a direct and important message from a representative of one of the most active movements from civil society, the student movement Otpor. The movement's spokesperson warned the opposition leaders: "you must remain united . . . not squabble among each other. Ten thousand students will demonstrate under the window of any opposition leader . . . who betrays that unity" (Cohen 2001, 359). Otpor was formed in 1998, soon after the draconian University Law was passed. It was a product of students' culminated frustration with continuous opposition, infighting, and the failure of past protests. Throughout the 1990s, on several occasions students organized their demonstrations simultaneously with the opposition's protests. Bieber argues that "their failure mostly did not lie in the protests themselves (e.g. low turnout), but rather in the inability of the political opposition to successfully challenge the regime on the basis of these protests" (Bieber 2003, 83). Aware that mass protests were not generating expected results, students turned to more targeted performances of mocking the regime and characterizing Milošević as a "falling star." They called for a "more open rebellion," stating: "the emperor is naked, and there will be no more games. There is just us and them in the street, and one of us has to go" (Otpor leader, qtd. in Cohen 2001, 256).

What was unique about Otpor was its lack of hierarchical structures, which made it quite difficult to contain by the regime apparatus but at the same time allowed it to avoid co-optation by the opposition parties (Bieber 2003, 84). Founding members of Otpor argued that the best model for a successful democratic movement was not democracy, but a military operation that can take advantage of the regime's mistakes (Dobson 2013, 182). By the end of 1999 Otpor became a truly insolent opponent of the regime, inducing the authorities to introduce a series of repressive measures against its members. However, as the number of arrested and beaten students (even those who just wore an Otpor T-shirt) increased, the movement's support among the general populous was increasing as well. Thanks to their activities and a disproportionate reaction by the authorities, Otpor and its symbol of a clenched fist became the true signs of resistance to Milošević's regime. Over time, numerous public figures started embracing Otpor's symbolism as a way of signaling their dissatisfaction with Milošević, while still not ready to align themselves with any of the opposition parties (Cohen 2001, 356).

Otpor's ability to generate nationwide support from all segments of the society made this movement one of the most admired youth movements globally. Following the success in ousting Milosevic's regime, many of the Otpor leaders organized the Centre for Applied Nonviolent Action and Strategies (CANVAS), where young activists from more than fifty countries around the world were trained and advised on how to take on some of the most authoritarian governments in the world (Rosenberg 2011, 2). In fact, the 6 April youth movement in Egypt was greatly inspired by the Serbian example. Mohamed Adel, a member of 6 April who attended a CANVAS workshop in 2009, pointed out: "The April 6 movement's logo—the outline of a clenched fist—was a copy of the Serbian group's own stencil. Even some of the slogans they spray-painted on the streets of Cairo—for example "Mubarak is over"—were borrowed from Otpor" (Dobson 2013, 182). More importantly, Otpor's experienced leaders explained to 6 April activists the difference between a protest movement and a resistance movement (182). As noted by Rosenberg (2011, 3), "CANVAS has built a durable blueprint for nonviolent revolution: what to do to grow from a vanload of people into a mass movement and then use masses to topple a dictator."

While constantly challenging the authorities, Otpor also tried to motivate the opposition parties to refrain from any cooperation with the regime. On 17 February 2000, they held their first congress, and in front of numerous opposition leaders,[4] they read their "Declaration on the Future of Serbia," in which they demanded that "all the institutions, organizations as well as the political parties willing to truly fight and give resistance to this regime unite around the following demands" (Otpor 1999). They emphasized that "it is of most importance to form a unified block of all relevant democratic forces in Serbia with the principal objective of replacing Milošević and his government on the basis of Declaration." The unified block was to struggle for elections (supervised by the international community, primarily OSCE, Organization for Security and Co-operation in Europe). During the elections, the unified block "shall be materialized through joint electoral list 'For Salvation and Future of Serbia' as well as constituting a government of experts named in advance, whose first task would be the removal of [current] laws of the system, primarily laws on the university and on information."

While the opposition parties were still struggling to formulate a clear vision for the future, Otpor's "Declaration" gave a number of suggestions: democratic principles, rule of law, territorial decentralization, cooperation with the international community (especially the International Criminal Tribunal for the former Yugoslavia), market economy, and protection of private property. While the list indicated students' preference for liberal-democratic values, some analysis warned that the movement was also flirting with a strong nationalist ideology (Martinov 2000; Zlatić 2000).

CeSID

While Otpor started as a grassroots movement of disillusioned student activists, the Center for Free Elections and Democracy (CeSID) consisted of distinguished social scientists and academics specialized in electoral processes. The organization was formed in 1997, putting together a group of electoral experts committed to unmasking the existing electoral system of all its potential flaws. CeSID was dedicated to building up the necessary monitoring infrastructure by training local volunteers (the existing legislation did not allow foreign observers) who would be stationed at the polling places, collect the raw voting data, and send the information back to CeSID, where the experts would compute instant preliminary results to share with the public. CeSID was also engaged in improving the voting lists, providing information about the voting process, and monitoring public opinion (Bunce and Wolchik 2012, 102).

These contributions were of crucial importance for the eventual electoral victory of the opposition forces. A few hours after the polling stations were closed, CeSID held widely publicized press conferences where they announced the preliminary results. The evident discrepancy between CeSID's results and those offered by the regime caused an unprecedented panic reaction by Milošević, who at first claimed victory, only to change his mind and call for a second round. CeSID's credibility and the activity of Otpor and other civil society groups brought Serbian citizens to the streets to demand that Koštunica be allowed to take office (Bunce and Wolchik 2012, 102).

SYNERGY BETWEEN CIVIL SOCIETY AND POLITICAL PARTIES

In the first half of 2000 Otpor's membership doubled to forty thousand, with more than 120 local branches opened all over Serbia, and as its public appeal grew, opposition leaders quickly started associating themselves with the movement (*Glas javnosti* 4 May 2000, 1 June 2000). The movement came to be perceived as the most prominent vehicle for mobilizing resistance to the regime (ICG 2000b, 18). Especially significant was its appeal for young first-time voters (introduced to the voting lists thanks to CeSID's initiative to update the lists), who according to the opinion polls were most dissatisfied with the current regime (90 percent of respondents) (*Blic* 14 April 2000). Initially, opposition roundtables called soon after the big rally of 14 April produced few results. On the one side, SPO argued that the united opposition should wait for the regime's reaction to their proposal of organizing elections, and in case of no reaction they should put more pressure on the authorities by organizing mass protests and rallies. Parties close to DS were more eager and urged that opposition activists collect the one hundred thousand signatures needed for a popular referendum on the issue of early parliamentary elections. DSS, on the other hand, was primarily focused on strengthening the opposition's nationalist cause, insisting that all opposition meetings be attended by Serb delegates from Kosovo (*Glas javnosti* 27 and 28 April 2000). Dissonant ideas were creating a deadlock in intra-opposition negotiations.

Aware of the situation, on 2 May Otpor requested permission to attend future opposition meetings, justifying this request on the grounds of increased repression by the regime against student activists (*Glas javnosti* 3 May 2000). A few days earlier in Milošević's hometown, Pozarevac, several members of Otpor were brutally beaten by the police during one of their many street performances. At the meeting, representatives from Otpor urged the opposition leaders to join them in a series of protests under the slogan "Stop the terror—for free elections" (*Glas javnosti* 4 May 2000). After a failed attempt to arrange a protest in Pozarevac, the opposition managed to organize a mass demonstration in Belgrade on 15 May. Most of the leaders wore Otpor T-shirts as they addressed an audience of twenty thousand, unanimously condemning the regime's repressive measures against student activists.

Otpor activists saw themselves as the "glue that kept the opposition together" (*Glas javnosti* 23 May 2000). They had only one request: oppositional unity. Otpor was ready to coordinate with the opposition but was very careful to avoid co-option by political parties, as many parties were offering a more institutionalized cooperation (ICG 2000b, 19–20). The continuous failure of opposition parties to find a common language and offer a platform for the elections frustrated Otpor to the point of considering "first changing the opposition, and only then the regime" (20). It proposed strategies of civil disobedience and networks of civic self-defense against the regime's repressive measures. Otpor's proposal was unanimously accepted by opposition leaders on 1 June 2000, but the same meeting marked the end of opposition unity created in January.

INTRA-OPPOSITIONAL SPLIT

Soon after the first rally in April, first sparks of disunity (especially between Koštunica's DSS and Nenad Čanak's League of Social Democrats of Vojvodina (LSV)) publically emerged, openly reflecting the Tactical Question. However, this clash over positions had a much deeper ideological meaning, and it was just the first illustration that parties were not upholding the agreement not to attack each other. High officials of both SPO and DS were quite unsuccessful in disguising their mutual distrust, and they did not hesitate to publically emphasize tainted roles from the past of their oppositional peers.[5]

One of the issues of coalition on which parties could not agree was the list of candidates for the elections. Đinđić of the DS promoted the idea that "the only logical thing" that the opposition could offer was a unified list of candidates. For SPO this idea was quite premature, as it could indicate unconditional acceptance of elections under any conditions. In fact, SPO was insisting on what was agreed to in January: that the regime agreed to organize elections on *all* levels, and that the conditions for the electoral process be fair and democratic. If the opposition leaders were to agree on a common list, then SPO wanted the criteria to be based on the parliamentary elections from 1997, when they won 18 percent of popular votes and forty-five seats. Such criteria were absolutely unacceptable for DS and many other parties, most of whom either boycotted those elections or were not even formed back then. As a counterproposal, DS suggested using local elections of 1996, when the DS (together with SPO and GSS) won a majority of votes in nearly half the municipalities in Serbia, as a reference point for quotas. These criteria would have greatly undermined SPO's position as the strongest party in the united opposition and as such were absolutely unacceptable (*Blic* 24 and 29 April 2000).

The inability to formulate a common list—a rather technical matter regarding the elections, which were not even scheduled yet—indicated just how far the opposition was from concluding negotiations for a coalition and formulating a common vision. After a series of roundtables that only reiterated and confirmed entrenched positions, the expert teams (established after the first conference in January) passed the decision to the summit of opposition leaders to decide whether they agreed to formulate a common list. The opposition leaders met on 1 June 2000 and overwhelmingly voted in favor of participating in any elections. According to their joint statement, the current electoral law for the local level gave solid chances for victory only to a united opposition front; thus the opposition leaders stressed their commitment to create as soon as possible "an unbiased analysis which will formulate the model that increases the chances of electoral victory and to use this model to formulate electoral list of candidates" (*Glas javnosti* 2 June 2000). The only negative vote came from SPO, reiterating its positions, and a few days later it announced its intention to stop attending further oppositional meetings, as the founding principle from January of unanimity for any decision was clearly breached (*Glas javnosti* 7 June 2000).

The final split between SPO and DS resulted in SPO's marginalization from the same coalition it helped create in January 2000. Ideological differences were slowly surfacing, and right after SPO's decision to continue boycotting the elections, an official from GSS publically admitted: "United opposition is an artificial product made to fight against Slobodan Milošević and his regime. It is unnatural because it unites parties of different political orientations, who are logically electoral enemies . . . but if we want a peaceful transition of power, elections are the only solution. I am afraid that SPO's move pushes the country toward civil war" (*Glas javnosti* 5 April 2000).

ELECTIONS AND REVOLUTION

With a divided opposition that lost its strongest party, Milošević no longer viewed the elections as a risky endeavor. In June and July 2000, Parliament changed the constitution to turn the Yugoslav presidency into an elected post, allowing him to bypass previous term limitations and run again for the federal presidency (Bujošević and Radovanović 2003; Thompson and Kuntz 2004, 166). He then called for early, simultaneous elections on the federal and local levels for 24 September, certain that a fragmented opposition without SPO would be unable to win at the local level, as the results of previous elections indicated (*Glas javnosti* 28 July 2000). He still wanted to use what was left of the patriotic sentiment after the NATO bombing to rally large support, and he calculated that a short election campaign of two months would not give the fractured opposition time to negotiate an effective coalition (Bunce and Wolchik 2012, 106).

Electoral victory over Milošević required a highly coordinated activity between the fragmented opposition and civil society's antiregime movements. However, neither side wanted to yield its influence and power. Thanks to unprecedented financial and logistical support from abroad, opposition parties and civil society movements were able to finalize a joint electoral list (without SPO) and to conduct an aggressive and effective campaign to convince a highly passive and disillusioned population that their votes would count and that they could dethrone Milošević (Bunce and Wolchik 2012, 107; *Glas javnosti* 4 August 2000).

With the list closed, the choice of a presidential candidate remained. Despite Đinđić's oppositional credentials and the fact that he was now the leader of the DS, the strongest opposition party in DOS, his chances at winning were undermined by his poor standing of 4 percent of support in the public opinion polls. The opposition leader with the greatest chances to challenge Milošević was DSS president Vojislav Koštunica, with 42 percent of support compared to 28 percent for Milošević (*Glas javnosti* 27 July 2000). Koštunica was widely perceived as an uncorrupted opposition figure who, in sharp contrast with Drašković and Đinđić, had never "pacted" with the regime and was a longtime foe of U.S. interference in Serbia, "a moderate or democratic nationalist who is also perceived as being independent of foreign ties, and thus difficult for the regime to demonize as a traitor or foreign collaborator" (Cohen 2001, 361) and who often praised himself for leading a party that combined observance of democratic principles with a defense of Serb national interests. The opposition chose Koštunica because he was most similar to Milošević and thus could serve as a credible alternative, able to grab his traditionally loyal nationalist voters (*Peščanik* 13 April 2012). Đinđić's acceptance of Koštunica's candidacy represented the turning point in establishing a unified opposition; his agreement to stand aside and assume a background role meant that the opposition would not exhaust itself over the question of who is number one, as it was quite clear that his DS was still the strongest party (Pavlović 2000, 3).

The DSS was one of the most active promoters of a nationalist platform within united opposition, inducing the rest of the coalition to strengthen its nationalistic credibility. Throughout the first half of 2000, opposition leaders managed to find common ground on their nationalistic values, which gained them valuable support from the Serbian Orthodox Church, influential nationalist intellectuals, and even the former Yugoslav and Serbian royal family Karađorđević (*Glas javnosti* 19, 22, and 24 April 2000). During the electoral campaign internal divisions in the DOS were still evident, as one part of the opposition was highlighting the dire economic situation in the country while the others were emphasizing the importance of the national question.

By mid-August DOS managed to adopt a platform for the future of Serbia by primarily formulating some broad short-term goals and transcending differences in the long term by refocusing on economic recovery (G17 2000). In the document DOS also guaranteed to adopt a new set of laws regarding the army and the police, with the aim of depoliticizing their role in society; a strong indoctrination made members of the police force believe that their position could be threatened by any change of the regime and hence to regard the opposition as the enemy (ICG 2000a, 9). The platform, however, never mentioned anything about the Serbian State Security apparatus, one of the basic pillars of Milošević's regime. An even more damaging split between the regime and security forces was evident in the case of the Yugoslav Army. The sobering experience of the "victory" over NATO forces induced changes especially among the mid-ranking officers: "mid-level officers have opted after their Kosovo experience for a peaceful solution to any future crises. They do not want and would not support a new war or the use of the army in suppressing popular dissent and demonstrations. Parts of the officer corps could become involved in, or even directly carry out, a coup d'état" (10). The change of attitude toward the regime by low- and mid-ranking officers of the security forces slowly grew as the elections were approaching. According to Miloš Vasić, during the campaign Đinđić along with several retired generals who formed their parties and joined the opposition took on the difficult task of approaching Milošević's allies, including the highest officials in the Serbian State Security and the Yugoslav Army (Vasić 2005). These early contacts intensified over time and proved to be of pivotal importance for the decision by security forces to stand aside during the popular unrest that followed the first round of elections, similar to the crucial role chosen by the armies in Tunisia and Egypt.

The preliminary results of the 24 September elections projected Koštunica's victory already in the first round, with 52.54 percent of the vote against Milošević's

35.01 percent. CeSID's results were immediately refuted by Milošević's SPS, but after a few days of hesitation, the Federal Electoral Commission officially stated that Milošević was in fact trailing behind Koštunica, who, however, did not manage to obtain more than 50 percent (exactly 48.95 percent) of the votes. As a result, the commission called for a second round of elections on 8 October. For DOS, these results were "a blatant fraud," pointing out that the commission "overlooked" some six hundred thousand votes counted by DOS, and it refused to participate in a second round (Cohen 2001, 416). As the news of an imminent electoral defeat was spreading, people started realizing that Milošević lost the basis of exercising power—popular support, "a discredited and delegitimized leader without any legal authority" (Cohen 2001, 419).[6]

POWER TAKEOVER

Refusing to accept a second round of elections, DOS decided on 28 September to increase the pressure on Milošević by organizing mass protests and waves of civil disobedience across Serbia in close coordination with Otpor (*Glas javnosti* 29 September, 1 and 4 October 2000). As the opposition's request for the transfer of power was perceived as legitimate, the task of motivating the people to join the protests became less difficult. Numerous public companies and institutions—such as the State Electric Company and countless schools, universities, and factories—followed the opposition's calls for "disobedience" and joined the wave of strikes (*Glas javnosti* 1 and 2 October 2000). According to some accounts, an unprecedented number of more than five hundred thousand people protested in the streets of Belgrade on 5 October.

The massive popular protests that so quickly ended the Milošević era can be understood as "both premeditated and spontaneous actions" (Bunce and Wolchik 2012, 112). In fact some of the unfolding events had no apparent connection or organizing linkage—for instance, the unexpected strike by the miners of Kolubara that threatened to paralyze Serbia and the refusal of security forces to follow Milošević's instructions and contain the "situation." However, the opposition leaders were careful enough to prepare for a potential counterprotest by Milošević's supporters and more importantly focused on containing a feared reaction by the security forces still under Milošević's control.

Contacts with the Police and Army

Already on 2 October there were news reports of antiriot police officers quitting their jobs because they refused to be engaged in potential antidemonstration activities and numerous "friendly elements" from the police managing to find common language with DOS (*Glas javnosti* 2 October 2000). For several years numerous opposition leaders had maintained close relations with members of the police force, and the unfolding events served to strengthen those relations and put them to use (*Vreme* 19 October 2000). Some oppositional leaders openly admitted that their close contacts with the police forces allowed them to progress with rioters toward the Federal Parliament building, where the protesters from all over Serbia were supposed to convene. Velimir Ilić, mayor of Čačak, even stated that his police contacts encouraged him and his followers to persevere in their task, as they expected a wave of vacillation among the police forces to start once the riots culminated in the late afternoon of 5 October (*Vreme* 12 October 2000). "Friendly elements" from the police supplied the opposition forces with weaponry as they were preparing for Milošević's retaliatory measures. The weapons were stored on the outskirts of Belgrade at the Metal Products Factory, whose director, Nebojša Čović, was one of the opposition leaders. On 4 October, at the same place, there was a secret meeting between some leaders of DOS, including Đinđić, Perišić, and Obradović, who already had contacts with different Special Forces, including the State Secret Service's elite Unit for Special Operations (JSO), to discuss joint strategies for the upcoming days, eventually agreeing on a nonaggression pact (*Vreme* 19 October 2000).

Although the accounts were rejected by DOS's chief of security, Slobodan Pajić, the unfolding events unquestionably indicate that there was strong contact between DOS and security services. Elite units of the police and the army, such as the Special Anti-Terrorist Unit (SAJ), and the sixty-third parachute brigade of the Yugoslav Army stood by, while the famous Red Burettes (JSO's pseudonym) openly joined the protesters (Bujošević and Radovanović 2003, 128; *Vreme* 19 October 2000).[7]

The fact that the police were ill-prepared for the events in front of the Parliament has been interpreted in two ways. According to one theory, this was done intentionally by "friendly elements" in the police force in order to facilitate the opposition's power takeover (*Vreme* 19 October 2000). However, to others this might have been a part of Milošević's plan: he needed the Parliament building to fall in order to justify deployment of army troops against the protesters (Bujošević and Radovanović 2003, 97). Once the Parliament building was set on fire, he contacted the Army Chief of Staff, asking the army to separate the demonstrators and the police and seize the Parliament building. General Nebojša Pavković evaded this command arguing, "I replied that the state was not under threat, that the constitutional order was not endangered and neither was the army. The orders I was receiving could not influence me to engage, or rather misuse, the army by supporting either side or any person in an attempt to influence the electoral will of the citizens. I wasn't prepared to carry out orders" (qtd. in Bujošević and Radovanović 2003, 103), a statement echoed by the Tunisian and Egyptian chiefs of staff a decade later.

DOS leaders had no doubts that the high-ranking officers were loyal to Milošević, but they also knew that middle- and low-ranking cadres were quite unwilling to protect the regime by force. In fact, according to some internal reports, the opposition claimed that around 80 percent of the military vote went to Koštunica (Cohen 2001, 417). This could be attributed to a painstaking electoral campaign—which included former generals—throughout which DOS assured the army officers (and the police) that protecting the state and the people does not mean protecting the interests of the regime (*Vreme* 26 October 2000). However, convincing the high-ranking army staff to stand aside, as the events were unfolding, was not as simple. Prior to the elections Pavković referred to 24 September as "D Day," indicating that the army was resolute to prevent any attempt of power takeover from the streets (*Vreme* 26 October 2000). In other words, Koštunica's nationalist credentials and moderate political views made him sufficiently suitable in the eyes of Pavković and those close to him to assume his taking the role of the president would not alter the course of current affairs (*Vreme* 16 October 2000). Induced by such advice, Pavković and his General Staff kept quite a low profile from 24 September until 5 October, while devising an adequate approach for convincing the new president "that any change among high army echelons would be catastrophic and unacceptable for the army" (*Vreme* 16 October 2000). Once it was clear that Milošević's rule was delegitimized by the people, Pavković used the opportunity to prove himself indispensible for the new establishment.

Contacts with the Regime

Koštunica used his first public speech as the new president, on the evening of 5 October, to promote his moderate and nonretaliatory political platform. As a stickler for legality, he called for an orderly state, continuity of the government, and democratic procedures (Bujošević and Radovanović 2003, 153–154), an approach that characterized the Short Track transitions of Egypt and Tunisia. When angry protesters started shouting for Milošević's arrest, he declined, stating, "we're not going to march on Dedinje [Belgrade neighborhood where Milošević resided]. We're going to stay here. We're going to stay here because these are the people's institutions, the assemblies, one, two, three of them." (Bujošević and Radovanović 2003, 153). While Đinđić was concerned that the regime would use the night to strike back, Koštunica argued that the only way to avoid violence was to establish contact with former authorities (155). The same night, the Constitutional Court of Yugoslavia ruled that Koštunica was officially the president of Yugoslavia (164). This decision had a twofold effect: Koštunica could legally assume the office already one day after the revolution, and he could use it as leverage in his upcoming meeting with Milošević.

On his first day as president, Koštunica received General Pavković, an indication that people from both Koštunica's and Pavković's camps were in close contact. Pavković summarized the position of the General Staff: congratulating Koštunica on his election as legal president and commander-in-chief, he indicated that he would accept any presidential decision regarding his own future status, but that it would be wise to postpone any decision about personnel changes until the new legal bodies have been constituted (*Vreme* 26 October 2000). Most of the opposition leaders wanted Pavković to be discharged right away, as he emblemized one of the most important pillars of Milošević's rule. Koštunica, however, was more interested in establishing stability and continuity.[8] Koštunica's firm aspiration for continuity allowed Pavković to retain his post until 24 June 2002, a decision that would be seen as one of the core reasons for DOS to split by 2001 (*Vreme* 8 July 2004).

As one of the first orders of business, Koštunica requested Pavković to arrange a meeting with Milošević (Bujošević and Radovanović 2003, 170). At first Milošević was reluctant, but later he yielded, offering to meet at his house without any witnesses, waiters, or any one else: "only him and me." While Koštunica preferred to have the meeting in the presidential building, he eventually agreed to meet in Dedinje, with Pavković as a mediator, indicating his long-lasting confidence in the army (171). He was escorted by army jeeps, which increased suspicion and fear by other DOS leaders that in case something happened the revolution would lose the only institution that it had managed to conquer. The conversation lasted for an hour, without any record or witnesses. According to Koštunica's account, Milošević spent most of the time arguing that regardless of the election results his term in office was supposed to last until July 2001, and he accused DOS of demolishing Belgrade and destroying governmental buildings. However, once Koštunica pointed out the ruling of the Constitutional Court and the fact that the *Government Gazette* already made the act legally binding, the conversation was over. Milošević allegedly stated: "I haven't seen it, but if that's the case, then I concede." He congratulated Koštunica and escorted him out (Bujošević and Radovanović 2003, 171–172). A few hours later Milošević gave a public speech in which he officially accepted electoral defeat and pointed out his intention to retire and devote more attention to his grandson. The other oppositional leaders were neither informed nor consulted about Koštunica's decision to meet with Milošević, and they still remain puzzled about the real intentions of Koštunica to make such a move. Many of them have argued that in the meeting Koštunica and Milošević actually discussed conditions for the transfer of power, with Milošević requesting that Koštunica maintain the current state apparatus (especially Serbian State Security and the army) in exchange for peaceful transition (B92, 2010).

FIRST MONTHS IN POWER

Even after Koštunica was sworn in, on 7 October, Đinđić still feared retaliation by the Old Order (*Glas javnosti* 8 October 2000). Although the opposition had won the elections, they in fact won "only" the federal elections, while Milošević's

SPS and their allies still held power on the republic (Serb) level. However, they did possess a revolutionary momentum and, most importantly, an unequivocal sign from the people that Milošević's regime did not have legitimacy to run the country any longer. In fact, Koštunica was the only opposition leader who held an office of power. He was now widely seen as the symbol of 5 October as "the man who overthrew Milošević" (Budding 2002). Overnight his leverage within DOS dramatically increased; not surprisingly, his moderate preference for upholding legality, stability, and continuity in further actions prevailed within DOS.

Right after the events on 5 October, DOS leaders started devising a strategy of extending their power to the republic level, seeking elections for the Serbian Parliament as soon as possible. Aware that they lacked institutional leverage, they unanimously opted to offer a creation of transitional government to the incumbent regime, which would be in charge of administering the country in the interregnum period until the new round of elections. During DOS-initiated negotiations in the office of the Serbian president, Milan Milutinović, on 9 October, Đinđić emphasized that the transitional government did not represent any type of coalition, but rather a technical body that would provide adequate functioning of the country so that the elections could take place. In order to provide the necessary degree of legitimacy for the transitional government, DOS was ready to accept the involvement of both the regime parties and SPO, as these parties still had a legitimate hold on power, under the condition that "controversial persons which emblemized Milošević's regime" not be part of the government (*Glas javnosti* 11 October 2000). The primary source of power of the Old Order was not in the ruling party but in its leader, because the whole system was structured around the personality of Slobodan Milošević (Vuković 2011, 88). Accordingly, the electoral results were not taken as just Milošević's personal defeat but also as a collective defeat of the whole regime.[9]

The negotiations generated two results: early parliamentary elections were scheduled for 23 December, and in the meantime the country would be run by a transitional government composed of officials from DOS, SPO, and SPS. Since SPS still had a legitimate majority in the Parliament, the negotiators agreed that SPS would assign a prime minister, while the two deputy prime ministers would come from DOS and SPO. Each of the four key ministries—police, justice, finance, and information—would be run by a collective body of three representatives or coministers, one from each political grouping.[10] The model was quite similar to the format of "roundtables" that several postcommunist states in Eastern Europe instituted during the period of communism collapse (*Vreme* 26 October 2000).

One of the most discussed issues in the aftermath of 5 October was the fate of the regime's state security structures and the people who ran them, which caused a serious rift between its two strongest parties. Đinđić depicted Milošević's regime after 5 October as "a headless hydra with functioning tentacles" (*Vreme* 2 November 2000). He feared that numerous controversial elements of the former regime would use the confusion after the revolution to blend in with the new structures. For this reason he strongly promoted the opening of police archives and files and a process of lustration that would first depose the current heads of the State Secret Service and the army, Rade Marković and General Pavković. He saw the cleanup of state security structures as a necessary precondition for the new phase of rebuilding Serbia.

Initially SPS quite adamantly defended Marković. Many in DOS saw this as SPS's attempt to consolidate before the elections and buy time necessary to dispose of all the compromising evidence. At the same time they suspected that Marković still represented an extended arm of Milošević's power and as such would allow him to run the system even when out of the office, as Ali Saleh was to do in Yemen (*Vreme* 9 November 2000). However, SPS had a well-placed ally in Koštunica on this matter. He strongly opposed any shuffling within the security structures, as this would threaten the stability and continuity of the new government. He argued that especially in the period of institutional vacuum, the country needed someone "who would guard the guardians" (after the Latin phrase *Quis custodiet ipsos custodes*?) until the new Serbian government was elected in December (*Vreme* 14 December 2000). The internal disagreement between the two most influential DOS leaders created a two-month vacuum during which the security apparatus worked diligently to destroy most of the evidence that could compromise them after the elections (B92 2009). Moreover, the intra-oppositional disagreement over security structures was just one of many issues that dominated the debate within DOS. Just as before the federal elections, ideological difference and personal animosities started surfacing, only this time between Koštunica and Đinđić.

PREPARATION FOR THE DECEMBER ELECTIONS

The elections in December 2001 proved to be a formality. As Đinđić remarked, "our advantage is that we do not have a counter candidate . . . we are both the government and opposition because there is no government or opposition" (*Vreme* 2 November 2000). Before the elections Đinđić pointed out that only when the new government was formed and elements of the Old Order deinstitutionalized could DOS dissemble according to component ideological affiliations (*Vreme* 2 November 2000). Thus the elections represented the final opportunity to tear down Milošević's authoritarian system.

On 17 November, opposition leaders negotiated a "gentlemen's agreement" on the principle that DSS and DS should have an even number of candidates on the DOS electoral list. Soon after, the media started speculating that they had also agreed on Đinđić as the DOS candidate for prime minister, which produced a reaction from DSS. Aware of Koštunica's popularity, and unwilling to give premature support to Đinđić for fear that the new coalition could be identified with him and jeopardize Koštunica's leadership position, DSS set two conditions for their coalitional participation with the rest of DOS. In order to contain Đinđić's ambition to take the leadership within DOS, DSS demanded that the list be led by Koštunica (thus the official name of the coalition for the elections was "DOS—Vojislav Koštunica") and that the choice of a new prime minister be made after the elections (*Vreme* 23 November and 7 December 2000). Even though both requests were accepted by oppositional leaders, it was an indication of yet another intra-oppositional split.

LIMITS OF MODERATION IN NEGOTIATED TRANSITIONS

As expected the elections were won with an overwhelming majority of 64 percent of the vote, which yielded 176 seats. The new government was indeed headed by Đinđić, who still enjoyed widespread support within DOS. It promised a fast and effective eradication of the Old Order structures (*Vreme* 25 January 2000). Reports had indicated that both corruption and organized crime were deeply rooted within state security structures, which Koštunica had refused to reform in the aftermath of 5 October (*Vreme* 15 and 29 March 2000).

The key source of conflict between DSS and DS was the pace of change, with Đinđić, the pragmatist, generally advocating greater speed even at the expense of the legalities, and Koštunica, a legalist by both temperament and training, taking a more cautious approach (Budding 2002, 163), a milder version of the Tactical Question.[11] His position led members of the previous regime still working for state institutions to perceive Koštunica as a true patriot and defender of the Serbian national cause. At the same time, media close to former state structures and Koštunica started depicting Đinđić as a puppet of organized crime, suggesting that getting rid of Đinđić would be the ultimate act of patriotism. After a series of scandals involving state security structures, DSS left the government and openly started attacking Đinđić. The new government, however, continued to dismantle the old state security apparatus and to collaborate with the International Civil Tribunal on Yugoslavia (ICTY). On 12 March 2003 Đinđić was assassinated by the same disbanded JSO unit with which he had negotiated the night before 5 October. As of this writing, there are speculations that Koštunica's close associates were involved (B92, 2009). It perhaps was the culmination of ideological and programmatic differences between the two leaders.

Silence regarding the operationalization of basic values was "a critical tactical maneuver" for DOS: "It could not rely on a common vision of Serbia's future because such a vision didn't exist; indeed the coalition partners did not even have a common understanding of the past" (Pešić 2009, 73). Thus the coalition focused on ousting Milošević, since "everyone was against him" (73). In a broad and ideologically diverse coalition such as DOS, reasons for wanting him removed from power were just as diverse, including economic collapse, recent military defeats, international isolation, increased levels of criminal activities, and brain drain. Regardless of the reasons that motivated political actors to join DOS, the coalition was still unable to avoid the debilitating split between reform-liberals and conservative-nationalists that has characterized most of Serbian political history. "With these two irreconcilable world views ruling together, the division became a struggle for control over untransformed institutions of power of the old regime, with the aim of putting 'force' into the service of one's own vision of Serbia" (Pešić 2009, 74).

The case of Serbia shows how moderation might actually complicate the transition process. While it can be a useful element in the process of negotiating a coalition, as it accommodates ideologically diverse groups under one umbrella structure, it can backfire in the process of formulating a vision of a future system. The opposition platform during the electoral campaign avoided any confrontation with nationalism, the key source of Milošević's legitimacy. According to Cohen (2001), this flirtation with nationalism was a "serpent in the bosom"; in other words, the alternative to Milošević's nationalism became democratic nationalism. In fact, the justification of Koštunica's candidacy was in his appeal to voters who traditionally supported Milošević or were dependent on his rule. At the same time, his candidacy suggested that the legitimacy of the former regime would not be disputed. While this strategy helped DOS overthrow Milošević, it greatly complicated matters in the long run as the New Order had fewer methods and even less support to clean the institutions of compromised elements from the Old Order. At the same time, the Serbian events also show how early contacts with particular authorities, especially the security forces, could smooth the process during the most crucial moments of protests.

The case also indicates several essential features for a successful overthrow. First, the isolation of spoilers—in this case marginalization of SPO—proved to be of crucial importance for the achievement of internal unity of the forces engaged in contesting the regime. At the same time, party politics proved to be insufficient to fight the authoritarian system, and a broader interaction with civil society was needed to oust the regime. Given their lack of partisan impediments and their unconventional methods of contesting the regime, civil movements are important as a mass mobilizer and a force of intimidation during the crucial times of protests and mass uprising. Free of the interests of party politics, they provide a credible source of information dissemination regarding the prospects of contesting the incumbent regime. Such forces are able to extend negotiations for coalition over and beyond the established political parties and develop negotiations to formulate a vision that justifies the uprising. For this, they need a focused organization of their own, along with an ability to use demonstrations to wield the threat of violence. Unfortunately, they then turn over official power in the New Order to the very parties that were unable to unite on either a lasting coalition or a durable dream for replacing the Old Order with the New.

Notes

1. Taxonomy put forward by Bieber (2003, 75).

2. There were several attempts to form a broad antiregime coalition; however, all failed to produce a clear program and broke up even before the elections. Most importantly, they never included all the major opposition forces (Bieber 2003; Milošević 2000).

3. While the popular dissatisfaction was slowly mounting, the opposition hoped that the system might also start weakening from inside. Goran Svilanović, chairman of the Civic Alliance and one of the opposition leaders, stressed that "Milošević cannot promise anything to anyone any more. He cannot offer a type of financial security to those around him as before, and I'm afraid he will not be able to guarantee their physical security either. I hope that those who contributed to his rise and power—and meanwhile stolen a lot of money from the people—will ask themselves where they are leading their families to" (Svilanović, qtd. in Cohen 2001, 320–321).

4. The opposition leaders that attended the event were Dragoslav Avramović, Zoran Đinđić, Goran Svilanović, Vladan Batić, Milan St. Protić, Vesna Pešić, Anđelko Tripković, Ognjen Pribićević, and Rebeka Srbinović (*Glas javnosti*, 17 February 2000).

5. For a debate between Đinđić and Ognjen Pribicević from SPO: Peščanik 10, emisija, 5 April 2000, available at http://pescanik.net/2000/04/10-emisija/.

6. Slowly, various domestic actors—such as the Serbian Orthodox Church and even Milošević's coalition partner, the Serbian Radical Party (SRS)—started voicing their approval of Koštunica's victory and asked Milošević to step down. On 26 September, Patriarch Paul (Pavle) of the Serbian Orthodox Church received Kostunica and invited the police and army forces to "protect the people and not an individual" (*Blic*, 27 September 2000).

7. The role of JSO during the events will be long discussed and scrutinized. Vasić (2005) argues that, despite alleged previous meetings with Đinđić and DOS, it was still quite unclear under what pretext JSO left its headquarters, and he speculates that JSO's commander Milorad Ulemek (also known as Legija) had incomplete information about what was going on but was quite mesmerized by the events and the number of protesters. Once they entered the mob, they sought an opportune moment to pledge their allegiance to the new establishment, creating a pretext for their future glorification for saving the revolution (Vasić 2005).

8. Koštunica, in fact, did not see 5 October as a revolution but rather as a transition of power. Therefore he believed that the fragile post–5 October situation would not benefit from major personnel changes. Later he explained his position: "In such unstable times it was very important to secure a continuity of state structures, most importantly of the army and the police. Imagine if in such instability, really with all the surprises we were experiencing in the south of Serbia [Kosovo], we started some major shuffling of the army and police personnel. What would that look like?" (see B92 2004).

9. In the negotiations DOS opposed the possibility of early elections for the president of Serbia, because Milutinović's term was supposed to last for two more years, at the same time suggesting that Milošević's defeat cut off the party from a suitable alternative that could represent the regime in a new race against the opposition. Overall, according to Đinđić, "there was a great deal of readiness among all to reach an agreement" (*Glas javnosti*, 10 October 2000).

10. The other twenty ministries were divided between the three groups. As still the strongest parliamentary party SPS would oversee the ministries of local self-governance, agriculture, infrastructure, trade, tourism, economic and ownership transformation, family welfare, science and technology, education, environment, and sport. DOS would be responsible for the ministries of mining and energy, labor, welfare, university education, health, and international economic relations. Finally SPO controlled the ministries of industry, traffic, culture, religious affairs, and

diaspora (*Glas javnosti*, 17 October 2000). It could be argued that DOS did not want to give an image of legitimizing the wrongdoings of the incumbent regime, as they feared that SPS wanted a coalition to "socialize" their past mistakes with DOS.

11. When Đinđić's government acted on the ICTY indictments and arrested Milošević on 30 March, Koštunica, who opposed cooperation with ICTY, defined the situation as a coup d'état.

References

B92. 2004. "Rukopisi ne gore." Episode 1 of *Insajder*. Documentary. B92, Belgrade. http://www.b92.net/insajder/arhiva/arhiva.php?nav_category=985&nav_id=400260 (accessed 6 February 2015).

———. 2010. *Bajka o Petom Oktobru*. Documentary by R. Despotović. B92, Belgrade.

Bieber, Florian. 2003. "The Serbian Opposition and Civil Society: Roots of the Delayed Transition in Serbia." *International Journal of Politics, Culture and Society* 17, no. 1: 73–90.

Budding, H. Audrey. 2002. "The Man Who Overthrew Milošević: Vojislav Koštunica, One Year Later." *Fletcher Forum of World Affairs* 26, no. 1: 159–166.

Bujošević, Dragan, and Ivan Radovanović. 2003. *The Fall of Milošević: The October 5 Revolution*. New York: Palgrave Macmillan.

Bunce, Valerie J., and Sharon L. Wolchik. 2012. *Defeating Authoritarian Leaders in Postcommunist Countries*. Cambridge: Cambridge University Press.

Cohen, Lenard J. 2001. *Serpent in the Bosom: The Rise and Fall of Slobodan Milošević*. Boulder, Colo.: Westview Press.

Dobson, William J. 2013. *Dictator's Learning Curve: Tyranny and Democracy in the Modern World*. London: Random House.

Drašković, V. 2010. *Meta*. Belgrade: Srpska reč.

G17. 2000. Unity Program. www.vojvodina.com/prilozi/g17.html.

Goati, Vladimir. 2001. "The Nature of the Order and the October Overthrow in Serbia." In *R/Evolution and Order: Serbia after October 2000*, edited by Ivana Spasić and Milan Subotić, 45–58. Belgrade: Institute for Philosophy and Social Theory.

ICG (International Crisis Group). 2000a. "Serbia: The Milošević Regime on the Eve of the September Elections." Balkans Report no. 99. Brussels: International Crisis Group.

———. 2000b. "Serbia's Embattled Opposition." Balkans Report no. 94. Brussels: International Crisis Group.

Martinov, Zlatoje. 2000. "Otpor ili smrt: Rađanje novog nacionalizma." *Republika*, no. 230–231 (February): 1–29.

Milošević, Milan. 2000a. "Pažljiva opozicija." *Vreme*, no. 472 (22 January).

———. 2000b. *Politički vodič kroz Srbiju*. Belgrade: Medija Centar.

Ninčić, Roksanda. 2000. "Opozicija na okupu." *Vreme*, no. 471 (15 January).

Nodia, Ghia. 2000. "The End of Revolution." *Journal of Democracy* 11, no. 1: 164–171.

Otpor. 1999. "Declaration on Future of Serbia." Belgrade, 25 August.

Pavlović, Dusan. 2000. "Populisticki katanc." *Vreme*, no. 517 (30 November).

Pešić, Vesna. 2009. "Nationalism of an Impossible State: A Framework for Understanding the Unsuccessful Transition to Legitimacy in Serbia." In *Between Authoritarianism and Democracy*, vol. 3: *Serbia at the Political Crossroads*, edited by Dragica Vujadinović and Vladimir Goati, 71–87. Belgrade: CEDET.

Popov, Nebojša. 2000. "Snaga drustva i sila vlasti." *Republika*, no. 230–231 (February): 1–29.

Rawls, John. 1987. "The Idea of an Overlapping Consensus." *Oxford Journal of Legal Studies* 7, no. 1: 1–25.

Rosenberg, Tina. 2011. "Revolution U: What Egypt Learned from the Students Who Overthrew Milosevic." *Foreign Policy*, 16 February.

Thompson, Mark R., and Phillip Kuntz. 2004. "Stolen Elections: The Case of the Serbian October." *Journal of Democracy* 15, no. 4: 159–172.

Vasić, Miloš. 2005. *Atentat na Zorana*. Belgrade: Narodna knjiga.

Vuković, Ivan. 2011. "Diverging Party Outcomes in Hybrid Regimes: The Cases of Croatia, Serbia and Montenegro." *Romanian Journal of Political Science* 11, no. 2: 81–104.

Zartman, I. William, and Tanya Alfredson. 2010. "Negotiating with Terrorists and the Tactical Question." In *Coping with Terrorism: Origins, Escalation, Counterstrategies, and Responses*, edited by Rafael Reuveny and William R. Thompson. Albany: State University of New York Press.

Zlatić, Ivan. 2000. "Buntovnici sa rđavim razlogom." *Republika*, no. 230–231 (February): 1–29.

Newspaper Archives

Blic: www.blic.rs/arhiva
Glas javnosti: http://arhiva.glas-javnosti.rs/arhiva/srpski/arhiva-index.html
Vreme: www.vreme.com/arhiva.php
Republika: www.republika.co.rs/arhiva/
Pescanik: www.pescanik.net

South Africa

Negotiated Transition to Democracy

MARK ANSTEY

AT THE END OF APRIL 1994, after four years of negotiation punctuated by violent breakdowns, 19.7 million South Africans across race groups queued peacefully together to vote the nation into a constitutional democracy. In a remarkable political trade-off the white minority ceded power in a context that would see it, as a racially defined identity group, forever relegated to the political sidelines; and the black majority took power in a manner that extended rights, freedoms, participation, and protections to those who had previously oppressed it. There was a rapid transition in political power, but it was recognized that economic empowerment would be a longer-term project. The constitution contains an expansive bill of rights and seeks national unity through tolerance and accommodation (syncretist or fruit-salad approach) rather than imposing a single uniform national identity through assimilation (Jacobinism or fruit-blend approach). Critical as these four years were, they can only really be understood in the context of the choices made over the previous decade; and the value of the negotiated agreement on a constitution and elections achieved at the end of 1993 can only really be evaluated to the extent that it has served to consolidate democracy in the period since.

The South African experience was different from that of Arab Spring countries in many ways. There was no symbolic dictator to chase out; politics and oppression were racial, not simply authoritarian; and the negotiated revolution was preceded by periods of unsuccessful liberalization and frustration. On the other hand, particularly like the Short Track cases in the Arab Spring, the South African ruling elite negotiated its own transition, the notion of the state was maintained, the opposing forces repeatedly affirmed its moderation, and violence was relatively minimal. Obviously, no two situations are the same, but significant difference in cases can be instructive and insightful (George and Bennett 2005). In this case, the comparison is useful for understanding contrasting dynamics of Arab Spring but also the posttransition challenges common to both.

Since 1994 four further free and fair elections have been held—and in 2013, despite a host of internal problems, the nation was still rated as "free" by Freedom House. South Africa is an outlier in the wider experience of the African continent where neither elections nor constitutions have been guarantors of peace or democracy. In a period of wider democratic recession (Diamond 2008), South Africa's transition has proved amazingly resilient but, for many reasons, remains vulnerable.

IN RETROSPECT: A MODEL TRANSITION

A great deal of work on negotiated transitions has been conducted (O'Donnell, Schmitter, and Whitehead 1986; Munck 1989; Ethier 1990; Hethy 1992; Friedman 1994; Harris and Reilly 1998), and the evolving South African story has been captured in several works (Sparks 2004; Slabbert 2006; Horowitz 1991; Price 1991; de Villiers 1993; de Villiers and Anstey 2000; Anstey 1998, 2005, 2006b). Passages to democracy may occur through military defeat by an external force (Japan and Germany after World War II); internal restoration after defeat of a conqueror (Europe post–World War II); after revolution; and internal dissensus and negotiation (Stepan 1986). O'Donnell, Schmitter, and Whitehead (1986) propose that negotiated transitions move through clear phases of *regime deterioration*; *internal division* in which soft-liners supplant hard-liners; soft-liners implement *liberalization* measures; opposition groups use newly provided political space to launch a *popular upsurge*; a period of *threat* by extremists on all sides; *pacting* (at political, social, and military levels) between key actors to stabilize the process and avert risks of a coup by regime conservatives or revolutionary overthrow by opposition extremists; *elections*; and then a period of democratic *consolidation* (Sisk 1995).

Partly perhaps because it reflects these phases, the South African transition to democracy in retrospect appears quite orderly and coherently managed. At the time, it did not feel like that on the ground. Across the population there was huge insecurity about where the process was going; leaders struggled sometimes to hold their constituencies together while reaching out to those of others; negotiations deadlocked over seemingly insurmountable issues of principle; there were breakdowns in trust as spoiler tactics took effect; and it often felt as if the process was on the edge of collapse. There was no certainty that parties would be able to cross the deep ideological divides separating them, move beyond a long history of racial repression, or overcome the volatile mixes of fear and conservatism, anger and extremism, across groups at times. There was no upfront assurance that the major parties would actually find one another and keep finding one another through periodic crises in relations; there were third forces in operation, spoilers, murderers, and "loose cannons." Many helpful events occurred almost by chance—but it takes wise leadership to see opportunity in chance events and to use them for nation-building purposes. South Africa's leaders did not enter negotiations with a shared vision for the shape of a future nation, but they did share an understanding that a future formula must encompass rights, freedoms, participation, and protection for everyone involved, that negotiation was the preferred route forward, and that negotiations would have to be inclusive to hold prospect.

This chapter builds on the proposed transition framework proposed by O'Donnell, Schmitter, and Whitehead (1986), illustrating the points made with a short historical narrative of the South African transition process.

SYSTEM DETERIORATION AND EXPLORATORY NEGOTIATION

A regime that has recognized it cannot continue in its current form must make choices—inevitably in the first instance it will seek to change in ways that secure its position. The early reform question is—"if we must share power, how can do it in a manner that ensures retention of control?" Consequently design outcomes are commonly perceived by opposition groups as too little too late, or co-optive even as they produce a division between regime conservatives and reformists. In the mix, social space is opened, and a popular upsurge often occurs with activists using new freedoms to push for further, more comprehensive change. And so it was in South Africa. Reforms occurred at a civil society level and more clumsily at a political level—and were responded to with increased militancy.

From the 1970s there was *deterioration* in the apartheid system in the face of demographic pressures, slowed economic growth, rising internal dissent, international isolation, and differences within the regime as to how to manage an increasingly unworkable and costly policy framework. In the 1970s South Africa's economic growth rate, which had been second only to Japan's after World War II, stalled in the face of demographic realities. It became steadily evident that apartheid was unsustainable. The economic slowdown was aggravated by the flights of capital that followed each wave of internal unrest—the Sharpeville shootings in 1969, a strike wave in 1973, the student-led Soweto uprising in 1976, and rising levels of insurrection within black communities. The white buffer states in Rhodesia and Mozambique fell, and South Africa became increasingly isolated as arms and oil sanctions and disinvestment drives took hold, international loans dried up, and sports teams and academics were refused international hospitality (Price 1991; Horowitz 1991). The South African regime was increasingly aware that its apartheid policy was in a cul-de-sac.

CIVIL SOCIETY REFORMS

At a civil society level, "hard" apartheid had slowly dissipated. Following a wave of strike action in 1973, the government set up a commission of inquiry into labor reform under Professor Nic Wiehahn. In 1979 in accordance with his recommendations, trade union and collective bargaining rights were extended to black workers, and an industrial court was established. If there was hope within the government that labor reforms would placate black workers as they had done white workers in the 1920s, they were mistaken. Black workers were still politically excluded. Reform did not result in grateful compliance—a powerful social movement unionism arose spearheading the internal liberation struggle through massive strike and stay-away action through the 1980s. Reforms (bold on the labor front; clumsy and limited on the political front) simply opened political space, spurring not acquiescence but greater resistance.

Important as the political agenda was, the new unions retained a strong workplace focus. They used the strike weapon but also negotiation to improve their wages and conditions. They fine-tuned the use of industrial action to leverage bargaining processes. Trade unions became nurseries for democracy for many black workers. This was where they acquired experience in forming legitimate self-governed organizations and could engage in collective bargaining with employers. For many the first experience of a vote was for their union representatives; their first experience of operating under a constitution was in the union; their first experience of a court as a protective rather than a repressive institution was the industrial court. In a separate society workplaces provided the only arena of daily interracial contact—it was where white managers and black workers began to "find" one another, acknowledge their common interests and humanity, and recognize each other's integrity. It is no surprise in retrospect then that trade unionists played such an important role not only in leading the political upsurge but also in stabilizing it through pacting arrangements, the negotiation of South Africa's new democracy, and the early design of its labor policies. In 1989 organized business and organized labor entered a bilateral accord to resist a threatened government rollback of advances in labor legislation—the SACCOLA/COSATU/NACTU Accord (Adler and Webster 2000; de Villiers and Anstey 2000; Landman, leRoux, and Piron 1990; Valenzuela 1989). Political transitions without roots in civil society tend to fail (Bratton and van der Walle 1997; Anstey 2004).

POLITICAL REFORM—NEO-APARTHEID

In 1984 the government embarked on a clumsy political reform initiative designed to preserve white dominance in a tricameral parliament (of whites, coloureds, and Indians) excluding black interests. In the long term, of course, the formulation mutated into the one F. W. de Klerk took with him into negotiations with the African National Congress (ANC)—that of a group-based dispensation within a single parliament. The reform generated major resistance and served to unite opposition groups under the United Democratic Front (UDF). Efforts to contain militancy through successive states of emergency failed. Liberalization is often accompanied by popular upsurge—it is a high-risk period when transitions can be stalled by either a right-wing coup or collapse into revolution. Historically neither result in viable democracies. Negotiated transitions tend to be stabilized through political and social pacts between power holders and opposition groups (Ethier 1990; O'Donnell, Schmitter, and Whitehead 1986). The importance of proposed government reforms lay not only in their shortcomings and their one-sided non-negotiated nature as a formulation, but the fact that they signaled a government in trouble looking for a solution. In this, South Africa differed in a major way from the authoritarian Arab regimes.

INTERNAL DIVISION AND EXPLORATORY NEGOTIATION

There was *division* within the regime, but the shift in government policy was not simply one of a soft-liner faction supplanting hard-liners and introducing reforms. It was, in fact, the hard-liner P. W. Botha (the "*groot krokodil*") who initiated exploratory talks. He never personally "crossed the Rubicon" of releasing opposition political leaders and entering negotiations before suffering a stroke in 1989 and being displaced as leader of his party and the nation, but he made the early running that enabled F. W. de Klerk's momentous political move in February 1990. Cautious talks with Nelson Mandela while in custody were started in 1985, and a dozen or so exploratory offshore meetings between the government and the ANC in exile took place. While P. W. Botha was in office, up to seventy-five meetings occurred between South African whites and the ANC in exile.

Beyond that there was a decade of *liberalization* at a civil society level (extending civil rights and protections but not votes) before formal political negotiations. Workers used the space provided to mobilize bus boycotts, school boycotts, rent boycotts, and huge stay-away and strike action, but their unions were also nurseries for democracy where workers were able to form and join democratic organizations and practice the skills of negotiation and the use of mediation, arbitration, and the courts. A decade of learning and relationship building at the civil society level later assisted in stabilizing the transition process when political negotiations broke down at various points. By the time de Klerk made his speech, a great deal had happened: apartheid had softened; the government, business, and the ANC were reaching out to one another; workplaces had become important sites not only of struggle but also of mutual discovery across race lines and a nursery for democracy. Along with the strikes came negotiations, contracts, due process, and court credibility. Into the 1990s the value of these civil society initiatives became apparent—exploratory pacts were firmed and expanded (Zartman 1994).

Botha's co-optive political reforms in 1984 failed—but they signaled a regime recognizing a problem and seeking a new solution, and served to unify opposition groups across race lines in the United Democratic Front (UDF). The pressures of internal popular upsurge, international sanctions and isolation, and the absence of workable political or military solutions prompted the initiation of the "unthinkable alternative"—the parties started talking with each other. The government was caught in a clumsy dance between unworkable reform and repression as it sought to contain rising levels of internal dissent; the ANC knew it could not win a military victory. In short, as the adversaries implicitly, and jointly, recognized that they were at an impasse, and the potential costs of ongoing no-win political struggle, they had the courage to initiate and sustain a covert, exploratory dialogue. The critical factor was the recognition by the leaderships of the regime and the ANC that they were in a political cul-de-sac—a mutually hurting stalemate—and a willingness to explore the idea of negotiation with "the enemy"—a way out.

A QUIET POLITICAL *TOENADERING:* SECRET TALKS ABOUT TALKS

When it became clear that co-optive political reform would simply polarize relations, a covert initiative was embarked on in the mid-1980s. Mandela in his jail cell and regime leaders exchanged signals of interest in the potentials for negotiation for a new formulation. The first signs of a *toenadering* (Afrikaans for "coming closer") among actors in both civil society and politics were evidenced. In the writing of history there is some contest over the significance of who did what with whom at which levels to start the great thaw in relations (Slabbert 2006). I make no attempt here to try to evaluate whose initiatives mattered more. Suffice it to record that in the late 1980s numerous formal and informal outreaches were made to the ANC in exile from the regime, and members of white civil society—and, critically, that the ANC responded. All of it mattered.

After the student uprising in Soweto in 1976, the government banished Nelson Mandela's troublesome wife Winnie to the small Karoo town of Brandfordt. There she befriended by chance the family of a local lawyer, Piet de Waal, who in turn was an old university friend of Kobie Coetzee, who became minister of the Department of Justice, Police and Prisons in 1980. De Waal urged a review in thinking about the Mandelas. In 1982 Nelson Mandela and a small group of leaders were moved from Robben Island to Pollsmoor Prison. In 1984 Mandela wrote to Coetzee asking for a meeting with P. W. Botha to explore potentials for a dialogue that might lead to negotiations—possible "talks about talks." In 1985 Mandela needed medical care and was hospitalized. Coetzee visited him in the hospital. On his return to Pollsmoor he was given a room of his own to facilitate meetings with Coetzee. It was delicate stepping. In the polarized political environment of the 1980s both ran the risk of being accused of selling out, failing to consult, and acting beyond their mandate. Adv Bizos, with the blessing of Coetzee, made two trips to Lusaka to assure the ANC leadership that Mandela was not selling out and to secure endorsement for his exploratory discussions. Discussions progressed. Winnie Mandela was released from exile in Brandfordt.

In 1986 a Commonwealth Eminent Persons Group (EPG) visited South Africa to evaluate prospects for change. Its visit included a meeting with Mandela. It put forward proposals almost exactly the same as those eventually contained in de

Klerk's 1990 speech. The proposals split the regime, with soft-liners seeing opportunity to use the moment to negotiate, but hardliners wanting to crush black resistance movements before any such moves. On 19 May Minister of Defence Magnus Malan ordered attacks on ANC bases in Zambia, Zimbabwe, and Botswana—effectively scuttling the initiative of the EPG while it was still busy in the country and prompting a shift in its recommendations from dialogue to comprehensive mandatory economic sanctions on South Africa (Sparks 1994, 35). Despite this, Mandela reached out asking for further discussions with the government, and a series of meetings ensued with Coetzee and a small committee of top Nationalist Party leaders—forty-seven in all. "Thus for four years before the rest of the world knew anything of it, the future of South Africa was being explored in secret conversations in hospitals, prisons and a cabinet minister's home between government officials and their principal political prisoner" (36). Mandela was taken on secret drives in the countryside to ready him for the outside world. P. W. Botha was searching for a way to release Mandela that would not make him appear weak or as having sold out the Afrikaner.

On another track there were quiet outreaches between the P. W. Botha government and the ANC in exile from 1986. Two Stellenbosch University professors, Sampie Terblanche and Willie Esterhuyse, met with the ANC in London, the latter as an emissary of P. W. Botha, to explore potentials for negotiation with Thabo Mbeki. An indirect dialogue was established enabling exploration of views and possibilities of talks between regime and opposition leaders. Twelve meetings sponsored by the British mining group Consgold took place at Mells Park House between November 1987 and May 1990 (Sparks 1994, 82) with an expanding group of Afrikaner leaders being introduced to the process. Formal exploratory discussions accompanied informal time together—all helping to break stereotypes, enable clearer understanding of the issues, and build confidence between those in the regime and those in exile.

In 1985 several captains of industry and the media visited the ANC in exile in Lusaka. Business wanted assurances. Attention to economic policy was demanded. It would help none of the stakeholders if a flight of capital occurred or policies were adopted that frightened off future investors. Then were meetings between the ANC in exile and Afrikaner leaders in Dakar in 1987 organized by Breyton Breytenbach and Frederik van Zyl Slabbert. A group of 115 white members of the civil society participated in four days of wide-ranging discussion between 29 June and 2 July 1989 in Lusaka under the auspices of the Five Freedoms Forum and the ANC. Louw (1989) reported that by 1989 at least seventy-five significant meetings had taken place between white South Africans and the ANC.

On the basis of all these exploratory talks the ANC felt confident enough to clarify a formal proposal at the Organization of African Unity Conference on 21 August 1989—the Harare Declaration. Five preconditions for negotiations were explicated: lifting of the state of emergency, free political activity, legalization of all political organizations, release of all political prisoners, and an end to all political executions. Under these conditions the ANC committed to suspending armed violence while negotiations for constitutional principles were conducted followed by a mechanisms for drafting a new nonracial constitution.

P. W. Botha's stroke in 1989 ended his leadership of the National Party and the nation. F. W. de Klerk was elected to lead the party, assuming the presidency in August 1989. Not being in Botha's inner circle, he was a surprised newcomer to the political exchanges that had been underway over the previous four years, though his brother Wimpie had been involved in the MellsPark meetings (Sparks 1994, 113). Sparks suggests he was a conservative, but his commitment to party was absolute—in 1986 when the National Party basically relinquished its commitment to territorial division and the evolution of a unified South Africa, so did he. Of course, at the time the P. W. Botha vision was one of a power-sharing formula among racial groups. De Klerk made the choice to lead the soft-liners rather than the hard-liners into the next phase. Moving away from the formula of separate parliaments, he proposed a single parliament in which minorities would have protections in a group-based dispensation. His reformism was reinforced by Gorbachev's actions in the USSR, and by the fact that neighboring Namibia did not collapse into chaos after independence in 1989.

FORMAL POLITICAL NEGOTIATIONS AND THE SHAPING OF A DEMOCRATIC SOUTH AFRICA

President de Klerk's parliamentary speech on 2 February 1990 in which he announced the release of political prisoners, lifted the ban on political parties, and opened the door to engage in negotiations for a future South Africa took his own cabinet, political party, and opposition groups by surprise (Slabbert 2006). At one level it had all the elements of the *unconditional concession*—simply doing the right thing without preconditions, releasing all parties from a long-standing political gridlock. It removed the rationale for armed struggle, clearing the way for negotiations. However, the ANC had already signaled its willingness to engage in negotiations under such conditions in the Harare Declaration of 1989. The move was a surprise in terms of timing, but the covert dialogue and the Harare Declaration made it less a high-risk leap into the unknown than an unexpected "next big step." De Klerk made his move when the old adversary was vulnerable in a unique historical *context* after its ideological and support system collapsed with communism in 1989. This does not diminish the significance of de Klerk's speech—the fact his timing was strategic does not detract from the boldness of the act, his courage in taking the leap, or its value in triggering a formal public negotiated transition. The outcome ultimately was not what he envisaged, but he saw opportunity offered by a unique "wormhole" in the national and global political firmament—a moment when all major actors in the apartheid war were in a crisis of direction and decision. The National Party had long recognized apartheid had no future but could not find a workable alternative formula. The ANC faced a crisis of ideology and resources with the collapse of the Communist empire. Recognizing the moment is, of course, quite different from having the courage to use it—and step into the unknown.

De Klerk's ambush of the system he led was made possible by the fact that the apartheid system was in a crisis for which its leaders had no solutions. The regime was at no risk of a military defeat, but its very powerful military establishment had recognized it was in a struggle that demanded a political rather than a military solution. The best efforts of regime politicians had produced no workable political formula—advanced apartheid in the form of a tricameral government that sustained the Bantustans had served to unite anti-apartheid opposition groups into the United Democratic Movement (UDM). The security forces felt betrayed and exposed and for this reason remained a risk factor for the transition right up to elections in 1994. However, security force leaders had been the tools of the apartheid system rather than its philosophers, harbored no political ambition of their own, and recognized that despite their capacity to stage a coup they (rather like the dog chasing a car) would have little idea how to run the country if they took it (Slabbert 2006).

De Klerk not only took his own party by surprise; he blindsided opposition groups internally and in exile. The collapse of the Communist empire in 1989 created a crisis of ideological direction and resources for the ANC and South African Communist Party and aggravated existing divisions over the negotiated change option, and over external and internal leadership issues. Umkonto we Sizwe (MK), its military wing renowned more for its courage than its victories on the ground, presented little military threat. Activists in the townships could render townships ungovernable and stop factories operating for short periods, but such actions stopped someway short of toppling the regime.

De Klerk made no demands in exchange for his concessions. Opposition groups were simply offered freedom and the opportunity to negotiate. It was an extraordinarily powerful move. He used the political opening created by the collapse of communism creatively, but it was a brief victory as international support flowed largely toward the ANC as the process unfolded. Neither the government nor the ANC arrived quite where they had planned in the outcome—a liberal democratic constitution and a market economy (Slabbert 2006, 36).

EARLY PROGRESS . . . AND COLLAPSE

If the informal preparations and the sudden opening for a negotiation process marked a South African difference from the Arab Spring and a prelude to a gradual transition, subsequent moves contributed to keeping that process on track.

The early process was managed through a series of *confidence-building pacts*—the release of political prisoners, the return of exiles, amendments to security laws (Groote Schuur Minute, signed on 4 May 1990), suspension of the armed struggle (Pretoria Minute, signed on 7 August 1990), and a deal not to disband Umkhonto we Sizwe before transition (D. F. Malan Minute, signed in February 1991). The parties agreed on a venue, participation, and structure to initiate an inclusive negotiation process. In short, a great deal of work had to be done before engaging in formal negotiations for a new political dispensation. It was agreed that the process should be widely inclusive—twenty-six political parties met under the umbrella of the Convention for a Democratic South Africa (CODESA) in December 1991.

The second element was the establishment of phased negotiations, in which the basic formula for the New Order was established, and then details of these basic constitutional principles were negotiated after the first election. Despite the *toenadering* that had evolved, an early difference was experienced. The Nationalist Party (NP) wanted a new constitution negotiated in a convention of political groupings—reducing the representative power of the ANC; the ANC wanted negotiation by "legitimate—i.e., elected—representatives" of the people—a scenario that would have rendered the NP a small-part player from the start. This "either-or" impasse was overcome through a sequencing of processes: the route to a constituent assembly and an interim constitution would be negotiated by an all-party convention, leading to the election of the assembly by universal franchise. The assembly would then negotiate a final constitution on the foundation of binding principles laid down in the interim constitution on the question of majorities required for decision-making purposes. On 21 and 22 December 1991 the twenty-six parties came together in CODESA 1 to start negotiations under the chairmanship of two judges. Gatsha Buthelezi, leader of the Inkatha Freedom Party (IFP), boycotted the first meeting because his request for an IFP delegation as well as one for the Zulu king had been refused. The convention ended with tensions between Mandela and de Klerk over the D. F. Malan Accord.

It was hard going when the parties reconvened in May 1992 at CODESA 2 to continue negotiations, with the ANC pushing for a short process while the government saw value in prolonging it. Decisions in the multiparty negotiation were made on the basis not of a majority but of "sufficient consensus" (basically agreement between the government and the ANC). The government was assisted in its slowing-down strategy when it was accused by the right wing of acting without a mandate; in March 1992 de Klerk called for a whites-only referendum to check backing for continuing negotiations. If conservative elements were hoping for a back door out of negotiations, it was not provided. A two-thirds majority favored ongoing negotiations. The referendum infuriated opposition groups, who saw it as a delaying and possibly derailing tactic, but the outcome in the end helped get the process back on track (Zartman 1995).

When they reconvened, however, the parties were unable to find agreement over the size of majority required for constitutional change by the deadline of 15 May—the ANC proposed 66.7 percent, the government 75 percent. The ANC moved to 70 percent and 75 percent on Fundamental Human Rights clauses, but the government would not budge. The minority group feared loss of control and exclusion; the majority was frustrated by the ANC's obduracy and feared it would be unable to govern—that it was in danger somehow of being locked permanently into an interim constitution. The ANC proposal that any deadlocks be determined by popular referendum did not help. Talks broke down.

THE SPECTER OF FAILURE: HOLDING TO NEGOTIATION, DEFEATING THE SPOILERS

Not surprisingly, despite some heady periods of progress, the process was dogged throughout by mutual suspicion. The ANC leaders in exile had feared trickery in which they'd all be arrested once back in the country; although political parties had been unbanned, individuals remained on wanted lists, and the National Intelligence Service had to smuggle leaders into the country for the first round of talks. All had moved way out in front of their constituents deeply indoctrinated against one another. Mandela's release speech was a difficult event in which he had to reassure ANC members on the ground that he had entered no secret deal in exchange for his release and that he remained a loyal member of the party, even as he tried to put white fears to rest. The ANC kept Operation Vula alive "in case" the government reneged, but its public exposure deepened mistrust, and a bold move was required to rebuild confidence in the process. In December 1990 the ANC suspended the armed struggle but did not disband its armed wing Umkhonto We Sizwe MK. On the other side, elements in the regime, with or without de Klerk's direct knowledge, kept "third forces" in operation.

When CODESA 2 broke down, the hawks came to the fore. The ANC returned to "rolling mass action." There was an increase in violence. Spoilers saw opportunity. Polarization occurred, and the negotiation process was put at risk. There were fears of all progress being lost in a flurry of revolutionary anger, or a security force coup. Violent tensions had arisen between supporters of the ANC and Chief Buthelezi's IFP in Kwa-Zulu Natal and on the Witwatersrand, with strong suspicions of "third force" collusion between the killers and the police for the latter group. On 17 June 1992 a group of armed Zulus attacked people in their homes in Boipatong township, killing thirty-eight in an orgy of violence. When de Klerk visited the scene later, all hell broke loose—more died. When Mandela visited, an angry mob basically accused the ANC of standing idly by while they were being slaughtered. The ANC formally withdrew from negotiations in the context of a polarized environment, listing fourteen demands for the resumption of talks. It was the end of CODESA.

The ANC turned its attention to the "independent homelands" still obstructing ANC political activity. Despite the absence of recognition from the rest of the world, the government still saw these as independent territories, as did those who took office in them. South Africa funded their parliaments and administrations, and over time deeply embedded systems of entitlement and corruption developed. On 7 September the ANC leader Ronnie Kasrils recklessly defied a court order in trying to lead a group into Bisho, breaking from a defined route during a planned protest march. Ciskei soldiers opened fire, killing twenty-eight protestors. Judge Goldstone discovered evidence of a "third force" dirty tricks unit in November 1992. Shortly afterward de Klerk fired or suspended twenty-three senior Defence Force officers. Goldstone's ongoing investigations turned up hard evidence of Kwazulu-Natal death squads linked to the IFP and receiving support from "elements in the regime."

This period of horror in which extremist elements briefly held sway sobered the principals—Mandela and de Klerk met to try to find a way to end the violence. A Record of Understanding was signed on 26 September, and negotiations resumed. A new round of formal talks began by the new Negotiating Council beginning in March 1993.

Spoiler activity was far from over, however. On 10 April 1993 Chris Hani, the hugely popular general secretary of the Communist Party, was assassinated by a white right-wing fanatic. The rage that followed was effectively managed through the leadership of Mandela, who appealed to people across race groups to see the negotiation process through, pointing out that Hani had been murdered by a white man, but that his murderer had been brought to justice by the actions of a courageous white Afrikaner woman (Retha Harmse, who saw the killing, remembered the car registration number, and called the Flying Squad). Labor leader Cyril Ramaphosa and South African Communist Party (SACP) leader Joe Slovo called for negotiations to be speeded up rather than called off. On 25 June 1993 three thousand right-wingers, many armed, drove a vehicle through the glass windows into the World Trade Centre to disrupt negotiations. It did not help their cause. On 25 July 1993 five black men attacked worshippers in Cape Town's St. James Church with automatic weapons and grenades. Twelve were killed and fifty-six injured. The armed wing of the Pan African Congress (PAC) had previously claimed responsibility for similar armed attacks in the Eastern Cape and Cape Town, but it denied allegations of responsibility for this attack. Investigations went nowhere, and counter allegations held that it was the work of agents provocateurs. A month later a young peace activist from the United States Amy Biehl, was killed by black youths in Cape Town. If anything, these extremist acts served only to consolidate a common revulsion by moderates across the spectrum and to reignite a sense of urgency to complete negotiations (Sparks 1994). The violence in Boipatong and Bisho confronted the negotiators with the implications of a failure to see the transition through. By now the hopes of the National Party in achieving a group-based democracy had been dashed; but the ANC also was not where it had started—a more liberal interpretation of the Freedom Charter had supplanted aspirations of the communists. Klein (2007) has argued that the transition was hijacked by neoliberal forces.

A NEW CONSTITUTION AND A FORMULA FOR A GOVERNMENT OF NATIONAL UNITY

On 18 November 1993 an interim constitution was agreed, ending "eight years of negotiating that had begun in Nelson Mandela's hospital ward, continued through prison cells and a cabinet minister's home, through intelligence networks and secret brotherhood channels, through underground communication systems and covert couriers, and finally concluded in a formal diplomatic forum involving as many as twenty-six political parties and government bodies" (Sparks 1994, 194). The striking feature of the process, absent in the Arab Spring, was the establishment of a consensual formula of principles to frame the ensuing negotiations on the details. The constitutional drafting process itself took less than four years, quite comparable to the various records (and anticipations) in Tunisia, Egypt, Libya, Yemen, and Morocco.

The interim constitution provided the foundations for a constitutional democracy, guaranteeing universal suffrage and fundamental rights to be protected by a constitutional court. A Government of National Unity (GNU) would come into effect after elections to stabilize relations in the new South Africa, and a final constitution would be approved by the constitutional assembly (a four-hundred-member national assembly and a senate comprising ten senators from each of nine provinces, both elected by proportional representation, and a national executive headed by a president from the party with the majority of votes). Cabinet posts were allocated proportionally to national assembly seats. Nine provincial legislatures were to be elected on the basis of proportional representation, making decisions by majority vote. Local governments were to be autonomous within the bounds of conferred powers. Houses of traditional leaders at national and provincial levels would advise parliament on traditional and customary law.

Two key factors that enabled final agreement were *contingent consent* and *bounded uncertainty*. Those resisting a deal gave their consent on the basis of certain assurances that responded to their fears. There would be two vice presidents, with one post going to the party that came second in the election, and the other to a third party that gained more than 20 percent of the vote—failing that the post would go the winner of the elections. Cabinet seats were promised to minorities on a proportional basis for the first five years, and the jobs and pensions of white civil servants, police, and military personnel were protected. Other assurances existed in the form of an entrenched Bill of Fundamental Rights and a powerful constitutional court. A creative new anthem melding that of the past with "Nkosi Si'kelel iAfrika" was composed; a new flag agreed upon. De Klerk delayed progress briefly pushing unsuccessfully for a further assurance—that the new cabinet should achieve a majority of two-thirds for any major changes. Importantly, although the government remained in place until elections, a Transitional Executive Council (TEC) was created, drawn from parties involved in the negotiating process. Negotiations, however, were not over—there was resistance to the transition right up to elections.

APARTHEID'S FINAL KICKS: DEALING WITH THREATS OF SECESSION, COUPS, AND BOYCOTTS

As negotiations drew to a close, resistance to the transition coalesced into a new group in the Negotiating Council—the Concerned South African Citizens Group (COSAG), comprising the IFP, leaders of Ciskei and Bophutatswana, and white rightist Conservative Party. Their demand was for a system of federalism that would see a continuation of the independent homelands and a new homeland for whites. In the dying days of apartheid this resistance became a serious threat. Sparks (1994, 197) writes, "What nobody realized at the time, and most South Africans still do not, is that this (getting these groups on board) meant overcoming an armed operation that threatened a massive secessionist rebellion, perhaps even a civil war." The Negotiating Council had agreed that all black people would have their citizenship restored on 1 January 1994 and that the homelands would be reabsorbed back into South Africa on election day (27 April 1994), with the end of their administrations.

White right groups formed the Volksfront, including the Conservative Party (CP) and the Afrikaaner Weerstandbeweging (AWB), to call for an Afrikaner homeland. General Constand Viljoen had emerged as a leader of the right but refused to leave the negotiations, feeling this would leave only an unworkable military option—eventually it was agreed that the Conservative Party would withdraw from negotiations, but the Volksfront generals would engage with the ANC in bilateral negotiations *outside* the Negotiating Council. Because meetings would cause great difficulty in their own caucuses, they met secretly—Viljoen's twin brother Braam, "a tribal dissident" who had been involved in meeting the ANC in exile, facilitated. Mandela acknowledged the ANC could not win a war but pointed out that neither could Volksfront forces, which faced the reality of overwhelming numbers and international support for the ANC. Twenty meetings followed. It became complex—the volkstaat the right-wingers wanted was ambitiously large; the NP objected that it had not been included; the CP would not agree to a basic principle of nonracialism.

Things came to a head in Bophutatswana. Its president, Lucas Mangope, decided not to participate in the April elections but to stay with the independence achieved under apartheid in 1977. When twenty-two thousand civil servants and police facing the uncertainty of the April election went on strike demanding advance wages and pension payouts, there was looting and a breakdown of order. A ragtag AWB militia entered Bophutatswana shooting wildly at civilians. It was quickly defeated, with some of its members shot by local security forces under the full glare of television cameras. The ANC pushed for Mangope to go before elections. On 22 March Ciskei's Brig Gqozo, faced with a similar set of demands from his civil servants, resigned. It was the end of the homelands.

The IFP and CP refused to participate in the election. Viljoen was left with a choice—join the election or lead a coup. Ten minutes before cutoff he broke with the CP and registered a party—the Freedom Front. Despite having long campaigned for the release of Mandela and against the total independence of the homelands, Chief Buthelezi (of the IFP) played out a spoiler role right to the eve of the election. Although he had always played out a role as the moderate nonviolent, anticommunist alternative to the ANC, his forces had been revealed in the Goldstone Report as playing a role in "third force" activities. His demands for self-determination by the Zulu people were secessionist in form. On 8 April, well past the deadline for registration of parties, Mandela and de Klerk failed in their attempt to entice Buthelezi and King Zwelithini into the election process. The IFP continued military training and now demanded international mediation—an effort to delay the election. The Transitional Executive Council (TEC) would have none of it. A week before the election, Buthelezi blinked—realizing nonparticipation would see him marginalized and the collapse of his administration, he decided to participate. Inclusiveness was critical. Eighty million ballots had already been printed—eighty million IFP stickers now had to be printed and attached to each ballot by hand.

THE CONTRIBUTION OF CIVIL SOCIETY, 1990–1994

Civil society was highly developed in South Africa and continued to play a vital role in the transition process as formal political negotiations got underway, then fell apart, and then reignited for a successful conclusion. The Congress of South African Trade Unions (COSATU) entered an embryonic social pact with business and the state in the National Economic Forum (NEF) and the National Manpower Commission (NMC), maintaining an independent labor identity even as it entered an alliance with the ANC and SACP. Business supplied a vital secretariat service to the political parties through the multiparty talks. A Local Government Negotiating Forum convened to develop a viable democratic local government system. The National Education and Training Forum was created to agree to a restructuring of the education system. The business community provided secretariat services to the political negotiation process.

In 1991 the Police Board, comprising political and civil society representatives, was established to review policy and recommend the structure and shape of a police service into the future. In 1992 organized business, the labor movement, and the churches brokered the National Peace Accord as a nonaggression pact among major stakeholders in the transition process, allowing a level of civilian control over the police and armed services and extending participation in peace committees to every level of society (Anstey 1993). It was a bold effort to contain political violence in the country, making provision for codes of conduct for political parties, police, and security forces and guidelines for the reconstruction and development of communities. The accord committed all parties and government agencies to respecting fundamental rights and freedoms underpinning a multiparty democracy and provided for a system of peace committees to be established at all levels in society. The success of these structures was, of course, uneven across activity areas and regions, but the critical thing was that people at every level in South African society became involved in the change process—it was not simply a top-down process conducted at the political level. There was a momentum in civil society that helped carry the process through when there were breakdowns at the political level.

A great deal of South Africa's successful transition can be credited to the strength of its civil society, and the fact that it laid the foundations (albeit it perhaps unwittingly) for its political process through civil reform for years before political negotiations began. In this sense South Africa "grew" its democracy.

ELECTIONS

The Independent Electoral Commission was established in December 1993. It started work for the nation's founding elections only two months before the April election. A short lead time was not its only problem—there were no voters' roll, no electoral infrastructure in many parts of the country, very few trained personnel, and inadequate demographic data. In the event, elections were run through 8,493 ordinary voting stations, supplemented by 950 mobile, 1,047 special, and 187 foreign voting stations in seventy-eight other countries. Over 30 percent of voting stations had no electricity or regular telephone services; there were last-minute shortages of voting materials, attempted sabotage of the counting process, and systems failures. At moments it seemed the election might be lost at the moment of its delivery. Very able internal and external support, some creative problem solving, and a huge popular impetus saw the process through to the finishing post. The good faith and creativity, in the middle of a promising transition process, provided the two elements that made for a successful event and would be needed in the Arab Spring countries two decades later.

THE POST-ELECTION PHASE: CONSOLIDATING DEMOCRACY

The achievement of a free, fair, and peaceful election in South Africa was remarkable. However, elections are no guarantee of a constitutional democracy. The post-election phase is the period in which the real test for democracy becomes evident. Populations as a whole must settle in for the long haul of nation building, affording each other freedoms, allowing their parties to win and lose power peaceably, and sustaining an independent judiciary and a free press. Many new democracies face threats to consolidating their new status as "free" nations. Diamond observes: "Emerging democracies must demonstrate that they can solve their governance problems and meet their citizens' expectations for freedom, justice, a better life and a fairer society. If democracies do not more effectively contain crime and corruption, generate economic growth, relieve economic inequality, and secure freedom and the rule of law, people will eventually lose faith and turn to authoritarian alternatives" (2008, 37).

Functional states are able to effectively broadcast power (design and implement laws); collect revenues and deliver public goods protecting and serving citizens; maintain accountable democratic structures; maintain legitimacy; ward off predatory neighbors; develop a shared sense of national identity; build a culture of constitutionalism and a rule of law; and reflect an acceptance by citizens and leadership groups who will continue to play the democracy game whether they win or lose elections, secure in the belief that all others will as well—it is a game of contingent consent (Fukuyama 2004; Herbst 2000; Anstey 2006b; Diamond 2008).

SOUTH AFRICAN CONSOLIDATION: THE POLITICAL TRACK

The final constitution became law in 1996. At the institutional level the National Assembly and the National Council of Provinces sit in Cape Town. Government ministries are based in Pretoria; the Constitutional Court sits in Johannesburg; Bloemfontein is the seat of the Appeal Court. In terms of control, a clear transfer of power has occurred in South Africa. The ANC won the 1994 elections with a 63 percent majority and has sustained its political dominance in all later elections: 66 percent in 1999, 70 percent in 2004, 66 percent in 2009, and 62 percent in 2014. A 67 percent majority is required to change the constitution. Support for the National Party (architect of apartheid) collapsed after it was in political control for nearly five decades, and in 2005 it dissolved itself into the ANC. The Democratic Alliance, as the current major opposition, has risen to 22 percent of the vote.

Sustained dominance of a political system by a single massively dominant majority party carries many risks. A rising centralization of power may allow it to progressively ignore and marginalize opposition parties, to deal with contentious matters as private internal issues rather than matters for the public domain, and to ignore or hide corruption, and it can lead to economic opportunity becoming vested in political connections rather than competence, facilitating a rise in crony capitalism. The ANC's political hegemony has given rise to unease not only among opposition parties but also within the "alliance" where the SACP and COSATU, the trade union federation, have periodically voiced disquiet over the manner in which their views are so easily sidelined on matters such as the economic policy, job creation, the Zimbabwe issue, corruption, and responses to the HIV/AIDS pandemic. There are concerns then that the ANC's overwhelming political dominance may inhibit the vibrant public exchange that characterizes healthy democracies (Sole 2004). The ANC itself is deeply concerned about levels of corruption within government.

INSTITUTIONS

"For democracy to triumph, the natural predatory tendencies of rulers must be restrained by rigorous rules and impartial institutions . . . fundamental innovations are necessary to transform closed, predatory societies into open, democratic ones" (Diamond 2008, 44). Strong commitments to ensuring consolidation of South Africa's new democracy were made by those who negotiated it. A number of state institutions were established including the public protector; Human Rights Commission; Commission to Promote and Protect Rights of Cultural, Religious and Linguistic Communities; Commission for Gender Equality; auditor general; and Independent Electoral Commission. The performance of these individuals and structures has been varied. The public protector's office has been dogged by controversy, as was the special police unit—the Scorpions—set up to root out corruption. It was later disbanded. The South African Police Service was severely set back by the appointment of Commissioner Selebi, who later was found guilty of criminal charges. Appointments to the judiciary have been fraught with controversy over political agendas and racial issues, as have appointments to the governing body of SABC/TV, the public broadcaster.

The new government moved swiftly to institutionalize social dialogue around social and economic policy making, transforming the fledgling NEF (established during the transition period in 1992) into a statutory body, the National Economic Development and Labour Council (NEDLAC), in 1994. Through this forum organized business, labor, and the state reached consensus on a suite of new labor laws intended to drive social transformation by the following:

- promoting economic development, social justice, and workplace democracy through orderly collective bargaining, workplace participation, and dispute resolution (Labour Relations Act);
- regulating rights to fair basic conditions of employment and their variation (Basic Conditions of Employment Act);

- achieving workplace equity through the removal of discriminatory practices and affirmative action of designated groups to ensure equitable representation in all occupational groups (Employment Equity Act); and
- providing an institutional framework for accelerated skills development of the country's workforce to enable competitiveness in a global economy (Skills Development Act).

Social dialogue has borne fruits, as has the project to persuade the social partners to resolve their disputes within rather than outside a regulatory framework. The statutory Commission for Conciliation Mediation and Arbitration (CCMA), set up in 1996 to handle 45,000 cases a year, has received over 125,000 referrals a year. However, there are serious concerns over the cost of the CCMA, as well as the cost of the "industry of dispute settlement" to the wider economy. Also, after a period in which industrial action fell, strikes have again become ubiquitous in a context of frustrated expectations, with a huge loss of workdays in 2010 and 2012. The behavior of certain public sector workers during these actions showed little respect for the rights of others and reflects deeply frustrated expectations and hopes in South African society. The crisis at Marikana on the platinum belt in which thirty-four workers died following a confrontation with police brought the extent of breakdown in labor-management relations in some sectors sharply into focus.

RECONCILIATION

Reconciliation is key to trying to ensure there is not a reversion to violent conflict. South Africa's much-vaunted Truth and Reconciliation Commission (TRC), despite some disappointment in its outcomes, was critical to the transition process, but its reach was limited. It must be understood at several levels. During the transition process the promise of the TRC was critical to removing the threat of security force resistance to the process; in the immediate post-apartheid period it sought to surface the truth of apartheid atrocities and to "kick-start" long-term reconciliation to avert a return to open conflict. Offering the prospect of amnesty for politically motivated acts, the TRC gave the opportunity for victims of apartheid atrocities to air their pain and for perpetrators to confess and repent their deeds in public forums. In often harrowing hearings more than twenty thousand people told their stories to the TRC, including eight thousand perpetrators. The pain of individuals was public, the tales of loss and suffering dreadful and tragic.

Inevitably, however, the process fell short of expectations for some. There were perceptions that some seeking amnesty offered a technical truth without showing remorse. Leaders tried to exonerate themselves by pleading ignorance of the activities of foot soldiers; foot soldiers claimed they were following orders. There was resistance from political parties. On the National Party side, P. W. Botha refused to appear. F. W. de Klerk was seen to adopt a route of "technical compliance" without really accepting responsibility for suffering under apartheid, or responding to Mandela's reconciliatory outreach. He successfully interdicted findings against him in the TRC report on the eve of its presentation to the president, resulting in a blacking out of this section in the presentation copy. The ANC, unhappy with reports of its own human rights abuses in camps of exiles, was not successful in its application to the court to prevent the release of the report and findings against it (Villa-Vicencio 2010, 160). Critics felt that the TRC never established proper identity, leaving victims and accused alike feeling betrayed (Slabbert 2000), and that it simply "degenerated into a game of racial name-calling" (Mangcu 2003, 116).

After the TRC experience, Alex Boraine (2000), who cochaired the TRC with Archbishop Tutu, and Frederik van Zyl Slabbert (2000) argued (sensibly) that reconciliation was less about perfect harmony than about a restoration of relations sufficient for parties to move on in peace while accepting each other's integrity in a climate of mutual trust. For all its flaws the TRC played a critically important enabling role in the transition process and in formalizing post-apartheid reconciliatory intent. Reconciliation remains a long-term process beyond confessions of the past, moments of forgiveness, and one-off payments for purposes of reparation. The cession of political power to a black majority helped white credibility, but more is expected. As Achmat (2010) has pointed out, the effectiveness of the reconciliation process will determine whether South Africa's miraculous transition represented a revolution averted, or simply deferred. He argues the TRC failed to deal with the depth of social deprivation incurred by apartheid and that there will not be reconciliation until this has been properly addressed. In his view sufficient reparation costs have not been paid, in particular by big business. The government, in fact, only made reparation payouts in 2011, in the form of a one-time payment of thirty thousand rands (about three thousand U.S. dollars) to each of twenty-two thousand individuals identified as being direct victims of apartheid. Compensation of this sort presents complex problems—inter alia, how reparations might be made to wider populations that suffered under a system of repressive inequality, how individuals should be identified for payouts and the criteria to be used, linking monetary payouts to actual suffering and how long-term structural disadvantages should be redressed (Achmat 2010; Ntsebeza 2010; Mamdani 2000).

SOCIAL TRANSFORMATION: THE RISING CRISIS OF POVERTY, DUALISM, AND SOCIAL DELIVERY

South Africa's democratic transformation is consolidated in the sense that the political kingdom now resides in the hands of political parties subject to accountability through regular elections. Despite the problems associated with the hegemony of a single party, voters have voice and choice. Very important work remains to be done in the areas of poverty, job creation, perceptions of social equity, and boundaries of social rights.

In the years it has enjoyed power, the ANC government has delivered a mixed scorecard. An average annual economic growth rate of about 3 percent is below the level required but positive; inflation and debt have been reasonably controlled; and some, but not enough, foreign direct investment has been attracted. It has delivered about three million subeconomic Reconstruction and Development (RDP) houses; over 70 percent of people now have access to electricity and 93 percent to safe water (about five million people have gained access to running water for the first time); social grants have been extended to fourteen million people (as many as are in formal employment); public works schemes have given rise to 240,000 jobs; matriculation rates have improved, markedly rising (though controversially) from 58 percent in 1994 to 67 percent of the population in 2010. Much of this has been underpinned by improved efficiencies in tax collection.

But South Africa faces serious problems. Official unemployment stands at 27 percent, but the picture is bleaker than this—almost 40 percent of its workforce population is not in formal wage employment. A sharp dualism has arisen between those who enjoy privileges and protections within a formal work environment and those outside the formal sector. Jobs have become a scarce resource. This has informed several waves of xenophobic attacks on Zimbabwean and other exiles. Those in poverty put huge pressures on those with jobs at the poorer end of South African society, with high dependency ratios eroding the wages of those with employment and in turn feeding the ambitious wage demands that inform industrial action in a struggling collective bargaining regime. Negatively then, the country's economy is not creating sufficient jobs; land reform has been slow and contentious; violent crime and corruption are at deeply worrying levels; HIV/AIDS saw life expectancy in the country fall from sixty-three to forty-eight, a decline only now being slowly reversed.

EQUITY AND DEMOGRAPHIC TRANSFORMATION

Democratic consolidation requires that political hegemony be translated into social delivery. Democracies are about constituencies. A previously excluded black population (the ANC's primary constituency) is demanding that the transfer of political power be translated into social benefits: education, jobs, transfers of wealth, business opportunities, social security. Reconciliation across racial lines will, of course, be best served through rapid access to social services and work opportunities within a growth economy. The South African government, however, is driving an ambitious program of demographic restructuring into a job-stressed environment in a cruelly competitive struggling global economy.

Quick success was achieved in the legislature and in the civil service. In 1979 racial employment policies under apartheid saw 90 percent of key civil service positions held by Afrikaners (Lapping 1987). By 2004, 85 percent of employees in the public service were black, with the percentage in the management echelon having risen to 66 percent from a base of 6 percent in 1994. Powerful and very contested pushes for demographic transformation continue in the judiciary, in universities, and in the private sector at levels of ownership, supply chains, and workforces. Although analysts such as Rumney (2004), Southall (2004), and Herman, du Plooy, and Calido (2007) suggest that black ownership in the economy has risen in various forms far more rapidly than commonly understood, black interests perceive and have become frustrated by the slow pace of change. Government is committed to driving Black Economic Empowerment strongly at all levels into the future.

Affirmative action is motivated by needs for redress but is also critical to political and social stability into the future and therefore to democratic consolidation (Dupper 2005). As early as the 1970s employers recognized that sustainable economic growth required a stable black middle class and expanding black consumerism (Lipton 1986). The problem is really less one of will than of context. A jobs growth economy would allow opportunity for many more; full employment would mute identity-based competition. The crisis in the job market may turn an ambitious social transformation project into a scarce resource conflict. Realistically there is a sharp contrast between affirmative action initiatives in the United States seeking to integrate a minority group of about 15 percent into a full employment economy, and South Africa seeking to absorb an 80 percent majority into an economy reflecting an almost 40 percent level of unemployment. It is not a matter than can be deferred morally or politically; neither can it be easily managed in the current shape of the economy.

In addition, there are disconnects between the conceptual acceptance of the need for affirmative action at a macro level and its implications for individuals in the workforce—if members of one ascriptive group (whites, but also to an extent other minorities) experience affirmative action as a process of multiple individual injustices, what are the implications for the larger project of a just and reconciliatory social transformation project? Across race groups there is a divide as to the meaning of "nonracialism." Where for many whites it simply implies removal of obstacles to opportunity for all, for many blacks it implies eliminating, in every sector, a colonial past of racial dominance. The manner in which it is implemented has important implications for a government struggling to achieve balance between demands for competent delivery of public goods and opportunity for members of a previously disadvantaged black population. Equity targets put pressure on organizations to cut "competency corners." As in the apartheid era, people may secure senior positions less by virtue of individual competence than through a collective ascriptive wave. Clan and connection come to outweigh competence. The ANC is becoming keenly aware of the problems associated with appointing people to posts beyond their competence, as it translates into poor social delivery to voters. This and perceived corruption have seen angry attacks on councilors in some townships.

INTO THE FUTURE

South Africa's transition is well advanced on many fronts—the formal structures of the apartheid state are long gone; all its people have been released from a repressive system of white minority government; elections to date have been peaceful, frequent, free, and fair; public institutions are demographically representative; the economy has been sensibly rather than creatively managed, and some real progress has been made on delivery to social needs. But it remains a transition in process, and its democracy remains fragile. Poverty, unemployment, and inequality are fundamental threats to sustainable democracy, as is hegemony by a single party. Apartheid is dead, but racial tensions remain alive on many fronts. Reconciliation across identity groups is more difficult in a context of scarcity that encourages mobilization around ethnic markers. Adherence to apartheid's racial categories ensures that the residual structural imbalances of apartheid receive focused attention, but they perpetuate the conflict categories of the past and race as *the* defining factor in a fast-changing South African society. Such policies carry the risk of progressively locking South Africa's transformation at every level into a game of racial proportionalism and becoming a polity more color bound than color blind. The ANC has strong credentials as the party that led the black majority to freedom on a platform of nonracialism. On ascriptive grounds it enjoys the support of the huge majority of South Africa's peoples, and this support seems resilient despite their anger over poor social delivery. Breakaway groups fare poorly. But despite this security, there remains a tendency under pressure to resort to identity-based politics by influential individual leaders.

South African society is far more nuanced than its official race group classifications suggest. Within each of the major identity groupings there is diversity—as reflected in Vahed and Jeppie's (2004) study of the country's Muslim population of 650,000. If South Africa's politics become locked into racial identity, it will limit the prospects of new groupings emerging based less on race than on values, class, religion, occupation, consumer preferences, or circumstance in an open society. There are class migrations underway evidenced in the emergence of a black middle class, reflecting shifts in access to opportunity and wealth. Burgess (2002), in a study involving over fifteen thousand respondents, suggested the emergence of sixteen South African "tribes" based on identity characteristics and living standards, within four major groupings: rural survivalists, emerging consumers, urban middle class, and urban elite.

If South Africa falls back to race-based politics after a long struggle for a nonracial polity, will it matter, and if so, to whom? If people across identity groups sustain a larger sense of national identity, acknowledge their common humanity, respect one another at individual and group identity levels, and accord one another democratic rights and freedoms, the ambition of unity through diversity might well be realizable. If racial identity is simply the ticket for accessing power and wealth through ascription within a scarce resource society, however much one recognizes a repressive past, identity-based tensions will continue. Democratic societies are evaluated by their constitutions, judicial systems, commissions, forums, laws, structures, and civil society freedoms, but the social glue that coheres them in diverse societies is a mix of inclusion, tolerance, accommodation (Gutmann 1995), and a shared preference for nonviolent settlement of disputes. They are characterized by nonviolent competition for power, universal rights to vote and run for office, to assemble, to move freely, to form political parties, trade unions, and other civic organizations, to voice opinions, to a free press (alternative sources of information), to protection from the courts, to freedoms from fear and want (Anstey 2006b; Diamond, Linz, and Lipset 1989; Dahl 1982). A workable social contract requires that every individual submits to conditions they would impose on others—all are (and feel) equal under laws founded in the general will and regulated through an impartial judicial system. In short, individuals and groups see greater benefit from accommodating one another's interests than in going to war over them.

South Africa has moved through the classical phases of a political transition. Beyond the technical expertise required to self-manage such a process (the parties did not use external assistance), it required a profound change of heart across its population. In escalated conflicts, identity groups polarize positions and perceptions, build in-group solidarity, demonize each other, and diminish communications. Those proposing negotiation, tolerance, or accommodation across groups are at risk of being declared sellouts in the context of "if you are not with us, you are against us" sentiments. As parties use increasingly coercive tactics to achieve their ends, the process becomes self-sustaining. Anger, desires for revenge and settling accounts, and inflicting pain on the other overwhelm motives for peace, harmony, and cooperation. Original issues may become forgotten as each responds to the tactics of the other. Parties take up arms and become afraid to suspend hostilities lest they be momentarily lulled and defeated by force. As parties become steadily entrapped, offensive action is argued away as self-preservation (rights to "anticipatory defense" and "preemptive strikes"). And then, of course, there are elements across sides who have little identity other than through open conflict (Anstey 2006b; Pruitt and Rubin 1986; Coser 1956). Unwinding this dynamic is an extraordinarily difficult task. In the first instance those advocating negotiation must convince their people that suspending hostilities will not see them simply defeated; people do not just suddenly become tolerant; people brutalized through conflict bring baggage of anger and need for revenge; then ways have to be found to prevent a return to conflict. Reconciliation becomes a critically important preventive negotiation process. If there is regression in the form of parties mobilizing around old identity groupings and struggles to secure power in later political exchanges, the risk of a reopening old wounds becomes salient, and the wider transformation process may be put at risk.

It is not sufficient, then, to understand South Africa's transition simply as a progression through a series of typical phases for authoritarian rule through to democracy. What greases the process is a conflict transformation process in which adversaries begin to see each other differently, use their power differently, and commit progressively to joint solution searches across the table in defiance of internal hard-liners. There is a shift from zero-sum thinking to system design that seeks to accommodate diverse interests; new levels of trust emerge; people "re-humanize" one another. To the extent that these shifts extend beyond simply political exchange and are underpinned by shifts in relations at a civil society level, the transition is strengthened. All these shifts have been evidenced in South Africa over the last thirty years of change, but there are forces in play that threaten the positive energy of its earlier period. There is no threat of a reversion to repressive rule under an ethnic minority—in this sense South Africa's transition is completed. It was Mandela's politics of reconciliation that facilitated the transition. It will be the politics of development that enable its consolidation. There will be tragedy if the politics of identity come to prevail over the politics of policy and performance. On these fronts the struggle continues.

References

Achmat, Z. 2010. "No Reconciliation without Social Justice." In Du Toit and Doxtader, *In the Balance*, 110–117.

Adler, G., and E. Webster, eds. 2000. *Trade Unions and Democratisation in South Africa, 1985–1997*. London: Macmillan.

Anstey, M. 1992. "Mediation in the South African Transition: A Critical Review of Developments, Problems and Potentials." *Genève-Afrique* 30, no. 2: 141–163.

———. 1993. *Practical Peacemaking*. Cape Town: Jutas.

———. 1998. "South Africa's Political Transition." In *Democracy and Deep-Rooted Conflict: Options for Negotiators*, edited by P. Harris and B. Reilly, 49. Stockholm: International Institute for Democratic and Electoral Assistance.

———. 2004. "African Renaissance: Implications for Labour Relations." *SA Journal of Labour Relations* 28, no. 1: 106–126.

———. 2005. "Social Transformation in South Africa: Workplace Tensions and Interventions." Paper presented at the 13th International Conference on Conflict Resolution, St. Petersburg, Russia, May.

———. 2006a. "Can a Fledgling Democracy in the Democratic Republic of Congo Take Flight?" *African Journal of Conflict Resolution* 6, no. 2: 35–68.

———. 2006b. *Managing Change, Negotiating Conflict*. 3rd ed. Cape Town: Jutas.

Boraine, A. 2000. "The Language of Potential." In *After the TRC: Reflections on Truth and Reconciliation in South Africa*, edited by W. James and L. van der Vijver, 73–81. Cape Town: David Philip.

Bratton, M., and N. van der Walle. 1997. *Democratic Experiments in Africa: Regime Transitions in Comparative Perspective*. Cambridge: Cambridge University Press.

Burgess, Steven M. 2002. *SA Tribes: Who We Are, How We Live and What We Want from Life in the New South Africa*. Cape Town: David Philip.

Coser, L. 1956. *The Functions of Social Conflict*. New York: Free Press.

Dahl, Robert. 1982. *Dilemmas of Pluralist Democracy: Autonomy vs. Control*. New Haven: Yale University Press.

Daniel, J., R. Southall, and J. Lutchman, eds. 2004. *State of the Nation: South Africa, 2004–2005*. Cape Town: HSRC Press.

de Villiers, David. 1993. "Transition by Transaction: A Theoretical and Comparative Analysis of Negotiated Transitions with Special Reference to South Africa." D.Phil. thesis, University of Port Elizabeth.

de Villiers, D., and M. Anstey. 2000. "A Comparative Analysis of the Role of Trade Unions in Transitions to Democracy in South Africa, Spain and Brazil." In *Trade Unions and Democratisation in South Africa 1985–1997*, edited by G. Adler and E. Webster. London: Macmillan.

Diamond, Larry. 2008. "The Democratic Rollback: The Resurgence of the Predatory State." *Foreign Affairs*, March/April: 36–48.

Diamond, Larry, Juan Linz, and Seymour Martin Lipset, eds. 1989. *Democracy in Developing Countries*. Boulder, Colo.: Lynne Rienner.

Dupper, O. 2005. "Remedying the Past or Reshaping the Future? Justifying Race-Based Affirmative Action in South Africa and the United States." *International Journal of Comparative Law and Industrial Relations* 21, no. 1 (Spring): 89–130.

Du Toit, F., and E. Doxtader, eds. 2010. *In the Balance: South Africans Debate Reconciliation*. Auckland Park: Jacana Media.

Erasmus, Z. 2004. "Race and Identity in the Nation." In Daniel, Southall, and Lutchman, *State of the Nation*, 9–33.

Ethier, D., ed. 1990. *Democratic Transition and Consolidation in Southern Europe, Latin America, and South East Asia*. London: Macmillan.

Freedom House. 2013. "Freedom in the World." http://freedomhouse.org.

Friedman, Edward, ed. 1994. *The Politics of Democratization: Generalizing East Asian Experiences*. Boulder, Colo.: Westview Press.

Fukuyama, Francis. 2004. *State-Building: Governance and World Order in the 21st Century*. London: Profile.

George, Alexander L., and Andrew Bennett. 2005. *Case Studies and Theory Development in the Social Sciences*. Cambridge: MIT Press.

Guest, R. 2004. *The Shackled Continent: Africa's Past, Present and Future*. London: Macmillan.

Gutmann, A. 1995. "Democracy." In *A Companion to Contemporary Political Philosophy*, edited by R. E. Goodin and P. Pettit. Oxford: Blackwell.

Harris, P., and B. Reilly. 1998. *Democracy and Deep-Rooted Conflict*. Stockholm: IDEA.

Herbst, Jeffrey Ira. 2000. *States and Power in Africa: Comparative Lessons in Authority and Control*. Princeton, N.J.: Princeton University Press.

Herman, D., T. du Plooy, and F. Calido. 2007. "The Truth about Employment Equity in South Africa." Johannesburg: Solidarity Report.

Hethy, L. 1992. "Hungary's Changing Labor System." In *Labor Relations in Transition in Eastern Europe*, edited by G. Szell, 229–321. Berlin: de Gruyter.

Horowitz, Donald. 1991. *A Democratic South Africa? Constitutional Engineering in a Divided Society*. Oxford: Oxford University Press.

Huntington, S. P. 1997. *The Clash of Civilisations and the Remaking of the World Order*. London: Simon and Schuster.

James, Wilmot Godfrey, and Linda Van de Vijver, eds. 2000. *After the TRC: Reflections on Truth and Reconciliation in South Africa*. Cape Town: David Philip.

Kaplan, Robert S., and David P. Norton. 2004. *Strategy Maps: Converting Intangible Assets into Tangible Outcomes*. Boston: Harvard Business School Press.

Klein, N. 2007. *Shock Doctrine: The Rise of Disaster Capitalism*. New York: Picador.

Landman, A. A., P. A. K. leRoux, and J. Piron. 1990. "The SACCOLA/COSATU/NACTU Accord." *Labour Law Briefs* 3, no. 2: 86.

Lapping, B. 1987. *Apartheid: A History*. London: Paladin.

Levy, A. 2005. "Tied Up in Technicalities." *Financial Mail* (Johannesburg), 18 February, 34–35

Lipton, Merle. 1986. *Capitalism and Apartheid: South Africa, 1910–1986*. Aldershot, UK: Wildwood House.

Lodge, Tom. 2003. *Politics in South Africa: From Mandela to Mbeki*. 2nd ed. Cape Town: David Philip.

———. 2006. *Mandela, A Critical Life*. Oxford: Oxford University Press.

Louw, Raymond, ed. 1989. *Four Days in Lusaka: Whites in a Changing Society*. Five Freedoms Forum—African National Congress Conference, Lusaka, Zambia, 29 June–2 July. Johannesburg: Forum.

Mamdani, M. 2000. "A Diminished Truth." In James and Van de Vijver, *After the TRC*, 58–61.

Mangcu, X. 2003. "The State of Race Relations in Post-apartheid South Africa." In *State of the Nation: South Africa, 2003–2004*, edited by J. Daniel, A. Habib, and R. Southall, 105–117. Cape Town: HSRC Press.

Mayer, Bernard S. 2000. *The Dynamics of Conflict Resolution: A Practitioner's Guide*. San Francisco: Jossey-Bass.

Mntambo, V. 2004. "Message from the Governing Body Chairperson." *2003/4 Annual Report of the Commission for Conciliation, Mediation and Arbitration*. Johannesburg: Commission for Conciliation, Mediation and Arbitration.

Modiano, G. 1996. "The Old and the New Concept of Race." In *Racism, Xenophobia and Ethnic Conflict*, edited by S. Bekker and D. Carlton, 139–157. Durban: Indicator Press.

Molahlele, E. 2004. *2003/4 Annual Report of the Commission for Conciliation, Mediation and Arbitration*. Johannesburg: Commission for Conciliation, Mediation and Arbitration.

Munk, R. 1989. *Latin America: The Transition to Democracy*. London: Zed Books.

Myburgh, J. Mbeki's Revolutionary Nationalist Agenda. *Focus* 29:2–4.

Ntsebeza, L. 2010. "Reconciliation and the Land Question." In *In the Balance: South Africans Debate Reconciliation*, edited by F. Du Toit and E. Doxtader, 85–92. Auckland Park: Jacana Media.

O'Donnell, Guillermo, Philippe C. Schmitter, and Laurence Whitehead, eds. 1986. *Transitions from Authoritarian Rule: Comparative Perspectives*. Baltimore: Johns Hopkins University Press.

Polley, J. A. 1988. *The Freedom Charter and the Future: Proceedings of the National Conference on the Freedom Charter and the Future*. Institute for a Democratic Alternative for South Africa. Johannesburg: A. D. Donker.

Power, M. 2005. "Equity Crackdown." *Sunday Times, Business Times* (Johannesburg), 20 February, 1.

Price, Robert M. 1991. *The Apartheid State in Crisis: Political Transformation in South Africa, 1975–1990*. New York: Oxford University Press.

Pruitt, Dean G., and Sung Hee Kim. 2004. *Social Conflict: Escalation, Stalemate, and Settlement*. 3rd ed. Boston: McGraw-Hill.

Pruitt, Dean G., and Jeffrey Z. Rubin. 1986. *Social Conflict: Escalation, Statemate, and Settlement*. New York: Random House.

Rumney, R. 2004. Who Owns South Africa: An Analysis of State and Private Ownership Patterns. In Daniel, Southall, and Lutchman, *State of the Nation*, 401–422.

Sisk, Timothy. 1995. *Democratization in South Africa*. Princeton: Princeton University Press.

Slabbert, Frederik van Zyl. 2000. "Truth without Reconciliation, Reconciliation without Truth." In James and Van de Vijver, *After the* TRC, 73–81.

———. 2006. *The Other Side of History: An Anecdotal Reflection on Political Transition in South Africa*. Johannesburg: Jonathon Ball.

Sole, S. 2004. "The State of Corruption and Accountability." In Daniel, Southall, and Lutchman, *State of the Nation*, 86–111.

Southall, R. 2004. "Black Empowerment and Corporate Capital." In Daniel, Southall, and Lutchman, *State of the Nation*, 455–478.

Sparks, Allister Haddon. 1994. *Tomorrow Is Another Country: The Inside Story of South Africa's Negotiated Revolution*. Sandton, South Africa: Struik Books.

Stepan, Alfred. 1986. "Paths toward Redemocratization: Theoretical and Comparative Considerations." In *Transitions from Authoritarian Rule: Comparative Perspectives*, edited by Guillermo O'Donnell, Philippe C. Schmitter, and Laurence Whitehead, 64–84. Baltimore: Johns Hopkins University Press.

Vahed, G., and S. Jeppie. 2004. "Multiple Communities: Muslims in Post-apartheid South Africa." In Daniel, Southall, and Lutchman, *State of the Nation*, 252–286.

Valenzuela, J. S. 1989. "Labour Movements in Transitions to Democracy: A Framework for Analysis." *Comparative Politics* 21, no. 4 (July): 445–473.

van der Merwe, Adrian, ed. 1995. *Industrial Sociology: A South African Perspective*. Johannesburg: Lexicon.

Villa-Vicencio, C. 2010. "Reconciliation: A Thing That Won't Go Away." In Du Toit and Doxtader, *In the Balance*, 160–168.

Zartman, I. William. 1994. "Local Negotiations." In *South Africa: The Political Economy of Transformation*, edited by Stephen John Stedman. Boulder: Lynne Rienner.

———. 1995. "Negotiating the South African Conflict." In *Elusive Peace: Negotiating an End to Civil Wars*, edited by I. William Zartman. Washington: Brookings Institution.

Lessons for Theory: Negotiating for Order and Legitimacy

I. WILLIAM ZARTMAN

IN SIMPLE TERMS, we posited that the purpose of the *intifadat* was/is to remove the Old Order and replace it with the New, and we posed a simple model of the Arab Spring transitions, asking why events went stray. The analysis has been made in terms of negotiation.[1] The authoritarian ruler has to be talked out of his office, as occurred in Tunisia, Egypt, and Yemen, and even when he cannot be persuaded to leave and needs to face force (as in Libya, Yemen, and Syria), negotiation is still required to pursue its conditions and consequences. Through it all negotiation, in terms of coalitions and formulations, is the path to setting up the New or Renewed Order. The evidence also shows that the approach is supported empirically, unevenly, and differently according to cases, taking the model as a measure for analysis, not a picture of reality.

The simple model proposed for analytical purposes and also aspired to by participants and observers considered the surprising overthrow of Arab authoritarian rulers as the opening for a newly liberated population to build a New Order of justice and dignity based on a consensus of legitimacy through participation. Negotiations for coalition would bring existing and new groups of civil society together to pursue negotiations for formulation over the shape and scope of the New Order. Such a course of events would not produce a Garden of Eternity on earth but would at least open the societies affected to normal politics of demands and supplies. As in the case of all ideal types, reality has deviated, in varying degrees. What are the causes and conceptual lessons of that variation?

In the beginning, as the *intifada* arose, there was little negotiation for coalition, in the sense of "what will you give me if we join?" but vigorous negotiation over the formulation. All uprisings began aimed at redress for substantive grievances but soon turned to the procedural goal of overthrow. However, even with that focusing objective, negotiations continued into how much overthrow was necessary—the authoritarian ruler alone, his family, his colleagues, his supporters, his party, or more. Overthrow as a unifying goal was never even proposed in Morocco, Algeria, and (until later) Bahrain, but negotiation over broad lustration measures in Egypt, Tunisia, Libya, and Yemen continued well into the transition.

But at the same time as the uprisers debated over "more and more," many of them turned to the New Order, and there the focusing unity over the goal broke down. More negotiations broke out over whom to associate with and over what, and since both subjects were open ended into the future, agreement was hard to reach and hold. The parties dug in on their own positions, with more effort to consolidate their own identities than to reach the broad consensus that the subject and moment required. The very sources of bargaining power in the Arab Spring—legitimacy, organization, and the threat or use of violence—pushed the parties against and away from each other rather than together, as is discussed later. These considerations return to the refined question, What was required and what was actually done in the Arab Spring?

Two approaches follow from the analysis to provide concluding lessons—a structural explanation based on the parties that result from negotiations for coalition and a process explanation based on the negotiations for formulation. They might be called Lessons for Theory and Lessons from Theory, respectively.

THE SEASONS: LESSONS FOR THEORY

The Arab Spring opens new perspectives on negotiation analysis in many ways, primarily structural. One way, as noted, is to expand the field of study to encompass negotiation at all *levels*, moving up and down from individuals through groups and parties to institutions, not just on one (diplomatic or legislative) level or even two, but welling up through many levels of society and polity as the Old Order, reluctantly and piecemeal, collapses. Even when negotiations did not move up from the lower levels, as in Yemen, they reached down to popular levels as adjuncts from the elites, as in Egypt and Tunisia. In some cases, vertical negotiations between government and civil society, as in Tunisia and also in Egypt, actually replaced the horizontal negotiations between elites. This complexity is different from the work on two-level negotiations, which is much more clearly structured (Evans, Jacobson, and Putnam 1993). Clear structures are not the matter of Arab Spring negotiations, and "lower-level" negotiators do not often stay on the "lower level." This presents an enormous tableau to handle. It means, however, that consideration of negotiations, or even politics, limited to the upper level, as between government and uprising or within a constitutional commission, is incomplete without consideration of the lower components that have gone into it. Negotiation, notably in such times of transition, should be analyzed bottom up, as a three-dimensional exercise.

Consideration of such negotiations must also be expanded to include more marginal *types* such as tacit and vertical negotiations and even nonnegotiation. By sticking only to explicit negotiations, analysis of the Arab Spring would have missed important elements and left much unexplained. The seesaw relations within the pacted societies sometimes involve direct exchanges and bargaining but frequently are conducted tacitly; the parties state their positions, invoke their threats, and then one party puts forward a decision that it believes will constitute the basis for acceptance or agreement, given the previous elements, and the other party responds.[2] Furthermore, it is hard to achieve a full picture of the negotiations without considering the disinterest of the *muntafadin* in negotiation per se, on one hand, but their importance to other parties' negotiations through their demonstrations or threat of violence, on the other. Usually parties that abjure negotiations are not included in negotiation analysis. But in the Arab Spring they nudge the negotiated transition along to meet the demands and interests of other parties who have the advantage of organization.

Negotiation analysis often assumes the existence of constituted *parties* to the negotiation (much as formerly economic analysis assumed the existence of given initial positions for its theories [Edgeworth 1881; Zeuthen 1930; Cross 1969]). Not only are there many levels, but parties are often shifting, kaleidoscopic, and engaged in internal negotiations while facing other organizing parties. Analysis has to dig below that comfortable surface and enter into the negotiations *within* parties, usually referred to as negotiations among factions, a relatively new field of study (Kenny 2010; Cunningham, Bakke, and Seymour 2012; Bapat and Bond 2012; Fjelde and Nilsson 2012; Fontini 2012; Zartman 2009; Zahar 2012; Lilje 2012; Lefkowitz 2015). Parties in internal negotiations are often inchoate, forming and dissolving during the process; in a word, they don't hold still.

To play a full role in negotiations, parties need bargaining *power*. There is no established conceptualization of the sources of bargaining power in negotiations. Power has been defined as "an action by one party intending to produce movement by another" or "value added to a particular outcome," but analysis needs to move to what it is that enables that action or value (Habeeb 1988; Zartman and Rubin 2000). In the Arab Spring the sources of bargaining power are organization, legitimacy, and the threat or use of violence. Parties pit the relative strength of the three components against each other, and it is important to judge how each plays out against the others. Legitimacy is arguably the primus inter pares among the sources of power in negotiating order and also the basis of order itself (Zartman 2009). It is legitimacy that makes violence acceptable and organization official and constitutes their power in turn. Legitimacy is the right to rule, and each side in the broader confrontation of the Arab Spring has a different source of legitimacy rather than merely contending for the award on the same basis. Effective governance and popular approval as secular legitimization vie with revelation and ex cathedra (*sic*) interpretation in religious legitimization as both subjects and sources of power in negotiation.

Arab Spring negotiations show the importance of violence and therefore the threat of violence, as an adjunct rather than an alternative to negotiation. Although often considered the opposite of negotiation—Churchill's "jaw, jaw, jaw rather than war, war, war."[3]—violence does not replace or destroy negotiation. It reinforces positions, gives an impetus to negotiation (as an element in the creation of a mutually hurting stalemate), and indicates seriousness in the search for outcomes. Conversely, even when violence takes over as the primary means of conducting the conflict, as in Libya, Syria, Bahrain, and at times Egypt, with the purpose of elimination rather than of reconciliation with the other party, negotiations are required to bring the violent confrontation to a conclusion.

Organization is also important, not merely as a characteristic of various parties but as a source of power. The success of the Islamic formations was above all the result of their ability to organize their followership, prepared under duress under the Old Order and expanded when the Old Order fell. While the other parties were trying to get their act together, the Islamic movements were busy recruiting, providing social services, benefiting from an attractive identity message and from the claim of having suffered most under the Old Order. Held together under repression by organization for their beliefs, they bided their time as the *intifadat* rolled in, jumping on the train and then taking over the locomotive when it appeared to be the vehicle of the future. On the other side, the whole liberal party scene is a poor player—disorganized and far from even the threat of violence, armed only with their claim to rational legitimacy. Lacking the discipline and conviction of the Islamists, the secular parties had been crushed by the *mukhabarat* (intelligence services) of the Old Order in Tunisia, Egypt, Syria, Libya, and Algeria, and have not yet recovered. The *mukhabarat* effect was doubly destructive: destructive of operating organization and also of the ability to make realistic plans for the future day when the regime would be gone.

But it takes two to negotiate. The opposing forces—the Egyptian military, the Yemeni Salehists, the Moroccan monarchy, the Algerian junta—remained in the ring because of their organization, their claim to legitimacy, and their control of violence. The *intifadat* attacked above all the legitimacy of the Old Order, gained steam when the state monopoly over the legitimate monopolization of violence collapsed, and succeeded when they were able to puncture the organization of the Old Order and produce defections from it.

THE STRUCTURE OF TRANSITION

Beyond these elements that broaden the consideration of negotiation, the analysis shows three patterns of transition, with their evolving subgroups, that emerge from the three tracks of the *intifada*. The three tracks—identified in the introduction and throughout the case studies as the Short Track Transition, the Long Track Transition, and the Short Track Reaction—yield different outcomes, roughly corresponding to the tracks themselves. The Short Track, in which the overthrow was produced in a matter of weeks, opened up a *competition* among a number of forces vying to define and control the New Order. The Long Track, which took months to produce an overthrow, if at all, produced disorder, a collapse of the state—even where it purported to exist, as in Syria and Yemen—and a *fragmentation* of political forces. The Short Track Reaction was a response of domination that left the state intact and the authoritarian Old Order in place, either by handling the uprisers adaptively or by repressing them or both. These patterns evolved in different ways inherent in the initial structures. They are not immutable; they evolve and can be changed, from within or without. But they evolve from where they are, limiting and channeling the further possibilities of evolution (Brynen et al. 2012). Thus the evolution of the uprising produced outcomes that can be structurally identified.

The Lally-Tolendal Theorem (1789, 8:515; cited in Elster 2000, 135), pronounced in the French Constituent Assembly, holds that "A single power will necessarily end by devastating everything. Two powers will fight until one of them has crushed the other. But three will maintain themselves in perfect equilibrium, . . . when two are fighting each other, the third, being equally interested in maintaining the one and the other, will join the oppressed against the oppressor, and thus restore peace among all." The theorem does not cover all structural situations, but it gives an insight into a way of thinking even about those not covered. It seizes the dynamics inherent in the patterns of transition and the setup for negotiation found in the Arab Spring. It has broad applications, including the Balance of Power and the Cold War in international relations. An advantage of the Balance of Power was that its alliances were temporary and not intended to harden into a bipolar system (Talleyrand in Orieux 1970, 249; in Waresquiel 2003, 351, 386). This understanding can also depend on external forces if not inherent in the main parties; the Neutral and Non-Aligned kept the bipolar Cold War from being an all-encompassing two-power system. The single power situation grasps succinctly the authoritarian regime and the dangers facing the Short Track Reactions. The other two situations contain a framework for the analysis of both tracks of transitions. The number of cases in the Arab Spring is limited, so there will often be only single examples of the situation and evolution analyzed.

The Short Track Transition produced a *competitive* system whose evolution was conditioned by the number of forces involved. As long as there are a number of political parties and other forces, the sense of the three-power situation is that they will keep each other in balance, continually jockeying for power while maintaining an interest in the preservation of the system that gives them a chance to play a role. Awareness of the curse of a two-power situation serves to maintain the system. In Tunisia, the new identity current and its leading organization, al-Nahdha, won nearly two-fifths of the seats in the 2011–2014 National Constituent Assembly, but the party's need for partners to govern encouraged it to preach cooperation and practice coalition.[4] This necessity entered into the party's self-image and reinforced

Table 1. Transition Tracks, Patterns, and Outcomes, by Country

Track	Cases	Characteristics	Pattern	Outcomes
Short Track Transition	Tunisia	Aged ruler Army not fire	Competition Pluralist	Normal Politics
	Egypt	Elites negotiate Moderate opposition Commitment to state	Dualist	Fragile Seesaw Authoritarian Return
Long Track Transition	Libya, Syria, Yemen	Long violence State collapse Foreign intervention	Fragmentation	Fragmented Politics Regional Breakup Civil War
Short Track Reaction	Morocco, Algeria	Strong Old Order Weak uprising Reforms adopted State continuity	Domination Adaptation	Normal Politics?
	Bahrain	Confrontation	Repression	Polarization

its collaborative wing. Despite the sharp opposition between the al-Nahdha and its liberal-left, in the following election, in 2014, it was the secular counterweight Nida Tunis that won two-fifths of the seats and al-Nahdha less than 30 percent, each short of a majority, and both sharing the need to continue the play of negotiation for a governing coalition, and in this way defined the New Order.

But where the pluralist structure of the political system devolves into a bipolar confrontation, the outcome is different, as the theorem indicates. It began with a pacting pattern that has an appearance of dynamic stability, with two dominant forces holding each other in check in a seesaw relationship (O'Donnell and Schmitter 1986). As long as neither could eliminate the other, the two continually negotiated distributively over formulaic terms of procedure—elections and constitution. But Arab Spring pacting is inherently unstable because its very dynamic incites each party to try for a permanent advantage to unseat the other, if only in defense against the other's presumed tactic in the same direction—a veritable security dilemma, as in Egypt. The Supreme Council of the Armed Forces (SCAF) moved the fulcrum of the seesaw in August 2012 when it took over interim constitutional functions, but President Mohamed Morsi—legitimately elected—kicked the fulcrum twice in the opposite direction in December 2012 when he claimed full powers and promulgated a hastily written constitution, imposing the Islamists' own notion of legitimacy and exploiting it. The fact that the Egyptian Freedom and Justice Party (FJP) and its Islamist allies held three-quarters of the parliamentary seats, and their candidate was elected president (barely, but no matter), led them to adopt a winner-take-all policy; the SCAF responded in kind, and the two fought "until one of them crushed the other" and ended up "devouring everything." When the SCAF responded by simply removing Morsi and issued *its* constitution, all sources of legitimacy lost.

Short Track Reactions are less well addressed by the Lally-Tolendal Theorem. The regime overcame the *intifada*, either by buying off and coopting the messages and messengers or by repressing them, and reasserted its form of order. The buying/co-opting reaction leaves the Old Order in place but with the adoption of a milder version of the *intifada*'s moderate demands. Since the contesting groups are weak, the state actually provides the legitimacy (monarchial in Morocco, a postrevolutionary junta in Algeria) as a basis for reform. But because the *intifada* accepts that basis and is too weak, absolutely and relatively, to keep the reforms on track, as in Morocco and Algeria, or in Serbia in a control case, exterior pressure is necessary. If the reforms are neglected, the weak *intifada* could turn stronger, much as in the repressing case. The repressing reaction maintains the centralized system of order, but it leaves the uprisers unsatisfied, gearing up for a second *intifada*, back to square one but with both sides better prepared. The polarized effects of the first round make it more difficult for moderates to stand up and seek joint solutions; the contest is highly combative since it involves the very existence of the uprising. External pressure is needed to move the "victorious" repressors to reforms on their own and toward opening up the system.

Long Track Transitions produce a fragmentation of the political forces, whether the authoritarian ruler is overthrown or successfully clings to power. Application of the theorem hangs on its assumption that in the case of three (or more) powers the sides are "equally interested in maintaining the one and the other." When the insurgent forces operate over a long time in a field vacated—wholly or regionally—by central authority, the politics turn to violence and elimination, not only of the other side but also of others on the same side, destroying the unifying impulse of the original *intifada* and preventing effective negotiations for coalition or for future visions. The long ebb and flow of the conflict washes out soft-liners, leaving the hard-liners in charge to turn inward to their small group interests. Fragmentation eats up the moderates and opens up the fissures among identity claims—ethnic, religious, regional, generational, personal—with little "interest in maintaining each other" (Zartman 1980). Attempts to create New Order through elections and constitutions are pushed aside by New Disorder until some sort of dominance is established on the battlefield, as in Libya and Syria. The Longer the Track, the more irresolvable the fragmentation.

Fragmentation poses the greatest challenge for external assistance. Foreign forces pick their own sides to help, the more militant naturally attracting more radical support. The struggle for each party to win tends to overcome the need to consolidate in order to win, with the effect of hardening a rigid, repressive regime. Support for moderates is imperative if the goals of the *intifadat* are to be preserved.

Each of these patterns contains further evolutions of its own, some in the short run, some in the long, beyond the immediate effects of the *intifadat* analyzed here. Each has its inherent dangers—competition that degenerates into a bipolar confrontation, domination that turns into repression and rebellion, fragmentation that finally ends in totalitarian terror. Awareness of the structural dynamics of the situation can lead domestic participants and international assistance to take measures to move the dynamics in favorable directions.

THE LEGITIMACY: LESSONS FROM THEORY

There may be a number of approaches to identifying best practices and to relate process to goal. One might look profitably at types of tactics or at use of power or at agencies of persuasion. But a basic conceptual grounding that underlies such elements of process hangs on the distinction, amply illustrated in the Arab Spring experiences, between *integrative* and *distributive* or positive- and zero-sum negotiations (Walton and McKersie 1965; Lax and Sebenius 1986; Zartman and Kremenyuk 2005). To say that integrative negotiations are positive does not say much: all successful negotiations are minimally positive sum in that they produce an outcome that the parties prefer to the status quo. But integration in the case of creating a political New Order has a meaning both broader and more specific. It refers to the creation of an undergirding procedural order and sense of legitimacy that is of value to all parties and offers opportunities to all to join in the processes of governance. This was to be the order of the day in the Arab Spring negotiations, as the parties undertook the task of setting up the rules and principles for a New Order by which they would then make governing decisions, a fundamental formula for a new sociopolitical contract. Negotiating the terms of trade and bargaining out the details of the formula is to be expected, but consensus on the basic notions is to be desired, and this requires integrative negotiations. Nowhere in the Arab Spring has this existed.

Yet, in some way, the conditions for integration existed with the overthrow. Once the initial goal of the uprising, however defined, was accomplished, a single focus returned as all action was aimed at setting up a new constitution. Party organization, elections, constitutional debates, even interim governance—all were shaped by their impact on creating the framework of the New Order, also variously defined. A defining characteristic of Short Track Transitions was the parties' commitment to state continuity through regime change; in Long Track Transitions the state was fragmented along with the contending forces, but its reimposition is the final goal. Of course, in the Short Track Reactions (Adapting and Repressing Patterns) the state and indeed the Old Order remain, even if revised or reformed. In all these cases, this commitment is a singular element of stability, in two senses—continuity and reform. Continuity provides an integrative frame for the transition, while reform indicates presumably stabilizing changes large or small in response to demands from the uprising and grievances from the larger society it represents.

Long Track Transitions faced the need to rebuild a state structure out of the shambles of a state. State institutions were gone and with them the notion of what the proper institutions are. The idea of a country with boundaries remains (despite the pretentions of an Islamic State operating in Iraq and Syria), but it is an empty shell, to be filled. The means of filling need to be worked out, pulling the arena for negotiation back to basics, without guidelines, themselves to be negotiated on the job, inductively. The only institution in these cases is the National Transitional Council or its equivalent. Yet in Libya the NTC was a secret and weak body that did its best but was pushed aside as new institutions came into being by election and by force, and in Syria the struggle for one NTC among several of them continued as long as the uprising itself. It is here that the two types of negotiation—for coalition and for formulation—and the basis of bargaining power—organization, legitimacy, and violence—most starkly come into play, and it is here that integrative negotiations are most strongly needed.

That said, the very characteristics of the transition—power, organization, violence, elections, legitimacy, criteria, governance—worked, almost inherently, to destroy consensus and impose distributive dynamics on the negotiations. *Bargaining power* with its three sources in the Arab Spring of legitimacy, organization, and the threat of violence is based on elements that are by nature conflictual and noncooperative. The *threat of violence* implies diminution of the targeted party and so is inherently zero-sum. Violence itself, as a decision-making mode, eliminates a party rather than building alternatives, and the threat of violence poses elimination as a goad to compliance. The same implication is also present in the other elements of bargaining power. Key to the evolution of the different patterns of the Arab Spring is the ability to create a coherent and cohesive *organization* for participation in the transition. But organization means giving a tangible, durable structure to leaders and followers, distinguishing them from other people. Their nature, and hence their negotiation, are highly distributive. The situation was reinforced by the negotiations against the Old Order regime, and, counterintuitively, they kept their distributive approach as they turned against each other in search of the New Order, unable to make solid coalitions and consensual formulations.

Thus, counterintuitively, negotiations for coalition were much more actively pursued within groups than between them; that is, in case of both organizational weakness and strength, groups negotiate to *keep their own followers in line rather than to build up allies*. In Tunisia, at one extreme, the parties—Islamic, secular, socialist—debated their appropriate courses individually and negotiated within the membership to keep their ranks in order; in Syria, at the other extreme, the militias negotiated over supplies and tactics—means and ends—to maintain their individual membership and participation in the fight. Fragmentation kills the ability to conduct negotiations for formulation as much as for coalition, leaving the participants weak and exhausted when the struggle is over and open to having the revolution snatched from them by better-organized groups awaiting the opportunity; this was characteristic of the diverse forces on the outbreak of the *intifada* and also, in the relevant cases, as the violent struggle dragged on. In Syria, where the eighteen-month search for an umbrella organization ended in a National Coalition of Syrian Revolutionary and Opposition Forces, whose contrived name and unpronounceable acronym testified to its cobbled nature (through Western intervention, in addition) and its rapid failure; Libya's National Transitional Council's imposed unity fell completely into pieces once the elected General National Congress and then the elected House of Representatives took over, as noted.

But even in competing and pacting (as well as adaptive) societies, parties stuck apart rather than together. Once the overthrow was achieved, the groups were still unable to coalesce into a single movement. In Tunisia, eighteen months after the *intifada*, an attempt at forming an opposition "big tent party" in Nida Tunis elicited a rival countercoalition, and then a third one that sought to fill the gap between the first two. These were the parties that competed with al-Nahdha another eighteen months later at the 2014 National Assembly elections that resulted in two large, three middle-sized, and ten tiny parties. It took Egypt two years to see a National Salvation Front contain the squabbling non-Islamic parties, and two years later, attempts to make a "big tent" party (to imitate the organization of politics under Mubarak) to compete with the virtual opposition of the banned Freedom and Justice Party produced four competing parties in the 2015 elections. At least, Lally-Tolendal's two-power curse was avoided. Important internal tactical splits in the Islamic parties rooted in different understandings of their religious missions and their place in the political order were found in Egypt and Tunisia, as al-Nahdha and the FJP pained over their relations with their extremist flankers, the Salafists and also the secular parties. In Morocco the Justice and Charity (JC) movement could not decide whether to join the 20 February Movement, both as a cause and an effect of the latter's waning fortunes. This focus on internal cohesion has had an ambiguous effect on the Islamist organizations' bid for the political center and their efforts to present themselves as moderates and nationalists as well as parties of a religious identity. Regardless of their leanings, the organizational imperative worked on the parties to stay separate, avoid integrative construction, and negotiate distributively among each other.

The distributive nature of the transition evolves toward a New Order of sorts. The first institutionalizing step toward the creation of the New Order is *election*. It is rarely recognized that elections are above all distributive exercises working against national integration: the parties compete against each other, show how different they are from the others, and outbid each other for public support, as in Serbia. The first election after an overthrow is usually one of testing individual and group strengths rather than rushing into alliances and coalitions; normally, when the strength of various groups is established, they then turn to negotiating common fronts and larger groupings, usually against an external enemy. This has not taken place in the Arab Spring, despite the presence of the Islamists as a focalizing opponent, and it sets the stage for accentuated distributive politics.

It might be expected that the *intifadat* would produce a new influx of participants on the political scene. Uprisings are a sudden outburst of participation, the entry of a new group of citizens into the political process. Revolutions spawn revolutionaries and revolutionary parties, which then push others aside as they take over politics, imposing their own ostensibly integrative organizations and visions on the search for a New Order. This element has been missing in the Arab Spring, leaving a vacuum that only sets the stage for further distributive politics. After the overthrow, the negotiation process has been marked by the defection of an important player—those who made the revolution: Universally, the spontaneously demonstrating young people, unemployed or making do in middle- and lower-class jobs, university graduates or dropouts who had no job future, the social media generation, the people who sought above all *karama* (dignity) and meaning for their lives—all have been bypassed, and by their own and others' actions. By themselves, first al all, because they have no faith in organized politics, as the Old Order had trained them to do. They have their goals and demands, their formulations for the future, but they do not know how to get them. They want immediate action, in ways they could not comprehend but only demand, and when new and leftover politicians arose to exploit the situation—whether from an understanding of how organized politics is practiced or for the benefit of their own organization—the uprisers saw further reason to turn their backs on parties, elections, votes, and organization, falling back on demonstrations and threats of violence, or simply on reinforced alienation. As a result, the *muntafadin* have opted out, making demonstrations for others, as in Yemen and Egypt, or simply sinking into their reinforced alienation.

Furthermore, the *muntafadin* were formed to avoid formation by their own social media, excellent for bringing people together and executing flexible strategies but inappropriate for structured organization. In social media, leadership, message nodes, and direction are shifting, transient, and replaceable; their structure is one of fluid multimode networking but not of established line and staff with clear command and control; ideology and visioning is under continual and disjointed discussion, if at all. Their basic approach or ideology is thus reinforced by their technology. While the technology is correctable, it is habit forming and reinforced by the ideology. In the absence of organizations, the only negotiating partner is civil society, heir to the *muntafadin*, reduced to tacit (albeit effective) negotiations, as in Tunisia. In sum, the withdrawal of the *muntafadin* from the political negotiations has contributed to the predominance of distributive bargaining among those who remain in the ring, despite a possibility to the contrary at the beginning of the process.

The newcomers' activities were warily welcomed by the organized forces of the transition, brandished for their purposes in the political interplay to negotiate coalitions and formulations, whether this occurred in a transition that moved toward competitive coalition politics and even normal politics, as in Tunisia, or in one that dissolved into adapting, repressing, or fragmenting, violently as in Syria and Libya, but also politically in Morocco. These demonstrations were carefully watched and restricted by the evolving organizations; no party would allow itself to be blindsided by spontaneous disorganized eruptions, lest it lose control. Parties new and old were little interested in these new cohorts as leadership trickled up to the older generations, topped by Qaid es-Sebsi, elected in Tunisia at eighty-eight. Only the Islamic movements such as al-Nahdha and the Brotherhood had their youth wing, held in hand by the older leadership. Only in the politics of fragmentation do the young leaders and activists find their place, in a position to effectively challenge the older generation's dominance. However, the nature of the armed struggle keeps them focused on the immediate goal, local organization, and the constraints of clandestinity, and away from integrative negotiation for coalition or for formulation (al-Zubaidi 2012; Quandt 1969).

The sidelining of the *muntafadin* may only be temporary. They have four options: to join normal politics through established political parties; to establish one of their own; to sink deeper into their alienation that was the mark of their relationship in the Old Order; or to take to the streets again. All four are possible. The last is most immediately so, and it has serious destabilizing effects on attempts at integrative negotiations for a New or Renewed Order. When it fails, it leads to the third possibility, more alienation. The second is most interesting, if less likely, although it is what the Islamists did and had difficulty in having accepted. A brand-new party that elbows its way into the political system or a gradual infiltration of youth negotiating their way into established parties would take another decade, and at the cost of a loss of integrative idealism and enthusiasm.

But it is in the overarching elements in the construction of a New Order—*legitimacy* and *formulation*—that the distributive rather than integrative nature of the negotiation process for a New Order has appeared most strongly to destroy the model. To move from the unity of overthrow toward the consensus of a new constitution, the actors need to establish a common basis for their construction. In South Africa during the miraculous process of system transformation in 1990–1994, the opposing parties established a set of basic principle on which the constitution would later guide the final constitution, as was explained by Mark Anstey in this book (also Sisk 1995). This has not been done in the Arab states. Instead, negotiations for formulation are a contest between the two different sources of legitimization, carried out inductively through debates on articles of a new constitution.

It might be expected that the parties negotiating a New Order would wrap themselves in the legitimacy bestowed by the *intifada*, akin to Weber's revolutionary legitimacy. But with the *muntafadin* out of the negotiating picture, none of the contending parties were those who made the uprising; they were all bystanders eager to benefit from the change in the political situation. What remains is a battle between traditionalist and legal-rational formulas for legitimization, a "Formula for all" versus a "Formula of all," or, in the key words of the conflict, an Islamic State or a Civil State. The first takes a given—indeed a God-given—set of substantive principles, defined and interpretable by revelation and inspiration, and imposes them on everyone; the other operates within an empirically verifiable and accountable set of procedural principles, defined and revisable by practice and review, and validates them by the subject population. Confronted with an ideology, the liberals and modernist society have values but no doctrine; confronted with the pragmatists and elections, the Islamists have no program. Instead of starting from a consensual basis for the integrative negotiation of a New Order, negotiations become a contest over its referent principles.

Thus, the negotiations continue over procedural details of the evolving order. Already in Tunisia, Egypt, and sporadically Libya and Yemen, these negotiations began—as negotiations do—with internal negotiations within the parties and groups over positions and then go on searches for overlap between groups' positions ("zones of possible agreement" or ZOPAS) and finally come up with acceptable outcomes in a new constitution. The process is accompanied by vertical pressures in various forms from the public outside the chambers, including the *muntafadin*, but the negotiations are mainly horizontal among the parties, in forms that then produce the type of transition—competitive, pacted, adapted, fragmented. The process yields incremental distributive changes. If the negotiated transitions, as stated in the introductory chapter, are able to restore order, make progress toward providing economic growth, and build political relationships based on a commitment to a vision of a mutually bearable future, the process can result in a dynamic stability among moderate ideological differences. If not, however, the process returns to a search for any form of order and will open to ideological absolutism or authoritarian regression or simply a return to a Revised Order close to the Old one.

The societies of the Arab Spring are understandably uneasy, and the conduct of the Islamist parties has neither confirmed nor at least dispelled the unease. The record of Morsi as president in Egypt aped the behavior of Mubarak, in a very determined winner-take-all policy; the refusal of the Islamist General People's Congress (GPC) to recognize the secular HoR that it had authorized was fought for the body (oil) and soul of Libya; and the insistence of Ghannouchi to hang onto the government in Tunis until the passage of the constitution "because we won the election" is a much paler replica of the same attitude. Despite assertions of moderation and protestations of a Civil State goal, and commendable, repeated concessions in the constitutional negotiations, statements of some Nahdha spokesmen and reluctance of the government to control Salafists and provide security have raised a hue and cry from Tunisian society. In Yemen, Syria, and Libya, secular tendencies and regional nationalisms have been compounded by religious fanaticism. As a result, even attempts to bridge the two bases of legitimacy are locked into a distributive concession or compensation process rather than the construction of a common base. Constitution making in this situation takes the form of zero-sum distributive negotiations (or refusals to negotiate at all), not of an integrative positive-sum consensus. Hugh Roberts, in his chapter on Algeria in this book, is eloquent about the way political forces view legitimacy as something one monopolizes, exclusively, not something a party shares in a national system. It is to Tunisia's exceptional credit that it has emerged from this process with a relatively coherent contract for a Civil State and a general (even if not universal) consensus that all could play the game of politics.

More surprising is the confirmation of the same characteristic in the fragmented transitions, where the intensity of the struggle might be expected to produce sharp and clear visions of the future order. Militants in the camps and trenches in other struggles were often immersed in dreams about the future of their country after it would be all over (Quandt 1969; Zartman 1956; Michel 1962). Instead, the violent fragmented conflict in a few Arab Spring countries continues to focus the uprisers on one clear and proximate goal, the elimination of the Old Order and of the other rebel groups, with an inability to think beyond that point (al-Zubaidi 2012). Fragmentation kills the ability to conduct negotiations for formulation just as it does for negotiations for coalition, leaving the participants weak and exhausted as the struggle degenerates. Just as in the case of the Short Track *intifada*, the *muntafadin* are then open to having the revolution snatched from them by better-organized groups awaiting the opportunity. Some of them in Syria, Lebanon, and Yemen do have sharp and clear visions of the future New Order and are making these divisions the front lines of the civil war.

As a result, the ideological orientation of society has shifted, or at least compounded, as a result of the uprisings, to include religious politics (Brynen et al. 2012). Whether this shift is left or right, or forward or backward, is a subject of the ongoing debate over identity underneath the negotiations for formulation, and indeed it is all of these directions in some measure. The introduction of Islam as a political identity cuts across these classical dimensions. The usual spectrum of right and left has been overlain with a new spectrum of loose or rigid Islam. How much of a shift is present is not only a matter of debate but of future evolution; as already noted, parties—including the minority parties—take their positions of the moment as a result of their situation, which they previously created, not as a result of a preestablished plan of action. Identity should be assumed and consensual, not a subject of continual debate about shades and requirements, so that an inclusive social contract can be established. What is involved is an added dimension rather than a total shift. The sea change that the Islamists hoped would establish a new basis for formulation has not taken place, but it has imposed a three-dimensional chessboard for the game of politics, leaving much of society—in varying proportions in each case—demanding confirmable results toward dignity, jobs, and justice. But this makes integrative negotiations unusually difficult because the identitarian basis is up for debate or, indeed, up for grabs.

There have been a few negotiatory innovations and corrections that offer some small alternatives to the distributive process. *Tacit* and *vertical* negotiation have already been mentioned. *Tacit negotiations*, simple offer-response-decision exchanges usually left out of negotiation analysis, were used in Egypt, Tunisia, and Yemen for specific decisions, unencumbered by underlying ontological debate. *Vertical negotiations* were especially significant for their ability to break through the horizontal layer, as in Tunisia. Vertical negotiation between government and civil society is not two-level negotiation between an international and a domestic level, but rather a tilting of the level so that civil society negotiates directly with officialdom. It has the effect of perpetuating the original negotiation process of the *intifada*, and of building the basis for future organized participation and the gestation of involved parties.

A third is the introduction of *dialogue* in the years after the original *intifadat* in Tunisia and Yemen when fatigue over the stalemate set in among the parties; dialogue has been proposed for Libya and was imitated in sham sessions in Egypt and Syria. In these cases, it was a realization of the stalemate and its negative consequences of its continuation that led the parties to soften their distributive demands and look for an outcome of general benefit. Dialogues are all-participatory, not dependent on representation or elections, and open to a more informal and creative exchange than constituent assemblies. They take the partisan onus out of concession and facilitate a search for new ideas. It takes patience and persistence to keep a dialogue on track, a role played by the government in Libya and Yemen and by the labor UGTT and other unions in Tunisia. All of these help move the process toward integrative negotiations, even though they do not overcome the basic legitimacy problem. But dialogue works only after the authoritarian ruler has been removed; before, in the midst of a fragmenting Long Track, there is no chance of an integrative reconciliation.

A final corrective is *mediation* when the parties cannot talk to each other effectively or at all. The Arab Spring was not only weak in negotiations in many of the patterns; it also lacked third parties who could bridge gaps and help parties talk. The UGTT and its other partners in the Quartet—the bar association, business association, and civil rights league—were an effective exception that made a major contribution to making the whole Tunisian experience an exception. Saleh's role in Yemen could also have been as an internal string-pulling mediator who was central to the system and left the tribal pieces in a vacuum when he was removed. When domestic mediators are absent, international negotiators have to step in. Intervention is often considered a foreign military exercise, as in Libya and Syria, but the more frequent type is one of external diplomatic intervention to try to restore or influence the negotiation process and put the uprising on a shorter track, hastening a smooth transition. External negotiators tried to broker an early transition in Libya, Syria, and Yemen; only the GCC in Yemen made any progress. Thereafter, foreign states and many NGOs have tried to help negotiations to overcome some of the structural problems noted above. When negotiations between the parties of the *intifada* are needed most, in fragmented uprisings and transitions, foreign efforts have been ineffective. One important instance was the multiple efforts in mid-2013 to bring the two pacting forces in Egypt to cooperate in an effective transition, to no avail. Another was the 2012 effort of Qatar and U.S. secretary of state Hillary Rodham Clinton to bring together a National Transitional Council in Syria; it succeeded only momentarily because the United States did not follow through with material support and Qatar did, behind sectarian Sunni forces. Another similar attempt was made in 2015 by the Arab League and the African Union to bring the two "governments" of Libya into one and to move ahead on drafting a constitution. Such foreign intervention is not welcome, even though the parties may admit that it—or its result—is necessary. The biggest challenge is to bring the hostile fragments of a Long Track uprising together into a working relationship.

So, in sum, why did the *intifadat* of the Arab Spring in only varying degrees follow the ideal type of evolution from a grassroots uprising, marked with negotiation at every stage and level, to provide working coalitions and a consensual formula for a New Order through a new constitution? And what kind of order has been negotiated across contending legitimacies? The ingredients for an answer have been laid out: when the negative procedural consensus over the elimination of the authoritarian figure reached its goal, it fell asunder with the introduction of the religious question, the disarray of the proponents of liberal legitimacy still reeling from the numbing effects of the *mukhabarat*, and the disinclination of the *muntafadin* to organize. The more the negotiations slipped into distributive bargaining, the further they moved away from a consensual formulation. Above—or beneath—all was the chasm separating the two sources of legitimacy—transmitted or tested—and the degree of rigidity with which their partisans hung onto either of them.

Yet in a short time, that confrontation evolved into a different one that is the immediate heritage of the Spring, as the nature of the models suggests. In Syria, Egypt, Libya, and Yemen, the confrontation has turned into civil and even turf warfare to be decided by force of arms and a murderous martial order. In Tunisia, Algeria, and Morocco, the confrontation was decided by negotiated concessions—admission of the Islamists as legal players among the others in the political order, in exchange for the maintenance of a pluralist order (under control in Morocco and Algeria, open and free in Tunisia) and an implicit admission by the Islamists that they were not going to take it over. Strong forces from the Old Order, reprocessed, remain to constitute significant parts of the New Order in Tunisia, Egypt, and Yemen. While the personalized form of the Old Order is undoubtedly swept away, the underlying structure and behavior of the political society is manifest in tribal Libya and Yemen, not to speak of *makhzen* Morocco, junta Algeria, and the "power body" monarchy in Syria and Bahrain. The notions of an Islamic order versus a liberal order are still at the forefront of the negotiations, where they take place, and more broadly of the events.

Notes

1. Another promising approach, still in an underdeveloped stage, is network analysis (Freeman 2004; Jasny, Zahn, and Marshall 2009).

2. This is captured in Rubenstein's (1982) two-move game, generally considered quite theoretical. See Schelling (1957).

3. "War" must be pronounced as Churchill did—"waw, waw, waw"—for full effect.

4. This statement suggests that Rachid Ghannouchi would have acted like Morsi if al-Nahdha had received a majority, but counterfactuals are hard to prove.

References

Bapat, Navin, and Kanisha Bond. 2012. "Alliance between Militant Groups," *British Journal of Political Science* 32, no. 4: 793–824.

Brynen, Rex, Pete W. Moore, Bassel F. Salloukh, and Marie-Joëlle Zahar. 2012. *Beyond the Arab Spring: Authoritarianism and Democratization in the Arab World*. Boulder, Colo.: Lynne Rienner.

Cross, John G. 1969. *The Economics of Bargaining*. New York: Basic Books.

Cunningham, Kathleen, Kristin Bakke, and Lee Seymour. 2012. "Shirts Today, Skins Tomorrow." *Journal of Conflict Resolution* 56, no. 1: 67–93.

Edgeworth, Francis Y. 1881. *Mathematical Physics: An Essay on the Application of Mathematics to the Moral Sciences*. London: Kegan Paul; rpt., New York: A. M. Kelley, 1967.

Elster, Jon. 2000. *Ulysses Unbound: Studies in Rationality, Precommitment, and Constraints*. Cambridge: Cambridge University Press.

Evans, Peter B., Harold K. Jacobson, and Robert D. Putnam. 1993. *Double-Edged Diplomacy: International Bargaining and Domestic Politics*. Berkeley: University of California Press.

Fjelde, Hanne, and Desire Nilsson. 2012. "Rebels against Rebels." *Journal of Conflict Resolution* 56, no. 4: 604–628.

Fontini, Christia. 2012. *Alliance Formation in Civil Wars*. Cambridge: Cambridge University Press.

Freeman, Linton C. 2004. *The Development of Social Network Analysis: A Study in the Sociology of Science*. Vancouver: Empirical Press.

Habeeb, William Mark. 1988. *Power and Tactics in International Negotiation: How Weak Nations Bargain with Strong Nations*. Baltimore: Johns Hopkins University Press.

Hopmann, P. Terrence. 1996. *The Negotiation Process and the Resolution of International Conflicts*. Columbia: University of South Carolina.

Jasny, Barbara, Laura Zahn, and Eliot Marshall. 2009. "Connections: Complex System and Networks." *Science* 325 (24 July): 405–428.

Jönsson, Christer. 1981. "Bargaining Power." *Cooperation and Conflict* 16, no. 2: 249–257.

Kenny, Paul. 2010. "Structural Integrity and Cohesion in Insurgent Organizations." *International Studies Review* 12, no. 4: 533–555.

Lally-Tolendal, Comte de. 1789. *Archives Parlementaires, série I: 1789–1799*. Imprimerie Nationale 1875–1888.

Lax, David A., and James K. Sebenius. 1986. *The Manager as Negotiator: Bargaining for Cooperation and Competitive Gain*. New York: Free Press.

Lefkowitz, Joshua. 2015. "Picking Up the Pieces: Mediation in Fragmented Conflicts." Paper prepared for the Academic Advisory Council for the Mediation Initiative, Department of Political Affairs, UN Secretariat.

Lilja, Jannie. "Outbidding the Decision to Negotiate." In Zartman, Anstey, and Meerts, *Slippery Slope to Genocide*, 126–153.

Michel, Henri. 1962. *Les courants de pensée de la Résistance*. Paris: PUF (Presses universitaires de France).

O'Donnell, Guillermo, and Philippe Schmitter. 1986. *Transitions from Authoritarian Rule: Tentative Conclusions about Uncertain Democracies*. Baltimore: Johns Hopkins University Press.

Orieux, Jean. 1970. *Talleyrand; ou le sphinx incompris*. Paris: Flammarion.

Quandt, William B. 1969. *Revolution and Political Leadership: Algeria, 1954–1968*. Cambridge: MIT Press.

Rubenstein, Ariel. 1982. "Perfect Equilibrium in a Bargaining Problem." *Econometrica* 50, no. 1: 97–110.

Schelling, Thomas. 1957. "Bargaining, Communication and Limited War." *Journal of Conflict Resolution* 1, no. 1: 1936.

Sisk, Timothy D. 1995. *Democratization in South Africa: The Elusive Social Contract*. Princeton, N.J.: Princeton University Press.

Walton, Richard E., and Robert B. McKersie. 1965. *A Behavioral Theory of Labor Negotiations: An Analysis of a Social Interaction System*. New York: McGraw-Hill.

Waresquiel, Emmanuel de. 2003. *Talleyrand, ou le prince immobile*. Paris: Fayard.

Zahar, Marie-Joëlle. "Handling Spoilers and the Prospect of Violence." In Zartman, Anstey, and Meerts, *Slippery Slope to Genocide*, 173–192.

Zartman, I. William. 1956. "From the Resistance to the Revolution: French Neutralism after the War." PhD thesis, Yale University.

———. 1980. "Toward a Theory of Elite Circulation." In *Elites in the Middle East*, edited by I. William Zartman, 84–115. New York: Praeger.

———. 1997. "Justice in Negotiation." *International Political Science Review* 18, no. 2: 121–138.

———. 2005. "Analyzing Intractability." In *Grasping the Nettle: Analyzing Cases of Intractable Conflict*, edited by Chester A. Crocker, Fen Osler Hampson, and Pamela Aall. Washington, D.C.: United States Institute of Peace Press (USIP).

———. 2008. *Negotiation and Conflict Management: Essays on Theory and Practice*. London: Routledge.

———. 2009a. "Negotiation as a Choice of Partners." *PINPoints* 33:13–17.

———. 2009b. "The Quest for Order in World Politics." In *Imbalance of Power: US Hegemony and International Order*, edited by I. William Zartman. Boulder, Colo.: Lynne Rienner.

Zartman, I. William, Mark Anstey, and Paul Meerts, eds. 2012. *The Slippery Slope to Genocide: Reducing Identity Conflicts and Preventing Mass Murder*. New York: Oxford University Press.

Zartman, I. William, and Victor Kremenyuk, eds. 2005. *Peace versus Justice: Negotiating Forward- and Backward-Looking Outcomes*. Lanham, Md.: Rowman & Littlefield.

Zartman, I. William, and Jeffrey Z. Rubin, eds. 2000. *Power and Negotiation*. Ann Arbor: University of Michigan Press.

Zeuthen, Frederik. 1930. *Problems of Monopoly and Economic Warfare*. London: Routledge and Sons.

al-Zubaidi, Layla. 2012. "Syria's Revolution: Society, Power, Ideology—Statehood & Participation." *Perspectives* no. 3 (February). Heinrich Böll Foundation report. http://lb.boell.org/en/2012/02/03/perspectives-3-february-2012-syrias-revolution-society-power-ideology (accessed 16 February 2015).

Lessons for Policy

FEN OSLER HAMPSON AND BESSMA MOMANI

THE ARAB SPRING is a cautionary tale for scholars and policymakers alike. Its speed and ferocity were unforeseen, although with the benefit of hindsight some now say that they saw the writing on the wall. The long-term political consequences of the Arab Spring remain as yet unclear. What we do know, however, is that its trajectory has been erratic, and the political tsunami unleashed by the Arab world's great awakening is far from being a spent force.

Drawing on the other contributions to this volume, this chapter identifies some provisional "lessons learned" for practitioners—in particular, diplomats and senior policymakers—about negotiation processes and regime transformation in Arab Spring countries. It poses the question whether external actors can play a constructive role through diplomacy to help advance negotiations for a new political order among local actors during the Arab Spring transition or whether a "hands-off" approach is really the only viable course.

At the beginning of his presidency, Barack Obama gave his now famous speeches in Istanbul and Cairo where he urged a hands-off approach to developments in the Muslim and Arab world. First, he sought to define "a new beginning" in U.S.-Arab relations, although whether this particular stance was substantively new or not is open to debate: the president's predecessor had often declared "we are not at war with Islam," although Obama added "and never will be." Second, while reiterating the familiar and usual goals of democracy and religious and electoral freedom, Obama conveyed the impression that regime change was not an active policy goal; countries would decide upon their own regime and form of government, which the United States would then deal with and live with (Ailboni 2011, 8–9; Dadush and Dunne 2011, 133; Ajami 2012). This was a theme that would reoccur with the overthrow of democratically elected Mohamed Morsi of Egypt in summer 2013.

The substance and tone of Obama's remarks were strikingly different from the "hands-on" approach of the Bush administration. George Bush's speech at the National Endowment for Peace in 2003 called for democratization in the Middle East as a geostrategic and moral imperative. Similarly, recall the diplomatic warning shot that then–secretary of state Condoleezza Rice fired across the bow of Arab regimes in June 2005 after the U.S. invasion of Iraq when she called for democratic reforms and singled out Egypt and Saudi Arabia, criticizing them for cracking down on dissidents and also in Egypt's case for failing to ensure that presidential and parliamentary elections were "free and fair." While the Mubarak regime allowed another candidate to run against him in the 2005 elections, true electoral reform was ignored with obvious consequences later on for one of its targets, President Mubarak of Egypt. But there was also little follow-through on U.S. urgings for reform, not just by the Bush administration, but even more by the Obama administration (see Morey et al. 2012).

The Obama administration was eventually forced to become more hands-on as the Arab Spring rapidly shifted into high gear. The United States cut itself loose from Mubarak just as he was being forced out the door. U.S. credibility with the Egyptian public was undermined by what was perceived in the streets of Cairo as "too little, too late" in helping get rid of Mubarak in spite of the fact that the administration worked vigorously behind the scenes to avert a bloodbath and again in slowly coming to accept the coup that overthrew Egypt's government led by Mohamed Morsi. Following Morsi's own overthrow by the Egyptian military, the United States exerted pressure on Egypt's generals to hold new elections and limit the use of violence and reprisals against the Muslim Brotherhood and its supporters. The United States provided critical logistical and military support to its NATO allies when they took to the skies to bomb Qadhafi into submission even though it chose to lead the mission "from behind" (Gause and Lustick 2012). It has been actively involved along with its allies in helping Libya's new government rebuild the country. The United States and the Gulf Cooperation Council (GCC) was also instrumental in bringing about regime change in Yemen. But the United States has generally taken a hands-off approach to other conflicts in the region (Ailboni 2011, 8), such as the bloody civil war in Syria (Hinnebusch 2012, 111).

With the escalation of conflict in the region, which now includes mounting sectarian strife in Iraq and Syria, there are mounting pressures on Washington and other Western capitals to become more deeply engaged through a combination of military action and aggressive diplomacy (Gause and Lustick 2012). The question of how much intervention should Western capitals exert is of considerable debate both within governments and with their citizens. The fear of some is that Western intervention will be ineffective at best and counterproductive at worst if it further alienates the local populace or encourages more terrorist attacks against Western interests.

It is at this juncture of international intervention that this chapter examines the contradictory hands-on versus hands-off lessons of negotiation and diplomacy in the Arab Spring.

CHALLENGES OF SHORT VERSUS LONG TRACK ENGAGEMENT

As the introductory chapter indicates, for those countries where regime transformation followed the Short Track and violence was generally kept to a minimum, the speed with which regime change occurred has left something of a political vacuum, giving organized Islamist groups in some countries the upper hand in the building of a new political order.[1] This presents its own unique challenges for diplomatic engagement, democracy promotion, and the advancement of human rights, but it does not mean that Western countries should turn their backs on Islamist regimes, which, notwithstanding their religious roots and affiliations, are generally center-right. As these countries look to rebuild their economies and build new social and political compacts, they will need significant foreign aid and investments if their newly elected governments are to succeed and extremists are to be kept in check. This runs in line with the introduction's observation that two types of Short Track outcomes "competing" and "pacting" should be accompanied by external support meant to keep the evolution on track. This would have been well applied to the 2013 coup in Egypt, where the Morsi government was overthrown due to deteriorating economic situations. Had the United States used its security relations as leverage with the Egyptian army, this might have avoided the coup and prompted Egyptian stakeholders to negotiate. Moreover, as Halperin, Siegle, and Weinstein (2010) note, democratic backtracking is most vulnerable in the early years of democratization, particularly when challenged by economic stagnation, inflation, rising national debt, and low income levels. Both Tunisia and Egypt are and were clearly vulnerable with decreasing income from tourism, rising debt levels, and overall economic malaise.

For those countries that are on what the introduction refers to as the Long Track, there has been a pattern of escalating violence that has stymied political negotiations among local actors and hindered the possibilities for reform and regime change. This is because the onset of violent conflict has led to a hardening of positions, or "fragmentation," which in turn has given extremists and hard-liners on all sides of the political divide the upper hand and thwarted the possibility of peaceful negotiations. In the Long Track uprisings where the international community intervened, it did so through informal agreement with others to act jointly to resolve conflict. However, where there has been collective action, it has not evolved into any kind of enduring pattern of cooperation among collaborating partners. Instead, initiatives taken have largely been ad hoc and improvised. The NATO mission in Libya was disbanded after the intervention occurred, and subsequent efforts to negotiate a similar operation to deal with another Long Track conflict—namely the civil war in Syria—have so far come to naught.

a) Regional support is a necessary but clearly insufficient condition for military intervention to break the "long track."

It is an accepted axiom of diplomacy that prolonged conflicts (including those that seem intractable) require mediators who can break logjams, redefine the issues, and coax the parties into reaching some kind of negotiated political settlement. Such conflicts also require multiple track mediation strategies that are directed at both elites and various factions within society. Mediation, as argued below, can also bring about regime change. Comparing the international community's engagement with Libya and Syria reveals different lessons about the use of force and coercive diplomacy to foster political change in two countries that were or are on the Long Track. In the Libyan case, diplomatic and military intervention occurred because negotiations to forge a consensus among key international *and* regional actors were successful in creating a joint basis for collective action.[2] This included negotiations about the use of force where a regional stamp of approval was essential to securing international support for military action to help topple Qadhafi. However, the precedent set by Libya proved to be short-lived because key members of the Security Council—Russia and China—did not want the precedent set by Libya to be followed in Syria, where they had a major stake in supporting the Asad regime (see Landis 2012; Barry 2011, 5–6; Gause and Lustick 2012).

In the case of Libya, two regional organizations took quick action a few weeks after the public uprisings began. Condemning the government of Libya's violent tactics against the uprisings, the Arab League suspended Libya's membership on 22 February 2011. The African Union also issued a strong denunciation of the Libyan government. Qadhafi had few friends in the Arab world so the Arab League's condemnation came as no surprise. In the case of the African Union, Qadhafi had more friends, but his actions clearly did not sit well with those African states that had turned to democracy. Both statements were recognized by UN Security Council Resolution 1970, which objected to the Qadhafi government's actions, referred the case to the International Criminal Court, and reminded the Libyan government of its responsibility to protect its civilians. Despite this resolution, Security Council members were not unified in their positions when it came to following up with stronger action (Barry 2011, 6): several members of the Security Council expressed reservations about using force, while France and Britain urged much more intensive international engagement (Dalacoura 2012, 77), and the United States and Germany held back.

However, a month later, after lengthy negotiations and as Libya's situation deteriorated further, the Security Council authorized member states to "take all necessary measures . . . to protect civilians" under Chapter VII of the UN Charter, establishing a no-fly zone (NFZ), an arms embargo, and economic sanctions. According to Alex Bellamy and Paul Williams, the galvanizing force behind this resolution was the action taken by regional organizations. The GCC called for UN action on 7 March, the Organization of Islamic Cooperation called for the same the next day, and on 12 March, the Arab League asked the UN to "impose a no-fly zone against any military action against the Libyan people." The rationale for the imposition of a NFZ over Libya was ostensibly to avert a blood bath by Qadhafi's forces (Barry 2011, 5–6; Toensing 2012), specifically in the cities of Benghazi and Tobruk. But it was apparent that the Arab League also wanted to tip the military scales toward the rebels, who were on the defensive. This explicit call to arms gave the interventionists among Security Council members and within the Obama administration the ammunition they needed to push through the resolution as discussed by Johannes Theiss in his chapter.[3]

The United Nations Security Council Resolution 1973 was passed on 17 March 2011. On 19 March, the United States joined with Britain, Canada, France, and Italy in engaging militarily with Libya. On 27 March, NATO took over from the coalition of countries involved in the Libyan operations, which by now also included Belgium, Denmark, the Netherlands, Norway, and Spain, and undertook a mission to protect the embargo, patrol the no-fly zones, and protect civilians. The NATO campaign was supported actively by Qatar, Jordan, and the United Arab Emirates and was also joined by Sweden (Barry 2011, 6). By August 2011, the Libyan National Transitional Council, with NATO's support, had taken over the country and killed Qadhafi. Presented to the world as a success, the mission ended on 31 October.

In terms of regionalism and conflict management, the Libyan intervention was a mixed approach. It involved the ad hoc utilization of NATO resources that was negotiated by a coalition of the capable and willing, as Johannes Theiss argues in his chapter. Moreover, as seen in high-level public statements, agreeing to openly disagree did not, in the end, prevent NATO's activists from mounting an effective air campaign and or prevent it from recruiting non-NATO participants to join the effort. Its elements also included regional organizations from two regions: Europe/transatlantic and the Middle East. In fact, the combination of the two regional initiatives gave the operation strength in terms of legitimacy, and its management and governance (Bobbitt 2011), even though such initiatives tested the tactical coordination of these partners (Barry 2011, 7–8).

The call from the Arab League, Gulf Cooperation Council and the Organization of the Islamic Council for the imposition of a no-fly zone over Libya gave a regional stamp of approval to the responsibility-to-protect norm, which lay behind the intervention (See Bellamy 2011). It also served to give critical legitimacy to the air campaign that followed, given that Western nations were, in effect, attacking an Arab country. The subsequent participation of three Arab states in the campaign only served to increase its legitimacy. The fact that another regional organization, the African Union, was much more guarded in its stance (Jones 2011, 51) and several Arab countries objected to the intervention did not seem to challenge the notion that the initiative had a strong endorsement by the regional players. In terms of operations, NATO's assumption of responsibility for the intervention provided the management and governance necessary to the complex, multiparty military endeavor and essentially moved the initiative from a loose coalition of a group of friends into a robust coalition of treaty partners and allies (Barry 2011, 7–9; Bobbitt 2011).

Digging a bit deeper, however, one uncovers significant rifts between the Security Council and NATO over the operations. The UN Security Council Resolution 1973 for the NFZ was notable not by who voted for it, but who abstained: Russia, Germany, India, Brazil, and China. There was clearly little appetite among the so-called emerging powers of the international system for this undertaking (Jones 2011, 53–57). With enough domestic worries and apprehensions over the principle of foreign intervention, many of the middle powers were not nearly that supportive. But because the Arab League seemed to support it, the skeptics did not stand in the way of those who felt that a NFZ was warranted (Bobbitt 2011, 1). By using the carefully negotiated words "all necessary means," the resolution also gave those engaged in the NFZ a license to do more than just patrol the skies over Libya, and as discussed below, this created a backlash when the Security Council addressed the possibility of engaging in the Syrian situation. As for the NATO coalition, Turkey and many of NATO's eastern European members shared Germany's reservations about the mission (Barry 2011, 6). Turkey also had significant trade and investment linkages with Libya, to add another complicating layer (Gause and Lustick 2012). The Libyan mission was thus a NATO-led mission without many of its members. NATO a la carte was convenient in this instance. The longer-term effects on the alliance itself are unclear (Toensing 2012).

In the Syrian case, the Arab League went straight to the UN to secure a UN resolution, hoping for a similar response and outcome to what had been achieved in Libya (Hinnebusch 2012, 111). The league's proactive overture to the UN complemented its own efforts under the Arab League Action Plan of 22 November 2011 to achieve a peaceful resolution of the crisis, including the deployment of a League of Arab States observer mission in Syria, which ultimately was unable to carry out its monitoring mission effectively and was eventually suspended (Ryan 2012).

The UN Security Council draft resolution on Syria was months in the making and the result of painstaking, behind-the-scenes negotiations (Hinnebusch 2012, 111; Ryan 2012). In all, nine countries voted for it. Brazil, India, Lebanon, and South Africa abstained. Although the draft resolution did not call for immediate sanctions, it laid out some clear markers for Bashar al-Asad's embattled regime to change its ways and included harsh measures to follow if it did not. The Americans, French, and the British thought they had finally secured the support of Russia and China in the careful wording of the resolution. It turned out they were wrong: Russia and China vetoed it.

The Friends of Syria initiative was a regionally inspired, collective response to the deadlock in the UN Security Council over Syria, although it ultimately failed to break that deadlock. Friends of Syria was formally initiated by France following the veto by Russia and China of Chapter VII action on Syria; some seventy countries attended a hastily convened meeting of foreign ministers and representatives of international organizations in Tunis in February 2012 in a bid to raise the pressure on Syria's Asad regime. It was supposed to be a show of unity by the international community on how to deal with Asad and help build up Syria's opposition. Despite their hopes, Arab League countries failed in their efforts to achieve an agreement to arm Syria's opposition and to begin planning for an international peacekeeping force—a mission that nonetheless would have had to be approved by the United Security Council and thereby run up against another Russian and Chinese veto.

The Tunis communiqué called on the Syria government "to cease all violence and to allow free and unimpeded access by the UN and humanitarian agencies." It also demanded that the regime "permit humanitarian agencies to deliver vital relief goods and services to civilians affected by the violence." In addition to enforcing existing sanctions, Friends of Syria agreed to introduce new ones, including banning travel, freezing assets, ceasing oil purchases, reducing Syria's diplomatic ties by closing embassies and, finally, preventing the shipment of arms. The Syrian National Council (SNC) also got the nod to serve as "a legitimate representative of Syrians seeking peaceful democratic change."

However, although it has convened a number of times since and issued further communiqués, the Friends of Syria grouping has proven to be more of a wailing Greek chorus than a spur to coordinated, collective action to bring regime change to Syria. Although UN-sponsored sanctions have hurt the Asad regime, Russian opposition and outright circumvention of the arms embargo against Syria—combined with Syria's porous borders with neighboring countries—has meant that Asad has been able to secure the resources and materiel he needs to keep on fighting (see also Landis 2012). These same porous borders allowed both Iran and Hezbollah to send support troops to fight along with the Syrian army.

The Syrian National Coalition for Syrian Opposition and Revolutionary Forces COS, and its predecessor the Syrian National Council, an umbrella organization of opposition groups, has had difficulty gaining ground because it has no real internal leadership (Hinnebusch 2012, 107–110). The Syrian National Council was criticized for having low legitimacy and connection with its own people, since it is largely composed of expatriate Syrians. The expanded and more inclusive National Coalition remains challenged by infighting among different stakeholders and the presence of external benefactors jostling for power and influence. Moreover, the Free Syrian Army (FSA), which initially did much of the fighting against Asad's forces (despite the fact it is outmanned and outgunned), had appeared to be gaining ground as arms flow into Syria and as Syria's neighbors exploit the conflict for their own ends (Ryan 2012). The FSA, however, has now been joined by al-Qaeda–inspired jihadist groups, such as Jubhat al-Nusra and Shams Brigade, and is better organized, funded, and determined than its secular FSA counterparts. The entry of

Lebanon's Hezbollah party in summer 2013 on the side of the Asad regime turned the tide, as regime forces were able to retake ground in key border towns with Lebanon.

It is in the area of precedent setting that the Libya approach or "model" for intervention has run into trouble, as the situation in Syria makes clear. Russia and China believed that NATO had vastly extended its reach in using the NFZ as a pretext to attack Qadhafi's forces and support the opposition in its efforts to topple his regime (Hinnebusch 2012, 111–112; Ryan 2012). The Russians, in particular, did not want a repeat of the Libyan experience in Syria, where they have direct strategic interests and have done everything to ensure that Asad remains in power (Ryan 2012).

Although regional support may be crucial to the legitimacy of international interventions in today's world—and especially among the deeply skeptical public of the Arab world—collective action still depends on negotiated compromises and sustained unity among the five permanent members of the UN Security Council. As the introduction points out, despite a breakdown in internal negotiations, it took the NATO "outsiders" to create a "working alliance" before handing it over to the "insiders." But that must be cemented from the inside to last, or else it will crumble under persistent inside differences after the outsiders have released their pressure. This alliance building process is a key element in a successful hands-on strategy. The Libyan intervention thus stands as a "one off" example of a successful hands-on intervention. It is not precedent setting for the simple reason that some Security Council members did not like the precedent, and there is still profound disagreement about how to deal with Syria (Landis 2012; Ryan 2012).

b) Mediation accompanied by coercive diplomacy can help promote regime change by breaking the Long Track cycle.

Yet, negotiated interventions confront a crucial dilemma. When violence is low or has yet to escalate, parties may be more receptive to interventions by a wide range of mediators, but less willing to compromise at the negotiating table because they believe they can still accomplish their goals through violent means if negotiations fail. Leverage is often limited because the parties continue to believe that they can gain more from continued fighting than they can through negotiations. However, when violence is high and has continued for a long time, positions are usually entrenched and attitudes hardened, which create obstacles to accommodation and settlement. Even a prolonged stalemate in a conflict is no guarantee that the parties are prepared to come to the table and make concessions. Protracted conflicts have a way of staying in this comfort zone because the parties simply keep on fighting—indeed, they have the resources to do so, and they cannot see any other way out. Such conflicts typically need third parties who can bring a combination of carrots and sticks to move parties from their entrenched positions.

The continuation of violence in such conflicts is also associated with a breakdown in governance and leaders who have lost much of their political legitimacy. Such situations typically involve longer-term issues that are not easily addressed in short-term or one-off negotiations. Instead, they require a complex negotiation strategy and willingness on the part of mediators and other third parties to use a wide range of tools in order to foster and sustain dialogue and promote political change.

Although a succession of mediated interventions by Britain, France, the United States, and Turkey failed to get Qadhafi to step down, mediated intervention in the Long Track Transition in Yemen lends support to the proposition that a hands-on approach involving mediation and coercive diplomacy can help to break deadlocks, end violent protest, and promote regime change when leaders see themselves backed into a corner. As Abdullah Hamidaddin shows in his chapter in this volume, for much of the first decade of the twenty-first century, Yemen was embroiled in a costly civil war between tribes in upper northern regions of the country and the south. In 2004, these wars erupted into a full-scale conflict between the Yemeni army and the followers of Husayn al-Huthi. Not only did these wars result in the deaths of thousands of civilians, but they also led to wide-scale population displacement by those fleeing the conflict. The situation escalated further as opponents to President Ali Abdullah Saleh's regime—a regime that had been in power since 1978 with the strong backing of Saudi Arabia—took to the streets, emboldened by protests in other Arab countries. Although there were many rounds of mediation to end Yemen's civil war, Saleh's intransigence hampered negotiations (Ajami 2012). Even though he could not defeat his opponents, Saleh had few incentives to make concessions to reduce or relinquish his power.

Two elements gradually changed the situation. The street protests in Yemen following the public uprisings in Tunisia and Egypt had an important impact on the country's overall political equation (Peutz 2012; Ajami 2012). Those who had backed Saleh in his war against the Huthis turned on him, and his fragile ruling coalition began to fracture. As Hamidaddin explains, "What seemed at the start to be a youth revolution against a corrupt and authoritarian order would turn out to be a war of attrition between Saleh, the Ahmars, and Ali Muhsen." As the violence in the streets of Yemen's major cities intensified, members of Saleh's own governing apparatus, including several influential ministers and diplomats, defected from the regime. Nonetheless, Saleh clung to power (Ajami 2012; Dalacoura 2012, 65–66).

The second element of change was the U.S. and UN Security Council's active engagement. Worried that an escalating civil war in Yemen would strengthen the position of one of al-Qaeda's most dangerous chapters (Dalacoura 2012, 78), the al-Qaeda in the Arabian Peninsula (AQAP), the United States increased its diplomatic pressure to get President Saleh to talk to his opponents and also to consider giving up the presidency under a transition plan that had been proposed by the

GCC. Indeed, as Zartman in his introduction to this volume notes, the U.S. ambassador in Yemen helped stakeholders to recognize that they existed in a "mutually hurting stalemate."

For its part, the GCC used it own elite networks to pressure Saleh to reconsider his resistance to a power transition (see Hill and Nonneman 2011). Following a bombing attack on Saleh, there were further negotiations as he recuperated in a hospital in Saudi Arabia. On his return to Yemen, Saleh tried to restructure the terms of the deal under an arrangement in which he would leave office only after new elections for the presidency were held. However, the proposal was rejected by the GCC and the UN Security Council, which called on him to leave office immediately, under a quid pro quo that gave amnesty to Saleh and his immediate family members.

On 24 November 2011, Saleh resigned and handed over the presidency to his vice president, Abdo Robo Mansour al-Hadi. Exactly why Saleh decided to relinquish power when he did remains something of a mystery. Some speculate it was so he could receive needed medical treatment in the West after the botched assassination attempt left his body with significant burns. However, the prospect that the UN might freeze his personal assets and those of his family might well have played into his own personal calculation, along with the promise of amnesty and the fear that if he did not take up the offer, he might suffer the same fate as Libya's Qadhafi.

Sanctions also played a role in propping up Yemen's transitional government. In June 2012, the UN Security Council approved a resolution threatening nonmilitary sanctions, including the freezing of financial assets and travel bans on key opposition leaders and key members of Yemen's al-AQAP (UN Threatens 2012). The resolution condemned "all terrorist and other attacks against civilians, oil, gas, and electricity infrastructure and against the legitimate authorities." It also demanded "the cessation of all actions aimed at undermining the government of national unity and the political transition," including interference with decisions relating to the restructuring of the armed and security forces and obstruction of military and civilian appointments.

Yemen launched into countrywide negotiations by engaging in a National Dialogue with opposition groups around the country, as urged by the UN, in order to create a broad consensus on a New Order. The completion of a new Constitution was planned for late 2013, to be followed by general elections in February 2014. President Hadi also moved to reform Yemen's security forces, still controlled by Saleh loyalists. Economic aid and donor attention to the socioeconomic crisis, particularly a looming food crisis, facing Yemen is resonating in a number of European capitals that have also committed financing during the transition process (Breisinger et al. 2012). Unfortunately these plans, including the constructive work of the National Dialogue, were put on hold, if not trashed, by the reemergence of the Huthi rebellion in 2014 and its penetration into the capital Sanaʿa in 2015.

The lesson of Yemen is that the parties can only be dislodged from their "existential positions" when they find themselves locked into what Hamidaddin describes as a "hurting stalemate," and there is active intervention by third parties who are prepared to use carrots as well as sticks to accelerate regime change and political reform—otherwise known as "mediation with muscle."

c) Without strong third-party intervention, negotiations can all too easily fall prey to extremists and thwart the prospects for political change and reform.

The story of Bahrain's failed "assertion of popular sovereignty" points to a third lesson: Where there is no third party willing and able to break negotiating deadlocks and promote regime change, stalemate will only strengthen the position of entrenched extremists and hard-liners, benefiting as well from third parties who would help their cause. As Roel Meijer and Maarten Danckaert report in their contribution to this volume, Bahrain's Shiʿite youth took to the streets in February 2011 to protest against the corrupt dynastic rule of a Sunni minority led by Bahrain's royal family. Protests reached a feverish pitch by early March 2012, threatening the stability of the regime.

Bahrain's version of the Arab Spring had its roots in long-standing sectarian tensions between the country's Sunni minority and the Shiʿite majority, although the country had weathered a series of popular uprisings dating back to the 1950s (Ajami 2012; Karolak 2012, 5–6; Dalacoura 2012, 65, 67, 71). The last *intifada* before 2010 erupted in the mid-1990s. Although King Hammad bin Isa Al Khalifa and his son Crown Prince Salman bin Hamad Al Khalifa were considered the voices of moderation in the royal family—they had granted concessions to prop up their rule in a series of political reforms at the beginning of the twenty-first century that extended political rights to women, turned Bahrain into a constitutional monarchy, and strengthened the role of the legislature—they were at odds with hard-liners like Bahrain's prime minister, Khalifa bin Salaman Al-Khalifa, who were not interested in making concessions to protestors. As Meijer and Danckaert argue, reform was especially difficult for Bahrain's ruling elites because members of the royal family occupied many of the key positions in government, from the ministerial level on down. Further, the regime's survival depends on the country's oil wealth and a deep-rooted system of patronage that is the source of its legitimacy (benevolence) and power. The fact that Bahraini police and security forces are made up of foreign-hired forces also made it easier for the government to turn its guns on its own people.

As opposed to Libya and Yemen, Bahrain appealed to outside intervention to quash the revolt, as the protests grew increasingly violent and threatened to topple the regime. Saudi forces entered the small kingdom on 14 March, arresting the leaders of the protest and enforcing a ban against any future public gatherings in the streets and city squares of Bahrain. The United States, which maintains its Fifth

Fleet in Bahrain, chose not to become actively involved in promoting negotiations between the government and the opposition or in encouraging regime change, as it had done in Yemen and Libya. Although the United States enjoyed close ties with moderates in Bahrain's government and with some members of the opposition movement, "[a]ttempts by of the American embassy to support the opposition and [mediate] with the ruling family faltered" (Dalacoura 2012, 78). For strategic reasons, perhaps, the United States was disinclined to do anything that would jeopardize its rights to bases in Bahrain, especially at a time of growing tensions with Iran over its nuclear program and suspicions that Iran was giving clandestine support to rebel Shiʿite groups in Bahrain. As Meijer and Danckaert point out, however, the consequence of Bahrain's failed rebellion was a backlash: moderates in Bahrain's government were unceremoniously pushed aside, and Bahrain's majority Shiʿite underclass is becoming more radicalized. The only real winners in Bahrain's relatively short-lived Arab Spring moment have thus been extremists and hardliners on both sides of the sectarian divide.

d) Some dynastic regimes in the Arab world appear to have greater political legitimacy and resiliency than others and have been able to mediate and deflect popular discontent from within.

Morocco and Jordan's experience with the Arab Spring points to a fourth lesson: some societies have sufficiently robust internal intermediary or arbitration mechanisms that they don't require other "hands" to help manage their internal disputes and processes of political change—a phenomenon that the introduction refers to as "adapting." If the monarchy was resilient to the uprisers' demands in both cases, the protesters also demanded less than in the other Arab Spring countries by not calling for the monarch to step down.

As Amy Hamblin argues in her chapter, Morocco confronted many of the same social and economic problems as its neighbors, including high levels of youth unemployment, poverty, income inequality, and corruption. The general populace was also underrepresented in the country's political institutions and a parliament that, though popularly elected, serves at the dictates of Morocco's king. On 20 February 2011, tens of thousands of Moroccans took to the streets to demonstrate for change. In response to their demands, King Mohammed VI announced a series of major constitutional reforms and the beginning of a controlled process of political evolution and economic reform. He also dissolved the parliament and called new elections to signal his commitment to change (Benchemsi 2012, 57–58; 64–65; Dalacoura 2012, 72–73, 79).

Unlike other Arab countries, however, Morocco's Alaouite dynasty enjoys unusually high levels of political legitimacy, respect, and authority (Benchemsi 2012, 67; Anderson 2011). As Hamblin notes, the dynasty "stretches back more than 350 years. The royal family's resilience in the face of shifting political winds derives in part from its alleged descent from the prophet Mohammed." In addition to controlling the armed forces, the king is also the "Commander of the Faithful." The monarchy's unique status and political legitimacy not only protects him from direct political challenges but also "allows him to act in the role as arbiter of the political system, intervening to quell public anger when it threatens the system's political stability." By dissolving parliament, the king has used a "scapegoat tactic" to deflect public criticism and rise "above the political fray."

Similarly in Jordan, the Hashemite monarchy's response to the Arab Spring was to engage in a process of domestic give and take. Schwedler (2011) notes that Jordan's protests are best viewed as a form of discourse with the state. Protestors have used sanctioned public demonstrations to elicit concessions and policy reforms with the ruling monarchy. With laws preventing criticism of the king and any calls for his deposition, Arab Spring protestors in Jordan have focused their aims on achieving incremental government reform.

On the heels of protests in Egypt, Jordanian protests were initiated by East Bank Jordanians and not Palestinian inhabitants or citizens. This garnered protestors a greater political legitimacy to demand concessions from the king and allowed East Bank Jordanian protesters to take advantage of their privileged political status to call for political reform and loosening of royal authority (Tobin 2012). Yet, as many of the protesters were East Bankers and traditionally loyal to the monarchical system—in fear of having the Palestinian inhabitants who form a majority call for an "alternative state" to Palestine in Jordan—the protestors did not call for the end of the monarchy (Tobin 2012). Nevertheless, Jordan did not escape the kinds of protests calling for economic justice. Indeed, in later stages of Jordanian protests, the increase in gas prices in fall 2012 did embolden a wider variety of Jordanians to participate, including Palestinian, Syrian, and Iraqi refugees in Jordan.

The ruling monarchy responded to protestors' demands with a number of political and economic concessions. The king first reacted to protestors by dismissing Prime Minister Bakhit in February 2011, further deflecting blame for economic and political problems on the appointed prime minister. A month later, King Abdullah also initiated a national dialogue toward enhanced political reforms. A number of reforms were eventually enacted, including the establishment of an Independent Election Commission, widening opportunities for national political parties to compete and gain seats in Parliament, and added seats for women. The results of these, albeit limited and cosmetic, reform efforts were successful enough to stave off further protests.

In January 2013, Jordan held a successful and peaceful national election. While the electoral process was deemed relatively fair, the electoral system continued to disadvantage Palestinian Jordanian communities in urban areas and to privilege East Bank communities in rural areas. While 70 percent of eligible voters had registered to vote, only 53 percent of those actually went to the polls. This effectively meant that approximately 30–40 percent of eligible voters had participated in the election. Nevertheless, the relatively high voter turnout in the 2013 elections was viewed as an endorsement of the king's reform efforts. The result of the 2013 election was little different from previous elections, but it effectively quelled internal demands for political reform as the king's internal intermediation achieved the kind of stability it had envisioned. Furthermore, as the conflict in Syria escalated into violent civil war and the influx of Syrian refugees into Jordan intensified, protestors and reform advocates softened their tone and were effectively quelled by the king's approach of intermediation and arbitration. The king's approach to political reforms is viewed as preferable to the alternative of chaos or civil war as in neighboring Syria.

The monarchies of Morocco and Jordan, therefore, may be unique cases of internal political management and internal intermediation, and their apparent success in weathering the storms of the Arab Spring is not necessarily transferable to other settings in the Arab world. Yet, both these countries are darlings of the West, and there are strong Western and Arab Gulf domestic sentiments not to allow either the Moroccan or Jordanian monarchy to fall. The international community has supported these two countries and used plenty of carrots to keep reforms on track. The G8 initiated its Deauville Partnership with Arab Countries in Transition on 26–27 May 2011 to connect its developed economies with the Arab countries undergoing the political and economic transition to good governance and inclusive economic growth. The Deauville Partnership envisioned developing an economic agenda to assist Arab governments undergoing rapid social and political transitions. The International Monetary Fund (IMF) and the World Bank were tasked further with assessing the region to help G8 members formulate coordinated economic policies with an expanded list of Deauville Partner countries: Egypt, Tunisia, Libya, Jordan, and Morocco. These international financial institutions' assessments concluded that there were regional and domestic economic opportunities that could be seized with good governance, coordinated economic and foreign donor policies, and stronger intraregional economic integration and coordination. Here the international community has feared that without strong policy support, both Jordan and Morocco could be susceptible to popular revolt. In theory, this could precipitate a hands-on approach, but both have effectively navigated out of their political crises using internal deflection and cooptation.

PERSISTENT LESSONS FROM THE SHORT TRACK

There are also some important persistent lessons from the Short Track uprisings of the Arab Spring that warrant closer consideration by policymakers.

a) Breakdown in negotiations between authoritarian regimes and mobilized interests can be an early warning indicator that a regime is in trouble.

Much of the literature on early warning indicators of impending political unrest and instability in failed states focuses on aggregate social and economic variables such as mounting demographic pressures, unemployment (especially among youth), uneven economic development, economic decline (as reflected in rapidly rising prices for basic foodstuffs), and the deterioration of public services (L20 2014). Many of these warning signs were evident and indeed prevalent in many countries of the Arab Spring. However, as noted in Zartman's introduction and the chapters in this volume, the massive uprisings of *intifadat* of the Arab Spring were preceded by the failure of particular sectors to secure change in negotiations with their employers and the government in what was clearly an early indicator of the fraying of the social compact, which generally tended to be fragile anyway. Some of these tensions were the inevitable result of neoliberal market reforms introduced by governments in the Arab world in the 1990s and the early 2000s (Dahi 2011, 4). In Egypt, for example, not only were food subsidies cut in half by the Mubarak regime at the beginning of the previous decade, but other social services, including public health care, were also clawed back (Anderson 2011). A similar trend was also evident in Tunisia (Adely 2012; Anderson 2011; Chomiak 2011, 70–73; Schraeder and Redissi 2011, 7–10).

Moreover, public opposition to President Mubarak's decision to run for reelection in 2005 was accompanied by growing protests and strikes by workers over wages and workplace conditions (Beinin 2012; Dahi 2011, 4–5; Dalacoura 2012, 68; see also Alterman 2011, 108–109). Demonstrations in al-Mahala were notably organized and effective. According to one estimate, "between 2004 and 2010, there were more than 3,000 labor actions in Egypt notwithstanding the fact the Egypt's workers were underinstitutionalized and its unions and civil society were weak. The clothing and textile sectors were the first to be hit by strikes, but building workers, transport workers, food processing workers, and even the workers on the Cairo metro system soon followed" (Maher 2011). Egypt's social contract, which for many years had included generous subsidies to lower-income Egyptians, was severely tested by the liberalized economic policies of the Mubarak government. However, the downside of these reforms was increased income disparities, growing levels of corruption, and a growing sense of insecurity among Egypt's working class.

The situation was not all that different in Tunisia, where the Ben Ali regime was also taking measures to liberalize Tunisia's economy (Adely 2012; Anderson 2011; Chomiak 2011, 70–73; Schraeder and Redissi 2011: 7–10). For more than two decades, Tunisia had a unique system of unified contract negotiations to "preserve social peace." However, in 2005 the Tunisian General Trade Union (UGTT), which represented 3.5 million workers in negotiations on fifty-one collective bargaining private and public sector contracts, broke ranks with the government. As a confidential report from the U.S. Embassy in Tunis published by Wikileaks noted:

> [UGTT's Secretary General] Jerad has partially returned to his militant roots and has staked out a more confrontational role for the union. A March 26 [2005] UGTT Politburo communiqué confirmed the union's independence from the government and

> called on employers to engage in direct negotiations. . . . [T]he union's March regional elections in Kairouan, Sfax, and Gabes placed real labor militants in positions of power. . . . [T]he new leaders are ready for the union to take the government to task on not only traditional labor issues such as wages and worker benefits, but also on elements of economic and political policy."[4]

The years that followed saw mounting labor unrest against Ben Ali's government and a breakdown in the social contract between unions and the government and a clear breakdown in the relationship that had existed in previous years (Anderson 2011; Chomiak 2011, 72–73; 80–83).

Popular social movements in the Arab world lack organizational capacity and structures that enable them to be effective power brokers and play a critical role in negotiations for a New Order. The new political order in Arab Spring countries has been driven and shaped by a youth movement that, empowered by social media, took to the streets in protest of existing regimes (see also Aouragh and Alexander 2011; Bellin 2012; Chalcraft 2012; Chomiak 2011, 73–75; Eltantawy and Wiest 2011; Hassan 2012; Khamis, Gold, and Vaughn 2012; Tufekci and Wilson 2012). But the power and speed of the Internet and mobile phones has not been able to bring different groups to work together to build viable political coalitions, nor has it translated the power of the street into concrete plans of action based on a shared vision of the future (Aday et al. 2012; Wolfsfeld, Segev, and Sheafer 2013). As instruments of political communication and vehicles for collective action, Facebook and Twitter have their limitations (Aday et al. 2012, 4–5, 7; Alterman 2011, 103–104; Dajani 2012, 2–3, 5–6; Dalacoura 2012, 69; Hassan 2012).

However, it is not simply the limitations of technology that constrain these new social movements, but also history and ideology. As discussed by Aly El Raggal and Heba Raouf Ezzat's chapter in this book, many of Egypt's young revolutionaries eschew traditional style political negotiations and concepts of coalition building for essentially ideological reasons. Like the anarchist movement of the nineteenth and early twentieth centuries, Egyptian youth want to continue with their revolution without falling captive to old-style politics where they would be forced to make concessions and engage in direct talks with established political power structures, like the Muslim Brotherhood or the military. These protesters actively resist "structures of domination" and believe that they are in a constant struggle against the state, which they consider to be a relic of a bygone era (see also Chalcraft 2012). They also seek social and economic transformation and not just political change.

El Raggal and Ezzat also observe that in a very significant sense, workers are not an organized political force: "Egypt did not have strong labor unions before the revolution, . . . and although it had witnessed many factional revolts, none of them succeeded in institutionalizing themselves in society, and none of the many social movements were independent and influential." The lack of strong civil society organizations is proving to be a kind of Achilles' heel in Egypt's revolution as it goes through its various twists and turns following the overthrow of Mohamed Morsi. That is because, according to El Raggal and Ezzat, a succession of autocratic rulers has limited the working classes' and the masses' capacities for negotiated change. This situation is by no means unique to Egypt and is clearly prevalent throughout much of the Arab world, where civil society has been actively repressed by autocratic regimes. But it has also meant that, at least up to now and notwithstanding their power to bring people into the streets and topple dictators, popular social protest movements have shown limited ability to shape the subsequent course of political events and critical negotiations to construct new institutions and a new political order.

However, external actors and interests should be careful about jumping to the conclusion that what underdeveloped civil society in the Arab World needs are generous doses of hands-on support to strengthen and grow. Wariness in a country like Egypt toward entrenched elites and traditional power structures extends to foreigners, who are generally seen as having played a key role in propping up the ancien regime. It is therefore important to listen, respect, and understand the local situation before extending a helping hand. As the Council for a Community of Democracies urges in a handbook for diplomats: "It should be mandatory at the outset to seek advice from local civil society on how best to support their efforts. Respecting and understanding the different roles and interests of all partners in the democratic development process is a basic requirement for productive relationships and successful support. Outsiders also have to understand and respect the ways in which the local reform process needs to take account of traditional values: social and political practices common in one country can be abrasive in another" (Kinsman and Bassuener 2013, 36).

b) There are stronger incentives for negotiation and compromise among rival interests, including the military, when no single group or force can dominate the political process.

Another axiom of politics is that incentives to negotiate, forge coalitions, and reach accommodation across the political divide are greater when no single group can dominate the political process versus situations where one group has decisive majority or monopoly control over the use of force that it is prepared to use to achieve its goals. Voting results in Egypt's presidential election underscored the country's deep polarization, but also the weakness of its key political groupings. The Muslim Brotherhood's candidate, Mohamed Morsi, barely won against his opponent, Ahmed Shafik, a former air force commander who served briefly as prime minister after the fall of Mubarak.

As in Tunisia, the outcome of Egypt's election has created incentives for negotiation between Egypt's power structures in what the introduction to this volume has identified as a pacting pattern, given that no group, neither the military nor the Muslim Brotherhood, could dominate the political process after the fall of Mubarak (see Cole 2012; Karawan 2011, 45). The Brotherhood and the military remained cautious in their dealings with each other during Egypt's political transition (Karawan 2011). Morsi negotiated the forced retirement of General Tantawi, who headed the Supreme Council of the Armed Forces (SCAF), and secured agreement on a new division of powers between the executive and the military. But when the seesaw between the two organizations escalated, and Morsi claimed full powers in December 2012 and imposed his constitution, he overstepped the balance; the SCAF claimed "even fuller" power by removing him from the presidency seven months later.

The 2013 coup against Morsi was a failure on his part to create a viable pact with Egypt's military to ensure that they stay in the barracks and out of politics. It has been argued that the military could no longer live with Morsi and the Brotherhood because of the latter's interference in security matters on the Sinai Peninsula. The military favored rooting out radical Islamist forces among Sinai Bedouin, while Morsi favored restraint (Hendawi 2013). This was despite Morsi's having permitted the SCAF and the generals to keep some of their perks (including the 25 percent control they exercise over the economy) and granted immunity from prosecution for their past sins.

Economic development has always been key to Egypt's political stability. Although the Egyptian economy in the final years of Mubarak's rule was experiencing a respectable rate of growth in the range of 4–5 percent GDP, it tanked during and after the revolution. Growth has been anemic, at 1.4 percent in 2012. This is far below the 7–8 percent needed to provide jobs for young Egyptians who are entering the workforce in massive numbers. The state of the country's public finances is tenuous after a $4.8 billion IMF loan has continued to stall over Egyptian failure to increase prices and remove subsidies; Morsi's government was unable to secure the loan for failing to meet the IMF's preconditions. The Qataris, in an implicit support to the Muslim Brotherhood, supported the Morsi government with billions in foreign aid and central bank support. But it was not enough to pay the bills that kept coming due and, more importantly, to stave off another attempt at a revolution on 30 June 2013 that was initiated by the Tamarrod movement. Morsi had a lot on his plate and not much time to deliver the results. Ordinary Egyptians were increasingly worried about a higher crime rate, insecurity on their streets owing to underfunded police services, and continued consolidation of Morsi's presidential powers. The Interior Ministry still controlled the police services, which have been plagued by corruption and inadequate due process in arrests. Calls for reforming the security sector have been made both from within the former Morsi government and by his opponents. Reform of the security sector would be strengthened by a democratically elected Parliament that can translate these populist demands into policy action (Brumberg and Sallam, 2012). Morsi failed to get stakeholders to agree to a parliamentary election as many opted to plan for his very downfall.

The Muslim Brotherhood tried to navigate a delicate course by pursuing a policy of neoliberalization with social safety nets, but this proved difficult to sustain because lower- and middle-class Egyptians are anti-neoliberal in outlook. The military-appointed government that took over from Morsi was keen to adopt many neoliberal policies. Yet, many Egyptians rejected the so-called Washington consensus. Privatization and the removal of subsidies was one of the reasons Egyptians (and Tunisians) took to the streets against their rulers (Adely 2012; Anderson 2011; Chomiak 2011, 70–73; Dalacoura 2012, 73–74). Surveys of Egyptian religious attitudes also show strong anti-secularist leanings (Brown 2012), with most Egyptians believing that religious scholars should interpret the law. Egypt's new social contract will not be easily constructed given the country's profound economic challenges and deep-rooted social tensions and cleavages. Persistent negotiation and the propensity to simply muddle through will be the operative political condition.

POLICY RECOMMENDATIONS

For scholars and policymakers alike, the Arab Spring is in many ways a study of contradiction—a lesson in hands-on and hands-off approaches to diplomacy in a region currently undergoing unprecedented transformation. This chapter has identified some provisional "lessons learned" regarding regime change and upheaval in the countries of the Arab Spring. At its core, it argues that there can be no singular approach to international intervention in countries so characterized by their own unique challenges for diplomatic engagement, not to mention an international environment so often divided about its role in intervening in the Middle East. At the same time, such complexity should not act as a deterrent or be used as a pass for the West to turn away from its obligations to provide much-needed diplomatic involvement where it is needed and where it is welcome.

As this chapter has shown, the *kind* of intervention that should be undertaken in Arab Spring countries (i.e., joint military action, aggressive diplomacy)—and, perhaps more importantly, *how much*—is of considerable debate. However, as this chapter has also shown, a good place to start before extending a helping hand in any negotiation is from a position of respect, both for the issues and the local situation at hand.

There is an overwhelming acceptance that non-inclusive economic growth leading to socioeconomic and then political frustration is a key part of the puzzle in searching for determinants of the Arab Spring. The Arab Spring started in countries that had economic growth and that were lead economic reformers. Tunisia, Egypt, Libya, and even Syria were "successfully liberalizing" their economies. But the revolutions hit these same countries where economic growth did not reach citizens at a pace that met the rising expectations of its people, and the demographic group hit hardest by unemployment and underemployment were the educated, interconnected, and middle-class youth. Simply, the Arab people demanded inclusive economic growth that would allow them to achieve their latent economic potential. The G8 can support the Arab region through increased investment, coordinated foreign aid programs, and opening G8 economic markets for Deauville partners.

Transition countries in the Arab world need to create labor-intensive jobs to meet the political and economic demands of its youth, augment the technical and postsecondary education sector to better prepare Arab youth for the global knowledge economy, and invest in infrastructural development projects needed in meeting urbanization challenges, such as improved public and private transportation systems, expanded affordable housing, better integrated health care systems, adequate food security through a modernized agricultural sector and distribution links, and upgraded sewage systems. There are plenty of respected studies, particularly by the IMF, World Bank, and the United Nations (*Arab Human Development Report* for 2002, 2003, 2004, 2005, 2009) that reiterate these points. Members of the G8 and its companies have the global comparative advantage in skills, resources, and capital to act as vital investors and partners in supporting the economic development of the Deauville members in the Arab world. To assist the Arab transition countries, G8 leaders need to encourage and promote their private investors to initiate or participate in private-public partnerships that can provide Arab countries with the technological know-how and innovation in short supply throughout the region's production value chains, energy facilities, and infrastructural development.

To help increase the productive capacity, economies of scale, and capital accumulation of the Arab world, the G8 members can help by opening their markets to Arab goods and services. Existing intraregional or bilateral trade agreements between G8 members and with many of the Deauville partners need to be further deepened, strengthened, and expanded to other Arab countries. The United States and Canada have bilateral free trade agreements with Jordan and Morocco that could be expanded to include Egypt, Tunisia, and Libya, for example, and could further promote integration among these partners by permitting them to share rules of origin in exports to the large market of the North American Free Trade Agreement. The Gulf Cooperation Council, a strong and liquid economic market, could further strengthen economic trade ties with the Middle Eastern countries, improve and facilitate Arab labor mobility to the GCC, and enhance its foreign direct investment into productive economic sectors that have a key objective to spur inclusive economic growth. Turkey, as a leading economic powerhouse in the region, could participate in and coordinate with G8 efforts to promote increased economic integration with Deauville partners. The European Union's Neighborhood Policy with a number of transition countries could be deepened with the ratification and implementation of the Deep and Comprehensive Free Trade Areas proposal. Arab countries in transition would benefit from increased trade and investment from G8 members, and a positive step forward would be to expand and deepen existing arrangements.

The political awakening of the Deauville partners should also provide an important lesson for G8 countries interested in investing and coordinating donor programs in the Arab region. Popular demands for accountability and transparency of the public purse and international economic transitions involving Arab transition countries will require governments to adopt the best practices of good governance. This can be further assisted by G8 countries by insisting on transparent and accountable procurement proposals and by enacting regulatory standards on labor and environmental protection. A challenge for the G8 will be to ensure that members' companies and donor agencies are not complicit in the political trappings of the inefficiencies of the Arab bureaucracies and of currying favor with the crony-capitalists of the region. These measures will ensure long-term and positive public diplomacy between the G8 and Deavuille partners while meeting the needs and aspirations of the Arab people. There is immense regional opportunity for inclusive economic growth with an educated and eager workforce; the G8 leaders can help facilitate this with enhanced economic trade and investment ties and with support for best practices in the Arab world using the Arab Spring as a Western Awakening to the need to preempt violence and collapse and to foster peaceful integration and evolution in the Middle East.

Notes

1. According to I. William Zartman in his introduction to this volume, Short Track Transitions are cases of "relatively rapid and negotiated overthrow" and "evolve through negotiated courses struggling to stay pluralistic." Conversely, Long Track Transitions are identifiable by relatively long "periods of violence . . . before overthrow" and "produce highly fractured systems" with more negotiations within the uprising than with the incumbents.

2. Elements of the discussion about NATO's intervention in Libya are based on Crocker, Aall, and Hampson (2012).

3. Interestingly, the African Union did not join with other regional organizations in urging the UN to take enforcement action and, in fact, made desultory and widely criticized efforts to mediate between Qadhafi and the Libyan rebel forces. However, this lack of AU support had little impact on the deliberations, perhaps because Gabon, Nigeria, and South Africa—all members of the AU—supported the resolution despite the reservations of their regional organization. Another possibility is simply that the proponents of military intervention privileged the opinions of the regional organization that agreed with their own. See Bellamy and Williams (2011).

4. "Tunisian Labor Update: UGTT Shows a More Independent Streak," confidential cable from U.S. embassy in Tunis, 25 March 2005, leaked to Wikileaks, http://www.cablegatesearch.net/cable.php?id=05TUNIS768.

References

Aday, Sean, et al. 2012. *New Media and Conflict after the Arab Spring*. Washington, D.C.: United States Institute of Peace.

Adely, Fida. 2012. "The Emergence of a New Labor Movement in Jordan." *Middle East Report* 264 (Fall): 34–37.

Ailboni, Roberto. 2011. "The International Dimension of the Arab Spring." *International Spectator* 46:5–9.

Ajami, Fouad. 2012. "The Arab Spring at One: A Year of Living Dangerously." *Foreign Affairs* 91, no. 2: 56–65.

Alterman, Jon B. 2011. "The Revolution Will Not Be Tweeted." *Washington Quarterly* 34, no. 4: 103–116.

Anderson, Lisa. 2011. "Demystifying the Arab Spring: Parsing the Differences between Tunisia, Egypt, and Libya." *Foreign Affairs* 90, no. 3: 2–7.

Aouragh, Miriyam, and Anne Alexander. 2011. "The Arab Spring: The Egyptian Experience: Sense and Nonsense of the Internet Revolution." *International Journal of Communication* 5:1344–1358.

Barry, Ben. 2011. "Libya's Lessons." *Survival: Global Politics and Strategy* 53, no. 5: 5–14.

Beinin, Joel. 2012. "Egyptian Workers and January 25: A Social Movement in Historical Context." *Social Research* 79, no. 2: 323–350.

Bellamy, A. J. 2011. "Libya and the Responsibility to Protect: The Exception and the Norm." *Ethics and International Affairs* 1, no. 1: 1–7.

Bellamy, Alex J., and Paul D. Williams. 2011. "The New Politics of Protection? Côte d'Ivoire, Libya and the Responsibility to Protect." *International Affairs* 87, no. 4: 825–850.

Bellin, Eva. 2012. "Reconsidering the Robustness of Authoritarianism in the Middle East: Lessons from the Arab Spring." *Comparative Politics* 44, no. 2: 127–149.

Benchemsi, Ahmed. 2012. "Morocco: Outfoxing the Opposition." *Journal of Democracy* 23, no. 1: 57–69.

Bobbitt, Philip. 2011. "Libya Shows the Way the West Can Now Intervene." *Evening Standard*, 23 August. http://www.standard.co.uk/news/libya-shows-the-way-the-west-can-now-intervene-6436005.html (accessed 14 February 2013).

Breisinger, Clemens, Olivier Ecker, Perrihan Al Riffai, Wilfried Engelke, and Abdulmajeed Al-Bataly. 2012. "Managing Transition in Yemen." Washington, D.C.: International Food Policy Research Institute.

Brown, Nathan. 2012. "Contention in Religion and State in Postrevolutionary Egypt." *Social Research* 79, no. 2: 531–552.

Brumberg, Daniel, and Hesham Sallam. 2012. "The Politics of Security Sector Reform in Egypt." Special Report, United States Institute of Peace. http://edoc.bibliothek.uni-halle.de/servlets/MCRFileNodeServlet/HALCoRe_derivate_00006289/usip_SR318_0.pdf (accessed 12 January 2015).

Chalcraft, John. 2012. "Horizontalism in the Egyptian Revolutionary Process." *Middle East Report* 262 (Spring): 6–11.

Chomiak, Laryssa. 2011. "The Making of a Revolution in Tunisia." *Middle East Law and Governance* 3, nos. 1–2: 68–83.

Cole, Juan. 2012. "Egypt's New Left versus the Military Junta." *Social Research* 79, no. 2: 487–513.

Crocker, Chester, Pamela Aall, and Fen Osler Hampson. 2012. "Jumpstarting Conflict Management: Regional Organizations, Hybrid Groups, and Security." Paper presented at the Annual Convention of the International Studies Association, San Diego, 1 April.

Dadush, Uri, and Michele Dunne. 2011. "American and European Responses to the Arab Spring: What's the Big Idea?" *Washington Quarterly* 34, no. 4: 131–145.

Dahi, Omar S. 2011. "Understanding the Political Economy of the Arab Revolts." *Middle East Report* 259 (Summer): 2–6.

Dajani, Nabil. 2012. "Technology Cannot a Revolution Make: Nas-book Not Facebook." *Arab Media and Society* 15. http://www.arabmediasociety.com/index.php?article=782&p=1 (accessed 12 January 2015).

Dalacoura, Katerina. 2012. "The 2011 Uprisings in the Arab Middle East: Political Change and Geopolitical Implications." *International Affairs* 88, no. 1: 63–79.

Eltantawy, Nahed, and Julie Wiest. 2011. "Social Media in the Egyptian Revolution: Reconsidering Resource Mobilization Theory." *International Journal of Communication* 5:1207–1224.

Gause, F. Gregory, III, and Ian S. Lustick. 2012. "America and the Regional Powers in a Changing Middle East." *Middle East Policy* 19, no. 2: 1–9.

Halperin, Morton H., Joseph T. Siegle, and Michael M. Weinstein. 2010. *The Democracy Advantage: How Democracies Promote Prosperity and Peace*. Rev. ed. New York: Routledge.

Hassan, Robert. 2012. "'Not Ready for Democracy': Social Networking and the Power of the People; The Revolts of 2011 in a Temporalized Context." *Arab Media and Society* 15. http://www.arabmediasociety.com/articles/downloads/20120410215415_Hassan_Robert.pdf (accessed 12 January 2015).

Hendawi, Hamza 2013. "Disputes between Morsi, Military Led to Egypt Coup." Associated Press, 18 July. http://bigstory.ap.org/article/disputes-between-morsi-military-led-egypt-coup-0 (accessed 12 January 2015).

Hill, Ginny, and Gerd Nonneman. 2011. *Yemen, Saudi Arabia and the Gulf States: Elite Politics, Street Protests and Regional Diplomacy*. London: Chatham House.

Hinnebusch, Raymond. 2012. "Syria: From 'Authoritarian Upgrading' to Revolution?" *International Affairs* 88, no. 1: 95–113.

Jones, Bruce D. 2011. "Libya and the Responsibilities of Power." *Survival: Global Politics and Strategy* 53, no. 3: 51–60.

Karawan, Ibrahim A. 2011. "Politics and the Army in Egypt." *Survival: Global Politics and Strategy* 53, no. 2: 43–50.

Karolak, Magdalena. 2012. "Bahraini Women in the 21st Century: Disputed Legacy of the Unfinished Revolution." *Journal of International Women's Studies* 13, no. 5: 5–16.

Khamis, Sahar, Paul B. Gold, and Katherine Vaughn. 2012. "Beyond Egypt's 'Facebook Revolution' and Syria's 'YouTube Uprising': Comparing Political Contexts, Actors and Communication Strategies." *Arab Media and Society* 15 (Spring). http://www.arabmediasociety.com/?article=791 (accessed 16 December 2014).

Kinsman, Jeremy, and Kurt Bassuener. 2013. "The Diplomat's Toolbox," chapter 3 in *A Diplomat's Handbook for Democracy Development Support*. 3rd ed. Waterloo, Ont.: Centre for International Governance Innovation; Washington, D.C.: Council of the Community of Democracies. http://www.diplomatshandbook.org/pdf/Handbook_CH3.pdf (accessed 16 December 2014).

Landis, Joshua. 2012. "Why the Assad Regime Is Likely to Survive to 2013." *Middle East Policy* 19, no. 1: 72–84.

L20 (Leaders 20). 2014. L20 University Course Package: Lesson 8, Failing States. http://www.l20.org/lessons/Lesson%208%20Failing%20States.pdf (accessed 12 January 2015).

Maher, Stephen. 2011. "The Political Economy of the Egyptian Uprising." *Monthly Review* 63, no. 6 (November). http://monthlyreview.org/2011/11/01/the-political-economy-of-the-egyptian-uprising (accessed 16 December 2014).

Morey, Daniel S., Clayton L. Thyne, Sarah L. Hayden, and Michael B. Senters. 2012. "Leader, Follower, or Spectator? The Role of President Obama in the Arab Spring Uprisings. *Social Science Quarterly* 93, no. 5: 1185–1203.

Peutz, Nathalie. 2012. "Revolution in Socotra: A Perspective from Yemen's Periphery." *Middle East Report* 263 (Summer): 14–16.

Ryan, Curtis. (2012). "The New Arab Cold War and the Struggle for Syria." *Middle East Report* 262 (Spring): 28–31.

Schraeder, Peter J., and Hamadi Redissi. 2011. "Ben Ali's Fall." *Journal of Democracy* 22, no. 3: 5–19.

Schwedler, Jillian. 2011. "The Geography of Political Protests." In *Revolution in the Arab World: The Long View*, by L. Khalili, J. Schwedler, I. W. Zartman, and K. Eid, 9–14. Georgetown: Center for Contemporary Arab Studies, Georgetown University.

Tobin, Sarah. 2012. "Jordan's Arab Spring: The Middle Class and Anti-Revolution." *Middle East Policy* 19, no. 1: 96–109.

Toensing, Chris. 2012. "Libya's Lessons." *Middle East Report*, 5 March. http://www.merip.org/newspaper_opeds/oped030512 (accessed 12 January 2015).

Tufekci, Zeynep, and Christopher Wilson. 2012. "Social Media and the Decision to Participate in Political Protest: Observations from Tahrir Square." *Journal of Communication* 62, no. 2: 363–379.

United Nations Development Programme. 2002. *Arab Human Development Report 2002: Creating Opportunities for Future Generations.* http://www.arab-hdr.org/ (accessed 16 December 2014).

———. 2003. *Arab Human Development Report 2003: Building a Knowledge Society.* http://www.arab-hdr.org/ (accessed 16 December 2014).

———. 2004. *Arab Human Development Report 2004: Towards Freedom in the Arab World.* http://www.arab-hdr.org/ (accessed 16 December 2014).

———. 2005. *Arab Human Development Report 2005: Towards the Rise of Women in the Arab World.* http://www.arab-hdr.org/ (accessed 16 December 2014).

———. 2009. *Arab Human Development Report 2009: Challenges to Human Security in the Arab Countries.* http://www.arab-hdr.org/ (accessed 16 December 2014).

"UN Threatens Sanctions against Yemen Opponents." Associated Press, 12 June. http://www.foxnews.com/world/2012/06/12/un-threatens-sanctions-against-yemen-opponents/#ixzz2A2Td1P6O.

Wolfsfeld, Gadi, Elad Segev, and Tamir Sheafer. 2013. "Social Media and the Arab Spring: Politics Comes First." *International Journal of Press/Politics* 20, no. 10: 1–23.

CONTRIBUTORS

Samir Aita is president of the Circle of Arab Economists and former editor in chief and general manager of *Le Monde Diplomatique*, Arabic edition. He teaches political economy at the University of Paris–Dauphine. He is currently active in Syrian affairs. His books include *Les travailleurs arabes* and *The Road Ahead for Syria.*

Alice Alunni is a PhD candidate at the School of Government and International Affairs at Durham University (UK). She was based in Libya between September 2013 and June 2014 as a consultant for civil society programs at the British Council in Tripoli. Her PhD research focuses on theories of nationalism, diaspora, and civil society in the Arab world with an emphasis on Libya. She received her master's degree in international relations and international economics from the Johns Hopkins University School of Advanced International Studies (SAIS).

Mark Anstey is an emeritus professor with Nelson Mandela Metropolitan University in South Africa and a senior visiting fellow of Clingendael, where he serves on the steering committee of the Processes of International Negotiation (PIN) Program. He served on the structures of the National Peace Accord during South Africa's transition and was director of monitoring (Eastern Cape) for the Independent Electoral Commission in the country's historic 1994 elections.

Abdelwahab ben Hafaiedh is an associate professor of sociology at the University of Tunis. He is the founder of the Arab Observatory of Education (2000), director of the Middle East Research Competition (2006–11), and presently president of the Applied Social Science Forum (ASSF) in Tunis.

Maarten Danckaert is head of the Department of Education and Capacity Building at the European-Bahraini Organization for Human Rights (EBOHR). Before joining the EBOHR, he was a research assistant at the Norwegian Centre for Human Rights (NCHR), University of Oslo, Norway, at which he was working on a project titled, "The Re-birth of Arab Citizenship? The Arab Uprisings and State-Society Relations in the Arab World."

Aly El Raggal is a political sociologist. He studied peace, development, security and international conflict transformation at the University of Innsbruck, Austria. He has been a political activist before and during the Egyptian revolution. His work on social movements, security topics, and especially the Egyptian revolution has been published in various academic outlets. He writes regularly for the newspapers *Assafir* (Lebanese) and *Al Shourok* (Egyptian).

Abdullah Hamidaddin is a writer and commentator on Middle Eastern societies, politics, and religion with a special focus on Saudi Arabia and Yemen. He chaired the Zayd bin

Ali Cultural Foundation, a Yemeni NGO concerned with the preservation of the country's Islamic Zaydi and Mu'tazili heritage. He is currently a columnist for alarabiya.net and a PhD candidate at King's College London. Hamidaddin's books in Arabic include *Harmonious Being: The Quest for God in Our Liquid Lives*, *Strategic Mediums of Development*, and *Zaydism: A Reading of the Project and an Exploration of Its Component Parts.*

Amy Hamblin is an analyst of Middle Eastern affairs, with a particular focus on social movements and democratization. She holds a master's degree in Middle East studies and conflict management from the Johns Hopkins University School of Advanced International Studies (SAIS).

Fen Osler Hampson is Chancellor's Professor at Carleton University, Ottawa, Canada, and concurrently Distinguished Fellow and Director of Global Security at the Centre for International Governance Innovation in Waterloo, Ontario. He is a member of the steering committee of the Processes of International Negotiation (PIN) Program at Clingendael NL. His latest book, with William Zartman, is *The Global Power of Talk: Negotiating America's Interests.*

Roel Meijer teaches history of the Middle East at Radboud University, Nijmegen, the Netherlands. He has written articles on the Islamist movement, the Gulf, and the history of political thought in the Middle East. He has edited *Global Salafism: Islam's New Religious Movement* and *The Muslim Brotherhood in Europe*. He is involved in a project on the history of citizenship in the Middle East and is editing a two-volume book, *Citizenship in the Middle East and North Africa: History, Theory, and Practice.*

Karim Mezran is a resident senior fellow with the Atlantic Council's Rafik Hariri Center for the Middle East. He also currently serves as an adjunct professor at the Johns Hopkins University School of Advanced International Studies (SAIS) and was previously director of the Center for American Studies in Rome. His latest publication is "Libya in Transition: From *Jamahiriya* to *Jumhuriyyah*?" in *The New Middle East*, edited by Fawaz Gerges.

Bessma Momani is an associate professor at the University of Waterloo's Balsillie School of International Affairs and a senior fellow at the Centre for International Governance and Innovation. She is a Fulbright Scholar and a former fellow at the Brookings Institution and Georgetown University's Mortara Center. The author and editor of seven books and over sixty academic journal articles and book chapters, she examines the intersection between international economics, the Middle East, and international politics.

Heba Raouf Ezzat is a lecturer of political theory at Cairo University and the American University in Cairo. She was a visiting fellow at the University of California, Berkeley in 2010 and at Georgetown University in 2012 and is currently a visiting fellow at the London School of Economics (2015–16). She has published widely in English and Arabic on notions of citizenship, global democracy, and global civil society; on the epistemology of Islam; and on issues of women and gender from an Islamic perspective. Her recent publications in Arabic include *The Political Imagination of Islamists* and *Towards a New Civility.*

Hugh Roberts is the Edward Keller Professor of North African and Middle Eastern History at Tufts University. He previously was director of the North Africa Project of the International Crisis Group. He is the author of *The Battlefield: Algeria, 1988–2002—Studies in a Broken Polity*; *Berber Government: The Kabyle Polity in Pre-colonial Algeria*; and *Algérie-Kabylie: Études et interventions*.

Johannes Theiss is an associate at the strategic advisory Steltemeier and Rawe European Affairs in Brussels specializing in negotiation analysis, security, and energy and climate policies. He holds a master's degree in EU international relations and diplomacy studies from the College of Europe in Bruges and a master's in political science from the Otto-Friedrich University of Bamberg. He has worked at the Latin-American Center for Relations with Europe in Santiago de Chile (2009–10), at the press office of the federal government in Berlin (2008), and at Siemens in Erlangen (2005–9).

Siniša Vuković is a lecturer in international mediation at the Johns Hopkins University School of Advanced International Studies (SAIS) and an assistant professor at Radboud University Nijmegen, the Netherlands. He has a PhD in international relations from the University of Leiden. His most recent book is *International Multiparty Mediation and Conflict Management*.

I. William Zartman is Jacob Blaustein Distinguished Professor Emeritus at the Johns Hopkins University School of Advanced International Studies (SAIS) and senior fellow and member of the steering committee of the Processes of International Negotiations (PIN) Program at Clingendael NL. He was the president and founding executive secretary of the Middle East Studies Association and founding president of the American Institute of Maghrib Studies and the Tangier American Legation Institute for Moroccan Studies. His recent books include *Cowardly Lions*, *Negotiation and Conflict Management*, and *Ripe for Resolution*.

INDEX